Arctic Ocean

Lapps

SWEDEN
FINLAND
ESTONIA
(Rus.) LATVIA
LITHUANIA
GERMANY POLAND BELARUS
CZECH REP.
SLOVAKIA UKRAINE
AUS. HUNG. ROMANIA MOLDOVA
ITALY BULGARIA
GREECE TURKEY
CYPRUS
TUNISIA SYRIA
LEBANON ISRAEL
JORDAN
IRAQ
IRAN

RUSSIA

Europe-Asia
Boundary

KAZAKHSTAN

MONGOLIA

ARCTIC CIRCLE

Tungus

80°N

60°N

Abkhasians

GEORGIA
ARMENIA AZERBAIJAN
TURKMENISTAN

UZBEKISTAN

Kazak

KYRGYZSTAN
TAJIKISTAN
AFGHANISTAN

40°N

NORTH
KOREA
SOUTH
KOREA

JAPAN

Kurds

Pacific
Ocean

LIBYA
EGYPT

SAUDI
ARABIA

PAKISTAN

CHINA

NEPAL
BHUTAN

TAIWAN

BAHRAIN
QATAR
U.A.E.
OMAN

BANGLADESH

INDIA

MYANMAR
(BURMA)

LAOS

HONG KONG
MACAU
(Port.)

TROPIC OF CANCER

NIGER

SUDAN
ERITREA
YEMEN
DJIBOUTI

THAILAND
VIETNAM
CAMBODIA

Agta
PHILIPPINES

NORTHERN
MARIANA
ISLANDS
(U.S.)

20°N

REPUBLIC OF THE
MARSHALL ISLANDS

Nuer

Nayar

Moken

lani
Jruba
Mandari

CHAD
CENTRAL
AFRICAN REP.

Toda

SRI LANKA

Marshall
Islanders

ko
Tiv

Azande

ETHIOPIA

MALDIVES

Semang

Trukese

CAMEROON

Jie Gabra

Somali

BRUNEI

Dusun

FEDERATED STATES
OF MICRONESIA

GABON

Lugbara

Dodoth
Samburu

Minangkabau

MALAYSIA

Borneo

Arapesh

EQUATOR

0°

CONGO

Ganda
Mbuti

Nyoro

Mijikenda

Sumatra

SINGAPORE

Manus

Malaita
Kwaio

Kiribati

DEMOCRATIC
REPUBLIC
OF THE CONGO

KENYA

Luo

Kipsigis

Dani

PAPUA
NEW GUINEA

ola)

Tutsi
Hutu
Hadza

RWANDA
BURUNDI

Kikuyu
Masai
Abaluyia

INDONESIA

Tchambuli

SOLOMON
ISLANDS

nda

TANZANIA

SEYCHELLES

Trobriand
Islanders

TUVALU

ANGOLA

Kaguru Gusii
Nyakyusa

COMOROS IS.

Balinese

Tikopia

ZAMBIA

Yao

MALAWI

Indian Ocean

Tiwi

Vanatinai

FIJI

VANUATU

V'hoansi
Herrero

NAMIBIA
BOTSWANA

ZIMBABWE

MADAGASCAR

MAURITIUS

NEW
CALEDONIA
(Fr.)

20°S

Swazi

MOZAMBIQUE

AUSTRALIA

TROPIC OF CAPRICORN

Zulu

SWAZILAND

SOUTH
AFRICA
LESOTHO

S. BAY
to be
lined)

NEW
ZEALAND

40°S

1. SLOVENIA
2. CROATIA
3. BOSNIA AND HERZEGOVINA
4. ALBANIA
5. MACEDONIA

Maori

60°S

ANTARCTIC CIRCLE

ANTARCTICA

80°S

20°E   40°E   60°E   80°E   100°E   120°E   140°E   160°E   180°

Cultural Anthropology

TENTH EDITION

Cultural Anthropology

An Applied Perspective

Gary Ferraro

Susan Andreatta

CENGAGE
Learning®

Australia • Brazil • Japan • Korea • Mexico • Singapore • Spain • United Kingdom • United States

Cultural Anthropology: An Applied Perspective, **Tenth Edition**
Gary Ferraro and Susan Andreatta

Product Director: Jon-David Hague

Content Developer: Lin Gaylord

Content Coordinator: Sean Cronin

Product Assistant: Chelsea Meredith

Media Developer: John Chell

Marketing Manager: Shanna Shelton

Content Project Manager: Tanya Nigh

Art Director: Caryl Gorska

Manufacturing Planner: Judy Inouye

Rights Acquisitions Specialist: Roberta Broyer

Production Service and Compositor: Integra

Photo and Text Researcher: PreMedia Global

Copy Editor: Integra

Illustrator: Graphic World, Inc.

Text Designer: Lisa Buckley

Cover Designer: Lee Friedman

Cover Image: George Steinmetz/National Geographic Stock

For product information and technology assistance, contact us at **Cengage Learning Customer & Sales Support, 1-800-354-9706.**

For permission to use material from this text or product, submit all requests online at **www.cengage.com/permissions.** Further permissions questions can be e-mailed to **permissionrequest@cengage.com.**

Library of Congress Control Number: 2013939557

ISBN-13: 978-1-285-73849-9

ISBN-10: 1-285-73849-7

Cengage Learning
200 First Stamford Place, 4th Floor
Stamford, CT 06902
USA

Cengage Learning is a leading provider of customized learning solutions with office locations around the globe, including Singapore, the United Kingdom, Australia, Mexico, Brazil and Japan. Locate your local office at **www.cengage.com/global.**

Cengage Learning products are represented in Canada by Nelson Education, Ltd.

To learn more about Cengage Learning Solutions, visit **www.cengage.com.**

Purchase any of our products at your local college store or at our preferred online store **www.cengagebrain.com.**

Printed in the United States of America
1 2 3 4 5 6 7 17 16 15 14 13

To Stefan and Stephanie—aka "The Steffersons"—who embody the values of multiculturalism, cross-cultural understanding, and the insights of cultural anthropology.

GPF

For Tim—Thank you for your love and for understanding the value of anthropological fieldwork.

SLA

Brief Contents

Detailed Contents

Danita Delimont/Gallo Images/Getty Images

Strauss/Curtis Corbis

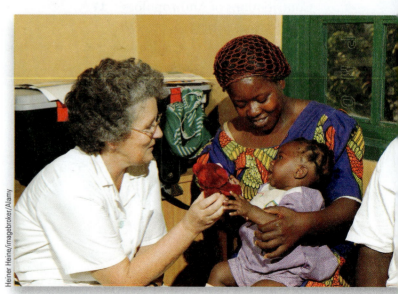

Heiner Heine/imagebroker/Alamy

© Tim Graham/Getty Images

© Richard Lord

Pinkyone/Shutterstock.com

Keren Su/China Span/Alamy

Sukree Sukplang/Reuters

Juanmonino/E+/Getty Images

Courtesy of Gary Ferraro

© Paul Conklin/PhotoEdit

Florian Kopp/Glow Images

Paul Almasy/Corbis

© David Samuel Robbins/Corbis.

PhotoviewPlus/Getty Images

© Joerg Boething/Peter Arnold, Inc.

Feature Contents

Preface

Applied cultural anthropology has become increasingly multifaceted, making it necessary to introduce material from new collaborators with diverse, yet complementary, backgrounds, experiences, and research interests. Both authors share a strong applied focus in their work as well as a similar, compatible vision of the importance of an applied perspective within the discipline and, particularly, the need for an applied focus in introductory-level anthropology courses.

Whereas Gary Ferraro has concentrated for the past several decades on the applied areas of the anthropology of business, education, and organizational structures, Susan Andreatta has focused her professional attention on environmental and medical anthropology. Since 2008 Ferraro and Andreatta have co-conducted five workshops at the annual meetings of the Society for Applied Anthropology and the American Anthropological Association dealing with how anthropology courses can be made more applied in their focus. And in 2013, Andreatta and Ferraro collaborated on a briefer version of this introductory textbook in cultural anthropology titled *Elements of Culture: An Applied Perspective.*

From the beginning, this text has had two major purposes. First, the book is designed to introduce university undergraduates to the field of cultural anthropology by drawing on the rich ethnographic examples found within the discipline. With its comparative approach to the study of cultural diversity, the text provides a comprehensive overview of the discipline. Second, the text goes beyond the basic outline of introductory materials by examining how the theory, insights, and methods of cultural anthropology have been applied to those contemporary situations that students, both majors and non-majors, are likely to encounter in their professional and personal lives.

The popularity of applied anthropology has grown steadily in the past two decades, largely as a result of the discipline's recognition of the need to become more relevant to our everyday lives. Now that we are more than two decades into the age of globalization, few would deny the need for our students to become culturally competent, irrespective of what occupation(s) they might pursue. Enabling today's undergraduates to cope more effectively with cultural diversity is hardly an empty catchphrase. Because cultural anthropology, even in its traditional (nonapplied) form, has always been the academic discipline best positioned to educate for cultural competency, it only makes sense to make our introductory courses as relevant and applied as possible.

The theme of applied anthropology runs throughout this text. While providing a comprehensive introduction to the field, *Cultural Anthropology: An Applied Perspective*, Tenth Edition, goes beyond the presentation of academic anthropology and thoroughly integrates the application of anthropological theory, methods, and examples to contemporary situations that students are likely to encounter in the world around them. The applied perspective is further highlighted by the chapter opening cases and the features called *Applied Perspectives* and *Cross-Cultural Miscues*. In addition, *Contemporary Issues* boxes draw attention to issues in the field and events, as well as helps students relate to the anthropological perspective in everyday life. The Applied Perspectives, which appear in boxed format in all sixteen chapters, demonstrate how cultural anthropology actually has been used to solve specific societal problems in such areas as medicine, the environment, education, government, architecture, business, and economic development. There are a total of thirty new boxed features in the tenth edition, including twelve new Applied Perspective boxes. For example, in Chapter 3 students learn about the use of cook stoves in Peru and the local health implications of food preparation, and in Chapter 11 students are introduced to a shelter for abused woman in Kenya. And in Chapter 16 a new Applied Perspective box illustrates how research findings from an environmental anthropologist helped in the development of a drought insurance program in Ethiopia.

Over the past decade a number of leading introductory textbooks in the field have, to one degree or another, included some applied case studies in boxed format. We consider this imitation to be the sincerest form of flattery. Nevertheless, the Applied Perspective case studies in this text differ in some important respects. For example, each case study is selected to illustrate how *certain understandings from each chapter have been applied to the solution of significant societal problems*; there are more in-depth applied case studies in this text than in the others; and each of the case studies is followed by *Questions for Further Thought*, designed to encourage students to think critically about the broader implications of the applied case.

The second applied feature of this textbook is Cross-Cultural Miscues. These short scenarios, which also appear in all sixteen chapters, illustrate the negative consequences of failing to understand cultural differences. There are fourteen new Cross-Cultural Miscues in the tenth edition. To illustrate, one new miscue box from Chapter 2 shows how even an anthropologist (who should know better) can ask culturally inappropriate questions when operating abroad, and in Chapter 3 a traveler in Indonesia may have benefitted from some knowledge of medical anthropology before panicking when seeing people using train-tracks for electric therapy. And in Chapter 16, students see how a failure to understand how what motivates one's culturally different workforce can cause a US business person to shoot himself in the foot when operating in an overseas context.

A third applied feature of this tenth edition is short, chapter-opening case studies designed to catch the attention of students and remind them that the study of cultural anthropology really is relevant to our lives. These introductory case studies (like the Applied Perspectives and the Cross-Cultural Miscues) are designated with the "SWAP" feature icon. This acronym stands for "share with a parent" (or a friend) and directly illustrates to students the importance and necessity for understanding culture—what it is and how it changes—as an individual living in today's world. Students should use these SWAP features to counter the inevitable questions from their parents and friends: "You're taking what? What possible benefit can you get from studying cultural anthropology? How will anthropology get you a job?" Accompanying the Applied Perspectives, the Cross-Cultural Miscues, and the chapter-opening case studies, the SWAP icon appears 45 times throughout the text. Thus, there is more than an adequate number of illustrations to show why tuition money is not being wasted when undergraduates take courses in, or even major in (heaven forbid!), cultural anthropology.

Please note that Chapters 1 and 16 start with letters (rather than opening scenarios) written to the students by us. The opening letter to students in Chapter 1 tells students essentially what we are telling you in this preface—namely, the nature of the book's applied perspective, what it is designed to accomplish, and how to get the most from the book. Because most professors do not require their students to read the preface, we decided to put this information in the beginning of the first chapter so that they would understand from day one what we are trying to do with the applied focus. And, we open Chapter 16 with a closing letter to the students designed to introduce them to the capstone chapter, remind them of the importance of the applied features of the text, and show them how anthropological understandings and sensitivities are absolutely essential for the resolution of those really big human challenges of the twenty-first century facing all people—namely, climate change, overurbanization in developing countries, environmental degradation, the spread of world health pandemics, the rise of militant religious fundamentalism, and the widening gap between the rich and the poor throughout the world.

There are also five new Contemporary Issue boxes in the book, dealing with such topics as "Water, Culture, and Power: When Is It Too Late to Act?" (Chapter 4), the competition for high levels of academic achievement between rich and poor students in the United States (Chapter 12), and the conflict between secular values in the United States and religious values in the Islamic World (Chapter 14).

In addition to the smooth integration of applied illustrations into the overall text, an applied perspective (using both positive and negative case studies) is tied to a wide range of professional areas, including, but not limited to, the following:

International businesspeople	Product designers
International development workers	Public health officials
Market researchers	Public school educators
Medical caregivers	Social workers
Postwar nation builders	University professors

Because our case studies are tied to a variety of occupational areas, students will be more likely to relate the concepts, findings, methods, and theories of cultural anthropology to their own future work lives in the twenty-first century. Tying anthropological insights to specific jobs is particularly important in the increasingly tight job market in the twenty-first century. And, in fact, hiring criteria in most free market economies have changed. By and large employers no longer hire on the basis of what a job candidate knows or whether one's degree is from a first-rate institution. Instead, they want to know: *Can you add value to the organization?* Do you have the skills and competencies needed to be creative and to solve future problems which do not even exist yet? Although it is true that many of the skills needed by today's employers are not being taught explicitly at institutions of higher learning, many are being taught.

So, if young people are to be successful in the school-to-work transition, they need to learn as much as possible about our rapidly changing workplace in addition to (not instead of) their chosen fields of study. Applying anthropology in the work place, such as using their acquired cultural sensitivity to multiethnic differences, immigration, and globalization are needed in today's workforce. Yet, some students may be interested in getting involved in nongovernmental organizations and working on applied projects that facilitate making a difference in local communities here and abroad, this text provides numerous examples inspiring such thinking and action. Students must "know themselves" well enough to identify what future professions or jobs would be most satisfying to them.

Given the present-day realities of transitioning from school to work, we feel that the applied focus of this textbook is particularly germane for today's students. Each of our applied case studies deals with using anthropological insights for the solution of problems and challenges faced by people from a variety of professions and occupying a wide range of jobs. All features, including the Applied Perspectives, Cross-Cultural Miscues, Contemporary Issues, and chapter-opening scenarios encourage students to appreciate the types of skills and competencies needed by people who work in jobs that require interacting with culturally different people. In today's global marketplace it is difficult to imagine any job that would not require cross-cultural skills and sensitivities when dealing with customers, clients, patients, or students, either at home or abroad.

Over the past decade an increasing number of cultural anthropologists have agreed with our basic premise: that an introductory text with an applied focus was long overdue. Anthropology instructors at many different types of institutions—public and private, large and small, two-year and four-year—have adopted the first nine editions of this book. As well received as the previous editions have been, however, there is always room for improvement. Responding to many helpful suggestions of reviewers, we have made the following changes in the tenth edition.

General Changes

As previously discussed, the tenth edition of *Cultural Anthropology: An Applied Perspective*, speaks more directly to students with more contemporary examples that deal with nonacademic career opportunities and the application of anthropological concepts in the workplace and in one's personal life. The revision further strengthens the themes of economics and environment as well as community and social responsibility that run throughout the text. In addition, global changes include:

1. Full integration of applied anthropology and applying anthropology examples into every chapter;
2. New Critical Thinking Questions at the end of chapters and the Suggested Readings have been eliminated;
3. A 10-percent reduction in overall length, with most chapters trimmed;
4. Reframing Chapter 3, Applied Anthropology, to eliminate redundancies with Chapters 4 and 5 on theory and methods, and to refocus the chapter on practical applications, emphasizing the role of anthropology and applying anthropology, including nonacademic careers and ethics;

5. The updating and improvement of the art program with new photos, tables, graphs, and maps.

Changes by Chapter
Chapter 1: What Is Anthropology?

1. Added a new section explaining the difference between *applied* anthropology and *applying* anthropology.
2. The chapter includes a new Applied Perspective box dealing with an applied archaeologist working in post-Katrina New Orleans.
3. A new section has been introduced on how archaeologists are now studying contemporary urban garbage dumps in the United States to determine consumption patterns and to provide data used by urban policy makers.
4. A new example of ethnocentrism has been added.
5. The discussion of cultural relativism has been reorganized to make it more understandable.
6. The section on anthropology's role in enhancing understanding has been streamlined.
7. New data have been added on the percentage of those accepted to college who choose to defer admission to college to take a gap year in some other culture.
8. The final section of the chapter titled "The Bottom Line" was rewritten with an eye toward succinctness and clarity.

Chapter 2: The Concept of Culture

1. The section dealing with the definition of "culture" now includes an additional early-twentieth-century definition offered by independent scholar FitzRoy Richard Somerset (1885–1964).
2. The section on cultural universals has been reorganized to make it both more comprehensive and user friendly.
3. A new cross-cultural scenario focusing on different world views between Italians and North Americans on how to conduct a vacation has been added to this chapter.
4. The entire section dealing with altering one's physical appearance for aesthetic reasons has been updated.
5. A new final section has been added dealing with the development of twenty-first-century information technology that will revolutionize how we study the concept of culture, culture change, and the flow of ideas.
6. Sixty four percent of the photos in Chapter 2 are new images.

Chapter 3: Applied Anthropology

1. Ethics is introduced in this chapter.

2. Introduced the Human Terrain System and its conflict with the professional code of ethics.

3. Included Mark Schuller's research in the Haitian camps postdisaster and the $5.3 billion dollars pledged for rebuilding Haiti. Internally displaced people remain in campus without proper sanitation, drinkable water, access to health clinics, and regular employment.

4. Added a new Applied Perspective that focuses on the use of more efficient cookstoves to reduce mortality rates in impoverished regions of the world that rely on biomass and coal for fuel and which contributes to environment, climatic and health benefits as well.

5. Added a new Cross-Cultural Miscue in Medical Anthropology on how the Indonesia poor turn to train-track electric therapy.

6. Added a second new Cross-Cultural Miscue on research and ethics in Mali.

Chapter 4: The Growth of Anthropological Theory

1. Noted that not all theoretical perspectives are offered in this chapter because most departments offer a course or two in anthropological theory.

2. Tightened up some of the theoretical sections. Introduced the terms *human ecology* and *political ecology*, which will be further defined and used in Chapters 7 and 8.

3. Reduced time spent on Levi-Strauss French Structuralism.

4. Added material on political economy.

5. Added material on political ecology.

6. Added material on Praxis, which is appropriate for applied research and applying anthropology to the real world.

7. New Contemporary Issue box on "Water, Culture and Power: When Is It Too Late to Act?"

Chapter 5: Applied Anthropology: Methods in Cultural Anthropology

1. Removed ethics from this chapter to introduce it in Chapter 3.

2. Tightened up the Case Study from Andreatta's research in Jamaica in the section on fieldwork.

3. Introduced community-based participatory research.

4. Introduced recommendations from Shirley Fiske on how to obtain government employment with an interest in applied anthropology.

5. Introduced a final section on accountability.

6. Added a new Applied Perspective box on climate change.

Chapter 6: Language and Communication

1. Added a new Cross-Cultural Miscue on the use of Facebook in the office as an appropriate means of group communication.

2. Added a new Applied Perspective on language preservation as a way to draw attention to saving endangered languages using digital technology and software apps from smartphones.

3. Introduced an applied linguistics example with the work of Pam Innes and language preservation examples among the Apache.

4. Added cell phone text-messaging examples to illustrate culture change and new means of communicating.

Chapter 7: Subsistence Patterns

1. Added a new chapter-opening case study on pastoralism and climate change, drawing on the work of Terry McCabe in East Africa.

2. Added a discussion of food deserts in the United States.

3. Added examples of changing environments and the impact on subsistence strategies for groups such as the Sami, Inuit, and Ju/'hoansi, as well as fishing communities and small island states.

4. Introduced the concepts of locavores and freegans as alternative means of sourcing food.

5. Added a discussion of using small-livestock such as goats to manage grassland regions around the airport in the United States.

6. Added a discussion of resistance to industrial agriculture using small-scale food production with examples from Slow Food, use of farmers markets, community-supported agriculture, the back of the land movement, World Wide Opportunities on Organic Farms (WWOOF), and a number of other programs.

7. Added an Applied Perspective box on eating insects to evade hunger.

Chapter 8: Economics

1. Introduced a new Cross-Cultural Miscue on learning how to change money in a foreign country.

2. Introduced a new Contemporary Issue box on alpacas in the Andes.

3. Added examples from Afghanistan in the section on division of labor that addresses women gaining employment.

4. Updated statistics for international labor and the use of children.

5. Introduced a new Applied Perspective box on what happens to used hotel soap and how nongovernmental organizations are using the business of recycling soap to help people around the world.

6. Introduced another Applied Perspective box on cruise ships in Alaska and increased pollution.

Chapter 9: Marriage and the Family

1. Introduced a new chapter-opening case study on same-sex families adopting children.

2. Introduced a new Applied Perspective box on preparing for resettlement because of climate change.

3. Introduced an example of Sumburu women in Kenya and the development of a village for abused women only, changing the traditional division of labor; here women do men's work as well.

4. Updated statistics of children with HIV and AIDS and the impact AIDS has on the children and added examples from orphaned children with AIDS.

5. Added an example of dowry deaths in India.

6. Added examples of the modern family in the United States changing composition with college-age students moving back home.

Chapter 10: Kinship and Descent

1. A new Cross-Cultural Miscue box about an incident of intercultural misunderstanding that occurred in Saudi Arabia between a North American woman and her local Saudi landlord, has been added to the chapter.

2. A new Contemporary Issues box now introduces the idea that the gender of the cultural anthropologist can influence the extent to which patrilineal descent groups are male oriented.

3. Added a new discussion of how kinship roles and obligations in western countries are being "outsourced" on a "fee-for-service" basis.

4. There is a new expanded section on twenty-first-century information technology useful for tracking kinship relations.

5. An expanded discussion has been added on reproductive technologies (e.g., in vitro fertilization, surrogate motherhood), which are making our traditional notions of parenthood more difficult to define.

6. A new case study has been added describing how a recent college senior learned (through new kinship-specific information technology) that she was the great-great-great-great granddaughter of the college's first graduate in 1814.

Chapter 11: Sex and Gender

1. Added discussion on same-sex relationships.

2. Added examples of stay at home fathers and fatherville.

3. Added examples of women in the developing world risking everything for an education, (e.g., example from Pakistan of girl who was shot by the Taliban for speaking out for girls getting an education).

4. Added examples of women in the developing world and their poor reproductive health.

5. Introduced a Cross-Cultural Miscue that focuses on humor in the work place at an international women's crisis shelter.

6. Introduced an Applied Perspective box on Umoja, Kenya a women's village (shelter) that emerged for abused women.

7. Introduced an Applied Perspective box on "Son Preference: New Reproductive Technologies and Family Building Strategies in India."

Chapter 12: Social Stratification

1. A new Cross-Cultural Miscue box has been added dealing with a culture clash between an American and his Japanese joint venture partners which ended badly.

2. A new Contemporary Issues box discussing how there is never a level playing field when rich and poor students in the United States compete for high levels of achievement in education.

3. The data on the relationship between educational attainment and annual income has been updated using the most recent census data.

4. The latest (2013) *Fortune* data on the world's wealthiest billionaires (and their nationalities) has been incorporated into this chapter.

5. The latest data on income inequities in the United States (since the "great recession of 2008") have been included.

6. A new discussion has been added on the changing nature of traditional ethnic neighborhoods in New York City.

7. The discussion on occupational prestige in the United States has been updated to show how people rank certain occupations after the financial meltdown of 2008.

8. The latest data from the World Bank (2011) has been used to update the ten wealthiest and the ten poorest nations in the world (according to gross national income).

Chapter 13: Political Organization and Social Control

1. The applied Perspective box on the Poarch Creek Tribe from Alabama has been updated to show the significant changes in the community's economic development that have occurred in the twenty-first century.

2. The section on "Gender and the Modern State" has been updated to show the modest advances in women's participation in government worldwide during the twenty-first century.

3. The section on "Changing State Systems of Government" has included the most recent data on the relationship between democracies and autocracies in world governments.

4. This same section now includes a major addition on the findings and methodologies of the 2012 Failed States Index published annually since 2005 by the Fund for Peace.

5. The multipage section dealing with social control has been reorganized by dividing the various mechanisms of social control into those found in (a) all types of societies, (b) small-scale societies, and (c) state societies.

6. New to Chapter 13 is an Applied Perspective case study showing an applied anthropologist's role as an expert witness in two court cases involving American Indians.

7. Chapter 13 now contains a new Cross-Cultural Miscue illustrating how a United States diplomat failed to understand the symbolism of touching his Kuwaiti counterpart with his left hand.

Chapter 14: Belief Systems

1. A new Cross-Cultural Miscue dealing with the Chinese belief system of *feng shui* has been added to this edition.

2. Updated information on the growing popularity of the Wiccan movement has been included in this edition.

3. A new section has been added on the relative religious knowledge of practitioners of various religious denominations in the United States based on the Pew Forum on Religion and Public Life (2010).

4. The tenth edition now includes an interesting example of a French city's (Bussy Saint Georges) response to new immigrant religions by building an "esplanade (campus) of religions" housing several Buddhist temples, a Jewish synagogue, and an Islamic mosque.

5. In the section on "globalization of world religions," a new discussion appears on the demographic shift in the Roman Catholic Church from Europe to the "Global South" (comprised of Latin America, Africa, and South Asia).

6. There is now a brief update on the relationship between religion and politics in the United States since the 2004 presidential election.

7. A new Contemporary Issues box has been added that illustrates the conflict between secular values in the United States and religious values in the Islamic world.

Chapter 15: Art

1. The case of the Denver Museum taking the lead in researching and posting the names of artists from small-scale societies has been added to this chapter, illustrating how some museums are ending the practice of putting more importance on who owns a piece of nonwestern art than on the artist who made it.

2. To illustrate how relatively segregated (by class) some forms of art are in the United States, we have included an example of a "random act of culture," whereby the Philadelphia Opera Company held an impromptu performance of the "Toreador Song" from "Carmen" at the crowded Reading Terminal Market.

3. To illustrate how music can play a role in disrupting the status quo, the music of one courageous rapper from Tunisia was shown to be the major impetus for the series of revolutions occurring in the Middle East known as the Arab Spring.

4. The contemporary issue box dealing with the return of a tattooed Maori head by the Museum of Rouen, France, was updated to include information about the actual repatriation of the body part.

5. A new Cross-Cultural Miscue has been added to Chapter 15 showing how humor often does not translate smoothly from one culture to another.

Chapter 16: Global Challenges and the Role of Applied Anthropology

1. Two new Cross-Cultural Miscues have been added. The first involves a US businessman working in Singapore who fails to realize the meaning of a hand gesture he uses when conversing with his Singaporean employees. The second new miscue involves the president of a US timber company working in Latin America who fails to understand the proper incentives for recruiting local workers.

2. The chapter also contains two new Applied Perspective boxes. One involves how environmental anthropologist Nicole Peterson applied her research findings to the design of a drought insurance program for small-scale farmers in Ethiopia. The second examines how a major US company, which develops and administers economic development programs in developing countries, recruits its expatriate program officers with an eye toward cross-cultural experience, sensitivities, and coping skills rather than technical expertise alone.

3. The economic data on former African colonies has been updated.

4. A number of new examples of globalization have been added to this edition.

5. The human rights efforts on behalf of the Ngobe of Panama by Cultural Survival have been brought up to date.

Chapter Features

As discussed, this edition contains a number of pedagogical features designed to enhance student learning. These include What We Will Learn introductory questions alerting the student to the key concepts of the chapter, chapter-opening scenarios that illustrate just how important culture is for understanding the world around us, concise chapter summaries, a list of key terms, a running glossary as well as a cumulative glossary, Applied Perspective boxes, Contemporary Issues boxes, and Cross-Cultural Miscues, all designed to illustrate the relevance of cultural anthropology to our everyday lives. Questions for Further Thought also appear at the end of the Applied Perspective boxes and are designed to stimulate critical thinking about the applied cases.

Supplements for Instructors

Online Instructor's Manual with Test Bank for Ferraro/Andreatta's *Cultural Anthropology: An Applied Perspective*, **Tenth Edition** An online Instructor's Manual accompanies this book. It contains information to assist the instructor in designing the course, including learning objectives, chapter outlines, key terms, critical thinking questions, class activities, Internet exercises, and suggested films. For assessment support, the updated test bank includes true/false, multiple-choice, short-answer, and essay questions for each chapter.

Cengage Learning Testing Powered by Cognero for *Cultural Anthropology: An Applied Perspective*, **by**

Ferraro/Andreatta, Tenth Edition This assessment tool is a flexible, online system that allows you to author, edit, and manage test bank content from multiple Cengage Learning solutions. You can create multiple test versions in an instant and deliver tests from your LMS, your classroom or wherever you want.

Wadsworth Anthropology Video Library Qualified adopters can select full-length videos from an extensive library of offerings drawn from such excellent educational video sources as *Films for the Humanities and Sciences.*

AIDS in Africa DVD Expand your students' global perspective of HIV and AIDS with this award-winning documentary series focused on controlling HIV and AIDS in southern Africa. Films focus on caregivers in the faith community; how young people share messages of hope through song and dance; the relationship of HIV and AIDS to gender, poverty, stigma, education, and justice; and the story of two women who are HIV-positive helping others.

Online Resources for Instructors and Students

Anthropology CourseMate for *Cultural Anthropology: An Applied Perspective*, **by Ferraro/Andreatta, Tenth Edition** Interested in a simple way to complement your text and course content with study and practice materials? Cengage Learning's Anthropology CourseMate brings course concepts to life with interactive learning, study, and exam preparation tools that support the printed textbook. Watch student comprehension soar as your class works with the printed textbook and the textbook-specific web site. Anthropology CourseMate goes beyond the book to deliver what you need and includes an interactive eBook that allows students to take notes, highlight, bookmark, search the text, and use in-context glossary definitions; as well as interactive teaching and learning tools including quizzes, flashcards, videos, and more.

Anthropology CourseReader. Anthropology Course Reader allows you to create a fully customized online reader in minutes. Access a rich collection of thousands of primary and secondary sources, readings, and audio and video selections from multiple disciplines. See the Author's Choice for selections of applied anthropology articles edited by Gary Ferraro, editor.

To access these resources and additional course materials and companion resources, please visit www.cengagebrain.com. At the CengageBrain.com home page, search for the ISBN of your title (from the back cover of your book) using the search box at the top of the page. This will take you to the product page where free companion resources can be found.

Supplements for Students

For a complete listing of our case studies and readers go to www.cengage.com/community/fromthefield

Classic Readings in Cultural Anthropology, **Third Edition** (ISBN: 978-1-111-29792-3) Practical and insightful, this concise and accessible reader by Gary Ferraro presents a core selection of historical and contemporary works that have been instrumental in shaping anthropological thought and research over the past decades. Readings are organized around eight topics that closely mirror most introductory textbooks and are selected from scholarly works on the basis of their enduring themes and contributions to the discipline.

Globalization and Change in Fifteen Cultures: Born in One World, Living in Another, **edited by George Spindler and Janice E. Stockard.** (978-0-534-63648-7) In this volume, fifteen case study authors write about culture change in today's diverse settings around the world. Each original article provides insight into the dynamics and meanings of change, as well as the effects of globalization at the local level.

Case Studies in Cultural Anthropology, **edited by George Spindler and Janice E. Stockard.** Select from more than sixty classic and contemporary ethnographies representing geographic and topical diversity. Newer case studies focus on culture change and culture continuity, reflecting the globalization of the world and include a legacy edition of Napoleon Chagnon's *Yąnomamö,* and a fourth edition of Richard Lee's *The Dobe Ju/'hoansi.* Recent publications include *Shadowed Lives,* by Leo Chavez.

Case Studies on Contemporary Social Issues, **edited by John A. Young.** Framed around social issues, these new contemporary case studies are globally comparative and represent the cutting-edge work of anthropologists today. Recent publications include *Slaughterhouse Blues* by Donald Stull and Michael Broadway and *Seeking Food Rights: Nation, Inequality and Repression in Uzbekistan* by Nancy Rosenberger.

Acknowledgments

To one degree or another, many people have contributed to this textbook. Some have made explicit suggestions for revisions, many of which have been incorporated into various editions over the past eighteen years. Others have contributed less directly, yet their fingerprints are found throughout the text. We are particularly grateful to the many professors with whom we have studied at Syracuse University (Ferraro) and Michigan State University (Andreatta). We owe a similar debt to the many colleagues over the years who have shared with us their thinking on anthropological research and teaching. Although there are far too many names to fit into a small preface, they have had an important impact on our thinking and our careers as anthropologists and, thus, on the content of this book. They have always responded graciously to our requests for information in their various areas of expertise and have taught us a great deal about teaching introductory anthropology. We are confident that they know who they are and will accept our most sincere gratitude.

Since its first appearance in 1992, this textbook has benefited enormously from excellent editorial guidance and the comments of many reviewers. We want to thank our original editor, Peter Marshall, for his encouragement to write an introductory textbook with an applied focus before it was fashionable. We also want to thank our Senior Content Developer, Lin Marshall Gaylord, for her vision, counsel, and many excellent suggestions for improving the tenth edition. Thanks are also extended to the entire Cengage Learning editorial, marketing, and production team composed of Chelsea Meredith, Product Assistant Editor; Sean Cronin, Content Coordinator; John Chell, Media Developer; Tanya Nigh, Senior Content Production Manager; Integra, Production Services; and Venkat Narayanan, Photo Researcher.

As with the previous editions of this book, many reviewers have made valuable and insightful suggestions for strengthening the text. For this tenth edition we would like to express our gratitude to the many colleagues who wish to remain anonymous.

We also want to thank the many unsolicited reviewers—both professors and students—who have commented on various aspects of the text over the years. We trust that these reviewers will see that many of their helpful suggestions have been incorporated into the tenth edition. We encourage any readers, professors, or students to send us comments, corrections, and suggestions for future improvements via e-mail at the following addresses:

gpferrar@uncc.edu
s_andrea@uncg.edu

After nearly a half-century (cumulative) of full-time university teaching, we want to express our deepest gratitude to our many students who have helped us define and refine our anthropological perspectives and, consequently, the concepts and interpretations in this book.

Gary Ferraro
Susan Andreatta

About the Author

Gary Ferraro, Professor Emeritus of Anthropology at the University of North Carolina–Charlotte, received his BA in history from Hamilton College and his MA and PhD from Syracuse University. He has been a Fulbright Scholar at the University of Swaziland in Southern Africa (1979–1980) and again at Masaryk University in the Czech Republic (2003), and he has served twice (1983, 2003) as a visiting professor of anthropology in the University of Pittsburgh's Semester at Sea Program, a floating university that travels around the world. He has conducted research for extended periods of time in Kenya and Swaziland and has traveled widely throughout many other parts of the world. He has served as a consultant and trainer for such organizations as USAID, the Peace Corps, the World Bank, IBM, G.E. Plastics, and Georgia Pacific, among others. From 1996 to 2000 he served as the Director of the Intercultural Training Institute at UNC–Charlotte, a consortium of cross-cultural trainers and educators from academia, government, and business, designed to help regional organizations cope with cultural differences at home and abroad. He is the author of

The Two Worlds of Kamau (1978),
The Cultural Dimension of International Business (1990, 1994, 1998, 2002, 2006, 2010, and
    2013 with co-author, Elizabeth K. Briody),
Anthropology: An Applied Perspective (1994),
Applying Cultural Anthropology: Readings (1998),
Global Brains: Knowledge and Competencies for the Twenty-First Century (2002), and
Classic Readings in Cultural Anthropology (2004, 2009, 2012).

Susan Andreatta, Professor of Anthropology at the University of North Carolina–Greensboro, received her BA in anthropology and Spanish at the University of Delaware, her MA in anthropology from Iowa State University, and her PhD in anthropology from Michigan State University. Andreatta also did a two-year post-doc in England at the University of Hull. During the past twenty-five years she has conducted fieldwork in Costa Rica, Jamaica, St. Vincent, Barbados, Antigua, Dominica, Mexico, Uganda, China, Peru and North Carolina. Her theoretical orientation lies in political economy and political ecology as applied to the environment and health. Since 1985 she has participated in a wide range of applied projects, including those that focused on tourism, migration and resettlement, health and nutrition, agriculture, agroforestry, fishing, and marketing of fresh local produce and seafood. Her interests in small family farms, rural communities, fishing communities, and their transformation or resistance to the expansion of agribusiness and the globalization of agriculture have enabled her to work both overseas and domestically. In addition, she has been examining traditional and Western approaches to health care in changing economic and political systems. Her work has been published in *Human Organization, Culture and Agriculture, Southern Rural Sociology, Urban Anthropology,* and *Home Health Care Management & Practice.* Andreatta is the Director of Project Greenleaf at University of North Carolina–Greensboro, a project she started in 2001 that provides undergraduate students with hands-on applied research experiences. She is a past board member and former secretary for the Society for Applied Anthropology (SfAA) as well as a past president of the Society for Applied Anthropology (2007–2009).

A young girl from Guatemala peers from behind a tree to see what is going on in the world around her, an activity in which students of cultural anthropology also engage.

What Is Anthropology?

A LETTER TO STUDENTS

Greetings! We would like to welcome you to the 10th edition of *Cultural Anthropology: An Applied Perspective.*

We are proud of this textbook and the difference we bet it will make in your lives after reading and learning from the text. To be certain, all introductory textbooks in cultural anthropology are designed to introduce the reader to the content of cultural anthropology. But this textbook, with its "Applied Perspective," goes beyond the content of the discipline by showing you how the research findings, theories, methods, and insights of cultural anthropology can be useful in your *everyday* personal and professional lives.

The study of cultural anthropology, in other words, is far more than the study of the similarities and differences among the thousands of distinct and discrete cultures of the world and, in today's interconnected world, it is far more relevant. The *applied* orientation of this book illustrates (through distinct examples and scenarios) how understanding the ideas and behavior patterns of culturally different people, both at home and abroad, enables us to better meet our personal and professional objectives. Conversely, when we fail to take our cultural environments seriously, we are likely to commit some serious cultural faux pas.

The book's applied orientation is woven into each chapter through three unique features: chapter-opening real-world scenarios, Applied Perspective features, and Cross-Cultural Miscues. First, an introductory mini-case study that is actual, and not hypothetical, begins each chapter and illustrates why it is important to understand the basic concepts in the chapter. The second feature that highlights applied anthropology is the Applied Perspective boxes. These are longer case studies based on actual anthropological research that demonstrate how cultural anthropology has been used to solve specific societal problems in such work-related areas as medicine, government, architecture, education, economic development, and business. Finally, the Cross-Cultural Miscues, which appear in each chapter, illustrate the negative consequences of failing to appreciate cultural differences in one's everyday interactions. All three of these features are highlighted with the SWAP (an acronym for "Share with a Parent" or a friend) icon to direct your attention to key examples in the text that illustrate the importance of applied anthropology.

We are writing to you in Chapter 1 so that you know from the outset that this book has a twofold purpose: (1) It introduces you to the basic field of

WHAT WE WILL LEARN

- How does anthropology differ from other social and behavioral sciences?
- What is the four-field approach to the discipline of anthropology?
- What do anthropologists mean by *holism*?
- What is meant by *cultural relativism*, and why is it important?
- What skills will students develop from the study of anthropology?
- How can anthropology help solve social problems?

cultural anthropology, and (2) it demonstrates how cross-cultural awareness is extraordinarily relevant in the highly interconnected world of the twenty-first century. We also want to alert you that there are several important features of each chapter that should be taken seriously because they remind us of the relevance of cultural knowledge to our everyday lives. It is, in fact, these highly relevant scenarios and examples that you should cite to your parents and friends who never fail to ask the question: Why are you taking (or worse yet, majoring in) cultural anthropology? Because we all play out our lives in a cultural context—and, to an increasing degree, in a multicultural or cross-cultural context—an understanding of cultural anthropology is extremely important for maximizing our personal and professional success in the twenty-first century, irrespective of what line of work you might pursue.

We trust that you will find reading about living and working in other cultures (for example, see the Cross-Cultural Miscue in Chapter 1) or about anthropology and new product research in the developing world (see the Applied Perspective about cell phone technology in Chapter 8) interesting and thought provoking as you learn about the real impact culture has on your everyday life. Be sure to pay close attention to the SWAP icons that appear beside all mini-case studies throughout the book. It is these case studies that will help you to answer the questions from parents and friends about what you can possibly learn from cultural anthropology. ■

When most North Americans hear the word *anthropologist*, a number of images come to mind. They picture, for example:

- Dian Fossey devoting years of her life to making systematic observations of mountain gorillas in their natural environment in Rwanda
- A field anthropologist interviewing an exotic tribesman about his kinship system
- The excavation of a jawbone that will be used to demonstrate the evolutionary link between early and modern humans
- A linguist meticulously recording the words and sounds of a native informant speaking a language that has never been written down
- A cultural anthropologist studying the culture of unemployed men in Washington, D.C.
- A team of archaeologists in pith helmets unearthing an ancient temple from a rain forest in Guatemala

Each of these impressions—to one degree or another—accurately represents the concerns of scientists who call themselves anthropologists. Anthropologists do in fact travel to different parts of the world to study little-known cultures (cultural anthropologists) and languages (anthropological linguists), but they also study culturally distinct groups within their own cultures. Anthropologists also unearth fossil remains (physical anthropologists) and various artifacts (archaeologists) of people who lived thousands and, in some cases, millions of years ago. Even though anthropologists in these subspecialties engage in substantially different types of activities and generate different types of data, they are all directed toward a single purpose: the scientific study of humans, both biologically and culturally, in whatever form, time period, or region of the world they might be found.

Anthropology—derived from the Greek words *anthropos* for human and *logos* for study—is, if we take it literally, the study of humans. In one sense this is an accurate description to the extent that anthropology raises a wide variety of questions about the human condition. And yet this literal definition is not particularly illuminating because a number of other academic disciplines—including sociology, biology, psychology, political science, economics, and history—also study human beings. What is it that distinguishes anthropology from all of these other disciplines?

Anthropology is the study of people—their origins, their development, and contemporary variations wherever and whenever they have been found. Of all the disciplines that study humans, anthropology is by far the broadest in scope. The subject matter of anthropology includes fossilized skeletal remains of early humans, artifacts and other material remains from prehistoric and historic archaeological sites, and all of the contemporary and historical cultures of the world. The task that anthropology has set for itself is an enormous one. Anthropologists strive for an understanding of the biological and cultural origins and evolutionary development of the species. They are concerned with all humans, both past and present, as well as their behavior patterns, thought systems, and material possessions. In short, anthropology aims to describe, in the broadest sense, what it means to be human (Peacock 1986).

In their search to understand the human condition, anthropologists—drawing on a wide variety of data and methods—have created a diverse field of study. Many specialists in the field of anthropology often engage in research that is directly relevant to other fields. It has been suggested (Wolf 1964) that anthropology spans the gap between the humanities, the social sciences, and the natural sciences. To illustrate, anthropological investigations of native art, folklore, values, and supernatural belief systems are primarily humanistic in nature; studies of social stratification, comparative political systems, and means of distribution are common themes in sociology, political science, and economics, respectively; and studies of comparative anatomy and radiocarbon dating are central to the natural sciences of biology and chemistry.

The global scope of anthropological studies has actually increased over the past century. In the early 1900s, anthropologists concentrated on the non-Western, preliterate, and technologically simple societies of the world and were content to leave the study of industrial societies to other disciplines such as sociology and economics. In recent decades, however, anthropologists have devoted increasing attention to cultural and subcultural groups in industrialized areas while continuing their studies of more exotic peoples of the world. It is not uncommon today for anthropologists to apply their field methods to the study of the Hutterites of Montana, rural communes in California, or urban street gangs in Chicago. Only when the whole range of human cultural variation is examined will anthropologists be in a position to test the accuracy of theories about human behavior.

Traditionally, the discipline of anthropology is divided into four distinct branches or subfields: *physical anthropology*, which deals with humans as biological organisms; *archaeology*, which attempts to reconstruct the cultures of the past, most of which have left no written records; *anthropological linguistics*, which focuses on the study of language in historical, structural, and social contexts; and *cultural anthropology*, which examines similarities and differences among contemporary cultures of the world (see Table 1.1). All four subfields of the discipline of anthropology engage in both (1) theoretical research (describing and comparing cultural features among and between cultures) and (2) more practical forms of research designed to solve specific societal problems. This more problem-oriented endeavor is itself comprised of two broad streams: first, "applied anthropology" involves conducting applied research projects designed to generate policy recommendations for addressing societal problems; and the second, which is known in the field as "applying anthropology," involves using already existing anthropological data, methods, theories, and insights to inform government programs and nongovernment organizations (NGOs) that promote, manage, and assess social programs and social policies.

Although cultural anthropology is the central focus of this textbook, a brief discussion of all four branches will provide an adequate description of the discipline as a whole.

TABLE 1.1

Branches of Anthropology

Physical Anthropology	Archaeology	Anthropological Linguistics	Cultural Anthropology
Paleoanthropology	Historical archaeology	Historical linguistics	Development anthropology
Primatology	Prehistoric archaeology	Descriptive linguistics	Psychological anthropology
Human variation	Contract archaeology	Ethnolinguistics	Environmental anthropology
Forensic anthropology	Applied archaeology	Sociolinguistics	Medical anthropology
Applied physical anthropology	Cultural resource management	Applied linguistics	Urban anthropology
			Political anthropology
			Applied anthropology

Physical (Biological) Anthropology

The study of humans from a biological perspective is called *physical anthropology* (biological anthropology). Essentially, physical anthropologists are concerned with three broad areas of investigation. First, they are interested in reconstructing the evolutionary record of the human species; that is, they ask questions about the emergence of humans and how humans have evolved up to the present time. This area of physical anthropology is known as *paleoanthropology*. The second area of concern to physical anthropologists, known as primatology, focuses on our nearest living relatives, namely apes, monkeys, and prosimians. And the third area, known as human variation, studies how and why the physical traits of contemporary human populations vary throughout the world. Unlike comparative biologists, physical anthropologists study how culture and environment have influenced these two areas of biological evolution and contemporary variations.

Evolutionary Record of Humans

In their attempts to reconstruct human evolution, paleoanthropologists have drawn heavily on fossil remains (hardened organic matter such as bones and teeth) of humans, protohumans, and other primates. Once these fossil remains have been unearthed, the difficult job of comparison, analysis, and interpretation begins. To which species do the remains belong? Are the remains human or those of our prehuman ancestors? If not human, what do the remains tell us about our own species? When did these primates live? How did they adapt to their environment? To answer these questions, paleoanthropologists use the techniques of comparative anatomy. They compare such physical features as cranial capacity, teeth, hands, position of the pelvis, and shape of the head of the fossil remains with those of humans or other nonhuman primates. In addition to comparing physical features, paleoanthropologists look for signs of culture (such as tools) to help determine the humanity of the fossil remains. For example, if fossil remains are found in association with tools, and if it can be determined that the tools were made by these creatures, then it is likely that the remains will be considered human.

physical anthropology (biological anthropology) The subfield of anthropology that studies both human biological evolution and contemporary physical variations among peoples of the world.

paleoanthropology The study of human evolution through fossil remains.

primatology The study of nonhuman primates in their natural environments for the purpose of gaining insights into the human evolutionary process.

The work of paleoanthropologists is often tedious and must be conducted with meticulous attention to detail. Even though the quantity of fossilized materials is growing each year, paleoanthropologists have little data to analyze. Much of the evolutionary record remains underground. Of the fossils that have been found, many are partial or fragmentary, and more often than not, they are not found in association with cultural artifacts. Consequently, to fill in the human evolutionary record, physical anthropologists need to draw on the work of a number of other specialists: paleontologists (who specialize in prehistoric plant and animal life), archaeologists (who study prehistoric material culture), and geologists (who provide data on local physical and climatic conditions).

In addition to reconstructing the human evolutionary record, paleoanthropology has led to various applications of physical anthropology. For example, forensic anthropology for years has used traditional methods and theories from physical anthropology to help identify the remains of crime and disaster victims for legal purposes. Forensic anthropologists can determine from skeletal remains the age, sex, and stature of the deceased as well as other traits such as physical abnormalities, traumas (such as broken bones), and nutritional history. In recent years, forensic anthropologists have been called on to testify in murder trials. On a larger scale, some applied forensic anthropologists have headed international teams to study the physical remains of victims of mass human rights abuses. For example, in 1984 forensic anthropologist Clyde Snow helped identify some of the nine thousand people murdered by the government of Argentina between 1976 and 1983. Snow's forensic research and subsequent testimony in an Argentinean court were crucial in convicting some of the perpetrators of these mass murders. Similarly, forensic anthropologists have been working in Bosnia and Kosovo to identify the victims of Slobodan Milosevic's programs of ethnic cleansing during the 1990s. More recently, the life and work of Kathy Reichs, a forensic anthropologist and best-selling crime novelist, have inspired the prime-time TV series *Bones* (Figure 1.1).

Primatology

Since the 1950s, physical anthropologists have developed an area of specialization of their own that helps shed light on human evolution and adaptation over time and space. This field of study is known as *primatology*—the study of our nearest living relatives (apes, monkeys, and prosimians) in their natural habitats (Figure 1.2). Primatologists study the anatomy and social behavior of such nonhuman primate species as gorillas, baboons, and chimpanzees in an effort to gain clues about our own evolution as a species. Because physical anthropologists do not have the luxury of

FIGURE 1.1 Dr. Kathy Reichs, a forensic anthropologist, works with police, the courts, medical examiners, and international organizations to help identify victims of crimes, disasters, and genocide. She also served on the forensic recovery team for victims of the World Trade Center disaster of September 11, 2001.

FIGURE 1.2 Primatologist Birute Galdikas holds an orphaned adolescent orangutan at the Oranutan Foundation International Care Center in Borneo, Indonesia. Galdikas has spent more than three decades braving tropical diseases and violent encounters in the forests of Borneo to study and defend some of the world's last remaining oranutans.

observing the behavior of human ancestors several million years ago, they can learn how early humans could have responded to certain environmental conditions and changes in their developmental past by studying contemporary nonhuman primates (such as baboons and chimps) in similar environments. For example, the simple yet real division of labor among baboon troops can shed light on role specialization and social stratification in early human societies, or the rudimentary tool-making skills found among chimpanzees in Tanzania may help explain early human strategies for adapting to the environment.

Sometimes the study of primatology leads to findings that are both startling and eminently practical. While studying chimps in their natural habitat in Tanzania, primatologist Richard Wrangham noticed that young chimps occasionally ate the leaves of plants that were not part of their normal diet. Because the chimps swallowed the leaves whole, Wrangham concluded that they were not ingesting these leaves primarily for nutritional purposes. Chemical analysis of the leaves by pharmacologist Eloy Rodriquez indicated that the plant contains substantial amounts of the chemical compound thiarubrine-A, which has strong antibiotic properties. Wrangham concluded that the chimps were medicating themselves, perhaps to control internal parasites. Seeing the potential for treating human illnesses, Rodriquez and Wrangham applied for a patent. Interestingly, they use part of the proceeds from their new drug to help preserve the chimpanzee habitat in Tanzania. In Wrangham's words, "I like the idea of chimps showing us the medicine and then helping them to pay for their own conservation" (quoted in Howard 1991).

Physical Variations among Humans

Although all humans are members of the same species and therefore are capable of interbreeding, considerable physical variation exists among human populations. Some of these differences are based on visible physical traits, such as the shape of the nose, body stature, and color of the skin. Other variations are based on less visible biochemical factors, such as blood type or susceptibility to diseases.

For the first half of the twentieth century, physical anthropologists attempted to document human physical variations throughout the world by dividing the world's populations into various racial categories. A *race* was defined as a group of people who share a greater statistical frequency of genes and physical traits with one another than they do with people outside the group. Today, however, no anthropologists subscribe to the notion that races are fixed biological entities whose members all share the same physical features. Despite an enormous amount of effort devoted to classifying people into discrete racial categories during much of the twentieth century, most anthropologists do not consider these categories to be particularly useful. Today we know that the amount of genetic variation is much greater within racial groups than between racial groups. Thus, most anthropologists view these early-twentieth-century racial typologies as largely an oversimplification of our present state of genetic knowledge. (For more on race and racism, see Chapter 12.)

race A subgroup of the human population whose members share a greater number of genes and physical traits with one another than they do with members of other subgroups.

Although contemporary anthropologists continue to be interested in human physical variation, they have turned their attention to examining how human physical variations help people adapt to their environment. Physical anthropologists have found that populations with the greatest amount of melanin in their skin are found in tropical regions, whereas lighter-skinned populations generally reside in more northern latitudes. This suggests that natural selection has favored dark skin in tropical areas because it protects people from dangerous ultraviolet light. In colder climates people tend to have considerable body mass (less body surface), which is a natural protection from the deadly cold. And sickle cells, found widely in the blood of people living in sub-Saharan Africa, protect people against the ravages of malaria. These three examples illustrate how physical variations can help people adapt to their natural environments. In their investigations of how human biological variations influence adaptation, physical anthropologists draw on the work of three allied disciplines: *genetics* (the study of inherited physical traits), *population biology* (the study of the interrelationships between population characteristics and environments), and *epidemiology* (the study of the occurrence, distribution, and control of disease in populations over time).

(ideas and behavior patterns) held by people thousands, and in some cases millions, of years ago.

Archaeologists work with three types of material remains: artifacts, features, and ecofacts. *Artifacts* are objects that have been made or modified by humans and that can be removed from the site and taken to the laboratory for further analysis. Tools, arrowheads, and fragments of pottery are examples of artifacts. *Features*, like artifacts, are made or modified by people, but they cannot be readily carried away from the dig site. Archaeological features include such things as house foundations, fireplaces, and postholes (Figure 1.3). *Ecofacts* are objects found in the natural environment (such as bones, seeds, and wood) that were not made or altered by humans but were used by them. Ecofacts provide archaeologists with important data concerning the environment and how people used natural resources.

The data that archaeologists have at their disposal are selective. Not only are archaeologists limited to material remains, but also the overwhelming majority of material possessions that may have been part of a culture do not survive thousands of years under the ground. As a result, archaeologists search for fragments of material evidence (such items as projectile points, hearths, beads, and postholes) that will enable them to

Archaeology

Experts in the field of *archaeology* study the lifeways of people from the past by excavating and analyzing the material culture they have left behind. The purpose of archaeology is not to fill up museums by collecting exotic relics from prehistoric societies. Rather, it is to understand cultural adaptations of ancient peoples by at least partially reconstructing their cultures. Because archaeologists concentrate on societies of the past, they are limited to working with material culture including, in some cases, written records. From these material remains, however, archaeologists are able to infer many nonmaterial cultural aspects

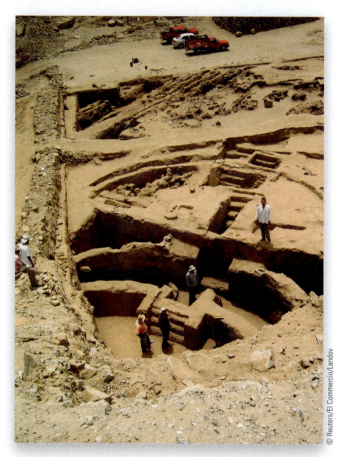

FIGURE 1.3 The archaeological ruins at Sechin Bajo, discovered in 2008, is located several hundred miles north of Lima, Peru. Build 5,500 years ago, this site is considered one of the oldest structures ever unearthed in the Americas.

genetics The study of inherited physical traits.

population biology The study of the interrelationships between population characteristics and environments.

epidemiology The study of the occurrence, distribution, and control of disease in populations.

archaeology The subfield of anthropology that focuses on the study of prehistoric and historic cultures through the excavation of material remains.

Artifacts A type of material remain (found by archaeologists) that has been made or modified by humans, such as tools and arrowheads.

features Archaeological remains that have been made or modified by people and cannot easily be carried away, such as house foundations, fireplaces, and postholes.

Ecofacts Physical remains—found by archaeologists—that were used by humans but not made or reworked by them (for example, seeds and bones).

piece together a culture. A prehistoric garbage dump is particularly revealing because the archaeologist can learn a great deal about how people lived from what they threw away. These material remains are then used to make inferences about the nonmaterial aspects of the culture (that is, values, ideas, and behaviors) being studied.

Once the archaeologist has collected the physical evidence, the difficult work of analysis and interpretation begins. By studying the bits and pieces of material culture left behind (within the context of both environmental data and anatomical remains), the archaeologist seeks to determine how the people supported themselves, whether they had a notion of an afterlife, how roles were allocated between men and women, whether some people were more powerful than others, whether the people engaged in trade with neighboring peoples, and how lifestyles have changed over time.

Present-day archaeologists work with both historic and prehistoric cultures. Historic archaeologists help to reconstruct the cultures of people who used writing and about whom historical documents have been written. For example, historical archaeologists have contributed significantly to our understanding of colonial American cultures by analyzing material remains that can supplement such historical documents as books, letters, graffiti, and government reports.

Prehistoric archaeology, on the other hand, deals with the vast segment of the human record (several million years) that predates the advent of writing about 5,500 years ago. Archaeology remains the one scientific enterprise that systematically focuses on prehistoric cultures. Consequently, it has provided us with a much longer time frame than written history for understanding the record of human development.

The relevance of studying ancient artifacts often goes beyond helping us better understand our prehistoric past. In some cases, the study of stone tools can lead to improvements in our own modern technology. To illustrate, while experimentally replicating the manufacture of stone tools, archaeologist Don Crabtree found that obsidian from the western part of the United States can be chipped to a sharp edge. When examined under an electron microscope, the cutting edge of obsidian was found to be two hundred times sharper than modern surgical scalpels. Some surgeons now use these obsidian scalpels because the healing is faster and the scarring is reduced (Sheets 1993).

Another area of applied archaeology is called *cultural resource management*. During the 1960s and 1970s, a number of preservation and environmental protection laws were passed to identify and protect cultural and historic resources (for example, landmarks, historic buildings, and archaeological sites) from being bulldozed. The laws require environmental impact studies to be conducted before the start of federally funded projects such as dams, highways, airports, or office buildings. If the building project would destroy the cultural resource, then the law requires that archaeological research be

conducted to preserve the information from the site. In response to these laws, archaeologists developed the specialty of cultural resource management (also known as *public archaeology* or *contract archaeology*).

The goal of this form of applied archaeology is to ensure that the laws are properly followed, that high-quality research is conducted, and that the data from archaeological sites are not destroyed by federally funded building projects. Cultural resource management has grown so rapidly in recent years that by the turn of the millennium about half of all professionally trained archaeologists were working in this field.

Although, typically, archaeology focuses on prehistorical and historical peoples, some archaeologists are using their techniques to study contemporary societies. For example, archaeologist William Rathje of the University of Arizona, one of the world's best known "garbologists," seeks to better understand prehistoric, historic, and *contemporary* peoples by studying what they throw away (Figure 1.4). For example, in his study of garbage in Tucson, Arizona, Rathje found some

Jim Sugar/corbis

FIGURE 1.4 Archaeologist William Rathje, shoveling debris in a landfill in San Francisco, seeks to understand cultures (both prehistoric and contemporary) by studying their waste.

cultural resource management A form of applied archaeology that involves identifying, evaluating, and sometimes excavating sites before roads, dams, and buildings are constructed.

Applying Archaeology in Post Katrina New Orleans

❃ Although we usually think of archaeology as focusing exclusively on history and prehistory, some archaeologists are finding ways to help people living in the twenty-first century. In the immediate aftermath of hurricanes Katrina and Rita, Shannon Lee Dawdy, an archaeologist from the University of Chicago, served as the liaison between the Federal Emergency Management Agency (FEMA) and Louisiana's Historic Preservation Office. Her mission was to prevent the rebuilding of New Orleans from further destroying what remained of its past and current cultural heritage. One such urban treasure damaged during the hurricanes was Holt Cemetery, the final resting place for many poor residents of a city that has had strong ties with its dead. For generations Holt Cemetery has been the gathering spot, particularly on All Souls' Day, for the living to pay their respects to the dead by decorating and adorning their grave sites with votive objects (everything from children's teddy bears to flowers to plastic jack-o'-lanterns). Dawdy tried (unsuccessfully) to convince FEMA and other officials that these votive objects, many of which were scattered throughout the cemetery by the floodwater, should not be considered debris. Rather, she argued, every effort should be made to restore the damaged site by replacing as many of these votive objects as possible. If this important place (which connects people to their dead ancestors and friends) was not restored, residents driven from New Orleans by the hurricanes would be much less likely to return to rebuild their homes and their lives. Jean Comaroff, chairperson of the University of Chicago's Department of Anthropology, summed up the value

of Dawdy's work: "The threat is great that much that was unique about New Orleans as a social and cultural world—qualities that are at once creative, poignant, and fragile—will be lost in its reconstruction" (J. Schwartz 2006: D-I). The importance of Daudy's work can be better appreciated by viewing the critically acclaimed HBO series titled *Treme*, which portrays New Orleans culture and social structure in the immediate aftermath of hurricanes Katrina and Rita.

Questions for Further Thought

1. In a single sentence, how would you describe the *significance* of Dawdy's research in post-Katrina New Orleans?

2. What areas—other than cemeteries—might contemporary archaeologists, like Dawdy, investigate in the aftermath of a natural disaster such as a hurricane or an earth quake?

3. How could archaeological research in your home community possibly lead to information that could help formulate public policy?

© Shannon Lee Dawdy, University of Chicago

---

interesting consumption patterns that had important implications for urban planners in charge of solid waste facilities. Moreover, this research supported the notion that there is always some discrepancy between what people say they do and what they actually do. When surveyed by questionnaire, 15 percent of his interviewees claimed to be beer drinkers. Yet analysis of the garbage of these same people revealed that approximately 80 percent of the households consumed beer. This sizeable discrepancy (533 percent) between real and reported behavior is useful to sociologists, medical anthropologists, and public health officials who need to address issues of health and dietary patterns.

---

anthropological linguistics The scientific study of human communication within its sociocultural context.

Historical linguistics The branch of anthropological linguistics that studies how languages emerge and change over time.

Anthropological Linguistics

The branch of the discipline that studies human speech and language is called *anthropological linguistics*. Although humans are not the only species that has systems of symbolic communication, ours is by far the most complex form. In fact, some would argue that language is the most distinctive feature of being human because without language we could not acquire and transmit our culture from one generation to the next.

Linguistic anthropology, which studies contemporary human languages as well as those of the past, is divided into four distinct branches: historical linguistics, descriptive linguistics, ethnolinguistics, and sociolinguistics.

Historical linguistics deals with the emergence of language in general and how specific languages have diverged over time. Some of the earliest anthropological interest in language focused on the historical connections between languages. For example, nineteenth-century linguists working with European languages demonstrated similarities in the sound systems between a particular language and a previous parent language from which the language was derived. By comparing contemporary languages, linguists have been able to identify certain language families and can approximate when two related languages began to diverge from each other. Today these historical linguistic techniques are used in conjunction with archaeological and biological evidence (for example, DNA). As an example, Cecil Brown (2006) established the prehistoric linguistic chronology of the common bean in the New World, which both complemented and supplemented archaeological dating techniques.

Descriptive linguistics is the study of sound systems, grammatical systems, and the meanings attached to words in specific languages. Every culture has a distinctive language with its own logical structure and set of rules for putting words and sounds together for the purpose of communicating. In its simplest form, the task of the descriptive linguist is to compile dictionaries and grammar books for previously unwritten languages.

Cultural linguistics (also known as *ethnolinguistics*) is the branch of anthropological linguistics that examines the relationship between language and culture. In any language, certain cultural aspects that are emphasized (such as types of snow among the Inuit, cows among the pastoral Maasai, or automobiles in US culture) are reflected in the vocabulary. Moreover, cultural linguists explore how different linguistic categories can affect how people categorize their experiences, how they think, and how they perceive the world around them.

The fourth branch of anthropological linguistics, known as *sociolinguistics*, examines the relationship between language and social relations. For example, sociolinguists are interested in investigating how social class influences the particular dialect a person speaks. They also study the situational use of language—that is, how people use different forms of a language depending on the social situation they find themselves in at any given time. To illustrate, the words and grammatical structures a US college student would choose when conversing with a roommate are significantly different from the linguistic style used when talking to a grandparent, a rabbi, or a potential employer during a job interview.

Anthropological linguists also engage in applied activities. After describing the structure of a language, descriptive linguists frequently take the next logical step and work with educators to plan effective strategies for teaching English as a second language. Some anthropological linguists serve as consultants to government and educational leaders responsible for setting language policy in a state or country. Anthropological linguists sometimes work with local (small-scale) minority groups whose languages are spoken by so few people that they are in danger of becoming extinct. Still other applied linguists help design foreign language and culture programs for people who are preparing to live and work abroad. Moreover, linguists like Deborah Tannen (see Chapter 11) apply their knowledge of gender differences in language to help men and women better understand one another.

For most of the twentieth century, anthropological linguists documented the vocabularies, grammars, and phonetic systems of the many unwritten languages of the world. At this point, most of the hitherto unwritten languages have been recorded or have died out (that is, lost all of their native speakers). This has led some anthropologists to suggest that the field of anthropological linguistics has essentially completed its work and should no longer be regarded as one of the major branches of anthropology. Such a view, however, is shortsighted. Because languages are constantly changing, anthropological linguists will be needed to document these changes and to show how they reflect changes in the culture as a whole. Moreover, in recent years anthropological linguists have expanded their research interests to include television advertising, linguistic aspects of popular culture, and computer jargon.

Cultural Anthropology

The branch of anthropology that deals with the study of specific contemporary cultures (*ethnography*) and the more general underlying patterns of human culture derived through cultural comparisons (*ethnology*) is called *cultural anthropology* (see Table 1.2). Before cultural anthropologists can examine cultural differences and similarities throughout the world, they must first describe the features of specific cultures in as much detail as possible. These detailed descriptions (ethnographies) are the result of extensive field studies (usually a year or two in duration) in which the anthropologist observes, talks to, and lives with the people he or she is studying. The writing of large numbers of ethnographies over the course of the twentieth century has

---

Descriptive linguistics The branch of anthropological linguistics that studies how languages are structured.

ethnolinguistics The branch of anthropological linguistics that studies the relationship between language and culture.

sociolinguistics The branch of anthropological linguistics that studies how language is used in different social contexts.

ethnography The anthropological description of a particular contemporary culture by means of direct fieldwork.

ethnology The comparative study of cultural differences and similarities.

cultural anthropology The scientific study of cultural similarities and differences wherever and in whatever form they may be found.

TABLE 1.2

Two Facets of Cultural Anthropology

Ethnography	Ethnology
Descriptive	Comparative
Based on direct fieldwork	Uses data collected by other ethnographers
Focuses on a single culture or subculture	Generalizes across cultures or subcultures

provided an empirical basis for the comparative study of cultures. In the process of developing these descriptive accounts, cultural anthropologists may provide insights into questions such as: How are the marriage customs of a group of people related to the group's economy? What effect does urban migration have on the kinship system? In what ways have supernatural beliefs helped a group of people adapt more effectively to their environment? Thus, while describing the essential features of a culture, the cultural anthropologist may also explain why certain cultural patterns exist and how they may be related to one another.

Ethnology is the comparative study of contemporary cultures, wherever they may be found. Ethnologists seek to understand both why people today and in the recent past differ in terms of ideas and behavior patterns and what all cultures in the world have in common with one another. The primary objective of ethnology is to uncover general cultural principles, that is, the "rules" that govern human behavior. Because all humans have culture and live in groups called societies, there are no populations in the world today that are not viable subjects for the ethnologist. The lifeways of Inuit living in the Arctic tundra, Greek peasants, Maasai herdsmen in Tanzania, and the residents of a retirement home in southern California have all been studied by cultural anthropologists.

Ethnographers and ethnologists face a daunting task because they describe and compare the many peoples of the world today. A small number of cultural anthropologists must deal with enormous cultural diversity (thousands of distinct cultures where people speak mutually unintelligible languages), numerous features of culture that can be compared, and a wide range of theoretical frameworks for comparing them. To describe even the least complex cultures requires many months of interviewing people and observing their behavior. Even with this large expenditure of time, rarely do contemporary ethnographers describe total cultures. Instead, they usually describe only the more outstanding features of a culture and then investigate a particular aspect or problem in greater depth.

paleopathology The study of disease in prehistoric populations.

Areas of Specialization

Because the description of a total culture is usually beyond the scope of a single ethnographer, in recent decades cultural anthropologists have tended to specialize, often identifying themselves with one or more of these five areas of specialization:

1. *Urban anthropology.* Cultural anthropologists during the first half of the twentieth century tended to concentrate their research on rural societies in non-Western areas. In the immediate post–World War II era, however, anthropologists in greater numbers turned their attention to the study of more complex urban social systems. With increases in rural-to-urban migration in many parts of the world, it was becoming more difficult to think of rural populations as isolated, insulated entities. With this increase in rural-urban interaction during the 1950s and 1960s, cultural anthropologists began to assess the impacts that cities were having on traditional rural societies. From that point it was a natural development to follow rural people into the cities to see how the two systems interacted. Thus was born the subdiscipline of urban anthropology.

   By focusing on how factors such as size, density, and heterogeneity affect customary ways of behaving, urban anthropologists in recent decades have examined such important topics as descriptive accounts of ethnic neighborhoods, rural-urban linkages, labor migration, urban kinship patterns, social network analysis, emerging systems of urban stratification, squatter settlements, and informal economies. Urban anthropology has also focused on social problems such as homelessness, race relations, poverty, social justice, unemployment, crime, and public health. Some recent studies have described the modern urban subcultures of truck drivers, cocktail waitresses, street gangs, drug addicts, skid-row alcoholics, and prostitutes. Interestingly, few studies have been conducted in the middle-class suburbs, where various forms of social problems are also found.

2. *Medical anthropology.* Another recent area of specialization is medical anthropology, which studies the relationship of biological and sociocultural factors to health, disease, and illness—now and in the past. Medical anthropology (which is only about thirty-five years old) includes a variety of perspectives and concerns, ranging from a biological pole at one end of the spectrum to a sociocultural pole at the other. Medical anthropologists with a more biological focus tend to concentrate on interests such as the role of disease in human evolution, nutrition, growth and development, and *paleopathology* (the analysis of disease in ancient populations). Medical anthropologists with more social or cultural interests focus their studies on ethnomedicine (belief

systems that affect sickness and health), medical practitioners, and the relationship between traditional and Western medical systems. Contemporary medical anthropology represents both the biological and the sociocultural approaches, but we should not think of them as separate and autonomous. In actual practice, theory and data from one approach are often used in the other.

Medical anthropology, like many other specialty areas, deals with both theoretical and applied questions of research. Because beliefs and practices about medicine and healing are part of any culture, they deserve the same type of study as other features of culture, such as economics or family patterns. Many medical anthropologists are motivated by the desire to (a) apply theories, methods, and insights to programs designed to improve health services at home and abroad and (b) serve as cultural brokers between healthcare professionals and their culturally diverse patients (Figure 1.5).

3. *Development anthropology.* Dating back to the nineteenth century, colonial powers were interested in the economic development of their colonies—which in the early days meant building infrastructure such as power plants, roads, railroads, and communication systems to support new, viable industries. Later other development projects were initiated in such areas as agriculture, education, medicine, and job training. Although anthropologists were sometimes consulted on these multimillion dollar projects, it was not until the 1960s (when development anthropology became a recognized subdiscipline) that they played a more active and comprehensive role in the development process. In the early

1960s development anthropologists focused their efforts on pointing out why and how development programs were unsuccessful because they failed to account for local cultural factors. By the 1970s and 1980s, however, development anthropologists were becoming more involved in the entire development cycle, which included project identification, design, budgetary considerations, implementation, and evaluation.

The development anthropology that has emerged in the twenty-first century is more critical and people-focused (rather than economy-focused). Many development anthropologists no longer start by asking: "How can I make this large development project successful?" Rather, they are asking: "Will this project benefit the target population?" If the answer is yes, then the new breed of twenty-first century development anthropologists will likely become involved in various aspects of the project by providing the vital local cultural information needed to make it successful. The focus is no longer on the international development agencies, governments, or multinational corporations financing the development project. Rather, the criteria for success depend on the benefits for the local populations, such as less poverty, equitable economic growth, environmental protection, and respect for human rights.

4. *Environmental anthropology.* Tracing its roots to such early ecological anthropologists as Julian Steward and Roy Rapport, environmental anthropology examines how human populations interact with the environment and, by so doing, develop solutions to current and future environmental problems. Environmental anthropologists are concerned with two fundamental questions that date back to the founding of anthropology in the nineteenth century: What role does the physical environment play in the formation and evolution of specific cultures? and How do specific sociocultural groups perceive, manage, and modify their environments? Most of the leading ecological anthropologists have demonstrated repeatedly that culture and environment cannot be treated in isolation because they are so intimately interconnected.

For much of its history, ecological/environmental anthropology focused primarily on how non-Western societies (composed of foragers, pastoralists, and small-scale farmers) conceptualized, adapted to, and transformed their natural environments. Although anthropologists in the twenty-first century are still interested in the relationships between culture and the natural environment per se, they have expanded their research interests to include theories and approaches useful for addressing contemporary problems of environmental degradation. These concerns include (but are not limited to) conflicts over

Gilles Peress/Magnum Photos

FIGURE 1.5 Physician and medical anthropologist, Dr. Paul Farmer, examines an AIDS patient at the Partners in Health Hospital in Cange, located in the central plateau of Haiti. For more than two decades Dr. Farmer has been working with the Haitian people on a successful treatment program for infectious diseases such as tuberculosis and AIDS.

land use, biodiversity conservation, air and water pollution, deforestation, soil erosion, human rights issues, sustainable development, mineral extraction, and the effects of biochemicals on the health of local populations. Often working collaboratively with scholars from many other disciplines, environmental anthropologists assist policy makers and planners by providing valuable insights into the local cultures of the people who are negatively affected by environmental changes.

5. *Psychological anthropology.* Psychological anthropology, one of the oldest subspecialty areas of cultural anthropology, looks at the relationship between culture and the psychological makeup of individuals and groups. Concerned with the relationships between psychological processes and cultural factors, psychological anthropologists examine how culture may affect personality, cognition, attitudes, and emotions.

The early practitioners of psychological anthropology between the 1920s and 1950s—namely, Ruth Benedict, Franz Boas, and Edward Sapir— were interested in the relationship between culture and personality. Many of these early theorists studied the effects of cultural features (such as feeding, weaning, and toilet training) on personality; but some, led by Abraham Kardiner, were interested in how *group* personality traits could be reflected in entire cultures. Stimulated by the need to know more about America's allies and enemies during World War II, some psychological anthropologists turned their attention to "national character studies" of Russia (Geoffrey Gorer and John Rickman in 1949), whereas Benedict wrote her classic study of the Japanese national character in 1946. Today these studies are not taken seriously because of the methodological difficulties involved in generalizing about large and diverse societies. Since the 1960s, psychological anthropology has moved away from these broad national character studies and has focused on a more narrowly drawn set of problems, such as symbolism, cognition, and consciousness in specific societies. Methodologies have become more varied, statistics have been more widely used, and psychological anthropologists have collaborated with those from other disciplines, such as psychology and linguistics.

These five areas are only a partial list of the specializations within cultural anthropology. Other specialties include agricultural anthropology, legal anthropology, educational anthropology (Figure 1.6), the anthropology of religion, business anthropology, economic anthropology, political anthropology, the anthropology of tourism, the anthropology of work, and nutritional anthropology.

Bonnie jacobs/iStockphoto.com

FIGURE 1.6 Some applied anthropologists conduct research in multicultural and multi-racial classrooms such as this one in the United States. Their findings enable teachers to better understand the cultural backgrounds of their students.

Despite this four-field division, the discipline of anthropology has a long-standing tradition of emphasizing the interrelations among these four subfields. One of the major sections of the American Anthropological Association is the General Anthropology Division (GAD), founded in 1984 to foster scholarly exchange on the central questions unifying the four subfields of the discipline. Moreover, in recent years there has been considerable blurring of the boundaries among the four branches. For example, the specialized area known as medical anthropology draws heavily from both physical and cultural anthropology; educational anthropology addresses issues that bridge the gap between cultural anthropology and linguistics; and sociobiology looks at the interaction between culture and biology.

Although a four-field approach to anthropology has prevailed in academic departments for the past century, a growing number of anthropologists are raising the question of dividing anthropology along subdisciplinary lines. Some departments (such as those at Duke and Stanford) have already created separate departments of biological and cultural anthropology. On the other hand, other departments (such as those at Emory and the universities of Pennsylvania and Florida) have purposefully moved toward greater integration of cultural and biological anthropology. Whether a department divides or integrates will be determined by broad intellectual forces. Nevertheless, according to Mary Shenk (2006: 6), "Multiple paths appear to be both possible and desirable."

While on a trip to Taipei, Matt Erskine made plans to have dinner with his former college roommate John, who is Taiwanese. After they caught up on each other's lives, Matt learned that John was about to leave his present job to start his own consulting business. However, before launching the new business, John told Matt that he must wait until the telephone company granted him the proper telephone number. Given all of the work John had done to get his new business started, Matt thought that having the proper telephone number was a minor obstacle that need not delay the opening of the business. But John insisted that he could not start his new enterprise until he had the right telephone number. Matt got the impression that John, perhaps fearful of taking risks, was using the telephone number as a lame excuse for not launching the business. But Matt misinterpreted this situation because he failed to understand some basic features of contemporary culture in Taiwan.

Despite their great economic leap into the global economy, many Taiwanese still retain beliefs in supernatural forces. This is particularly true about certain numbers. Some primary numbers, associated with negative things such as death or excrement, are to be avoided at all costs. Other numbers, associated with positive things such as money, growth, and wealth, should be used in house addresses, license plates, and telephone numbers. In Taiwan the telephone company receives many requests for numbers that include the lucky numbers, leaving those with unlucky numbers unused. Thus, John believed strongly that unless he got a telephone number with lucky numbers in it, his business would be doomed from the start.

Guiding Principles

For the past century, cultural anthropology has distinguished itself from other disciplines in the humanities and social sciences by following several guiding principles. Although other disciplines have adopted some of these major themes over the decades, they remain central to the discipline of cultural anthropology.

Holism

A distinguishing feature of the discipline of anthropology is its holistic approach to the study of human groups. Anthropological *holism* is evidenced in a number of important ways. First, the anthropological approach involves both biological and sociocultural aspects of humanity—that is, people's genetic endowment as well as what they acquire from their environment after birth. Second, anthropology has the longest possible

time frame, from the earliest beginnings of humans several million years ago right up to the present. Third, anthropology is holistic to the extent that it studies all varieties of people wherever they may be found, from East African pastoralists to Korean factory workers. And, finally, anthropologists study many different aspects of human experience, including family structure, marital regulations, house construction, methods of conflict resolution, means of livelihood, religious beliefs, language, space usage, and art.

In the past, cultural anthropologists have made every effort to be holistic by covering as many aspects of a culture as possible in the total cultural context. More recently, however, the accumulated information from all over the world has become so vast that most anthropologists have needed to become more specialized or focused. This is called a *problem-oriented research approach*. To illustrate, one anthropologist may concentrate on marital patterns, whereas another may focus on farming and land-use patterns. Despite the recent trend toward specialization, anthropologists continue to analyze their findings within a wider cultural context. Moreover, when all of the various specialties within the discipline are viewed together, they represent a comprehensive or holistic view of the human condition.

Ethnocentrism

While waiting to cross the street in Mumbai, India, a US tourist stood next to a local resident, who proceeded to blow his nose, without handkerchief or tissue, into the street. The tourist's reaction was instantaneous and unequivocal: *How disgusting!* he thought. He responded to this cross-cultural incident by evaluating the Indian's behavior on the basis of standards of etiquette established by his own culture. According to those standards, it is considered proper to use a handkerchief in such a situation. But if the man from Mumbai were to see the US tourist blowing his nose into a handkerchief, he would be equally repulsed, thinking it strange indeed for the man to blow his nose into a handkerchief and then put the handkerchief back into his pocket and carry it around for the rest of the day.

Both the American and the Indian are evaluating each other's behavior based on the standards of their own cultural assumptions and practices. This way of responding to culturally different behavior is known as *ethnocentrism*: the belief that one's own culture is superior to all others. In other words, it means viewing the

holism A perspective in anthropology that attempts to study a culture by looking at all parts of the system and how those parts are interrelated.

ethnocentrism The practice of viewing the cultural features of other societies in terms of one's own.

rest of the world through the narrow lens of one's own cultural perspective.

Incidents of ethnocentrism are extensive. For example, we can see ethnocentrism operating in the historical accounts of the American Revolutionary War by both British and American historians. According to US historians, George Washington was a folk hero of epic proportions. He led his underdog Continental Army successfully against the larger, better-equipped redcoats; he threw a coin across the Potomac River; and he was so incredibly honest that he turned himself in for chopping down a cherry tree. What a guy! But according to many British historians, Washington was a thug and a hooligan. Many of Washington's troops were the descendants of debtors and prisoners who could not make it in England. Moreover Washington did not fight fairly. Whereas the British were gentlemanly about warfare (for example, standing out in open fields in their bright red coats, shooting at the enemy), Washington's troops went sneaking around ambushing the British. Even though the US and British historians are describing the same set of historical events, their own biased cultural perspectives produce two different interpretations.

And, ethnocentrism is still very much in evidence in the twenty-first century. Sometimes our own ethnocentrism can startle us when we find ourselves in a different cultural setting. A particularly revealing episode occurred when a US educator visited a Japanese classroom for the first time. On the wall of the classroom was a brightly colored map of the world. But something was wrong: directly in the center of the map (where he had expected to see the United States) was Japan. To his surprise, the Japanese did not view the United States as the center of the world. Because this was a map produced by Japanese, rather than US, cartographers, the Japanese placed Japan in the center of the map with North America in the outlying fringes.

It should be quite obvious why ethnocentrism is so pervasive throughout the world. Because most people are raised in a single culture and never learn about other cultures during their lifetime, it is only logical that their own way of life—their values, attitudes, ideas, and ways of behaving—seems to be the most natural. Our ethnocentrism should not be a source of embarrassment because it is a natural by-product of growing up in any society. In fact, from a functionalist perspective, ethnocentrism may serve the positive societal function of enhancing group solidarity. Even though ethnocentrism is present in all cultures, it nevertheless serves as a major obstacle to the understanding of other cultures, which is, after all, the major objective of

cultural anthropology. Although we cannot eliminate ethnocentrism totally, we can reduce it. By becoming aware of our own ethnocentrism, we can temporarily set aside our own value judgments long enough to learn how other cultures operate.

Cultural Relativism

Since the beginning of the twentieth century, the discipline of anthropology has led a vigorous campaign against the perils of ethnocentrism. As cultural anthropologists began to conduct empirical fieldwork among the different cultures of the world, they recognized a need for dispassionate and objective descriptions of the people they were studying. Following the lead of Franz Boas in the United States and Bronislaw Malinowski in Britain, twentieth-century anthropologists have participated in a tradition that calls on the researcher to strive to prevent his or her own cultural values from coloring the descriptive accounts of the people under study.

According to Boas, the father of modern anthropology in the United States, anthropologists can achieve that level of detachment by practicing *cultural relativism*. This is the notion that any part of a culture (such as an idea, a thing, or a behavior pattern) must be viewed in its proper cultural context rather than from the viewpoint of the observer's culture. Rather than asking, How does this fit into *my* culture?, the cultural relativist asks, How does a cultural item fit into the rest of the cultural system of which it is a part? First formulated by Boas and later developed by one of his students, Melville Herskovits (1972), cultural relativism rejects the notion that any culture, including our own, possesses a set of absolute standards by which all other cultures can be judged. Cultural relativity is a cognitive tool that helps us understand why people think and act the way they do.

Perhaps a specific example of cultural relativity will help to clarify the concept. Anthropologists over the years have described a number of cultural practices from around the world that appear to be morally reprehensible to most Westerners. For example, the Dani of western New Guinea customarily cut off a finger from the hand of any close female relative of a man who dies; the Kikuyu of Kenya routinely remove part of the genitalia of teenage girls to suppress their maleness; and the Dodoth of Uganda extract the lower front teeth of young girls in an attempt to make them more attractive. Some Inuit groups practice a custom that would strike the typical Westerner as inhumane at best: When aging parents become too old to carry their share of the workload, they are left out in the cold to die. If we view such a practice by the standards of our Western culture (that is, ethnocentrically), we would have to conclude that it is cruel and heartless, hardly a way to treat those who brought you into the world. But the cultural relativist would look at this form of homicide in the context of

---

cultural relativism The idea that cultural traits are best understood when viewed within the cultural context of which they are a part.

the total culture of which it is a part. John Friedl and John Pfeiffer (1977: 331) provide a culturally relativistic explanation of this custom:

> It is important to know … that this … [custom] is not practiced against the will of the old person. It is also necessary to recognize that this is an accepted practice for which people are adequately prepared throughout their lives, and not some kind of treachery sprung upon an individual as a result of a criminal conspiracy. Finally, it should be considered in light of the ecological situation in which the Eskimos [sic] live. Making a living in the Arctic is difficult at best, and the necessity of feeding an extra mouth, especially when there is little hope that the individual will again become productive in the food-procurement process, would mean that the whole group would suffer. It is not a question of Eskimos not liking old people, but rather a question of what is best for the entire group. We would not expect—and indeed we do not find—this practice to exist where there was adequate food to support those who were not able to contribute to the hunting effort.

There is a problem with taking the notion of cultural relativism too literally. If cultural relativism is taken to its logical extreme, we would have to conclude that absolutely no behavior found in the world would be immoral provided that the people who practice it concur that it is morally acceptable or that it performs a function for the well-being of the society. Practicing cultural relativism, however, does not require that we view all cultural practices as morally equivalent; that is, not all cultural practices are equally worthy of tolerance and respect. To be certain, some cultural practices (such as genocide) are morally indefensible within any cultural context. Also, keep in mind that to practice cultural relativism does not require that you give up your own culture and practice another. In fact, it does not even require that you like, or approve of, the other culture. Yet, if our goal is to *understand* human behavior in its myriad forms, then cultural relativism can help us identify the inherent logic behind certain ideas and customs.

Emic versus Etic Approaches

Another feature of cultural anthropology that distinguishes it from other social science disciplines is its emphasis on viewing another culture from the perspective of an insider. For decades anthropologists have made the distinction between the *emic approach* and the *etic approach*, which are terms borrowed from linguistics. The emic approach (derived from the word *phonemic*) refers to the insider view, which seeks to describe another culture in terms of the categories, concepts, and perceptions of the people being studied. By contrast, the

etic approach (derived from the word *phonetic*) refers to the outsider view, in which anthropologists use their own categories and concepts to describe the culture under analysis. For the last half century, there has been an ongoing debate among anthropologists as to which approach is more valuable for the scientific study of comparative cultures.

A radically emic approach was taken by a group of US anthropologists (known as ethnoscientists) during the 1950s and 1960s. In an attempt to obtain a more realistic understanding of another culture, the ethnoscientists insisted on the insider approach. More recently the interpretive school of cultural anthropology has strongly supported the emic approach to research. This school, represented by the late Clifford Geertz and others, holds that because human behavior stems from the way people perceive and classify the world around them, the only legitimate strategy is the emic, or insider, approach to cultural description. At the opposite end of the debate are the cultural materialists, best represented by the late Marvin Harris. Starting from the assumption that material conditions determine thoughts and behaviors (not the other way around), cultural materialists emphasize the viewpoint of the ethnographer, not the native informant. There is no consensus on this issue, and each cultural anthropologist must make a decision about which approach to take when doing research. (More in-depth discussions of these three schools of anthropology are found in Chapter 4.)

Contributions of Anthropology

One of the major contributions of anthropology to the understanding of the human condition stems from the broad task it has set for itself. Whereas disciplines such as economics, political science, and psychology are considerably narrower in scope, anthropology has carved out for itself the task of examining all aspects of humanity for all periods of time and for all parts of the globe. Because of the magnitude of this task, anthropologists must draw on theories and data from a number of other disciplines in the humanities, the social sciences, and the physical sciences. As a result, anthropology is in a good position to integrate the various disciplines dealing with human physiology and culture.

---

emic approach A perspective in ethnography that uses the concepts and categories that are relevant and meaningful to the culture under analysis.

etic approach A perspective in ethnography that uses the concepts and categories of the anthropologist's culture to describe another culture.

Enhancing Understanding

In comparison with people in other countries, people from the United States generally have less knowledge about other countries and other cultures. The level of knowledge about other parts of the world has been dismal for decades and is not improving to any significant degree. Knowledge about the rest of the world is particularly important today because the world has become increasingly interconnected. Forty years ago it made relatively little difference whether North Americans spoke a second language, knew the name of the British prime minister, or held a passport. But now, in the twenty-first century, we live in a world in which decisions made in Geneva or Tokyo send ripples throughout the rest of the world.

For the past several decades, the world has experienced globalization, which involves rapidly growing free-market economies, the lowering of tariff barriers, and the worldwide use of high-speed information technology. This recent intensification of the flow of money, goods, services, and information to all parts of the globe has greatly accelerated culture change and has made the study of different cultures more complex.

Increasing numbers of people today are moving, both geographically and through cyberspace, outside their own familiar cultural borders, causing dramatic increases in cross-cultural contact and the potential for culture change. Through its distinctive methodology of long-term, intensive, participant-observation research, cultural anthropology offers a more in depth look at how local cultural groups are reacting to the process of globalization. Although many pundits discuss the consequences of globalization by talking to only government and business leaders, cultural anthropologists are more likely to see what is actually occurring on the ground and how the local people themselves talk about their life experiences in a time of rapid globalization.

Still another contribution of anthropology is that it helps us better understand ourselves. The early Greeks claimed that the educated person was the person with self-knowledge ("know thyself"). One of the best ways to gain self-knowledge is to know as much as possible about one's own culture—that is, to understand the forces that shape our thinking, values, and behaviors. And the best way of learning about our culture is to examine the similarities and differences between ourselves and others. The anthropological

APPLIED PERSPECTIVE

Applying Anthropology to the Field of Economic Development

❀ Ann Dunham Soetoro, a cultural anthropologist who spent many years studying local craftsmen and economically depressed peoples in rural Indonesia, provides a shining example of the type of understanding derived from anthropological fieldwork and how that understanding can be applied to the solution of societal problems. After fourteen years of living with and studying the inhabitants of an isolated rural village, she wrote a doctoral dissertation of more than a thousand pages in 1992 titled "Peasant Blacksmithing in Indonesia: Surviving Against All Odds."

Owing to her long-term, in-depth, participant-observation research, Soetoro was able to challenge many popular misperceptions about politically and economically marginalized people. For example, she demonstrated that the people she studied were not substantially different from more affluent Western capitalists in their economic needs, beliefs, and aspirations. Village craftsmen, she argued, were highly entrepreneurial and interested in profits and, in fact, had been this way for generations. Based on these findings, she concluded that the poverty of people in Central Java was not the result of a "culture of impoverishment" (passed on from generation to generation) but rather stemmed from a lack of capital to invest in their business enterprises. In other words, she did not blame the poor for their economic marginalization.

With such understandings, Soetoro's work had important implications for economic development programs in Indonesia and elsewhere throughout the world. The best approach for ameliorating poverty, according to Soetoro, was through micro-credit programs, whereby artisans and other small-scale entre-

preneurs were given small loans to finance their business operations. In fact, before her death in 1995, Soetoro was one of the pioneers of micro-financing programs for the poor, which have become widespread and successful in many parts of the developing world (see, for example, the description of the Grameen Bank in Bangladesh in Chapter 11).

Soetoro's work illustrates an important lesson from cultural anthropology. According to anthropologist Michael Dove (2009), a long-time friend and colleague of Soetoro:

> No nation—even if it is our bitterest enemy—is incomprehensible. Anthropology shows that people who seem very different from us behave according to systems of logic, and that these systems can be grasped if we approach them with the sort of patience and respect that Dr. Soetoro practiced in her work.

Oh, incidentally, did we mention that Soetoro was the mother of President Barack Obama? Do you think her anthropological perspective and cross-cultural sensitivities have had an influence on the thinking of her son?

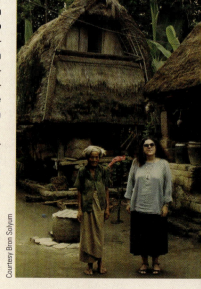

Courtesy Bron Solyum

perspective, with its emphasis on the comparative study of cultures, should lead us to the conclusion that our culture is just one way of life among many found in the world and that it represents one way (among many possible ways) to adapt to a particular set of environmental conditions. Through the process of contrasting and comparing, we gain a fuller understanding of other cultures as well as our own, which then allows us to operate more effectively (both personally and professionally) in our increasingly interconnected world.

Applying Anthropological Concepts to Social Problems

As we stated at the start of this chapter, cultural anthropology has relevance for all of us, in both our personal and professional lives. Cultural anthropology, like other social science disciplines, engages in both basic and applied research. Basic research is dedicated to gaining scientific knowledge for its own sake. Applied research, on the other hand, seeks to gain scientifically obtained knowledge for the sake of informing public policy and solving particular societal problems. In other words, the fields of applied (or practicing) anthropology are aimed at putting to use the knowledge anthropology has produced over the years. Interest in applying anthropology has increased over the past several decades. The number of graduate and undergraduate courses in applied anthropology has increased, as has the number of people with masters and doctorate degrees finding employment outside of academic settings. Applied and practicing anthropologists usually work in nonacademic settings such as hospitals, government agencies, international development agencies, public health organizations, law firms specializing in immigration law, and for-profit businesses. For a list of the types of nonacademic careers anthropology students qualify for, see Table 1.3.

Among the many practical (nonacademic) careers opening up to cultural anthropologists today is *new product developer* hired by design firms. Research and design firms, which develop new products, are actively recruiting anthropologists to help them gain deeper insights into their customers through ethnographic research. One such cultural anthropologist, Susan Squires, who has worked in product development for more than a decade, conducted participant-observation research on US families during breakfast time (National Association of Practicing Anthropologists [NAPA] website 2012, practicinganthropology.org). Her research not only has shed light on new ways of thinking about food consumption in the mornings, but it has also led to the development of a successful new breakfast food product. By actually sitting at the breakfast table with parents and their children, Squires learned a number of interesting features about

TABLE 1.3

Nonacademic Career Opportunities in Anthropology

Subfield	Examples
Physical anthropology	Forensic specialist with law enforcement
	Museum curator
	Genetic counselor
	Human rights investigator
	Zoologist or primatologist
	Public health official
Archaeology	Cultural resource manager
	Museum curator
	Environmental impact specialist
	Historical archaeologist
	Contract (salvage) archaeologist
Anthropological linguistics	English-as-a-Second Language teacher
	International business trainer
	Foreign language teacher
	Cross-cultural advertising or marketing specialist
	Translator or interpreter
Cultural anthropology	International business consultant
	Cross-cultural consultant in hospitals
	Museum curator
	International economic development worker
	Cross-cultural trainer
	International human resources manager
	School educator
	Immigration or refugee counselor

the morning meal for the modern US family in the twenty-first century:

- With both parents working, children have to be dropped off at school or day care relatively early, and consequently breakfast time is hectic. Children often eat "on the run" rather than sitting down to a large traditional breakfast.

- Because children are not hungry when they wake up at 6:30 in the morning, they often leave the house at 7:00 without eating much of anything.

- Both children and adults eat bananas because they are nutritious, portable, disposable, and fun to eat.

- Parents, children, and even grandparents, although agreeing that breakfast is an important meal, have different ideas about what constitutes a good breakfast. Mothers believe that breakfast food should be nutritious and free of preservatives; fathers prefer less nutritional "comfort food"; grandparents think that the best breakfast is warm and high in cholesterol (bacon, eggs, and buttered toast); and children prefer sweet foods such as Fruit Loops, donuts, or pancakes with plenty of maple syrup.

If a new breakfast food product were developed, it would have to meet the needs of a number of family members. For example, it would need to be nutritious, like a banana, portable, disposable, versatile, and fun to eat. Based on her ethnographic research—which determined *actual* eating patterns rather than asking people what they had for breakfast—Squires developed a new breakfast food product designed for the two-parent, working family on the go called "Go-Gurt." The first yogurt served in a tube, Go-Gurt is a healthy, high-protein food; it is smooth and creamy and comes in a number of fun and tasty flavors such as Strawberry Splash and Cool Cotton Candy (Figure 1.7). This alternative breakfast supplement, developed by an anthropologist and based on ethnographic research, had sales of more than $37 million during its first year on the market.

Is cultural anthropology practical for our everyday lives? Stay tuned for many other examples of how anthropological data, insights, research, methods, and theories inform a wide range of professions, some of which *you* might be practicing in the not-too-distant future.

Building Skills for the Twenty-First Century

As discussed in the preceding section, the study of cultural anthropology has relevance to our everyday lives. The data, concepts, and insights derived from the study of other cultures can help us better meet

FIGURE 1.7 Applied cultural anthropologist Susan Squires, by conducting participant-observation research on eating patterns of U.S. families at breakfast time, has contributed to the development of a new breakfast food product called "Go-gurts."

© Tom and Dee Ann McCarthy/Corbis

our professional goals and lead more satisfying lives in a multicultural society. But the process of studying cultural anthropology is also valuable because of the skills and competencies that it helps develop. Activities such as taking courses about different cultures, participating in local internships with international organizations, living in the university's international dormitory, and participating in study-abroad programs all combine to provide students with valuable carryover skills that go beyond the mere mastery of subject content.

Educators have written volumes concerning the behavioral traits, skills, and competencies needed for success in the twenty-first century. Although many of these writers have put a unique spin on their own list of competencies, there remains a basic core on which most can agree. These skills involve developing a broad perspective, appreciating other points of view, operating comfortably in ambiguous situations, working effectively as part of cross-cultural teams, and becoming emotionally resilient, open-minded, and perceptually aware. These traits have been identified as essential for coping with a world that has become increasingly interdependent. And because the study of cultural anthropology involves immersing oneself in other cultures, it is perhaps the best training ground for developing those competencies. How does the study of cultural anthropology help us develop the skills and competencies needed for the twenty-first century?

Develop a Broad Perspective

This skill involves seeing the big picture and the interrelatedness of the parts. A basic anthropological strategy for understanding other cultures is to look at a cultural feature from within its original cultural context rather than looking at it from the perspective of one's own culture. In other words, the student of anthropology is continually being asked to analyze a part of a culture in relationship to the whole. What better way to develop this type of systems thinking?

Appreciate Other Perspectives

Being inquisitive, nonjudgmental, and open to new ways of thinking is vital if we are to adapt to ever-changing environments. This involves, essentially, a willingness to learn and postpone making evaluations until more facts are known. Such a capacity also requires suppressing one's ego and letting go of old paradigms. It does not mean giving up one's cultural values in favor of others. But it does entail (at least temporarily) letting go of cultural certainty, learning how other cultures view us, and being willing to see the internal logic of another culture. This is exactly what students of cultural anthropology are encouraged to do in order to learn about other cultures.

Balance Contradictions

A major requirement for working and living effectively in a global society is to be able to balance contradictory needs and demands rather than trying to eliminate them. Contradictions and conflicts should be seen as opportunities, not as liabilities. Conflicting values, behaviors, and ideas are a fact of life in today's world. The study of cultural anthropology provides insights into the nature of the world's diversity and how each culture is a logical and coherent entity. When anthropology students are exposed to logical alternatives to their own ways of thinking and behaving, they learn to cope with differences and contradictions and actually use these differences for the sake of achieving synergy.

Emphasize Global Teamwork

Success in the twenty-first century requires an emphasis on cultural awareness and cross-cultural teamwork, not just personal awareness and individual mastery (Figure 1.8). Both private and public institutions are becoming increasingly more global in focus. For example, foreign subsidiaries, joint ventures with foreign firms, and overseas facilities are commonplace in the world of business. If young adults are to be successful at working within and leading these culturally complex organizations, they will need to know the underlying cultural assumptions of the diverse people on those multicultural teams. There is no academic discipline in higher education today that addresses this competency better than cultural anthropology.

FIGURE 1.8 The study of cultural anthropology prepares people for working in the global economy of the twenty-first century.

Develop Cognitive Complexity

Citizens of the new millennium need what is referred to as *cognitive complexity*, which is made up of the twin abilities of differentiating and integrating. Differentiation involves being able to see how a single entity is composed of a number of different parts; integration, on the other hand, involves the capacity to identify how the various parts are interconnected. The cognitively complex person is able to engage in both types of thinking and can move comfortably between the two. One must be able to focus on the unique needs of the local situation while at the same time understanding how it fits into the operations of the total organization. The study of cultural anthropology encourages one to examine another culture as well as one's own, compare the two, and understand the relationship of both cultures to the generalized concept of culture. Thus, the student of anthropology gets practice at becoming cognitively complex by moving from the specific parts to the whole and back again.

Develop Perceptual Acuity

Living and working in the twenty-first century require people to be perceptually acute. We need to accurately derive meaning from interactions with others from a wide variety of cultures and subcultures. This involves being attentive to both verbal and nonverbal communication by being an active listener, deriving meaning from social context, and being sensitive to the feelings of others and to one's effect on others. Studying other cultures—and particularly living in other cultures—forces the anthropology student to derive meaning not only from the words exchanged in cross-cultural encounters but also from the nonverbal cues, the social context, and the assumptions embedded in the other culture.

Thus, a number of skills and capacities that are considered essential for effective living and working in the twenty-first century can be mastered while studying cultural anthropology. Although a mere exposure to cultural anthropology does not guarantee that these skills will be developed, the comparative study of the world's cultural diversity and shared heritage is the single best classroom for acquiring these competencies. Even if you do not major in anthropology, however, you can develop skills for the twenty-first century by doing what anthropologists do—that is, throwing themselves into other cultures by traveling and living abroad, either before, during, or after college. For example, an increasing number of recent high school graduates are opting to take a "gap year," a time to travel and intern with organizations abroad before attending college. According to the Higher Education Research Institute, 1.2 percent of all students accepted to colleges and universities deferred admission to take a gap year

(Strauss 2012). In addition, it has become increasingly important for university students to have some type of experiential international learning opportunity during their undergraduate careers. Over the past decade, the number of students in US colleges and universities who study abroad has doubled, with approximately six thousand programs sending students to more than a hundred countries. Moreover an appreciable number of college graduates (both anthropology and nonanthropology majors) are beginning to figure out the value of immersing oneself in a different culture. It has been estimated (Chura 2006) that approximately thirty-five thousand recent US college graduates have taken a year or two off to travel and work in a culture different from their own. In most cases this is not frivolous "bumming around" but rather a way of developing vital global skills for the twenty-first century. For many it has been a way to leverage their position in the job market when they return home.

The Bottom Line: Understanding Other Cultures

This book, and indeed cultural anthropology as a discipline, focuses on understanding other cultures, wherever they may be found. Although a large part of gaining this understanding involves acquiring accurate information on the world's cultures, it also involves learning about one's own culture. However, what we know, or think we know, about our own culture is not necessarily perceived in the same way by culturally different people. In other words, we may see ourselves as holding a particular value or cultural trait, but then we describe that trait in only the most positive ways. Those looking at us from the outside, however, are more likely to see some of the negative implications as well.

These different interpretations of our values by people from other cultures can be illustrated in a number of ways. For example, whereas people in North America place a high value of individualism and independence, people from other cultures often place a higher value on collectivism, cooperation, and interdependence, and therefore, tend to see us as selfish, unloyal, superficial in our relations, and unwilling to meet our social obligations to others and to our society in general. Or North Americans tend to be youth-oriented to the extent that young people are held in higher esteem than old people. It is believed that the young are energetic, resourceful, enthusiastic, resilient, forward-thinking, and more tech-savvy than their elders—all traits that are associated with high levels of productivity. This high value on youth, however, is not universally held by many cultures in Asia, Africa, or South America, where older people are afforded the highest status because they are thought to be the wisest, most thoughtful, and most trustworthy segment of society. People from societies that hold elders in the highest esteem, cannot understand why we North Americans have younger people supervising older people in the workplace, make jokes about older people and the aging process, and generally treat our elders with such disrespect, or perhaps even worse, neglect. In short, they view our emphasis on youth as both immoral and counterproductive because we are not using the wisdom, experience, and competencies of older citizens for the betterment of society.

Thus, if cultural anthropology is to help us function more effectively in an increasingly interconnected world, we will have to focus on accomplishing three tasks: understanding culture-specific information about other cultures, understanding our own culture, and understanding how culturally different people view us and our cultural patterns. (For excellent ethnographic accounts of how foreign scholars view US culture, see DeVita and Armstrong 2001 and Fujita and Sano 2001.)

Summary

1. The academic discipline of anthropology involves the study of the biological and cultural origins of humans. The subject matter of anthropology is wide-ranging, including fossil remains, nonhuman primate anatomy and behavior, artifacts from past cultures, past and present languages, and all of the prehistoric, historic, and contemporary cultures of the world.

2. As practiced in the United States, the discipline of anthropology follows an integrated four-field approach comprising physical anthropology, archaeology, anthropological linguistics, and cultural anthropology. All four subdisciplines have both theoretical and applied components.

3. The subdiscipline of physical anthropology focuses on three primary concerns: paleoanthropology (deciphering the biological record of human evolution through the study of fossil remains), primatology (the study of nonhuman primate anatomy and behavior for the purpose of gaining insights

into human adaptation to the environment), and studies in human physical variations (race) and how biological variations contribute to adaptation to one's environment.

4. The subfield of archaeology has as its primary objective the reconstruction of past cultures, both historic and prehistoric, from the material objects the cultures leave behind.

5. Anthropological linguistics, which studies both present and past languages, is divided into four major subdivisions: historical linguistics (studying the emergence and divergence of languages over time), descriptive linguistics (analyzing the structure of phonetic and grammar systems in contemporary languages), ethnolinguistics (exploring the relationship between language and culture), and sociolinguistics (understanding how social relations affect language).

6. Cultural anthropology focuses on the study of contemporary cultures wherever they are found in the world. One part of the task of cultural anthropology involves describing particular cultures (ethnography), and the other part involves comparing two or more cultures (ethnology). Cultural anthropologists tend to specialize in areas such as urban anthropology, medical anthropology, development anthropology, environmental anthropology, and psychological anthropology, among others.

7. A long-standing tradition in anthropology is the holistic approach. The discipline is holistic (or comprehensive) in four important respects: It looks at both the biological and the cultural aspects of human behavior; it encompasses the longest possible time frame by looking at contemporary, historic, and prehistoric societies; it examines human cultures in every part of the world; and it studies many different aspects of human cultures.

8. There are essentially two ways to respond to unfamiliar cultures. One way is ethnocentrically—that is,

through the lens of one's own cultural perspective. The other way is from the perspective of a cultural relativist—that is, within the context of the other culture. Cultural anthropologists strongly recommend the second mode, although they are aware of certain limitations.

9. Cultural anthropologists distinguish between the emic (insider) approach, which uses native categories, and the etic (outsider) approach, which describes a culture in terms of the categories, concepts, and perceptions of the anthropologist.

10. The study of anthropology is valuable from a number of different viewpoints. From the perspective of the social and behavioral sciences, cultural anthropology is particularly valuable for testing theories about human behavior within the widest possible cross-cultural context. For the individual, the study of different cultures provides a much better understanding of one's own culture and develops valuable leadership skills. From a societal point of view, the understanding of different cultures can contribute to the solution of pressing societal problems.

11. This textbook takes an *applied* perspective. This means that, in addition to surveying the content material of cultural anthropology, this book takes a number of opportunities to emphasize how the theories, methods, and insights of cultural anthropology can be used to help solve societal problems, both at home and abroad.

12. The discipline of cultural anthropology helps students develop the skills and competencies needed to live in the twenty-first century, including developing a broad perspective, appreciating other perspectives, balancing contradictions, emphasizing global teamwork, developing cognitive complexity, and developing perceptual acuity.

Key Terms

physical anthropology (biological anthropology)
paleoanthropology
primatology
race
genetics
population biology

epidemiology
archaeology
artifact
features
ecofacts
cultural resource management

anthropological linguistics
historical linguistics
descriptive linguistics
ethnolinguistics
sociolinguistics
ethnography
ethnology

cultural anthropology
paleopathology
holism
ethnocentrism
cultural relativism
emic approach
etic approach

Critical Thinking Questions

1. In a single unambiguous sentence, how are the concepts of ethnocentrism and cultural relativism polar opposites of one another?

2. One of the new subspecialties of cultural anthropology is the anthropology of tourism. What type of research do you think this new type of anthropologist typically conducts, and how can the findings from this research be applied to contribute to the solution of societal problems?

3. The discipline of anthropology studies the human condition from a cultural *and* a biological perspective. Can you think of some examples of the interrelatedness of culture and biology from your own life?

Online Study Resources

CourseMate

Access chapter-specific learning tools including learning objectives, practice quizzes, videos, flash cards, glossaries, web links, and more in your Cultural Anthropology CourseMate. Login to www.cengagebrain.com to access the resources your instructor has assigned and to purchase materials.

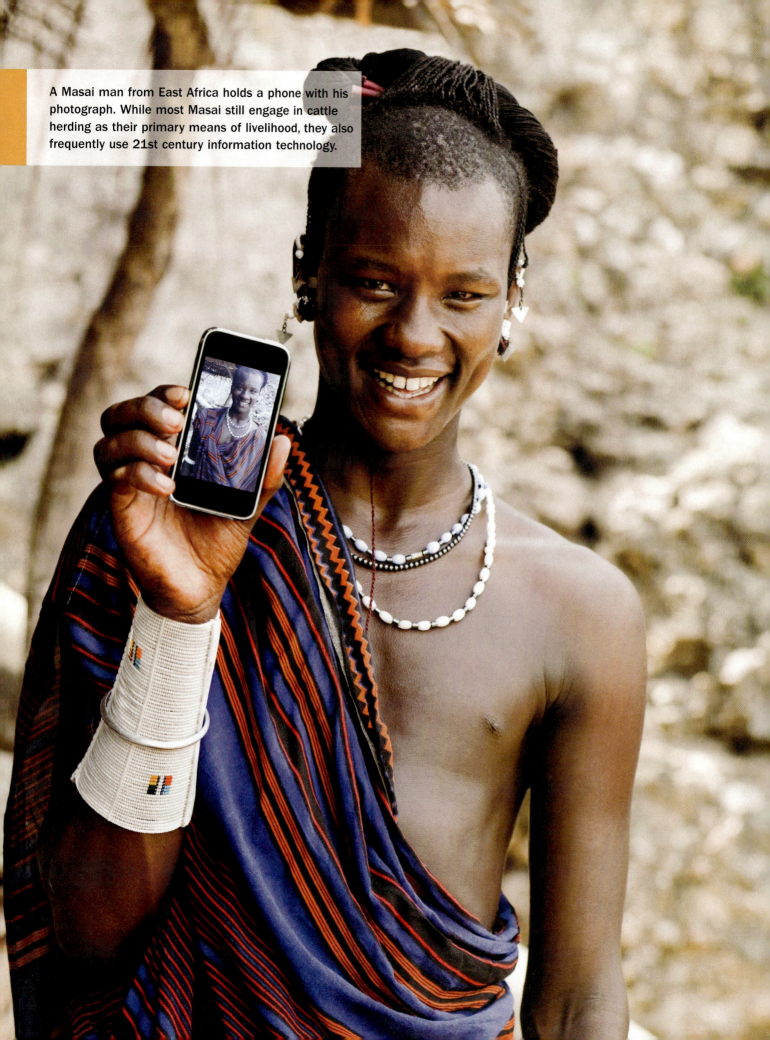

A Masai man from East Africa holds a phone with his photograph. While most Masai still engage in cattle herding as their primary means of livelihood, they also frequently use 21st century information technology.

The Concept of Culture

Jason, an associate in an internationally known architectural firm in Philadelphia, was assigned to head up a project designing public housing units in Nairobi, Kenya. Working with a small team of colleagues, Jason spent about three months preparing the schematics for a large, nine-building project consisting of more than two hundred separate units. The units were laid out in much the same way that public housing units are designed in Philadelphia, Atlanta, or Chicago—that is, with two bedrooms, a large bathroom, a living room, and a dining area with an adjoining open kitchen. The plans were accepted by the Nairobi City Council, and the buildings were constructed over a period of several years.

Once completed, the units were rented (with substantial government subsidies) to needy families. Unfortunately, many of the new residents, although grateful to live in new housing with modern conveniences, were not at all satisfied with one particular design feature. Jason and his team of Western architects had designed every unit with a dining room that opened up into the kitchen. Such a design reflects the typical US lifestyle of using the kitchen for both preparing food and socializing. It is, in other words, not at all unusual for dinner guests in the United States to socialize in the kitchen (with or without drinks) while the host puts the final touches on the dinner. For Kenyans (most of whom retain strong ties to their traditional rural cultures), however, the place where food is cleaned, prepared, and cooked is considered unclean and is totally unsuitable for entertaining one's guests or, for that matter, even letting them see. To serve dinner to guests in the dining room while they can look into the "unclean" place where food is prepared is as unthinkable as having a bathroom without a door next to the dining room. After residents complained to the public housing officials, the units were modified by the addition of a door between the dining room and kitchen.

Jason and his design team were guilty of failing to remove their cultural blinders. They assumed that people the world over deal with their personal domestic space in similar ways. Perhaps the municipal government of Nairobi could have been spared the needless expense of altering the kitchens if Jason had enrolled in a cultural anthropology course while he was studying architecture. ■

WHAT WE WILL LEARN

■ What do anthropologists mean by the term *culture*?

■ How do we acquire our culture?

■ Despite the enormous variation in different cultures, are some features common to all cultures of the world?

■ Do cultures change over time, and if so, how do they change?

■ How does culture inform one's thoughts and behaviors?

■ How can the understanding of the concept of culture help us more effectively address societal challenges?

Although the term *culture* is used by most of the social sciences today, over the years it has received its most precise and comprehensive definition from the discipline of anthropology. Whereas sociology has concentrated on the notion of society; economics on the concepts of production, distribution, and consumption; and political science on the concept of power; anthropology has focused on the culture concept. From anthropology's nineteenth-century beginnings, culture has been central to both ethnology and archaeology and has been an important, if not major, concern of physical anthropology. Anthropology, through its constant examining of different lifeways throughout space and time, has done more than any other scientific discipline to refine our understanding of the concept of culture.

Our discussion of the concept of culture in this chapter will examine such topics as how anthropologists define culture, how culture is acquired, the relationship between culture and biology, cultural universals, and how culture changes over time.

Culture Defined

In nonscientific usage, the term *culture* refers to personal refinements such as classical music, the fine arts, world philosophy, and gourmet cuisine. For example, according to this popular use of the term, the cultured person listens to Bach rather than Lady Gaga, orders escargot rather than barbecued ribs when dining out, can distinguish between the artistic styles of Monet and Toulouse-Lautrec, prefers Grand Marnier to Kool-Aid, and attends the ballet instead of professional wrestling. The anthropologist, however, uses the term in a broader sense to include far more than just "the finer things in life." The anthropologist does not distinguish between cultured people and uncultured people. All people have culture, according to the anthropological definition. An Australian aboriginal, living with a bare minimum of technology, has as much culture as Yo-Yo Ma or Placido Domingo (Figures 2.1 and 2.2). Thus, for the anthropologist, projectile points, creation myths, and mud huts are items of culture as legitimate as a Beethoven symphony, a Kandinsky painting, or a Sondheim musical.

Over the past century, anthropologists have formulated a number of definitions of the concept of culture. In fact, in the often-cited work by Alfred Kroeber and Clyde Kluckhohn (1952), more than 160 different definitions of culture were identified. This proliferation of definitions should not lead to the conclusion that anthropology is a chaotic battleground where no consensus exists among practicing anthropologists. In actuality, many of these definitions say essentially the same thing. One early definition was suggested by nineteenth-century British anthropologist Edward Tylor. According to Tylor, culture is "that complex whole which includes knowledge, belief, art, morals, law, custom, and any other capabilities and habits

Miva Stock/DanitaDelimont/Alamy

FIGURE 2.1 According to anthropologists, this Australian aborigine playing the didgeridoo has as much culture as the conductor of this symphony orchestra.

Ferenc Szelepcsenyi/Shutterstock.com

FIGURE 2.2

acquired by man as a member of society" ([1871] 1958: 1). In the early twentieth century, the soldier and independent scholar FitzRoy Richard Somerset (1885–1964), the 4th Baron Raglan, is reputed to have defined culture as "roughly everything we do and monkeys don't." Although this was a clever and catchy definition for its time, it has become much less relevant today because we now know that monkeys and other nonhuman primates engage in some cultural or quasi-cultural behavior unknown to Somerset and his contemporaries. Since then culture has been defined as "a mental map which guides us in our relations to our surroundings and to other people" (Downs 1971: 35) and perhaps most succinctly as "the way of life of a people" (Hatch 1985: 178).

Adding to the already sizable number of definitions, we will define the concept of culture as "everything that people have, think, and do as members of a society." This definition can be instructive because the three verbs (*have, think,* and *do*) correspond to the three major components of culture. That is, everything that people *have* refers to material possessions; everything that people *think* refers to the things they carry around in their heads, such as ideas, values, and attitudes; and everything that people *do* refers to behavior patterns. Thus, all cultures are composed of material objects; ideas, values, and attitudes; and patterned ways of behaving (see Figure 2.3).

Although we compartmentalize these components of culture, we should not conclude that they are unrelated. In fact, the components are so intimately connected that it is frequently hard to separate them in real life. To illustrate, a non-American anthropologist studying the mainstream culture of the United States would observe people engaged in writing in a wide variety of contexts. Middle-class North Americans fill out job applications, pen letters to loved ones, scribble messages on Post-it notes, write books, and compose e-mail and text messages, to mention only a few examples. When we write, we are using tangible *things* (or artifacts), such as pens, pencils, computers, word-processing software, hard drives, and paper. Although these artifacts are both obvious and visible, they represent only one part of writing. If we are to understand the full significance of writing in US culture, it is imperative that we look below the surface to those other components of culture, such as ideas, knowledge, attitudes, and behavior patterns. For example, for a New Yorker to use English in its written form, he or she must know the alphabet, correct spelling, basic English grammar and syntax, and the rule that words are written from left to right and from top to bottom. He or she must know how to manipulate a writing implement (pen or pencil) or have basic computer skills. He or she needs to know a wealth of cultural information to communicate written messages coherently. In addition, he or she must follow certain behavioral conventions, like not writing while sitting nude in a public library. Thus, the cultural process of writing involves an intimate knowledge of the three fundamental components of culture: things or artifacts, ideas and knowledge, and patterns of behavior.

Perhaps the most fundamental aspect of culture, and what makes humans unique in the animal world, is the capacity to symbolize. A *symbol* is something that stands for (represents) something else. When North Americans see a Nazi swastika, a multitude of images come to mind, including the Holocaust, Adolf Hitler, concentration camps, and goose-stepping storm troopers. Most citizens of the United States have a generally positive feeling when they see the red, white, and blue stars and stripes of the US flag. That particular arrangement of colors and shapes symbolizes, among other things, democracy, the Bill of Rights, due process, and the war on terrorism. Yet, as we have seen in recent years, the US flag represents a host of different meanings for angry young men who delight in burning it in the streets of Tehran, Djakarta, and Karachi. Whether the US flag symbolizes positive or negative images, it is true that all human behavior begins with the use of symbols.

As Leslie White (1959) stated so eloquently more than half a century ago, the ability to symbolize is the single most important hallmark of humanity. It is this capacity to create and give meaning to symbols that helps people identify, sort, and classify things, ideas, and behaviors. When people symbolize by using language, they are able to express experiences that took place at a previous time or suggest events that may happen in the future. Without symbols we would not be able to store the collective wisdom of past generations, and consequently we would be prone to repeating the mistakes of the past. Symbols tie together people who otherwise might not be part of a unified group. The power of our shared symbols becomes clear when we meet others from our own culture in a far-off country. We generally are drawn to them because

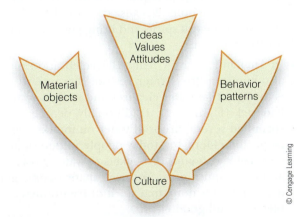

FIGURE 2.3 **The three components of culture.**

© Cengage Learning

symbol Something, either verbal or nonverbal, that stands for something else.

we share a common set of symbols—for example, language, nonverbal forms of communication, and material culture such as clothing. It is the shared meaning of our symbols that enables us to interact with one another with the least amount of ambiguity and misunderstanding.

In everyday usage the term *race* often is used as a synonym for *culture*. But anthropologists consider these to be two *different* concepts. A *race* is an interbreeding population whose members share a number of important physical traits with one another, such as blood types, eye color and shape, skin color, and hair texture, to mention just a few (for a fuller discussion of race, see Chapter 12). By way of contrast, *culture* refers to our *nonbiological* and *nongenetic* characteristics. All people can be classified according to their physical traits and according to their acquired or cultural characteristics. And even though many groups share both a common culture and a similar set of physical traits, these two concepts vary quite independently of each other.

Another popular misunderstanding involves the confusion between culture and civilization. Again, the concepts of civilization and culture are not interchangeable. Although all civilizations are cultures, not all cultures are civilizations. The concept of *civilization*, as used by anthropologists, refers to a specific type of culture that first appeared around 5,500 years ago in the Fertile Crescent (present-day Iraq). Civilizations are essentially cultures that have developed cities. Based largely on the definition of archaeologist V. Gordon Childe (1936), civilizations (or urban societies) are characterized by traits such as monumental architecture, centralized (hierarchical) governments, fully efficient food production systems, and writing. Although we sometimes hear such statements as "Oh, how uncivilized!" modern anthropologists do not use the term *civilization* to designate a superior type of culture.

An inescapable conclusion from studying cultural anthropology is that there are an enormous number of discrete societies with their own unique cultures. Just how many distinct cultures there are depends largely on how one defines the term *culture*, an issue on which there is no absolute consensus among anthropologists. Many scholars equate the number of discrete cultures with the number of mutually unintelligible languages; that is, they assume that if two groups speak mutually unintelligible languages, then other parts of their cultures are sufficiently different to consider them distinct (unique) cultures. Using this equation, we can get a rough estimate of world cultural variation by realizing

that approximately 850 separate cultures (speaking mutually unintelligible languages) are on the continent of Africa alone and more than 5,000 throughout the world.

But in addition to linguistic differences, there are literally hundreds of cultural features that vary from one society to another, including ideas, values, ideologies, religions, material objects, and behavior patterns. To illustrate the magnitude of cultural diversity in today's world, we can look at how the beginning of a new year is celebrated in different cultures. In most cases, the rituals symbolize doing away with the old year and welcoming in the good fortune of the new year. Here are some examples from around the world (Peterson 2008):

- As a harbinger of good fortune, people in Venezuela carry a suitcase around the house on New Year's Day if they want to travel during the new year.

- New Year's Day in Italy, called *Capodanno*, is a time of feast and festival for family and friends, including such symbolic foods as lentils and pork (considered to bring prosperity and good luck in the new year). Dancing, fireworks, and white sparkling Italian wine (Prosecco and Spumante) add to the festivities.

- In Denmark people save old dishes year round and throw them at the homes of their friends on New Year's Eve. Having a pile of broken dishes outside one's front door on New Year's Day symbolizes that the homeowner has many friends and will have good fortune in the new year.

- In the Philippines people in rural villages beat pots and pans to drive away evil forces and ensure good fortune in the new year.

- As a way of securing twelve happy months in the coming year, people in Spain follow the custom of eating twelve grapes at midnight, one grape for each chime of the clock.

- People celebrate New Year's Day in China by placing paper cuttings (a popular folk art) on all the windows of the house because they are thought to scare away the evil spirits and bring good fortune for the new year.

- In Thailand the New Year's Day celebration is also known as the "Water Festival" because it is thought that water cleanses and washes away bad luck (Figure 2.4). Traditionally, people sprinkled several drops of water on monks and respected elders, but today people wet down any passers-by with cups or buckets of water, hoses, and even squirt guns. Although many people get drenched, it is done in a spirit of friendliness, blessing, and good cheer.

civilization A term used by anthropologists to describe any society that has cities.

FIGURE 2.4 Thai children in Bangkok dump water on a tourist during the New Years celebration known as "Water Festival."

Culture Is Shared

The last phrase in our working definition—*as members of a society*—reminds us that culture is a shared phenomenon. For a thing, idea, or behavior pattern to qualify as being cultural, it must have a meaning shared by most people in a society. It is this shared nature of culture that makes our lives less complicated. Because people share a common culture, they are able to predict, within limits, how others will think and behave. For example, when two people meet for the first time in Toronto, it is customary for them to shake hands. If both people grew up in Toronto, neither party will have to wonder what is meant by an outstretched hand. They will know, with nearly absolute certainty, that the extended hand is a nonverbal gesture signifying friendship rather than a sexual advance, a hostile attack, or an attempt to steal one's wallet. It is when we step outside our familiar cultural setting—where meanings are not shared with other people—that misunderstandings occur. In fact, the uncertainty one experiences when trying to operate in an unfamiliar culture often leads to *culture shock*, a form of psychological distress that can result in depression, overeating, or irritability (see Chapter 5).

The degree to which people within any given society share their culture varies from culture to culture. Even in small-scale, homogeneous societies, one can expect to find a certain amount of differentiation based on gender, class, age, religion, or ethnicity. The daughter of a wealthy physician in Athens, for example, is likely to have a somewhat different set of values and behavioral expectations than the daughter of a rural Greek farmer. Moreover societal rules are never adhered to strictly. Although culture exerts a powerful influence, people continue to exercise free will by reinterpreting rules, downplaying their consequences, or disregarding them altogether (such as the Catholic who practices birth control or the conscientious objector who flees the country rather than serve in a war).

In larger, highly complex societies, such as the United States or Canada, one is likely to find a number of subcultural groups in addition to the mainstream culture. The use of the terms *subculture* and *mainstream culture* should in no way imply that subcultures are inferior or any less worthy of study. Rather, subcultures are subsets of the wider culture. They share a number of cultural features with the mainstream, but they retain a certain level of cultural uniqueness that sets them apart. Examples of subcultural groups include American communities such as Japanese Americans in Seattle, Cuban Americans in Miami, and Islamic Americans in Detroit, as well as the Amish communities of Pennsylvania, Indiana, and Wisconsin. Subcultures can also include students at universities and colleges.

Many societies, such as Canada and the United States, are called *pluralistic societies* because they are composed of a number of subcultural groups. Pluralistic societies are not without their difficulties. When different subcultural groups operate with different sets of values and behaviors, misunderstandings (or outright hostilities) are always possible. To illustrate the type of culture clash that can occur, Norine Dresser (1996) recounts an incident that took place in a sixth-grade classroom in the United States. The teacher noticed that one of his students, a Vietnamese girl, had strange red marks on her neck and forehead. Without giving the girl a chance to explain, the teacher notified local authorities, who accused the girl's parents of child abuse. What the teacher did not understand was that in many Asian countries, and in Vietnam in particular, rubbing a coin vigorously on the back, neck, and forehead is a common folk remedy for headaches, colds, and respiratory problems. Unfortunately, the resulting red marks from this remedy were misinterpreted by school officials as signs of abuse.

culture shock A psychological disorientation experienced when attempting to operate in a radically different cultural environment.

subculture A subdivision of a national culture that shares some features with the larger society and also differs in some important respects.

pluralistic societies Societies composed of a number of different cultural or subcultural groups.

Culture Is Learned

Culture is not transmitted genetically. Rather, it is acquired through the process of learning or interacting with one's cultural environment. This process of acquiring culture after we are born is called *enculturation*. We acquire our culture (ideas, values, and behavior patterns) by growing up in it. When an infant is born, he or she enters a cultural environment in which many solutions already exist to the universal problems facing all human populations. The child merely needs to learn or internalize those solutions to make a reasonable adjustment to his or her surroundings. A male child who is born in Kansas will probably watch a good deal of TV; attend schools with books, desks, and professionally trained teachers; eventually learn to drive a car; and marry one wife at a time. In contrast, a male child who is born among the Jie of Uganda is likely to grow up playing with cows, learn most of what he knows from peers and elders rather than teachers, undergo an initiation ceremony into adulthood that involves being anointed with the undigested stomach contents of an ox slaughtered for the occasion, and look forward to having at least three or four wives at one time. Even though these children are born into radically different cultures, they have something important in common: Both children are born into an already existing culture, and they have only to learn the ways of thinking and acting set down by their culture.

If we stop to think about it, a great deal of what we do during our waking hours is learned. Brushing our teeth, eating three meals a day, sweeping the floor, attending school, wearing a wristwatch, knowing to stop at a red light, sleeping on a mattress, and waving goodbye are all learned responses to our cultural environment (Figure 2.5). To be certain, some aspects of our behavior are not learned but are genetically based or instinctive. For example, a newborn infant does not need to attend a workshop on the "art of sucking." Or if someone throws a brick at your head, you do not have to be taught to duck or throw your hands up in front of your face. Nevertheless, the overwhelming majority of our behavioral responses are the result of complex learning processes.

Learning versus Instincts

During the first half of the twentieth century, psychologists and other social scientists tended to explain human behavior in terms of various instincts or genetically based propensities. Gypsies traveled about because they were thought to have "wanderlust" in their blood; black people were musical because they were believed to have natural rhythm; and some people, owing to their genetic makeup, were supposedly born criminals. Today

Jamie Grill/The Image Bank/Getty Images

FIGURE 2.5 Children learn their culture from their parents and others in their society, as shown here by a mother and daughter practicing yoga.

the discipline of anthropology has dismissed this type of biological determinism. Instead, though acknowledging the role of biology, most social scientists support the notion that humans are born with little predetermined behavior. If humans are to survive, they must *learn* most of their coping skills from others in their culture. This usually takes a number of years.

By the beginning of the twenty-first century, it is safe to say that, as a discipline, anthropology has taken a strong stand in favor of the learned (rather than the biological) nature of human behavior. In a statement on race adopted in 1998 by its executive board, the American Anthropological Association weighed in on this topic:

> At the end of the twentieth century, we now understand that human cultural behavior is learned, conditioned into infants beginning at birth, and always subject to modification. No human is born with a built-in culture or language. Our temperaments, dispositions, and personalities, regardless of genetic propensities, are developed within a set of meanings and values that we call "culture." Studies of infant and early childhood learning and behavior attest to the reality of our cultures in forming who we are.

Learning Different Content

Even though there is an enormous range of variation in cultural behavior throughout the world, all people acquire their culture by the same process. People often

---

enculturation The process by which human infants learn their culture.

assume erroneously that if a Hadza adult of Tanzania does not know how to solve an algebraic equation, then she or he must be less intelligent than we are. Yet there is no evidence to suggest that people from some cultures are fast learners and people from others are slow learners. The study of comparative cultures has taught us that people in different cultures learn *different* cultural content (attitudes, values, ideas, and behavioral patterns) and that they accomplish this with similar efficiency. The traditional Hadza hunter has not learned algebra because such knowledge would not particularly enhance his adaptation to life in the east African grasslands. However, he would know how to track a wounded bush buck that he has not seen

for three days, where to find groundwater, and how to build a house out of locally available materials. In short, people learn (with relatively equal efficiency) what they need to know to best adapt to their environment.

Some degree of learning is nearly universal among all animals. Yet no other animal has a greater capacity for learning than do humans, and no other animal relies as heavily on learning for its survival. This is an extraordinarily important notion, particularly for people who are directly involved in the solution of human problems. If human behavior was largely instinctive (genetic), there would be little reason for efforts aimed at changing people's behavior—such as programs in agricultural development, family planning, or community health.

APPLIED PERSPECTIVE

Cross-Cultural Coaching

An increasing number of organizations are beginning to employ cultural anthropologists to help valued foreign employees adjust to the organization's culture. In 2000 the author (Ferraro) was hired by a US-based multinational company to coach one of its foreign research scientists who was having difficulty becoming part of a research team located in rural Georgia. The researcher, whom we will call "Kwanda," grew up in French-speaking Zaire (today the Democratic Republic of Congo), completed his undergraduate degree in France, and earned a PhD from a Canadian university. Kwanda's supervisor described him as someone who, though highly competent, (1) was not a good team player (that is, collaborative researcher), (2) did not take criticism well, and (3) was seen as aloof and arrogant by his colleagues. Ferraro, in his role as cross-cultural coach, met with Kwanda on five different occasions over a three-month period (with each session lasting three to four hours).

A major issue addressed in the coaching sessions was the "prima donna" factor. Arriving at his first job with a brand new PhD, Kwanda, no doubt, held his academic credentials (that is, the highest level of training in his field) in high esteem. He was not prepared, like most new PhDs, for the fact that US society in general does not share his high opinion of a doctoral degree. Moreover he was raised in Zaire (a country one-third the size of the United States), which when it gained its independence from Belgium in 1960 had a total of eight college graduates employed in its government. For youngsters growing up in Zaire, education of *any* type was limited and competition to get into school was fierce. Thus, anyone who managed to receive even a secondary education in Zaire was truly a rare, fortunate, and highly competent student. To then go on to college and graduate school at

excellent foreign universities must have been a heady experience. Clearly, Kwanda had overcome enormous odds to achieve his high level of education. It is little wonder that he held his academic credentials in higher esteem than most people in corporate America.

Thus, part of the cross-cultural coaching challenge was to help Kwanda become more comfortable with the fact that his degrees did not automatically give him instant celebrity. Within the corporate culture of Kwanda's employer, people earned respect and credibility by accomplishing things, rather than by resting on their academic degrees. He eventually came to realize that he was not being discounted simply because his colleagues in Georgia did not want to bow down and kiss his ring. His view of education and the view of his colleagues are simply two different ways of approaching the world, and neither is better than the other.

Through coaching, Kwanda came to understand that he could continue to feel pride in his educational accomplishments, but at the same time he would gain credibility and respectability within the organization only through his tangible accomplishments.

Another issue addressed in the coaching sessions was communication—that is, the sending and receiving of messages. Part of Kwanda's difficulty involved linguistic style (see Chapter 6). Growing up in French-speaking Zaire, Kwanda had learned not only the French language but also the attitudes that go along with speaking French. French speakers, perhaps to a greater degree than any other linguistic group in the world, believe that their language is far more than just a mechanism for sending and receiving messages; rather, they perceive it as an art form and a thing of beauty. This is why the French do not appreciate attempts to speak their language. They feel that if you cannot speak their language eloquently, it is better

(Continued)

Cross-Cultural Coaching (*Continued*)

not to speak it at all. Coming from such a linguistic tradition, Kwanda had difficulty with typically terse, functional US English. The function of language in the United States (other than in formal academic settings) is to communicate as quickly and effectively as possible. The words need not be beautifully constructed; they simply need to do the job efficiently. So, when Kwanda received a cryptic two-word e-mail response to his eloquently crafted letter, he immediately interpreted this as a linguistic "slap in the face." Kwanda viewed this type of communication as offensive because he interpreted it as being sent by someone who did not care enough about the intended receiver to use the proper level of eloquence. Again Kwanda needed to see that the US sender was not purposefully trying to be rude. Kwanda simply came from a different linguistic tradition, one in which linguistic style communicates respect for the recipient of the message. Neither party, in other words, is right or wrong. Nevertheless, such cultural differences can cause communication breakdowns, hurt feelings, and hostility. Although Kwanda may never stop cringing at overly terse ways of communicating in the United States, he came to understand the nature of this linguistic difference and learned that he should not take it as a personal affront.

During the early coaching sessions, Kwanda came to understand the nature of the cross-cultural differences that were preventing him from making a smooth adjustment to his new work environment. After identifying behavioral changes that he could make to facilitate his adjustment, Kwanda was asked to keep a journal of his new behaviors in the workplace, as well as his thoughts and feelings about them. And because communicating across cultures is a two-way process, it was also recommended that Kwanda's supervisor and colleagues learn more about the cultural differences that were operating within their laboratory setting.

Questions for Further Thought

1. Can you think of any *other* cultural issues in this case that may have impeded Kwanda from making a smooth adjustment to the corporate culture?

2. Should Kwanda be solely responsible for modifying his attitudes and behavior so as to adjust to the corporate culture, or does the corporation have a responsibility to make certain accommodations?

3. In what other situations could you envision a cross-cultural coach working?

Culture Is Taken for Granted

Culture is so embedded in our psyche that we frequently take it for granted. We live out our lives without thinking too much about how our culture influences our thinking and behavior. How we act and what we think are often so automatic and habitual that we rarely give them any thought at all. Unfortunately, this leads to the uncritical conclusion that how we live out our lives is really no different from how people from other cultures live out theirs. The job of cultural anthropology is to heighten our awareness of other cultures, as well as our own, in hopes that we will be less likely to take our own culture for granted. Learning *not* to take our own culture for granted is the best way to combat ethnocentrism.

Perhaps an example of taking one's culture for granted will be helpful. Anthropologist Edward T. Hall devoted much of his career to the study of time across cultures. He identified a useful model for understanding how various cultures deal with time throughout the world. Hall distinguished between two fundamentally different ways of dealing with time: monochronically and polychronically. People from *monochronic cultures*—such as the United States, Germany, and Switzerland—view time in a linear fashion, prefer to do one thing at a time, place a high value on punctuality, and keep precise schedules (Figure 2.6). Most middle-class North Americans would never think of leaving the house without that little gadget strapped to their wrist that tells them, no matter where they may be, exactly what time it is.

Other cultures tend to be *polychronic cultures*, preferring to do many things at the same time. Unlike Americans, they see no particular value in punctuality for its own sake. Rather than reacting to the hands of a clock, polychronic people strive to create and maintain social relationships. Their de-emphasis on schedules and punctuality should not be interpreted as being lazy. Rather, owing to their cultural values, they *choose* to place greater worth on social relationships instead of completing a particular task on time. In fact, polychronic people often interpret the typical North American's

---

monochronic cultures A culture in which people view time in a linear fashion, place great importance on punctuality and keeping on schedule, and prefer to work on one task at a time.

polychronic cultures A culture in which people typically perform a number of tasks at the same time and place a higher value on nurturing and maintaining social relationships than on punctuality for its own sake.

listening to music, and sending text messages at the same time are prone to making more mistakes than they would if they did these three things separately. According to a recent study of Microsoft employees by Shamsi Iqbal and Eric Horvitz (2007), it took workers on average 15 minutes to return to their task at hand (like writing a report) after being distracted by an incoming e-mail or text message. Rather than taking just a few seconds to read an e-mail message, workers, once interrupted, strayed off to reply to other messages, browse news items, or start other tasks. So, multitaskers beware! Doing two or more tasks at once is associated with (1) spending more, not less, time and (2) decreasing the quality of the work product.

Culture Influences Biological Processes

Human existence, by its nature, is biocultural—that is, the product of both biological and cultural factors. All animals, including humans, have certain biologically determined needs that must be met if they are to stay alive and well. We all need to ingest a minimum number of calories of food each day, protect ourselves from the elements, sleep, and eliminate wastes from our body, to mention a few. It is vital for us to distinguish between these needs and the ways in which we satisfy them. To illustrate, even though all people need to eliminate wastes from the body through defecation, how often, where, in what physical position, and under what social circumstances we defecate are all questions that are answered by our individual culture. Thus, to say that life is biocultural means that our bodies and their accompanying biological processes are heavily influenced by our cultures.

A dramatic example of how culture can influence or channel our biological processes was provided by anthropologist Clyde Kluckhohn (1949), who spent much of his career in the US Southwest studying the Navajo culture. Kluckhohn tells of a non-Navajo woman he knew in Arizona who took a somewhat perverse pleasure in causing a cultural response to food. At luncheon parties she often served sandwiches filled with a light meat that resembled tuna or chicken but had a distinctive taste. Only after everyone had finished lunch would the hostess inform her guests that what they had just eaten was neither tuna salad nor chicken salad but rather rattlesnake salad. Invariably, someone would vomit on learning what he or she had eaten. Here, then, is an excellent example of how the biological process of digestion was influenced by a cultural idea. Not only was the process influenced, it was reversed! That is, the culturally based *idea* that rattlesnake meat should not be eaten triggered a violent reversal of the normal digestive process.

FIGURE 2.6 North Americans, who tend to be monochromic, place a high value on punctuality, schedules, and deadlines.

obsession with time as being antithetical to meaningful social relationships. Monochronic types are seen as wanting to rush through their personal encounters so they can move on to the next item on their list. In other words, this rigid adherence to schedules and the insistence on doing only one thing at a time are seen by polychronic people as being rude and dehumanizing.

How we deal with time varies greatly from culture to culture. Middle-class North Americans pay close attention to their watches, take deadlines seriously, move rapidly, start their meetings on time, and eat because it is time to eat. Polychronic cultures, on the other hand, are much less attentive to the hands of a clock, view deadlines much less rigidly, build in a lot of socializing time before starting the business portion of their meetings, and eat because there are others with whom to share food. When we uncritically expect everyone to operate according to our sense of time, we are taking our own culture for granted.

Although North Americans have been traditionally monochronic, the information technology (IT) revolution in recent decades has turned many people in the United States and Canada into multitaskers. Recent research in neuroscience and psychology (Lohr 2007) has suggested, however, that people who are studying,

Our Bodies and Culture

The nonmaterial aspects of our culture, such as ideas, values, and attitudes, can have an appreciable effect on the human body. Culturally defined attitudes concerning male and female attractiveness, for example, have resulted in some dramatic effects on the body. Burmese women give the appearance of elongating their necks by depressing their clavicles and scapulas with heavy brass rings, Chinese women traditionally had their feet bound, men in New Guinea put bones through their noses, and scarification and tattooing are practiced in various parts of the world for the same reasons that women and men in the United States pierce their ear lobes (that is, because their cultures tell them that it looks good). People intolerant of different cultural practices often fail to realize that had they been raised in one of those other cultures, they would be practicing those allegedly disgusting or irrational customs.

Even our body shape is related to a large extent to our cultural ideas. In the Western world, people go to considerable lengths to become as slender as possible. They spend millions of dollars each year on running shoes, diet plans, appetite suppressants, and health spa memberships to help them lose weight. However, our Western notion of equating slimness with physical beauty is hardly universally accepted. In large parts of Africa, for example, Western women are perceived as emaciated and considered to be singularly unattractive. This point was made painfully obvious to me (Ferraro) when I was conducting fieldwork in Kenya. After months of living in Kenya, I learned that many of my male Kikuyu friends pitied me for having such an unattractive wife (five feet five inches tall and 114 pounds). Kikuyu friends often came by my house with a bowl of food or a chicken and discreetly whispered, "This is for your wife." Even though I considered my wife to be beautifully proportioned, my African friends thought she needed to be fattened up to be beautiful.

Altering the body for aesthetic purposes (what is known euphemistically as "plastic surgery") has become increasingly widespread in US culture over the last decade. To illustrate, according to the American Society for Aesthetic Plastic Surgery (www.surgery.org), more than 1.6 million plastic surgeries (for example, liposuction, breast augmentation, and tummy tucks) were performed in the United States in 2011 as compared to only 939,192 in 1997. Moreover, nonsurgical procedures designed to alter one's physical appearance (for example, Botox injections, acid peels for the skin, and laser hair removal) increased from 740, 751 in 1997 to more than 7.5 million in 2011, a tenfold increase in fourteen years. In fact, surgical and nonsurgical altering of our physical appearance is now so widespread and routine that it has become a popular form of TV entertainment. One such show (in 2004), *The Swan*, featured seemingly unattractive people who voluntarily submitted to a host of cosmetic surgical procedures (such as nose jobs, lip and breast augmentation, chin implants, and forehead lifts), emerging at the end of the show transformed to enjoy rave reviews from friends, family members, and the sizable viewing audience. A particularly popular

CROSS-CULTURAL MISCUE

❋ Eric Britt, the headmaster of a New Hampshire prep school for boys, was entertaining a group of Taiwanese parents and their sons who were interested in attending the school. As a recruiting tool, Eric made a point of presenting each father and son with a green baseball cap representing the school's colors. After receiving the caps, none of the male Taiwanese put the caps on their heads, and many of the fathers looked embarrassed when receiving their gift. Surprisingly, none of the Taiwanese boys applied for admission to the school.

Unfortunately, Britt failed to realize that in Taiwan the expression "He wears a green hat" conveys the meaning that a man's wife or girlfriend has been unfaithful. Clearly, no self-respecting Taiwanese male would want to be seen in public wearing a green hat. Britt's choice of a gift was an unfortunate one.

reality show since 2004 has been NBC's *The Biggest Loser*, which features overweight contestants attempting to lose (through dieting and exercise) the most weight for a cash prize of $250,000.

Cultural Universals

Since the early twentieth century, hundreds of cultural anthropologists have described the wide variety of cultures found in the contemporary world. As a result, the discipline of anthropology has been far more effective at documenting cultural differences than at showing similarities among cultures. This preoccupation with different forms of behavior and different ways of meeting human needs was the result, at least in part, of wanting to move away from the premature generalizing about human nature that was so prevalent a century ago.

This vast documentation of culturally different ways of behaving has been essential to our understanding of the human condition. The significant number of cultural differences illustrates how flexible and adaptable humans are in comparison with other animals because each culture has developed its own set of solutions to the universal human problems facing all societies. For example, every society, if it is to survive as an entity, needs a system of communication that enables its members to send and receive messages efficiently. That there are thousands of mutually unintelligible languages in the world today certainly attests to human flexibility. Yet, when viewed from a somewhat higher level of abstraction, all of these different linguistic communities have an important common denominator; that is, they all have developed some form of language. Thus, it is important to bear in mind that despite their many differences, all cultures of the world share a number of common features (*cultural universals*) because they have all worked out solutions to the whole series of problems that face all human societies. We can perhaps gain a clearer picture of cultural universals by looking in greater detail at the universal societal problems or needs that give rise to them.

Basic Needs

One of the most fundamental requirements of each society is to see that the basic physiological needs of its people are met. Clearly, people cannot live unless they receive a minimum amount of food, water, and protection from the elements. Because a society will not last without living people, every society needs to work out systematic ways of producing (or procuring from the environment) absolutely essential commodities and then distributing them to its members. In the United States, goods and services are distributed according to the capitalistic principle of "to each according to his or her capacity to pay." In classic socialist countries of the mid-twentieth century, distribution took place according to the principle of "to each according to his or her need." The Hadza of Tanzania distribute meat according to how an individual is related to the person who killed the animal. The Mbuti of Central Africa engage in a system of distribution called silent barter, whereby they avoid having face-to-face interaction with their trading partners.

Many societies distribute valuable commodities as part of the marriage system, sending considerable quantities of livestock from the family of the groom to the family of the bride. Even though the details of each of these systems of distribution vary greatly, every society has worked out systems of production and distribution ensuring that people get what they need for survival. As a result, we can say that every society has an *economic system.*

All societies face other universal needs besides the need to produce and distribute vital commodities to their members. For example, all societies need to make provisions for orderly mating and child-rearing that give rise to patterned *systems of marriage and family* (Figures 2.7). If a society is to endure, it will need to develop a systematic way of passing on its culture from one generation to the next. This universal societal need for cultural transmission leads to some form of *educational system* in all societies. A prerequisite for the longevity of any society is the maintenance of social order; that is, most of the people must obey most of the rules most of the time. This universal societal need to avoid chaos and anarchy leads to a set of mechanisms that coerce people to obey the social norms, which we call a *social control system.* Because people in all

---

cultural universals Those general cultural traits found in all societies of the world.

FIGURE 2.7 Although marriage practices differ considerably between this North Korean couple and this North American couple, both sets of practices are responses to the universal societal need to have an orderly system of mating and child rearing.

societies are faced with life occurrences that defy explanation or prediction, all societies have developed systems for explaining the unexplainable, most of which rely on some form of supernatural beliefs such as religion, witchcraft, magic, or sorcery. Thus, all societies have developed a *system of supernatural beliefs* that serves to explain otherwise inexplicable phenomena. And because all societies, if they are to function, need their members to be able to send and receive messages efficiently, they all have developed *systems of communication*, both verbal and nonverbal.

Sometimes the similarities (or universal aspects) of different cultural features are not obvious. To illustrate, in the middle-class in the United States it is customary to spend a certain proportion of one's income on various types of insurance policies, including life insurance, medical insurance, and fire insurance. In many parts of the world today, such as rural Swaziland, these forms of insurance are virtually unknown. This is not to suggest, however, that rural Swazis do not experience misfortunes such as death, illness, or accidents. Nor do they suffer misfortunes without any support or safety net. Whereas most North Americans view the insurance company as their first line of security against such calamities as death or serious illness, Swazis have their extended family for support. If a husband dies prematurely, the widow and her children are provided for (financially, socially, and emotionally) by the relatives of the deceased. In Swaziland the extended family is the insurance company. Thus, the function of providing security and support in the face of misfortune is performed in both Swazi and North American cultures. Indeed such security systems are found in all cultures and consequently are universal. What differs, of course, are the agencies that provide the systems of support—in this case, either insurance companies or extended families.

Despite what may appear to be an overwhelming amount of cultural variety found in the world today, all cultures, because they must meet certain universal needs, have a number of traits in common. Those just mentioned are some of the more obvious cultural universals, but many more could be cited. Anthropologist George Peter Murdock (1945: 124) compiled a list of cultural universals that our species has in common, including bodily adornment, courtship, decorative arts, dream interpretation, etiquette, food taboos, kinship terminology, status systems, and tool making. Despite the fact that cultural anthropologists (since Murdock's list first appeared) have tended to emphasize cultural differences rather than similarities, cultural universals nevertheless exist, are

numerous, and are theoretically significant for carrying out the work of anthropology.

Culture Is Adaptive and Maladaptive

Culture represents the major way by which human populations adapt or relate to their environments so that they can continue to reproduce and survive. Most living organisms other than humans adapt to their environments by developing physiological features that equip them to maximize their chances for survival. For example, certain species of predators, such as wolves, lions, and leopards, have developed powerful jaws and canine teeth to be used for killing animals and ripping the flesh of the animal. Humans, on the other hand, have relied more on cultural than on biological features for adapting to their environments. Through the invention and use of cultural tools such as spears, arrows, guns, and knives, humans are able to kill and butcher animals even more efficiently than an animal can with its massive jaws and teeth. The discovery of chemical substances such as penicillin, quinine, and the polio vaccine has provided the human species a measure of protection against disease and death. The proliferation of agricultural technology over the past century has dramatically increased humans' capacity to feed themselves. Because humans rely much more heavily on cultural adaptation than on biological adaptation, we are enormously flexible in our ability to survive and thrive in a wide variety of natural environments. Because of the *adaptive nature of culture,*

FIGURE 2.8 Culture enables humans to adapt to the most hostile climates, as illustrated by a colony of scientists living at this research station in Antarctic.

---

adaptive nature of culture The implication that culture is the major way human populations adapt or relate to their specific habitat in order to survive and reproduce.

people are now able to live in many previously uninhabitable places, such as deserts, the polar regions (Figure 2.8), under the sea, and even in outer space.

Culture provides humans with an enormous adaptive advantage over all other forms of life. Biological adaptation depends on the Darwinian theory of natural selection. According to this theory, nature selects those members of a species that happen to already possess certain biologically based features that make them better adapted to a particular environment. But what if those adaptive characteristics do not exist in the gene pool? Then evolutionary change in the traits of the species will not happen over time, and as a result, the species may become extinct. Moreover, even when natural selection works, it works slowly. But because culture is learned, humans can produce certain technological solutions to better adapt to the environment. For example, when one's environment becomes increasingly colder over a number of years, nonhumans (relying on Darwinian natural selection) must wait generations to develop more protective body hair. Humans with culture, however, need only to develop methods for making clothing and shelters to protect people from the elements. Thus, culture is a much quicker and more efficient means of adaptation than is a purely biological approach.

The notion that culture is adaptive should not lead us to the conclusion that every aspect of a culture is adaptive. It is possible for some features to be adaptively neutral, neither enhancing nor diminishing the capacity of a people to survive. Moreover it is even possible for some features of a culture to be maladaptive or dysfunctional. To illustrate, the large-scale use of automobiles coupled with industrial pollutants is currently destroying the quality of the air in our environment. If this set of cultural behaviors continues unchecked, it will destroy our environment to such an extent that it will be unfit for human habitation. Thus, it is not likely that such a maladaptive practice will persist indefinitely. Either the practice will disappear when the people become extinct, or the culture will change so that the people will survive. Whichever outcome occurs, the maladaptive cultural feature will eventually disappear.

An understanding of the adaptive nature of culture is further complicated by its relativity. What is adaptive in one culture may be maladaptive or adaptively neutral in another culture. For example, the mastery of such skills as algebra, word analogies, and reading comprehension is necessary for a successful adaptation to life in the United States because these skills contribute to succeeding in academics, landing a good job, and living in material comfort. However, such skills are of little value in helping the Nuer herdsman adapt to his environment in the Sudan. Furthermore the adaptability of a cultural item varies over time within any particular culture. To illustrate, the survival capacity of traditional Inuit hunters living on the Alaskan tundra would no doubt be enhanced appreciably by the introduction of guns and snowmobiles. Initially, such innovations would be adaptive because they would help the Inuit hunters to obtain caribou more easily, thereby enabling people to eat better, be more resistant to disease, and generally live longer. After several generations, however, the use of guns and snowmobiles would, in all likelihood, become maladaptive because the newly acquired capacity to kill caribou more efficiently would eventually lead to the destruction and disappearance of a primary food supply.

Cultures Are Generally Integrated

To suggest that all cultures share a certain number of universal characteristics is not to imply that cultures comprise a laundry list of norms, values, and material objects. Instead, cultures should be thought of as integrated wholes, the parts of which, to some degree, are interconnected with one another. When we view cultures as integrated systems, we can begin to see how particular culture traits fit into the whole system and, consequently, how they tend to make sense *within that context*. Equipped with such a perspective, we can begin to better understand the "strange" customs found throughout the world.

One way of describing this integrated nature of cultures is by using the *organic analogy* made popular by some of the early functionalist anthropologists, most notably Herbert Spencer and Bronislaw Malinowski. This approach makes the analogy between a culture and a living organism such as the human body. The physical human body comprises a number of systems, all functioning to maintain the overall health of the organism; these include the respiratory, digestive, skeletal, excretory, reproductive, muscular, circulatory, endocrine, and lymphatic systems. Any anatomist or surgeon worth her or his salt knows where these systems are located in the body, what function each plays, and how parts of the body are interconnected. Surely no sane person would choose a surgeon to remove a malignant lung unless that surgeon knew how that organ was related to the rest of the body.

Cultural Interconnections

In the same way that human organisms comprise various parts that are both functional and interrelated, so too do cultures. When conducting empirical field research, the cultural anthropologist must describe the various parts of the culture, show how they function, and explain how they are interconnected. When

organic analogy The early functionalist idea that cultural systems are integrated into a whole cultural unit in much the same way that the various parts of a biological organism (such as a respiratory system or a circulatory system) function to maintain the health of the organism.

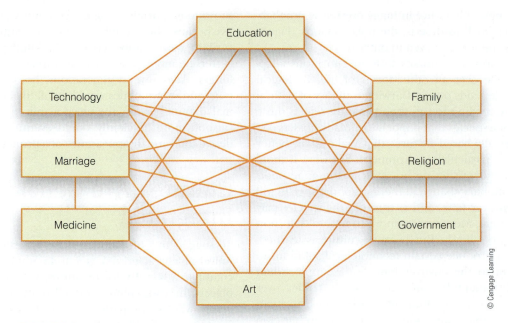

FIGURE 2.9 Interconnectedness of the parts of culture.

describing cultures, anthropologists often identify such parts as the economic, kinship, social control, marriage, military, religious, aesthetic, technological, and linguistic systems—among others. These various parts of a culture are more than a random assortment of customs. Even though more often than not anthropologists fail to spell out clearly the nature and dimensions of these relationships, it is believed that many parts of a culture are to some degree interconnected (see Figure 2.9). Thus, we can speak of cultures as being logical and coherent systems.

The integrated nature of culture enables anthropologists to explain certain sociocultural facts on the basis of other sociocultural facts. When we say that cultures are integrated, we are suggesting that many parts not only are connected to one another but in fact influence one another. To illustrate this point, consider that Japan has the second largest economy in the world, yet Japanese scholars have received only 14 Nobel Prizes since 1901 compared with 116 for the United Kingdom, 126 for Germany, and 320 for the United States (Coutsoukis 2010). If we want to explain or understand this phenomenon, it is important to seek answers in other parts of the culture. For example, Japanese culture is steeped in Confucianism, which emphasizes piety toward elders, age-graded promotions, and a general penchant for incremental advances rather than bold experimentation. Moreover, in a society that has always valued cooperation and harmony, Japanese scholars avoid the intense peer review that has stimulated creativity and experimentation in other industrialized nations. Professional advancement for Japanese scholars has been based more on seniority than on actual contributions, and relationships among

scientists are cordial, friendly, and nonconfrontational. Thus, if we are to understand why the Japanese have received relatively few Nobel Prizes over the years, we need to look at other related parts of the Japanese culture that have influenced the behavior (and the creativity) of Japanese scientists.

The notion of integrated cultures has important implications for our understanding of culture change. If the parts of any given culture are integrated, then we might expect that a change in one part of the cultural system will bring about changes in other parts of the system. To illustrate, since Coca-Cola was introduced into the southern Mexican state of Chiapas in the 1950s, the soft drink has influenced (that is, stimulated changes in) a number of other features of the local culture. The local power structure has been headed by a family that became the sole distributor of the soft drink nearly a half-century ago. Because this enormously popular carbonated beverage accounts for a large part of the total sales of local shopkeepers, this powerful family distributorship, for all practical purposes, determines who will or will not be a successful retailer in Chiapas. At the same time, Coke has become a major status symbol in Chiapas at family celebrations such as baptisms. Serving Coca-Cola has replaced the local alcoholic beverage (called *pox*) as the highest form of hospitality. In fact the number of servings of Coke offered to a guest is directly proportional to his or her social status. The introduction of Coke into Chiapas has even influenced the state government, which over the past several decades has used Coke in its campaign to curb the consumption of alcohol. Thus, as this example illustrates, a change in one part of the culture system (the introduction of Coke) has been responsible for changes in

❀ One might think that cultural anthropologists are immune from cultural gaffes. When one of your authors (who will remain anonymous, but his initials are "Gary Ferraro") was vacationing in Northern Italy with his two college-age children, he spent four nights in a small hotel in Santa Margarita run by Roberto and his wife Anna. As the three US tourists were checking out and saying their farewells to Roberto and Anna, the "interculturally savvy" cultural anthropologist asked Roberto a question that revealed his US values: "How long will it take us to drive to our next destination, the town of Bergamo?" Looking surprised, Roberto responded, "What difference does it make, you're on vacation?"

Immediately the cultural anthropologist realized that he had exposed himself as the fairly naïve US tourist that he was. For Americans, with their high value on the precise reckoning of time, one feature of a successful vacation is how little time is "wasted" on getting from one place to another. But for many Italians, the journey can be, and often is, as pleasurable as the destination itself, and thus, should be explored and enjoyed because unless you take your time, you will never know what unexpected experiences you could have along the way. The anthropologist should have realized that it was, after all, the Italians who started the "Slow Food" movement.

other parts of the system—namely, the economic power structure, symbols of social status, and the operation of government programs (Borden 2004).

Although the organic analogy is a useful model for looking at culture, it should not lead us to believe that *all* parts of a culture are intimately interconnected with all other parts. If this were the case, every culture would be a smooth-running operation, like a well-oiled machine, with all of the parts working in harmony with one another. But cultures, like machines, often have parts that are out of sync and detract from the well-being of the whole. And yet the culture, or the machine, does not come to a grinding halt. There are, in other words, parts of culture that may not be mutually supportive, or may even be in conflict with one another. For example, the goals of a family are not always compatible with those of the workplace. Moreover, within the workplace itself, there are built-in conflicts between labor (interested in maximizing wages) and management (interested in maximizing profits). To be certain, cultures can be viewed as systems, but they also have certain parts that grind against one another. Thus, cultures are characterized by both harmony and conflict.

The concept of integrated cultures is directly related to the concept of cultural relativism (discussed in Chapter 1), which involves viewing any item from within its proper cultural context rather than from the perspective of the observer's culture. The fact that all cultures are composed of interrelated parts prompts us to explore how a feature from a new and different culture fits into its original cultural context.

Cultures Change

Thus far we have presented culture as a combination of things, ideas, and behavior patterns transmitted from generation to generation through the process of learning. This view of culture, focusing as it does on continuity among the generations, tends to emphasize its static rather than dynamic aspects. And yet a fundamental principle underlying all cultures is that there is nothing as constant as change. Some cultures—those that remain relatively insulated from the global economy—change quite slowly, whereas for others change occurs more rapidly. Despite the wide variation in the speed with which cultures change, one thing is certain: No culture remains completely static year after year.

One need not be a scholar of cultural change to notice that cultures have been changing more rapidly with each passing decade. In contrast to our hectic existence, the everyday lives of our grandparents seem simple and slow moving. Today many people are overwhelmed by how quickly their cultures are changing. In 1970 Alvin Toffler coined the term *future shock*, which he defined as the psychological disorientation resulting from living in a cultural environment that is changing so rapidly that people feel they are constantly living in the future. In the second decade of a new millennium, Toffler's notion of future shock rings truer than ever before.

Cultural change occurs at such an accelerated pace today that it is often difficult to keep up with the latest developments. The recent revolution in transportation and electronic communications has made the world seem smaller. Today it is possible to travel to the other side of the earth in a commercial airliner in about the same time it took our great-grandparents to travel fifty miles using a horse and carriage. Via satellite we can view instant transmissions of live newscasts from anywhere in the world. Indeed the global exchange of commodities and information is bringing the world's population closer to the notion of living in a global village. Because of this rapid and dramatic increase in our capacity to interact with people in other parts of the world, the likelihood of cultures diffusing (or spreading) has increased dramatically in recent decades.

In a real sense, any ethnographic description of a specific group of people is like a snapshot at one particular time. If the ethnographer studies the same group again five years later, it is likely that some cultural features will have changed. Some cultures (usually small-scale, preliterate, and technologically simple societies) tend to change slowly. Modern, complex, highly industrialized societies tend to change much more rapidly. Whatever the rate of change, however, we can be sure of one thing when dealing with cultures: Nothing is as constant as change.

Cultural change is brought about by both internal and external factors. Internal factors include inventions and innovations, and external factors include cultural diffusion (spreading) between cultures. Although diffusion is responsible for the greatest amount of cultural change, it is important to examine both processes of change in greater detail.

Inventions and Innovations

Any new thing, idea, or behavior pattern that emerges from within a society is an *invention* or an *innovation*. Some inventions are deliberate and purposeful, whereas others are unconscious and unintentional. Ralph Linton, one of the most prominent scholars of cultural change in the twentieth century, suggested that over the long run, the unconscious inventor has had a greater impact on cultural change than has the conscious inventor. The unconscious or accidental inventor contributes to cultural change without being driven by an unmet societal need or even realizing that she or he is making a contribution. As Linton (1936: 311) puts it, "Their inventions are, as a rule, of little individual importance, but they loom large in the aggregate."

These numerous unintentional inventors sometimes go unnoticed and unrewarded, even though they may be making a significant cumulative contribution to their culture. (An example of an unintentional invention—which actually had an important impact—was the scientist at 3M who, while trying to invent a strong adhesive, failed and produced instead a weak adhesive that was ideal for Post-it notes.) Most often it is the deliberate, intentional inventor who is recognized and rewarded. From our own recent history, Eli Whitney was sufficiently motivated by the need to produce more cotton to invent the cotton gin, Jonas Salk discovered the polio vaccine to eradicate a crippling disease, and hundreds of other inventors have come up with new discoveries, gadgets, and ideas because they wanted to do something better or more efficiently.

© Chicago Tribune/MCT/Landov

FIGURE 2.10 Professional inventor Ron Popeil has made hundreds of millions of dollars marketing such products as his Showtime Rotisserie on TV infomercials. ("Just set it and forget it.")

Sometimes inventions occur as a result of a person simply following his or her chosen profession of inventor. One of the most widely known (and successful) professional inventors is the television pitchman, Ron Popeil, president of Ronco Products (Figure 2.10). Popeil spends a lot of time in his kitchen thinking up new kitchen appliances that are time-saving, convenient, efficient, and affordable and will help people prepare delicious and nutritious meals for their families. Over the years he has invented slicing and dicing devices, food dehydrators, automatic pasta and sausage makers, and meat smokers, and then he has sold them via TV infomercials in which the product is the star of the show, not Popeil. Popeil's most successful invention is his Showtime Rotisserie, which may be the best kitchen appliance ever invented, with sales in the hundreds of millions of dollars (Gladwell 2009: 3–31).

Cultural Diffusion

In addition to changing as a result of inventions and discoveries, cultures change through the process of *cultural diffusion*: the spreading of a thing, an idea, or a behavior pattern from one culture to another. As important as inventions and discoveries are to cultural change, the total number of inventions in any given society is generally quite small. In fact, Linton (1936) estimates that no more than 10 percent of all the cultural items found in any culture—including our

---

invention A new combination of existing cultural features.

innovation A change brought about by the recombination of already existing items within a culture.

cultural diffusion The spreading of a cultural trait (that is, a material object, idea, or behavior pattern) from one society to another.

own—originated in that culture. If every culture had to rely solely on its own inventions, human progress over the centuries would indeed be slow. Cultures have been able to develop rapidly because the process of diffusion has enabled humans to pool their creative/inventive resources.

To illustrate how cultural diffusion actually works, we need only refer back to the example of traditional views of physical attractiveness among Africans discussed in a previous section of this chapter. In precolonial times (nineteenth century) most sub-Saharan African societies viewed thin women as unattractive and substantial woman as beautiful. But owing to the twentieth-century IT revolution, contemporary African women (with the assistance of government health officials) are getting the message that being obese, or even overweight, not only is unhealthy but also will dash whatever hopes they might have of participating in the "Miss Universe" contest held in the major capitols of the world. As one indicator of these changing values, women in Mauritania—where women have routinely been "force fed" to make them more corpulent—are now seen going on power walks at local sports stadiums to lose weight (LaFraniere 2007: 4). Although many Africans continue to hold onto their traditional values, Western values are beginning to take hold through the process of cultural diffusion.

Because diffusion plays such a prominent role in cultural change, it is appropriate to examine this process in some detail. Even though cultural diffusion varies from situation to situation, a number of generalizations about the process are worth mentioning.

The Process of Diffusion Is Selective

When two cultures come into contact, they do not exchange every cultural item. If that were the case, there would be no cultural differences in the world today. Instead, only a small number of cultural elements are ever diffused from one culture to another. Which cultural item is accepted depends largely on the item's use and compatibility with already existing cultural traits. For example, it is not likely that men's hair dyes designed to "get out the gray" will diffuse into parts of rural Africa where a person's status is elevated with advancing years. Even when an innovation is consistent with a society's needs, there is still no guarantee that it will be accepted. For example, most people in the United States have resisted adopting the metric system even though making such a change would enable US citizens to interface with the rest of the world more efficiently.

Diffusion Is a Two-Way, Reciprocal Process

We should not assume that cultural items diffuse only from technologically complex societies to simpler societies. The anthropological record from many parts of the world clearly shows that cultural traits are diffused in both directions. European contact with Native Americans is a case in point. Even though Europeans introduced much of their culture to American Indians, the Europeans nevertheless received a number of cultural features in return, including articles of clothing such as ponchos, parkas, and moccasins; medicines such as quinine, pain relievers, and laxatives; and food items such as corn, beans, tomatoes, squash, yams, avocados, and the so-called "Irish" potato.

Cultural Elements May Be Modified.

Once a cultural element is accepted into a new culture, it may undergo changes in form or function. Pizza is a good example of how a cultural item can change form as it diffuses. Pizza, which diffused from Italy to the United States in the late nineteenth century, has been modified in significant ways to conform to U.S. tastes. It is unlikely that its Italian originators would recognize a pizza made of French bread, English muffins, or pita bread and topped with pineapple, tuna, or jalapeño peppers.

Sometimes the reinterpretation process involves a change in the way an item is used. While living in Kenya, the author (Ferraro) observed a stunning example of functional reinterpretation. The Maasai of Kenya and Tanzania practice the custom of piercing the earlobes and enlarging the hole by inserting increasingly larger round pieces of wood until a loop of skin is formed. Rather than using pieces of round wood for this purpose, one group of Maasai was observed using Eveready flashlight batteries discarded by tourists. In this case the form of the batteries was the same, but the function definitely had been reinterpreted.

Some Parts of Culture Are More Likely to Diffuse than Others

As a general rule, items of material culture are more likely candidates for diffusion than are ideas or behavior patterns. For example, a traditional farmer in Senegal is more likely to be convinced of the advantages of using a tractor over a hoe for plowing his field than he is of substituting Shintoism for his traditional form of ancestor worship.

Diffusion Is Affected by Other Important Variables

These variables include the duration and intensity of contact, the degree of cultural integration, and the similarities between the donor and recipient cultures. To illustrate, owing to changing demographics in

California, an institution as "red-blooded American" as McDonald's is being transformed by cultural diffusion. According to US Census Bureau data, the number of Asians in Hacienda Heights, California (population 53,000), increased from 27 percent in 1990 to 36 percent in 2000. To appeal to this growing population of Asians, the owners of a local McDonald's decided to renovate and redecorate his fast-food restaurant with the help of an expert in *feng shui*, the Chinese practice of creating harmonious surroundings. The new feng shui McDonald's includes such design features as two silently flowing waterfalls, curved walls painted in soothing earth tones, a vase filled with bamboo at the entrance, booths arranged in a semicircle, and ceiling and floor tiles turned at a distinctive angle (Figure 2.11). The doors have been designed to swing in both directions to keep good luck inside the building. And the number 4 (considered to be bad fortune in Asian cultures) has been removed from the restaurant's address and telephone number. All of these feng shui–inspired design features have been added as a way of attracting new customers from the ever-expanding Asian population (Steinhauer 2008).

FIGURE 2.11 To appeal to a growing number of Asian residents, elements of the Chinese philosophy *feng shui* are built into this McDonald's restaurant in Hacienda Heights, California.

© Monica Almeida/The New York Times

acculturation A specific form of cultural diffusion in which a subordinate culture adopts many of the cultural traits of a more powerful culture.

linked changes Changes in one part of a culture brought about by changes in other parts of the culture.

Before we leave the topic of cultural diffusion, it is important to distinguish between it and a related term that anthropologists use: acculturation. The concepts of diffusion and acculturation have some things in common. In fact, *acculturation* is a special type of diffusion that takes place as a result of sustained contact between two societies, one of which is subordinate to the other. Thus, both diffusion and acculturation involve cultural change as a result of contact with another group. But whereas diffusion involves a single trait or a complex set of traits, acculturation involves the widespread reorganization of one or both cultures over a short period of time. Both the dominant and subordinate cultures may experience changes, but the subordinate culture always changes more dramatically. Acculturation can have a variety of consequences. The subordinate culture may become extinct, it may be incorporated as a distinct subculture of the dominant group, or it may be assimilated (blended) into the dominant group. But whatever form it takes, acculturation is *forced* borrowing under conditions of external pressure.

Linked Changes

In the previous section, we introduced the idea that cultures are more than the sum of their parts. Rather cultures are systematic wholes, the parts of which are, to some degree, interconnected. If cultures truly are integrated wholes, it would follow that a change in one part of the culture would be likely to bring about changes in other parts. In other words, most changes that occur in cultures tend to be *linked changes*. The introduction of a single technological innovation may well set off a series of changes in other parts of the culture.

An example of linked cultural changes is the boom in cell phone usage that has occurred throughout the world. A mere twenty years ago, anyone using a cell phone on the streets of Chicago would, in all likelihood, have been a wealthy investor who was calling his stockbroker on a mobile phone the size of a gallon container of milk. Today, however, it seems as though there are more people than not walking the streets of our cities either speaking, or more frequently texting, on their cell phones. One change linked to the cell phone has been the increase in auto accidents caused by multitasking Americans wanting to make business calls or chat with friends while driving to work. Moreover, in some of our major cities the number of traffic accidents has further increased because of inattentive pedestrians talking or texting on their cell phones. In fact the New York

TABLE 2.1

Features of the Concept of Culture

Culture defined	Culture is everything that people have, think, and do as members of a society.
Culture is symbolic	The capacity to use such symbols as language and art (which is the hallmark of humanity) enables people to better understand the world around them.
Culture is shared	The shared meanings connected to things, ideas, and behavior patterns make life less ambiguous and more predictable for members of the same cultural group.
Culture is learned	Culture is transmitted not genetically but through interacting with one's cultural environment.
Culture is taken for granted	Our own culture is so ingrained in us that we are often unaware that it even exists.
Culture influences biological processes	Our bodies and biological processes are influenced by culture.
Cultural universals	Despite variations in specific details, all cultures have certain common features such as systems of governing, patterns of producing and distributing food, forms of enculturation, and family patterns.
Culture is adaptive	Culture enables people to adapt to their environments and thus increase their chances of survival.
Cultures are integrated	The various parts of a culture (that is, things, ideas, and behavior patterns) are interconnected to some degree. Thus, a change in one part of the culture is likely to bring about changes in other parts of the culture.
Cultures change	The things, ideas, and behavior patterns of some cultures change more rapidly than others, but all cultures experience change, both internally and externally.

City Department of Transportation has sponsored campaigns warning cell phone-toting pedestrians of the dangers of not paying attention when crossing the streets (Belson 2004).

"Primitive" Cultures

A fundamental feature of the discipline of cultural anthropology is its comparative approach. Whether studying religions, economic systems, ways of resolving conflicts, or art forms, cultural anthropologists look at these aspects of human behavior in the widest possible context, ranging from the most technologically simple foraging societies at one end of the continuum to the most highly industrialized societies at the other. Societies with simple technologies, once called "primitive," are described by contemporary cultural anthropologists as *preliterate, small-scale, egalitarian,* or *technologically simple.* Because of the misleading implication that something primitive is both inferior and earlier in a chronological sense, we will not use the term *primitive* in this book. Instead we will use the term *small-scale society,* which refers to societies that have small populations, are technologically simple, are usually preliterate (that is, without a written form of language), have little labor specialization, and are not highly stratified. Making such a distinction between small-scale and more complex societies should not be taken to imply that all societies can be pigeonholed into one or the other category. Rather, it is more fruitful to view all of the societies of the world along a continuum from most small-scale to most complex.

Culture and the Individual

Throughout this chapter we have used the term *culture* to refer to everything that people have, think, and do as members of a society. All cultures, both large and small, have shared sets of meanings that serve as a collective guide to behavior. Because people from the same culture learn essentially the same set of values, rules, and expected behaviors, their lives are made somewhat less complicated because they know, within broad limits, what to expect from one another. To illustrate, when people walk down a crowded hallway in the United States, there is a general understanding that they will keep to the right. Because most people share that common understanding, the traffic flows without serious interruption. If, however, someone walks down the left-hand side of the hallway, traffic will slow down because people will be unsure how to cope with the oncoming person. Such an incident is disruptive and produces anxiety for the simple reason that normal, expected, and predictable behavior has not occurred.

small-scale society A society that has a small population, has minimal technology, is usually preliterate, has little division of labor, and is not highly stratified.

Young Male Japanese Shut-Ins: A Culture-Specific Disorder.

Although culture enables people to adapt in a general sense to their environments, it is also possible for certain features of a culture to combine at a point in its history that causes some people to become socially dysfunctional. A particularly powerful example of a *culture-specific* syndrome is found in twenty-first-century Japan. Known as *hikikomori*, this culture-bound disorder is characterized by severe withdrawal by an alarming number of teenage boys and young men in Japan. Those suffering from hikikomori sequester themselves in their rooms for months and years at a time, cutting themselves off socially from the rest of society. Occupying themselves with television, video games, and Internet surfing, they rarely leave their rooms other than for early morning visits to all-night convenience stores where they can avoid all but the most superficial social interaction. Although many cases go undetected, it has been estimated that as many as a million Japanese males are shunning work and social contact by shutting themselves in their rooms (Jones 2006).

Medical and psychological experts see hikikomori largely as a social disease stemming from certain features of contemporary Japanese culture. First, for decades Japanese culture has put enormous pressure on Japanese youth, particularly males, to succeed in school and later in the corporate structure. Highly competitive cram schools preparing students for high school and college entrance exams are a major industry in post–World War II Japan. Many Japanese believe that their sons will be failures if they are not admitted to a leading university and subsequently hired by a prestigious corporation. This social pressure on Japanese males to succeed is intensified by a second feature of Japanese society—namely, conformity. In other words, a failure will "stick out like a sore thumb." Since the economic downturn in the 1990s, many young Japanese men, having become weary or fearful of the intensified competition, are dropping out, refusing to play the game, and withdrawing to their bedrooms. A third feature of Japanese culture that contributes to the rise of hikikomori is the normal relationship between parents and children. Because unmarried children normally live with their parents well into their twenties or thirties, parents often enable their children to drop out of society by continuing their economic support well into adulthood.

Young people in every culture experience difficulties adjusting to adult expectations. In Western cultures, the pressure of parental and societal expectations may cause teenagers to live on the streets (see the Applied Perspective on homeless youth in Chapter 10) or join a drug culture. In the United States, a serious (sometimes deadly) disorder among young women is anorexia nervosa, the relentless pursuit of thinness. Laboring under the *culturally based* assumption that beauty is directly proportional to slimness, young girls and women in the United States literally starve themselves to become as thin as possible. Unlike hikikomori, which affects mostly males, anorexia nervosa affects predominantly females between the ages of ten and twenty.

Both hikikomori and anorexia nervosa affect approximately 1 percent of the population and are culture specific. Hikikomori, voluntarily taking oneself out of the game of life, results from the fear of failing to reach high levels of success in school and career, which Japanese values tend to encourage. Anorexia nervosa, on the other hand, is a potentially deadly eating disorder resulting from taking a basic US value (that is, that slimness equals female attractiveness) to its illogical conclusion. Both disorders remind us how an irrational reaction to one's own cultural values can lead to dysfunctional behavior.

Our cultures exert a powerful influence on our conduct, often without our even being aware of it. However, to assert that culture *influences* our behavior is hardly the same as asserting that it *determines* our behavior. Deviance from the cultural norms is found in all societies. Because individual members of any society maintain, to varying degrees, a free will, they have the freedom to say no to cultural expectations. Unlike the honeybee, which behaves according to its genetic programming, humans can make a range of behavioral choices. Of course, choosing an alternative may result in unpleasant consequences, but all people have the option of doing things differently from what is culturally expected

People sometimes choose to go against cultural conventions for a number of reasons. In some cases where adherence to a social norm involves a hardship, people may justify their noncompliance by stretching the meaning of the norm. Or sometimes people flout a social norm or custom to make a social statement. Whatever the reason, the fact remains that social norms rarely, if ever, receive total compliance. For this reason, cultural anthropologists distinguish between ideal behavior (what people are expected to do) and real behavior (what people actually do).

New Twenty-First-Century Tools for the Study of Cultures

In the previous chapter we mentioned how the process of *globalization,* which is thought to have started with the fall of the Berlin Wall in 1988, has intensified the interconnectedness of the various peoples of the world in the last three decades because of lowering of tariff barriers, the expansion of free market economies, and the explosion of communication and information technology. Moreover, we will be revisiting this notion of globalization in a number of our substantive chapters coming up. But it is important to end this chapter on the concept of culture by discussing briefly how this recent revolution in information technology has developed exciting new tools for the study of *ethnography* (descriptions of individual cultures), *ethnology* (analysis of cultural comparisons), and culture change.

The Internet has provided easy access for hundreds of (keyword) databases that enable anyone from professional anthropologists to seventh graders to access specific cultural data suitable for analysis. For example, the American Anthropological Association (AAA; aaanet.org) has developed AnthroSource, a digital searchable database containing all past, present, and future AAA publications, more than 250,000 journal articles, and 24/7 access to anthropological information. In addition, the AAA website contains links to anthropological listservs, discussion groups, and blogs that enable anyone interested in the study of culture to share data and collaborate on research. But in addition to those tools developed by professional anthropologists and the AAA, there are also some ambitious data sources that are extremely helpful for generating profiles on different cultures through different points in time. Although space does not permit a complete survey of these new tools for the study of culture, we will consider one recent development that could vastly facilitate our understanding of cultural variability and how, and to what extent, cultures change over time.

In 2010 Google made available a free online data bank (and accompanying searching tools) comprised of words and short phrases, which was generated by digitizing 5.2 million books published between 1500 and 2008 in English, French, Spanish, German, Chinese, and Russian. For those of you who are counting, that represents a database of 500 billion words. Developed by Google Labs, this research tool, called Ngram, allows anyone to string together up to five words, and within several seconds, see a graph that charts how often each term is used in print over time. Of course, such a tool would be extremely useful for historical linguists (see Chapter 1) who are interested in determining when new words enter a language, how long they remained, and when they faded out or changed. Because of the enormity of this database, historical linguists now have a tool for measuring linguistic changes that occurred in six major languages in the world, and they can do it with incredible speed and precision.

Not only can Ngram transform our understanding of language and language change, but it can also track a wide range of other features of culture as well as the flow of ideas. To illustrate, enter the term *culture shock* in English, and with a simple click of the mouse you will be given a graph showing how the term, after being nearly non-existent in the database for over 450 years, showed a sharp spike of interest starting in 1960 and continuing through the turn of the century. This confirms (through statistically significant linguistic data) what we suspected: that 1960 was the year that the first journal article on culture shock by anthropologist Kalvero Oberg appeared in the literature; and it was one year before the creation of the Peace Corps, an organization that was faced with developing methods for minimizing the negative effects of culture shock on thousands of its young volunteers who were working under demanding conditions in developing countries.

If your research interests lay in the area of religious movements in twentieth century United States, Ngram can provide an accurate assessment of how long the idea that "God is dead" was a viable theological position. Although the phrase "God is dead" barely appeared in print until the 1950s, the heyday of this religious "movement" took off in 1958 and peaked in 1968 before leveling off for the remainder of the century at about 45 percent of its 1968 high point.

Although the Ngram Viewer is too recent an innovation to assess its true significance as an anthropological research tool, it does show enormous potential for testing hypotheses about cultural features, culture change, and the ebb and flow of human ideas. What we can say about it at this early stage of its existence is that it is a fascinating (and potentially addictive) pastime to statistically see the relative popularity of contemporary and historical words, material objects, ideas, and personalities. Now, with less effort than texting a friend, you will be able to assess (using the world's largest linguistic databases) whether Babe Ruth was more prominent than President Warren Harding or whether Lady Gaga was a more popular celebrity than Katy Perry.

Summary

1. For the purposes of this book, we have defined the term *culture* as everything that people have, think, and do as members of a society.

2. Culture is something that is shared by members of the same society. This shared nature of culture enables people to predict—within broad limits—the behavior of others in the society. Conversely, people become disoriented when attempting to interact in a culturally different society because they do not share the same behavioral expectations as members of that society.

3. Rather than being inborn, culture is acquired through a learning process that anthropologists call *enculturation*. People in different cultures learn different things, but there is no evidence to suggest that people in some cultures learn more efficiently than do people in other cultures.

4. Certain aspects of culture—such as ideas, beliefs, and values—can affect our physical bodies and our biological processes. More specifically, certain culturally produced ideas concerning physical beauty can influence the ways in which people alter their bodies.

5. Although cultures throughout the world vary considerably, certain common features (cultural universals) are found in all cultures. Cultural anthropology—the scientific study of cultures—looks at both similarities and differences in human cultures wherever they may be found.

6. Cultures function to help people adapt to their environments and consequently increase their chances for survival. It is also possible for cultures to negatively alter or even destroy their environments.

7. A culture is more than the sum of its parts. Rather, a culture should be seen as an integrated system with its parts interrelated to some degree. This cultural integration has important implications for the process of culture change because a change in one part of the system is likely to bring about changes in other parts.

8. Cultures—and their three basic components of things, ideas, and behavior patterns—are constantly experiencing change. Although the pace of culture change varies from society to society, no culture is totally static. Cultures change internally (innovation) and by borrowing from other cultures (diffusion).

9. Cultural diffusion is selective, it is a two-way process, it is likely to involve changes in form or function, some cultural items are more likely candidates for diffusion than are others, and it is affected by other important variables.

10. Acculturation is a specialized form of cultural diffusion that involves forced borrowing under external pressure.

11. Because the parts of a culture are to some degree interrelated, a change in one part is likely to bring about changes in other parts. This insight from cultural anthropology should be of paramount importance to applied anthropologists, who are often involved directly or indirectly with planned programs of cultural change.

12. Although culture exerts considerable influence on a person's thoughts and behaviors, it does not determine them.

13. With the vast changes in information technology over the past thirty years, a number of powerful tools (such as AnthroSource and Ngram) have been developed that greatly facilitate the study of culture, culture change, and the flow of ideas from one part of the world to another.

Key Terms

symbol	enculturation	organic analogy	linked changes
civilization	monochronic culture	invention	small-scale society
culture shock	polychronic culture	innovation	
subculture	cultural universals	cultural diffusion	
pluralistic societies	adaptive nature of culture	acculturation	

Critical Thinking Questions

1. Cultural diffusion is the spreading of a thing, idea, or behavior pattern from one culture to another. Look at your own culture and identify as many cultural features as possible that have been diffused from other cultures throughout the world. In other words, these cultural features were not invented by our culture.

2. In this chapter we learned that culture is both adaptive and maladaptive. How many cultural features in the United States can you identify which are maladaptive?

3. The United States and Canada are both pluralistic societies because they are composed of a number of subcultural groups. Look around your own town or city and identify the major subcultural groups that make your immediate community diverse. Which groups are the most powerful and which are the least powerful?

Online Study Resources

CourseMate

Access chapter-specific learning tools including learning objectives, practice quizzes, videos, flash cards, glossaries, web links, and more in your Cultural Anthropology CourseMate. Login to www.cengagebrain.com to access the resources your instructor has assigned and to purchase materials.

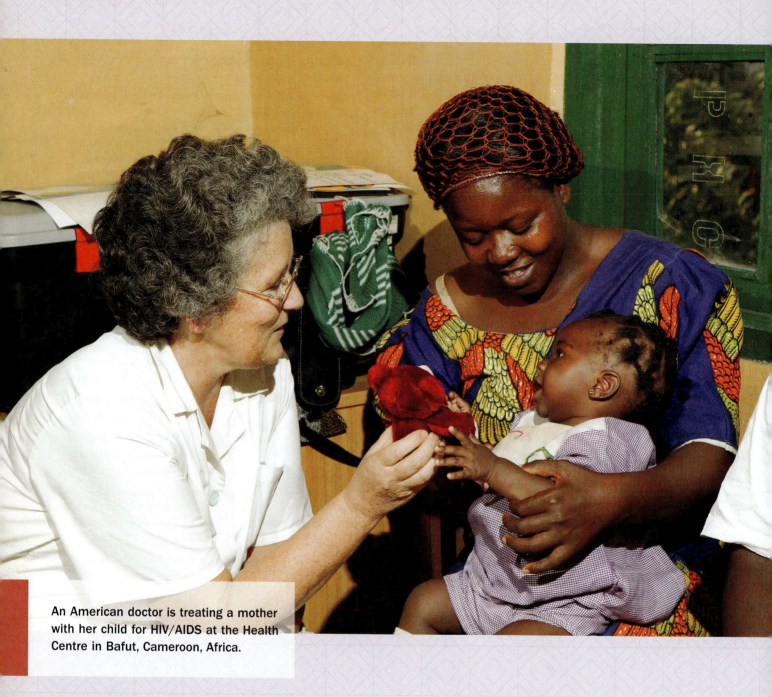

An American doctor is treating a mother with her child for HIV/AIDS at the Health Centre in Bafut, Cameroon, Africa.

Applied Anthropology

While visiting relatives with her husband in Boston for several weeks, Ngina Githongo, a twenty-three-year-old woman from Limuru, Kenya, was rushed to a local hospital for an emergency appendectomy. On the morning after the operation, the nurse brought Ngina a typical US breakfast consisting of two poached eggs, lightly buttered toast, and orange juice. When the nurse returned thirty-five minutes later, she noticed that Ngina had eaten everything except the two eggs, which were placed intentionally on the menu to ensure that Ngina received an adequate amount of protein needed for a speedy recuperation. The nurse commented that Ngina should eat her eggs if she wanted to leave the hospital as quickly as possible. Looking somewhat surprised, Ngina told the nurse, "Oh, I could never eat the eggs of a chicken!" After giving Ngina a less than friendly glare, the nurse picked up the breakfast tray and left the room.

Clearly the nurse was annoyed with Ngina for being either ungrateful for the food or too simple-minded to know that she needed a high-protein diet. But Ngina was neither ungrateful nor simple-minded. Rather, she was adhering to a widely held food taboo among the Kikuyu of east Africa. Kikuyu females grow up believing that they will be infertile if they ever eat the egg of a chicken. Moreover they believe this every bit as strongly as many Americans believe that bad things will happen to them if they sleep on the thirteenth floor of a hotel.

The nurse's response was both unprofessional and counterproductive. Rather than being offended, she should have learned why Ngina did not eat the chicken eggs. Even though the nurse (in all likelihood) would not have shared Ngina's belief that chicken eggs cause infertility, it is not part of her job description as a nurse to talk patients out of their strongly held beliefs. The nurse's primary responsibility is to provide the best possible medical care for the patient. Consequently, the more professional response would have been for the nurse, equipped with cultural knowledge about the patient, to substitute a piece of cheese or meat for the eggs so that the patient gets the appropriate amount of protein. Clearly this nurse is a prime candidate for a course in medical anthropology, a specialized subfield of applied cultural anthropology aimed at sensitizing medical professionals to the special features of their patients' cultures that can influence wellness and healing. ■

Heiner Heine/imagebroker/Alamy

Applied Anthropology

As we have pointed out in the first two chapters, cultural anthropologists are inquisitive and curious about people, their way of life, their beliefs and values, the way they do things and the material objects they make, use, collect, and discard over a lifetime. In general, these anthropologists may be considered ethnographic or descriptive anthropologists because their interests lay in principally describing another culture. Yet another distinction is made within anthropology between anthropologists who use or apply their anthropological training in real-world settings, versus those who are more descriptive or theoretical in their outcomes. Let us explain.

Among cultural anthropologists, another way of approaching one's research or career is to have an *applied perspective* from the outset. What is meant by this? Specifically, there are cultural anthropologists who purposefully conduct field research among populations experiencing serious societal problems with the goal of changing or improving these problems. They work on issues such as poor health, inadequate food production, high infant mortality, political repression, or rampant population growth, which are but a few concerns facing societies. In other settings anthropologists with an applied perspective might be employed to develop new products or organize a vaccination program in a developing country or facilitate team building in an international corporation. These cultural anthropologists are often referred to as applied anthropologists. Simply put, *applied anthropology* is characterized as being primarily aimed at changing human behavior to ameliorate contemporary problems. The applied anthropologist takes on an additional role in their research whereby they seek to improve specific social, economic, or political conditions.

In the discipline of anthropology some circles make a further distinction between applied anthropologists and practicing anthropologists. Applied anthropologists generally work at a university and also work as consultants for government or nongovernmental agencies or as principle investigators on their own research. Such applied anthropologists may also work with community partners to establish a community-based research project while also employed at a university. *Practicing anthropologists*, on the other hand, may be a specialist in a topical area of anthropology or a particular methodology, but they use their anthropological knowledge in their places of employment. These applied anthropologists are not employed by a university; rather they are practitioners applying anthropological concepts where they work and in the jobs they perform. For example, you may have heard about an anthropologist working in the human relations office for an international corporation or possibly came across a story about an anthropologist and their product development for Microsoft in the gaming industry or an anthropologist who has had their hand in technology device development for Apple.

Although, to some extent, anthropologists have always applied their findings to the solution of human problems, an increasing number of anthropologists since the mid-twentieth century have conducted research aimed explicitly at practical applications. These practitioners share the applied perspective, which is characterized by *problem-oriented research* among the world's contemporary populations. These pragmatic anthropologists attempt to apply anthropological data, concepts, and strategies to the solution of social, economic, environmental, and technological problems, both at home and abroad. Such applied anthropologists also have further specializations that they may have acquired in graduate school while completing advanced degrees.

As you have seen, a number of terms have been given to the variety of uses for applying anthropological research for the improvement of human conditions: *action anthropology, development anthropology, practicing anthropology*, and *advocacy anthropology*. For the purposes of this chapter, however, we will use the more widely accepted and generic term *applied anthropology* for all forms and interpretations of the term. As you read through this chapter we hope you may find ways in which you might include anthropological concepts in your careers, whether or not you declare a major or minor in anthropology. For some of you graduate school in anthropology might be the next logical step in a career, whereas for others this course in anthropology may be sufficient for your career plans. No matter what career you chose, however, you can carry your anthropological knowledge with you to help you better interact with people from around the world.

All Anthropologists Are Not Applied Anthropologists

The nature of anthropological research—which involves living with people, sharing their lives, and often befriending them—makes it difficult for cultural anthropologists to ignore the enormity of the problems these societies face on an everyday basis. It should therefore come as no surprise that many cultural anthropologists feel a sense of responsibility for helping to solve—or at least alleviate—some of these

---

applied anthropology The application of anthropological knowledge, theory, and methods to the solution of specific societal problems.

problem-oriented research A type of anthropological research designed to solve a particular societal problem rather than to test a theoretical position.

Stephen Dorey ABIPP/Alamy

FIGURE 3.1 Medical anthropologists can contribute to food and nutrition programs where they assist in a variety of capacities as researchers and advocates as in this feeding project in the village of Buli, Malawi.

chairs the Department of Global Health and Social Medicine at Harvard Medical School, earned both his MD and his Ph.D. in medical anthropology in 1990. Farmer is also one of the founding directors at a nonprofit organization established in Haiti, Partners in Health (PIH), twenty-five years ago. PIH has a long history treating the Haitian people for HIV/AIDS and tuberculosis. PIH was poised to provide health care when the devastating earthquake struck Haiti in 2010. Today PIH has its headquarters in Boston, and they have established clinics in Burundi, Guatemala, Haiti, Lesotho, Malawi, Mexico, Peru, Rwanda, and Russia.

Applying the Anthropological Perspective

pressing social problems (Figure 3.1). Given this understanding we also know that all anthropologists are not applied anthropologists, much like all anthropologists are not archaeologists. Anthropologists may specialize in a subfield of anthropology and that subfield may be applied anthropology. As was discussed in Chapter 1 some anthropologists consider applied anthropology to be a fifth subfield to anthropology, whereas other anthropologists recognize that applied concepts are embedded in all of anthropology's four major subfields. Either way understanding a particular culture is at the heart of being able to engage in applied anthropological work.

Most anthropologists who identify with an applied perspective are cultural anthropologists, but the other three traditional subfields (archaeology, biological or physical, and linguistics) are certainly involved in their share of applied activities. For example, an archaeologist may develop a career around cultural resource management; a biological anthropologist may be involved in forensic anthropology where they work on crime scenes and testify in court, or they may assist in disaster work with DNA analysis and body recovery. A linguist may work on language preservation among speakers of an endangered language (one with a small number of speakers).

Some applied anthropologists share both an interest in biological and cultural anthropology and may combine these interests in the form of medical anthropology. To illustrate, there are some medical anthropologists who have a degree in nursing or in medicine. In fact, Paul Farmer, a renowned medical doctor who

Previously in the chapter we made the distinction between ethnographic or theoretical research and applied or problem-oriented research. However, we want to temper this contrast. If we take the ethnographic or applied distinction too literally, we might conclude that applied anthropologists are devoid of any theoretical concerns and that ethnographers have no concern for the practical implications of their work. In actual practice, neither of these is true. Applied anthropology, when it is done effectively, takes into account theories, methods, and data that have been developed by the discipline as a whole. And similarly, the more theoretically oriented anthropologists are indebted to applied anthropologists for stimulating their interest in new areas of research and, in some cases, for contributing to the development of new theory. For a more well-developed discussion of how applied and theoretical anthropology can inform one another, see the article by Barbara Rylko-Bauer, Merrill Singer, and John Van Willigen (2006: 184-85).

It is not surprising that the line between ethnographic and applied anthropology is so murky because both groups receive the same form of training and draw on the same methods—notably, participant-observation and interviewing (Figure 3.2). The line is blurred still further by the fact that the two have experienced parallel development, have been mutually supportive, and often work in the same university departments.

Thus, it would be misleading to think of cultural anthropology as being neatly divided into *ethnographic* or *theoretical anthropology*, on the one hand, and *applied* or *problem-oriented anthropology*, on the other. Rather, we should think more in terms of a continuum, with five different types of cultural anthropology ranging from most theoretical to most applied. Alexander Ervin

FIGURE 3.2 Dr. Paul Farmer has devoted his life to treating infectious diseases and is one of the founders of Partners In Health (PIH), an international health and social justice organization. Farmer meets with a student group, Students Helping Honduras, at Virginia Tech and shares how working in one impoverished Haitian village grew into an organization with projects addressing health and poverty issues on multiple continents.

(2005: 2-5) suggests such a model comprised of the following five types of cultural anthropology (see also Table 3.1 and 3.2):

1. *Ethnography* or *ethnology*. For the past century, traditional ethnography (describing) and ethnology (comparing or theorizing) have accounted for most of the anthropological studies conducted on cultures and subcultures throughout the world. These wide-ranging studies have examined everything from nomadic pastoralists in Uganda to schoolchildren in New York City, and from subsistence farmers in New Guinea to an urban street gang in Chicago. The meticulousness with which these many and varied cultural groups have been described, analyzed, and compared has led to the development of the accumulated knowledge (cultural practices, behaviors, values, ideologies, and institutions) of cultural anthropology.

2. *Studies of social issues.* The ethnographic study of contemporary social issues often generates findings that have relevance to policy makers. For example, Shirley Fiske who has worked in executive and legislative branches of the federal government including the National Oceanic and Atmospheric Administration (NOAA) has promoted the value of social sciences and anthropology for ocean governance, marine fisheries, coastal communities, and the human dimension of climate change. Her work in large part has been in support of promoting policies for common property use of shared natural resources.

3. *Policy studies.* The purpose of policy research is to provide information to those in position to make decisions on behalf of others, formulate policy, implement it, or possibly conduct evaluations on policy. It is policy that we look to for the strategies of action or making choices that we use to achieve desired goals. So whether one is engaged in public policy, food policy, industrial policy, social policy, or environmental policy, they are all strategies designed for action or choices used by government, nongovernmental agencies, or other organizations. Conducting an evaluation on the effectiveness of postdisaster funding to Haiti in its earthquake aftermath, Mark Schuller (2012) found critical examples in how funding was distributed to government and nongovernmental

TABLE 3.1

Comparison of Ethnographic and Applied Anthropology

	Ethnographic Anthropology	Applied Anthropology
Primary objective	Test hypotheses and describe ethnographic reality	Help solve societal problems
Research methods	Participant-observation and interviewing	Rapid ethnographic assessment (see Chapter 5)
Time frame	A year or longer	Several weeks to several months
Collaboration	Seldom collaborative	Usually collaborative

TABLE 3.2

A Continuum of Ethnographic and Applied Cultural Anthropology

Ethnographic Polarity				Applied Polarity
Ethnography/ethnology	Studies of social issues	Policy studies	Applied anthropology	Practicing anthropology

organizations for water and sanitation. His findings shed light on the rampant spread of infectious diseases facing the Haitian peoples who remain in the tent cities.

4. *Applied anthropology.* Applied cultural anthropology is most often commissioned by organizations (businesses, governments, and nonprofits) that are interested in receiving concrete recommendations for solving specific problems. For example, an international aid agency may be interested in knowing how best to establish a health clinic in a rural area that has been experiencing high incidence of infectious diseases related to chronic hunger and poor sanitation, or a nongovernmental organization that is involved in environmental awareness campaigns might be developing plans among coastal low lying communities for future rising waters and more extreme climatic events.

5. *Practicing anthropology.* The term *practicing anthropology* has become popular since the 1970s to refer to that group of professionally trained anthropologists (at the MA or PhD level) who work full-time outside of academia by applying their cultural expertise to advance the goals of their employing organizations. Unlike their academically based counterparts, practicing anthropologists not only conduct needs assessments, program evaluations, and social impact studies, but frequently implement and administer the programs as well. For example, the Center for Disease Control employs anthropologists to use their medical anthropology training to assist in public health education, intervention programs, and assist in field and laboratory research.

The work of applied anthropology involves (to varying degrees) three major products: information, policy, and action. The first of these products is the collection of solid sociocultural *information* on the people under study—the so-called project beneficiaries. This information, obtained by conducting research with community partners (see Chapter 5) can range from raw ethnographic data, different levels of analyses, to general anthropological theories (Figure 3.3). Using research findings as a foundation, the applied anthropologist next develops *policy*, which can be used to help lessen a problem or condition identified during the information-gathering phase. Although anthropologists may, in fact, be involved in the policy-making process, it is more likely that they will include the policy implications in their findings, or even make policy recommendations. The final product of the applied anthropologist is a plan of *action*, or intervention, designed to correct the problem or undesirable condition. Thus, as John Van Willigen (2002: 11) reminds us, "information is obtained through research, information is used to formulate policy, and policy guides action."

Recent History of Applied Anthropology

Applied anthropology has always been a part of the discipline of anthropology. In fact, applied and ethnographic or theoretical anthropology have developed alongside each other. Anthropologists with applied interests were involved in shaping the professional organizations from the beginning. To illustrate, from its founding in 1902, the American Anthropological Association (AAA; today's largest professional organization of anthropologists) was linked to the Anthropological Society of Washington (founded in 1879), an organization that helped organize applied research on inequities in low-income housing in Washington, D.C., during the nineteenth century. Also, some of the major subfields of anthropology evolved out of early applied research, including political, urban, medical, agricultural, educational, and environmental anthropology. Thus, as we can see, applied anthropology has played a key role in shaping the entire discipline of anthropology (Rylko-Bauer, Singer, and Van Willigen 2006: 179).

Throughout the history of anthropology, its anthropologists have been concerned

FIGURE 3.3 Indonesia Sulawesi Kaledupa Island Ambuea Project Darwin employee talking to Indonesian environmental researcher.

with the use of their findings for solving social problems. For example, in the early 1930s the Applied Anthropology Unit of Indian Affairs was created by President Franklin Roosevelt's Commissioner of Indian Affairs, John Collier (an anthropologist himself). The aim of this unit was to study the progress of self-governing organizations among some American Indian groups as called for in the 1934 Indian Reorganization Act. As part of the Interdisciplinary Committee on Human Relations at the University of Chicago, anthropologists W. Lloyd Warner, Burleigh Gardner, and others conducted applied research in the areas of industrial management, productivity, and working conditions. Moreover World War II provided vast opportunities for anthropologists to apply their skills and insights to the war.

Even though anthropologists have been applying their insights since the beginning of the twentieth century, the real stimulus came in the 1940s, when many of the leading cultural anthropologists were asked to participate in efforts related to World War II. Margaret Mead (1977), herself a government employee during the war years, estimated that 95 percent of all professional anthropologists in the United States contributed to the war effort.

Anthropologists were recruited by the National Research Council to examine national morale during wartime, to learn about food preferences and wartime rationing, and to perform national character studies on our adversaries—the Germans, Italians, and Japanese. After the war most anthropologists left government service and returned to academia and more theoretical concerns (Figure 3.4). This trend continued throughout the 1950s and 1960s. Any applied anthropology that was conducted during those decades was carried out by academic anthropologists engaged in short-term projects outside the university setting.

From the 1970s to the present, however, a new brand of applied anthropology has emerged. These new applied anthropologists are not university professors but full-time employees of the hiring agencies. Data from a recent survey conducted by the American Anthropological Association (AAA) indicate that approximately 30 percent of all anthropologists with doctorate degrees work outside an academic setting for government organizations or nonprofit or private-sector firms. This trend is largely the result of two factors essentially external to the discipline of anthropology. First, over the past four decades, the market for most academic jobs has declined dramatically. The abundance of jobs that marked the 1950s and 1960s turned into a shortage of jobs in the 1970s and afterward. Second, increased federal legislation has mandated policy research that can be accomplished effectively by cultural anthropologists. For example, the National Historic Preservation Act of 1966 (aiming to preserve the historical and cultural foundations of the nation), the National Environmental Policy Act of 1969 (requiring impact assessments of federally funded construction projects on the cultural environment), and the Foreign Assistance Act of 1961 (establishing USAID, the foreign aid arm of the federal government) all provide for policy research of a cultural nature. As a result of these two factors (fewer academic jobs and more applied research opportunities), more anthropologists with doctorates are finding permanent employment outside academia. This trend has been accompanied by increases in the number of master's programs in applied anthropology (see the national Consortium for Practicing and Applied Anthropology programs for a listing http://www.copaa.info/) and growing membership in applied anthropology organizations, such as the Society for Applied Anthropology (SFAA) and the National Association of Practicing Anthropologists (NAPA).

The Ethics of Cultural Anthropology: Ethnographic and Applied

All field anthropologists—both those who do applied work and those who do descriptive ethnographic fieldwork—find themselves in social situations that are varied and complex because they work with and have different role relationships with a wide range of people. For example, they are involved with and have responsibilities to their subjects, their discipline, their colleagues (both in and outside anthropology), their host governments, their own governments, and their sponsoring agencies.

Under such socially complex conditions, it is likely that the anthropologist, having to choose among

© Michael Pole/Corbis

FIGURE 3.4 After World War II, many anthropologists left government service and returned to colleges and universities. This trend, which continued throughout the 1950s and the 1960s, accompanied a return to more theoretical concerns.

conflicting values, will face a number of ethical dilemmas. For example, how do you make your findings public without jeopardizing the anonymity of your informants? Can you ever be certain that the data your informants gave you will not eventually be used to harm them? How can you be certain that the project you are working on will benefit the people with whom you worked? To what extent should you become personally involved in the lives of the people you are studying? Should you intervene to stop illegal activity? These are just a few of the ethical questions that arise in anthropological research. Though recognizing that anthropologists continually face such ethical decisions, the profession has made it clear that each member of the profession is ultimately responsible for anticipating these ethical dilemmas and for resolving them in a way that avoids causing harm to their subjects or to other scholars.

Today US federal law and policies at most research-oriented universities require that any faculty research (in which human beings are subjects) must comply with accepted ethical and professional standards. Generally academic anthropologists are required to submit a description of their research to their university's internal review board (IRB), a committee dedicated to research on human and animal subjects, and obtain

approval for the methods to be used in conducting the research. Many granting agencies refuse to fund anthropological research unless the proposed research has been reviewed for potential ethical pitfalls.

Concern for professional ethics is hardly a recent phenomenon among anthropologists. As early as 1919 Franz Boas, the guru of the first generation of US anthropologists spoke out adamantly against the practice of anthropologists engaging in spying activities while allegedly conducting scientific research. Writing in *Nation*, Boas (1919:797) charged that someone who uses science to cover for political spying should not be called a scientist. Although anthropologists have been aware of ethical dilemmas, it was the Society for Applied Anthropology (SfAA) that first developed an ethics statement in 1949 and was the first within the field of anthropology to do so. In 1971 the AAA adopted its "Principles of Professional Responsibility" and established a Committee on Ethics. The SfAA published a revision of its "Statement on Professional and Ethical Responsibilities" in 1975. See the websites of the AAA (http://www.aaanet.org) and the SfAA (http://www.sfaa.net), for the most recent versions of these statements.

Although the SfAA first published its statement of ethics in 1949, because of events that transpired during World War II the independent publication of these professional codes of ethics in the 1970s was, to a large degree, precipitated by several controversial events that occurred in the 1960s. One controversy revolved around the allegation that US anthropologists secretly had engaged in counterinsurgency research for the Pentagon during the Vietnam War. Another ethical crisis arose around *Project Camelot (1964–1965)*, a $6-million research project funded by the US Army to gather data on counterinsurgency that would enable the US Army to cope more effectively with internal revolutions in foreign countries, primarily in Asia, Latin America, Africa, and Europe. Project Camelot, which had hired the services of a number of prominent anthropologists, was canceled by the secretary of defense shortly after the project director was hired. Word about this clandestine operation in Chile was brought to the attention of the Chilean senate, which reacted with outrage over the apparent US. interference in its internal affairs.

Although the project never really got under way, it had enormous repercussions for the discipline of anthropology. The heated debate among anthropologists that followed revolved around two important questions. First, was Project Camelot a legitimately objective attempt to gather social science data, or was it a cover for the US Army to intervene in the internal political

CROSS-CULTURAL MISCUE

✿ A medical researcher received an opportunity to work in Mali at a Malaria Research and Training Center. Filled with enthusiasm, but limited cultural experience, she was confident she would have a malaria research program up and running in a month's time. Her research experience had been in New York City where she was accustomed to speaking with individuals; however, she had no background in Africa, let alone Malian culture. Used to the individualism of US culture, where everyone can make decisions by themselves, she headed out visiting individuals in the Malian village. To move the research program forward she needed participants and their informed consent. What she did not realize is the village works together as a unit; the social structures demand that decision making be done more communally than in the West. Had she held a communal meeting or focus groups among men and women or spoken to the village elders she may have made more headway. One thing is for certain, the process would take much longer than a month to get a research program running of any kind. It requires more discussion and more ground work to generate mutual understanding of a project for the participants and their entire community. How might the medical researcher have prepared for her overseas experience differently? What anthropological and ethical consequences might she have considered before rushing out to individuals in the village? How would this project have benefitted from hiring a medical anthropologist?

Project Camelot (1964–1965) An aborted US Army research project designed to study the causes of civil unrest and violence in developing countries; created a controversy among anthropologists about whether the US government was using them as spies.

affairs of sovereign nations? And second, were the participating anthropologists misled into thinking that scientific research was the project's sole objective, while they were really (and perhaps unwittingly) serving as undercover spies?

One practical and immediate consequence of the alleged activities of US anthropologists in both Vietnam and Project Camelot was the cloud of suspicion that fell over all legitimate anthropological research. For years afterward many US anthropologists experienced difficulties trying to prove that they were not engaged in secret research sponsored by the Central Intelligence Agency (CIA) or the Department of Defense. And history has a tendency to repeat itself.

Profound changes occurred in the United States and elsewhere in the world after September 11, 2001, subsequent to the loss of life and destruction of the twin towers in New York City, the Pentagon in Arlington, Virginia, and the downed plane in Pennsylvania. These simultaneous events have had major implications for everyone in general, and in particular for a number of researchers working in the Middle East, be they archaeologists, linguists, cultural or biological anthropologists. Not only has air travel changed since 9/11, these past events continue to influence where, how, and why research is conducted. For example, post-9/11 has brought on a new era for field anthropologists. Some linguists and other social scientists are employed in military intelligence for the United States Army in a program referred to as the *Human Terrain System (HTS)*. Such anthropologists, who are specialists of the Middle East region have been hired to provide military commanders and staff with an understanding of the language and culture of the local population resulting in a map of the "human terrain." According to Anthropologist Montgomery McFate (2011), from 2007, HTS has grown from a program with five deployed teams and a $20 million two-year budget to one that has become a permanent US Army program with 31 deployed teams and a $150 million annual budget by 2010.

Coming off the distant heels of Project Camelot and Vietnam, the HTS program has caused great controversy within the anthropological academy among anthropologists who believe working with or aiding the military violates both the SfAA and AAA code of professional responsibility. There are others who see things differently and believe they have a moral obligation to assist because their cultural understandings

of the region may contribute to peaceful resolutions in the region.

The public debate surrounding HTS has received widespread coverage in the media, at annual SfAA and AAA conferences, and has been the topic of numerous articles in academic journals. All controversy aside, today's anthropologists specializing in the Middles East, Islamic studies, and Arabic culture and language may find employment teaching cultural anthropology in a range of places that provide assistance to people working in the region. In addition, Peace and Conflict Studies programs established at universities also hire anthropologists with language and cultural expertise.

As we discussed previously, the discipline of anthropology learned an important but costly lesson from Vietnam and Project Camelot: Anthropologists have a responsibility to their subjects, their profession, their colleagues, and themselves to become much more aware of the motives, objectives, and assumptions of the organizations that sponsor their research. Also, professors and instructors cannot control what students do with the information and skills might be imparted in a classroom setting. However, they can equip men and women with cross-cultural understandings that may allow them to do their jobs and carry out their orders in a more culturally informed and sensitive fashion (Figure 3.5). Yet at the end of the day, maintaining the SfAA and AAAs' code of professionally responsibility to do no harm is paramount to working with in any population.

All anthropologists have an ethical responsibility to avoid being hired by or receiving funds from any organization that might use their research findings in morally questionable ways. These lessons learned from past experiences need to be considered and re-evaluated by anthropologists working in Afghanistan, Iraq, and elsewhere that is politically contested, and especially by those working within the Human Terrain System (HTS). The AAA recently revised their code of ethics in response

---

Human Terrain System (HTS) A US Army, military intelligence support program in which personnel are hired from the social science disciplines—such as anthropology, sociology, political science, regional studies, and linguistics—to provide military commanders and staff with an understanding of the local population (that is, the "human terrain") in the regions in which they are deployed.

Courtesy of United States Department of Defense

FIGURE 3.5 U.S. Army Maj. Robert Holbert takes notes as he talks and drinks tea with local school and Andar Special Needs School administrators in Nani, Afghanistan.

to anthropologists' participation in the HTS and the opposing views some anthropologists have of their colleagues' participation. The AAA website will have the most current version (http://www.aaanet.org/). Here is a synthesis of the code of ethics shared by SfAA and AAA that help guide one's professional responsibility as an anthropologist.

Anthropologists' Major Areas of Ethical Responsibility

The codes of professional ethics adopted by the AAA and the SfAA are not appreciably different. Both codes identify major areas of responsibility for all anthropologists, including the following:

- *Responsibility to the people studied.* According to the AAA and the SfAA, the anthropologist's paramount responsibility is to the people he or she studies. Every effort must be made to protect the physical, psychological, and social well-being of the people under study. The aims and anticipated consequences of the research must be clearly communicated to the research subjects so they can decide for themselves whether they wish to participate in the research. Participation is to be voluntary and should be based on the principle of informed consent. Informants should in no way be exploited, and their rights to remain anonymous must be protected.
- *Responsibility to the public and to the communities affected by our actions.* Anthropologists have a fundamental responsibility to respect the dignity, integrity, and worth of the communities that will be directly affected by the research findings. More generally, anthropologists have a responsibility to the general public to disseminate their findings truthfully and openly. They are also expected to make their findings available to the public for use in policy formation.
- *Responsibility to the discipline and social science colleagues.* Anthropologists bear responsibility for maintaining the reputation of the discipline and their colleagues. They must avoid engaging in any research of which the results or sponsorship cannot be freely and openly reported. Anthropologists must refrain from any behavior that will jeopardize future research for other members of the profession.
- *Responsibility to students, interns, and trainees.* Anthropologists should be fair, candid, and non-exploitive when dealing with their students. They should alert students to the ethical problems of research and should acknowledge in print the contributions that students make to anthropologists' professional activities, including both research and publications.
- *Responsibility to sponsors, employers, and funders.* Anthropologists have a professional responsibility to be honest about their qualifications, capabilities, and purposes. Before accepting employment or research funding, an anthropologist is obligated to reflect sincerely on the purposes of the sponsoring organizations and the potential uses to which the findings will be put. Anthropologists must retain the right to make all ethical decisions in their research while at the same time reporting the research findings accurately, openly, and completely.
- *Responsibility to one's own and the host governments.* Anthropologists should be honest and candid in their relationships with both their own and the host governments. They should demand assurances that they will not be asked to compromise their professional standards or ethics as a precondition for research clearance. They should not conduct clandestine research or write secret reports.

Ethical Consideration in Private and Public Sectors

With the growth in applied anthropology in recent decades, many cultural anthropologists are finding employment in the private and public sectors. This raises some important ethical dilemmas because, as employees, such applied anthropologists may not have control over their own research. To illustrate, it is possible that an employer could ask the applied anthropologist to engage in research that could be harmful to a specific population, such as how best to market cigarettes or alcohol. Even in cases where the products are not harmful, it is possible that anthropological research can be applied not to developing better products but rather to devising new ways to encourage consumers to buy one product rather than a competitor's. Also, suppose an applied anthropologist was prohibited from publishing important scientific findings based on his or her proprietary research because the employing firm felt it might give an advantage to a competitor. Fortunately, these and many other potential conflicts of interest are explicitly covered by the general guidelines of either the AAA or the SfAA.

Similarly in academia, anthropologists must have their research approved by their University's Internal Review Board (IRB) when working with human subjects. The IRB assumes no project or questionnaire is benign. For example, asking what might be thought of as a harmless question, "how many children do you have," may provoke unpleasant memories for a mother who has lost a child because of accident, miscarriage, violence, war, or something else. The outsider, the anthropologist, who would not have known the family history, may have thought they were only collecting information on household size when in fact they could be rekindling an old wound. Careful consideration is needed in learning how and when to ask questions while doing community-engaged research. We will talk more about methods used in ethnographic anthropology and applied cultural anthropology in Chapter 5.

Funding Applied Research

Much of the applied anthropology carried out in recent decades has been supported by large public and private organizations seeking to better understand the cultural dimensions of their sponsored programs. These organizations include international agencies such as the:

- US Agency for International Development (USAID)
- the World Bank, the World Health Organization (WHO)
- National Oceanic Atmospheric Administration (NOAA)
- Center for Disease Control and Prevention (CDC)
- the Ford Foundation, and the Population Council
- certain national organizations such as the National Institutes of Health (NIH)
- the Bureau of Indian Affairs
- the US Department of Agriculture, and on a more local level, various hospitals, private corporations and foundations, school systems, urban planning departments, substance abuse programs, facilities for the aged, and family planning clinics

These private and public agencies not only are interested in what applied anthropologists' research has to offer, but in some cases they are the funding agencies that the researchers apply to for financing their research or developing their project. A useful skill for an applied anthropologist is to know how to write grant proposals to secure funding for the desired projects. Such technical writing can be helpful in community-based partnerships because often the applied social scientist may be the one assisting in the grant-writing process. Some grants help fund the anthropologist for short-term work from a few weeks to a couple of months; other contracts might be for much longer period, employing them for half a year to a year, and possibly longer.

Experience tells us there is no such thing as a free lunch, thus being a successful grant writer may help to provide the necessary funding for a project and help keep the applied anthropologist employed. Knowing where your funding source is also makes one accountable to their funders. Sometimes being ethically responsible is saying "no" to the funding or even not applying to certain funding agencies. So whether one is an independent contractor working on a project or one is employed at a university and working on a project over the summer months or taking time off from teaching and involved in a project all projects need to be funded in some way. While involved in the particular project an applied anthropologist may be hired for a special role or several roles, depending on the nature of the project and the expertise. Some of the roles an applied anthropologist may take on during their involvement in the project are discussed next.

Specialized Roles of Applied Anthropologists

Applied anthropologists also play a number of specialized roles, which are more thoroughly described by John Van Willigen (2002: 3–6):

Policy researcher: This role, perhaps the most common role for applied anthropologists, involves providing cultural data to policy makers so that they can make the most informed policy decisions.

Evaluator: In another role that is also quite common, evaluators use their research skills to determine how well a program or policy has succeeded in fulfilling its objectives.

Impact assessor: This role entails measuring the effects of a particular project, program, or policy on local peoples. For example, impact assessors may determine the consequences, both intended and unintended, that a federal highway construction project might have for the community through which the highway runs.

Planner: In this fairly common role, applied anthropologists actively participate in the design of various programs and policies.

Needs assessor: This role involves conducting research to determine ahead of time the need for a proposed program or project.

Trainer: Adopting what is essentially a teaching role, the applied anthropologist imparts cultural knowledge about certain populations to different professional groups working in cross-cultural situations (such as Peace Corps volunteers or international businesspeople).

Advocate: This rare role involves becoming an active supporter of a particular group of people. Usually involving political action, this role is most often combined with other roles.

Expert witness: This role involves the presentation of culturally relevant research findings as part of judicial proceedings through legal briefs, depositions, or direct testimony.

Administratory manager: An applied anthropologist who assumes direct administrative responsibility for a particular project is working in this specialized role.

Cultural broker: This role may involve serving as a liaison between the program planner and administrators on one hand and local ethnic communities on the other, or between mainstream hospital personnel and their ethnically distinct patients.

These specialized roles are not mutually exclusive. In many cases, applied anthropologists play two or more of these roles as part of the same job. For example, an applied anthropologist who is working as a policy researcher may also conduct a needs assessment before a program is initiated and carry out an impact assessment and evaluation after the program has concluded. It is not uncommon for an applied anthropologist to be working at their university during the academic year and be involved in a short-term project over the summer. It is also possible to maintain local projects during the academic year while also teaching. This makes for a busy year but possibly one that also offers opportunities for students to participate in as part of their course requirements.

One place that tends to hire a number of anthropologists is the federal government. According to Shirley J. Fiske (2008), an applied anthropologist, the federal government is the largest employer of anthropologists outside of the academy, employing nearly 7,500 social scientists in 2006. Writing for the NAPA Bulletin, Fiske offers recommendations and lessons learned from other federal employees that she interviewed. She found that along with their advanced degree (an advanced degree in anthropology or another social science) federal employees or short- or long-term contractors for international projects or programs should have a secondary specialty. For those planning to work in international development, specialties in data collection and analysis, which we will talk more about in Chapter 5, are useful skills to have for research and evaluation. Substantive specialties such as public health, agriculture, public policy, or any number of topical areas are also important. No one is hired just because they are an applied cultural anthropologist.

Having experience is equally important before applying to the federal government. Working for a non-governmental agency when one first graduates would be akin to a doctorate graduate going onto a post-doc for additional training or mentoring experiences before seeking employment at a university. In this case, the applied anthropologist who goes on to work for a non-governmental organization is getting additional and valuable training and mentoring before applying for a federal position such as USAID or the World Bank. Those applicants with more hands-on experience have a greater chance of being considered for a position because of their additional training.

Fiske identifies three areas which could help applied anthropologists as well as other social scientists who want to be or who are already employed by the federal government. She recommends:

1. "Get methodological and statistics training." Most of the anthropologists mentioned that in addition to graduate school, many anthropologists were expected in their jobs to have this training.

2. "Utilize internships, fellowships, and networking." Networking is a life-long skill and these programs allow prospective job seekers to make employment contacts.

3. "Prepare with training specific to government work." Receive training in federal laws applicable to your specialty and practical skills such as how to create, read and interpret a budget. Although most skills are learned on the job; you can find workshops, classes or courses on various topics to keep current.

Examples of Applied Anthropology

An Ethnographic Study of Postdisaster Relief (Development Anthropology)

Haiti experienced a devastating earthquake on January 12, 2010. As many as 300,000 people lost their lives; equally as many were severely injured and more than a million were orphaned. Port-au-Prince along with Léongâne, Jacmel, Petit-Goâve, and Grand-Goâve were devastated. With no building or housing codes, most structures collapsed with the 7.0 seismic quake. Nearly two million people became internally displaced. Questions were quickly raised about where the Haitian people would now reside and how they would survive.

At a United Nations conference held in March 2010, 58 donor agencies pledged $5.3 billion over the next year and a half. Within the first weeks US citizens contributed hundreds of millions of dollars, mostly to large nongovernment organizations such as the Red Cross. By March 2011 world citizens, including those in the United States, contributed $1 billion. Plans for repairing the infrastructure, rebuilding homes, places of work and schools that could double as future hurricane shelters better than before was the motto for everyone. The aftermath of the quake was the emergence of tent cities or camps housing hundreds to thousands of internally displaced persons (IDP) in open spaces (parks, stadiums, and parking lots). As one would image the displaced persons thought these to be temporary living conditions. By midsummer 2010 the International Organization for Migration identified 1.3 million IDPs living in 1,300 camps, with more than 800 camps within the greater Port-au-Prince metropolitan area. As of May 2011, more than 600,000 people remained living in the camps (Schuller 2012). Applied anthropologist Mark Schuller is asking the important questions as it has now been two years since the earthquake: (1) where did all the money go? (2) Where is the promised funding for development, rebuilding, and repairing for the Haitian people? And (3) for how much longer will there be "temporary" camps?

In an attempt to learn more about the conditions in which the Haitian victims find themselves, Schuller (Figure 3.6) and eight students surveyed more than100 of the 861 metropolitan camps for IDPs in the summer of 2010. He and his team found that despite the billions in aid pledged to the Haitian people, the living conditions for the 1.5 million IDPs is appalling. For example, there is a lack of clean water for drinking, bathing, and cooking. The tents or tarps people are living in are too hot during the day, leak when it rains, and provide no protection during the hurricane season (May–November). IDPs in camps also suffer with poor sanitation and drainage. With no running water or a sewer system or drainage the rain events can cause sickness to spread rapidly. After the rains there are huge pools of muddy water harboring mosquitoes, flies, and other diseases, which cause illness and helped contribute to a cholera outbreak in October of 2010.

The conditions in the temporary camp are beyond capacity. Schuller and student researchers also discovered there are an insufficient number of latrines for the

FIGURE 3.6 A view of a tent city is seen on January 8, 2013 in Marassa, a suburb of Port-au-Prince, Haiti, three years after the earthquake that devastated Haiti and 360,000 people still live under tarps. About 5,000 people coexist in three Marassa makeshift camps under the permanent threat of a large river that runs through the neighbourhood.

number of residents in each of the camps they visited. There are certain public health standards for large groups of people living under temporary conditions as outlined by the Sphere Minimum Standards. These standards are the result of the 1997 sphere project designed to improve the quality of assistance provided to people affected by disasters, and they state that no more than 20 people may share a toilet. And imagine in one camp they found the ratio to be thirty toilets to 30,400 people. Schuller and his students also found that most camps do not have a system for cleaning the latrines after daily or weekly use. In fact, some IDP camp residents reported their latrines had never been cleaned and others had no latrines at all and instead they use the land or streams behind their camp. The combined stench of the latrines, pools of stagnating water, and rising refuse heaps made living in the camps far worse than if one had built a shelter at a garbage dump situated in a swamp. In addition to poor living conditions, the camp residents suffer from skin rashes and other health conditions after residing in the camps.

Clearly Schuller's research raises more questions than answers. For example, with all the money that came pouring into Haiti, what happened to the development and the rebuilding process? How long will IDPs be in these camps? Will IDPs be able to withstand epidemics, hurricanes, and other maladies that are frequently found in refugee camps such as lawlessness, rape of men, women, the old, and young, and the spread of infectious diseases and despair.

In postdisaster situations how can applied cultural anthropologist play a significant role? First, applied anthropologists can gather the necessary *information* that highlights the problem(s) at hand. Second, they can take this information to help move beyond the problem and to identify the needs or materials necessary for solutions to reduce the problems at hand. This list can be quite long and involve a lot of money, people, and needs. Third, in some cases the applied anthropologist may help with changes in *policy* or contribute to the *action*s necessary for change to occur. In both cases a policy approach or action oriented approach, it is acting on the information gathered from the postdisaster situation to make a difference in bettering people's quality of life.

FIGURE 3.7 Co-author Susan Andreatta found that the continued use of insecticides and herbicides on such export crops as bananas had negative health and environmental effects on the Caribbean Islands of Antigua, Barbados, and St. Vincent.

Agrochemical Effects on the Human and Natural Environments (Environmental Anthropology)

As the world became increasingly industrialized and globalized during the twentieth century, environmental anthropologists became more and more interested in the effects of technology on both the natural and human environments. In the late 1990s, one of the authors (Susan Andreatta) studied the impact of the use of agrochemicals (that is, insecticides, fungicides, and herbicides) on the health of both local farmers and their physical environments (Figure 3.7) in the Caribbean islands of Antiqua, Barbados, and St. Vincent (1998). Andreatta collected her data in 1994–1995 from a network of players in the agricultural sector of these three island nations, including farm owners, farm laborers, government officials, and international corporations.

Andreatta found that the increased use of chemical biocides was driven by a number of factors: a world marketplace demanding blemish-free fruits and vegetables, international chemical companies wishing to expand their markets into developing countries, growers

interested in producing the most marketable produce possible, and a lack of government control of the importation and use of potentially dangerous chemical biocides. Andreatta's findings confirmed that the continued use of agrochemicals over the decades in Antigua, Barbados, and St. Vincent has had harmful consequences for the health of local producers as well as the

quality of their physical environments. Farm workers were at risk of overexposure to toxic chemical biocides as a result of both use and misuse. Because most of the chemical products did not come with mixing instructions, farm workers often used more powerful concentrations of the chemicals than were necessary. Moreover, workers often mixed and applied the chemicals without wearing adequate protective clothing. Direct exposure to the biocides used on banana trees caused eye damage, skin rashes, and fingernail loss. The literature on other banana-producing nations, such as Costa Rica, indicates that overexposure or continued exposure to such biochemicals could lead to lower sperm counts and sterility for men, whereas women reported increased reproductive problems, including producing infants with serious birth defects.

The widespread use and misuse of biocides also had major negative effects on the natural environments of these three Caribbean islands. First, the use of biocides on banana crops often contaminated other food crops as well, such as peppers, tomatoes, broccoli, and strawberries. Second, farmers who used biocides were unable to raise chickens because chickens die from exposure to the chemicals. Third, biocides often leached into natural drinking water supplies. And finally, chemical run-off into streams and rivers killed off fish populations, thereby endangering a source of protein in the diets of local populations.

After documenting the risks of agrochemicals on both human and environmental health, Andreatta offered some useful suggestions to help ameliorate some of the more negative consequences of using agrochemicals. To illustrate, there was a pressing need for the departments of agriculture on these three islands to take a more proactive role in regulating both the importation and use of these biocides. Some products could be banned from entering the country because they are simply too toxic. The governments could require by law that biocide products contain explicit instructions on their packaging for mixing and application. The governments need to ensure that local producers receive adequate training (and perhaps even certification) on the safe use of agrochemicals, including wearing protective clothing, marking recently sprayed fields with appropriate signs or flags, and adhering to a safe re-entry schedule.

The Greater Use of Anthropological Knowledge

This book focuses on how anthropological knowledge can be used to solve problems of architects, government officials, businesspeople (Figure 3.8), medical personnel, educators, foreign aid personnel, court officials, family planners, and others. Although this applied perspective demonstrates how anthropology has contributed to the solution of societal problems, much still needs to be done to increase the extent to which anthropological knowledge can actually be used by policy makers. It is one thing to point out the potential uses of anthropological information, and it is quite another to actually apply that information to make a difference in public policy and the quality of peoples' lives.

© Charles Gupton/Getty Images

FIGURE 3.8 The study of cultural anthropology prepares people for working in the global economy of the twenty-first century.

Before, and particularly during, World War II cultural anthropologists played prominent roles in setting governmental policy in a variety of areas, including American Indian affairs, food-rationing programs, and how best to deal with our allies and our enemies during wartime. Many of the biggest names in the field—such as Edward Spicer, Margaret Mead, Conrad Arensberg, and Ruth Benedict—conducted research for the federal government for the specific purpose of informing public policy. After the war, however, most cultural anthropologists returned to university employment and lost their "public policy voice." Despite the growth of applied anthropology within the discipline over the last thirty-five years, cultural anthropologists are not widely sought out as public policy experts. Today, it is much more likely that when we hear an expert being interviewed on CNN or NPR, it is a sociologist or a political scientist, not a cultural anthropologist.

Will anthropologists be able to reclaim their public policy "mojo" in the twenty-first century? Cultural anthropology as a discipline—and recent research by many of its practitioners—certainly has policy relevance for a number of issues facing the nation and the world. More cultural anthropologists' voices need to be heard and contribute to the pressing policy issues of our time. Drawing on anthropological data and their own sharp analytical skills, a number of leading anthropologists take on many of the leading pundits in the United States on some of the most controversial topics of the day. For example, cultural anthropology, to a greater extent than any other social science, is in the best position to reframe the current debate on gay marriage and family life. In a publication titled *Why America's Top Pundits Are Wrong: Anthropologists Talk Back*, Gusterson and Besteman point out (2005: 31), it is cultural anthropologists who have collected "ethnographic information on the diversity of gender identities and marriage arrangements around the world—a diversity that would quickly puncture glib claims about what constitutes a 'natural' nuclear family."

Free-market economies, same-sex marriage, and religious differences in the Muslim world debates are areas in which anthropologists can contribute to public policy debate. They also have a good deal to say on other areas of public concern such as globalization, the environment and equitable access to resources, the culture wars, nation building and the spread of democracy, migration, family violence, issues of racism, ethnic conflicts, equitable food access and social justice, and poverty. Clearly, cultural anthropologists—with their cross-cultural perspective—are in a unique position to help people from all cultures navigate effectively and humanely through this twenty-first-century world—a world that is growing increasingly more interdependent each year. But before this can happen, there needs to be a considerably larger group of cultural anthropologists willing to re-engage in politically significant issues and be a part of the conversations.

Career Opportunities in Applied Anthropology

With the cost of a college education continuing to skyrocket, more and more parents are asking their college-aged children why they are majoring in anthropology. Behind such a question, of course, is the more pragmatic question: What kind of job can you get with a bachelor's degree in anthropology? It is important to bear in mind that a bachelor's degree in cultural anthropology is a liberal arts degree, not some type of professional certification. An undergraduate degree in anthropology does not prepare a person to become a professional research anthropologist any more than an undergraduate degree in economics equips a person to be the chairman of the Federal Reserve Bank. The bachelor's degree in anthropology does provide excellent background for graduate study in anthropology, which is the normal route to becoming a professional anthropologist.

For those not interested in pursuing a traditional career as an academic anthropologist, the bachelor's degree in anthropology provides valuable skills and insights that can be relevant for a wide variety of other professions. The terms *applied anthropologist* and *cross-cultural expert* are not standard job categories in the employment section of a newspaper's classified ads. In recent decades, however, the governmental, industrial, and nonprofit sectors have created jobs that require sensitivity to cross-cultural issues and involve working with people from different cultural backgrounds. To illustrate, anthropological skills and insights are being used with increasing frequency to (1) help architects design culturally appropriate housing and neonatal care settings, (2) enable agronomists to implement successful local seed saving and planting breeding programs, (3) educate healthcare providers about the public health aspects of the AIDS and tuberculosis epidemics, and (4) provide criminal justice officials with culturally relevant information for the resolution of legal cases, to mention but a few applications. As we discussed in this chapter and the rest of the textbook, this text contains many case studies that illustrate the wide variety of occupational domains in which anthropological data and insights are being used. Many other areas are drawing on the insights and skills of applied anthropologists, as shown in Table 3.3.

TABLE 3.3

Recent Growth Areas for Careers in Applied/Practicing Anthropology

Agriculture	Fisheries research	Missions
Alcohol and drug use	Forestry	Nutrition
Architectural design	Geriatric services	Policy making
Community action	Health and medicine	Population and demography
Coastal management	Housing	Public administration
Criminal justice and law enforcement	Human rights	Recreation and tourism
Disaster research	Industry and business	Resettlement
Economic development	Land use	Urban affairs
Education and training	Language policy	Water resource management
Employment and labor	Media and broadcasting	Wildlife management
Environment	Military	

As more and more doctorate-level anthropologists are working in nonacademic jobs, employment opportunities for those with less than doctorate training in anthropology are also increasing. Today people with training in cultural anthropology are putting their observational and analytic skills to work in the public (government), private (business), and nonprofit sectors of the economy. In fact more professionally trained anthropologists are employed in nonacademic positions today than in colleges and universities. As you consider your own career options, entertain several important questions. Are you more interested in an academically based job that permits some part-time applied research or in a full-time job with a government agency, a nonprofit, or a business that involves using anthropological skills on an everyday basis? If you are interested in a nonacademic career, how much additional education (beyond the bachelor's degree) will you need? Do you want to work in the private, public, or nonprofit sector of the economy? Do you want to work for a local, regional, national, or international organization or a funding agency? Do you see yourself working as a full-time, permanent employee of an organization or as an independent, contracting consultant to larger organizations? Because jobs in public or nonprofit organizations generally have lower salaries than jobs in the private (business) sector, what are your realistic income expectations? And because academic anthropologists tend to work alone and control the pace of their own research, how comfortable would you be with working on collaborative research projects with a number of colleagues and having many aspects of that research controlled by your employing organization? Once you have answered these questions (and perhaps others as well), you will be in the best position to embark on a career path based on applied anthropology or one that allows you to apply anthropological perspectives in other settings. This involves (1) applying for posted jobs seeking the skills of an applied cultural anthropologist and (2) presenting oneself (with your valuable anthropological perspective and competencies) as the best candidate for a wide variety of traditional jobs within an organization, such as a human resources director for a large multinational corporation.

How to Start to Become an Applied Anthropologist

On finishing a bachelor's degree, a student will need to complete a master's thesis and doctoral dissertation. The higher degree of specialization may provide the necessary experience(s) that will open doors

to future applied projects and a career in applied anthropology. For example, someone with a bachelor's degree in anthropology might have a master's degree in accounting and work in the accounting department for an international auto company. Another student may speak Laotian and also have a double major with an undergraduate degree in nursing and anthropology with a concentration in medical anthropology. Her cross-cultural understanding of Hmong culture, Hmong health, and traditional healing practices might land her a nursing position in a hospital located near a large Hmong community. Although the student did not have a higher degree in anthropology, she would be able to apply her cultural anthropology at her place of work.

Combining anthropology and another area of study such as biology, ecology, business, a second language, and statistics could be the building blocks for a career in anthropology. Take for example this scenario of a graduate student in medical anthropology who examined the transmission of tuberculosis in a South American community. Maybe his research methods and findings, and language skills will enable him to work on additional health-related projects in South America. For example on graduating with his Ph.D. in hand, the now graduate might find a postdoctoral position as an applied medical anthropologist and expand his career to learning about the spread of other infectious diseases such as *dengue fever* or HIV/AIDS and help to develop community-base prevention programs in affected areas. Such a career path may take this applied medical anthropologist not only to other regions in South America, but anywhere there might be socially infectious diseases. This example is not so different for Dr. Jim Jong Kim, the current president of the World Bank. Dr. Kim has both degrees from Harvard, his Ph.D. in anthropology and MD. He too specialized in infectious diseases and was the former director of the department of HIV/AIDS at WHO. Building on experiences and developing an array of skills sets may open many doors that lead to exciting careers as applied anthropologists. Here are a few examples to consider when developing an applied perspective in anthropology.

Medical Anthropology

Medical anthropology is a subfield of sociocultural, biological anthropology, and applied anthropology. Medical anthropology is an interdisciplinary and complex field, which studies human health, illness and disease, curing, healing and healthcare systems, and biocultural adaptation from multiple perspectives. Some medical anthropologists come from health professions such as medicine or nursing, whereas others come from backgrounds such as psychology, social work, education, human geography, or sociology.

---

dengue fever An infectious tropical disease caused by the dengue virus that is transmitted by the mosquito *Aedes aegypti*. Dengue fever also is known as breakbone fever. Symptoms include a high fever, headache, muscle and joint pains, and a skin rash.

Medical anthropologists normally acquire a master's degree and a doctoral degree. Some graduates train for employment in medical administration, nursing, public health as well as the Center for Disease Control (CDC). Medical anthropologists may desire to work on projects requiring them to engage in empirical research in learning more about health, illness, curing, and caring practices from a cross-cultural perspective. Still others may study the effects of aging cross-culturally or examine body image, mental health, or midwifery practices in different cultures. Medical anthropologists, who might be more applied in their research approach, might work with patients with AIDS, drug addicts, those exposed to pesticides, or who have contracted tuberculosis or other socially infectious diseases to develop interventions programs. The Society for Medical Anthropology provides information on careers and graduate programs in Medical Anthropology; their website is http://www.medanthro.net/.

CROSS-CULTURAL MISCUE

A traveler walking on the outskirts of capital city in Jakarta, Indonesia, came across dozens of people stretched out train tracks. The traveler panicked searching for help as he heard the distant train approach. What is wrong with all of these people he exclaimed as he went up to the ticket master's booth? Why the massive suicide?

Well unknown to the traveler, poorer members of the city are turning to electric therapy for health care. Laying on the tracks is a free way to obtain treatment.

The ticket master informed the traveler every day people come to lay on the tracks and for him not to worry; they know when to get up. He suggested after the train passes that may be one of them would speak to the traveler about their experience and explain why they do it?

Ethnomedicine is a local approach people use for health care. In this case electric therapy is used to feel comfort or relief from what ails them. Although there is no scientific evidence that train track electric therapy does anything, users contend it offers pain relief, lowers the blood pressure, and helps with sleeplessness and high cholesterol. Medical anthropologists spend a lot time researching local belief systems and health, and have learned that believing in a particular treatment makes a difference in the outcome.

This cultural miscue came about because the traveler had never heard of electric therapy before and certainly did not recognize any benefit from laying on a train track while a train was approaching. Understanding that other cultures have different ways of approaching wellness and healing from a course in medical anthropology may have helped the traveler to understand what he saw as well as recognize his own culture may have its own *unusual* approaches to health care.

Environmental Anthropology

Environmental anthropology is a subspecialty within the field of anthropology that takes an active role in examining the relationships between humans and their environment across space and time. Drawing on political ecology (which will be discussed in Chapter 4), this perspective integrates culture, politics and power, globalization, localized issues, and more. The focus and data interpretation is often used for arguments for and against the creation of policy and to prevent corporate exploitation and damage of land, water, and forested areas. In fact, applied anthropologists are involved in protecting lands in the United States from fracking for natural gas, mining, and pollution both at home and abroad (Simonelli 2012).

Most environmental anthropologists get advanced degrees, be that at the masters or doctoral level, to provide them with skill sets to work in the field knowledgably. Some environmental anthropologists are employed with USAID, NOAA, USDA, or EPA as well as with state and federal agencies for agricultural, fisheries, and health. Helpful sources for careers in environmental anthropology can be found at the National Association for Practicing Anthropologists (NAPA) http://practicinganthropology.org/, and through the AA – the Anthropology and Society website (http://www.aaanet.org/sections/ae/index.php/internet-resources/).

International Business and Business Anthropology

International business and business anthropologists work both at home and abroad in international development agencies such as the World Bank and USAID. They also work in private organizations like the Red Cross, Oxfam, or Americore or for international corporations such as automobile, textiles, coffee, cocoa, and other manufacturers and food processors. Business anthropologists apply anthropological theories, methods, and skills to research and identify solutions to solve all kinds of business- and industry-related problems. Some business anthropologists are involved in management, operations, marketing, advertising, consumer behavior, organizational culture, and human resource management. Knowledge of social organization, culturally appropriate behavior, and applying business principles are concepts key to how business anthropologists help business organizations develop ways of doing business better with suppliers, business partners, clients, and customers. The National Association of Practicing Anthropologists (NAPA) holds a career expo annually at the American Anthropology Association (AAA) meetings. The NAPA website is available for assistance for mentorship programs, internships and how to craft a resume (http://practicinganthropology.org/).

If the Food Won't Kill You, the Cooking Will

Cooking on a cookstove can be hazardous to one's health in many homes around the world. The World Health Organization (WHO) lists indoor household cooking fires as a leading environmental cause of death in the world with as many as 2 million deaths annually, which is more deaths than are caused each year by malaria (Martin et al. 2011). Almost half of the world's population lives in poverty, and those households generally use biomass (wood, crop residues, charcoal, or dung) or coal as fuel for cooking and heating. Typically, fires fill the homes with dense smoke and sicken those within, especially women and children. Researchers say it is as if those exposed were lifelong tobacco smokers (Martin et al. 2011). Women and children are at higher risk for adverse health outcomes from exposure to the indoor air pollution from these fires because they are at home more, and the women are responsible for cooking meals and heating the home. Men, spouses, and fathers tend to spend more time outdoors, and therefore, suffer less from exposure chronic. The two leading causes of death are acute pneumonia in children under age of five and chronic obstructive pulmonary disease for adults (Martin et al. 2011).

For those households at the bottom of the energy ladder, reliance on biomass fuels and coal contributes to local and regional

Horizons WWP/Alamy

environmental degradation and deforestation. A 2011 World Bank report underscores the health benefits for a cookstove intervention and highlights the other benefits to the environment and climate. Improved and more efficient stoves reduce fuel use and carbon dioxide emissions. Interventions then would contribute to people's health and their surrounding environment.

Educational Anthropology

Educational anthropology is a specialty in anthropology that relies on applying methods and theory of cultural anthropology to the educational setting. Whether assisting immigrant populations or refugees acculturate to their new home or children from these same relocated household do better in school anthropologist can help to minimize certain issues that arise from cross-cultural misunderstandings. Educational anthropologists come with diverse backgrounds to be able to address issues of cross-cultural understanding in learning, ethnic identity, ethnic change and the transmission of cultural knowledge and behavior between generations. Some educational anthropologists further specialize and get trained in teaching English as a second language (ESL) or in teaching English as another language (EAL) for those students who come to the United States speaking multiple languages (see Chapter 6). Another area of specialization is learning American Sign Language (ASL) as a cross-cultural approach to education anthropology. The Council on Anthropology and Education (http://www.aaanet.org/sections/cae/) is available for more information on careers and employment opportunities.

CROSS-CULTURAL MISCUE

Sometimes the way some words are spoken or the words selected in us English are different from British English. For example, an American may grown up knowing to put garbage in a trashcan, whereas an English-speaking person would toss rubbish in a bin. Michelle, an English-as-a-second-language teacher, had a similar experience describing her love of peanut butter and jelly sandwiches to her new students at an elementary school in Cuenca, Spain. Michelle had learned one word for peanut in her university training, and it was not *mani*. She had learned *cacahuate*, an indigenous Nahautl word for peanut common to those speaking Mexican-Spanish. The funny thing is that she used only part of the word and ended up describing her favorite sandwich as creamed pooh mixed with grape jelly to her students, who burst out laughing. They could not imagine their teacher's fascination with such a sandwich. This example illustrates there are differences between language and culture, word use, and word meaning and that a slip of the tongue, or a slightly different word use can change a meaning as well as who might share your sandwich.

Past projects for improving stoves or fuels have been around for decades. For any number of reasons, though, there have been a variety of obstacles interfering in a smooth transition for a technology transfer and adoption. Some challenges stem from lack of the public's awareness of the health-related problems associated with indoor air pollution made from the existing style of cookingstoves used by local community members or the international community. Another reason great strides have not been made is that there has been limited health research in determining the minimal levels of exposure needed to reduce the health risks associated with the indoor smoke. And lastly, funding a global cookstove project of this magnitude is problematic. The lack of affordable improved stoves or fuels that reduce exposures to safer levels and the logistics of trying to solve this problem that affects nearly 3 billion people is an enormous and daunting project (Martin et al. 2011).

To address this problem, the United Nations Foundation launched the Global Alliance for Clean Cookstoves (http://cleancookstoves.org). It is a public–private partnership aimed at creating a global market for clean and efficient cookstoves and fuels in the developing world. Their goal is to have 100 million homes adopt the new cookstoves and fuels by 2020. Several small-scale projects have been started in Guatemala and Peru.

There is a role for applied anthropologists to contribute on any number of levels to facilitate this process of efficient cookstove adoption. From a community-based approach anthropologists could work with community members to better understand gendered division of labor, technology access, and adoption. Women and girls typically gather fuel for home use, sometimes at great distances from their villages, and they may have to travel to places that may not be safe to secure materials for cooking and heating. A more efficient cookstove could reduce the time spent in collecting fuel to burn, saving time, and requiring fewer trips.

However, providing just a new cookstove is not enough for successful adoption. Users must receive training on how to use the stove and being taught that fuel saving would follow with proper and sustained use. Most importantly though, promoting changes in the way food is prepared to reduce exposure to poor indoor air requires fundamental understanding of traditions, social interaction, and family dynamics, which vary widely across cultures. Successful implementation will involve women designing the stove, training, use in the home, and follow-up with the community.

Questions for Further Thought

1. Based on this reading, what role do you see for the applied anthropologist in working with people from the United Nations on a cookstove project?

2. What challenges do you see face the anthropologist involved in this project?

3. What ethical considerations need to be considered with a cookstove project?

Development Anthropology

Development anthropology takes international development and international aid as primary focus. Within this specialization of anthropology the term *development* refers to the social action made by different institutions, business, enterprise, states, and independent volunteers, who are trying to modify the economic, technical, political, and social life of a given place in the world, especially in impoverished areas. Anthropologists who specialize in development anthropology often are part of multidisciplinary teams. They are able to use anthropological knowledge, theory, and methods to help with a project's design, its implementation, or its evaluation.

Development anthropologists tend to be involved in projects that seek to improve the economic well-being of marginalized communities and to illuminate poverty. Projects are generally aimed at putting people first by focusing on, for example, improving health care, providing access to education, creating jobs or new cottage industries, and improving the quality of environment such as with water purification or digging of wells for increasing water access and many other kinds of projects. For example, other projects are aimed at agriculture and development for improved food security and food access and as you can imagine the list of possible development project is endless.

Development anthropologists work both at domestically and abroad in international development agencies such as the World Bank, the United Nations, or USAID. They might also be employed in nongovernmental organizations. Some anthropology students interested in development anthropology volunteer through Peace Corp upon graduation to see if this is the kind of work is what they are interested in doing. Being that Peace Corp is a two-year commitment in which you are trained in language and culture and the job you would be performing in the host country in which you would be working. It is an opportunity to test yourself it this is the work you are interested in doing. Like training to be a surgeon there is no sense studying medicine for eight years and on your first surgery you find out that you are afraid of blood by fainting after the first incision.

There are many career paths to becoming an applied anthropologist. Just remember it is a lifelong journey. One does not become an applied practitioner over night. Building on experiences, applying your anthropological knowledge, and language and writing abilities will help you in the long run in securing employment with an applied perspective.

Summary

1. Applied anthropology is characterized by problem-oriented research among the world's contemporary populations. These pragmatic anthropologists attempt to apply anthropological data, concepts, and strategies to the solution of social, economic, environmental, and technological problems, both at home and abroad.

2. World War II provided many opportunities for anthropologists to turn their efforts to applied projects related to the war. The postwar boom in higher education lured many anthropologists back into academic positions during the 1950s and 1960s. But the decline in the number of academic positions for anthropologists since the 1970s has resulted in more applied types of employment outside the academic environment.

3. Cultural anthropologists in general—but particularly applied anthropologists—face ethical problems when conducting their research. One important ethical issue to which applied anthropologists must be sensitive is whether the people being studied will benefit from the proposed changes. Both the AAA and the SfAA have identified areas of ethical responsibility for practicing anthropologists, including responsibilities to the people under study, the local communities, the host governments and their own government, other members of the scholarly community, organizations that sponsor research, and their own students.

4. Cultural anthropology can make unique contributions as a policy science. For example, anthropologists bring to a research setting their skills as participant-observers, the capacity to view sociocultural phenomena from a holistic perspective, their regional and topical expertise, a willingness to see the world from the perspective of the local people (emic view), and the value orientation of cultural relativism.

5. Applied anthropologists work in a wide range of settings, both at home and abroad. Moreover they play a number of specialized roles, including policy researcher, impact assessor, expert witness, trainer, planner, and cultural broker.

6. Examples of applied anthropology include Mark Schuller's work where he and his students examined the sanitary conditions after the earthquake in Haiti and Susan Andreatta's research on the effects of agrochemicals on the human and natural environments in three Caribbean island nations.

7. Today there is a growing need for applied anthropologists to develop strategies that will increase the likelihood of their research findings being used by policy makers.

8. In the last several decades there has been significant growth in areas that have attracted applied and practicing anthropologists. These include architecture, environmental studies, fisheries research, geriatric services, the military, tourism, and water resource management.

Key Terms

applied anthropology

problem-oriented research

Project Camelot (1964–1965)

Dengue fever

Human Terrain System (HTS)

Critical Thinking Questions

1. The discipline of anthropology is holistic and offers many opportunities to understand change over time. Can you think of examples in your community in which an applied anthropologist might find employment?

2. Can you think of examples in which an applied anthropologist might contribute to a project in a developing country? What kind of project and what would the anthropologist being contributing?

3. What ethical considerations should an anthropologist be mindful of when engaging in applied research?

Online Study Resources

CourseMate

Access chapter-specific learning tools including learning objectives, practice quizzes, videos, flash cards, glossaries, web links, and more in your Cultural Anthropology CourseMate. Login to http://www.cengagebrain.com to access the resources your instructor has assigned and to purchase materials.

Photo of Indonesian woman in traditional dress.

The Growth of Anthropological Theory

Carl Tyler, a chemical researcher for a large plastics company in Los Angeles, was planning to submit a proposal to deliver a research paper at an international chemistry conference in the Netherlands in Amsterdam. According to the literature on the conference, proposals were due no later than 6/5/12. Tyler submitted his proposal on May 20, more than two full weeks before the deadline; however, he was shocked and confused when he received an e-mail message the next day from the conference organizers expressing their regret that they could not accept his proposal because it was submitted after the deadline.

The misunderstanding occurred because people in the United States write the date differently than people do in Europe. To illustrate, in the Netherlands the date is written in the order day, month, year, a seemingly logical system that moves from the smallest to the largest unit of time. For Europeans 6/5/12 means May 6, 2012. People in the United States, however, write the date in the order month, day, and year. For the typical North American, 6/5/12 means June 5, 2012. Thus, the conference organizers published the proposal deadline as May 6, but Tyler's US cultural mind-set caused him to read the date as June 5. So, Tyler was not a couple weeks early but in fact, according to the conference organizers, was more than two weeks late!

This cross-cultural scenario—which is played out regularly throughout the world—should serve as a reminder that people from different cultures have different ways of conceptualizing and expressing such things as how they keep track of time. Ethnographic studies for more than a century have demonstrated that culture and language have an appreciable influence on how humans perceive and organize the world around them. And, it is through this understanding that helps us understand why Tyler misunderstood the deadline date set by his colleagues in the Netherlands. ■

© Tim Graham/Getty Images

As anthropologists began to accumulate data on different cultures during the nineteenth century, they needed to be able to explain the cultural differences and similarities they found. This desire to account for vast cultural variations gave rise to anthropological theories. A *theory* is a statement that suggests a relationship among phenomena. Theories enable us both to explain or postulate that certain behaviors occur as a result of a certain set of similar circumstances

WHAT WE WILL LEARN

- What is a theory, and how can it be useful?

- Who have been the important theorists in cultural anthropology since the mid-nineteenth century?

- What theories have anthropologists used to explain cultural differences and similarities among the peoples of the world?

- How can anthropological theory be used to help solve societal problems?

in different cultures. Theories help to guide one's research and allow for making sense out of a variety of ethnographic information from different parts of the world. A good theory is one that can both explain and predict. In other words, theories provide models for what we learn and know about cultures and enable us to bring some measure of order to a vastly complex world.

Theories are useful for research because they guide empirical (hands-on) research and may contribute to generating *hypotheses* (unproven propositions that can provide a basis for further investigation) to be tested in the research investigation. In tests of a hypothesis, it is possible to determine how close the actual findings are to the expected findings. If what is found is consistent with what was expected, the theory will be strengthened; if not, the theory will probably be revised or abandoned. Anthropological theory changes as new data become available. But, either way, the original theory serves the important function of guiding empirical research.

Anthropological theories attempt to answer such questions as Why do people behave as they do? and How do we account for human diversity? These questions guided nineteenth-century attempts to theorize, and they continue to be relevant today. In this chapter we will explore—in roughly chronological order—the major theoretical schools of cultural anthropology that have developed since the mid-nineteenth century. Some of the previous theoretical orientations no longer attract much attention; others have been modified and reworked into something new; and still others continue to command some popularity. It is easy, with the advantage of hindsight, to demonstrate the inherent flaws in some of the early theoretical orientations. We should keep in mind, however, that contemporary anthropological theories that appear plausible today have been built on what we learned from those previous theories. We will limit our discussion here to an overview because most departments devote an entire course on the history of anthropological theory.

While training, all anthropologists learn about various anthropological theories and the importance of theory in guiding their research. For example, an anthropological theory or theoretical framework (also known as school of thought) is necessary because it provides an explanatory framework for the research to be conducted on past or present cultures, or in a particular topical area. What theory is chosen, how it is used or why it is used is related to the type of anthropological questions the researcher is interested in exploring. Take for an example an ethnographic anthropologist who may be interested in why people of a particular culture share in a symbolic understanding of something that is linked to identity or ethnicity. For this anthropologist, deconstructing meaning to understand a symbol or sign within a culture is important. Yet, this line of inquiry often avoids social justice or a human rights dimensions of the people they study. Other ethnographic anthropologists may take an existing theoretical framework and modify it with new information or new insights gathered from their own fieldwork or from synthesizing the written works of others. In other words, theoretically driven research helps to build new insights into our understanding of peoples' culture.

Applied anthropologists also use theory. In Chapter 3 we learned that applied research is stimulated by a real-world social problem, such as a social issue or possibly a response to a disaster or event. In comparison to the previous example in which the anthropologist was interested in the meaning of a symbol or sign, an applied cultural anthropologist may see the importance of a symbol by focusing on the collective attraction to a symbol from a particular segment of a society, and then look for ways the symbol may provide an understanding of inequality and unequal access to power, capital and other resources. This applied approach to understanding the importance of a symbol may lead to first an explanation for a social problem and second to developing an intervention to minimize the disparity emanating from the social problem.

In general, both ethnographic and applied anthropologists rely on theory to guide their research and interpret their findings. This chapter has a brief history of different theoretical frameworks that are at the foundation of anthropology. It is far from an exhaustive list, but we invite you to read more in this area and take more classes in anthropology to learn how to use theory in your own research.

Evolutionism

Trying to account for the vast diversity in human cultures, the first group of early anthropologists, writing during the last half of the nineteenth century, suggested the theory of cultural *evolutionism*. Their basic premise was that all societies pass through a series of distinct evolutionary stages. We find differences in contemporary cultures because they are at different evolutionary stages of development. This theory, developed by Sir Edward Tylor in England and Lewis Henry Morgan (Figure 4.1) in the United States, placed Euro-American cultures at the top of the evolutionary ladder and "less-developed" cultures on the lower rungs. The evolutionary process was thought to progress from

---

theory A general statement about how two or more facts are related.

hypotheses An educated hunch about the relationship among certain variables that guides a research project.

evolutionism The nineteenth-century school of cultural anthropology, represented by Sir Edward Tylor and Lewis Henry Morgan, that attempted to explain variations in world cultures by the single deductive theory that they all pass through a series of evolutionary stages.

FIGURE 4.1 Lewis Henry Morgan, a nineteenth-century evolutionist, held that all societies pass through certain distinctive evolutionary stages.

simpler (lower) forms to increasingly more complex (higher) forms of culture. Thus the "primitive" societies at the bottom of the evolutionary ladder had only to wait an indeterminable length of time before eventually (and inevitably) rising to the top. It was assumed that all cultures would pass through the same set of preordained evolutionary stages.

Although this evolutionary scheme appears terribly ethnocentric by today's standards, we must remember that it replaced the prevailing theory that small-scale, preliterate societies were composed of people whose ancestors had fallen from God's grace. Hunters and gatherers, it had been argued previously, possessed simple levels of technology because their fall from favor had made them intellectually inferior to peoples with greater technological complexity.

While Tylor (1832–1917) was writing in England, Morgan (1818–1881) was founding the evolutionary school in the United States. Morgan, a lawyer in Rochester, New York, was hired to represent the neighboring Iroquois Indians in a land grant dispute. After the lawsuit was resolved, Morgan conducted an ethnographic study of the Seneca Indians (an Iroquois group). Fascinated by the Seneca Indians (who trace their family lines of descent and inheritance rights through the mother's line only), Morgan circulated questionnaires and traveled around the United States and elsewhere gathering information about kinship systems among native North Americans and other native cultures. This kinship research—which may be Morgan's most enduring contribution to the comparative study of culture—was published in his book, *Systems of Consanguinity and Affinity of the Human Family*, in 1871.

Six years later Morgan wrote his famous book, *Ancient Society* (1877). In keeping with the general tenor of the times, he developed a system of classifying cultures to determine their evolutionary niche. Morgan, like Tylor, used the categories *savagery*, *barbarism*, and *civilization* but was more specific in defining them according to the presence or absence of certain *technological* features. Subdividing the stages of savagery and barbarism into three distinct subcategories (lower, middle, and upper), Morgan (1877: 12) defined seven evolutionary stages—through which all societies allegedly passed:

1. *Lower savagery.* From the earliest forms of humanity subsisting on fruits and nuts
2. *Middle savagery.* Began with the discovery of fishing technology and the use of fire
3. *Upper savagery.* Began with the invention of the bow and arrow
4. *Lower barbarism.* Began with the advent of pottery making
5. *Middle barbarism.* Began with the domestication of plants and animals in the Old World and irrigation cultivation in the New World
6. *Upper barbarism.* Began with the smelting of iron and the use of iron tools
7. *Civilization.* Began with the invention of the phonetic alphabet and writing

The theories of Tylor and Morgan have been criticized by succeeding generations of anthropologists for being ethnocentric because they concluded that Western societies represented the highest levels of human achievement. Also, Tylor and Morgan have been criticized for being armchair speculators, putting forth grand schemes to explain cultural diversity based on fragmentary data at best. Although there is considerable substance to these criticisms, we must evaluate the nineteenth-century evolutionists with an eye toward the times in which they were writing. As David Kaplan and Robert Manners (1986: 39–43) remind us, Tylor and Morgan may have overstated their case somewhat because they were trying to establish what Tylor called "the science of culture," whereby human behavior was explained in terms of secular evolutionary processes rather than supernatural causes.

In defense of Tylor and Morgan, we should acknowledge that they firmly established the notion (on which

savagery The first of three basic stages of cultural evolution in the theory of Lewis Henry Morgan; based on hunting and gathering.

barbarism The middle of three basic stages of a nineteenth-century theory developed by Lewis Henry Morgan holding that all cultures evolve from simple to complex systems: savagery, barbarism, and civilization.

civilization A term used by anthropologists to describe any society that has cities.

modern cultural anthropology now rests) that differences in human lifestyles are the result of certain identifiable cultural processes rather than biological processes or divine intervention. Moreover Morgan's use of techno-economic factors to distinguish among fundamentally different types of cultures remains a viable concept.

Evolutionism in Brief

- All cultures pass through the same developmental stages in the same order.
- Evolution is unidirectional and leads to higher (better) levels of culture.
- A *deductive approach* is used to apply general theories to explain specific cases.
- Evolutionism was ethnocentric because evolutionists put their own societies at the top.

Diffusionism

During the late nineteenth and early twentieth centuries, the diffusionists, like the evolutionists, addressed the question of cultural differences in the world but came up with a radically different answer. Evolutionism may have overestimated human inventiveness by claiming that cultural features have arisen in different parts of the world independently of one another, as a result in large measure of the *psychic unity* of humankind. At the other extreme, *diffusionism* held that humans were essentially uninventive. According to the diffusionists, certain cultural features were invented originally in one or several parts of the world and then spread, through the process of diffusion, to other cultures.

Represented by Grafton Elliot Smith (1871–1937) and William James Perry (1887–1949) in England and Fritz Graebner (1887–1934) and Wilhelm Schmidt (1868–1954) in Germany and Austria, diffusionism had run its course by the early part of the twentieth century. To be certain, the diffusionists started with a particularly sound anthropological concept—that is, cultural

---

deductive approach The act or process of reasoning from general propositions to specific cases, used by the cultural anthropologists of the late nineteenth and early twentieth centuries.

psychic unity A concept popular among some nineteenth-century anthropologists who assumed that all people, when operating under similar circumstances, will think and behave in similar ways.

diffusionism See *cultural diffusion* in Chapter 2.

American historicism Headed by Franz Boas, a school of anthropology prominent in the first part of the twentieth century that insisted on the collection of ethnographic data (through direct fieldwork) before making cross-cultural generalizations.

inductive approach The act or process of reasoning that involves the development of general theories from the study of a number of specific cases. Boas insisted on this approach.

---

diffusion—but they either took it to its illogical extreme or left too many questions unanswered. Few cultural anthropologists today would deny the central role that diffusion plays in the process of culture change. But some of the early diffusionists, particularly Smith and Perry, took this essentially valid concept *ad absurdum* by suggesting that everything found in the world could ultimately be traced back to the early Egyptians. Moreover, even though they collected considerable historical data, the diffusionists were not able to answer a number of important questions concerning the process of cultural diffusion. For example, when cultures come into contact with one another, what accounts for the diffusion of some cultural items but not others? What determines the rate at which a cultural item spreads throughout a geographic region? Diffusionists failed to raise certain important questions, such as why certain traits arose in the first place. Despite these limitations they were the first to point out the need to develop theories dealing with contact and interaction among cultures.

Diffusionism in Brief

- All societies change as a result of cultural borrowing from one another.
- A deductive approach is used, with the general theory of diffusion being applied to explain specific cases of cultural diversity.
- The theory overemphasized the essentially valid idea of diffusion.

American Historicism

In the early twentieth century, *American historicism*, which was a reaction to the deductive approaches just discussed, began under the leadership of Franz Boas (1858–1942; Figure 4.2). Coming from an academic background in physics and geography, Boas was appalled by what he saw as speculative theorizing masquerading as science. To Boas's way of thinking, anthropology was on the wrong path. Rather than dreaming up large, all-encompassing theories to explain why particular societies are the way they are, Boas wanted to put the discipline on a sound footing using an *inductive approach*; that is, Boas planned to start by collecting specific data and then move on to develop general theories. Boas felt that the enormous complexity of factors influencing the development of specific cultures rendered any type of sweeping generalization, such as those proposed by the evolutionists and diffusionists, totally inappropriate. Thus, Boas and his followers insisted on collecting detailed ethnographic data through fieldwork and at the same time called for a moratorium on theorizing.

FIGURE 4.2 Franz Boas, the teacher of the first generation of cultural anthropologists in the United States, put the discipline on a firm empirical basis.

Bettmann/Corbis

Some of Boas's more severe critics claimed that this antitheoretical stance was responsible for retarding the discipline of anthropology as a science. Yet, in retrospect, most commentators would agree that his experience in the areas of physics and mathematics enabled Boas to bring to the young discipline of anthropology both methodological rigor (such as in the form of systematic and thematic data collection) and a sense of how to define problems in scientific terms. Even though Boas himself did little theorizing, he left the discipline on a sound empirical footing so that those who followed him could develop cultural theories.

The impact Boas had on anthropology is perhaps most eloquently demonstrated by the long list of anthropologists he trained. As one of the earliest anthropologists in the United States, Boas trained virtually the entire first generation of US anthropologists. The list of Boas's students reads like *Who's Who in Twentieth-Century US Cultural Anthropology:* Margaret Mead, Robert Lowie, Alfred Kroeber, Edward Sapir, Melville J. Herskovits, Ruth Benedict, Paul Radin, Jules Henry, E. Adamson Hoebel, and Ruth Bunzel.

In recruiting graduate students to study anthropology with him at Columbia University, Boas, from the beginning, was purposeful about attracting women to the discipline. Recognizing that male fieldworkers would be excluded from observing certain aspects of a culture because of their gender, Boas felt that the discipline needed both male and female ethnographers to describe cultures more completely. Today, compared to other academic disciplines, cultural anthropology has been producing more female professionals than males, a legacy that can be traced back to Boas's methodological concerns when the discipline was in its formative period.

American Historicism in Brief

- Ethnographic facts must precede the development of cultural theories (induction).
- Any culture is partially composed of traits diffused from other cultures.
- Direct fieldwork is absolutely essential.
- Each culture is, to some degree, unique.
- Ethnographers should try to get the view of those being studied (emic), not their own view (etic).

Functionalism

While Franz Boas was putting anthropology on a more empirical footing in the United States, Bronislaw Malinowski (1884–1942) was also proceeding inductively by establishing a tradition of firsthand data collection in the United Kingdom. Like Boas, Malinowski (Figure 4.3) was a strong advocate of fieldwork. Both men insisted on learning the local language and trying to understand a culture from an insider's perspective (*emic approach*). They differed, however, in that Malinowski had no interest in asking how a cultural item got to be the way it is. Believing that little could be learned about the *origins* of small-scale societies, Malinowski concentrated on exploring how contemporary cultures operated or functioned. This theoretical orientation, known as *functionalism/functional theory*, assumed that cultures provided various means for satisfying both societal and individual needs. According to Malinowski, no matter how bizarre a cultural item might at first appear, it had a meaning and performed some useful function for the well-being of the individual or the society. The job of the anthropologist is to become sufficiently immersed in the culture and language to be able to identify these functions.

emic approach A perspective in ethnography that uses the concepts and categories that are relevant and meaningful to the culture under analysis.

functionalism/functional theory A theory of social stratification holding that social stratification exists because it contributes to the overall well-being of a society.

FIGURE 4.3 During one of the longest uninterrupted fieldwork experiences on record, Bronislaw Malinowski not only set the standard for conducting fieldwork but also developed an important new way of looking at contemporary cultures known as functionalism.

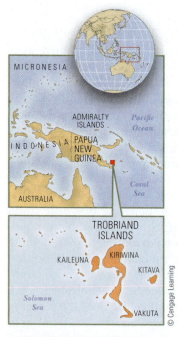

Locator map of Trobriand Islands

Not only do all aspects of a culture have a function, but, according to Malinowski, they are also related to one another. This functionalist tenet is no better illustrated than in Malinowski's own description of the *kula* ring, a system of trade found among the Trobriand Islanders. The kula not only performs the function of distributing goods within the society but is related to many other areas of Trobriand culture—including political structure, magic,

technology, kinship, social status, myth, and social control. To illustrate, the kula involves the exchange of both ceremonial necklaces and bracelets and everyday commodities between trading partners on a large number of islands. Even though the exchanges are based on the principle of reciprocity, usually long periods of time elapse between repayments made by trading partners. Alvin Gouldner (1960: 174) suggested that during these periods debtors are morally obligated to maintain peaceful relationships with their benefactors. If this is the case, we can see how the kula ring maintains peace and thereby functions as a mechanism of social control as well as a medium of material exchange. Thus, by examining a cultural feature (such as the kula ring) in greater depth, the ethnographer, according to this functionalist perspective, will begin to see how it is related to many other aspects of the culture and what it contributes to individuals and society as a whole.

Another form of functionalism was developed by the British anthropologist Alfred Reginald Radcliffe-Brown (1881–1955). Like Malinowski, Radcliffe-Brown held that the various aspects of a society should be studied in terms of the functions they perform. Whereas Malinowski viewed functions mostly as meeting the needs of the *individual*, Radcliffe-Brown saw them in terms of contributing to the well-being of the *society*. Because of this emphasis on social functions rather than individual functions, Radcliffe-Brown's theory has taken the name *structural functionalism*.

The functionalist approach, most closely associated with Malinowski and Radcliffe-Brown, is based on two fundamental principles. First, the notion of *universal functions* is that every part of a culture has a function. For example, the function of a hammer is to drive nails into wood, the function of a belief in an omnipotent god is to control people's behavior, and the function of shaking hands in the United States is to communicate nonverbally one's intentions to be friendly. The second principle, known as *functional unity*, is that a culture is an integrated whole composed of a number of interrelated parts. As a corollary to this second principle, it follows that if the parts of a culture are interconnected, then a change in one part of the culture is likely to produce change in other parts.

Even though anthropologists such as Malinowski and Radcliffe-Brown fought vigorously for the acceptance of the functionalist approach, the most effective revisions of functionalist theory came from sociologists, most notably Robert Merton (1910–2003). For example, in his influential book *Social Theory and Social Structure* (1957), Merton suggests that although every cultural item may have a function, it would be premature to

structural functionalism A school of cultural anthropology, associated most closely with Alfred Reginald Radcliffe-Brown, that examines how parts of a culture function for the well-being of the society.

universal functions The functionalist idea that every part of a culture has a particular function.

functional unity A principle of functionalism stating that a culture is an integrated whole consisting of a number of interrelated parts.

assume that every item *must* have a function. As a result, Merton proposed the notion of *dysfunction* as a source of stress or imbalance in a cultural system. According to Merton, whether a cultural trait is functional or dysfunctional can be resolved only by empirical research.

Functionalism in Brief

- Through direct fieldwork, anthropologists seek to understand how the parts of contemporary cultures contribute to the well-being of the individual and the society.
- Society is like a biological organism with many interconnected parts.
- With this high level of integration, societies tend to be in a state of equilibrium; a change in one part of the system brings change in other parts.
- The existing institutional structure of any society performs indispensable functions without which the society could not continue.

Psychological Anthropology

As early as the 1920s, US anthropologists became interested in the relationship between culture and the individual. Radcliffe-Brown, warning against what he called psychological reductionism, looked almost exclusively to social structure for his explanations of human behavior. A number of Boas's students, however, were asking some theoretically powerful questions: What role do personality variables play in human behavior? Should personality be viewed as a part of the cultural system? If personality variables are part of culture, how are they causally related to the rest of the system? Wanting to relate some of the insights of Gestalt and Freudian psychology to the study of culture, the early psychological anthropologists looked at child-rearing practices and personality from a cross-cultural perspective. They held that child-rearing practices (which are an integral part of a culture) help shape the personality structure of the individual, which in turn influences the culture. Thus, they saw an interactive relationship among child-rearing practices, personality structure, social structure, and culture.

Although best known for his linguistic research, Edward Sapir (1884–1939) was interested in the area of culture and personality. Individuals learn their cultural patterns unconsciously, Sapir suggested, in much the same way that they learn their language. Rejecting the notion that culture exists above the individual, Sapir believed that the true locus of culture could be found within the interactions of individuals. Even though Sapir did no direct fieldwork himself in this area of culture and personality, his writings and lectures stimulated interest in this topic among other anthropologists, most notably Ruth Benedict and Margaret Mead. Adherents of *psychological anthropology*, which studies the

relationship between culture and personality, would be interested in such questions as How do the video-gaming habits of US children affect children's personality structures? and How do these personality structures, in turn, affect other parts of the culture?

Ruth Benedict (1887–1948), a student of Boas, was one of the earliest anthropologists to suggest each society produces it own personality characteristics. In *Patterns of Culture* (1934) she claimed that each society unconsciously chooses a limited number of cultural traits and that individuals within society internalize them through a wide range of enculturation practices. Collectively, Benedict suggested, this results in similar ways of thinking and behaving that form a group personality pattern. To illustrate her perspective, Benedict analyzed the basic personality traits of two societies: the Kwakiutl Indians of the Pacific Northwest and the Zuñi Indians of the US Southwest (Figure 4.4). She claimed the Kwakiutl were an aggressive people that were prone to excess and competition. In contrast,

FIGURE 4.4 A photograph of Ruth Benedict whose theories influenced on cultural anthropology, especially in the area of culture and personality.

dysfunction Stress or imbalance caused by cultural traits within a cultural system.

psychological anthropology The subdiscipline of anthropology that looks at the relationships among cultures and such psychological phenomena as personality, cognition, and emotions.

the Zuñi were described as peaceful, restrained, and distrustful of excesses and disruptive disputes. As you can imagine, Benedict's ideas have been sharply criticized as stereotyping. However, at the time she was promoting this theoretical framework, she attracted the attention of the Office of War Information where she served as an adviser from 1943 to 1945 to help with the people of occupied territories and enemy lands. In the end, and to this day there is little evidence that any society has a modal or group personality. However, characterizing a group by its cultural style continues to be of interest to *interpretive* anthropologists, which we will introduce shortly.

Margaret Mead (1901–1978), a student of both Benedict and Boas, was one of the most prolific writers in the field of culture and personality. After completing her graduate training under Boas and Benedict at Columbia University, Mead became fascinated with the general topic of growing up —enculturation—and the emotional disruption that seemed to accompany adolescence in the United States. Psychologists at the time maintained that the stress and emotional problems found among US adolescents were a biological fact of life and occurred at puberty in all societies. But Mead wanted to know whether this emotional turbulence was the result of being an adolescent or of being an adolescent in the United States. In 1925 she left for Samoa to try to determine whether the strains of adolescence were universal (that is, biologically based) or varied from one culture to another. In her first book, *Coming of Age in Samoa* (1928), Mead reported that the permissive family structure and relaxed sexual patterns among Samoans were responsible for a calm adolescence (Figure 4.5). Thus, she concluded that the emotional turbulence found among adolescents in the United States was culturally rather than biologically based because US adolescent sexuality was (at the time) strictly monitored.

From the turbulence of adolescence, Mead next turned to the question of gender roles. Based on her research among the Arapesh, Tchambuli, and Mundugumor of New Guinea, she attempted to demonstrate that there were no universal temperaments that were exclusively masculine or feminine. More specifically, Mead reported that among the Arapesh both men and women had what Westerners would consider feminine temperaments (that is, nurturing, cooperative, non-aggressive, maternal). Both Mundugumor men and women displayed exactly the opposite traits (that is, ruthless, aggressive, violent demeanors), whereas among the Tchambuli there was a complete reversal of the male-female temperaments found in North American culture. Based on these findings, Mead concluded in her *Sex and Temperament in Three Primitive Societies* (1935) that our own Western conception of masculine and feminine is not genetically based but rather is culturally determined.

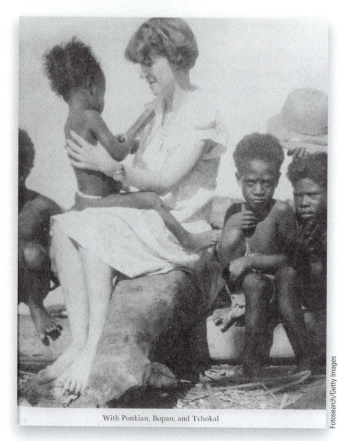

With Ponkiau, Bopau, and Tchokal

Fotosearch/Getty Images

FIGURE 4.5 Margaret Mead devoted much of her long and distinguished career in anthropology to the study of how culture affects the process of growing up. Here she is conducting fieldwork in the Admiralty Islands in 1953.

Psychological Anthropology in Brief

- Anthropologists need to explore the relationships between psychological and cultural variables.
- Personality is largely the result of cultural learning, but there is no modal cultural personality type for a particular society.
- Universal temperaments associated with males and females do not exist.

Neoevolutionism

As we have seen, Boas and others were extremely critical of the nineteenth-century evolutionists, in part because they made sweeping generalizations based on inadequate data. Despite these criticisms, no one, including Boas himself, was able to demonstrate that cultures do *not* develop or evolve in certain ways over time.

As early as the 1930s, Leslie White (1900–1975), a cultural anthropologist trained in the Boasian tradition of collecting detailed ethnographic data based on an emic perspective, resurrected the theories of the nineteenth-century evolutionists. Like Tylor and Morgan,

White believed that cultures evolve from simple to increasingly more complex forms and that cultural evolution is as real as biological evolution. It was White's position that Tylor and Morgan had developed a useful theory, but their major shortcoming was that they lacked the data to demonstrate it. White's unique contribution to anthropological theory was to suggest the cause (or driving force) of evolution, which he called his "basic law of evolution." According to White (1959), as the amount of energy harnessed annually increases or as putting energy to work becomes more efficient, a culture evolves.

According to White's *neoevolutionism* model, culture evolves when people are able to increase the amount of energy under their control. For most of human prehistory, while people were hunters and gatherers, the major source of energy was human power. But with the domestication of animals, and the invention of agriculture, the steam engine, the internal combustion engine, and nuclear power (Figure 4.6), humans began to dramatically increase the levels of energy at their disposal. To illustrate, the daily average energy output for a healthy human is a small fraction of a horsepower per day; the amount of energy produced from a kilogram of uranium in a nuclear reactor is approximately 33 billion horsepower! For White, the significant equation was $C = ET$, where C is culture, E is energy, and T is technology. Therefore, White's mathematical equation offers an explanation of the mechanics for cultural evolution. In other words, cultural evolution is caused by advancing levels of technology and a culture's increasing capacity to "capture energy" and control it.

Another anthropologist who rejected the particularist orientation of Boas in the mid-twentieth century was Julian Steward (1902–1972). Like White, Steward was interested in the relationship between cultural evolution and adaptation to the environment. But White's approach—which focused on the whole of human culture—was far too general for Steward. Even though Steward rejected Boasian historicism, he was equally unaccepting of approaches that were overly abstract. For Steward the main problem with White's theory was that it cannot explain why some cultures evolve by having more energy under their control, whereas others do not. One way of characterizing the difference between these two prominent neoevolutionists is that White was interested in the broad concept of culture and Steward was more interested in developing propositions about specific cultures or groups of cultures.

Steward distinguished among three different types of evolutionary thought. First, there is *unilinear evolution* (Tylor and Morgan), which attempts to place

© Corbis/SuperStock

FIGURE 4.6 According to the neoevolutionist theory of Leslie White, a society that produces nuclear power has reached an advanced stage of cultural evolution.

particular cultures into certain evolutionary stages. Second, Steward called White's approach *universal evolution* because it is concerned with developing laws that apply to culture as a whole. Third, in contrast to these two previous forms of evolutionism, Steward called his own form *multilinear evolution*, which focuses on the evolution of specific cultures without assuming that all cultures follow the same evolutionary process.

Steward held that by examining sequences of change in different parts of the world, one could identify paths of development and some limited causal principles that would hold true for a number of societies. To test out his hypothesis, Steward selected areas of the world that had produced complex societies (civilizations), such as Egypt and the Middle East in the Old World and Mexico and Peru in the New World. In all of these cases, Steward tried to show certain recurring developmental

neoevolutionism A twentieth-century school of cultural anthropology, represented by Leslie White and Julian Steward, that attempted to refine the previous evolutionary theories of Sir Edward Tylor and Lewis Henry Morgan.

unilinear evolution A theory held by anthropologists such as Sir Edward Tylor and Lewis Henry Morgan that attempts to place particular cultures into specific evolutionary stages.

universal evolution Leslie White's approach to cultural evolution, which developed laws that apply to culture as a whole and argued that all human societies pass through similar stages of development.

multilinear evolution The mid-twentieth-century anthropological theory of Julian Steward, who suggested that specific cultures can evolve independently of all others even if they follow the same evolutionary process.

sequences from earliest agriculture up through large, complex, urbanized societies. For example, in all of these areas, people were faced with dry environments that required them to develop methods of irrigation to obtain water for farming.

Steward's approach was based on analysis of the interaction between culture and environment. He argued that people who face similar environmental challenges (such as arid or semiarid conditions) are likely to develop similar technological solutions, which, in turn, lead to the parallel development of social and political institutions. Even though environment is a key variable in Steward's theory, he was not an environmental determinist because he recognized the variety of human responses to similar environmental conditions. By focusing on the relationships among people, environment, and culture, Steward was the first and leading proponent of *cultural ecology*, a theory to which many anthropologists rely on today as they begin their research on political ecology (discussed later in this chapter).

Neoevolutionism in Brief

- Cultures evolve in direct proportion to their capacity to harness energy.
- Culture is shaped by environmental conditions.
- Through culture, human populations continuously adapt to techno-environmental conditions.
- Because technological and environmental factors shape culture, individual (personality) factors are de-emphasized.

French Structuralism

No single theoretical orientation is as closely associated with a single person as *French structuralism* is associated with Claude Lévi-Strauss (1908–2009). Although both Radcliffe-Brown and Lévi-Strauss are called structuralists, their approaches to cultural analysis are vastly different. Whereas Radcliffe-Brown focused on identifying how the parts of a society function as a systematic whole, Lévi-Strauss concentrated on identifying the mental structures that undergird social behavior. For Lévi-Strauss, ethnology (comparing cultures) tends to be more psychological or cognitive than sociological.

cultural ecology An approach to anthropology that assumes that people who reside in similar environments are likely to develop similar technologies, social structures, and political institutions.

French structuralism A theoretical orientation holding that cultures are the product of unconscious processes of the human mind.

binary oppositions A mode of thinking found in all cultures, according to Claude Lévi-Strauss, based on opposites, such as old-young, hot-cold, and left-right.

The approach taken by Lévi-Strauss draws heavily on the science of linguistics. After assuming for decades that language is purely a learned response, many linguists have hypothesized that basic grammatical structures are pre-programmed in the human mind. Likewise Lévi-Strauss argues that certain codes programmed into the human mind are responsible for shaping cultures. Cultural differences occur, according to Lévi-Strauss, because these inherent mental codes are altered by environment and history. Although he recognizes these surface differences, Lévi-Strauss suggests that in the final analysis the mental structure of all humans is essentially the same. The content of a cultural element may vary from one society to another, but the structure of these elements is limited by the nature of the human mind. In essence, Lévi-Strauss has reintroduced his own version of the psychic unity of humankind first put forth by diffusionism.

One of the basic characteristics of the human mind for Lévi-Strauss is that it is programmed to think in *binary oppositions*, or opposites. All people have a tendency to think in terms of pairs of opposites such as male–female, hot–cold, old–young, night–day, and right–left. It is these dichotomies that give shape to culture. Consider, for example, Lévi-Strauss's interpretation of totemism, a belief system found in many parts of the world that states a relationship between social groupings (such as clans or lineages) and aspects of the natural world (such as plants or animals). Lévi-Strauss suggests that totemic beliefs are complex mental devices that enable people to classify the units of their culture and relate them to the natural world. For example, in the northwest of the United States there are American Indian groups that label their ancestral lineage as the bear, wolf, and eagle clans.

Lévi-Strauss's structuralism has been criticized for being overly abstract. Because his theories are not inclined to empirical testing, many anthropologists have rejected them. He chose to focus on the grand questions that anthropologists, in their modern-day quest for specialization, have largely abandoned: How does the human mind work? Even with the world's vast cultural variations, is there a psychic unity for all of humankind? Even though French structuralism does not appeal to more empirically oriented anthropologists, Lévi-Strauss has made a major contribution by directing our attention to the relationship between culture and cognition.

French Structuralism in Brief

- Human cultures are shaped by certain preprogrammed codes of the human mind.
- Theory emphasizes repetitive structures rather than sociocultural change.
- Rather than examining attitudes, values, and beliefs, structural anthropologists concentrate on what happens at the unconscious level.
- It is assumed that the human mind categorizes phenomena in terms of binary oppositions.

Ethnoscience

The theoretical approach of Lévi-Strauss is similar in several significant respects to that of the ethnoscientists, a small but vocal group of US cultural anthropologists who gained fleeting recognition during the 1950s and 1960s. For example, both approaches draw on a linguistic model, seek explanations in the human mind, and view human behavior from a logical or rational perspective. However, the methods used are radically different. Whereas the French structuralists infer mental structures or codes from cultural traits, ethnoscientists attempt to understand a culture from the point of view of the people themselves by speaking to them directly about their culture and language. Proponents of *ethnoscience* include Ward Goodenough (1956) and William Sturtevant (1964).

In an effort to make ethnographic description more accurate than in the past, ethnoscientists try to describe a culture in terms of how it is perceived, ordered, and categorized by the members of that culture (an emic approach) rather than by imposing the categories of the ethnographer (an etic approach). To illustrate, traditionally Western ethnographers used categories from their own cultures for describing another culture. Whereas most middle-class North Americans would divide all of the items in the fresh produce department of a supermarket into either fruits or vegetables, people from some other cultures would not. Whereas English speakers have different words for turquoise, aqua, and teal, other cultures might include them all under a single color term, and still others would have thirty or more different words for various shades of blues and greens. Whereas some cultures have different linguistic categories for mother's brother's daughter and mother's sister's daughter, in the United States these two family members are lumped together under the single kinship category *cousin*. Thus, the primary aim of ethnoscience is to identify the implicit rules, principles, and codes that people use to classify the things and events in their world.

Ethnoscientists have been criticized on several fronts. First, though admitting that it may be desirable to get the natives' viewpoint, some anthropologists feel that one's own conditioning and preconceptions make it impossible to get into the minds of culturally different people. Second, even if it is possible to understand another culture from the natives' point of view, how does one communicate one's findings to others in one's own linguistic or cultural group? Third, if every ethnographer described specific cultures using native categories, there would be little or no basis for comparing different societies. And fourth, ethnoscience is extremely time-consuming. To date, ethnoscientific studies have been completed on limited domains of culture, such as kinship terms and color categories. The completion of an ethnoscientific study of a total culture would, no doubt, be beyond the time capabilities

CROSS-CULTURAL MISCUE

A major legacy of the ethnoscientists is that they remind us to use the native categories (emic view) when trying to understand people from another culture. We can get ourselves into trouble if we assume that people from different cultures categorize the world around them exactly as we do. This point is well illustrated in the following cross-cultural misunderstanding.

Harold Josephson, an electronics engineer, had spent weeks negotiating with a Japanese parts distributor in Yokohama. The Japanese executive, Mr. Kushiro, was tough in the negotiations, so progress had been slow. Eventually Josephson felt that they had found common ground and an equitable deal could be worked out to the advantage of both companies. On the final day of negotiations, Josephson was pleased to announce to Kushiro that their thinking on the contract negotiations was parallel. Kushiro pleasantly thanked Josephson for his time and left the meeting without further discussion.

What Josephson failed to realize is that the word *parallel* has a different meaning to Japanese than it does to Americans. We think of the word as meaning compatible, proceeding on the same track, going in the same direction, or being in agreement. However, to the Japanese, *parallel* means a lack of agreement—positions that will always remain apart, never to meet, like two train tracks. When Josephson stated that their thinking was "parallel," Kushiro mistakenly thought that Josephson was saying they would never reach an agreement.

of a single ethnographer. Despite its impracticality, the ethnoscientific approach has served as a useful reminder of a fundamentally sound anthropological principle: People from different cultural and linguistic backgrounds organize and categorize their worlds in essentially different ways.

Ethnoscience in Brief

- This theory attempts to make ethnographic description more accurate and replicable.
- Ethnoscience describes a culture by using the categories of the people under study rather than by imposing categories from the ethnographer's culture.
- Because it is time-consuming, ethnoscience has been confined to describing small segments of a culture.

ethnoscience A theoretical school popular in the 1950s and 1960s that tries to understand a culture from the point of view of the people being studied.

Feminist Anthropology

Feminist anthropology developed alongside the wider women's movement in the 1960s and 1970s and has its roots in psychological anthropology with previous contributions from Mead and Benedict. The feminist critique of anthropology and past theoretical orientations was centered on the fact that anthropology has been androcentric (male-centered). Critics argued that, although some anthropologists were women, the women in those societies studied by anthropologists were often neglected as objects of study or imbedded with gender neutral terms such as the farmer or the peasant where it could not be discerned if one was speaking about a man or a woman. Even when women were put under the anthropological lens, they were often portrayed as passive objects rather than as prime players in the mainstream of social life.

As a long-overdue corrective to this neglect, marginalization, and misrepresentation of women in anthropology, *feminist anthropology* called for a systematic reanalysis of the role women play in the social structure. As recounted by Micaela di Leonardo (1991: 8), feminist anthropologists in the 1970s responded enthusiastically to the challenge of reanalyzing and rewriting previous ethnographies "as if gender really mattered." Feminist anthropologists such as Louise Lamphere (1974; Figure 4.7), Sherry Ortner (1974), Eleanor Burke Leacock (1978), and Michelle Zimbalist Rosaldo (1974), among others, tried to rectify this male bias by focusing on women's positions within society. Many of the early feminist studies concentrated on explaining female subordination (which some scholars saw as a cultural universal). More recent studies, however, have looked at the social construction of gender, work and production, reproduction and sexuality, body image variations between different groups of women, and how gender influences economic, political, and social power (see Lewin 2006; Scheper-Hughes and Lock 1998).

Although feminist anthropology is diverse in terms of areas of investigation and theoretical indebtedness, a number of basic features are generally agreed on. First, feminist anthropology takes as a given that gender is an important, albeit previously neglected, variable when studying any aspect of cultural life. That is, just as economics, politics, and religion vary according to status, class, power, and age, they also vary according to gender. Second, the feminist critique rejects *positivism* because the language of science (that is, hypotheses, objective measures, generalizations from empirical

Photograph by Margaret Randall

FIGURE 4.7 This is a photo of Louise Lamphere in the field with a research colllaborator; she is also a past president of the American Anthropological Association.

evidence, and so on) is seen as repressive and serving the interests of the elites. Instead, feminist ethnographies are more subjective and collaborative in their perspective, with the line between the researcher and the subject less distinct. Third, this antipositivist approach leads to a preference for qualitative methods (based on empathy, subjectivity, and a dialogue between the anthropologist and the informant), so as to eventually better understand the inner world of women. In fact most feminists avoid the term *informant* because it implies an unequal relationship between the anthropological "expert" and the subordinate "lay person." Instead, the feminist methodology seeks to eliminate status and power differences between the researcher and the subject, thereby creating a more equal and collaborative relationship. And finally, there is little or no attempt in feminist anthropology to assume a value-neutral position; it is aimed at consciousness-raising and empowerment of women and, in the words of Stanley Barrett (1996: 164), "unapologetically promotes the interests of women."

The new attention given to gender issues by the feminist anthropologists of the 1960s and 1970s led some anthropologists to return to sites where previous studies had been conducted from a largely male-centric perspective. Annette Weiner (Figure 4.8) is an excellent example of a feminist anthropologist who returned to look at none other than Malinowski's classic study of the Trobriand Islanders. According to Malinowski's (1922) original ethnography, Trobriand men gave gifts of yams at harvest time to their sisters' husbands. Malinowski

---

feminist anthropology A theoretical approach that seeks to describe and explain cultural life from the perspective of women.

positivism A philosophical system based on observable scientific facts and their relationships to one another.

Courtesy of Dr. William E. Mitchell

FIGURE 4.8 Feminist anthropologist Annette Weiner with two Trobriand Islanders and harvested yams.

viewed these gifts as a type of tribute from the girl's family to her husband's family, and thus as a way of consolidating male power, but Weiner (1976) had a different interpretation. She found that, because the yams are given *in the wife's name*, the gift is as much a symbol of the high value placed on women as it is a symbol of power and status for men. Moreover, because Malinowski paid limited attention to the world of women, he failed to record that this gift of yams had to be reciprocated. Rather than reciprocating to his wife's brother, however, the recipient of the yams was expected to give *directly to his own wife* a unique form of wealth consisting of women's skirts made from banana leaves, which she used in important funeral ceremonies. If the husband failed to provide his wife with these skirts, his own brother-in-law might reduce or eliminate altogether his gift of yams, which would negatively affect the husband's chances of ever elevating his status in becoming a *big man*. Thus, in her restudy of Trobriand culture, Weiner was able to show that men were much more dependent on women for their status and power than Malinowski's previous description would have us believe.

Feminist Anthropology in Brief

- All aspects of culture have a gender dimension that must be considered in any balanced ethnographic description.
- Feminist theory represents a corrective to male bias in traditional ethnographies.
- Feminist anthropologists are more subjective and collaborative in their research, rather than objective and scientific.

Cultural Materialism

Most closely associated with Marvin Harris (1927–2001), *cultural materialism* is the theoretical position based on the concept that material conditions or modes of production determine human thoughts and behavior. According to this approach (Harris 1968, 1979b, 1999), the primary task of anthropology is to provide *causal* (cause and effect) explanations for the similarities and differences in thought and behavior found among human groups. Cultural materialists accomplish this task by studying material constraints that arise from the universal need to produce food, technology, tools, and shelter. These material constraints are distinguished from mental constraints, which include such human factors as values, ideas, religion, and aesthetics. Harris and the cultural materialists see the material constraints as the primary causal factors accounting for cultural variations.

Harris has been criticized for devaluing the importance of ideas and political activities as sources of cultural change and variation. But rather than ignoring these nonmaterial factors, Harris suggests that they have a secondary, or less important, role related to cultural changes and variations: Ideas and political ideologies can either accelerate or retard the process of change but are not themselves causes of the change.

Cultural materialists rely heavily on an etic research methodology—that is, one that assumes the viewpoint of the anthropologist rather than the native informant. This research strategy uses the scientific method, logical analysis, the testing of hypotheses, measurement, and quantification. Using these scientific methods, cultural materialists attempt to explain the similarities and differences among various sociocultural structures by focusing on the material and economic factors.

Although cultural materialism has much in common with the ideas of Karl Marx (in particular, a materialist interpretation), the two schools should not be equated. Cultural materialists reject the Marxist notion of materialism, which was to result in the destruction of capitalism by an empowered working class. Cultural materialism does not have a particular political agenda, however, and is committed to the scientific study of culture. At the same time, Harris is critical of cultural idealists, anthropologists who rely on an emic approach (the natives' point of view) and use ideas, values, and ideologies as the major explanatory factors for thought and behavior. As Harris (1979b) argued, codes and rules (à la ethnoscientists) are not at all helpful in explaining phenomena such as poverty, underdevelopment, imperialism, population explosions, minorities, ethnic and class conflict, exploitation, taxation, private property, pollution, the military-industrial complex, political repression, crime, urban blight, unemployment, and war.

cultural materialism A contemporary orientation in anthropology holding that cultural systems are most influenced by such material things as natural resources and technology.

The New Hope Antipoverty Program

✿ As pointed out in Chapter 3, it is misleading to think of all cultural anthropology as being either applied or pure. In reality applied anthropologists use theoretical propositions to guide their research, whereas pure or academic anthropologists are informed by practical studies. A particularly good example of the use of theory to guide an applied study was a research project conducted by Christina Gibson and Tom Weisner (2002) evaluating the New Hope antipoverty program in Milwaukee, Wisconsin. (For a comprehensive look at the workings of the New Hope Poverty Program, see Duncan, Houston, and Weisner [2007]).

Based on the notion of "workfare" rather than "welfare," the New Hope program offered participants a package of benefits in exchange for a demonstrated work effort. If participants worked thirty hours per week, the program would make available to them wage subsidies, child-care subsidies, health insurance, and even temporary community service jobs. Like many welfare programs established since the mid-1990s, the Milwaukee program was predicated on "rational choice theory," which stipulates that people make decisions based on an objective cost-benefit analysis. In other words, people will avail themselves of the benefits offered by the program if the benefits outweigh the costs. Rational choice theory, however, rests on the assumptions of materialism, maximizing one's financial gain, and self-interest; that is, a person will opt for health insurance or a child-care subsidy because it makes financial sense to do so. Gibson and Weisner, however, found that the extent to which program participants opted for the benefits package varied greatly from family to family. The purely economic incentives of the program were too narrow to motivate all of the participants.

Typically, evaluation research on social service programs such as New Hope is conducted by using survey methods. Although Gibson and Weisner used demographic and opinion surveys for both their experiment and control groups, they also used participant observation as the basis for an ethnographic study of forty-six participating families. These urban ethnographers listened to parents tell their stories over meals, visited the children's schools,

and accompanied the families to church, family visits, and shopping trips. By combining the quantitative survey data with the more qualitative information gained through participant observation, Gibson and Weisner were able to use participants' own words to understand why they opted for some benefits and not others.

Testing of the rational choice theory in this program evaluation research led the researchers to suggest another theory to partially explain their findings, which they call *ecocultural theory*. Rational choice theory does not take into account beliefs, emotions, or other cultural factors. Availing oneself of program benefits is not just a matter of maximizing one's material benefits, as the rational choice theory suggests. Instead, Gibson and Weisner found that some people made choices about program benefits based on whether they thought the benefit would sustain their daily routine. Others used a cost-benefit analysis but did not define costs in largely materialistic or financial terms. For them, costs included nonfinancial factors such as family well-being, their children's mental health, or the effects on other social relationships. The researchers concluded that if we are to understand why participants opted for some program features and not others, it is imperative that we use a wider theoretical model than the rational choice theory. They acknowledge that rational choice is involved in the decision-making process of low-income families but argue that the rational choice model does not account for all of the choices made. What is needed, according to Gibson and Weisner, is both rational choice theory (based largely on financial cost-benefit analysis) and ecocultural theory (based on the need to sustain a familiar daily routine).

This study is significant on two levels: theoretical and applied. On the one hand, it tested the utility of the widely used rational choice theory to explain behavioral choices in a social service program for low-income families. That the theory, although viable, did not explain all of the behavioral data provides us with an excellent example of how theories can be refined and reworked by means of applied anthropology. On the other hand, this research project demonstrates the use of social theory for the applied enterprise of program evaluation. If the New Hope program (or others like it) is to continue to provide services to the poor, administrators will need to know why some people opt for program benefits and others do not. Program implementers should look beyond financial motivation and pay closer attention to the sociocultural circumstances of their target populations.

Questions for Further Thought

1. What data-gathering techniques did Gibson and Weisner use in their evaluation research on the New Hope project? In what ways did the different techniques yield different types of information for the researchers?

2. Compare and contrast the two theories used in this study: rational choice theory and ecocultural theory.

3. What other government-sponsored programs might benefit by using both theories to evaluate why some people participate and others do not?

Michael Ventura/PhotoEdit

Cultural Materialism in Brief

- Material conditions determine human thoughts and behavior.
- Theorists assume the viewpoint of the anthropologist, not the native informant.
- Anthropology is seen as scientific, empirical, and capable of generating causal explanations.
- Cultural materialism de-emphasizes the role of ideas and values in determining the conditions of social life.

Humanistic Anthropology

For much of the twentieth century, anthropology saw itself as essentially a scientific enterprise. The nineteenth- and early-twentieth-century founders of the discipline attempted to put anthropology on a solid scientific footing by offering an alternative to a theological explanation of human behavior and cultural variation. Although many of the schools of anthropology discussed so far varied between hard and soft scientific approaches, they never abandoned such scientific canons as gathering empirical data, testing hypotheses, looking for cause-and-effect relationships, and adhering to the scientific method. However, in the 1970s and 1980s a number of anthropologists, collectively referred to as *interpretive* anthropologists, questioned the scientific nature of anthropology itself. Gradually this school of anthropological thought evolved into another, that of *postmodernism*. Such anthropologists see cultural anthropology as more of a humanistic enterprise than a scientific one, having more in common with art and literature than with biology or psychology. Interpretative anthropologists and postmodernists are more interested in describing and interpreting particular cultures than formulating general patterns.

Interpretative Anthropology

Interpretive anthropology, advocated by Clifford Geertz (1926–2006), is a major force in this area of anthropology. Rather than searching for general propositions about human behavior, Geertz (1973, 1983) and fellow interpretive anthropologists take a more descriptive approach by examining how the people themselves (rather than the anthropologist) interpret their own values and behaviors. Cultures can best be understood by listening and recording the ways in which the natives (locals) explain their own customary behavior. Similar to ethnoscientists and some feminist anthropologists, interpretive anthropologists are strongly wedded to the emic, rather than the etic, approach to the discipline. According to Geertz, the job of the anthropologist is not to generate laws or models that will predict human behavior because these predictive devices tend to ignore the complexity of human cultures. Rather, Geertz would have anthropologists concentrate on cultural description, literature, folklore, myths, and symbols and their findings in the form of "thick description." Most importantly, the anthropologist is not present in his or her writings. In interpretive ethnographic accounts, we generally do not read about the anthropologists conducting their fieldwork or any other interaction they may have had while collecting narratives or observing daily routines.

Trained in the West as observers of foreign cultures, interpretive anthropologists believe they can never adequately describe another culture, but essentially articulate their own culture's response to the "other." In *Anthropology as Cultural Critique: An Experimental Moment in the Human Sciences*, George Marcus and Michael Fisher (1986) contend there are some ethnographies written with such detail that one almost feels as though they are reading literature or a good novel. In other instances the Western-trained anthropologist does not know what he or she is seeing or hearing to know how to adequately interpret actions or talk. You may have had a similar experience (or will) while you traveled to a place that speaks another language or does things differently from your own culture. For example, you will find learning Spanish in a classroom does not make one fluent in Mexican culture. Years of living in Mexico may help, but one is still not a native of the culture and may never fully understand some of the subtle nuances recognized by members of the culture. Social scientists who critique the interpretative approach do so because this form of anthropology rules out any possibility for generalizations, for comparisons between cultures, and for building on the cumulative nature of anthropological knowledge.

Interpretative Anthropology in Brief

- Interpretative anthropologists take a more descriptive approach by examining how the people themselves interpret their own values and behaviors.
- Interpretative anthropologists use thick description to describe a culture they observe.
- Often the anthropologist is not present in the written account of the research process.

Interpretive anthropology A contemporary theoretical orientation holding that the critical aspects of cultural systems are subjective factors such as values, ideas, and worldviews.

Postmodernism

Although *postmodernism* means different things to different people, it grew out of the traditions of structuralism, feminist anthropology, and interpretative anthropology. Essentially, postmodernists dispute the possibility that anthropology can construct a grand theory of human behavior. A basic tenet of postmodernism is that the "modernists" (scientific anthropologists) are extraordinarily arrogant to think that they can describe, interpret, and give meaning to the lives of people from other cultures. The modernists' enterprise for much of the twentieth century, they claim, was based on the privileged status of science (held by most developed countries) and reflected the basic power imbalances between the wealthy, colonial countries and those developing countries where much anthropological research was conducted. It is nearly impossible, they contend, for predominantly white, male, Euro-American anthropologists to step outside of their own culture so as to produce an objective view of another culture.

Rather than attempting to discover the truth about how the world works through empirical investigations, postmodernists hold that all ethnographic accounts are subjective because they are conditioned by the experiences and personal histories of the ethnographer. Instead of the ethnographer being the sole authority, postmodernists call for a collaborative approach like the feminists to the study of culture. For the postmodernist, written ethnography should have multiple contributors, thereby creating a dialogue between the anthropologist and the people being studied. It involves relinquishing sole authorship to include the voice of the research subjects themselves. Postmodernists contend that only through this dialogical process will meaning and interpretations emerge.

Similar to interpretive anthropology, another tenet of the postmodernist philosophy involves the rejection of generalizing from data and developing predictable theories. By emphasizing the uniqueness of every culture, postmodernists view culture as a changing set of individual meanings that require continual reinterpretation. According to postmodernists, for anthropologists to think that they can single-handedly develop general theories of culture that have any level of predictability is both misguided and unethical. They contend it is misguided because it cannot be done. It is unethical because grand theories tend to support the dominant ideology that promotes order and consistency at the expense of individual autonomy and variation.

Admittedly, the postmodernist perspective is relativistic and designed to sensitize anthropologists to their own views and values as well as those of the informant. They advocate combining self-knowledge with knowledge of the people under study so that anthropologists learn something about themselves as they are learning about the culture of the informant. In fact, a reading of a postmodernist ethnography usually reveals as much about the anthropologist as it does about the people being studied. The writings of Cuban American anthropologist Ruth Behar of the University of Michigan are an excellent example of postmodernism in anthropology.

In her book *Translated Woman: Crossing the Border with Esperanza's Story* (1993), Behar tells how she started her research by listening to the life story of Esperanza, a Mexican woman she had befriended. Before long Behar found that learning about Esperanza's life history was causing her to reflect on her own life. Behar began to question aspects of her own life and work, including the role of the ethnographer, the validity of comparing her life with Esperanza's, and her achievements as an affluent and successful academic. The book turned out to be two life stories rather than one.

The most radical postmodernists contend that because objectivity is impossible and all interpretations are relative, generalizations are unwarranted, and anthropology should be treated as literature rather than as science. In fact, purists, in the postmodern sense, believe all anthropologists carry with them their own cultural baggage; they would argue that from the beginning their research will be subjective in nature. It will be an interpretation from their own cultural lens. Fortunately, few anthropologists today hold such an extreme view, which would, in effect, reject all past attempts to make generalizations about cultural differences and similarities. As you can well imagine, postmodernists have had many heated discussions with their more traditional, scientifically oriented colleagues. However, even their strongest critics should realize that the postmodernists have raised the consciousness of all anthropologists to consider issues such as how we generate knowledge, how we come to know what we think we know, and whose story we are telling in ethnographic accounts—theirs or ours.

Postmodernism in Brief

- Postmodernism calls on anthropologists to switch their focus from cultural generalizations and predictable laws to description, interpretation, and the search for individual meaning.

---

postmodernism A school of anthropology that advocates the switch from cultural generalization and laws to description, interpretation, and the search for meaning.

- Ethnographies should be written from several voices—that of the anthropologist along with those of the people under analysis.

- Postmodernism involves a distinct return to cultural relativism.

Political Economy

Although valued by ethnographers in general, a major theoretical framework used by many applied anthropologists, and more so than any of the theoretical perspectives that have been discussed previously, is *political economy*. Political economy is not a new theoretical perspective chronologically, in that it did not come after postmodernism. In fact, it has a long history dating back to eighteenth-century philosophers Thomas Malthus, Marx, and Adam Smith. Today, prominent scholars whose research is closely aligned with political economy are Eric Wolf (Figure 4.9), Pierre Bourdieu, Sidney Mintz, Phillip Bourgois, June Nash, and Marshal Sahlins.

As a theoretical framework its use is a rather curious one. At the core of political economy theoretical perspectives are the abstract issues of conflict, ideology, and power. Anthropologists whose research relies on this framework do so to explain, in part, the relationship between economic production and political processes. It is often used when there is a hierarchical social order

with one group dominating or controlling another within a culture and among cultures. Conceptually it leads to multiscaled research that can start in a local village, connect to a more dominant regional government, and reach all the way to the international arena.

Political economy scholars challenge capitalism for its inequality and the marginalizing effects it has on local people, ethnic minorities, the poor, and disenfranchised. To illustrate, Eric Wolf's work, *Europe and the People without History* (1982) provides an in-depth account of the political-economic perspective in anthropology. He provides insight into people's responses and resistance to the process of control by elite groups. Other anthropologists have taken a slightly different perspective detailing how political and economic structures govern a labor force, or worker and capitalist relations, or discussions of war and violence. Anthropologists find political economy helpful to examine the increasing presence of poverty, the limited access to education, health care, and growing unemployment. Still others, such as Pierre Bourdieu (1977) use the political economy framework to examine the production of cultural meaning and symbols. For Bourdieu, a society's cultural construction of meaning and symbols has political and economic interests, especially when there is conflict over the meanings or when they prove to be provocative in their interpretation. For example, understanding the different positions groups (that is, governments, different tribes, special interests, etc.) have during a time of war.

Political economy has the potential to be widely used to frame research that focuses on social injustice, human rights, and marginalization, which is appealing to applied anthropologists. Unequal access to power, resources, and capital poses challenges preventing some people to have a better quality of life than others. For applied anthropologists the political economy perspective guides the research process so as to unravel the political and economic barriers, to confront them, develop a project, get it funded, and implement it. Political economy has applications in business, education, health care, development, and urban planning. For example, a medical anthropologist might use a political economy approach to examine malnutrition, unequal access to health care, and diseases and illnesses related to poverty, to name a few social issues that receive attention nationally and internationally. Someone in business might examine workers' rights, organizational structure, and the mediation process to avoid strikes within an industry or company.

One need not travel far to see an opportunity to employ a political economy perspective. In 2011 the

Courtesy of Sydel Silverman Wolf

FIGURE 4.9 Anthropologists such as Eric Wolf and other scholars challenge capitalism for its inequality and the marginalizing effects it has on local people, ethnic minorities, the poor, and disenfranchised through a political economy perspective.

political economy Political economy at its core examines the abstract issues of conflict, ideology and power.

"Occupy Wall Street" protesters illustrated all too clearly the unequal access to power and capital there is in the United States (Figure 4.10). When local people voiced their concerns and protested against the banks' bailouts on Wall Street and elsewhere, the police were called to intervene, and they effectively dismantled the protesters' months'-long occupation. Such an event is perfect for analysis using a political economy perspective.

Just like all the other theoretical frameworks discussed previously, political economy is frequently critiqued. One negative critique of political economy is that some research is void of economics, and it places too much of its emphasis on policy, the political structure, and power and control over others. In other cases, there is sufficient economics in the research, but insufficient policy or political structure, or it is apolitical. So it all depends on the point of departure and the particular interests of the anthropologist as well as the nature of the topic and how it lends itself to being studied. Take for example the work by Phillip Bourgois. He is much in the thick of a political conflict when he tried to conduct his field research for his Ph.D. dissertation. It took him three tries and three countries before he could complete his research to earn his Ph.D. degree.

Bourgois started out with an examination of the indigenous population, the Moskitu in Nicaragua just after the overthrow of the Anastasio Somoza by the Sandinistas (Bourgois 1981) and the beginning of the Nicaragua revolution. He writes:

> Soon after I arrived in the heartland of Moskitu territory, the indigenous population began

mobilizing to defend their rights to land and autonomy in a tragic alliance with the [U.S.] Central Intelligence Agency. 'My' fieldwork village, accessible only by a full day's journey upstream in a dug-out canoe, became the central arena of a bloody conflict against the central government. Although the underlying causes for this indigenous war were the historical structures of racism and marginalization of the region dating back to the colonial period, the fighting itself was sponsored economically and was escalated militarily by the U. S. government, (Bourgois 2002:31)

He thought better of staying and after a harrowing couple of weeks left Nicaragua. Not long after he headed to Honduras. Again, because he was trained in political economy and history he chose to examine the context of radical political mobilization (Bourgois 2002:31). To gather his data he worked in a Salvadoran refugee camp in Honduras. This research experience did not bode well for him either; he had crossed the borders between the countries of El Salvador and Honduras, which was illegal. What he discovered and how he went about reporting it nearly ended up costing him his career, one that he had not even begun. On his third attempt, he went to Costa Rica and engaged in fieldwork among laborers working on a banana plantation for a large fruit company. As you can imagine, this research was also filled with controversy because he focused on labor rights and unfair working conditions. Political economy research, especially from an applied perspective, tends to focus on marginalized peoples, conflict and struggle with political and economic systems, and with an eye or the means to increase public awareness and where possible to do something to make a difference. Yet, as one gets involved in this kind research one also needs to be mindful of the safety of the people one is working with as well as one's own safety. Sometimes the work can be life-threatening, whereas on most cases it is not.

Political Economy in Brief

- Political economy at its core examines the abstract issues of conflict, ideology, and power.
- An ethnographic approach to political economy tends to be descriptive.
- An applied approach using a political economy framework focuses on making a difference for marginalized or disenfranchised groups of people.

FIGURE 4.10 Occupy Wall Street protesters' sign in front of the tent city at Zuccotti Park in the financial district, October 31, 2011, New York.

Dr. Alan Lipkin/Shutterstock.com

Water, Culture, and Power: When Is It Too Late to Act?

✿ Water lies at the heart of all development. Worldwide, water is an extremely relevant contemporary issue for us to explore. Many researchers believe that over time water will become as important as oil. As water becomes scarce in many parts of the world, it will increasingly be the cause of social and political conflict, most particularly where freshwater resources cross international boundaries. Access to drinkable water at the local level as well as the regional interconnections of a shared resource will become a global and local challenge. All living things need water for survival. Electricity generation in many countries is also highly dependent on water; without water, parts of the world experience regular power supply shortages and increased charges for electricity. Water could be the looming crisis for the twenty-first century.

Though generally regarded as an ecological or technical problem, the overuse or misuse of water is, above all, a social and political issue. Competition for water allocation between rural and urban users, between indigenous and nonindigenous groups, and between industrial and recreational users is a hot topic now and will become even more important in the future. In two issues of *Anthropology News* (January and February 2010), many of the commentaries written by anthropologists focused on water issues facing global inhabitants. The authors noted the important contributions made by anthropologists to the research agenda, policy formation, and action with respect to water. However, these anthropologists started not with an in-depth examination of a particular culture group or society, the traditional ethnographic approach, but with a focus on a natural resource—water. The authors reminded readers that as we explore such topics, we should engage in traditional ethnography or applied research much like studying a culture group, but with the added emphasis on how particular cultures use water in everyday life.

Anthropologists will still ground their research in anthropological theory, methods, and units of analyses, but they may also have to master new skills and methodologies relating to water. They may draw on political ecology or symbolic anthropology as theoretical orientations to provide the framework for their research design, but then focus on using their research findings to contribute to the effectiveness of water management systems or water conservation policies.

As Veronica Stang (2009: 5) points out:

> An understanding and appreciation of people's diverse relationships with water—and with each other—is vital for the resolution of conflicts, and for the development of more ecologically and socially sustainable forms of water use. There is a need to consider not just the formal institutions and structures involved, but all the ways that different groups control or influence the management and use of water as well as conceptual models and values that they apply in this process.

Standard anthropological methods are useful for such research endeavors, which include literature reviews, participant observation, interviewing, and archival research. Many anthropologists examine issues of social justice and marginalization that typically arise out of the unequal power relations that shape all governance systems. By examining the social and environmental relationships involved in engagement with water and responses to development in water policy and governance, social scientists can play a pivotal role in helping to design policy that emphasizes equitable access to a shared and vital resource.

According to Barbara Rose Johnson, who served as an advisor to UNESCO's International Hydrological Programme on water and cultural diversity, the United Nations millennium project defined water "as the essential lifeblood of our planet, with the power to generate, sustain, receive and ultimately to unify life. This vision reflected advisory concern for ancient waterworks; water and the arts; water ethics; indigenous knowledge, stewardship and customary management systems; the sanctity of water; water and sacred sites; values, norms and behavior that shape water culture of public health risk and strategies to transform behavior and reduce risk" (Johnson 2010: 6).

Keith Dannemiller/Alamy

Political Ecology

Previous anthropologists who framed their research with a political economy theoretical perspective often were not interested in the environment. In fact, their approach to ethnography pretty much ignored the environment and various repercussions because of political and economic factors. Since the late 1970s and 1980s research grounded in political economy began a resurgence of including environmental issues, giving an old term political ecology new life and a new following. Simply put, although it is far from simple to do or contemplate, *political ecology* is

---

political ecology Political ecology examines how unequal relations in and among societies affect the use of the natural environment and its resources, especially in the context of wide ranging ecological settings, and subsequent economic, policy, and regulatory actions.

the study of power relations among groups and how they are linked to the biophysical environment at the local, state, national, and international levels. Scholars whose work uses the political ecology perspective examine relationships among political, economic, and social factors with environmental issues and changes within a community and beyond. By paying attention to environmental interests, knowledge, beliefs, values, and practices of social groups, applied anthropologists and others can differentiate how resources are used, misused, and overused according to ethnicity, gender, and race or other factors.

Historically political ecology focused on marginalized conditions affecting the developing world. Rooted in neo-Marxism, political ecology picks up where political economy and cultural ecology left off. Political ecology incorporates political economy into its theoretical construct but then goes one step further by including the environment on an equal playing field as the political structure or economic systems. Similarly political ecology addresses issues of power and recognizes the importance of explaining environmental impacts on cultural processes as part of the political and economic context. For example, political ecology may be used to examine how unequal relations in and among societies affect the use of the natural environment. Resources (for example, access to water, fish, soils and land, oil, trees and timber, biodiversity, clean air), especially in the context of wide-ranging ecological settings, such as coastal, rainforests, deserts, high mountains, glaciers, and urban and rural communities, are particularly complex and get even more complicated with subsequent policy and regulatory actions favor certain groups over others.

Political ecology draws scholars and researchers from many academic disciplines, including anthropology, environmental studies, geography, history, and sociology. For anthropologists who integrate ecological social science with political economy, their work might emphasize topics such as sustainability, conservation, environmental conflict, environmental identities, marginalization, and social movements. The use of political ecology sees environmental degradation as a cause and effect of social marginalization.

Anthropologists recognized for the contributions in political ecology include Eric Wolf, Susan Stonich, Arturo Escobar, Diane Rocheleau, and Susan Paulson.

So whether we are examining where a new garbage dump is to be located or the next hydroelectric dam, in each case there are those with the power to decide on the future location and those who will be relocated with or without compensation or be forced to reside near the smells or potential for flooding. An example of political ecology helps to illustrate how the environment is brought to the forefront of the research. This example also illustrates the multiscalar approach (connecting the local level to the state or region and global level) frequently used in political ecology. Here, a hydroelectric dam was constructed in Patagonia, Chile, with the approval of the Chilean government (Figure 4.11). However, where the dam was to be constructed would flood the region inhabited by Mapuche Indians located in the southern regions of Chile. The Spanish utility company gained permission from the Chilean government to locate a dam for hydroelectric project along the river where the Mapuche families had been residing for centuries. As a cultural practice the Mapuche also use the river banks to intern their dead; to them the river and adjoining banks were sacred. However, it was necessary for the Spanish hydroelectric company to flood the river to generate the power needed to make the electricity. Yet, these decisions destroyed fourteen ancient cemeteries and an indigenous homeland.

In the end, the Mapuche lost their land, their way of life, and their ancestors' remains. Families were relocated into a barren region of Chile where they were without sufficient means to afford the electricity from the newly installed hydroelectric facility. Today the

Reuters/Corbis

FIGURE 4.11 A Pehuenche Indian, whose tribe is part of the Mapuche peoples in the Andes in south central Chile stands on a hill overlooking the construction site of a US$500 million hydroelectric dam. The hydroelectric dam, once constructed, flooded lands to which the Pehuenche Indians claim historical ownership rights.

Spanish electric company owns the hydroelectric dam in southern Chile and sells the electricity to Chileans. Clearly this example illustrates how unequal relations among societies and populations affect the use of the natural resources and the marginalization of those with less access and power.

Political Ecology in Brief

- Political ecology is the study of power relations among groups and how they are linked to the biophysical environment at the local, state, national, and international levels, a multiscalar approach.

- The use of political ecology sees environmental degradation as a cause and effect of social marginalization. Scholars whose work uses the political ecology perspective examine relationships among political, economic, and social factors with environmental issues and changes within a community and beyond.

- Political ecology is used to examine how unequal relations in and among societies affect the use of the natural environment and its resources (for example, access to water, fish, soils and land, oil, trees and timber, biodiversity, clean air) and marginalization of those with less access.

Theory, Practice, and Praxis

Anthropologists depend on theory at the beginning of their research to be able to frame their research questions, or at the end of the research to interpret their findings, and overall to contribute to be the body of anthropological knowledge. As you have read we continue to build on several hundred years of social science theory. Clearly we have not thrown out the baby with the bathwater, may only a few of its toys.

We noted when we began this chapter that anthropologists are curious about humans, their adaptive nature, and cultural beliefs and practices that hold them together, such as language, identity, spiritual beliefs, economic and political systems, and the environment in which they reside. Descriptive accounts presented by academic ethnographers are important for documenting the rich cultural heritage found around the world. In contrast, applied anthropologists are concerned with producing useful information that raises awareness for contemporary social problems and places those findings within a broader context of implementation (of projects and programs), thus contributing to making policy. These anthropologists

emphasize the practical aspects of their work rather than their theoretical contribution. The opposite tendency is true of ethnographic anthropologists who would prefer to emphasize their theoretical contributions and descriptive analyses over any practical or pragmatic application. Anthropologists working outside of academia altogether (practicing anthropologists), as described in Chapter 3, may also have to write for a particular audience such as a client or an employer, or colleagues working nongovernmental organizations as well as the public who may not know any anthropology. Their work is more general in nature, and a theory-driven or scholarly paper will probably not help them keep their job. Someone working for the World Bank, however, may need to understand kinship and family for their research, but they will probably not be writing about specific marriage patterns and descent groups like an academic anthropologist would. Anthropologists in general are trained to recognize and use various theoretical perspectives to accomplish their work.

Praxis in Anthropology

Integrating theory with practice is known as *praxis* and serves as a means to produce new knowledge. Although not always standard practice among some researchers, praxis is frequently used among applied anthropologists when combining their approach in data collection, data analysis, and application to an applied project. Applied business anthropologist, Marietta Baba reminds us, "praxis carries with it a strong sense of social critique that we find in political economy and political ecology, where by people with whom anthropologists work may be liberated from the exploitive and alienating circumstances of their lives" (2000:26). Praxis is an attainable ideal within anthropology that provides a balance that includes theory, method, and application. This balance is important to recognize, especially considering the continuum discussed in Chapter 3 that separates ethnographic theorists on the one hand, from practicing anthropologists on the other, where one extreme is mostly theoretical (and no empirical research) and the other mostly practice (and no theory). Anthropologist Jim McDonald (2002) reminds us that in striving for praxis, (combining theory with practice) that we always need to keep in mind the ethical considerations of our work and the people with whom we consult and interact, especially when engaged in applied research.

---

praxis Integrating theory with practice; serves as a means to produce new knowledge.

Concluding Thoughts on Anthropological Theory

This chapter was written with subheadings that divide the field of anthropological theory into discrete schools. Table 4.1 summarizes the primary anthropological theories and their proponents. These divisions can serve as a useful device to help track, in general terms and in roughly chronological order, the various emphases that anthropologists have taken since the mid-nineteenth century. It is important to note, however, that we should not think of these different schools (theoretical framework) as being superseded by those that came later. In other words, evolutionism was not replaced by American historicism, nor was functionalism replaced by political ecology theorists. Moreover, these schools of anthropology are not particularly relevant categories for distinguishing among the different approaches used by contemporary anthropologists. Few anthropologists today would tie themselves to a single school or theoretical orientation such as neoevolutionism, functionalism, cultural materialism, or political ecology.

Contemporary anthropologists tend to be more eclectic and problem oriented, focusing on explaining cultural phenomena while drawing on a wide variety of theories, research methods, and sources of data. Today it is generally recognized that many of these theoretical schools are not mutually exclusive. It is evident that anthropology is maturing as a discipline when its practitioners reject hard-drawn lines among themselves and thereby enrich one another's thinking.

TABLE 4.1

Anthropological Theories and Their Proponents

School	Major Assumption	Advocates
Evolutionism	All societies pass through a series of stages.	Sir Edward Tylor, Lewis Henry Morgan
Diffusionism	All societies change as a result of cultural borrowing from one another.	Fritz Graebner, Grafton Elliot Smith
American historicism	Fieldwork must precede cultural theories.	Franz Boas, Alfred Kroeber
Functionalism	The task of anthropology is to understand how parts of contemporary cultures contribute to the well-being of individuals.	Bronislaw Malinowski
Structural functionalism	Anthropology's task is to determine how cultural elements function for the well-being of the society.	Alfred Reginald Radcliffe-Brown
Psychological anthropology	Anthropology's task is to show relationships among psychological and cultural variables.	Ruth Benedict, Margaret Mead
Neoevolutionism	Cultures evolve in direct proportion to their capacity to harness energy.	Leslie White, Julian Steward
French structuralism	Human cultures are shaped by certain preprogrammed codes in the human mind.	Claude Lévi-Strauss
Ethnoscience	Cultures must be described in terms of native categories.	William Sturtevant, Ward Goodenough
Feminist anthropology	Social relationships should be viewed as being gendered.	Louise Lamphere, Sherry Ortner, and Michelle Zimbalist Rosaldo
Cultural materialism	Material conditions determine human consciousness and behavior.	Marvin Harris
Postmodernism	Human behavior stems from the way people perceive and classify the world around them.	Clifford Geertz
Political economy	Economic and political systems are critique to understand conflict, struggle, and power.	Eric Wolf, June Nash, Sidney Mintz, Pierre Bourdieu, Phillip Bourgois, Marshall Sahlins
Political ecology	Combining political economy with the environment and resource use.	Eric Wolf, Susan Stonich, Arturo Escobar, Diane Rocheleau, and Susan Paulson

Summary

1. Anthropological theory, which arose from the desire to explain the great cultural diversity in the world, enables us to reduce reality to an abstract, yet manageable, set of principles.

2. The first group of anthropologists used the notion of evolution to account for differences in human cultures. Nineteenth-century evolutionists such as Tylor and Morgan suggested that all societies pass through a series of distinct evolutionary stages. Although they have been criticized by their successors for being overly speculative and ethnocentric in their formulations, these early evolutionists fought and won the battle to establish that human behavior was the result of certain cultural processes rather than biological or supernatural processes.

3. The diffusionists explained cultural differences and similarities in terms of the extent of contact cultures had with one another.

4. In contrast to the evolutionists and diffusionists, Boas insisted on the collection of firsthand empirical data on a wide range of cultures before developing anthropological theories. Although he has been criticized for not engaging in much theorizing himself, the meticulous attention Boas gave to methodology put the young discipline of anthropology on a solid scientific footing.

5. The British functionalists Malinowski and Radcliffe-Brown, who, like Boas, were strong advocates of fieldwork, concentrated on how contemporary cultures functioned to meet the needs of the individual and perpetuate the society. Not only do all parts of a culture serve a function, but they are interconnected (functional unity) so that a change in one part of the culture is likely to bring about change in other parts.

6. The early psychological anthropologists, most notably Benedict and Mead, were interested in exploring the relationships between culture and the individual. By examining the configuration of traits, Benedict described whole cultures in terms of individual personality characteristics. Mead's early research efforts brought her to Samoa to study the emotional problems associated with adolescence and later to New Guinea to study male and female gender roles.

7. The theory of evolution was brought back into fashion during the twentieth century by White and Steward. White, like Tylor and Morgan before him, held that cultures evolve from simple to complex forms, but for White the process of evolution was driven by his "basic law of evolution" ($C = ET$). Steward's major contribution was the concept of multilinear evolution, a form of evolution of specific cultures that did not assume that all cultures passed through the same stages. Steward also introduced the concept of cultural ecology, formally bringing the environment into the discussion when describing a culture.

8. Drawing heavily on the models of linguistics and cognitive psychology, Lévi-Strauss maintained that certain codes or mental structures preprogrammed in the human mind are responsible for culture and social behavior. A fundamental tenet of Lévi-Strauss's theory is that the human mind thinks in binary oppositions—opposites that enable people to classify the units of meaning in their culture and relate them to the world around them.

9. The theoretical approach known as ethnoscience is cognitive in that it seeks explanations in the human mind. By distinguishing between the emic and the etic approaches to research, ethnoscientists attempt to describe a culture in terms of how it is perceived, ordered, and categorized by members of that culture rather than by the codes or categories of the ethnographer's culture.

10. Feminist anthropologists call for a systematic analysis of the role women play in the social structure. The feminist critique, by and large, does not embrace positivism, quantitative methods, or a value-neutral orientation.

11. Led by Harris, cultural materialists believe that tools, technology, and material well-being are the most critical aspects of cultural systems.

12. Diametrically opposed to the cultural materialists are the humanistic anthropologists: interpretive anthropologists and postmodernists, who advocate cultural description and interpretation rather than a search for generalizations and explanatory theories.

13. Anthropologists whose research relies on a political economy theoretical framework do so to explain the relationship between economic production and political processes, especially when there is a hierarchical social order with one group dominating or controlling another within a culture and among cultures.

14. Political ecology is the study of power relations among groups and how they are linked to the biophysical environment at the local, state, national, and international levels. This type of research examines how unequal relations in and among societies affect the use of the natural environment and its resources, especially in the context of wide ranging ecological settings, and subsequent economic, policy and regulatory actions.

15. Integrating theory with practice is known as *praxis* and serves as a means to produce new knowledge. It is an ideal that applied anthropologists strive to achieve in their application of their research.

Key Terms

theory
hypothesis
evolutionism
savagery
barbarism
civilization
deductive approach
psychic unity
diffusionism

American historicism
inductive approach
emic approach
functionalism/functional
theory
structural functionalism
universal functions
functional unity
dysfunction

psychological
anthropology
neoevolutionism
unilinear evolution
universal evolution
multilinear evolution
cultural ecology
French structuralism
binary oppositions

ethnoscience
feminist anthropology
positivism
cultural materialism
interpretive anthropology
postmodernism
political economy
political ecology
praxis

Critical Thinking Questions

1. Why is theory important to both ethnographic and applied anthropologists?
2. Can you identify a particular social problem that an applied anthropologist might want to get involved in and think about what theoretical perspectives would be useful to develop a research proposal?

Online Study Resources

CourseMate

Access chapter-specific learning tools including learning objectives, practice quizzes, videos, flash cards, glossaries, web links, and more in your Cultural Anthropology CourseMate. Login to http://www.cengagebrain.com to access the resources your instructor has assigned and to purchase materials.

Anthropologist Katherine Dolan uses a laptop and printer powered by a car battery in the field.

Applied Anthropology Methods in Cultural Anthropology

As we will see in some detail in this chapter, cultural anthropologists collect much of their data through participant-observer research, which involves living with and observing the people under study. A common concern of any anthropologist doing fieldwork, particularly in the early stages, is committing a cultural faux pas that will be embarrassing, offend the hosts, and possibly have negative consequences for the research itself. I would question any experienced cultural anthropologist who claims that he or she never had a regrettable, "foot-in-the-mouth" moment. Though not a cultural anthropologist himself, Thomas Crampton (2003), correspondent for the *International Herald Tribune* in Hong Kong, tells about a cultural blunder he committed while visiting the rural home of an English-speaking Thai acquaintance from Bangkok. This cross-cultural faux pas resonates with many cultural anthropologists because it is the type of mistake that any outsider, anthropologist or not, could make on an initial encounter with a radically different culture.

When Crampton arrived at his friend's family's house, both men were treated like celebrities. Although excited about having the weekend to learn about life in rural Thailand, Crampton was soon taken aback by the barrage of questions he was asked that, by Western standards, would be considered overly personal. Are you married? How much do you earn? How old are you? Particularly puzzling was the question, Would you like a bath? Unfortunately Crampton did not understand that this is a common Thai greeting.

Wanting to be a good guest, he finally took them up on their offer and retreated to the bathroom, which had a full-sized tub already filled with water. He got in, lathered up, shampooed his hair, and rinsed off. When he finished, he could not find a drain in the bottom of the tub to let out the dirty, soapy water. Feeling more than mildly perplexed, he scooped out the upper layer of soap scum and hair with a bowl he found in the bathroom until the water looked relatively clean. After concluding that the Thais must have a special system for draining the tub, he dressed and rejoined his hosts.

WHAT WE WILL LEARN

- How do cultural anthropologists conduct fieldwork?

- What types of data-gathering techniques do cultural anthropologists use?

- What are some of the problems that make fieldwork less than romantic for cultural anthropologists?

- What ethical dilemmas do applied anthropologists face when they conduct fieldwork?

The next morning, on his way to the bathroom, Crampton was greeted by a family member who led him to the house of a neighbor, where he was met by his host family and the neighbor's family in a bathroom resembling the one in which he had bathed the previous day. In front of both families, Crampton's friend, with a big smile on his face, made a broad scooping motion with the bowl into the tub, used the water to rinse his mouth, and spit it into the drain on the floor. In Crampton's own words, "horror and embarrassment welled up as I learned lesson No. 1 of life in rural Thailand: Do not bathe in the week's supply of drinking water."

This example should not suggest that journalists are less culturally sensitive than anthropologists. After reading this account, most experienced fieldworkers probably think, "and this could happen to me." ■

A distinctive feature of present-day cultural anthropology is the reliance on *fieldwork* as the primary way of conducting research. Cultural anthropologists carry out their research in other contexts as well—such as libraries and museums—but they rely most heavily on experiential fieldwork. Like any other professionals, cultural anthropologists want to describe the basic subject matter of their discipline. They are interested in documenting the enormous variety of ways of life found among the peoples of the world today. How do people feed themselves? What do different people like to eat? What do they believe? How do they legitimize marriages? In addition to learning the *what* and the *how* of different cultures, cultural anthropologists are interested in explaining *why* people in different parts of the world behave and think the way they do. To answer these questions by providing both description and explanation, cultural anthropologists collect their data on site by engaging in fieldwork, which in anthropology is also referred to as *ethnographic fieldwork*.

As a research strategy, anthropological fieldwork is eminently experiential, which means that cultural anthropologists learn while they work. Cultural anthropologists, be they ethnographic or applied researchers, collect their primary data by immersing themselves into the cultures they are studying (Figure 5.1). Specifically, this kind of data collection involves living with the people they study, learning their language, asking them questions, surveying their environments and material possessions, and spending long periods of time observing their everyday behaviors and interactions in their natural setting. Doing firsthand fieldwork has become a necessary rite of passage for the professional

anthropologist. Generally, to receive a doctorate in cultural anthropology in the United States, one must conduct extended ethnographic fieldwork in a culture or co-culture other than one's own.

FIGURE 5.1 The study of everyday life in the state of Bahia in Brazil (*top*) presents different problems and challenges to the field anthropologist than does the study of village life in Malawi (*bottom*). For example, the languages are different, as are the climate, dress, and housing.

fieldwork The practice in which an anthropologist is immersed in the daily life of a culture to collect data and test cultural hypotheses.

ethnographic fieldwork Research carried out by cultural anthropologists among living peoples in other societies and among subcultures of our own society.

The strong insistence on ethnographic fieldwork has not always been an integral part of the discipline. Much of the theorizing of nineteenth-century anthropology was based on secondhand information at best, and often, on the superficial and impressionistic writings of untrained observers. For example, Lewis Henry Morgan's classic work *Ancient Society* (1877), discussed in Chapter 4, was based largely on information collected by ships' captains, missionaries, explorers, and others who inadvertently came across cultures in their travels around the world. It was not until the early twentieth century—largely at the suggestion of Franz Boas and Bronislaw Malinowski—that extended fieldwork of a year or longer became the norm for collecting cultural data. Applied anthropologists also go through extensive training in ethnographic field methods identical to ethnographic field researchers.

Even though anthropologists routinely conducted fieldwork for most of the twentieth century, they did not explicitly discuss their field techniques until quite recently. Before the 1960s, it was usual for an anthropologist to produce a book on "his" or "her" people several years after returning from a fieldwork experience. Such a work is called an *ethnography*, an in-depth account of a people and their culture studied by the anthropologist who conducted the on-site fieldwork. Frequently these books did not contain a detailed description or explanation of field methods or of the fieldwork experience itself. A reader had no way of knowing, for instance, how long the anthropologist stayed in the field, how many people were interviewed and observed, how samples were selected, what data-gathering techniques were used, what problems were encountered, or how the data were analyzed.

Curiosity of the exotic and of on small-scale, non-Western cultures was the focus of much of the early-twentieth-century fieldwork studies for cultural anthropologists. Today we may find some contemporary anthropologists who study cultures closer to home as well as of those abroad. In recent decades cultural anthropologists have conducted fieldwork not only in rural settings, but also in domestic urban ethnic neighborhoods, in hospitals, elementary schools, and prisons.

Because the credibility of any ethnographic study depends on its methodology, cultural anthropologists since the 1960s have been producing excellent accounts of their own fieldwork experiences and data-collection methods. In more recent decades, a number of books and journal articles explore the methodological issues involved in designing a fieldwork study, collecting the data, and analyzing the results.

By the 1980s applied anthropologists, in particular, began to involve members of the cultural group they were studying with the project design, data collection, and data analyses. Involving local people in the applied research process is known as *participatory action research*. This is a critical methodological change in the discipline because it empowered local residents and those participating in research projects to be part of the research design and data-collection process and not just subjects who were interviewed in a study. Today this method is referred to as *community-based participatory research (CBPR)*. A CBPR approach is collaborative and involves partners from within a community in all aspects of the research process. Most importantly CBPR begins with a research topic of importance to the community. By working together and combining knowledge with action, CBPR project goals are aimed at achieving social change equitably.

Some anthropologists have dedicated their research to problem-oriented topics such as reforestation, nutrition, post-disaster events (earthquakes, tsunamis and hurricanes), and resettlement. For example, Anthony Oliver-Smith has researched disasters and involuntary resettlement for the past thirty years. His work has taken in him to Peru, Honduras, India, Brazil, Jamaica, Mexico, Japan, and the United States, where he has assisted in post-disaster recovery and resettlement. After many years in the field that resulted in contributing to policy, Oliver-Smith (2011) observed a change in the voices being heard—that of the victims of the events. He recounts these changes in *Defying Displacement: Grassroots Resistance and the Critique of Development* in which he describes how societies and cultures are taking action against development-forced displacement and resettlement. And rather than it being only a negative critique of development, he also reports on new ideas and alternatives to resettlement and displacement, many of which come from the people with whom he has worked.

Even though cultural anthropologists have studied Western societies such as our own, they have not abandoned the essential features of ethnographic research, specifically of living among the people they study. When conducting ethnographic research, anthropologists combine multiple methods to provide depth and breadth to the data they are collecting. Although ethnographic fieldwork is the favorite approach, anthropologists also borrow methods used by other social sciences (such as statistics and surveying) particularly sociology, economics, geography, political science, and psychology.

---

ethnography Both a strategy of anthropological research and its products, such as a written account reflecting the views of the people and those of the anthropologist.

participatory action research A mode of research in which the anthropologist and the community work together to understand the conditions that produce the community's problems to find solutions to those problems.

community-based participatory research (CBPR) A collaboration involving partners from within a community in all aspects of the research process. Most importantly CBPR begins with a research topic of importance to the community and works towards achieving social change equitably.

Why do anthropologists choose to primarily use the ethnographic approach? First, the ethnographic approach takes a holistic view (see Chapter 1) by studying complete, functioning societies (e.g., an urban neighborhood or a farming community). Second, the ethnographic approach depends on firsthand, experiential methods, which include face-to-face interactions with people within the culture. Sometimes the research or an applied project requires the anthropologist to engage with people who may affect the community being studied but may live outside the village; examples are interviewing government officials, agriculture extension agents, city planners, and others who may influence the local dynamics of a community.

To get a better handle on a particular culture, an anthropologist begins by listening to stories and other kinds of talk that give insight into the community. Anthropologists refer to this form of data as qualitative data. *Qualitative data* are gathered from personal interviews, oral histories, observations, and interactions with community members. These data are important to the research process and may be logged in anthropologists' *fieldnotes* or digitally recorded and transcribed for later text analyses. Being able to see the patterns in the shared worldviews within a culture provides perspective on the numerical data obtained from gathering quantitative data. *Quantitative data* are numerical data such as population trends, morbidity and mortality rates, household and community size, the numbers of births and marriages, landholding size, annual income and education levels, and any other data that can be counted. Anthropologists use these data to conduct statistical analyses. For example, if the anthropologist has been collecting data on household size, sex, and age, he or she can conduct simple descriptive statistical analyses. The anthropologist can determine from these data what percentages of the adult members of the community are female or male. Of course more complex quantitative data analyses may also be conducted from the data. For example, if the anthropologist had asked the appropriate questions and gathered other relevant measurements, he or she might be able to find out from the data how many women of childbearing age have children under five who are malnourished. More thorough ethnographic methods often blend qualitative and quantitative approaches to verify and validate patterns and trends.

Like ethnographic anthropologists, applied anthropologists use similar methods to conduct their research.

Applied anthropologists are grounded in ethnography—in the methods of gathering, coding, and analyzing data. Applied anthropologists, however, focus their research endeavors on contemporary problems and social issues, rather than examining the whole culture. Given the nature of their work, applied anthropologists often collaborate on projects with other scientists and community participants to help expedite the fieldwork. They may work as facilitators, assisting in project design, project implementation, or evaluation. They may be interested in such things as the incidence of malnutrition in a village, the rate at which deforestation is taking place in a region, or how a village has been able to retard the spread of tuberculosis. Each of these topics requires that the applied anthropologist specializes in something beyond the knowledge of a particular people's culture. Such specializations may include (but are not limited to) nutritional anthropology, environmental anthropology, or medical anthropology, which requires the specialist to undertake additional training in related methods of data collection and analyses (see below Cross-Cultural Miscue Box). Most important, though, the applied anthropologist's role is to provide a cultural understanding of how a problem came to be and how it may be removed, lessened, or resolved.

CROSS-CULTURAL MISCUE

❀ While conducting urban fieldwork in Kuala Lumpur, Malaysia, medical anthropologist Jennifer Roberts devoted the first several weeks of her research time to establishing her credibility, building social networks, and getting to know the local people. Her research assistant introduced Roberts to a woman who was accompanied by her five-year-old daughter. Roberts was so taken by the girl's beauty that she patted the girl on the head while commenting to the mother what a gorgeous child she had. Much to Roberts's surprise, the mother responded by saying that the girl was not pretty at all and then abruptly left. What had Roberts done? She was simply trying to pay the woman and her daughter a compliment.

In fact Roberts had inadvertently committed two cultural gaffes. First, in this part of the world, the head is considered to be the most sacred part of the body, where one's spiritual power resides. Although patting a child on the head in North America is a gesture of endearment, in Malaysia it is viewed as a violation of the most sacred part of the body. Second, complimenting a child on her beauty or health is regarded in Malaysia as inviting bad fortune for the child. If evil people or evil spirits believe that a child is particularly healthy or beautiful, they might become jealous and want to harm the child.

So, unlike parents in North America who often boast of their children's beauty, health, and intelligence, parents in Malaysia downplay those traits to protect their children from harm.

---

qualitative data People's words, actions, records, and accounts obtained from participant-observation, interviews, group interviews, and relevant documents.

fieldnotes The daily descriptive notes recorded by an anthropologist during or after an observation of a specific phenomenon or activity.

quantitative data The data that are counted and interpreted through statistical analyses.

Any general discussion of how to do fieldwork is difficult because no two fieldwork situations are the same. The problems encountered while studying the reindeer-herding Chukchee of Siberia are quite different from those faced when studying hard-core unemployed street people in Philadelphia or rural peasant farmers in Peru. Even studies of the same village by the same anthropologist at two different times involve different experiences because in the period between the two studies, both the anthropologist and the people being studied have changed.

Despite these differences, field anthropologists face some common concerns, problems, and issues. For example, everyone embarking on ethnographic fieldwork must make preparations before leaving home, gain acceptance into the community, select the most appropriate data-gathering techniques, understand how to operate within the local political structure, take precautions against investigator bias, choose knowledgeable *informants* (also known as "cultural consultants" or "participants"), cope with culture shock, learn a new language, and be willing to reevaluate his or her findings in light of new evidence. In this chapter we will explore these and other common concerns of the fieldworker, while recognizing that every fieldwork situation has its own unique set of concerns, problems, and issues.

Preparing for Fieldwork

The popular image of the field anthropologist tends to be overly romanticized. Field anthropologists are often envisioned as working in idyllic settings, listening to exotic stories, and taking pictures of native peoples. In reality, conducting anthropological fieldwork bears little resemblance to a carefree vacation. Like any scientific enterprise, it makes serious demands on one's time, patience, and sense of humor and requires a lot of hard work and thoughtful preparation. Although luck can be a factor, the success of a fieldwork experience is usually directly proportional to the thoroughness of one's preparations.

Any fieldwork project lasting a year or longer may well require a minimum of a year's preparation. For a fieldwork project to be successful, the anthropologist must attend to many essential matters during this preparatory period. First, because doing fieldwork is expensive, it is necessary to obtain funding from a source that supports anthropological research, such as the Social Science Research Council, the National Science Foundation, or the Wenner-Gren Foundation. Financial support (covering living expenses, transportation, and other research- and project-related costs) is awarded on a highly competitive basis to the proposals that have the greatest merit. Even though a proposal may require months of preparation, there is no guarantee that it will

be funded. Most anthropologists spend time writing and submitting more than one grant proposal with the hope at least one will take them to the field.

Second, preparation for fieldwork involves taking the proper health precautions. Before leaving home, a fieldworker should obtain all relevant immunizations. For example, a fieldworker traveling to a malaria-infested area must take the appropriate (region-specific) malarial suppressants before leaving home. It is also prudent to get information about available health facilities ahead of time in case the anthropologist or a family member becomes ill while in the field.

Third, if the field research is to be conducted in a foreign country (as is often the case), permission or clearance must be obtained from the host government. Because field projects usually last a year or longer, no foreign government will allow an anthropologist to conduct research without prior approval. Some parts of the world are simply off limits to US citizens because of travel restrictions established by the governments of either the United States or the particular countries involved. Even countries that are hospitable to Westerners require that the researcher spell out the nature of the proposed research in considerable detail. The host government officials often want to make sure that the research will not be embarrassing or politically sensitive, that the findings will be useful, and that the researcher's presence in the host country will not jeopardize the safety, privacy, or jobs of any local citizens. Moreover host governments often require cultural anthropologists to become affiliated with local academic institutions to share their research experiences with local scholars and students. Sometimes—particularly in developing countries—the approval process can be slow, which is another reason it can take nearly a year to prepare for a long-term field study.

A fourth concern that must be addressed before leaving for the field is proficiency in the local language. An important part of the tradition of anthropological fieldwork is that it must be conducted in the native language. If the anthropologist is not fluent in the language of the culture to be studied, he or she should learn the language before leaving home. That may not always be possible, however. Dictionaries and grammar books may not exist for some of the more unusual languages, and finding a native speaker to serve as a tutor while still at home may not be possible. In such cases the ethnographer will have to learn the language after arriving in the field. Building in time for learning a new language into the fieldwork timeline is important for the research design, for conducting the research, as well as for funding purposes—and it may, and for good reasons, lengthen one's stay in the field.

---

informants A person who provides information about his or her culture to the ethnographic fieldworker.

Finally, the soon-to-be field anthropologist must take care of a host of personal details before leaving home. Arrangements must be made for:

- the care of personal possessions such as houses, cars, and pets;
- what to ship and what to purchase abroad;
- children's education if families are involved;
- equipment to purchase and insure, such as cameras and recording devices;
- up-to-date passports and international driving license; and
- a schedule for transferring money between one's bank at home and a convenient bank in the host country.

Recognizing these predeparture details should put an end to the illusion that fieldwork is a romantic holiday.

Stages of Field Research

Although no two fieldwork experiences are the same, every study should progress through the same five basic stages:

1. Selecting a research problem
2. Formulating a research design
3. Collecting the data
4. Analyzing the data
5. Interpreting the data

Rather than describing these stages in abstract terms, we will discuss them within the framework of an actual fieldwork project: the Jamaica Agroforestry Project (JAP) conducted by Andreatta (one of the authors) during the early 1990s. This applied project examined a wide range of issues related to the contemporary farming practices of relocated farmers in a drought-prone area of Jamaica.

Stage 1: Selecting a Research Problem

In the early twentieth century, the major aim of fieldwork was to describe a culture in as much ethnographic detail as possible. In recent decades, however, anthropologists have moved away from general ethnographies of particular cultures to research that is focused, specific, and problem-oriented. Rather than studying all the parts of a culture with equal attention, contemporary cultural anthropologists are more likely to examine specific issues dealing with relationships among various phenomena, such as the relationship between gender socialization and employment opportunities or the relationship between nutrition and food-getting strategies. The shift to a problem-oriented approach lends itself to research that builds on a series of descriptive questions that are progressively more complex to better understand not only *how* and *why* particular problems have come to be, but also *what* may be done about them.

The problem-oriented issue that gave rise to the JAP sought answers to both a long-term problem and a short-term problem. The long-term problem was rapid soil erosion, and the short-term problem was the lack of fodder for livestock during the dry season. An agroforestry project to solve these problems was conceptualized whereby researchers focused on the possibility of planting nitrogen-fixing trees that would hold the soil against erosion and that also could be used to feed cattle and goats and provide green manure for crops and pastures. Andreatta's role as the applied anthropologist in this stage of formulating a research design was to identify which farmers in a particular community, which was located on a former sugarcane plantation, would be likely to plant and use nitrogen-fixing trees in their farming practices. These farmers lived in an area where drought was common, often leaving the fields barren for pasture and crops. Andreatta was hired by the JAP to learn who spends time with their cattle and goats and how much time they spend with them. It was thought that this information would help to identify the activities that were contributing to deforestation and soil erosion as well as what livestock management practices needed to be modified for the sake of the animals and animal owners. The ethnographic information collected would be used in designing a five-year project for planting nitrogen-fixing trees in a drought prone area, such trees and their leaf litter are particularly useful for crop producers and cattle farmers during the dry periods.

Andreatta conducted one year of fieldwork and the data and information obtained assisted a forestry student in where to the plant nitrogen-fixing trees that would provide fodder for cattle farmers during the drought period. This type of strategic tree planting within a farming system is known as agroforestry. Agroforestry is where trees are purposefully planted to feed livestock or provide green manure in the form of leaf litter for crop production as a form of fertilizer for the fields or kitchen gardens. Agroforestry projects in the 1980s that worked with farmers in developing countries tended to assume that the larger farmers were the ones most likely to be the innovators or risk takers willing to try new solutions.

Projects by Louise Fortmann (1985) in Africa and Gerald Murray (1987, 1988) were interested in how to integrate trees into farming systems as a solution. Would the assumption about innovators be true for the study site in Jamaica?

As it was, the JAP was a multidisciplinary, multiyear project. It required foresters to grow nitrogen-fixing trees and monitor which ones performed best in the particular climate and under management conditions. Andreatta's role as the applied anthropologist was to work with community members to discern how the nitrogen-fixing trees would fit into the existing farming practices and with which resettled farmers on former sugarcane plantation. So, although Andreatta was neither a forester nor a farmer, her training in Caribbean culture, tropical agriculture, forestry, medical anthropology, and political ecology provided her with a comprehensive understanding of tree care and use, which she could use to formulate a research design and implement a strategy for tree planting.

Stage 2: Formulating a Research Design

The *research design* is the overall strategy for conducting the research. In the research design stage, the anthropologist must decide how to identify who might be willing to participate in a project, such as planting trees for the JAP. The fieldwork was designed to examine the current farming practices, how farmers handled protracted dry spells, and how they used trees in their farming practices. From a series of questions, Andreatta wanted to learn who the farmers (men and women) were; how they interacted with their environment and animals; if their farming practices integrated vegetable crops and fruit trees along with livestock; and how a tree-planting project would have to take these activities into consideration for it to be a success.

Relying on political ecology as the theoretical framework, Andreatta's research was to identify what people were doing (behavior) on and off the farm and how a new farming technique, such as planting and caring for nitrogen-fixing trees, would fit into their farming practices. The project identified five specific categories of questions:

1. *Residence patterns:* How long had families lived in the resettlement area? Was their home located near their pastureland?
2. *Occupation:* Were they currently farmers? Had they always been farmers? What was their occupation before they lived in the resettlement area?
3. *Land tenure:* Did they own the land where their house was located? Did they have pastureland? How much land was in pasture? Did they own all the pastureland they used?

4. *Livestock ownership:* Did the household raise cattle, goats, or both? How long had they been raising the animals? What challenges did they face with their livestock, and how had they been handling the challenges?
5. *Tree use:* Did they have access to trees on their property? Did they plant trees? Did they harvest from the trees? What were the current uses for trees (charcoal production, timber, orchards, living fence line, feed for animals, green manure, etc.)?

Stage 3: Collecting the Data

Once a series of big-picture questions, driven by theory, have been developed, the next step—*collecting data*—involves selecting the appropriate data-gathering techniques. The JAP relied on multiple data-gathering techniques; however, the two principal techniques used were participant-observation and semi-structured interviews.

Through participant-observation and interviewing—the two primary field techniques used by cultural anthropologists—data and information were collected on crop production and livestock care. From interviews with farmers, data were gathered on the following topics: *land* (tenure, size, and use), *labor* (wage labor, family labor, frequency, and tasks), *livestock* (number and type), *trees* (species of fruit and fodder trees, location, and use), *markets* (crops, livestock, fruit, frequency of marketing, where products are sold, and means of getting goods to market), access to *agricultural information* (technology, markets, etc.), *technology* used in farming (inputs and tools used), and information on *natural environmental* (climate, seasonal variation, soils, erosion, and access to water), *political*, and *economic* factors that influence farming practices over time.

Stage 4: Analyzing the Data

Once data have been collected from any fieldwork experience, the process of *analyzing data* begins. The fieldworker starts by transcribing recordings of interviews and then taking the information from the surveys and putting the data into a computerized spreadsheet (Excel) to be coded in a way that helps her or him identify patterns and trends. For qualitative data, software such as ATLAS.ti helps facilitate the analysis. For quantitative data, most anthropologists (and social scientists for that matter) use the statistical package SPSS.

---

research design The overall strategy for conducting research.

collecting data The stage of fieldwork that involves selecting data-gathering techniques and gathering information pertinent to the hypothesis being studied.

analyzing data One of five stages of fieldwork in which the cultural anthropologist determines the meaning of data collected in the field.

© Susan Andreatta

FIGURE 5.2 Anthropologist Susan Andreatta worked with farmers on a tree-planting project to help feed livestock during the dry season. Here a Jamaican farmer is testing out a limb from a nitrogen-fixing tree on his cow to find out how he likes it!

For the JAP, Andreatta's analyses focused on a community of small-scale Jamaican farmers and identified patterns they shared with respect to livestock management practices and crop production. She linked this information to a tree-planting program and had hoped that my investigations would assist in identifying similar social conditions and limitations of small-scale farmers elsewhere in Jamaica and possibly in other communities of the West Indies that possessed similar management practices and biophysical environmental conditions (Figure 5.2).

When all of the data were coded and analyzed, patterns emerged among the residents of the resettlement area, and the composition of the resettlement area was found to be significant for several reasons. The resettlement area was made up of a combination of nonfarmers, wage earners, charcoal makers, livestock owners, cultivators of crops (permanent, cash, and garden crops), and fishermen. The residents therefore incorporated mixed production systems as an adaptive agrarian strategy that included: crops, livestock, trees, and wage labor activities. The residents who had come to depend on the community's natural resources (land, soils, water, trees, etc.) brought with them a wide range of experiences in resource use. Some had minimal experience with using and managing natural resources (as often happens with migrants); some managed natural resources using

practices better suited to different microclimates; and some had acquired knowledge based on a period of trial and error. Some households relied heavily on natural resources in their subsistence and commercial agrarian practices, whereas others relied more on off-farm activities to sustain their households, contending that they are not farmers. The differences were related to length of resource use in the community, age, off-farm income, time commitment to off-farm activities, and differential access to capital, information, labor, land, and markets. The data analysis provided insights into the formation of resettlement areas and resource use over time that were critical in implementing the strategic planting of nitrogen-rich trees for animal use and erosion control.

Stage 5: Interpreting the Data

Like any science, the discipline of anthropology does more than simply describe specific cultures. *Interpreting data*—perhaps the most difficult step—involves explaining the findings. Have the research questions been answered? What patterns and trends emerged from the analyses, and what do they mean? What factors can be identified that will help explain the findings? How do these findings compare with the findings of other similar studies? How generalizable are the findings to wider populations? Have these findings raised methodological or theoretical issues that have a bearing on the discipline? In applied cultural anthropology the questions may revolve around how the findings contribute to a project's design, implementation, or evaluation. These are the types of questions anthropologists must answer, usually after returning home from the fieldwork experience.

To draw on the JAP once again, interpreting the findings revealed differences in land and tree ownership among residents of the resettlement area. Because of the residents' different histories and reasons for living in the resettlement area, land ownership influenced their relationship to planting trees and managing natural resources. The data indicated that people who own land are more likely to plant a tree on it than are those who only lease or rent land. For example, orchards are established in the community by those who own their land. Most residents stated they would not plant a tree on rented land because the rental agreement is generally of a short and insecure duration. Leased land normally has a longer-term contract formalized with a legal document. If the resident is leasing land for an extended period of time, then the likelihood of planting trees on such land is greater.

---

interpreting data The stage of fieldwork, often the most difficult, in which the anthropologist searches for meaning in the data collected in the field.

The land and tree use in the community was noticeably transformed by new residents on the flatlands and hillsides. The short-term adaptive strategies contributed to physical deterioration and elimination of certain cultural and biophysical niches. The land-tenure and land-use systems were losing their capacities to provide subsistence both for residents who were farming and for those who had livestock. Therefore, identifying which farmers would be willing to participate in the tree-planting project was critical to the next phase of the project—implementation, which involved planting nitrogen-fixing trees, especially on the eroding hillsides.

In describing these five stages of field research, there is a risk of portraying the research process as a neat, precise, and systematic process. In reality, doing fieldwork is messier than is often admitted. Many personal and intellectual issues may interfere with this idealized scheme. To illustrate, in many cultures a male ethnographer may find it inappropriate to ask questions publicly or privately of women, and especially single women. In more general terms, an ethnographer might find it nearly impossible to conduct research among a particular group of people because the ethnographer is not the correct gender, age, or ethnicity. The ethnographic books and articles that emerge from field research usually emphasize the orderly, systematic, and scientific aspects of the research process, while downplaying the chaotic aspects such as people not showing up for an arranged interview time, language barriers, or setting one flat on their back from coming down with an illness.

FIGURE 5.3 Anthropologist Margaret Kieffer conducts an ethnographic interview in Guatemala, where she is doing her research among Mayan weavers. While weaving, the local woman is able to provide the anthropologist with cultural insights. Interviewing in this fashion is not too disrupting to local people who also need to carry on with their own work.

Peggy & Yoram Kahana/Peter Arnold, Inc./Photolibrary

Data-Gathering Techniques

A central problem facing any anthropological fieldworker is determining the most appropriate methods for collecting data. Some data-collection methods, such as interviewing with a digital recorder, that might work in one culture may be totally inappropriate for a neighboring culture. Given the wide variety of cultures in the world, it is important that anthropologists have a number of options so that they can match the appropriate set of data-gathering techniques to each fieldwork situation (Figure 5.3). There is a need to be flexible, however, because the techniques originally planned in the *research proposal* may prove to be inappropriate when actually used in the field. Whatever techniques are finally chosen, a variety of methods will be needed so that the findings from one technique can be used to check the findings from others.

Participant-Observation

It seems only fitting to start a discussion of data-gathering techniques with participant-observation because anthropologists use this method more than any other single technique and more extensively than any other social science discipline. Participant-observation—as the name implies—means becoming involved in the culture under study while making systematic observations of what people actually do. When anthropologists participate, they become as immersed in the culture as the local people permit. They share activities, attend ceremonies, eat together, and generally become part of the rhythm of everyday life. H. Russell Bernard (1995: 137) captured the complexity of participant-observation:

> It involves establishing rapport in a new community; learning to act so that people go about their business as usual when you show up; and removing yourself every day from cultural immersion so you can intellectualize what you've learned, put it into perspective, and write about it convincingly. If you

research proposal A written proposal required for funding anthropological research that spells out in detail a research project's purpose, hypotheses, methodology, and significance.

are a successful participant-observer, you will know when to laugh at what your informant thinks is funny; and when informants laugh at what you say, it will be because you meant it to be a joke.

From the first day of fieldwork, gaining entry into the community presents some challenges for the participant-observer. The anthropologist will begin by observing the community before fully participating in all aspects of social life, so as to gradually learn the appropriate behavior for participating in a local community in a non-obstructive way. Cultural anthropologists in the field can hardly expect to be accepted as soon as they walk into a new community. Under the best of circumstances, the anthropologist, as an outsider, will be an object of curiosity. More often, however, the beginning anthropologist encounters a wide variety of fears, suspicions, and hostilities of the local people that must be overcome.

Guidelines for Participant-Observation

By and large the anthropologist conducting participant-observation fieldwork for the first time has received little instruction in how to cope with these initial problems of resistance. In a sense it is not really possible to prepare the first-time fieldworker for every eventuality for the obvious reason that no two fieldwork situations, cultures, or ethnographers are the same (Figure 5.4). Nevertheless it is possible to offer some general guidelines that apply to most fieldwork situations, and it is helpful to take a cultural anthropology methods course before writing a grant proposal or conducting fieldwork.

First, because the participant-observer is interested in studying people at the grassroots level, it is always advisable to work one's way down the political hierarchy. Before entering a country on a long-term visa, the anthropologist must obtain *research clearance*, or permission, from a high level of the national government. For the JAP, research clearance came from a letter confirming funding by the Jamaica Agriculture Research Program and Jamaica's Ministry of Agriculture. This letter enabled Andreatta to work with local agricultural extension agents and forestry people as well as community leaders in the area where the research was going to take place. Because of the ongoing drought and farmers' concerns for their crops and livestock, it was relatively easy to get the research project under way.

Second, when introducing oneself, one should select a particular role and use it consistently. There are a number of ways that a field anthropologist could answer the question, Who are you? (a question, incidentally, that is asked frequently and requires an honest and straightforward answer). In Andreatta's case, when participating in the JAP, she could have said, with total honesty, that she was a student (she was finishing her doctorate), an anthropologist (her research was funded by the Jamaican government), a visiting research associate at the University of the West Indies-Jamaica, a teacher, and a number of other things. Yet many of these roles, though accurate, were not particularly relevant to the members of the community where she was working. Even though she was there because she was an anthropologist, that particular role would have little meaning to the local people. So she selected the role of a researcher, a role that was known to the residents. Andreatta had planned on a career working in applied research projects and teaching at the university level when she returned to the United States. So, when asked who she was and what was she doing in Jamaica, Andreatta always said that she was a researcher collecting information on the people's use of natural resources for their animals and for their general well-being. If time permitted she explained the tree-planting project. Always carrying copies of her questionnaire and a tape recorder, she landed many great interviews from chance meetings. If she had not standardized my introductions, but instead told one person that she was an anthropologist, another that she was a student, and still another that she was a researcher, the local people would have thought that she was lying or perhaps equally bad, that she had too much sun and did not know who she was.

FIGURE 5.4 Marjorie Shostak interviews San woman in the Kalahari Desert, Botswana.

Mel Konner/Anthro-Photo

research clearance Permission from the host country in which fieldwork is to be conducted.

A third general piece of advice for most fieldworkers is to proceed slowly. Coming from a society that places a high value on time, most US anthropologists do not take kindly to the suggestion to slow down. After all, because they will be in the field for a limited amount of time, most Western anthropologists think they must make the best use of that time by collecting as much data as they can as quickly as possible. The natural tendency for most Westerners is to want to "hit the ground running." There seems to be so much to learn and so little time.

There are compelling reasons for not rushing into asking highly specific questions from day one. First, because most fieldworkers have such an imperfect understanding of the culture during the initial weeks and months they live in a community, they often do not know enough to even ask the right types of specific questions. And, second, the quality of one's data will vary directly with the amount of social groundwork the anthropologist has been able to lay. In other words, fieldworkers must invest a considerable amount of time and energy generating rapport by allowing the local people to get to know them. For example, in the JAP, Andreatta spent the first months engaging in a number of activities that did not seem particularly scientific, including helping people move cattle from one pasture to another, collecting sugarcane tops to feed the cattle during a drought, planting and harvesting pigeon peas, selling eggs at the farmers market, and talking about life in the United States. These activities helped to demonstrate that she was interested in the locals as people rather than merely as sources of information and offered a way to give back to the people who were sharing information with me. Once the local people got to know and trust Andreatta, they were far more willing to give her the type of realistic cultural information she needed for the project.

Fourth, the anthropologist must communicate to the local people, in a genuine way, that she or he is like a student, wanting to learn more about a subject on which *they* are the experts. For example, anthropologists are not interested in simply studying the physical environment (rivers, grasslands, livestock, homes, and so on) of a pastoral people; instead they try to discover how the people define and value these aspects of their physical surroundings. To assume a student's role, while putting the local informant in the role of the teacher/resident expert, is a helpful way to elicit information. The reason the anthropologist is there is to gather information on the local culture, a subject on which he or she has an imperfect understanding. The local people, on the other hand, certainly know their own culture better than anyone else. When people are put in their well-deserved position of teacher/expert, they are likely to be more willing to share their cultural knowledge.

Advantages of Participant-Observation

Using participant-observation has certain methodological advantages for enhancing the quality of the data obtained. For example, people in most cultures appreciate any attempt on the part of the anthropologist to live according to the rules of their culture. No matter how ridiculous one might appear at first, the fact that the anthropologist takes an interest in the local culture is likely to improve rapport. And as trust levels increase, so do the quantity and quality of the data an anthropologist is able to obtain.

Another major advantage of participant-observation is that it enables the anthropologist to distinguish between normative and real behavior—that is, between what people *say they do* and what people *actually do*. When an anthropologist conducts an interview, there is no way to know for certain whether people behave as they say they do. The participant-observer, however, has the advantage of seeing actual behavior rather than relying on hearsay. To illustrate, as part of the JAP, informants were asked how often they spent time with their animals and the role trees played in their farming practices. Through participant-observation, however, it became apparent that not all farmers worked with their livestock in the same way or incorporated tree use into their everyday farming activities. The variations found were related to land and tree ownership: Did the farmers own the land and the trees on their property? If they were not the landowners, then they could not use the trees already on the land for themselves or their animals, nor could they plant trees on the lands they were using. Thus the participant-observer gains a more accurate picture of the culture by observing what people actually do rather than merely relying on what they say they do.

Disadvantages of Participant-Observation

On the other hand, participant-observation poses certain methodological problems that can jeopardize the quality of the data. For example, the nature of participant-observation precludes a large sample size. Because participant-observation studies are both in-depth and time-consuming, fewer people are actually studied than would be if questionnaires or surveys were used. A second problem with participant-observation is that the data are often hard to code or categorize, which makes synthesizing and comparing the data more challenging. Third, participant-observers face special problems when recording their observations because it may be difficult, if not impossible, to record notes while attending a circumcision ceremony, participating in a feast, or chasing through the forest after a wild pig. The more time that passes between the event and its recording

Methodological Advantages and Disadvantages of Participant-Observation

Advantages	Disadvantages
Generally enhances rapport	Practical only for small sample size
Enables fieldworkers to distinguish actual from expected behavior	Difficult to obtain standardized comparable data
Permits observation of nonverbal behavior	Incomplete data resulting from problems recording information
Enables fieldworkers to experience the behaviors being observed	Obtrusive effect on subject matter

in one's fieldnotes, the more details are forgotten. And, finally, a major methodological shortcoming of participant-observation is that it has an *obtrusive effect* on the thing that is being studied. Inhibited by the anthropologist's presence, many people are likely to behave in a way they would not behave if the anthropologist were not there.

Table 5.1 summarizes the methodological advantages and disadvantages of participant-observation.

Interviewing

In addition to using participant-observation, cultural anthropologists in the field rely heavily on ethnographic interviewing. Interviewing is used for obtaining information on what people think or feel (*attitudinal data*) as well as on what they do (*behavioral data*). Even though interviewing is used widely by many disciplines (including sociology, economics, political science, and psychology), the ethnographic interview is unique in three important respects. First, in the ethnographic interview, the interviewer and the participant almost always speak different

first languages. Second, the ethnographic interview is often broad in scope because it elicits information about the entire culture. Third, the ethnographic interview cannot be used alone but must be used in conjunction with other data-gathering techniques.

Structured, Semi-Structured, and Unstructured Interviews

Ethnographic interviews may be unstructured or structured, depending on the level of control retained by the interviewer. In *unstructured interviews*, which involve a minimum of control, the interviewer asks open-ended questions on a general topic and allows interviewees to respond at their own pace using their own words. At the other extreme are *structured interviews*, in which the interviewer asks all informants exactly the same set of questions, in the same sequence, and preferably under the same set of conditions. And in cases in which a fully structured interview is used, the subject selects a response from options provided by the interviewer. And in between structure and unstructured interviews are semi-structured interviews in which the anthropologist relies on an interview guide covering the topics he or she needs to address in a particular order during an interview. If an analogy can be drawn between interviews and school examinations, the fully structured interviews are comparable to multiple-choice exams, semi-structured interviews would be short-answer exams, and the unstructured interviews are more like lengthy open-book essay exams.

Structured, semi-structured, and unstructured interviews have advantages that tend to complement each other. Unstructured interviews, which are most often used early in the data-gathering process, have the advantage of allowing informants to decide what is important to include in their responses to anthropologist's questions. In an unstructured interview, for example, an informant might be asked to describe all of the steps involved in getting married in her or his culture. It is from the unstructured interview that the anthropologist may narrow in on a line of questioning in a semi-structured interview to obtain more detailed nuanced information from the participant on a specific subject. Structured interviews, on the other hand, have the advantage of producing large quantities of data that are comparable and thus lend themselves well to more rapid statistical analyses, yet much less qualitative data. Because structured interviews ask questions based on specific cultural information, they are used most commonly late in the fieldwork, if at all, and only after the anthropologist knows enough about the culture to ask highly specific questions.

It is important to be aware of the social situation in which the interview takes place. In other words, what effect does the presence of other people have on the answers given? The social context of the interview became an issue when Andreatta was collecting data

---

obtrusive effect The presence of the researcher causes people to behave differently than they would if the researcher was not present.

attitudinal data Information collected in a fieldwork situation that describes what a person thinks, believes, or feels.

behavioral data Information collected in a fieldwork situation that describes what a person does.

unstructured interviews An ethnographic data-gathering technique—most often used in the early stages of fieldwork—in which interviewees are asked to respond to broad, open-ended questions.

structured interviews An ethnographic data-gathering technique in which large numbers of respondents are asked a set of specific questions.

while accompanied by a local resident, an adult male and respected farmer of the community. During one of the interviews, the respondent claimed to own a lavish house that was being constructed. The following day when she questioned the farmer who accompanied her, Andreatta learned that the respondent was a property caretaker and not the owner, who was still residing in England. The farmer did not understand why his friend and neighbor chose to lie about what he did and did not own. The respondent was a great storyteller. She never found out exactly why he made up such a tale, but Andreatta determined that the presence of the farmer might have influenced his response. Therefore, from that time on, she conducted the interviews privately and allowed the respected farmer to help arrange the interviews when needed.

Table 5.2 offers guidelines for conducting ethnographic interviews.

Validity of the Data Collected

The cultural anthropologist in the field must devise ways to check the validity of interview data. One way to validate data is to ask a number of different people the same question. If all people independently of one another answer the question in essentially the same way, it is safe to assume that the data are valid. Another method of checking the validity of interview data is to ask a person the same question over a period of time. If the person answers the question differently at different times, there is reason to believe that one of the responses might not be truthful. A third way to determine validity is to compare the responses with people's actual behavior. As mentioned in the discussion on participant-observation, what people do is not always the same as what they say they do.

Additional Data-Gathering Techniques

Even though participant-observation and interviewing are the mainstays of anthropological fieldwork, cultural anthropologists use other techniques for collecting cultural data at various stages of the field study. These techniques include census taking, mapping, document analysis, collection of genealogies, and photography—although this list is hardly exhaustive.

Census Taking

Early on in the fieldwork, anthropologists usually conduct a census of the area under investigation. Because *census taking* involves the collection of basic demographic data, such as age, occupation, marital status, and household composition, it is generally not threatening to the local people. However, most anthropologists tag these questions onto their surveys or questionnaires so as not to over-interview people. It is important to update the census data because the anthropologist learns more about a culture, especially if a number of years are spent working among the people. Because things change in the short and long terms, the census should be updated with new information such as marriages and births as they occur.

Mapping

Another data-gathering tool used in the early stages of fieldwork is *ethnographic mapping*—attempting to locate people, material culture, and environmental features in space. To illustrate, anthropologists are interested in mapping where people live, where they pasture their

---

TABLE 5.2

Guidelines for Ethnographic Interviewing

- Obtain informed consent before interviewing; when appropriate get a signature from the respondent.

- Maintain neutrality by not conveying to the interviewee what may be the "desired" answer.

- Pretest questions to make sure they are understandable and culturally relevant.

- Keep the recording of an interview as unobtrusive as possible.

- Make certain that the conditions under which the interviews are conducted do not encourage the distortion of testimony.

- Use simple, unambiguous, and jargon-free language. Phrase questions to avoid yes or no responses. For example, ask "What is your favorite food?" rather than "Is pizza your favorite food?"

- Keep the questions and the interview itself short, preferable one page for questions handled in less than an hour.

- Avoid two-pronged (having two parts to the answer) questions.

- Save controversial questions for the end of the interview.

- Be sensitive to the needs and cultural expectations of the respondents.

- Remember that after each completed interview, respondents will talk to their friends and neighbors about the interview process. It may get more difficult to complete additional interviews once the curiosity wears off.

---

census taking The collection of demographic data about the culture being studied.

ethnographic mapping A data-gathering tool that locates where the people being studied live, where they keep their livestock, where public buildings are located, and so on, to determine how that culture interacts with its environment.

Climate Change: Food and Water Insecurity

✺ Food and water insecurity pose challenges for human health and well-being in many parts of the world. Climatic change combined with uncertain economic, political and social conditions have made equitable access to nutritious food and potable (drinkable) water a global crisis. There are some cultures, however, that face these uncertain conditions with some regularity. Social scientists want to know how they cope with food or water insecurity, and how it is possible to measure the degree of food or water insecurity? Is there a standard measure with which one should use to determine who is at risk? Researchers Hadley, Wutich, and McCarty (2009) conducted a study in Tanzania and Bolivia that focused on developing new measures to answer these questions. Such a tool would be valuable as away to head off future crises in areas known for food and water shortages.

Developing a better measure, the individual's experience of food insecurity can be better researched. Applied anthropologists, with their years of experience in community-based research, are uniquely poised to contribute to the growing need for development of locally appropriate tools to measure and monitor levels of community-based food and water insecurities. Food and water insecurity occur when there is insufficient and uncertain access to nutritious food and potable water to maintain a healthy and active lifestyle (Food and Agriculture Organization 2005). Generally, when studies are made of these situations they focus on caloric consumption, measures of actual daily water use, and anthropometric (body) measures. Medical and nutritional anthropologists rely on anthropometric indicators such as weight for age, height for age, and body mass index in their fieldwork. Although these data can provide insights into households or individuals experiencing food insecurity, such quantitative indicators do not measure individual's *experience* with food insecurity. In other words, previous measures did not illicit how people responded to or felt during those times of food or water shortage; their qualitative responses were not recorded as part of the data set.

Another approach was used in Sen's (1981) research in which he found that inequitable access to food—rather than the absolute scarcity of food—produced food insecurity. From this economic perspective a different line of questioning emerged to assess food access. Such questions focused on: the distance to food markets, the availability of land or livestock to produce food locally, household income, socioeconomic status, and food prices (Hadley, Wutich, and McCarty 2009: 452). A similar economic line for assessing water access tends to examine variables such as the distance to water sources, seasonality in water availability, water expenditures, time spent acquiring water, and storage capacity (Hadley, Wutich, and McCarty 2009: 452). This economic line of questioning still does not get at how people responded or what they felt when there was inequitable access to food and water.

Hadley, Wutich, and McCarty critiqued these methods because they each missed something. Specifically, the data collected and their analyses were incomplete because they did not help explain the *adequacy* of the quantity of food or water acquired or the *security* of access to those resources as well as how people respond

to food and water shortages. Hadley, Wutich, and McCarty (2009) used a different approach to measuring food insecurity that enabled them to focus not only on the physiological demands for food and water, the link between inequalities and access, and subsequent health impacts, but also on a people's culture and individual experience and perceptions to get a complete picture of food and water insecurities and health consequences. Hadley, Wutich, and McCarty (2009) illustrated the need for new models for measuring food or water insecurity in their research from Tanzania and Bolivia.

The Pimbwe of Tanzania are horticulturalists, and the Sukuma of Tanzania are agropastoralists. In each of these settings, the data revealed there was a *hunger season*, that is a period of time when a substantial portion of the population experienced food insecurity. Community members commented that children were the most affected, often going to bed with without having eaten. Insecure access to food and the presence of hunger are key dimensions to poverty, but the question remains how to measure food security systematically? The authors thought first measure when stores ran out of food, thus limiting households access to food items. They came to realize this measure was useless, especially for those who ran small shops or those employed in something other than farming. In other instances those with larger families depleted their stocks more quickly than those with smaller families or smaller social networks.

In the end the authors recognized if they reworded their questions to ask respondents how they acquired food other than through purchasing, modified the question on food frequency to include local dietary pattern, they would be moving in the right direction and be developing a survey instrument with greater reliability in capturing food insecurity in wet and dry seasons. More importantly they revealed the uncertainty and worry that goes with providing food for one's family was the burden carried by all of the mothers, which affected their mental health. The seasonal insecure access to food and the uncertainty of not being able to feed their children carried with it a psychosocial burden.

In Bolivia, the authors developed an ethnographically grounded measure for water insecurity. They worked in a semi-arid region of the Bolivian Andes, in a squatters' settlement located on the south side of the city of Cochabamba. Nearly 38 percent of the population is without municipal water service, forcing those households to collect rainwater, surface water, dig wells, or seek out private water sources for cooking, bathing, and

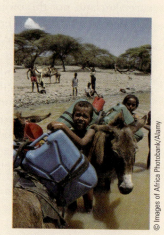

© Images of Africa Photobank/Alamy

Water is in short supply in many parts of the world. Children are expected to help with water collection and other chores from an early age. These children use their donkeys to transport the water they collect at Lake Langano, Ethiopia.

cleaning. "Because many of these alternative sources are vulnerable to climatic variability, year-round water insecurity intensifies during the dry season" (Hadley Wutich, and McCarty 2009: 454).

After spending five months living in the community, the authors learned to use water in culturally appropriate ways, and they observed how water insecurity affected people's lives (Hadley Wutich, and McCarty 2009: 455). They identified six categories in which water insecurity affected residents: (1) water quantity; (2) water quality; (3) water acquisition; (4) water conflicts; (5) economic issues; and (6) health outcomes. Using these six domains, they designed a survey that asked questions from each one. To interpret the responses, Hadley Wutich, and McCarty (2009) had to develop tools to scale the respondents' qualitative responses.

Their research reminds us of the increasing importance using multiple, integrated methods in applied research. There is no one measure that will work for all conditions when learning about (in)equitable access to food and water or the affects of chronic shortages. Rural or urban settings, highlands or lowlands, levels of poverty, education, access to employment, gender, age, and household size are only a few of the indicators that influence coping strategies for food or water insecurity. Developing measures that include multidimensional experiences as well as those of psychosocial trauma are necessary for understanding a local context for any kind of successful policy when facing water and food uncertainty and insecurity. Biological demands of food and water should not be separated from the cultural needs, which are deeply embedded in cultural system. Anthropological approaches have a great deal to offer in conceptualizing and measuring, and possibly alleviating food and water security in some communities. It is from these varied approaches that we can develop an understanding of how adaptations and coping strategies affect the incidence and experience of food and water security across cultures, and thus a single measure should not be the only measure.

Questions for Discussion

1. What is the different between quantitative and qualitative data collection?
2. Why is it important to develop a community-based tool to measure food or water insecurity?
3. How does an ethnographic approach inform applied research? Does this means there is only one way to collect empirical data?

livestock, where various public and private buildings are located, where playing fields and sacred places are located, how people divide up their land, and how the people position themselves in relation to environmental features such as rivers, mountains, and oceans (Figure 5.5). We can learn a good deal about a culture such as the Ju/'hoansi, who are African hunters and gatherers, by examining how they interact with their physical environment. Aerial and panoramic photographs are particularly useful for mapping a community's ecology. Advanced training in geographic information system (GIS), remote sensing, or collaborating with a geographer trained in these mapping techniques offers additional understanding of the people and how they interact with their environment, with space and with one another.

Document Analysis

Cultural anthropologists may do *document analysis* to supplement the information they collect through interviews and observation. For example, some anthropologists study personal diaries, colonial administrative records, newspapers, marriage registration data, deeds and property titles, government census information, and various aspects of popular culture, such as song lyrics and television programs. The advantage to using historical documents or reviewing popular culture is that neither is expensive nor time-consuming, and it is totally unobtrusive in providing the anthropologist with a cultural context for their research.

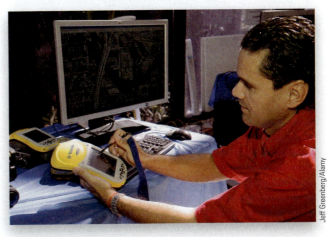

Jeff Greenberg/Alamy

FIGURE 5.5 Advanced training in geographic information system (GIS), remote sensing, or collaborating with a geographer trained in these mapping techniques offers additional understanding of the people and how they interact with their environment, with space and with one another.

Collecting Genealogies

Another technique used to collect cultural data is the *genealogical method*, which involves writing down all the relatives of a particular informant. Collecting this type of information is especially important in the small-scale societies that anthropologists often study because

document analysis Examination of data such as personal diaries, newspapers, colonial records, and so on.

genealogical method A technique of collecting data in which the anthropologist writes down all the kin of an informant.

© Jenny Matthews/Alamy

FIGURE 5.6 Ethnographers in the field are interested in studying all segments of a population, including these Salvadorian children as well as their parents. The anthropologist might want to learn about agricultural production, nutritional intake, education levels, and health status. By collecting data on all family members, and with parental consent, ethnographers can gain a thorough understanding of a culture.

kinship relationships tend to be the primary social ties in those societies (Figure 5.6). Whereas in Western societies much of our lives are played out with people who are not family members—such as teachers, employers, coworkers, and friends—in small-scale societies people tend to interact primarily with their family and extended familial relations. When using the genealogical method, the anthropologist asks each informant to state the name and relationship of all family members and how they are referred to, addressed, and treated. From this information the anthropologist can deduce how family

---

photography The use of a camera or video camera to document the ecology, material culture, and social interactions of people during ethnographic fieldwork.

proxemic analysis The study of how people in different cultures use space.

event analysis Photographic documentation of events such as weddings, funerals, and festivals in the culture under investigation.

members interact with one another and what behavioral expectations exist among different categories of kin.

Photography

A particularly important aid to the fieldworker's collection of data is *photography*, both still photography, videography, and ethnographic documentaries. Recent decades have brought a proliferation of ethnographic documentaries portraying a wide variety of cultures from all parts of the globe. Although ethnographic documentaries are valuable for introducing anthropology students to different cultures, they also have more specific uses in anthropological research. To illustrate, ethnographic documentaries can be extremely helpful in *proxemic analysis* (that is, the study of how people in different cultures distance themselves from one another in normal interactions) and *event analysis* (that is, documentation of who participates in events such as circumcision ceremonies, marriages, and funerals).

Photography has become such an important part of anthropological research that it is hard to imagine an anthropologist in the field without a camera. As a research tool, the camera can be put to many uses. First, as mentioned previously, the camera can produce a lasting record of land-use patterns and the general ecological arrangements in the community under study. Second, as the adage suggests, a picture is worth a thousand words. Photography can document the technology of the culture (tools, weapons, machines, and utensils), how these items are used (by whom, where, when, in what combinations, and so on), the sequences in a craft process, and the sex roles associated with different items of technology. Third, photography can be used as a probe in the interview process. Because the photograph becomes the object of discussion, the informant feels less like a subject and more like an expert commentator. And finally, photographs may be taken by members of the community. Allowing members of the community to photograph and document what is meaningful to them and their culture provides an insider's perspective. In the day of digital cameras, portable laptops, and printers, viewing the photographic images as well as making prints can be rapid. Leaving copies of these photographic images with the community members, if appropriate, is a way of sharing with the community (Figure 5.7).

Applied Field Methods

As pointed out in Chapter 3, there are fundamental differences in the research conducted by descriptive ethnographers and applied cultural anthropologists. When compared to more descriptive anthropological research, applied research is characterized as (1) more collaborative and interdisciplinary, (2) more inclusive of local people in all stages of the research, and (3) faced with real-time limitations (weeks or months rather than years). Data-gathering techniques that have

CROSS-CULTURAL MISCUE

Within the first several weeks of conducting fieldwork in rural Kenya, anthropologist Peter Sutton decided to photograph the physical surroundings of the village he was studying. He wanted to visually document the locations of houses and fields so as to better understand how the people used space. But within minutes of his photographing the environment (which unavoidably also included some people), several men in the village began shaking their fists and shouting angrily at him. Sutton retreated and rarely used his camera again during his eighteen months of fieldwork.

Sutton learned an important lesson from this incident: Photography has different meanings in different cultures. Even

though cameras can be useful for documenting cultural features, they must be used with caution. In addition to being an invasion of privacy—as may be true in our own society—there are other reasons East Africans are reluctant to have their pictures taken. For example, because some East Africans (particularly in the coastal region) are Islamic, they feel strongly about not violating the Koranic prohibition against making images of the human form. Moreover people who do not understand the nature of photography may believe that having one's picture taken involves the entrapment of their souls in the camera. In those societies where witchcraft is practiced, the prospect of having one's soul captured, particularly by a witch, can be terrifying.

been developed over the last century by ethnographic anthropologists have been described. Although all of these techniques are used by both ethnographers and

FIGURE 5.7 Photographs taken in the field can serve as probes during an interview as well as useful sources of information. Asking questions about activities or actions can provide insight into gender roles and other appropriate or inappropriate behaviors.

applied anthropologists, applied anthropologists tend to rely on data-collection techniques that are focused to the problem and expedite the data-collection process.

- *Community-Based Participatory Research (CBPR):* This process begins when members of a community recognize a problem they want to solve and they contact a professional researcher to help facilitate the change. The overall approach stresses a non-dominating orientation of the practitioner as well as community involvement in the process.

- *Participatory Rural Appraisal (PRA):* This is one of the most useful methods used by applied anthropologists because of its strong commitment to community participation. "It enables rural people to share, enhance and analyze their knowledge of life and conditions, to plan and to act" (R. Chambers 1994: 953). With the use of local mapping, PRA relies on the cooperation of community members, development professionals, including applied anthropologists, and can discover and document local conditions that are relevant to planning programs and projects that are culturally appropriate.

- *Rapid Ethnographic Assessment (REA):* As its name implies, REA requires much less time than traditional ethnographic fieldwork. The usual steps in an applied research project (such as problem identification, needs assessment, research plan design, data collection, intervention, and program evaluation) do not typically require long-term, total immersion in the culture. Ideally, applied anthropologists are already familiar with the culture, speak the local language, and are experts in the problems being investigated. The research tends to be narrowly focused on the problem area, and the sample size is small.

- *Surveys:* Applied anthropologists as well as ethnographers use survey methods to gather a large amount of attitudinal and behavioral data in a relatively short time frame. Surveys are particularly useful to anthropologists working in complex communities where there is not a single "native" point of view. Gathering both quantitative and qualitative data enable anthropologists to analyze data that have the additional advantage of being statistically comparable.

■ *Focus groups:* These are small groups (six to ten people) convened to discuss a particular topic. Topics focus on anything such as what people living with HIV/AIDS need in terms of community assistance, what women need to become entrepreneurs, or what a community needs for a water-well project. Although focus groups are helpful for getting a group perspective, applied anthropologists use them to generate insights not always available from merely interviewing individuals.

Choosing a Technique

Which data-gathering technique(s) will be used depends largely on the nature of the problem being investigated. For example, environmental studies on overuse of the commons (shared community lands that are not owned by anyone) may require gathering information on the natural resources used by a community. A medical anthropologist may look to indigenous (local) practices in health care but also may seek out where Western medicine may intersect local practices. And like the other examples, food and agricultural studies are likely to combine a number of methods in addition to participant observation and interviewing.

Another significant factor that influences the choice of techniques is the receptivity of the people being studied. It is important that the anthropologist carefully plan which techniques will be appropriate to use and what types of data to collect, as well as the segments of the population to study. If, after entering the field, the anthropologist finds that a technique is not working, he or she must be sufficiently flexible to revise the research design and creative enough to come up with a workable alternative. Whatever technique is selected, it should be used in conjunction with at least two other techniques. By using multiple techniques, the anthropologist can collect different types of data concerning the same set of issues, using the different sets of data to cross-check their validity.

The Pains and Gains of Fieldwork

It should be clear by now that the process of direct fieldwork is central to cultural anthropology. Unlike many other scientific endeavors, anthropological fieldwork tends to have a powerful impact not only on the community

studied but also on the life of the practitioner. Spending a year or longer living and working in an unfamiliar culture is bound to have life-altering consequences; the anthropologist is never quite the same after completing a fieldwork project.

The anthropologist in the field faces a number of anxiety-producing situations that can result in both stress and growth. For example, cultural anthropologists in the field rarely, if ever, follow their research design step by step in a cookbook fashion. Despite the most meticulous research design and predeparture preparations, fieldwork is fraught with unanticipated events. From day one, the fieldworker can expect to be surprised, as was the case with Barry and Bonnie Hewlett, who are no strangers to challenges in fieldwork. Their research on the emerging infectious disease Ebola hemorrhagic fever took them to the Baka people of Gabon (Figure 5.8). They write of their first stop at a village:

> We talked about Ebola with the chief, who provided details of Baka deaths that we assumed occurred in the 1994-95 Mékouka outbreak. Approximately half the people in his camp had died. After talking with him for about an hour, I came to an awful realization—he was describing deaths that had occurred earlier in 1997; in fact, these deaths had occurred only a few months before our arrival. My stomach churned and head started to ache as I listened attentively.... Physicians told us the area was safe, Ebola free, and open for travel to previous Ebola sites. (Hewlett and Hewlett 2007: 8)

© Associated Press

FIGURE 5.8 Jean-Claude Ndjibadi, on the right, turns over a tobacco leaf he is drying out on the embers of a fire in Mendemba, a small hunting village close to Makemba in northeastern Gabon. Ndjibadi has lost eight members of his extended family to the Ebola virus. He blames an ancient family feud involving tales of theft, murder, adultery, and vampires and accuses a cousin who lived next door of using witchcraft to poison those close to him.

The initial feeling of being overwhelmed by the fieldwork situation is more common than most anthropologists are willing to admit. And one does not have to travel to remote parts of the world to feel that way. One US anthropology student who was conducting fieldwork among farmers in Reidsville, North Carolina, experienced some challenges in the field, including hard manual labor and sunburn.

When I began working on the farm, we were harvesting lettuce heads, kale, turnips, peas and onions. The tomatoes were still very small, as were the bell peppers, eggplant and beans. My first few days were full of harvesting and mulching (putting a protective cover that is spread on top of the soil)… and more mulching. At some point during the summer, Pat promised to always save the mulching for me, because I love to do it so much. There is a bit of sarcasm in her statement, but the truth is, I enjoy it. On my second day, we had to come in early because of a storm. We went into the kitchen and weighed produce for their Community Supported Agriculture (CSA) customers. Brian has this uncanny knack for estimating…. I've never seen anything like it. He can pinpoint how much kale will fill how many bags, and the weight of each. It comes out to be nearly perfect. After the bagging, Pat brought out a big basket of cherries that she had picked. We pitted them all, and had a chance to talk. After a few hours, some great stories, and shared hopes, expectations and disappointments, I left for the day. Brian says that Pat is shy around new people, but she and I had great conversations almost immediately. On my third day, Brian asked me to aerate the garlic beds with a truly tiny hoe and a wheeled edging implement— also very small. I suppose I was there for an hour hoeing in that garlic bed, which smelled great. I inadvertently destroyed a few pieces of garlic, despite my conscious effort not to. I wasn't wearing a hat, and could feel the sunscreen melting off of my face. My thoughts continuously drifted between garlic, and my burning skin. Brian made the comment that most of the young people who go to farms, perhaps with the intention of learning how to grow food, mainly want to *say* that they worked on a farm. They want to be a part of this trend, without committing to the actual work that it entails, which is considerable. I left exhausted, and their day just got started (Donna Smith 2008, personal communication).

Sometimes cultural anthropologists in the field can be in life-threatening situations, not just uncomfortable ones. By conducting fieldwork in remote parts of the world, anthropologists may expose themselves to dangers from the physical environment that can be fatal. Contagious disease, as mentioned previously in the Hewetts' experience, has resulted in the serious illness and even death of anthropologists in the field. And, in certain situations, anthropologists are exposed to various forms of social violence, including civil wars, intergroup warfare, muggings, and other forms of crime. To illustrate, anthropologist Philippe Bourgois (the same anthropologist who you read about in Chapter 4), who studied the drug culture of East Harlem, New York, witnessed shootings, bombings, machine-gunnings, fire bombings, and numerous fistfights, and he was manhandled by New York City police who mistook him for a drug dealer. These risks, some of which can be fatal, make the conduct of fieldwork serious business. Those anthropologists who require high levels of comfort or safety might consider a different topic of study

Culture Shock

Not all introductions to fieldwork are as unsettling as these, of course. But even anthropologists whose fieldwork experience is less traumatic encounter some level of stress from *culture shock*, the psychological disorientation caused by trying to adjust to major differences in lifestyles and living conditions. Culture shock, a term introduced by anthropologist Kalervo Oberg (1960), ranges from mild irritation to out-and-out panic. This general psychological stress occurs when the anthropologist tries to play the game of life with little or no understanding of the basic rules. The anthropologist, struggling to learn what is meaningful in the new culture, never really knows when she or he may be committing a serious social indiscretion that might severely jeopardize the entire fieldwork project, such as using the wrong hand when giving a gift or sharing food, or speaking out of turn.

When culture shock sets in, everything seems to go wrong. Someone may become irritated over minor inconveniences. A person may begin to view things critically and negatively. For example, a person might think the food is strange, people do not keep their appointments, no one likes them, everything seems unhygienic, people do not look that person in the eye, and on and on. Even though culture shock manifests itself in many different symptoms, it usually has these characteristics:

- A sense of confusion over how to behave
- A sense of surprise, even disgust, after realizing some of the features of the new culture
- A sense of loss of old familiar surroundings (such as friends, possessions, and ways of doing things)
- A sense of being rejected (or at least not accepted) by members of the new culture
- A loss of self-esteem because the person does not seem to be functioning effectively
- A feeling of impotence at having so little control over the situation
- A sense of doubt when the persons' own cultural values are brought into question

culture shock A psychological disorientation experienced when attempting to operate in a radically different cultural environment.

TABLE 5.3

Symptoms of Culture Shock

Homesickness	Stereotyping of host nationals
Boredom	Hostility toward host nationals
Withdrawal (for example, spending excessive amounts of time reading, seeing only other Americans, and avoiding contact with host nationals)	Loss of ability to work effectively
Need for excessive amounts of sleep	Unexplainable fits of weeping
Compulsive eating	Physical ailments (psychosomatic illnesses)
Compulsive drinking	Feelings of isolation
Irritability	Weight loss
Exaggerated cleanliness	Feelings of helplessness
Marital stress	Tenseness, moodiness, and irritability
Family tension and conflict	Loss of confidence
Chauvinistic excesses	Fear of the worst happening

SOURCES: L. Robert Kohls, *Survival Kit for Overseas Living* (Yarmouth, ME: Intercultural Press, 1984), p. 65; Elizabeth Marx, *Breaking Through Culture Shock: What You Need to Succeed in International Business* (London: Nicholas Brealey Publishing, 1999), p. 32.

Table 5.3 lists twenty-two symptoms of culture shock. One would hope that undergoing the training to become an anthropologist and making specific preparations for entering the field would help to prevent anyone from experiencing extreme culture shock. Nevertheless every anthropologist should expect to suffer, to some extent, from the discomfort of culture shock. Generally the negative effects of culture shock subside as time passes, but it is unlikely that they will go away completely. The success or failure of an anthropological field project depends largely on how well the ethnographer can make the psychological adjustment to the new culture and overcome the often debilitating effects of culture shock.

Biculturalism

Not all of the consequences of fieldwork are negative. Culture shock is real and should not be taken lightly. Yet, despite the stress of culture shock (or perhaps because of it) the total immersion experience of fieldwork provides opportunities for personal growth and increased understanding of the nuances of culture—once talked about in a cultural anthropology class and now lived through fieldwork. Spending weeks and months operating in a radically different culture can provide new insights into how the local people think, act, and feel. In the process of learning about another culture, however, people unavoidably learn a good deal about our their culture as well (Gmelch 1994a). When learning about another culture in depth, people become bicultural and develop a much broader view of human behavior. This can be a consequence of successful fieldwork. Richard Barrett (1991: 20–21) captures

the essence of this *bicultural perspective*, which he claims enables cultural anthropologists

> to view the world through two or more cultural lenses at once. They can thus think and perceive in the categories of their own cultures, but are able to shift gears, so to speak, and view the same reality as it might be perceived by members of the societies they have studied. This intellectual biculturalism is extremely important to anthropologists. It makes them continually aware of alternative ways of doing things and prevents them from taking the customs of our own society too seriously.

When speaking of achieving biculturalism, it should not be assumed that the anthropologist, no matter how much fieldwork he or she does, will ever become a native. Roger Keesing (1992) reminds us that after many fieldwork encounters with the Malaita Kwaio of the Solomon Islands, he still considered himself little more than an informed outsider. Keesing relates a story of his unsuccessful attempts to convince the Malaita Kwaio not to eat a dolphin they had caught because, he argued, it was not a fish but a mammal like us. He used the argument that dolphins, like humans, are warm-blooded and red-blooded, but the Malaita Kwaio were unimpressed. He got their rapt attention when he informed the locals that dolphins should not be eaten because they actually communicate with one another, just as humans do. Keesing was then asked a series of questions he could not answer to their satisfaction: How do you talk to a dolphin? What language do they speak? How can they talk under water? Finally, as his informants were cooking the dolphin steaks on the fire, Keesing came to realize a basic fact about anthropological fieldwork: No matter how long one spends studying another culture, the anthropologist is little more than "an outsider who knows something of what it is to be an insider" (1992: 77).

bicultural perspective The capacity to think and perceive in the categories of one's own culture as well as in the categories of a second culture.

What Do You Do with a Degree in Anthropology?

❋ How do you answer the question "what are you going to do with a major in anthropology?" After reading this chapter we hope that you will have a number of ideas for a response. To illustrate, there are some anthropologists that are interested in doing ethnographic fieldwork to learn and describe people from another culture. Many of these ethnographic anthropologists are driven by a theoretical orientation, which guides their questioning and frames their scope of research. Over time these anthropologists may become experts in a culture and way of life and are able to denote changes across time in a particular and region. However, there are other anthropologists that are more applied in the research they do; they are interested in contemporary issues and problem solving at the grassroots level or in using their findings to influence policies on behalf of a people. As you see in this chapter, there are a wide range of projects applied anthropologists are involved in, many of which begin at the level of the community.

An interesting account of an applied medical anthropologist is found in "When Bamboo Bloom" by Patricia Omidian (2011) where she writes about working in Taliban-controlled Afghanistan. Omidian describes her experiences in Kabul, Hazaraja, and Herat pre-9/11. However, before working in Afghanistan, Omidian (an American who had married a man from Iran in the 1970s) worked with Afghan refugees from the mid-1980s in the United States as well as spent time living in Pakistan. Over the decades she has specialized in the region; this has lead to employment from governmental and nongovernmental organizations where she helps with field research dealing with disaster-response and development work.

In this monograph, Omidian recounts a number of choices she made based on her anthropological training and her particular interests in psychosocial wellness and the anthropology of emotions. As an applied medical anthropologist she relies heavily on her methods training, which is critical to both ethnographic and applied research. As she writes, "I have a strong background in 'training of trainers,' most of my work included some level of training and mentoring local staff, teaching them to conduct their own surveys, evaluations or training.... Each project I was hired to do was unique: to conduct training, to carry out a survey, or to facilitate a process – such as strategic planning" (Omidian 2011: 2).

Another important skill Omidian possesses is that she is fluent in the local language, Dari (the Persian dialect spoken in Afghanistan). Speaking the local language, which is not something most foreigners can do, as well as respecting the dress code and the limits on mobility imposed on women, enabled Omidian to fulfill her employment obligations and provide insights into the rural areas of Afghanistan. She was able to point out project needs in a culturally holistic manner. Thus, she has become an expert in training future local trainers to design surveys, collect and enter data as well as analyze it in a region without electricity, sophisticated technology, or freedom of movement.

Omidian shares her life and work experiences with us as she moves from one project to the next, each with a methodological or logistical challenge. She points out that life expectancy at birth is forty-three years of age for women and more than half the population is under the age of eighteen. Although improving, she comments that one finds the worst maternal and infant mortality records in the world in contemporary Afghanistan. She has heard the horrors of war from men and women alike. She saw and lived under the rural and urban conditions ruled by the Taliban, the impact their edicts had on the education, health and everyday life of men and women. She describes how men could be beaten or whipped if their beards were too short and how women could be punished (or their fathers, husbands and brothers) because their pants were the wrong color or they visited a market to get food for the family unescorted by male family members. Each time Omidian visited or interviewed Afghani families she was putting them and herself at risk because one never knew from day-to-day what the Taliban would decree next. What is clear from reading such a personal account is the wealth of cultural understanding she had acquired to navigate in Afghanistan while the Taliban were in control, and how hospitable those who hosted and protected her while she was "doing her job" were. In the end she was evacuated within a couple days following 9/11 and today she continues her work in the region but from Pakistan.

Questions for Discussion

1. What is the difference between the work of an ethnographic anthropologist and an applied anthropologist?
2. When asked what kind of anthropologist you are studying to be, how will you respond?
3. What are some key personal qualities one should possess to do good field work?

Recent Trends in Ethnographic Fieldwork

Much of this chapter on ethnographic field research discusses an essentially scientific approach. The various stages of the ethnographic process have been explored, as exemplified by the Jamaica tree-planting project. Developing a series of linked research questions, devising a set of complementary methods, minimizing observer bias, and using a range of data-gathering techniques has been discussed. The point of this chapter has been to demonstrate that cultural anthropology, like any scientific discipline, must strive toward objectivity by being sensitive to methodological issues.

Reflexive Methods

Despite the quest for scientific objectivity, conducting ethnographic fieldwork is quite different from doing research in a chemistry or biology laboratory. To reflect the native's point of view, the observer must interact with her or his subjects, which introduces a powerful element of subjectivity. Nowhere is the coexistence of subjectivity and objectivity more evident than in the data-gathering technique of participant-observation. Participation implies a certain level of emotional involvement in the lives of the people being studied. Making systematic observations, on the other hand, requires emotional detachment. Participant-observers are expected to be emotionally engaged participants while at the same time being dispassionate observers. Thus, by its nature, participant-observation carries with it an internal source of tension, because sympathizing with those people whom an anthropologist is trying to describe is incompatible with scientific objectivity.

Since the 1970s, however, the postmodernists (see Chapter 4) have ushered in a new type of ethnography that has become known as *reflexive or narrative ethnography*. Being less concerned with scientific objectivity, narrative ethnographers are interested in coproducing ethnographic knowledge by focusing on the interaction between themselves and their informants (Michrina and Richards 1996). In fact many ethnographers today use the term *collaborator* rather than *informant*, recognizing the role of the person who is providing the information to the anthropologist. These narrative ethnographers are no longer interested in producing descriptive accounts of another culture written with scientific detachment. Rather their ethnographies are conscious reflections on how their own personalities and cultural influences combine with personal encounters with their informants to produce cultural data.

The narrative or reflexive approach to ethnography involves a dialogue between informant and ethnographer. Such a postmodern approach, it is argued, is needed because the traditional ethnographer can no longer presume to be able to obtain an objective description of other cultures. In an effort to reclaim a more "scientific" methodology, Lawrence Kuznar (1996), Marvin Harris (1999), and many others have again harshly critiqued these reflexive methods. If these often ferocious debates on methods are taken too literally, people are led to believe that the discipline is in turmoil because it cannot agree on which

methodology is the correct one. But, as Ivan Brady (1998) noted, people should avoid drawing absolute lines between subjective and objective ethnographic methods. Instead, ethnography of the twenty-first century is moving toward a "methodological pluralism," whereby anthropologists use multiple methods in the data collection and analyses to help produce a richer and more accurate description of ethnographic reality.

Statistical Cross-Cultural Comparisons

During the first half of the twentieth century, anthropologists amassed considerable descriptive data on a wide variety of cultures throughout the world. Because of these many firsthand ethnographic field studies, sufficient data existed by mid-century to begin testing hypotheses and building theory inductively.

The development of statistical, cross-cultural comparative studies was made possible in the 1940s by George Peter Murdock and his colleagues at Yale University, who developed a coded data retrieval system known as the *Human Relations Area Files (HRAF)*. The largest anthropological data bank in the world, HRAF has vast amounts of information about more than three hundred different cultures organized into more than seven hundred different cultural subject headings. The use of the simple coding system enables the cross-cultural researcher to access large quantities of data within minutes for the purpose of testing hypotheses and drawing statistical correlations.

The creation of HRAF has opened up the possibility for making statistical comparisons among large numbers of cultures. Murdock himself used HRAF as the basis for his groundbreaking book *Social Structure* (1949), in which he compiled correlations and generalizations on family and kinship organization. John Whiting and Irvin Child (1953) used HRAF as the database for studying the relationship between child-rearing practices and adult attitudes toward illness. More recently a host of studies using HRAF data have appeared in the literature, including studies on the adoption of agriculture, sexual division of labor, female political participation, reproduction rituals, and magico-religious practitioners.

New Information Technology

Although anthropologists today continue to use traditional data-gathering methods, such as participant observation and interviewing, the revolution in information technology that has occurred during the past twenty years has greatly expanded the toolkit of twenty-first-century cultural anthropologists. New tools include, but are not limited to, the following examples:

- *Internet search engines:* These general mega search engines, available with a single mouse click, provide a wide variety of data relevant for research

---

reflexive or narrative ethnography A type of ethnography, associated with postmodernism, that focuses more on the interaction between the ethnographer and the informant than on scientific objectivity.

Human Relations Area Files (HRAF) The world's largest anthropological data retrieval system, used to test cross-cultural hypotheses.

in cultural anthropology (see, for example, Google Scholar, Jstor).

■ *Programs for ethnographic analysis:* Since the 1980s several excellent computer-assisted programs have been developed to facilitate the analysis of ethnographic data. ATLAS.ti and NVivo, two such software packages, allow ethnographers to import text-based qualitative data (such as interview transcripts, fieldnotes, and other text-based documents) into their personal computers for easier and more efficient data analysis.

■ *Internet reference pages:* Such websites as New York Times, Smithsonian Institution, and Library of Congress are excellent sources of information for conducting research in either ethnography or ethnology.

■ *Videoconferencing:* Several collaborating social scientists and other researchers can share information from one anothers' desktops while communicating face to face electronically. Skyping, Gmail Chat, and Face Time are useful for these face-to-face meetings, without really being there.

■ *Internet survey research:* Using such sites as Zoomerang and Survey Monkey, cultural anthropologists are able to create survey instruments, invite participants, administer the surveys, and tally and analyze the results. Although these tools do not provide the quality of data derived from actual fieldwork, they enable the researcher to obtain and analyze data without ever having to leave their personal computer.

Mining Social Networking Web sites for Sociocultural Data

Some social scientists are beginning to use social networking web sites, such as Facebook and LinkedIn, to mine large quantities of sociocultural data about the adults who frequent these sites. Every day millions of people in the United States get on Facebook.com to troll for cyberfriends; share videos, photos, stories, and opinions on a variety of topics, and continuously refine and update their public personas for the rest of the world to see. In 2008 Twitter emerged as an online and more rapid way to communicate with one's social network. Each communiqué on Twitter is known as a tweet and is limited to 140 characters. Anyone can follow a twitter page (unless it is private) or create a personal one to have instant messaging with friends or strangers who join their social network.

Facebook and Twitter have captured the interests of many from around the world. In the aftermath of the

Gilles Peress/Magnum Photos

FIGURE 5.9 Medical doctor and medical anthropologist Dr. Paul Farmer visits with patients at Clinique Bon Sauveur, Haiti.

2010 earthquake in Haiti, locals who were able to take photographs on their cell phones let the world know what was happening by logging on to their Facebook accounts and tweeting (Fig 5.9). The dramatic images informed the world instantly of the devastation that had occurred and helped to mobilize rescue workers from around the world to coordinate with agencies already established in Haiti.

Accountability

All anthropologists be they applied or ethnographic in their approach to fieldwork are accountable to the people with whom they study. Collecting data with or from participants in a field study needs to be carried out ethically as we discussed in Chapter 3. Moreover, it is not just about the getting the data or just writing the story. Novelists and journalists do that kind of writing or chasing a story for hype. Critical to ethnographic and applied research methods are the scientific approach, the application of sociocultural theory, and the role of praxis as discussed in Chapter 4. And in the end, the final analyses whether they are written up in journal article form, books or book chapters, monographs, or newspaper editorials, are not to violate the Professional Code of Ethics. The published insights from the research should never bring harm to the people who are the subject or beneficiaries of the field study. As read in Chapter 3, the code of professional responsibility is a euphuism for the code of ethics for any kind of anthropology practiced, be it applied or ethnographic in nature.

Summary

1. Since the beginning of the twentieth century, cultural anthropologists have conducted their research in a firsthand manner by means of direct ethnographic fieldwork. Explicit discussion of how anthropologists actually do their fieldwork is a much more recent phenomenon, however.

2. Preparations must be made before any fieldwork experience is begun, including securing research funds; taking adequate health precautions, such as getting immunizations; obtaining research clearance from the host government; gaining proficiency in the local language; and attending to a host of personal matters such as securing passports and visas, purchasing equipment and supplies, and making sure that one's affairs at home are in order.

3. Although every fieldwork project in cultural anthropology has its own unique character, all projects go through the same basic stages: selecting a research problem, formulating a research design, collecting the data, analyzing the data, and interpreting the data.

4. Because no two fieldwork experiences are identical, cultural anthropologists must match the appropriate data-gathering techniques to their own fieldwork situations. Among the tools at the anthropologist's disposal are participant-observation, interviewing, ethnographic mapping, census taking, document analysis, the collection of genealogies, and photography.

5. Two general guidelines are applicable to most fieldwork situations. First, when one introduces oneself to the local population, it is important to select a single role and use it consistently. Second, to firmly establish one's credibility with the local people, it is best to proceed slowly.

6. The participant-observation technique has certain methodological advantages, including building rapport and allowing the anthropologist to distinguish between real and normative behaviors. Participant-observation is not without its methodological shortcomings, however. It is time-consuming, poses problems of data comparability, presents difficulties in recording data, and may interfere with the thing that is being studied.

7. Ethnographic interviews, which are particularly useful for collecting both attitudinal and behavioral data, are of two basic types: unstructured and structured. In unstructured interviews, interviewers ask open-ended questions and permit interviewees to respond at their own pace. In structured interviews, interviewers ask the same questions of all respondents, in the same order, and under the same set of social conditions.

8. When cultural anthropologists conduct field research in cultures different from their own, they need to be flexible and should always expect the unexpected. Like anyone else trying to operate in an unfamiliar cultural setting, cultural anthropologists are susceptible to culture shock.

9. The twenty-first century has ushered in web-based tools for collecting large amounts of high-quality anthropological data. Such social networking sites such as Facebook provide attitudinal and behavioral data from people throughout the world.

10. All anthropologists be they applied or ethnographic in their approach to fieldwork are accountable to the people with whom they study. The published insights from the research should not bring harm to the people who are the subject of the field study or beneficiaries of a project.

Key Terms

analyzing data
attitudinal data
behavioral data
bicultural perspective
census taking
collecting data
community-based participatory research
culture shock

document analysis
ethnographic fieldwork
ethnographic mapping
ethnography
event analysis
fieldnotes
fieldwork
genealogical method

Human Relations Area Files (HRAF)
informant
interpreting data
obtrusive effect
participatory action research
photography
proxemic analysis

qualitative data
quantitative data
reflexive or narrative ethnography
research clearance
research design
research proposal
structured interview
unstructured interview

Critical Thinking Questions

1. Why is it necessary for applied anthropologist to have experience in ethnographic methods for their fieldwork?

2. What similarities and differences can you discern in the field methods used by applied and ethnographic anthropologists?

3. If you were to evaluate the success of a project what criteria would you use for your evaluation?

Online Study Resources

CourseMate

Access chapter-specific learning tools including learning objectives, practice quizzes, videos, flash cards, glossaries, web links, and more in your Cultural Anthropology CourseMate. Login to www.cengagebrain.com to access the resources your instructor has assigned and to purchase materials.

Whether on computer or a smart phone our means of communicating with others is changing. What might once have been private information is now shared with many.

Language and Communication

In recent years forms of communication between individuals have changed dramatically. Where we once relied on one-to-one conversations with others, sent private letters and cards of sentiment or inquiry, today's communicators act for the world to see and to know. Technological advances have played a key role in these new modes of communication, yet they are altogether different in how they enable us to communicate with friends, family, and complete strangers. Although computers, microchips, cell phones, and high-speed internet technology enable people to communicate more rapidly, social media has enabled users to share their feelings, thoughts, daily routines, and so on with everyone that befriends the user. What was once a private act written in one's personal diary or journal, until discovered by the teasing younger brother or posthumously and made into a novel, has been transformed into a culture of sharing globally. Today's communicators seem to be able to write and share whatever with complete strangers and sometimes without a care. Take for example Bob, an employee at a major corporation, who relies on current technology to stay in touch with friends, family, and anyone else who he happens to be linked in with on his social media site.

Bob is not unique, he is just many of us who use technology to communicate rather than speak one-on-one or send a letter to a friend. Bob came into work and fell into his normal routine. He had his cup of coffee and fired up his computer. As he settled into work mode he spent the first thirty minutes on Facebook communicating with friends and people from work. He learned what everyone was up to and also shared his unhappiness with his place of work. A friend replied "maybe that is why you are always out drinking after work, to forget about the job so to speak." On one gloomy Friday after a particularly taxing week, Bob shared all again. He had had it and could not wait for the weekend so that he could *distance* himself from the job. What Bob had not realized when he was sharing his feeling with his friends was his boss was a friend of a friend on Facebook.

On the following Monday his boss called him into his office and asked if Bob was satisfied with his position in the company and was this really where he wanted to work? What did Bob forget about social media? Did Bob remember who all his *friends* are on Facebook? Could it be that Bob forgot that friends of friends also get access to his posts and that things can often be taken out of context and misinterpreted? What does this example suggest about the social consequences of using these new modes of communication? How is the culture of language and communication changing, national and internationally? ■

Pinkyone/Shutterstock.com

WHAT WE WILL LEARN

■ How does human language differ from forms of communication in other animals?

■ How do languages change?

■ Do people from different cultures have different styles of linguistic discourse?

■ What is the relationship between language and culture?

■ How do people communicate without using words?

■ How has the recent revolution in communication technology influenced the way people communicate in the twenty-first century?

Understanding language is an important part of cultural anthropology in general and is especially so for linguistic anthropologists. Applied anthropologists rely heavily on understanding both language and culture too. This chapter will discuss the various ways you can use language as a tool in research as well as in understanding language as part and parcel of culture. Such areas as historical linguistics, sociolinguistics, paralinguistics, nonverbal language (body language), and the cultural use of space will be examined. Knowledge of such concepts can be critical in cross-cultural settings such as negotiating a business deal or settling a dispute between nations. One could easily mess things up, so to speak, just by using the wrong hand, positioning one's fingers in an inappropriate way, or even by revealing the sole of one's shoe.

In addition to the interesting topics mentioned, such topics as the differences between human and nonhuman communications, how languages change, the relationships between language and culture, and linguistic styles, among others will be considered. The SWAP example of technology and new forms of communication should remind us that language, and how it is used, can have profound effects on our thinking, behavior, quality of life, physical health, and even job security.

Perhaps the most distinctive feature of being human is the capacity to create and use language and other symbolic forms of communication. It is hard to imagine how culture could even exist without language. Fundamental aspects of any culture, such as religion, family relationships, and the management of technology, would be virtually impossible without a symbolic form of communication. Our capacity to adapt to the physical environment—which involves identifying usable resources, developing ways of acquiring them, and finally forming groups to exploit them—is made possible by language. It is generally held that language is the major vehicle for human thought because our linguistic categories (a shared collection of form-meaning associations in a given environment or cultural setting) provide the basis for perception and concept formation. Moreover it is largely through language that we pass on our cultural heritage and identity from one generation to the next. By translating our experiences into linguistic symbols, we are able to store them, manipulate them, and pass them on to future generations. Without the capacity to symbolize, we would not be able to practice religion, create and maintain systems of law, engage in science, or compose a symphony. Language, then, is such an integral part of the human condition that it permeates everything we do. In other words, humans are humans because, among other things, we can symbolize through the use of language.

The Nature of Language

Like so many other words we think we understand, the term *language* is far more complex than we might imagine. Language, which is found in all cultures of the world, is a symbolic system of sounds that, when put together according to a certain set of rules, conveys meanings to its speakers. The meanings attached to any given word in all languages are totally *arbitrary*; that is, the word *cow* has no particular connection to the large bovine animal that the English language refers to as a cow. The word *cow* is no more or less reasonable as a word for that animal than would be *kaflumpha*, *sporge*, or *four-pronged squirter*. The word *cow* does not look like a cow, sound like a cow, or have any particular physical connection to a cow. The only explanation for the use of the word is that somewhere during the evolution of the English language the word *cow* came to be used to refer to a large, milk-giving, domesticated animal. Other languages use different, and equally arbitrary, words to describe the same animal.

Nowhere is the arbitrariness of languages more evident than in how people in different language communities select names for their children. In some East African societies, boys are given the name of their grandfather. For centuries certain segments of the US population have named male children after their fathers, and in fact this may extend for multiple generations, as in the name Harold Bennett IV. People in the United States also have been known to name their children after celebrities (Kathryn, for Kathryn Hepburn), famous

CROSS-CULTURAL MISCUE

❊ Difficulties in communication can arise even between two people who ostensibly speak the same language. Although both New Yorkers and Londoners speak English, there are enough differences between US English and British English to cause communication miscues. Speakers of English on opposite sides of the Atlantic often use different words to refer to the same thing. To illustrate, Londoners put their trash in a dustbin, not a garbage can; they take a lift, not an elevator; and they live in flats, not apartments. To further complicate matters, the same word used in England and the United States can convey different meanings. For example, in England the word *homely* (as in the statement "I think your wife is very homely") means warm and friendly, not plain or ugly as in the United States; for the British, the phrase "to table a motion" means to give an item a prominent place on the agenda rather than to postpone taking action on an item, as in the United States; and a *rubber* in British English is an eraser, not a condom. These are just a few of the linguistic pitfalls that North Americans and Brits may encounter when they attempt to communicate using their own versions of the "same" language.

---

arbitrary The meanings attached to words in any language are not based on a logical or rational system but rather are arbitrary.

presidents (Jefferson), famous jewelry stores (Tiffany), or even scientists (Booker T). In Thailand children are given playful nicknames, such as Pig, Chubby, Crab, and Money, which usually stay with the person through adulthood (T. Fuller 2007: 4). And in Zimbabwe we can find people with the first names such as Godknows, derived from a person's early childhood days of grave illness when his parents were not sure whether he would survive; Smile, whose parents wanted to raise a happy child; and Enough, the youngest of thirteen children (Wines 2007: 4).

Human communication differs from other animal communication systems in at least two other important respects. One feature of human language is its capacity to convey information about a thing or an event that is not present. This characteristic, known as *displacement*, enables humans to speak of purely hypothetical things, events that have happened in the past, and events that might happen in the future. In contrast to other animals, which communicate only about particular things that are in the present and in the immediate environment, language enables humans to think abstractly. Another feature of human communication that distinguishes it from nonhuman forms of communication is that it is transmitted largely through tradition rather than through experience alone. Although our propensity (and our physical equipment) for language is biologically based, the specific language that any given person speaks is passed from one generation to another through the process of learning. Adults in a linguistic community who already know the language teach the language to the children.

Diversity of Language

Given the arbitrary nature of languages, it should come as no surprise that there is enormous linguistic diversity among human populations. Even though linguists do not agree on precisely how many discrete languages exist, a reasonable estimate is nearly seven thousand (Wiflord 2010). The criterion used to establish such estimates is mutual unintelligibility; that is, linguists assume that if people can understand one another, they speak the same language, and if they are unable to understand one another, they speak different languages. The application of this criterion is not as straightforward as it might seem, however, because there are differing degrees of intelligibility. Nevertheless, despite our inability to establish the precise number of discrete languages found in the world today, the amount of linguistic diversity is vast (Figure 6.1).

displacement The ability to talk about things that are remote in time and space.

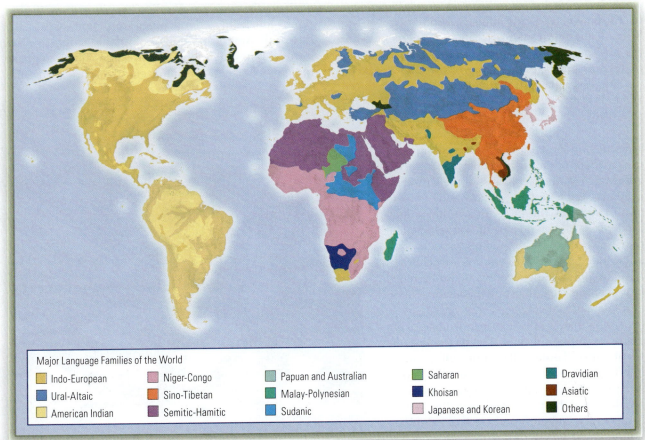

FIGURE 6.1 Major Language Families of the World.

TABLE 6.1

Major Languages of the World

Language	Primary Country	Number of Speakers
Chinese	China	1,213,000,000
Spanish	Spain/South America	329,000,000
English	United Kingdom/ United States	328,000,000
Arabic	Worldwide	221,000,000
Hindi	India	182,000,000
Bengali	Bangladesh	181,000,000
Portuguese	Portugal/Brazil	178,000,000
Russian	Russia	144,000,000
Japanese	Japan	122,000,000
German	Germany	90,000,000

SOURCE: *The World Almanac and Book of Facts 2013* (New York: World Almanac Education Group, 2013), p. 717.

Not only is there considerable variation in the number of languages of the world, but the size of the different language communities varies widely as well. It has been estimated that 95 percent of the world's people speak fewer than one hundred of the approximately six thousand different languages (Table 6.1). Mandarin alone accounts for about one in every five people on earth. When we add English, Hindi, Spanish, and Russian, the figure jumps to about 45 percent. Thus, the last 5 percent of the world's people speak thousands of discrete languages that have relatively few speakers.

Linguists today are particularly concerned about this last 5 percent of the world's languages, which are in danger of disappearing. The larger languages, which have both the power of the state and large numbers on their side, are in no danger of sliding into oblivion. Some linguists, such as Michael Krauss of the University of Alaska, estimate that as many as 90 percent of all languages will be extinct within a hundred years. If they do not die out altogether, they will become moribund—spoken by only a few older people and unknown to children (Dreifus 2001). Language loss is also hastened by war, ethnic cleansing, and mandatory education in a national language.

Traditional North American languages are tragic examples of how languages become moribund and eventually extinct. Of the many hundreds of languages that existed in North America when Europeans arrived, only about two hundred have survived into the twenty-first century, and most of these face a dubious future. How this loss of linguistic diversity has come about is not hard to understand. From the sixteenth century onward, American Indians were conquered, subdued, pacified, resettled, and moved onto reservations. After relegating them to the marginal areas of society, the Bureau of Indian Affairs, in a heavy-handed attempt to civilize the "savage beasts," took American Indian children from their families, put them into boarding schools, and forced them to speak only English. More recently American Indian children were punished or expelled from publicly funded schools if caught speaking their traditional languages. Clearly this is not an ideal environment in which children can learn their traditional languages.

Although many American Indian languages have become moribund or extinct, recently there have been attempts to revive some of these languages. Dr. Pam Innes, a linguistic anthropologist from the American Indians Language Study Program at the University of Wyoming, is active in language retention and revitalization work with members of the Muskogee and Seminole Nations of Oklahoma, the Apache Tribe of Oklahoma, and the Comanche Tribe of Oklahoma (Figure 6.2). Her applied research efforts have contributed to creating dictionaries, after-school programs for the youth, and to working among indigenous speakers to identify ways to facilitate future language programs for future generations.

Although such efforts to revive dying languages are admirable, the challenges facing those who would reverse the extinction process are daunting. Not all of the extinctions are the direct result of hostility and repression from a dominant government, as was the case with American Indians throughout most of US history. But where brutal repression failed to make indigenous languages and culture extinct, intense

Courtesy of Dr. Pamela Innes

FIGURE 6.2 Language programs are found in New Mexico. Seen here are classmates from the Mescalero Apache Tribe Language Program's Apache language class.

globalization since the 1980s has been more successful. The recent revolution in communications technology has provided powerful tools (through the airwaves and cyberspace) for the spread of mainstream Western culture and language. Yet, for some endangered languages the tide is changing through the digital revolution. As Rosenberg (2011) points out, digital technology, discussion groups, software companies and apps are life lines for language preservation for minority and endangered language communication needs. At one time technology forced some language speakers to adopt the dominant language of their community or nation. Now, new tools create the possibility for revitalizing a language and retaining language speakers of endangered languages.

Communication: Human versus Nonhuman

Communication is certainly not unique to humans because most animals have ways of sending and receiving messages. Various bird species use specific calls to communicate a desire to mate; honeybees communicate the distance and direction of sources of food accurately through a series of body movements; certain antelope species give off a cry that warns of impending danger; and even amoebae seem to send and receive crude messages chemically by discharging small amounts of carbon dioxide.

Communication among primates is considerably more complex. Some nonhuman primate species, such as gorillas and chimpanzees, draw on a large number of modes of communication, including various calls as well as nonverbal forms of communication such as facial expressions, body movement, and gestures (Figure 6.3). Yet despite the relative complexity of communication patterns among nonhuman primates, these patterns differ from human patterns of communication in significant ways. For example, because animal call systems are to a large extent genetically based, they are rigidly inflexible to the extent that each call always has the same form and conveys the same meaning.

Open and Closed Communication Systems

Chimpanzees make one sound when they have found a plentiful source of food, another when threatened, and a third when announcing their presence. Each of these three sounds is unique in both form and message. And each sound (call) is mutually exclusive; that is, the chimpanzee cannot combine elements of two or more calls to develop a new call. To this extent we speak of nonhuman forms of communication as being

© Susan Kuklin/Photo Researchers, Inc.

FIGURE 6.3 Joyce Butler of Columbia University shows famous chimpanzee Nim Chimpsky the sign configuration for "drink" and Nim imitates her. Even though Nim has been trained to use sign language, the differences between his form of communication and human language are vast.

closed systems of communication. Humans, on the other hand, operate with languages that are *open systems of communication* because they are capable of sending messages that have never been sent before.

Unlike nonhuman primates, humans use language to send an infinite array of messages, including abstract ideas, highly technical information, and subtle shades of meaning. Starting with a limited number of sounds, human languages are capable of producing an infinite number of meanings by combining sounds and words into meanings that may have never been sent before. To illustrate, by combining a series of words in a certain order, we can convey a unique message that has, in all likelihood, never been previously uttered: "I think that the woman named Clela with the bright orange hair left her leather handbag in the 1998 pink Mustang that was involved in a hit-and-run accident later in the day." This productive capacity of human language illustrates how efficient and flexible human communication is.

To suggest that the communication system of nonhuman primates such as chimps and gorillas is closed

closed systems of communication Communication in which the user cannot create new sounds or words by combining two or more existing sounds or words.

open systems of communication Communication in which the user can create new sounds or words by combining two or more existing sounds or words.

Endangered Languages Saved by Digital Technology

❀ It has been estimated that there are nearly seven thousand languages spoken in the world today. Yet, the majority of these languages are spoken by a limited number of speakers, which means these languages will become either endangered or extinct of some intervention is not put in place for each of these languages. In other words, if new speakers are not brought in to learn the language and share it with a next generation of speakers the language will die out. Some linguistic anthropologists are taking a proactive stance to identify these endangered languages, document them and where possible develop programs that revitalize an interest among the speakers as well as generate new speakers. These combined approaches may help to retain a significant number of speakers within the language so that it does not become moribund (see Dr. Pam Innes' work in this chapter).

Although we find a number of examples speakers of an endangered language found in remotes parts of the world such as in northern India, the jungles of the Amazon, and among some American Indian tribes in the southwest of the United States, some speakers are located in populated communities. Three different examples are discussed to illustrate how anthropological linguists approach language and culture from an applied perspective. One such example is the Endangered Language Alliance in New York City that is codirected by Linguistic Anthropologists Daniel Kaufman, Juliette Blevins, and Bob Holman. Their project is an urban initiative for endangered language research and conservation that takes place in New York City (http://endangeredlanguagealliance.org). An estimate from the 2000 census indicates there are more than 800 different first languages spoken in New York City. In Queens, which is the most diverse borough of the City, there are 176 different language spoken by students in the public schools and 138 different languages reported by the residents from the various immigrants groups that reside in the area, many of which are rare with few speakers remaining. Researchers who work for the Endangered Language Alliance plan to conduct door-to-door interviews in Queens to identify the endangered languages in the borough. It will be the first time that linguistic anthropologists will attempt an accurate account of the different languages spoken. They also invite other researchers and scholars whose work may overlap with theirs to contact them. It is from this research collaboration they will be able to document the range of endangered languages spoken in the city as well as develop community based language conservation programs in such a diverse urban setting.

In another example linguistic anthropologists were researching in northeastern India to identify and study little-known languages in remote areas. India is known to have 150 different languages spoken. Gregory Anderson, director of the Living Tongues Institute for Endangered Languages in Salem, Oregon, K. David Harrison, a linguist from Swarthmore College, and Ganash Murmu, a linguist at Ranchi University in India worked together on this expedition, "Enduring Voices Project," which is a National Geographic Society project for Disappearing Languages (http://travel.nationalgeographic.com/travel/enduring-voices/). Their expedition in 2010 to Arunachal Pradesh, India, was to document endangered languages in isolated villages. While engaged in this research and listening to the speakers of the Aka language, one that is common in that district, they came upon another language that sounded remarkably different. They identified this hidden language known locally as "Koro," a language that was actually unknown to the outside world. Interestingly, Harrison points out that Koro speakers "are thoroughly mixed

---

in contrast to the open system used by humans is an oversimplification. Some linguistic scholars, such as Noam Chomsky (1972), posited that because human language is so radically different from other forms of animal communication, humans must be endowed with certain genetically based mental capacities found in no other species. As we have learned more about the communication systems of nonhuman primates, however, a growing number of scholars have questioned this theory by claiming that certain species, such as chimpanzees and gorillas, have a latent capacity to learn language.

A major limitation to the development of language among gorillas and chimps is physical: They do not possess the vocal equipment for speech. In an effort to circumvent this physical limitation, recent researchers have taught some aspects of American Sign Language to chimpanzees and gorillas with some startling results. In four years Allen and Beatrice Gardner (1969) taught a chimp named Washoe (1965–2007) to use 130 different signs. Of even greater significance is the fact that Washoe was able to manipulate the signs in ways that previously had been thought possible only by humans. For example, Washoe was able to combine several signs to create a new word (having no sign for the word *duck*, she called it *waterbird*), thereby "opening up" her system of communication. In another research effort in nonhuman communication, a gorilla named Koko by age four was able to use more than 250 different signs within a single hour and, like Washoe, was able to name new objects by combining several different signs.

These recent developments suggest that chimps and gorillas have more complex powers of reasoning in with other local people and number perhaps no more than 800." Aka speakers with whom the Koro live among, number about 10,000 (Roberts 2010:D3). The research team is not sure how the Koro language survived living in such close relations with another linguistic group, but it has. The researchers further investigated the Koro language and compared it to other languages. Anderson and Harrison have determined it belongs to the Tibeto-Burman language family (which includes four hundred tongues), but Koro has never been recognized in any previous research (Wilford 2010).

These examples illustrate there are linguistic anthropologists actively documenting endangered languages and with an effort to developing initiatives on language conservation, revitalization, and retention. Yet, these researchers are also not alone in their quest for endangered languages and means to preserve them. To be certain the digital revolution has enhanced this process. For a good number of years English was the predominant language used to communicate with the Web and cell phones technology. In fact, such technology at one time fostered the learning of English globally. Today, however, the new smartphones with mobile apps and new software capabilities are encouraging the development of new software to accommodate many languages, including endangered languages (Canton 2012). Rosenberg (2011) suggests that the new technologies are inspiring people, especially younger generations to read and write in their native language, and the new language apps make it possible to do it many more languages than just English. In fact, Eatoni, a company in New York City is making not just one cell phone keyboard for texting, but three hundred different keyboards, with different symbols and characters to accommodate many different languages.

Linguistic projects using mobile phones and software technology (apps) to provide speakers of a heritage or an endangered language access to their language are increasing in Africa and Australia. Cell phone sales are taking off in both Africa and Australia, especially with the new smartphones. In Australia, there

are more than one hundred endangered languages among the aborigines. One of the heritage languages, Ma! Iwaidja, has two hundred speakers. A free mobile app has been created for Ma! Iwaidja to prevent its extinction (Canton 2012). In Guinea, Africa rather than rely on French to communicate to friends and family a mobile app for the N'Ko language speakers has been created. In this case there are millions are potentially tens millions of speakers of N'Ko, however, not everyone has the ability to read and write. The mobile app technology encourages people to retain their own language, which is much easier on a smartphone than the old cell phones without the apps (Rosenberg 2011). For linguistic anthropologists with an applied perspective, working with communities, software and technology companies and others has the potential for preserving heritage and endangered languages. The imminent threat of the rapid loss of so many languages may have been brought to an abrupt halt by a smartphone.

Bert Hoferichter/Alamy

Maasai woman using a smart phone in Tanzania, East Africa.

Discussion Questions

1. What opportunities are there for applied linguistic anthropologists?
2. Can you identify new ways, using technology such as smart phones that could assist with projects to help with endangered language revitalization and retention of language speakers?

than had been previously believed. Some have used this evidence to support the notion that chimpanzee and gorilla linguistic abilities differ from those of humans only in degree, not in kind. We must keep in mind, however, that nonhuman primates, despite their capacity to master several aspects of American Sign Language, do not have a language in the human sense of the term. Although nonhuman primate systems of communication are complex and functional, there are still many features of human language that nonhuman primates, left to their own devices, do not possess and never will. They deserve to be studied on their own terms, rather than with the false impression that chimps and gorillas are really incipient humans (linguistically speaking), who simply need a little more time and assistance before they are able to debate the sociopolitical complexities of globalization.

The Structure of Language

Every language has a logical structure. When people encounter an unfamiliar language for the first time, they are confused and disoriented, but after becoming familiar with the language, they eventually discover its rules and how the various parts are interrelated. All languages have rules and principles governing what sounds are to be used and how those sounds are to be combined to convey meanings. Human languages have two aspects of structure: a sound (or phonological) structure and a grammatical structure. *Phonology* is the study of the basic building blocks of a language,

---

phonology The study of a language's sound system.

units of sound called phonemes, and how these phonemes are combined. The study of grammar involves identifying recurring sequences of phonemes, called *morphemes*, the smallest units of speech that convey a meaning.

The *descriptive linguistics*, whose job is to make explicit the structure of any given language, studies both the sound system and the grammatical system of as many different human languages as possible.

Phonology

The initial step in describing any language is to determine the sounds that it uses. Humans have the vocal apparatus to make an extraordinarily large number of sounds, but no single language uses all possible sounds. Instead, each language uses a finite number of sounds, called *phonemes*, which are the smallest units of sound that signal a difference in meaning. The English language contains sounds for twenty-four consonants, nine vowels, three semivowels, and some other sound features—for a total of forty-six phonemes. The number of phonemes in other languages varies from a low of about fifteen to a high of about one hundred.

Clearly the twenty-six letters of the English alphabet do not correspond to the total inventory of phonemes in the English language. This is largely because English has a number of inconsistent features. For example, we pronounce the same word differently (as in the present and past tense of the verb *read*) and we have different spellings for some words that sound identical, such as *meet* and *meat*. (See Table 6.2) To address this difficulty, linguists have developed the International Phonetic Alphabet, which takes into account all of the possible sound units (phonemes) found in all languages of the world.

The manner in which sounds are grouped into phonemes varies from one language to another. In English, for example, the sounds represented by *b* and *v* are two separate phonemes. Such a distinction is absolutely necessary if an English speaker is to differentiate between such words as *ban* and *van* or *bent* and *vent*. The Spanish language, however, does not distinguish between these two sounds. When the Spanish word *ver* ("to see") is pronounced, it would be impossible for the English speaker to determine with absolute precision whether the word begins with a *v* or a *b*. Thus, whereas

---

descriptive linguistics The branch of anthropological linguistics that studies how languages are structured.

phonemes The smallest units of sound in a language that distinguish meaning.

morpheme The smallest linguistic forms (usually words) that convey meaning.

TABLE 6.2

English Is No Easy Language to Learn

The medic *wound* the bandage around the *wound*.

The dump was so full that it had to *refuse* more *refuse*.

The *Polish* woman decided to *polish* her dining room table.

He could not *lead* the way because his pants were full of *lead*.

The soldier decided to *desert* his *dessert* in the *desert*.

I did not *object* to the *object*.

The *invalid* had an *invalid* driver's license.

Two members of the Harvard crew team had a *row* about how to *row*.

They were too *close* to the door to *close* it.

The buck *does* funny things when the *does* are around.

After the dentist gave me a *number* of injections, my jaw finally got *number*.

I shed a *tear* when I noticed a *tear in* my new suit jacket.

I had to *subject* the *subject* to a series of tests.

How can I *intimate* this to my most *intimate* friend?

Or have you ever asked yourself these questions?

- If the plural of *tooth* is *teeth*, then why isn't the plural of *moose*, *meese*?
- Why are boxing rings square?
- Why do I push the *start* button when I want to *shut down* my computer?
- Why do we say that the alarm *went off* when in fact it *turned on*?
- How do we explain that eggplant contains no *eggs*, hamburgers contain no *ham*, and pineapple contains neither *pine* nor *apples*?
- Do you know the difference between *groundhog meat* (the flesh of an animal called a groundhog) and *ground hog meat* (ground pork)?

---

v and *b* are two distinct phonemes in English, they belong to the same sound class (or phoneme) in the Spanish language.

Morphemes

Sounds and phonemes, though linguistically significant, usually do not convey meaning in themselves. The phonemes *r, a,* and *t* taken by themselves convey no meaning whatsoever. But when combined, they can form the words *rat, tar,* and *art,* each of which conveys meaning. Thus two or more phonemes can be combined to form a *morpheme*.

Even though some words are made up of a single morpheme, we should not equate morphemes with

CONTEMPORARY ISSUE

Becoming a Teacher of English to Non-Native English Speakers

✿ As the United States becomes more diverse with more foreign-born nationals, and the world becomes more globally interconnected in places of business, education, health, and government, people are learning a second language, and in some cases multiple languages. Teaching English as a Second Language (ESL), Teaching English as a Foreign Language (TEFL), or Teaching English as an Additional Language (TEAL) are similar terms about teaching English to adults and children who are native speakers of another language. As an undergraduate student one can develop a major that would allow one to pursue a multicultural career teaching English but as a foreign language. Some specialists find work at a public school (K–12), community college or university, business, international tour companies, and government, depending on one's degree qualifications. Others, especially adventurous people, find teaching opportunities in foreign countries, where they can teach English also in a variety of setting and for different age groups.

Getting qualified is the key to being hired and being successful in a teaching and learning environment. Generally, a job in teaching ESL minimally requires a bachelor's degree in cultural studies, linguistics, English, or a related area. Many students actually double major to combine some aspect of language and culture studies to be more prepared for where

ever they end up teaching. In the United States, teachers who have ESL certification are typically qualified to teach non-English speaking adults and children, but each state has its own educational guidelines that have to be met. An ESL degree may allow an undergraduate to teach English abroad or increasing their chance of being hired in an international setting. Before completing one's undergraduate degree studying abroad for a semester or a year offers a similar experience of learning another language and culture, putting an ESL teacher in the enviable position of being empathetic to their future students learning another language and culture. As with all teachers, patience in teaching is necessary; however, an ESL teacher should also have the ability to relate to students from diverse cultural backgrounds, creating a supportive environment for all of the students. Today with the increasing demand for ESL there are face-to-face and online programs of instruction. Doing a Google search for ESL programs, the requirements at your university or college (should they have the ESL certification program), employment opportunities, and career paths is one way to being pulling available resources together. One never knows after teaching English in South Korea, China, Russia, Indonesia, Malaysia, or elsewhere where the experience may take you next.

---

words. In our example, the words *rat, tar,* and *art,* each a single morpheme, cannot be subdivided into smaller units of meaning. In these cases the words are made up of a single morpheme. However, the majority of words in any language are made up of two or more morphemes. The word *rats,* for example, contains two morphemes: the root word *rat* and the plural suffix *-s,* which conveys the meaning of more than one. Similarly, the word *artists* contains three morphemes: the root word *art;* the suffix *-ist,* meaning one who engages in the process of doing art; and the plural suffix *-s.* Some of these morphemes, like *art, tar,* and *rat,* can occur in a language unattached. Because they can stand alone, they are called *free morphemes.* Other morphemes, such as the suffix *-ist,* cannot stand alone because they have no meaning except when attached to other morphemes. These are called *bound morphemes.* (See Figure 6.4.)

Grammar

When people send linguistic messages by combining sounds into phonemes, phonemes into morphemes, and morphemes into words, they do so according to a highly complex set of rules. These rules, which are unique for each language, make up the *grammar* of the

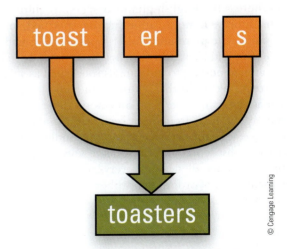

© Cengage Learning

FIGURE 6.4 Morphemes make up words. The word *toasters* is made up of the morphemes *toast,* *-er,* and *s.* Which morphemes are free and which are bound?

---

free morphemes A morpheme that can convey meaning while standing alone without being attached to other morphemes.

bound morphemes A morpheme that can convey meaning only when combined with another morpheme.

grammar The systematic rules by which sounds are combined in a language to enable users to send and receive meaningful utterances.

language and are well understood and followed by the speakers of that language. These grammatical systems, which constitute the formal structure of the language, consist of two parts: the rules governing how morphemes are formed into words (*morphology*) and the principles guiding how words are arranged into phrases and sentences (*syntax*). In some languages meanings are determined primarily by the way morphemes are combined to form words (morphological features), whereas in other languages meanings are determined primarily by the order of words in a sentence (syntactical features).

We can illustrate the distinction between morphology and syntax by looking at an example from the English language. From a grammatical point of view, the statement "Mary fix Tom phone" does not make much sense. The order of the words in the statement (the syntax) is correct, but clearly some revision in the way that the words themselves are formed (morphology) is required for the statement to make grammatical sense. For example, because the English language requires information about verb tense, we must specify whether Mary fixed, is fixing, or will fix the phone. The English grammar system also requires information about the number of phones and the nature of the relationship between the phone and Tom. To make this statement grammatical, we can add an *-ed* to *fix*, an *-s* to *phone*, and an *-'s* to *Tom*. The revised statement ("Mary fixed Tom's phones"), which is now grammatically correct, tells us that Mary has already fixed two or more phones that belong to Tom.

Whereas the English grammar system requires that tense, number, and relationship be specified, other language systems require other types of information. For example, in Latin or Czech, a noun must have the proper case ending to indicate its role (such as subject or direct object) in the sentence. In some languages, such as Spanish, the ending on a noun determines the noun's gender (masculine or feminine). In the Navajo language, certain verbs such as "to handle" take different forms depending on the size and shape of the object being handled. Thus, every language has its own systematic way of ordering morphemes within a word to give linguistic meaning.

Syntax, on the other hand, is the aspect of grammar that governs the arrangement of words and phrases into sentences. In our original example ("Mary fix Tom phone"), the syntax is correct because the words are in the proper sequence. The statement would be totally meaningless if the words were ordered "fix Tom phone Mary" because the parts of speech are not in the proper relationship to one another. Moreover, in English, adjectives generally precede the nouns they describe (such as "white horse"), whereas in Spanish adjectives generally follow the nouns they describe (such as "*caballo blanco*"). The order of the words, then, determines—at least in part—the meaning conveyed in any given language.

Language Change

When linguists look at the sound system or the structure of a language, they are engaging in *synchronic analysis* (that is, analysis at a single point in time). However, like all other aspects of culture, language is not static but rather is constantly changing. When linguists study how languages change over time, they are engaged in *diachronic analysis* (that is, analysis over a period of time). Languages can be studied diachronically or historically in various ways. For example, *historical linguists* may study changes in a single language, such as changes from Old English to modern English. Or linguists can look at changes that have occurred in related languages (comparative linguistics). Thus, historical linguists are interested in studying both the changes that have occurred in a single language over time and the historical relationship of languages to one another.

Changes in the meanings of words reflect changing cultural values. The value placed on being old in the United States, for example, changed dramatically between the eighteenth and nineteenth centuries. To illustrate, the English word *fogy* was a term of respect for a veteran in the 1700s. By the mid-1800s, however, the word took on a derisive meaning, largely because values and attitudes toward the elderly were changing from deference and respect to contempt and neglect. Later in the century (as we became more of a youth culture), the term *fogy* was joined with new disparaging terms for the elderly, including *codger, coot, fuddy-duddy,* and *geezer*. And the derogatory terms used for the elderly continue into the present with such words as *fossil, blue hair, senior, gray panther, golden ager, cotton-top,* and *gerry* (short for *geriatric*).

Just as languages change for internal reasons, they also are changed by external forces, or linguistic borrowing. It is generally thought that languages borrow from one another for two primary reasons: need and prestige. When a language community acquires a new cultural item, such as a concept or a material object, it

---

morphology The study of the rules governing how morphemes are formed into words.

syntax The linguistic rules, found in all languages, that determine how phrases and sentences are constructed.

synchronic analysis The analysis of cultural data at a single point in time, rather than through time.

diachronic analysis The analysis of sociocultural data through time, rather than at a single point in time.

historical linguists The study of how languages change over time.

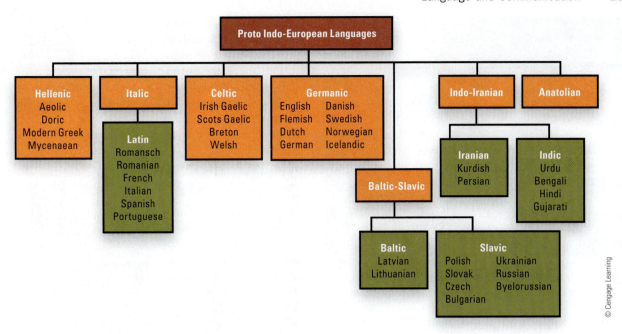

FIGURE 6.5 Proto Indo-European Languages.

needs a word to describe it. This explains why different cultures have similar words referring to the same item, such as automobiles, computers, and coffee. The other reason that words are borrowed from other languages is that they convey prestige to the speakers of the recipient language. To illustrate, the French word *cuisine* (from *kitchen*) was adopted into English because French food was considered more prestigious than English food during the period of French dominance (700 to 950 years ago). The proliferation of cell phones and text messaging has encouraged creative spelling and symbolic representation in coining terminology for the Web or Web language. In fact, the Oxford Dictionary includes lol (laugh out loud) and OMG (oh my gosh) as entries. Similarly we recognize :-) as something other than punctuation marks and sometimes the software autocorrects the key strokes into ☺, which is most likely the intended message.

Language and Culture

For the cultural anthropologist, the study of language is important not only for the practical purpose of communicating while doing fieldwork but also because of the close relationship between language and culture.

It would be difficult, if not impossible, to understand a culture without first understanding its language, and it would be equally impossible to understand a language outside of its cultural context. For this reason, any effective language teacher will go beyond vocabulary and grammar by teaching

students something about such topics as the eating habits, values, and behavior patterns of native speakers. This important relationship between language and culture—which is the subject matter of *cultural linguistics*—was recognized in the early twentieth century by the father of modern US cultural anthropology, Franz Boas (1911b: 73):

> The study of language must be considered as one of the most important branches of ethnological study, because, on the one hand, a thorough insight into ethnology cannot be gained without a practical knowledge of the language, and, on the other hand, the fundamental concepts illustrated by human languages are not distinct in kind from ethnological phenomena; and because, furthermore, the peculiar characteristics of language are clearly reflected in the views and customs of the peoples of the world.

How Culture Influences Language

Although little research has been conducted to explore how culture influences the grammatical system of a language, there is considerable evidence to demonstrate how culture affects vocabulary. As a general rule, the vocabulary found in any language tends to emphasize the words that are considered to be adaptively important

cultural linguistics The study of the relationship between language and culture.

Image © 2010 Ilka Mašik. Used under license from Shutterstock.com

FIGURE 6.6 Would this skier have a more robust vocabulary focusing on different words for snow than a nonskiing Floridian?

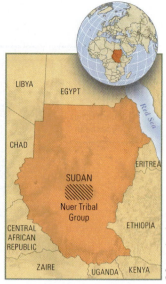

© Cengage Learning

in that culture. This concept, known as *cultural emphasis of language*, is reflected in the size and specialization of vocabulary (Figure 6.6).

In standard US English, a large number of words refer to technological gadgetry (such as *tractor, microchip,* and *intake valve*) and occupational specialties (such as *teacher, plumber, CPA,* and *pediatrician*) for the simple reason that technology and occupation are points of cultural emphasis in our culture. Thus, the English language helps North Americans adapt effectively to their culture by providing a vocabulary well suited for that culture. Other cultures have other areas of emphasis.

The Nuer

A particularly good example of how culture influences language through the elaboration of vocabularies is provided by the Nuer, a pastoral people of the Sudan, whose daily preoccupation with cattle is reflected in their language (Evans-Pritchard 1940). The Nuer have a large vocabulary to describe and identify their cattle according to certain physical features such as color, markings, and horn configuration. The Nuer have ten major color terms for describing cattle: *white (bor), black (car), brown (lual), chestnut (dol), tawny (yan), mouse-gray (lou), bay (thiang), sandy gray (lith), blue and strawberry roan (yil),* and *chocolate (gwir).* When these color possibilities are merged with the many possible marking patterns, there are several hundred combinations. And when these several hundred

cultural emphasis of language The idea that the vocabulary in any language tends to emphasize words that are adaptively important in that culture.

possibilities are combined with terminology based on horn configuration, there are potentially thousands of ways of describing cattle with considerable precision in the Nuer language.

US Example of Cultural Emphasis

In small-scale cultures such as the Nuer, where most people's lives revolve around herding, areas of cultural emphasis are fairly obvious. In middle-class US culture, which tends to be more complex occupationally, it is not always easy to identify a single area of cultural emphasis. Nevertheless, sports is one area of US culture that can be shared by people from a wide variety of occupational or class backgrounds. As Nancy Hickerson (2000: 165) pointed out, many colloquialisms in US English are taken from the game of baseball, our national pastime:

- He made a grandstand play.
- She threw me a curve.
- She fielded my questions well.
- You're way off base.
- You're batting a thousand (five hundred, zero) so far.
- What are the ground rules?
- I want to touch all the bases.
- He went to bat for me.
- He has two strikes against him.
- That's way out in left field.
- He drives me up the wall.
- He's a team player (a clutch player).
- She's an oddball (screwball, foul ball).
- It's just a ballpark estimate.

How Language Influences Culture

Another major concern of linguistic anthropology since the 1930s has been whether language influences or perhaps even determines culture. There is no consensus on this topic among ethnolinguists, but some have suggested that language is more than a symbolic inventory of experience and the physical world, and that it actually shapes our thoughts and perceptions—the way in which we see the world.

Edward Sapir (1929: 214) stated this notion in its most explicit form:

> The real world is to a large extent unconsciously built up on the language habits of the group. No two languages are ever sufficiently similar to be considered as representing the same social reality. The worlds in which different societies live are distinct worlds, not merely the same world with different labels attached.

The Sapir-Whorf Hypothesis

Drawing on Sapir's original formulation, Benjamin Lee Whorf, a student of Sapir, conducted ethnolinguistic research among the Hopi Indians to determine whether different linguistic structures produced different ways of viewing the world. Whorf's observations convinced him that linguistic structure was in fact the causal variable for different views of the world. This notion has come to be known as the *Sapir–Whorf hypothesis*.

Both Sapir and Whorf were suggesting that language is more than a vehicle for communication; it actually establishes mental categories that predispose people to see things in a certain way (Figure 6.7). For example, if my language has a single word—*aunt*—that refers to my mother's sister, my father's sister, my mother's brother's wife, and my father's brother's wife, it is likely that I will perceive all of these family members as genealogically equivalent and consequently will behave toward them in essentially the same way. Thus, Sapir and Whorf suggested that both perception and the resulting behavior are determined (or at least influenced) by the linguistic categories we use to group some things under one heading and other things under another heading.

When they focused attention on the relationship among language, thought, and culture, Sapir and Whorf neither used the term *hypothesis* nor attempted to support their idea with empirical evidence. Rather, it was subsequent linguistic scholars who assigned the term *hypothesis* to their writings. These later scholars focused on two main ideas: (1) a theory of linguistic determinism that states that the language you speak *determines* the way you perceive the world around you and (2) a weaker theory of linguistic relativism that states that your language merely *influences* your thoughts about the real world.

Testing the Hypothesis

Many ethnolinguists have attempted to test the Sapir-Whorf hypothesis. One creative test was conducted by Joseph Casagrande (1960), using a matched sample of Navajo-speaking children. Half of the sample, who spoke only Navajo, were matched on all significant sociocultural variables (such as religion, parental education, family income) with the other half, who spoke

FIGURE 6.7 Although the Navajo and English languages have different structures, these Navajo speakers can express abstract ideas every bit as effectively as native English speakers can.

both Navajo and English. Because the groups were identical on all important variables except language, it would be logical to conclude that whatever perceptual differences emerged between the two groups could be attributed to language.

Having a thorough knowledge of the Navajo language, Casagrande understood that Navajo people, when speaking about an object, are required to choose among a number of different verb forms depending on the shape of the object. When asking a Navajo speaker to hand you an object, you use one verb form if the object is long and rigid like a stick and another verb form if it is long and flexible like a rope. Based on this linguistic feature, Casagrande hypothesized that children who spoke only Navajo would be more likely to discriminate according to shape than the English-speaking children. English-speaking children would be

---

Sapir–Whorf hypothesis The notion that a person's language shapes her or his perceptions and view of the world.

more likely to discriminate according to other features such as size or color. This hypothesis was tested by having both groups of children participate in a number of tasks. The children were shown two objects (a yellow stick and a blue rope) and then asked to tell which of these two objects was most like a third object (a yellow rope). In other words, both groups of children were asked to categorize the yellow rope according to likeness with either the yellow stick or the blue rope. Casagrande found that the children who spoke only Navajo had a significantly greater tendency to categorize according to shape (yellow rope and blue rope) than the bilingual children, who were more likely to categorize according to color.

Sapir and Whorf were primarily concerned with the effects of language on perception. Whatever the exact nature of that relationship is, there is little disagreement among cultural linguists that people from different cultural groups do not see the world in exactly the same way. More recently, experiments have been conducted to define more accurately this relationship between language and perception. Lera Boroditsky (2009) of Stanford University has demonstrated that even frivolous aspects of language, like grammatical gender, can have significant effects on perception. In many languages, such as the Romance languages (such as Italian, French and Spanish), nouns are classified as either masculine or feminine, which means that masculine and feminine nouns are treated differently grammatically. In these languages, speakers must use the proper gender-related pronouns, adjectives, and verb endings depending on the gender of the noun. For example, in a language that designates the word *sofa* as masculine, to say "my sofa is old" requires that the words *my*, *is*, and *old* be used in their masculine forms to agree with the masculine noun. And, the same grammatical forms are used when speaking of a person, such as an uncle, since *uncle* is also a masculine noun. Likewise, when referring to a *table* or an *aunt* (which are both feminine nouns), one must use pronouns, verbs, and adjectives that have feminine endings.

Boroditsky asked the question: Does treating words as either masculine or feminine make speakers think of sofas and uncles as masculine (having the traits of males) and tables and aunts as feminine (having the traits of females)? In one of many studies, Boroditsky asked German and Spanish speakers to describe the characteristics of objects that have opposite gender assignments. To illustrate, she asked them to describe a key; the word for *key* is masculine in German and feminine in Spanish. In describing a key, German speakers used such words as *heavy, hard, jagged, metal,* and *serrated,* whereas Spanish speakers used such words as *lovely, intricate, golden, little, shiny,* and *tiny.* And, when asked to describe an expansion bridge, which is feminine in German and masculine in Spanish, German speakers used such descriptors as *beautiful, elegant, fragile, pretty,* and *slender,* whereas Spanish speakers used such words as *big, strong, dangerous, sturdy,* and *towering.* Boroditsky (2009: 116–129) concluded that "apparently even small flukes of grammar, like the seemingly arbitrary assignment of gender to a noun, can have an effect on people's ideas of concrete objects in the world."

The power of language can also be seen in the way people use language to alter other people's perceptions of various things. For example, language can be used to mislead by making things appear better than they actually are. Large organizations, such as corporations and branches of the federal government, are particularly adept at using euphemisms—forms of language that conceal something unpleasant, bad, or inadequate. Companies no longer *fire* employees; rather, employees are *outplaced, released, dehired,* or *non-renewed* (Figure 6.8). Corporate structures are *downsized, reengineered,* or *restructured.* Phrases like *reducing redundancy* and *enhancing efficiency* are designed to conceal the fact that the company is having problems.

The problem with the Sapir–Whorf hypothesis—and the reason it remains a hypothesis rather than a widely accepted fact—is causation. At times Sapir suggested that people are virtual prisoners of their

FIGURE 6.8 Euphemisms make things appear better than they are. How much better do these unemployed people feel because they were "outpaced" or "dehired" rather than "fired"?

Frances Roberts/Alamy

language, such as when he stated (1929: 209) that "human beings … are very much at the mercy of the particular language which has become the medium of expression for their society." At other times Whorf and Sapir suggested that language simply reflects, rather than determines, culture and perception. To be certain, language and culture influence each other in important ways. Yet problems arise when attempting to demonstrate that language actually *determines* culture, or vice versa, in any definitive way. What does seem obvious, however, is that all people, being constantly bombarded with sensory stimuli, have developed filtering systems to bring order to all of these incoming sensations. Sapir, Whorf, and more recent scholars have suggested that one such filtering system is language, which provides a set of lenses that highlight some perceptions and de-emphasize others. Today most scholars agree that language does influence perception in certain limited ways. We cannot conclude from this, however, that language forces or coerces people to have particular thoughts or perceptions, or prevents them from thinking in certain ways.

Whatever may be the precise effect of language on culture, the Sapir–Whorf hypothesis has served to focus attention on this important relationship. For interesting contemporary discussions of the Sapir–Whorf hypothesis, see David Thomson (1994) and Lera Boroditsky (2009).

Linguistic Style

When we state that there are approximately seven thousand mutually unintelligible languages spoken in the world today, we are implying that they all have unique vocabularies, grammar systems, and syntax. But each language group also varies in linguistic style. For example, some linguistic groups send explicit messages directly, whereas other groups communicate indirectly by sending more implicit messages. In Canada and the United States, where words and eloquence are highly valued, people strive to communicate in a way that is precise, straightforward, and unambiguous. We are expected to "tell it like it is" and avoid "beating around the bush." Communication in some Asian cultures, by way of contrast, is noticeably more ambiguous, implicit, and inexact. With much less emphasis placed on words, many Asian cultures rely heavily on nonverbal cues and social context to derive meaning.

These differing linguistic styles can lead to cross-cultural misunderstandings. The indirect style of the Japanese has been known to test the patience of Westerners, who mistakenly interpret it as sneaky and devious. In fact Japanese indirectness stems from a predominating concern to allow others to "save face" and avoid shame. Direct communicators, such as Americans, Canadians, and Germans, choose their words carefully because they want to be as clear and unambiguous as possible. Japanese, on the other hand, also choose their words carefully, but for different reasons. Their meticulous choice of words stems from their desire to avoid blunt, offensive language, which would cause others to "lose face."

This stylistic difference between directness and indirectness can be seen in TV commercials in the United States and Japan. Advertising in the United States clearly uses a hard-sell approach. Products are prominently displayed while viewers are bombarded with words aimed at convincing them to buy the product. How could we not buy a particular product if "nine out often doctors agree …" or if "studies at a leading university confirm …"? North Americans are likely to see the fast- and loud-talking announcer telling us why we must not miss this weekend's "48-Hour Sale-A-Thon" at the local car dealership. Television commercials in Japan, with their more subdued and indirect approach, are different from those seen on US or Canadian television. They do not preach or try to coerce the viewer into buying the product. They do not use strong, persuasive language. In fact sometimes it is not altogether clear what product is being advertised. Robert Collins (1992: 130–31) described one Japanese commercial in which a man is sitting in a folding chair on a beautiful sunny day at the beach, with a dog at his side. He is wearing jeans and drinking an amber liquid from a glass, while his head bobs back and forth, apparently in time to music from his earphones. Classical music is playing on the soundtrack. Toward the end of the commercial, the man holds up his glass to toast the camera, while a voice announces the name of the product. End of commercial. This was not an advertisement for beer or for designer jeans, but rather for stomach medicine. Clearly this is a subtle and indirect message. The intended message was that the man would not be having such a wonderful time at the beach if he was at home with stomach distress. Although much was left unsaid in this commercial, the typical Japanese viewer would have no difficulty understanding the indirect, implicit, and subtle message.

Another aspect of indirect versus direct linguistic style is the role of silence in communication. People from indirect societies see silence as useful; they tolerate intermittent periods of silence so as to gain a better understanding of their communication partners. Direct communicators, such as the majority of North Americans, avoid silence at all costs. Many American Indian groups use silence as an integral part of their normal mode of discourse. Keith Basso (1970) described the role of silence among the Apache of Arizona, who define silence as the proper way of dealing with certain categories of people. For example,

Basso found that silence was used with strangers, during the initial stages of courtship, with children coming home after a long absence, with people who "cuss them out," with people who are sad, and with those involved in curing ceremonies. Interestingly, what was common to each of these six categories of people was that they all involved relationships that were ambiguous and unpredictable. Thus, in some cultures silence (that is, whether or not a person actually uses words) is determined by the nature of the social relationship between people and their social context.

In addition, there are stylistic variations in the extent to which some linguistic groups assign greater importance to *words* (that is, the content of the message) than to *nonverbal cues* such as tone or body language. Keiko Ishii, Jose Alberto Reyes, and Shinobu Kitayama (2003), for example, have shown that Americans have greater difficulty ignoring the content of a message than ignoring how the message is intoned. However, their findings showed just the opposite for Japanese; that is, the Japanese had greater difficulty ignoring vocal tone than ignoring verbal content. Thus, the Americans had an attentional bias toward content, whereas the Japanese paid more attention to intonation (Figure 6.9). This stylistic difference between these two linguistic groups at least partially explains why both sides have a propensity to misunderstand each other. Americans are often perplexed because they think their Japanese counterparts do not seem to mean the same thing that they mean by the word *yes*. Many Japanese, conversely, feel perplexed by the fact that the Americans just do not seem to get it because they are failing to read the available nonverbal cues such as intonation (see next Cross-Cultural Miscue Box).

CROSS-CULTURAL MISCUE

❋ The best entrée into another culture is through its language. Linguistic competency, however, involves more than knowing vocabulary, grammar, and pronunciation. It also involves knowing something about the meaning of silence. For English-speaking North Americans, silence is seen as a negative and, in fact, makes most people uncomfortable. Sometimes our North American inability to deal with silence gets us into trouble when communicating across cultures. Take, for example, Rick Highsmith, an executive from Portland, Oregon, who was less than successful when negotiating an acceptable price for his company's product with a Japanese firm. After a thorough sales presentation, Rick made a price offer that he felt best represented the interests of both parties involved. The Japanese met his offer with silence, while casting their eye toward the table. After several moments of silence, Rick said that he thought his firm might be able to reduce the price a bit. This offer too was met with silence. Unable to disguise his frustration, Rick made his last and final offer of a reduced price, which the Japanese eventually accepted. Rick was startled when one member of the Japanese negotiating team told him that his first price offer was an acceptable offer. It was usual, however, for Japanese to consider the offer silently for several minutes before accepting and declaring their acceptance. Thus, by not understanding the meaning of silence in Japanese culture, Rick was much less successful in negotiating the contract than he could have been.

Sociolinguistics

Anthropological linguistics has devoted much of its time and energy to the study of languages as logical systems of knowledge and communication. Recently, however, linguists have taken a keen interest in how people actually speak to one another in any given society. Whereas other linguists tended to focus on uniform structures (morphology, phonology, and syntax), sociolinguists concentrate on variations in language use depending on the social situation or context in which the speaker is operating.

In much the same way that entire speech communities adapt their language to changing situations, so do the individuals in those speech communities. Bilingualism and multilingualism are obvious examples of the situational use of language. A Hispanic junior high school student in Miami, for example, may speak English in the classroom and Spanish at home. But often

FIGURE 6.9 Japanese and Americans use different communication styles, which can influence the outcome of negotiations.

© MIXA/Getty Images

people who are monolingual speak different forms of the same language depending on the social situation. To illustrate, the language that a college sophomore might use with a roommate is appreciably different from the language used when talking to grandparents; the expressions heard in a football locker room would hardly be appropriate to use in a job interview. In short, what is said and how it is said are often influenced by variables such as the age, sex, and relative social status of the people involved. Whether we are talking about selectively using either totally different language or variations on the same language, the process is known as *code switching*.

The major focus of sociolinguistics is the relationship between language and social structure (Figure 6.10). What can we tell about the social relationships between two people from the language they use with each other? Analyzing terms of address can be particularly useful in this regard. Professor Green, for example, could be addressed as Dr. Green, Ma'am, Professor, Ms. Green, Elizabeth, Darling, Doc, Prof, or Beth, depending on who is doing the addressing. One would not expect that her mother or husband would refer to her as Ma'am or that her students would call her Beth. Instead we would expect that the term of address chosen would reflect appropriately the relative social status of the two parties. That is, in middle-class US society, the reciprocal use of first names indicates a friendly, informal relationship between equals; the reciprocal use of titles followed by last names indicates a more formal relationship between people of roughly the same status; and the nonreciprocal use of first names and titles is found among people of unequal social status. We would also expect that the same person might use different terms of address for Professor Green in different social situations. Her husband might call her Beth at a cocktail party, Darling when they are making love, and Elizabeth when engaged in an argument.

Diglossia

The situational use of language in complex speech communities has been studied by Charles Ferguson (1964), who coined the term *diglossia*. Ferguson used this term to refer to a linguistic situation in which two varieties of the same language (such as standard form, dialect, or pidgin) are spoken by the same person at different times and under different social circumstances.

Ferguson illustrated the concept of diglossia by citing examples from a number of linguistic communities throughout the world, including the use of classical or Koranic Arabic and local forms of Arabic in North

FIGURE 6.10 What features of women's political discourse are culture-bound or what features transcend cultural or other social boundaries? Former Secretary of State Hillary Rodham Clinton continues to champion women's rights nationally and globally, as she meets with women of the Upendo Women's Cooperative group in Mlandizi, Tanzania.

Africa and the Middle East, the coexistence of standard German and Swiss German in Switzerland, and the use of both French and Haitian Creole in Haiti. In speech communities where diglossia is found, there is a long-standing connection between appreciably different linguistic varieties. Which form is used carries with it important cultural meanings. For example, in all cases of diglossia, one form of the language is considered to be high and the other low (see Table 6.3). High forms of the language are associated with literacy, education,

TABLE 6.3

Diglossia

High Form	Low Form
Religious services	Marketplace
Political speeches	Instructions to subordinates
Legislative proceedings	Friendly conversations
University lectures	Folk literature
News broadcasts	Radio/TV programs
Newspapers	Cartoons
Poetry	Graffiti

SOURCE: Charles A. Ferguson, "Diglossia," in *Language in Culture and Society: A Reader in Linguistics*, ed. Dell Hynes (New York: Harper & Row, 1964), pp. 429–39.

code switching When speakers of multiple languages combine words or elements of a language in a single conversation.

diglossia The situation in which two forms of the same language are spoken by people in the same language community at different times and places.

and, to some degree, religion. The high forms are usually found as part of religious services, political speeches in legislative bodies, university lectures, news broadcasts, and newspapers. Low forms are likely to be found in the marketplace, in instructions given to subordinates, in conversations with friends and relatives, and in various forms of pop culture, such as folk literature, television and radio programs, cartoons, and graffiti.

It is generally agreed that high forms of the language are superior to low forms, and often the use of the high form is associated with the elite and the upwardly mobile. This general superiority of the high form is at least partially the result of its association with religion and the fact that much of the literature of the language is written in the high form.

Specialized Vocabularies

Code switching is seen quite dramatically in complex societies made up of a number of special interest groups, each with its own specialized vocabulary. Jean Lave and Etienne Wenger (1991) introduced the concept of "community of practice," a group of people within a large society who interact regularly around specialized activities. They may be skateboarders or stockbrokers, prostitutes or politicians, or truck drivers or computer geeks. They may spend much time together, or they may have only limited contact with one another. Similarly, members of a community of practice may have contact with one another for decades, or their membership may be much more short lived. From a linguistic perspective, however, these "communities" develop unique ways of communicating, complete with their own signature expressions.

Code switching between two distinct languages involves a *blending* of the two languages simultaneously. So-called Spanglish (the blending of Spanish and English) has become a popular vernacular in places such as San Diego and Miami. Words from both languages are combined into a single sentence, such as "Vamos a la store para comprar milk." (Translation: "Let's go to the store to buy milk.") Though once disparaged by language purists, Spanglish is gaining considerable respectability among academics such as Amherst College professor Ilan Stavans, who recently published a Spanglish dictionary with 4,500 entries (Stavans 2003). Today Spanglish has become more mainstream, showing up in television and film scripts, in McDonald's advertisements, and even on a line of Hallmark greeting cards. As the use of Spanglish becomes increasingly widespread, a debate is emerging about whether Spanglish is a fleeting form of slang or an emerging new language. It may be too early to answer that question, largely because Spanglish is still highly spontaneous and fluid (Hernandez 2003). Interestingly, a similar composite

language called Denglish (a combination of Deutsch and English) is becoming commonplace in Germany and is finding its way into advertisements for such German companies as Lufthansa and Douglas Perfumes.

Dialects

The study of dialects is also the concern of sociolinguistics. *Dialects* are regional or class variations of a language that are sufficiently similar to be mutually understood. It is not uncommon for certain dialects in complex speech communities to be considered substandard or inferior to others. Such claims are based on social or political rather than linguistic grounds. That is, minority dialects are often assigned an inferior status by the majority for the purpose of maintaining the political, economic, and social subordination of the minority. People who are not from the South regard certain Southernisms such as "y'all" (as in the statement "Y'all come by and see us now") as quaint and colorful regional expressions (at best) or inferior and inappropriate incursions into Standard US English (at worst). A more obvious example is majority attitudes toward the non-Standard English dialect used by Black Americans in northern cities. Clearly such expressions as "You be goin' home" or "Don't nobody go nowhere" will never be used by major network newscasters. Although such expressions are considered to be inferior by speakers of Standard English, these forms demonstrate logically consistent grammatical patterns and in no way prevent the expression of complex or abstract ideas. Non-Standard English should not be viewed as simply a series of haphazard mistakes in Standard English. Rather it is a fully efficient language with its own unique set of grammatical rules that are applied consistently. Thus, in linguistic terms, the grammar and phonology of Black urban English are no less efficient than the language of the rich and powerful (Hecht, Collier, and Ribeau 1993; Rickford 1999).

Some linguists have suggested that during the last several decades of the twentieth century, regional dialects in the United States became less noticeable because of mass media, increased geographic mobility, and differing immigration patterns. Another possible explanation is that because regional dialects or accents are associated with certain socioeconomic classes, they are often dropped as people move up the social ladder. This seems to be the case with New Yorkese, the accent that the rest of the nation loves to hate. No matter where you are from, you will probably recognize some of these classic New Yorkese expressions:

- Didja (did you) or dincha (didn't you) go to the park?
- I need to go to the terlet (toilet).
- I understand you had a baby goil (girl).
- You wanna cuppa (cup of) kawfee (coffee)?
- Hey, alia (all of) youze (you) guys, get ovuh hee (over here).

---

dialects Regional or class variations of a language that are sufficiently similar to be mutually intelligible.

This last example of dropping the *r* sound in the word *here* is characteristic of New Yorkese. Several linguists have shown, however, that "*r*-lessness" is more common among lower-class than upper-class New Yorkers. William Labov (1972) conducted a series of spontaneous interviews with salespeople in three New York department stores: S. Klein's (a low-prestige store), Macy's (moderate prestige), and Saks Fifth Avenue (high prestige). Labov found that clerks in the high-prestige store were significantly more likely to pronounce their *r*'s than were clerks in the low-prestige store. The Labov study reminds us, first, that dialects can vary according to social class, and second, that these linguistic patterns are constantly changing. During the 1940s, for example, *r*-lessness was found widely in the speech of all New Yorkers. But over the last half-century, wealthy, fashionable, and upwardly mobile New Yorkers modified their twang for social reasons. It is no coincidence that there are twenty-eight listings for diction coaches in the Manhattan Yellow Pages.

Perhaps the accent that carries the highest status in the United States is not from the United States at all but from the United Kingdom. The so-called British accent is associated—often erroneously—with high levels of charm, sophistication, wealth, and education. British accents often are sought out for jobs as receptionists, voices on radio commercials, and employees of telephone message production companies. For some, it is considered classier than Standard US English and even a bit regal, depending on the speaker because just as in US English there are dialectical variations of high and low speakers. What English is spoken on an English Polo field may well indeed be different from the English spoken on a cricket pitch or rugby pitch (Figure 6.11).

CROSS-CULTURAL MISCUE

✳ An imperfect understanding of other languages has had some embarrassing consequences for North Americans engaging in international marketing. US chicken entrepreneur Frank Perdue decided to translate one of his successful advertising slogans into Spanish. Unfortunately the new slogan did not produce the desired results. The slogan "It takes a tough man to make a tender chicken" was translated into Spanish as "It takes a virile man to make a chicken affectionate."

The Pepsi-Cola Company, when attempting to use its catchy advertising slogan "Come alive with Pepsi" in Asia, learned that it was translated "Pepsi brings your dead ancestors back from the grave." And the Dairy Association's wildly successful US ad campaign of "Got milk?" had the unfortunate translation "Are you lactating?" when used in Mexico. Although all of these cross-cultural advertising blunders cause us to snicker, they can result in a loss of revenue and diminished product credibility.

FIGURE 6.11 (Top) Prince Charles playing cricket will use different sport terms on the pitch than those playing rugby (bottom).

Language, Nationalism, and Ethnic Identity

It should be recognized that language plays an important symbolic role in the development of national and ethnic identities. In some situations powerful political leaders or factions attempt to suppress local languages for the sake of standardization across a nation-state. The country of Tanzania is a case in point. When Tanzania became independent in the 1960s, its leaders were faced with the task of running a country that contained 120 mutually unintelligible languages. To administer a country with such linguistic diversity, the government adopted Swahili as the official national language. This meant that Swahili became the language of instruction in schools, government bureaucracies, and parliament. Although Swahili (an Arabicized Bantu language) is no one's first language, it has served as a unifying *lingua franca* (common language) for the many linguistic communities that reside in Tanzania. To be certain, each linguistic group would have preferred to have had its own language declared the official language, but the adoption of Swahili early in Tanzania's history as a sovereign nation enabled the country to standardize its national language and get on with the business of nation-building.

In many other situations, the establishment of official languages has not gone so smoothly. In an attempt to strengthen the power of the Spanish nation, the Francisco Franco government made a number of unsuccessful attempts to suppress the minority Basque and Catalan languages by forbidding people from speaking them in public or using them on signs or billboards. But people take their languages seriously, and languages often become a rallying point for expressing one's cultural identity. Each time a strong national government tries to suppress a minority language or establish the majority language as the official one, it is likely that minority populations will strongly resist. The government of India, for example, has had to abort its several attempts to establish Hindi as the official language of India because riots erupted in non-Hindi-speaking areas of the country. And closer to home, the French-speaking province of Quebec, which for decades has had laws restricting the use of the English language in schools and on signs, nearly won its independence from Canada in 1995 largely over the issue of language policy.

In 2004 official languages were a hot topic in the news when the European Union expanded from fifteen nations to twenty-five. The inclusion of ten new member nations increased the number of official languages from eleven to twenty and the number of translations needed from 110 to 380. Unlike the United Nations with its 191 members, which conducts its business in six official languages,

the European Union decided to adopt the democratic principle of allowing business to be conducted in *all* of the twenty official languages. The problems involved with 380 translations and interpretations are thought to be less objectionable than silencing any particular language, such as Maltese or Czech. Though cumbersome, the actual cost of salaries for all of these translators is estimated to be less than $2.50 per citizen. So, unlike many nations that have excluded certain languages from the conduct of business, the European Union has affirmed the democratic ideal of cooperation and linguistic parity (Riding 2004: 3). Similarly since 2007 the US Election Assistance Commission provides voter education material in six different languages, including Chinese, Japanese, Korean, Spanish, Tagalog, and Vietnamese. California, because of its diverse ethnic population, is one of the states that makes voter education material in multiple languages.

Nonverbal Communication

To comprehend fully how people in any particular culture communicate, we must become familiar with their nonverbal forms of communication in addition to their language. *Nonverbal communication* is important because it helps us to interpret linguistic messages and often carries messages of its own. In fact it has been suggested that up to 70 percent of all messages sent and received by humans are nonverbal (Figure 6.12).

Like language, nonverbal forms of communication are learned and therefore vary from one culture to another. Even though some nonverbal cues have the same meaning in different cultures, an enormous range

---

nonverbal communication The various means by which humans send and receive messages without using words (for example, gestures, facial expressions, and touching)

Myrleen Pearson/Alamy

FIGURE 6.12 Teenagers use verbal language and nonverbal language to communicate as they practice for the debate team.

of variation in nonverbal communication exists among cultures. In some cases a certain message can be sent in a number of different ways by different cultures. For example, whereas in the United States we signify affirmation by nodding, the same message is sent by throwing the head back in Ethiopia, by sharply thrusting the head forward among the Semang of Malaya, and by raising the eyebrows among the Dyaks of Borneo.

Humans communicate without words in a number of important ways, including hand gestures, facial expressions, eye contact, touching, space usage, scents, gait, and stance. A thorough discussion of these and other aspects of nonverbal communication, based on the recent literature, is beyond the scope of this textbook. A brief examination of three of the more salient types of nonverbal communication—hand gestures, posture, and touching—will help convey the importance of this form of human communication.

Hand Gestures

Consider how many hand gestures we use every day. We cup our hand behind the ear as a nonverbal way of communicating that we cannot hear. We thumb our noses at those we do not like. We can thumb a ride on the side of the highway. We can wave hello or good-bye. We tell people to be quiet by holding our forefinger vertically against our lips. We give the peace sign by holding up our forefinger and middle finger, but we send a different message when we flash half of the peace sign. Or, by making a circle with our thumb and forefinger, we can communicate that everything is A-OK. However, problems arise with these gestures when we cross national boundaries. Although the A-OK sign carries a positive, upbeat message in North America, it refers to money in Japan, zero (worthless) in France, male homosexuality in Malta, and obscenity in parts of South America. Thus, a single hand gesture carries with it many different meanings throughout the world. There are also many examples of the opposite phenomenon—namely, the use of different gestures to send the same message. For example, the nonverbal ways of communicating admiration for an attractive woman vary widely throughout the world. The Frenchman kisses his fingertips, the Italian twists an imaginary moustache, and the Brazilian curls one hand in front of another as if he is looking through an imaginary telescope.

Posture (Body Stance)

The way that people hold their bodies often communicates information about their social status, religious practices, feelings of submissiveness, desires to maintain social distance, and sexual intentions—to mention several areas. When communicating, people tend to orient their bodies toward others by assuming a certain stance or posture. A person can stand over another person, kneel, or "turn a cold shoulder," and in each

case the body posture communicates something different. The meaning attached to different body postures varies from one culture to another and is learned in the same way that other aspects of a culture are internalized. To illustrate this point, we can look at differences in body posture that people assume when relaxing. People in the United States, for example, are sitters, whereas people in some rural parts of Mexico are squatters. This basic cultural difference has actually been used by the US Border Patrol to identify illegal immigrants. According to Larry Samovar and Richard Porter (1991), while flying surveillance planes at low altitudes over migrant worker camps in southern California, the border patrol can tell which groups of campers are squatting and which are sitting, the implication being that the squatters are the illegal aliens.

Perhaps one of the most visible and dramatic nonverbal messages sent by posture is submissiveness. Generally submissiveness is conveyed by making oneself appear smaller by lowering the body (crouching, cowering, or groveling). As part of their religious practices, some Christians kneel, Catholics genuflect, and Muslims kowtow, an extreme form of body lowering in which the forehead is brought to the ground. Nowhere is bowing more important to the process of communication today than in Japanese society. Bowing initiates interaction between two Japanese, it enhances and embellishes many parts of the ensuing conversation, and it is used to signal the end of a conversation. As an indication of how pervasive bowing is in contemporary Japan, some Japanese department stores employ people whose sole function is to bow to customers as they enter the store. In fact bowing is so ingrained in the Japanese psyche that some Japanese actually bow to invisible partners at the other end of a telephone line.

Touching

Touching is perhaps the most personal and intimate form of nonverbal communication. Humans communicate through touch in a variety of ways and for a variety of purposes, including patting a person on the head or back, slapping, kissing, punching, stroking, embracing, tickling, shaking hands, and laying-on of hands. Every culture has a well-defined set of meanings connected with touching; that is, each culture defines who can touch whom, on what parts of the body, and under what circumstances. Some cultures have been described as high-touch cultures and others as low-touch. Some studies (Paige et al 2002) have suggested that eastern European, Jewish, and Arab cultures tend to be high-touch cultures, whereas northern European cultures such as German and Scandinavian cultures tend to be low-touch. The difference between high- and low-touch cultures can be observed in public places, such as subways or elevators. For example, Londoners (from a low-touch culture) traveling in a crowded subway are likely to assume a rigid posture, studiously avoid eye contact, and refuse to even acknowledge the presence of other passengers. The French (from a high-touch culture), on the other hand, have no difficulty leaning and pressing against one another in a crowded Parisian subway. It is surprising that there can be such significant differences in touching behavior between the English and the French, two groups separated by only a narrow channel of water.

Communication and Technology in the Twenty-First Century

The revolution in information technology (IT) has had profound consequences on the way humans communicate in the twenty-first century as well as for human societies in general. Most "twenty-somethings" today fail to realize how their parents communicated just a generation ago. Back in the "dark ages" of the 1980s, people could communicate (that is, send and receive messages) by writing letters or speaking either face to face or via such technology as the telephone, telegraph, radio, television, or carrier pigeon. It was not until the 1990s that the Internet and cell phones emerged as the communication technologies of choice. When viewed from this narrow time frame of several decades, the changes in the number of ways of communicating at our disposal today are truly revolutionary.

Innovations in Internet technology have revolutionized how information is delivered and how we produce and consume information. At the same time they have transformed our social lives and behaviors as citizens. Many IT commentators argue that the new technology of e-mail, online discussions, networking websites such as Facebook, and high-speed, web-powered information diffusion will lead to a more informed, engaged, and influential population. Others, however, contend that the recent communications revolution may instead spawn a population of impressionable, impersonal, and easily manipulated people. Although the impact of the Internet and cell phone technology on society is still widely debated, one thing is certain: The new twenty-first-century technologies are powerful vehicles for change in the way humans communicate and share information.

The new information technology—instant messaging, cell phones, smartphones, web sites, and blogs—has altered the way people are communicating. Because it is less expensive to text message than to actually speak on one's cell phone, there has been an explosion of text messaging in recent years (Figure 6.13). According to the International Association for the Wireless Telecommunications Industry (www.ctia.org), approximately 4.1 billion text messages were sent over US carrier networks every day in 2009, nearly twice as many as in the preceding year. Although an enormous number of text messages are being sent today, the

FIGURE 6.13 Young couple walking along the street using their mobile phones to text with others and not speak with one another.

messages themselves lack both intimacy and specific details. Because the typical cell phone screen accommodates only about 160 characters, the craze of text messaging encourages blandness, brevity, and superficiality. On the other hand, it does encourage creativity in devising such shorthand symbols as *gr8*, *2moro*, and *4ever*. (For an entire online dictionary of chat acronyms and texting shorthand, see www.netlingo.com/emailsh.cfm.)

Although text messaging has become widespread in the United States, it is even more widely used in Asia. This greater popularity in China is as a result, at least in part, of the nature of the Chinese language. Because in Standard Chinese the names of numbers sound similar to certain words, it is possible to send the message "I love you" by simply typing the number 520 or "Drop dead" by using 748. Moreover, in China leaving voicemails is considered both rude and humiliating to the sender whose message must be left with a machine. Using text messages enables both senders and recipients to save face by eliminating the human voice.

Because texting is second nature to teenagers and young people in general in the United States, it serves as a communication divide between children and the older generations. Because most people over age

Applied Anthropology and Internet Communication

❀ Do you tweet on twitter, blog, partake in a chat room to lol? Do you use the Internet to connect to Bing, Google, or some other Web browser? Are you part of a listserv or enjoy watching YouTube videos? If you have done any of these activities you will recognize that your own language and culture are changing, especially how we communicate to others.

Mark Zuckerberg, a young man who was given the honor of being named *Time* Magazine's Person of the Year for 2010, was recognized for creating a web site that has transformed the world on so many levels and in a short time span. What started out as an in-house project to help college students connect to one another in 2004 has expanded to Facebook, Inc., a global social network with more than one billion participants. This achievement is a historic transformation in human culture, especially in computing communication and technology.

Facebook is transforming the way friends, family members, and strangers communicate with one another. In the past, how did we breakup with a boyfriend or talk about our exes, remember our friends birthdays or make a date? Conversations with family and friends might have been held in private, sharing details of the unmentionable, the routine of everyday life, sad events and joyous moments. Now they are out there for anyone to view and exchange, if one is "linked" as a friend. Facebook has enabled communicating what was once "private" to communication that is "public" and interactive, even among total strangers and future employers.

This global social and cultural phenomenon of being on Facebook or for that matter part of any online social network is transforming the concept of "friend," and "community." Of course not everyone is connected to everyone as a network friend. However, even that concept of friend has morphed to include not physical beings, but entities. One can be a "friend" to CNN or to Aunt Sallie. So how does it work?

To be included in this social network, *users* create a personal profile where they can add other users as *friends* and exchange messages. They can share photographs, video clips, stories, anything digital and all uncensored. And if you do not add photos others may do it for you with a simple "tag." Users can join or create interest groups, organized by workplace, school, or college, or any other unifer, and be one with many. To be in the loop, connected to the social network, is to be kept up to date with the latest news and information, they claim.

Facebook has fundamentally changed the way people interact with each other. It allows people to stay in touch with others that might otherwise drift away either because of distance or time commitments. It allows people to talk to others without them being on the other end of anything, so to speak. It does not require a person to be at a computer, cell phone, iPod, or any of the other latest gadgetry we used to communicate digitally. Updates are made to our "friends" so they can be keep up with our activities. In fact, Facebook has been used in a variety ways beyond talking to friends. Some people use it to let others know they are trapped or lost, knowing that their friends are regular viewers and can get them help quickly. For others it is a way to interact and voice opinions. For example, Facebook has been used to launch political campaigns, fund-raise, and it is widely used in commerce and advertising. Yet, Facebook is not universally accepted as a good thing. As a global social network, it has been met with controversies and blocked (yet millions find a way around the ban) in several countries including the People's Republic of China, Vietnam, Iran, Pakistan, and Syria for political or religious reasons. It has also been banned at workplaces to avoid employee's wasting company time. Can you imagine your life without being connected to an online social network?

Questions for Discussion

1. The natural question, of course, is why has Facebook been able to transform how people communicate with one another?

2. What is it about this online service that seems to draw people in? Is it because people have a deep desire to feel part of a community?

3. Have some cultures lost the art of speaking face to face and storytelling?

4. From an applied cultural perspective, in what ways do you see language and culture changing in the future?

---

seventy do not engage in social texting, their grandchildren use it as a way to communicate with their friends out of earshot of their elders. Young people, having developed their own texting abbreviations, are now able to send and receive messages in school, at the dinner table, or even during church services without sacrificing their privacy. Teens in the United States, in other words, use text messaging as a way to exclude their parents from their youth culture.

Because of the need to be brief, text messaging frees us from having to communicate with intimacy or emotional content. One can flirt, make a date, or even break up with a "significant other" without having to divulge any emotions. In fact, this may be the major attraction of this new twenty-first-century mode of communication: It preserves the immediacy and efficiency of face-to-face communication without the burden of emotional self-disclosure.

Text messaging is widely used by young people in rural India as a way to circumvent the long-standing traditional barriers against premarital mingling. Unlike their counterparts in the United States, or even Mumbai or Delhi, singles in rural India can not flirt or "cruise for dates" at crowded bars or clubs. Unmarried women are expected to marry young, show no interest in men's flirtatious advances, and marry a person chosen for them by their families. And because most singles in India live with their families and share rooms with siblings, they have few opportunities to speak privately with a member of the opposite sex. Text messaging offers young Indian singles a way to overcome their awkwardness and lack of experience in interacting with the opposite sex. Singles are, in other words, able to communicate in private without having to worry about either violating traditional customs or revealing intimate feelings.

Twenty-first-century IT is affecting even the authenticity of our communications. With the dramatic growth of cell phone use over the past decade (more than a billion are in use worldwide), a new phenomenon has emerged, at least in many Western cultures—*faking cell phone conversations*. Some people in public spaces pretend to be talking on their cell phones to avoid social contact with panhandlers or unwanted approaches by men. Others, frequently men, conduct phony conversations to give themselves an air of importance while "checking out" women. Still others may engage in cell phone subterfuge just to communicate to others around them that they are sufficiently socially connected to at least have someone to call, even if they do not. And, who could forget the brazen woman who robbed four banks in northern Virginia in October 2005 while chatting on her cell phone the entire time?

Cell phone technology now makes it possible to send deceptive or false messages. For example, new applications now allow users to add various background sounds to phone calls to make it seem as if they are somewhere else, such as caught in traffic or near heavy machinery rather than in a singles' bar. It is now possible for video phone users to select a background of their choice before answering the phone, thus allowing a cheating husband or wife to answer a call with a photo of the office in the background. Cell phone users who want to get out of work or an unwanted social engagement now have a convenient excuse. According to Matt Richtel (2004), a group of several thousand cell phone users have formed an "alibi and excuse club" in which one member lies on behalf of another. Along the same lines, Cingular Wireless now offers a new technological mechanism for sending false messages called "Escape-A-Date." If you are going on a date with someone for the first time, you can arrange to have your cell phone ring at a prearranged time. A prerecorded message then guides you through a script that makes it sound to the unsuspecting first-time date as

though you must rush off. If the date is going well, however, you simply turn off your cell phone. All of these recently developed cell phone "functionalities" have affected the way Westerners send and receive messages (or, to use a contemporary euphemism, provide "disinformation").

And, finally, modern-day technology, such as the World Wide Web, has profound implications for the way we *define* the words in our language. In pre-Internet times, the hard-copy dictionary was the final authority for what a word means, how it is used and how to spell it. The authors of dictionaries (lexicographers) traditionally arrived at their definitions by carefully analyzing as many examples as possible of how a particular word is used. Even though some complex words found in any standard desk dictionary can have as many as nine or ten possible meanings, even these definitions fail to cover all possible usages. According to lexicographer Erin McKean (2009: 16), a recent study showed that in a set of randomly chosen passages from modern fiction, 13 percent of the nouns, verbs, and adjectives were used in ways not listed in large desk dictionaries. The major shortcoming of the traditional dictionary is that the limited space available permits the inclusion of only a sampling of how words are used. There are, in other words, many contemporary usages that never make it into a standard dictionary because of space limitations.

The beauty of the Internet, however, is that there are virtually no space limitations. As a result, it is possible for twenty-first-century lexicographers to define words by including every conceivable example of the word's use. These examples may be generated electronically not only from literature, nonfiction writings, and newspapers, but also from web sites, blogs, and social networking sites. In fact, this is what the online dictionary called Wordnik.com is currently doing—text-mining every available example of how a particular word in used in everyday standard English and then including these examples, along with the definitions, in the nearly infinite space of the World Wide Web. It may be that the widespread use of cell phone technology and software applications will be the life raft for preserving endangered languages by inspiring young and old to learn to read and write in their native language. In this regard the potential for applied perspectives that can be extended to language and culture may be endless.

Summary

1. Language—and the capacity to use symbols—is perhaps the most distinctive hallmark of our humanity.

2. Although there are approximately six thousand discrete languages in the world today, many languages from small-scale societies are becoming moribund or extinct at an alarming rate.

3. Although nonhumans also engage in communication, human communication systems are unique in important respects. First, human communication systems are open; that is, they are capable of sending an infinite number of messages. Second, humans are the only animals that can communicate about events that happened in the past or might happen in the future. Third, human communication is transmitted largely through tradition rather than experience alone.

4. All human languages are structured in two ways. First, each language has a phonological structure made up of rules that govern how sounds are combined to convey meanings. Second, each language has its own grammatical structure comprising the principles that govern how morphemes are formed into words (morphology) and how words are arranged into phrases and sentences (syntax).

5. Like other aspects of culture, languages change over time in response to internal and external factors. Historical linguists want to know not only how languages change but also why they change.

6. Cultures can influence language to the extent that the vocabulary in any language tends to emphasize words that are adaptively important in that culture. Thus, the highly specialized vocabulary in US English involving the automobile is directly related to the cultural emphasis that North Americans give to that particular part of their technology.

7. According to the Sapir–Whorf hypothesis, language influences perception. Language, according to Sapir and Whorf, not only is a system of communicating but also establishes mental categories that affect the way in which people conceptualize the real world.

8. Just as languages vary widely in terms of vocabulary, grammar systems, and syntax, they also vary in features of linguistic style such as directness and tolerance for silence.

9. Sociolinguists are interested in studying how people's use of language depends on the social situation or context in which they are operating.

10. Language plays an important symbolic role in the development of national and ethnic identities, as exemplified in Canada, Tanzania, and the European Union.

11. As important as language is in human communication, the majority of human messages are sent and received without using words. Human nonverbal communication—which, like language, is learned and culturally variable—can be transmitted through facial expressions, gestures, eye contact, touching, and posture.

12. The revolution in information technology (cell phones, instant messaging, e-mails, chat rooms, blogs, etc.) has had a profound impact on how humans communicate. Although these and other technological innovations in the last several decades have led to a proliferation of messages sent and received quickly and efficiently, many messages lack both specific detail and personal intimacy.

Key Terms

arbitrary nature of language

bound morpheme

closed system of communication

code switching

cultural emphasis of language

cultural linguistics

descriptive linguistics

diachronic analysis

dialects

diglossia

displacement

free morpheme

grammar

historical linguistics

language family

morphemes

morphology

nonverbal communication

open system of communication

phonemes

phonology

Sapir–Whorf hypothesis

synchronic analysis

syntax

Critical Thinking Questions

1. Analyze the factors that have contributed to language change in your life time.

2. How have these language changes impacted other aspects of culture?

3. What role does technology play in modifying language? How might you incorporate future technological changes in understanding language and culture?

Online Study Resources

CourseMate

Access chapter-specific learning tools including learning objectives, practice quizzes, videos, flash cards, glossaries, web links, and more in your Cultural Anthropology CourseMate. Login to www.cengagebrain.com to access the resources your instructor has assigned and to purchase materials.

Samburu tribeswoman with baby calf,
Samburu National Reserve, Kenya

Subsistence Patterns

East Africa is known for its many different nomadic tribal groups who raise livestock; they are referred to as *pastoralists*. Tribal groups such as the Maasai, Gabra, Rendille Sumburu, Arrial, Pokot, and Turkana are just but a few that reside in either Kenya or Tanzania. For centuries these patrilineal and patriarchal societies raised cattle, and in some cases also goats, sheep, and camels. Climate change has affected many parts of the world and is threatening east African pastoralists. The two strongest environmental challenges pastoralists face are flood and drought cycles, and the accompanying problems associated with these extreme events. Flooding for pastoralists brings about subsequent decreased mobility, which limits forage availability for the livestock. With both humans and their animals becoming more sedentary during the flooding period, there is the increase of disease and pollution of surface water. Drought also brings additional pressures with increased competition for food and water resources (for humans and their animals), which often lead to famine. Development agencies have assisted in teaching western ranching techniques (with fences and confined grazing areas), but not with great success for animals or pastoralists. Other projects assist in range management, dairying, and reforestation. In some cases pastoralists have been forced to abandon their ways for other trades.

Anthropologist, Dr. Terry McCabe, who has been working among peoples of eastern Africa for the past thiry years, examines the process of livelihood diversification as an adaptive strategy to changing climates. His years of experience among the east African pastoralists offers a rare opportunity to examine cultural, economic, and political changes in light of environmental changes that have occurred in the life ways of local pastoralists in sites located in Tanzania, Uganda, Namibia, and Botswana. For some like the Maasai, they have chosen to adopt cultivation as well as outward migration to lessen the impact on their fragile environment. Such knowledge is useful for development initiatives and programs to assist local populations. For example, the Rural Agriculture and Pastoralism Programme (RAPP) assists pastoralists in Eastern Africa. RAPP is working with local peoples on projects related to natural resource management and projects that strengthen nonagricultural activities. By working in partnership with local peoples and national governments, respectively, RAPP is able to incorporate indigenous knowledge in policy debates dealing with animal health, biodiversity, plant genetic resources as well as in development planning. Anthropologists like McCabe and local community partners can play an important role in assisting programs in the region to manage the natural resources for pastoralists and marginal farmers in eastern Africa as a means to improving their overall food security and economic security. ■

Keren Su/China Span/Alamy

WHAT WE WILL LEARN

■ What are the different ways by which societies get their food?

■ How do technology and environment influence food-getting strategies?

■ How have humans adapted to their environments through the ages?

■ What applied initiatives have taken place to foster support for local food systems?

Critical to any culture's survival is meeting the society's basic needs for shelter and access to food and drinkable water. In one form or another, every culture has a system for procuring food: growing it, raising it, trading for it, and even shopping for it. The pattern for obtaining one's food is known as a *subsistence strategy*. As we know, not all food-getting systems or subsistence strategies are equitable. Within societies and between societies, some people have greater access to more food than others. We see examples of extremes in access or lack of access in countries where people are severely malnourished or dying of starvation, whereas in other countries people are dying from overconsumption with obesity, which has become a global epidemic.

In all parts of the world, both culture and the environment influence the traditions that are passed on from one generation to the next in terms of how food is obtained, what is considered food and how it is eaten, and who gets to eat and when. There are some regions of the world where people engage in the production of nonfood items for trade to purchase their food, such as growing tobacco, cotton, or trees for timber. Such cultures also are intimately in tune with their environments. In most Western countries, the majority of people are not tied to the land or to the sea for their subsistence strategy; they are not likely to be involved in the actual production of their sustenance. In other words, they shop for their food, becoming the modern-day hunter-gatherers of the supermarkets. What is amazing in the twenty-first century is that people can eat foods from all over the world year-round, thanks to globalization, food preservation, transportation systems, and storage facilities.

Before we go on we should identify the various subsistence strategies that have emerged. Like other aspects of culture, food-getting practices vary widely from one society to another and change over time (Figure 7.1). Nevertheless, it is possible to identify five major food-procurement categories found among the world's populations:

1. *Food foraging* (hunters and gatherers) is living by hunting animals, fishing, and gathering wild plants.

2. *Horticulture* (subsistence agriculture or garden agriculture) is low-intensity, small-scale cultivation using small fields, plots, or gardens. Horticulturalists rely on human power and simple tools to work small plots of land to produce food primarily for household consumption.

3. *Pastoralism* is animal husbandry. Pastoralists breed and care for domestic and other animals (camels, cattle, goats, horses, llamas, reindeer, sheep, and yaks) and then use their products (such as milk, meat, and blood) as their major food source and as an item for exchange.

4. *Intensive agriculture* is a large-scale and complex system of farming and animal husbandry. It is a more productive form of cultivation of food plants than horticulture, owing to the use of animal power (wooden or metal plows), mechanical power (tractors, reapers, combines), irrigation systems, and fertilizers to produce surpluses.

5. *Industrial agriculture* is commercial farming on a much larger scale than intensive agriculture, relying on complex machinery, high-yielding germ-plasm (DNA from animals and plant seeds), and distribution of products for domestic and export

FIGURE 7.1 (Left) Student volunteers harvest chard and kale at the Ceres based Heifer International farm. Produce will be transported and sold at the West Modesto Certified Farmers Market. (Right) Pastoralists in Kenya, Samburu District such as this Samburu boy, will take care of goats in their arid environment.

markets. It also is linked to processing systems—the transformation of raw commodities into processed food and nonfood items (i.e., corn fructose used as a flavoring in soft drinks and corn biomass converted into ethanol, a biodiesel fuel).

As we move forward in this chapter we examine a number of different ways by which societies obtain their food. We also explore the various ways in which food-getting strategies are influenced by technology and the environment. As you know, culture is at the heart of what makes each society different, and it is culture that influences what different peoples eat as well as how they go about getting food in the environment in which they live.

Westerners often consider traditional means of procuring food, such as nomadic hunting and gathering and pastoralism, as markedly different from the sedentary food-procurement systems of intensive agricultural and industrial agricultural. Before concluding that one particular means is superior to all others, however, let us look at the inherent logic in each food-procurement system. When we do that, we are likely to recognize that each particular food-getting strategy is adapted for its unique environment and the people involved.

Human Adaptation

Anthropologists, particularly those specializing in environmental anthropology, have always had an interest in how humans adjust to their natural environments. They want to know how a particular environment influences people and their culture, and conversely how the culture (and people's activities) influences the physical environment (Sutton and Anderson 2009). Throughout history the various patterns of subsistence have had an impact on the environment, and culture has enabled people to adapt to changing conditions. Some anthropologists refer to this as cultural ecology or human ecology, first introduced by Julian Steward (see Chapter 4). It is recognized that political and economic systems also influence the manner in which people get their food, how much they have, and where it is from. Political ecology, a theoretical perspective also discussed in Chapter 4, helps us to explore this kind of research. I bet you never guessed there was politics behind your burger quest (Mac attack).

When we speak of human adaptation to a particular environment, we are referring to two types of adaptation: *cultural* and *biological*. Cultural responses to cold climates include "technological" solutions such as building fires, using animal skins as clothing and blankets, and seeking refuge from the elements in caves or constructed dwellings. And let us not forget using wood fires, coal-burning stoves, and gas and electric heating systems for keeping warm. Humans who live in cold climates also engage in certain behaviors that are adaptive. They tend to eat more food, particularly fats and carbohydrates, especially during the colder months; they engage in greater amounts of activity obtaining food and getting fuel for heat, which increases their internal body temperature; and they curl up when sleeping to reduce the surface area of exposure and resulting heat loss. Some would say many cultures have gone soft with today's modern housing and stocked refrigerators and food pantries. Members of such cultures now have a hard time going without such conveniences, which is especially noted when there are long power outages.

Recent economic changes coupled with environmental changes have made more communities, globally, less food secure. Ironically in the United States, traditionally known for over-production of many food items now has many communities living in food deserts. A *food desert* is generally an area found in an urban setting with little or no access to large grocery stores that offer fresh and affordable foods (fresh fruit, vegetables, meats, dairy, grains) needed to maintain a healthy diet (Smith 2012). Food deserts tend to have many more fast-food restaurants and convenience stores with limited, over-priced food items as a source of food stuffs. Using the US Department of Agriculture locator web site you can find your state and locate food deserts in your area (http://www.ers.usda.gov/data-products/food-desert-locator.aspx). Other web sites also exist that allow you to identify the nearest farmers markets or community-supported agricultural (CSA) farmers. Such web sites might be useful to combat food deserts by helping people learn how to source and eat seasonally local food products.

Adapting to One's Environment

In today's modern world, technology has enabled humans to adapt to a wide range of environments on earth, on water, and even in outer space; to produce vast amounts of food; and to protect ourselves from the heat and cold with air conditioners and furnaces. Yet many small-scale societies have made fitting adaptations to their natural environment without the benefit of modern science and technology. Many groups living in remote parts of the world are so well adapted to their surroundings that they have been able to manage their essential resources in highly efficient ways for millennia. They often have enormous knowledge of plant life that is useful for eating, building houses, and curing illnesses. They cultivate crops by managing

---

food desert An area found in an urban setting with little or no access to large grocery stores that offer fresh and affordable foods (fresh fruit, vegetables, meats, dairy, grains) needed to maintain a healthy diet and tend to have many more fast-food restaurants and convenience stores with limited, over-priced food items as a source of nutrition.

the soil, controlling moisture levels, preventing erosion, attracting certain organisms to reduce pests, and pacing their horticultural activities to correspond to seasonal cycles. In short, they use their accumulated knowledge to maximize the land's productivity and their own long-term benefits. And pastoralists also learn to manage their environment in such a way that their animals benefit directly from the available resources and thereby indirectly aid human adaptation.

We should not overly romanticize small-scale societies, however, by thinking that they always live in total harmony with their environments. Some cultures overfarm their soil, overgraze their pastures, pollute their waters, and severely jeopardize both their livelihoods and their environments. This has been particularly true in recent years as many small-scale societies enter modern-market economies or external pressures force rapid change that are not sustainable for the culture or the environment. When not dealing with colonial governments, strong world market forces, or pressures from others encroaching on their resource base, however, many small-scale societies develop and maintain a means of survival that is highly adaptive, productive, sustainable, and environmentally friendly.

A number of studies by anthropologists document highly successful adaptations to the environment among contemporary societies, and we now have archaeological evidence to demonstrate successful land management in prehistoric societies. According to Kevin Krajick (1998), archaeological research in Peru indicates that the Incas used conservation practices such as irrigation canals, terracing, and tree planting to build a highly efficient agricultural system in the Peruvian highlands. Archaeologists and geologists have found that between 2000 B.C.E. and 100 A.D., pre-Incan people had overfarmed the land, causing severe soil erosion and degradation. Core soil samples indicate that by the time the Incas took over the area, alder trees were beginning to proliferate, whereas soil was less eroded and seeds from maize began to appear. Terraces were built by people who hauled soil to the hillsides from the valley and riverbeds below. And the Incas built a 31.2-mile canal system that provided water to hillside cultivators from streams and lakes located at higher altitudes. Researchers have suggested (based on both archaeological evidence and written accounts after the Spanish conquest in the early 1500s) that the Incas actually practiced agroforestry by purposefully planting trees and managing them as part of the agricultural system.

Some of the ancient Incan farming practices are being revived for contemporary residents of the area. Since 1995, local Peruvian farmers have rebuilt the terraces, reconstructed the canal system, and put

FIGURE 7.2 Traditional Inca terraces still in use today by local small-scale farmers in Pisac, near Cuzco, Peru, South America.

160 hectares under cultivation (Figure 7.2). Preliminary reports suggest that crops are growing well and using less fertilizer than is required in other areas. One of the major grains produced by the Incas was quinoa. Today quinoa and a variety of Inca potatoes are found in Western supermarkets. Clearly the Incas had hundreds of years to develop an agricultural system that maximized the utility of the land without degrading it. This example illustrates how people in the past can provide lessons for people in the present.

Today worldwide consumer appetites for cash crops such as corn, coffee, tea, cocoa, sugar, pineapples, soybeans, tobacco, trees (pine, teak, and neem), and flowers (poppies, roses, and tulips) have led to dramatic changes in traditional subsistence strategies and to the demise of traditional ecosystems all over the globe. Examining the often disastrous effects of industrial agricultural influences has given anthropologists heightened respect for

the ways in which traditional peoples have adapted to their natural environments. Consumer demand for wood furniture has resulted in deforestation of tropical areas and the replanting of plantation monocultured (single species) forests. Drilling for precious metals, minerals, and fossil fuels (coal, gas and oil) has also led to environmental degradation and the alteration of habitats. In Ecuador, the Huaorani and their neighbors have been fighting to protect their lands from international corporations extracting oil. Even when Western governments have administered their "foreign aid" programs for disaster relief or economic development, inattention to how local people relate to their natural environments has produced unfortunate consequences.

The relationship between environment and culture is illustrated in Uzbekistan in Central Asia. The drying up of the Aral Sea in Uzbekistan is one of the planet's most shocking disasters ("Aral Sea" 2010). The Aral Sea, once the world's fourth-largest lake, has now shrunk by 90 percent. The lake started to get smaller in the 1960s, when the Soviet Union embarked on a vast irrigation project, diverting water from rivers that fed the Aral Sea to boost cotton production in the central Asian deserts. The impact has been devastating on a number of fronts. By the 1990s, the dry seabed had become a salt desert covering thousands of square kilometers. Such changes are altering the local climate and creating further economic and ecological damage. By 2010, the once vibrant fishing economy is now only a memory. Fishing trawlers have been left stranded in the dried seabed. The salty sands are carried as far away as Scandinavia and Japan and plague the local inhabitants with health problems. The rapid effects of environmental changes on cultures such as the residents of Uzbekistan (most of which, unfortunately, are negative) can be studied over the course of years or decades rather than centuries.

Similar examples of the drying up of lakes and rivers are also found in northern China, countries in western, southern and eastern Africa, as well as India, Pakistan, and Brazil (Figure 7.3). Around the world, experts in water-resource management attribute the shrinking of rivers and lakes to environmental change and to the overuse of groundwater supply and deep aquifers. Growing populations and rapid economic development also contribute to the lessening of clean water supplies, which have increasing threats for fishing communities, agricultural communities, pastoralists, and the tourist industries in each of the affected

Zhou Ke/Xinhua Press/Corbis

FIGURE 7.3 In 2012 the dried-up lake bed of Poyang Lake in Duchang County of China has few fish and 120,000 residents in the county struggle for drinking water.

countries. For example, the Han River in northern China, Shijiu Lake, and Poyang Lake (large freshwaters lakes in north, central China), Lake Manyara in Tanzania, and Lake Chilwa in Malawi, are a few examples of extreme cases where lack of water threatens every way of life.

Environment and Technology

Which food-getting strategy is actually developed by any given culture depends, in large measure, on the culture's environment, technology, and way of life. The relationship between the physical environment and food-getting methods is not tidy. For example, people could reside in a rural area with fantastic soils conducive to good farming but choose to rely on a grocery store as their food source. We also know that the earth cannot easily be divided into neat ecological zones, each with its own unique and mutually exclusive climate, soil composition, vegetation, and animal life. Geographers often divide the earth's land surface into categories, including grasslands, deserts, tropical forests, temperate forests, polar regions, and mountain habitats. Some of these environments are particularly hospitable to the extent that they support a number of modes of food acquisition. Others are more limiting in the types of adaptations they permit. Anthropologists generally agree that the environment does not determine food-getting patterns but rather sets broad limits on the possibilities, especially when we consider that culture defines what is considered a food item. For example, among some cultures in Africa, Asia, and Latin America, insects such as ants, grasshoppers, grubs, locusts, termites, and other larvae are regular fare or snack foods, whereas in other cultures these items are not considered food but something that ought to be avoided. In Uganda after the rains, live winged termites are sold in the markets because some Ugandans enjoy roasting and eating them (Figure 7.4). In some Japanese restaurants one can find on a menu aquatic fly larvae sautéed in sugar and soy sauce, and in Bali one can sample wingless dragonflies boiled in coconut milk with ginger and garlic (see Applied Perspective Box on page 157 for further discussion on insect consumption).

In part it is technology—a part of culture—that helps people adapt to their specific environment. In fact the human species enjoys a tremendous adaptive advantage over all other species precisely because it has developed a wide range of technological solutions to the problems of survival. In many cases, cultures with complex technologies have gained greater control over their environments and their food supplies. Coupled with technology it is the knowledge a group has of its environment that is passed down from one generation to the next that facilitates a people's approach to cultural survival.

FIGURE 7.4 In Uganda after the rains, live winged termites and grasshoppers are sold in the markets. Some Ugandans enjoy roasting and eating them.

carrying capacity The maximum number of people a given society can support, given the available resources.

optimal foraging theory A theory that foragers choose those species of plants and animals that maximize their caloric intake for the time spent hunting and gathering.

The specific mode of food getting is influenced by the environment itself and its interface with a people—both their culture and their technology. To illustrate, the extent to which a hunting-and-gathering society is able to procure food depends not only on the sophistication of the society's tools but also on the abundance of plant and animal life in the environment and the society's knowledge of what is edible and how to process it into something people will consume. Similarly the productivity of a society based on irrigation agriculture varies according to the society's technology as well as environmental factors such as the availability of water and the natural nutrients in the water and in the soil. These environmental factors set an upper limit on the ultimate productivity of any given food-getting system and the size of the population it can support. Cultural ecologists call this limit the environment's *carrying capacity* (Glossow 1978; Sutton and Anderson 2009).

A natural consequence of exceeding the carrying capacity is damage to the environment, such as killing off too much game or depleting the soil of its nutrients for growing crops or raising animals. Societies cannot easily increase their food-getting productivity beyond the carrying capacity. Thus, if a society is to survive, it must meet the fundamental need of producing or procuring enough food and water to keep its population alive for the long term while not exhausting its natural resources. But beyond satisfying this basic minimal requirement for survival, societies also satisfy their distinctive and arbitrary desires for certain types of food. To a certain degree, people regularly consume the foods that are found naturally (or can be produced) in their immediate environment. Often, however, people go out of their way to acquire some special foods while avoiding other foods that may be both plentiful and nutritious in their local habitats.

Although early anthropologists wrote off such behavior as irrational and arbitrary, cultural ecologists in recent years have examined these peculiar behaviors more carefully and have found that they often make sense in terms of the energy expended versus the caloric value of the foods consumed. This theory—known as the *optimal foraging theory*—suggests that foragers will choose the animal and plant species that tend to maximize their caloric return for the time they spend searching, killing, collecting, and preparing (E. Smith 1983; Sutton and Anderson 2009). In other words, when specific foraging strategies are examined in ethnographic detail, decisions to seek out one food source and not others turn out to be quite rational because they are based on a generally accurate assessment of whether the search is worth the effort. To illustrate, the Ache, a foraging group from Paraguay, prefer to hunt peccaries (wild pigs) rather than armadillos, even though armadillos are easier to find and easier to

APPLIED PERSPECTIVE

Fighting Hunger with Edible Insects

For decades people have been fighting hunger. Back in the 1960s the green revolution with its hybrid seeds was supposed to rid the world of poverty in hunger. Now, we are well into the twenty-first century and hunger and poverty still abound in all regions of the world. At nearly 9 billion, the world's population continues to be faced with finding sustainable protein sources for everyone, especially in light of climate change, water shortages and other factors impeding food production. At the forefront of many food assistance programs has been the Food and Agriculture Organization (FAO) of the United Nations. Drawing on the work of anthropologists, entomologists (people who study insects) as well as entomophagy—the practice of eating insects—the FAO is stepping up to the plate again with a new initiatives that focus on edible insects.

Insects have long been a common food item in many parts of the world: Southeast Asia, Central Africa, and Latin America. It is cultural. Just as snails or *escargot* is regular fare in France or in French cuisine, and fish eggs are consumed in many fishing communities as roe, or as *caviar*, a pricey delicacy in upper-class communities, insects have met food needs for many. There are 1,700 edible species of insects. Some of the more popular ones include grubs, termites, scorpions, weaver ant larvae, crickets, and meal worms. Insects take up less space and they require less water to produce. They also produce less waste, especially when compared to a cow, pig or chicken. As Schmidt (2011:16) points out, "bugs are a sustainable, inexpensive source of protein. And raising, harvesting and selling them can be an excellent small-business opportunity for people in the developing world."

Eating insects is not a new thing, especially in developing countries. For example, Paul Votmann and Ester Mertens (2012), a researcher for FAO's Forestry Department, found that during the Central African bush meat crisis, a result of deforestation and unsustainable hunting practices, 30 percent of people's protein during the rainy season came from insects such as the caterpillar, the mopane worm, or the Emperor moth. Vantomme noted during the rainy season that catapillars were gathered by hand by women and children, providing an excellent source of protein, calcium, niacin and riboflavin. It was customary to eat them stewed, fried or ground into nutrient-rich flour. Given these valuable micronutrients, children and pregnant or breastfeeding women in Central Africa would consume the mopane worm in some form to combat or ward off malnutrition.

Given the ease with which these caterpillars are gathered from trees and the ground, they also provide extra income for rural families. Schmidt (2011:18) reports on one study from Botswana that found "the mopane worm generates about 13 percent of household income for rural families but accounts for only about 6 percent of the labor output. Rural people often sell them to traveling merchants, who then sell them at urban markets."

Scientists, nutritionists, economists, and other development specialists are looking to expand the edible-insect market. There are opportunities in the West for new import-export businesses, but most likely customers would be consuming insects as a luxury item rather than one of necessity. It is easier to expand the edible insect market in developing countries where there is a cultural tradition for entomophagy, bug-eating practice. One example is from the Philippines, where the mole cricket and June beetle are wrecking havoc in agricultural fields and creating an environmental concern. Scientists are now promoting the idea of harvesting these insects for consumption on a large scale rather than blasting the fields with insecticides, which creates a different kind of environmental concern. Eating the insects seems to have a greater benefit over the cost of chemically treating the fields. In another case researchers are looking to expand silkworm farming in Thailand to develop a commercial production of silkworm snacks.

The range of opportunities for development of a new subsistence strategy around edible insects—be they wild caught or farmed raised—has the potential for providing a sustainable protein source and income for many in the developing world. FAO is currently working in Laos where 40 percent of Lao children are malnourished or stunted by inadequate protein consumption. "Many Lao children and adults also suffer from deficiencies in micronutrients like iron, iodine and many vitamins" (Schmidt 2011:19). FAO believes that eating insects in quantity on a regular basis could address all of these deficiencies. Lao culture does recognize insects as food and a high percentage of the population eat them regularly. Currently, FAO trainers teach how to raise and breed crickets, palm weevils, mealworms, and weaver ants for food with an eye toward increasing production to make edible insects more widely available. Laos and Thailand are moving into commercial insect farms as a way to fight poverty, hunger and malnutrition.

What might happen in other parts of the world? Would you try roasted cricket for your next snack? Awareness, education, and economic opportunities might be all that is needed for a cultural shift that transforms food production and food-eating traditions to one that includes insect farming, harvesting, and consumption.

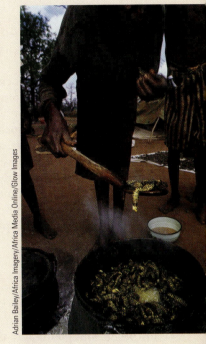

Masses of mopane worms hatch each year in Botswana. The worms are collected, boiled, dry roasted, and then sold as snacks or for cooking in traditional meals on the roadside.

Adrian Bailey/Africa Imagery/Africa Media Online/Glow Images

Questions for Further Thought

1. In working for the FAO on an edible-insect farming program what could an applied anthropologist contribute? What cultural information should be considered?

2. If you were a medical anthropologist or business anthropologist why would learning about edible insects be useful?

kill. This is a rational decision, however, because the peccaries produce considerably more calories of food per hour of hunting: 4,600 calories per hour for the peccaries compared to only 1,800 calories for the armadillos (Hill et al. 1987).

Major Food-Getting Strategies: Subsistence

The five forms of food procurement (hunting and gathering, horticulture, pastoralism, intensive agriculture, and industrial agriculture) are not mutually exclusive because most human societies use more than one strategy. Where this is the case, however, one form usually predominates. Moreover, in each category we can expect to find considerable variation largely because of differences in environment, historical experiences, technology, and cultural preferences. These five categories of food getting are explored in more detail in the following sections.

Hunting-and-Gathering Societies

Hunting and gathering (also known as *food collecting* or *foraging*)—as compared to food producing—involves the use of wild plants and animals that already exist in the natural environment. People have been hunting, gathering, and fishing for the overwhelming majority of the time they have been on earth. It was not until the *neolithic revolution*—approximately ten thousand years ago—that humans for the first time produced their food by means of horticulture or animal husbandry (B. Smith 1998). With the rise of food production and population expansion into many regions of the earth, the reliance on purely hunting and gathering as the means of a group's subsistence has been marginalized.

Even though most societies have become food producers, a handful of societies in the world today (with a combined population of less than a half million people) are still hunters and gatherers. Some hunter-gatherers are known to be food collectors; they live in differentiated environments where extreme weather differences (such as snow for months at a time) require them to exploit specific food resources and often store them in bulk (Binford 1980). Others are known as food

foragers, and they reside in undifferentiated environments where there are short-term weather events with limited seasonal variation that do not require them to store food. Their indigenous knowledge of when and where to go to obtain food items was traditionally sufficient to sustain them. Foraging and collecting societies vary widely in other cultural features and are found in a wide variety of environments (semi-deserts, tropical forests, and polar regions, among others). For example, some hunting-and-gathering societies, such as the Ju/'hoansi of the Kalahari Desert (formerly called the !Kung), live in temporary encampments, have small populations, do not store food. At the other end of the spectrum are groups such as the Kwakiutl of the Canadian Pacific coast, who live in permanent settlements, have relatively dense populations, and live on food reserves. Despite the considerable variations among contemporary foragers and collectors, it is possible to make the following four generalizations about most of them:

1. *Food-collecting/foraging societies have low population densities.* This is because they have thresholds for extraction that is using what is in their environment so that they do not overexploit their resources. Living below the carrying capacity at which they believe their environment can sustain them has enabled such populations to reside in particular habitats for millennia.

2. *Foraging and collecting societies are usually nomadic or semi-nomadic.* By and large, hunters and gatherers move periodically from place to place in search of wild animals and vegetation and usually do not recognize individual land rights. Hunters need to be sufficiently mobile to follow migrating game. Collectors are more likely to have a semi-permanent residence, however, with task groups going out to collect food items and then returning. Collectors, who need to store food, have limited mobility, whereas foragers, who do not store food, are more mobile.

3. *The basic social unit among foragers and collectors is the family or band, a loose federation of families.* The typical form of social organization among hunting-and-gathering families is small groups of kinsmen coming together at certain times of the year. These groups, sometimes referred to as bands, tend to be highly fluid in membership, with family members coming and going with considerable regularity.

4. *Contemporary foraging and collecting peoples occupy the remote and marginal areas of the earth.* These areas include the Alaskan tundra, the Kalahari Desert, the Australian outback, and the Ituri forest of central Africa. It is reasonable to suggest that these food-gathering, hunting-and-fishing societies,

---

foraging (Hunting and gathering) A form of subsistence that relies on using animal and plant resources found in the natural environment.

neolithic revolution A stage in human cultural evolution (beginning around ten thousand years ago) characterized by the transition from hunting and gathering to the domestication of plants and animals.

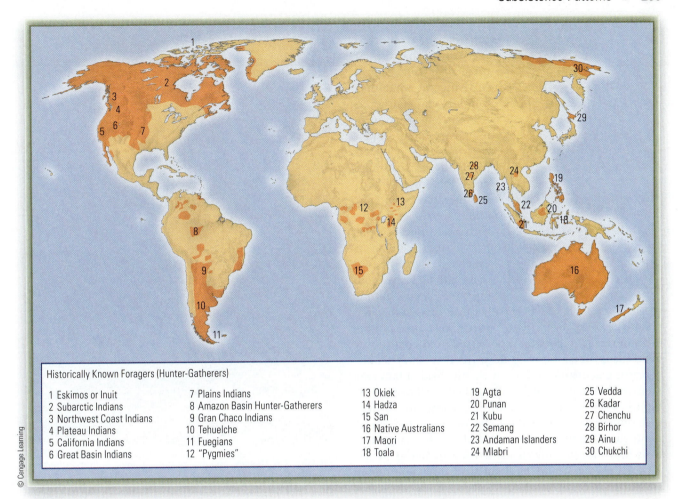

Historically Known Foragers (Hunter-Gatherers)

1 Eskimos or Inuit	7 Plains Indians	13 Okiek	19 Agta	25 Vedda
2 Subarctic Indians	8 Amazon Basin Hunter-Gatherers	14 Hadza	20 Punan	26 Kadar
3 Northwest Coast Indians	9 Gran Chaco Indians	15 San	21 Kubu	27 Chenchu
4 Plateau Indians	10 Tehuelche	16 Native Australians	22 Semang	28 Birhor
5 California Indians	11 Fuegians	17 Maori	23 Andaman Islanders	29 Ainu
6 Great Basin Indians	12 "Pygmies"	18 Toala	24 Mlabri	30 Chukchi

© Cengage Learning

FIGURE 7.5 **Historically known foragers.**

with their simple technology, have been forced into these marginal habitats by food producers, with their more complex technologies.

Early anthropological accounts tended to portray hunters and gatherers as living precariously in a life-or-death struggle with the environment. The association of hunting and gathering with an absence of social, political, and economic complexity is an accurate portrayal of the remaining hunting-and-gathering societies; most are small-scale, with no single individual or group specializing as a hunter of a particular animal or gathered item. Reciprocity and food sharing are critical to the group's survival. Archaeologists suggest that hunting-and-gathering societies in prehistoric times in all likelihood had considerably more social complexity and they are increasingly better able to interpret their findings (Price and Brown 1985). In the 1960s some anthropologists (Marshall Sahlins and Richard Lee) suggested that certain food-gathering groups are well off despite inhabiting some unproductive parts of the earth. The question of abundance within hunting-and-gathering societies became a topic

of heated debate at a major conference of seventy-five scholars on "Man the Hunter" held in Chicago in 1966. In fact Marshall Sahlins (1968) described hunters and gatherers as representing the "original affluent society." Hunters and gatherers, he argued, spent little time working, had all the food they needed, and enjoyed considerable leisure time. Although many scholars today take issue with such a formulation, considerable evidence suggests that hunters and gatherers are capable of adapting to harsh environments with creativity and resourcefulness (Sutton and Anderson 2009). Perhaps we can get a better idea of how foragers and collectors procure their food by examining two different contemporary groups—the Ju/'hoansi of present-day Namibia and the Inuit of the Arctic region—in greater detail.

The Ju/'hoansi of the Kalahari Region

One of the best-studied foraging societies, the Ju/'hoansi, inhabit the northwestern part of Africa in the Kalahari Desert, which straddles Namibia, Botswana, and Angola. In 1963, when Richard Lee

first visited the Dobe Ju/'hoansi, he observed that three-quarters of them lived in camps, surviving on what they hunted and gathered from their surrounding environment as well as what they gleaned from their pastoralist neighbors—the Herero and Tswanna, who kept small herds of cattle and goats. Because the Ju/'hoansi lived in a desert environment, they had to keep moving to keep eating because food and water resources are sparse. The Ju/'hoansi were classic hunter-gatherers (foragers) and possessed no domestic animals except their hunting dogs (R. Lee 2007). Food-procuring activities were fairly rigidly divided between men and women. Women collected 60 to 80 percent of the food (by weight) in the form of roots, nuts, fruits, and other edible vegetables and occasionally snared small game, and men hunted medium and large animals and occasionally brought back gathered items. Although women and men spent roughly equivalent amounts of time on their food-procurement activities, women provided two to three times more food by weight. The Ju/'hoansi's most important single food item was the mongongo nut, which accounted for about half of their diet. Nutritionally, the mongongo, which is found in abundance all year long, contains five times more calories and ten times more protein per cooked unit than cereal crops. However, unlike people in other arid regions, the Ju/'hoansi did not have any periods of plenty and they had no way of storing food supplies. When food shortages occurred, the Ju/'hoansi adapted by relying on pooling networks among their local groups to reduce their risk of starvation.

Even though the terms *affluence* and *abundance* tend to be relative, Richard Lee (1968) presented convincing evidence to suggest that the Ju/'hoansi were not teetering on the brink of starvation. In fact their food-gathering techniques were both productive and reliable. A measure of Ju/'hoansi affluence noted in the 1960s was their selectivity in taking foods from the environment. Lee (1968) estimated that the average Ju/'hoansi adult spent twelve to nineteen hours per week in the pursuit of food. Usually women could gather enough food in one day to feed their families for three days, which left a good deal of time for such leisure activities as resting, visiting, and entertaining visitors (Figure 7.6). If they had indeed been on the

FIGURE 7.6 Despite popular misconceptions, hunter-gatherers such as the Ju/'hoansi do not live on the brink of starvation. Their knowledge of their environment and where and what is edible, such as these mongongo nuts, is key to their survival. Having a wide range of plants and animals they traditionally identify as food enables them to adapt to a challenging environment.

brink of starvation, we would have expected them to exploit every conceivable source of food. But, in fact, they ate only about one-third of the edible plant foods and regularly hunted only 17 of the 223 local species of animals known to them (Lee 1968). Moreover, if the Ju/'hoansi had been in a life-or-death struggle with the natural environment, their survival rate and life expectancy would have been low, infant mortality would have been high, malnutrition would have been rampant, and the elderly and infirm would have been abandoned. This is hardly the demographic picture for the Ju/'hoansi. Based on fieldwork conducted in the 1960s, Lee (1968) found that approximately 10 percent of his sample population was sixty years of age or older, a percentage that was not substantially different from that in industrialized societies.

During the 1960s, when the first ethnographic studies were conducted, the Ju/'hoansi were general foragers, with the men hunting with bows and poisoned arrows and the women gathering edible plants. The band, the basic unit of social organization, was fluid in its membership to the extent that families could readily join other bands that were more successful at procuring food and water. By the mid-1970s, however, the Ju/'hoansi were adopting many of the lifeways of the neighboring Bantu peoples. Many families had begun to plant fields and keep goats, two agricultural pursuits that had been unheard of just a decade previously. Traditional grass huts were beginning to be replaced by more substantial (and permanent) mud structures. The Ju/'hoansi began to substitute manufactured clothing for their traditional skin garments, and even though bows and arrows were still made, they were primarily sold to the tourist market rather than used in hunting. All of these changes were accompanied by a major infusion of cash and consumer goods into Ju/'hoansi society.

Along with these changes in material culture, John Yellen (1990) found that the Ju/'hoansi began to place less emphasis on personal intimacy, sharing, and interdependence. Yellen also found increased hoarding of material goods purchased with the newfound cash. As the Ju/'hoansi accumulated more and more possessions, they became less mobile and less willing to continue their semi-nomadic, foraging lifestyle. These changes indicated that the Ju/'hoansi were retreating from their traditional values of sharing and interdependence. The major impetus for the relatively sudden changes in culture was not disenchantment with the foraging lifestyle but rather the civil war in the region, which forced some Ju/'hoansi into settlements.

The introduction of money, commodities, and wage labor expedited the process of culture change within the Ju/'hoansi culture. By the early years of the twenty-first century, their foraging, semi-nomadic way of life had, for all practical purposes, disappeared. Today the majority of the Ju/'hoansi get most of their food by raising small domestic livestock, tending small gardens, participating in government food programs, and purchasing items at food stores. The lands occupied by the Ju/'hoansi are now covered with trading markets, boreholes for water, schools, health clinics, airstrips, and government bureaucrats. And, of course, changes in their means of livelihood have resulted in other, often far-reaching, changes in their way of life (Lee 2003, 2007; Yellen 1990).

Today the Ju/'hoansi living in //Nhoq'ma village at Nhoma in the Tshumkwe are embarking on ecotourism and playing host to tourists. Neil Digby-Clarke (2007) reports that the owners of a nearby lodge and safari outfit have developed a close relationship with

© Frans Lemmens/Lonely Planet Images

FIGURE 7.7 Traditionally, hunters and gatherers of the Kalahari Desert interact with local pastoralists and other neighboring groups. Today, however, tourists from around the world visit the traditional bushmen in their villages in Namibia, Kalahari Desert.

the Ju/'hoansi (Figure 7.7). In 2000 they entered into an exclusive agreement with the village at // Nhoq'ma, and by 2003 they had built a tent camp for tourists and donated it to the villagers. Digby-Clarke describes the tourist accommodations as "five luxury double tents, complete with en-suite facilities" (Digby-Clarke 2007). The community is able to generate revenue from this arrangement. Once the income from accommodations, meals, and activities is paid, the costs of marketing and management are subtracted. In 2005 the villages received a total of N$105,000 (Namibian dollars), and in 2006 the amount increased to N$130,000 generated by two hundred tourists visiting the Ju/'hoansi. More than a decade has passed and the camp is still in operation. A number of web sites assist tourists making travel arrangements with local safari companies who lead expeditions to Nyae Nyae, where the //Nhoq'ma safari camp is located. There also are several development funds and conservancies established to protect the Ju/'hoansi and their local environment.

The Inuit

Like the Ju/'hoansi, the traditional Inuit of the Arctic region live in a delicate balance with their environment. Living in the barren Arctic and sub-Arctic regions stretching from Greenland in the east to Alaska in the west, the Inuit have had to adapt to a climate of bitterly cold temperatures, short summers, and a terrain almost devoid of vegetation. To adapt to this harsh environment, the Inuit developed creative survival strategies.

They were traditionally hunters and fishers living off of Arctic animal life. They fished as well as hunted for whales, walruses, caribou, and seals and would take down polar bears, birds, and any other edible animal if the opportunity presented itself. The Arctic has little edible vegetation, so the Inuit supplemented their diet with seaweed. They spent part of the year on the move, searching for food, and then part of the year at a central, more permanent camp. The Inuit divided the year into three hunting seasons, each revolving around a single animal: the seal, the caribou, and the whale.

Understanding the seasonal migratory patterns of animals is central to the Inuits' subsistence strategy. Under frozen conditions large social and hunting groups come together to hunt the sea. Inuit hunters station themselves at seal breathing holes in the ice and wait patiently, sometimes for hours, for a seal to surface and kill it. Seal meat is first shared through reciprocal exchanges within kinship lines and then among others within the community to ensure that no one goes hungry. As the ice begins to break up in April and May, game becomes more plentiful, and the Inuit hunt caribou with bows and arrows and fish for salmon and trout with pronged spears. During these summer months, people tend to live in smaller groups and their social interaction is less intense. The Inuit adapt to their environment by organizing their economic and social lives around the availability of different types of game and the strategies required for hunting them.

Much of what we have described about traditional Inuit hunting and fishing practices has changed over the last several decades. Today most contemporary Inuit live in villages, hunt with guns rather than spears and harpoons, and use snowmobiles rather than dogsleds (Figure 7.8). Some live in houses with modern conveniences such as telephones and TVs, and work for a living in wage employment. In the twenty-first century, Inuit hunters use ice floe maps, regularly updated by the European Space Agency, for tracking the rapidly changing ice edge conditions to determine where wildlife is most likely to be found.

Since the late 1970s, the Inuit have introduced legislation to protect their traditional ways and to maintain their subsistence lifestyle. Further legislation enabled the Inuit people to become masters over their own land when the Canadian government created a new territory called Nunavut ("our land" in the Inuit language) as of April 1, 1999. The territory is 1.2 million square miles—twice the size of Alaska and larger than all of western Europe—and comprises one-fifth of the entire Canadian landmass. Yet the population is only about twenty-seven thousand, roughly the size of a small suburban commuter town on the outskirts of Toronto. The creation of this territory gives the Inuit a measure of control over their own lives and an opportunity to preserve their traditional culture. Inuit culture over the centuries has been influenced by contact with the whaling industry, fur trappers, and even official government attempts to convert young Inuit by placing them in schools where only English was spoken. Nevertheless, much of Inuit culture remains intact. They have not abandoned their traditional system of food distribution, which ensures that no one goes hungry. Interestingly, unlike most other places in the world seeking self-determination, the Inuit were able to achieve theirs peacefully, without civil unrest.

These two ethnic groups—the Ju/'hoansi and the Inuit—have been used consistently for a number of decades as classic examples of hunting-and-gathering societies. In fact the traditional Ju/'hoansi have

FIGURE 7.8 Although the Inuit from Nunavut, Canada, have been using snowmobiles for more than a half century, they face new challenges as they adapt to the influences of global warming.

come to be regarded as the quintessential food foragers. Research since the 1980s, however, questions how well these two groups represent the world's hunters and gatherers. Researchers have been revising their view of hunter-gatherers as clever "lay ecologists" who live in an affluent society. To illustrate, studies indicate that members of some foraging groups spend as much as seven or eight hours per day working in subsistence pursuits, not the twelve to nineteen hours per week that Lee found to be typical for the Ju/'hoansi (Hawkes and O'Connell 1981; Hill et al. 1985). It also appears that some food-foraging groups experience seasonal fluctuations in their dietary intake; in fact some are chronically undernourished (see, for example, Howell 1986; Isaac 1990). Moreover the idyllic, nonviolent existence attributed to foragers has in all likelihood been overstated because they have been found fighting and raiding other groups for food, for revenge, or to defend territory (B. Ferguson 1984; Knauft 1987).

It is also important to keep in mind that although hunter-gatherers occupy remote habitats, they have always had contact with other people. For decades they have not lived in a pristine, isolated world. To illustrate, the traditional Sami, hunters and gatherers of the Scandinavian Arctic and sub-Arctic, who resided in the Sami, which today covers Norway, Sweden, Finland, and the Kola Peninsula of Russia, hunted and trapped the migratory reindeer for millennium. Yet, by the fifteenth century agricultural people slowly invaded the Samis' lands. Whereas some Sami left to go further north to maintain their traditional hunter-and-gatherer ways and to follow the reindeer, others remained. The gradual clearing of the forest for agricultural activities contributed to the loss of the reindeer habitat, yet the Samis' desire for reindeer meat and pelts was still present. By the seventeenth century the Sami took up pastoralism, choosing to raise reindeer and other domesticated animals, rather than follow them on their migratory path.

Today's hunters and gatherers face rapid change. Instead of living in isolation they are experiencing increased contact with a world of computers, civil wars, and the World Bank—sponsored development projects. Many people from hunting-and-gathering societies have interacted for years with neighboring groups through trade relations, wage labor, and intermarrying. As Robert Kelly (1995: 24–25) reminds us:

> Virtually no hunter-gatherer in the tropical forest today lives without trading heavily with horticulturalists for carbohydrates, or eating government or missionary rations…. Long before anthropologists arrived on the scene, hunter-gatherers had already been contacted, given diseases, shot at, traded with, employed and exploited by colonial powers, agriculturalists, and/or pastoralists.

Although hunting and gathering has been largely replaced by food production, there remains one important form of hunting that many world economies depend on—that is, fishing. Hunting and gathering is distinguished by its basic method: collecting or tracking down food. Fishing is different; it is distinguished by the type of animal rather than by the method of getting hold of the fish. Today's fishermen are equipped with Global Positioning System (GPS) technology to locate large schools of fish, high-tech equipment, and strong synthetic nets that are invisible to fish. Despite their enormous technological advantages, modern fishermen may well become victims of their own success. The rivers, lakes, and oceans of the world, which not too long ago seemed inexhaustible, can produce only a limited number of fish at the current rate of extraction. The Atlantic Ocean is a case in point. After World War II, commercial fishing boats from Europe and Asia began fishing the waters off the coast of the United States and Canada. By the 1960s the cod stock had declined so dramatically from overfishing that the governments of the United States and Canada extended their exclusive fishing rights to two hundred nautical miles from shore. Although this kept foreign fishing vessels out of the area, it encouraged the proliferation of domestic fishermen. Fishing became excessive, fish stocks shrank, and even future stocks were in jeopardy because fish populations could not sustain themselves. The problem remains today, with too many industrial commercial vessels fishing for a dwindling number of fish. Industrial commercial fishing—the last form of big-time "hunting"—illustrates the traditional dilemma of hunting-and-gathering people. Traditional hunters and fishers are in direct competition with large-scale commercialized fishing outfits for the wild caught, natural resource (Figure 7.9).

Value is placed on the quantity and frequency of fish caught and traded on an international scale among strangers. As the public demand for wild-caught seafood increases and fishermen become more efficient hunters, they run the risk of destroying their food supply and, in the process, eliminating biodiversity

FIGURE 7.9 Today's small-scale fishermen are finding it harder to compete with large-scale commercialized fishing outfits for the wild caught seafood. One way to make a fuller dollar is by selling directly to consumers off their boats and not paying middlemen.

and ruining the health of their ecosystem. As with so many aspects of the global economy, overfishing the oceans has had more negative consequences for some segments of the world's population than for others. Because fish populations in the Northern Hemisphere have been drastically reduced by commercial fishing interests in the United States, Canada, Japan, Russia, and northern Europe, many fishing companies from the developed world have moved south of the equator to the oceans around Africa and South America. Fleets of modern trawlers are now fishing within the two-hundred-mile limits of independent countries. Most are there legally because they pay cash-poor governments for fishing rights. A growing number of commercial fishing companies, however, are harvesting these waters illegally. Although scientists and government officials refer to this euphemistically as "illicit biomass extraction," the local fishermen, whose livelihoods are threatened, call it *piracy*. The consequence is that people in New York and Atlanta (for the present) can find all of their favorite seafood at the supermarket, whereas local fishermen in Angola are going out of business and their countrymen are deprived of a sorely needed source of protein (Salopek 2004). Some

small-scale fishermen in the United States, in particular the New England region, are trying to keep things afloat by catching and selling directly to consumers.

We have described the linkages between fishers and their environment and how globalization is forcing fishing vessels to explore waters all over the world to meet the public's increasing demand to have fresh fish on a regular basis. However, declining fishstocks as a result of overfishing is only part of the story in terms of the environment being able to support future generations of fishers working the waters. When humans continuously take from their natural environment as in the case with taking as much fish as one can without regard for environment or the fish species, there are additional consequences not only for the survival of fish species but also for those who make their livelihoods from fishing. For example, on April 20, 2010, BP produced a catastrophe when one of its oil-drilling platforms exploded and collapsed 40 miles off the Gulf Coast of Louisiana. Huge quantities of oil gushed into the Gulf of Mexico. The impact of this environmental crisis affects all marine life, coastal marshes, wildlife, the livelihoods of all the fishers and their families, the fishing industry, the coastal tourism industry, and the cultural traditions of coastal peoples, who were recently recovering from hurricanes Katrina, Rita, Gustav, Ike, and Ida.

The lives of coastal inhabitants and the surrounding area have changed in the aftermath of the Gulf Coast oil spill. The lifeways for the multigenerational fishing families and all those connected to the fishing industry hangs in a delicate balance. Many fishers interviewed by the media lost their livelihood and feared the environment would not recover quickly enough for them to resume shrimping or oystering. Climate change has also increased the strength and frequency of hurricanes in the area and will continue to keep coastal people on notice. Rising waters, loss of mangroves (necessary for spawning fish), stronger storms, and loss of fishing vessels and fleets are making the fishing industry vulnerable for artisan fishing families and commercial fleets.

Today's nonfood producing public continues to forage, but in grocery stores and at farmers' markets, instead of hunting and gathering their own food. Those shoppers are learning to eat in season and eat locally gathered foods. The Oxford English Dictionary added a new entry in 2007—*locavore*, a person who is committed to eating locally in the community or within a narrow radius or where one resides. In contrast to the locavores who hunt for their local foods at direct markets, freegans are in search of discarded foods. *Freegans*,

locavore A person who is committed to eating foods grown locally in the community or within a narrow radius or where one resides.

freegan Akin to the dumpster divers in that they are individuals gathering foods or reclaiming foods in as many ways as possible with the intent of not having to pay for food.

Niche Marketing for Local Commercial Fishermen

❋ Commercial fishing is critical to North Carolina's coastal heritage and local economy. For centuries, fishermen and their families have worked the waters, built boats and nets, and sold seafood. Early fishing communities were established in Carteret County, North Carolina, several hundred years ago by families who relied on the water for their livelihoods. Many of the descendants of these families still live in the area; however, few are able to continue the legacy as full-time fishermen. Today, quintessential fishing communities along Carteret County's coastline struggle to maintain a viable fishing industry. No one points to any one thing that has caused the decline of the fishing industry. Rather, a collection of events and conditions is making it impossible for local commercial fishermen to sustain their livelihood.

Fishermen will tell a tall tale, but it is not the one about the big fish that got away; it is the one about too few markets for their fish. Interviews with fishermen reveal that they have weathered storms, hurricanes, and government regulations. But today's fishermen are encountering additional pressures from higher fuel prices, more shark bites on nets, turtles squashing crab cages, and loss of markets in which to sell their catch. Competition from imported seafood displaces fresh, local seafood. These changes in environment, policy, and marketing conditions have negatively affected not only the local fishing industry but also those who own or are employed at the fish houses, the fish processors, drivers of refrigerated seafood trucks, and local restaurants. What was once a thriving way of life has now become a challenge with a questionable future.

In 2006 I (Andreatta) embarked on a multiyear applied project that focused on helping the fishermen in Carteret County increase their seafood sales. The project had several objectives, including: (1) to create a marketing program that would educate residents and visitors to seek out and purchase local seafood, (2) to develop niche marketing and direct-marketing opportunities for Carteret County fishermen, and (3) to expand these niche marketing opportunities to be used elsewhere. I worked with members of the fishing community and those who in 2005 established *Carteret Catch*™, a branding program with a logo used to identify seafood caught by commercial fishermen from Carteret County. Throughout the project we included fishermen and members of the community and *Carteret Catch*™. If any tinkering needed to be done in developing an alternative marketing approach, we wanted to hear from fishermen and others working in the industry.

Drawing on community-based participatory research, I developed a social marketing program. The primary goal of social marketing is to influence behavior or create behavioral change. It is a social change strategy that seeks to induce a behavioral change that will benefit the audience(s) (Van Willigen 2002). The behavior we were seeking to influence was consumers' intent to purchase local seafood and their recognition of local seafood in the county.

The inspiration for a direct-marketing strategy for the fishing industry came from working with local farmers in North Carolina—in particular, working among small-scale farmers who relied on farmers markets and community supported agriculture (CSA) plans to sell their local produce. CSAs are direct-marketing arrangements that have been operating in the United States since the 1980s; however, they began in Japan in the 1960s and made their way to Europe in the 1970s. In a CSA, families or individuals prepay a farmer in the winter for fresh produce they will receive when the harvest is available. This early payment helps the farmer buy seeds and maintain the farm at a time when no funds are coming in. These prepaying people are known as shareholders. Shareholders realize and accept that there will be lean weeks and bountiful weeks. They share the risk with the farmer and do not expect repayment or replacement food. Thus emerged community-supported fisheries (CSFs), a direct-marketing approach developed in 2006 (Andreatta and Parlier 2010).

In the summer of 2007 a group of fishermen came together to form a CSF. They worked as a buying club with primarily shrimp. Some of them went after the smaller sound shrimp, whereas others fished for the larger shrimp. Together they could help each other out and know who had what and when. A brochure was created to advertise their fishing operations. The group benefit from this brochure was that people heard about these fishermen. Those who had roadside stands saw their business increase; they sold more shrimp in a shorter time.

Several ways were identified for sustaining the local fishing industries, such as encouraging the public to prepay for a season of locally caught fish, buy directly from fish house dealers or from roadside vendors known to sell local seafood, and support restaurants known to purchase local seafood. Combining the *Carteret Catch*™ branding program with CSF arrangements helped the public to identify which roadside stands, fish houses, and restaurants served local seafood. The public plays an important role in sustaining local fisheries by choosing where they spend their money and in this case what seafood they purchase.

By 2012 CSFs and branding programs had expanded into other coastal areas in North Carolina, Maine, New Hampshire, South Carolina, California, Oregon, Australia, and Nova Scotia to list only a few locations. In addition one fish retailer and member of *Carteret Catch*™ began transporting seafood inland in North Carolina. This retailer now has four hundred members signed up for a weekly distribution. The buying club has started a new trend in the state as the public seeks to support local fishermen and eat local seafood.

© Susan Andreatta

Local *Carteret Catch*™ fishers are able to provide local seafood weekly to customers. The challenge for them is to get the public to look for it and ask for it. Community-supported fisheries—a term coined by Andreatta—is a direct-marketing approach to help the fishermen presell their catch to the seafood-eating public.

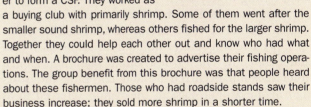

Questions for Further Thought

1. How are CSA arrangements different from CSF arrangements?

2. What ideas do you have to help small farmers and fishermen maintain their subsistence strategy? What suggestions do you have to protect the environment for farmers and fishers?

3. So that we do not lose the cultural knowledge of production in farming and fishing, what could be done to encourage future generations of farmers and fishers?

somewhat akin to the dumpster divers, are gathering foods or reclaiming foods in as many ways as possible with the intent of not having to pay for food. Clearly these modern-day hunter-gatherers (shoppers, locovores, and freegans) do not possess the same skill sets as those whose subsistence strategy depends on obtaining directly from the natural environment, but they are acquiring new skills and supporting those who are food producers.

Food-Producing Societies

Approximately ten thousand years ago, humans made a revolutionary transition from hunting and gathering to food production (the domestication of plants and animals). For reasons that are still not altogether clear, humans began to cultivate crops and keep herds of animals as sources of food. For the first time, humans gained a measure of control over their food supply. That is, through tilling of the soil and animal husbandry, humans were able to *produce* food rather than having to rely solely on what existed naturally in the environment. This shift from hunting and gathering to producing food, known as the *neolithic revolution*, occurred in several different areas of the world independently. The earliest known plant and animal domestication occurred around ten thousand years ago in the Middle East in the region referred to as the Fertile Crescent, including parts of Jordan, Israel, Syria, southeastern Turkey, northern Iraq, and western Iran. The first domesticated animal and plant species were dogs, sheep, goats, wheat, and barley. Other early centers of food production also emerged. By nearly ten thousand years ago, villagers in northern China were raising millet, and people farther south were growing rice (Loewe and Shaughnessy 1999).

Elsewhere in the world domesticated crops and livestock developed independently of the Fertile Crescent. Archaeologists have found evidence for the emergence of plant and animal domestication in Thailand around 8,800 years ago and in sub-Saharan Africa around 5,000 years ago. Archaeologists believe the people in central Mexico cultivated squash, chilis, and a

FIGURE 7.10 Modern day corn's ancestral form was a wild grass known as teosinte.

variety of millet by 5,000 years ago. Corn was developed as early as 7,000 years ago from a wild grass called teosinte. Teosinte looked different from our corn today; the kernels were small and were not close together like the kernels on the husked ears of modern corn (Figure 7.10). Indians throughout North and South America eventually came to depend on this corn, also known as *maize*, for much of their food even though some of their other grains were more nutritious. Beans and avocados also were domesticated in Mexico along with many other crops (B. Smith 1998). In South America the first cultivated potato appeared between 3,000 and 7,000 years ago in southern Peru and the northeast of Bolivia. Yuca, manioc, peanuts, sweet potatoes, and countless other crops spread throughout the Inca Empire.

A number of theories have been suggested to explain why the neolithic revolution occurred. Although no definitive explanation has emerged, most archaeologists agree that the shift to food production was a response to certain environmental or demographic conditions, such as variations in rainfall or population pressures. It is reasonable to suggest that most of the early foragers and collectors did not rush to adopt agriculture. Farming requires a greater expenditure of labor than does hunting and gathering, it also provides less security, and it usually involves a less varied (and less interesting) diet. Rather than hunter-gatherers purposefully choosing agriculture as a way of life, it is likely that food production serendipitously came about because of the need to feed an increasing number of people who could not be sustained by foraging alone and to meet the desire to stay in one place rather than migrating on a seasonal or as-needed basis.

Whatever the cause or causes may have been, there is little doubt about the monumental consequences of the neolithic revolution. What made the neolithic revolution so revolutionary was that it produced the world's first population explosion. Even though the early neolithic communities were small, they were far larger than any others in human prehistory had been. Throughout the Near East, Egypt, and Europe, thousands of skeletal remains have been unearthed from the neolithic period (10,000 to 5,500 years ago) compared to only a few hundred for the entire paleolithic period, even though the paleolithic lasted hundreds of times longer than the neolithic.

Changes Resulting from Food Production

That food producing, as compared to hunting and gathering, should result in a dramatic increase in population is not difficult to understand. As pointed out previously, subsistence food-procurement systems such as those of hunter-gatherers had built-in thresholds or quotas on what they could extract from the natural environment. For such people, over-extraction from the natural environment would destroy their natural food sources. Farmers, however, can increase the food supply (and thus support larger populations) simply by sowing more seeds and managing soil nutrients and irrigation systems. As farmers increased the amount of land under cultivation or cultivated for longer periods of time, they came to rely on their children for help. Children can be taught to perform useful tasks such as weeding fields, scaring off birds or other small animals, and tending flocks, and consequently family size increased.

Not only did populations become larger as a result of the neolithic revolution, but they also became more sedentary. Cultivators invest their time and energy in a piece of land, develop the notion of property rights, and establish permanent settlements. In other words, a gradual settling-in process occurred as a result of the neolithic revolution. This is not meant to imply that all, or even most, people became tied to the land after the neolithic revolution. Many remained hunters and gatherers, some became nomadic or semi-nomadic pastoralists, and still others became horticulturalists. Nevertheless the neolithic (or food-producing) revolution initiated the gradual trend toward a more settled way of life.

The cultivation of crops also brought about other important cultural changes. For example, farming can potentially generate more food per unit of land than hunting-and-gathering activities, especially if the farmer has intercropped multiple varieties of seed crops. This may have allowed farmers to store more food for times of scarcity and trade with others for goods they did not produce, while enabling other members to specialize in non—food-producing activities. The neolithic revolution also stimulated a greater division of labor. That is, people could for the first time become specialists, inventing and manufacturing the tools and machinery needed for a more complex social structure. Once some people were liberated from the food quest, they were able to make new farm implements such as the plow, pottery storage containers, metal objects, the wheel, stone masonry, and improved hunting and fishing technology. Without these and many other inventions that resulted from an increase in labor specialization, it is unlikely that we would have ever reached the second revolution: the rise of civilization.

The multitude of changes brought about by the neolithic revolution cannot be overestimated. The introduction of agriculture and animal husbandry ten

CROSS-CULTURAL MISCUE

✿ A British fertilizer company from Manchester, England, decided to venture into the potentially lucrative markets of sub-Saharan Africa. After conducting research on locally appropriate fertilizers, the company developed a marketing plan that involved giving, free of charge, hundred-pound bags of fertilizer to selected farmers in certain areas of Kenya. It was thought that those using the free fertilizer would be so impressed with the dramatic increases in crop output that they would spread the word to their friends, family, and neighbors.

Teams of marketers went from hut to hut offering each male head of household a free bag of fertilizer along with an explanation of how to use it. Though polite, every farmer contacted turned down the offer of free fertilizer. The marketing staff concluded that these Kenyan farmers were either not interested in growing more crops or too stupid to understand the benefits of the new product. But both of these conclusions failed to take into account the cultural realities of the small-scale farmers in Kenya. First, company officials tried to convince the village men to accept an agricultural innovation when, in fact, it was the women who were responsible for farming. Failure to understand this basic ethnographic fact did little for their overall credibility. Second, many East Africans have two important beliefs that can help explain their reaction: (1) the theory of limited good, which assumes that there is a finite amount of good in the world (such as fertility), and (2) witchcraft, the notion that evil forces embodied in people can be harmful. Given these two beliefs, the typical east African farmer would never participate in a scheme that promises to produce more crops than any of the neighbors because to do so would open you up to charges of having bewitched the fertility out of other peoples' soil. In short, to continue to grow the same amount as one had in the past is a preferable alternative to being killed for witchcraft.

thousand years ago set humankind on a radically different evolutionary path. Although it enabled humans to move toward civilization (urban societies), the industrial revolution, and eventually the global information age, these transformations had their downside. Recent discoveries by paleopathologists (physical anthropologists who study disease among ancient peoples) suggest that the transition to early agriculture from a hunting-and-gathering subsistence strategy actually led to a decline in overall health. To illustrate, skeletal remains of hunters and gatherers from Greece and Turkey at the end of the ice age (approximately twelve thousand years ago) indicate that the average height was five feet nine inches for men and five feet five inches for women; but by five thousand years ago, the predominantly agricultural people from the same region were appreciably shorter (averaging five feet three inches for men and five feet zero inches for women), indicating a nutritional decline. Findings from the excavation of burial mounds in the Illinois and Ohio river valleys point to negative health consequences for a population that changed from foraging to maize cultivation in the twelfth century. For example, when compared with the foragers who preceded them, the maize farmers had a 50 percent increase in tooth enamel defects (hypoplasia) caused by malnutrition, four times the incidence of iron-deficiency anemia, and a 300 percent increase in bone lesions, indicative of infectious disease (Cohen and Armelagos 1984). With the rise of agriculture in the area, the average life expectancy dropped from twenty-six to nineteen years.

There are reasons early farmers paid a high price for their newfound food-getting strategy. First, hunters and gatherers generally had a more balanced diet (composed of both plants and animal proteins) than did early farmers, who were often limited in the number of crops planted and time to still hunt and gather items to balance out their diet. Second, if early farmers were dependent on a small number of crops, they ran the risk of serious malnutrition or even starvation if those crops should fail. And finally, the increased population densities caused by the neolithic revolution brought people into closer contact with one another and consequently made everyone more susceptible to both parasitic and infectious diseases.

Food production also had some dramatic social effects. The egalitarianism of traditional hunting-and-gathering societies was replaced by increasing social

inequality and other problems such as poverty, crime, war, aggression, and environmental degradation. Thus, even though we often glorify the introduction of subsistence agriculture as a defining moment in human evolution, it certainly had some negative consequences.

Horticulture

Horticulture—also known as *subsistence agriculture* or *small-holder agriculture*—is small-scale, low-intensity farming on small plots. It involves basic hand tools such as the hoe or digging stick rather than plows or other machinery driven by animals or engines. Horticulturalists also use few, if any, purchased inputs such as fertilizer, seeds, pesticides, and other such items that help them to plant prepare and plant their fields. Because horticulturalists produce low yields, which are consumed directly by the household, they generally do not generate much of a surplus and thus do not develop extensive market systems. Some horticulturalists keep domesticated food animals, such as pigs or chickens, along with producing their household crop. Pigs, chickens, and other relatively small domesticated animals are often raised for both food and prestige. For example, the Swazi of Swaziland in southern Africa keep not only pigs but also a variety of other domesticated animals, including cows, goats, sheep, horses, and donkeys (Kuper 1986). Other horticultural societies are known to supplement their diet with occasional hunting and gathering of wild plants and animals, such as the Yanomamo, who live in the Amazon Basin of Venezuela and Brazil (Chagnon 1992). Still other horticultural groups, such as the Samoans, supplement their crops with protein derived from fishing, whereas the Miskitos, indigenous people of coastal Nicaragua in Central America, raise small domesticated livestock and fish along with their horticultural practices. Some horticulturalists not only are subsistence farmers but also produce a small surplus to sell or exchange in local markets for things they cannot produce themselves. In Central America, Mayan horticulturalists augment their crops with fruit-bearing trees such as papaya, avocado, and cacao. On their small-scale plots they plant multiple crops, such as corn, beans (using cornstalks as supports), squash, pumpkins, and chili peppers.

A major technique of horticulturalists, especially those found in tropical regions of the world, is *shifting cultivation*, sometimes called *swidden cultivation* or the *slash-and-burn method*. This technique involves clearing the land by manually cutting down the growth, burning it, and planting in the burned area. Even though the ash residue serves as a fertilizer, the soil nutrients are usually depleted within a few years (Figure 7.11). The land is then allowed to lie fallow until the natural vegetation is restored, or it may be abandoned altogether. Slash-and-burn cultivating can eventually destroy the environment if fields are not given sufficient time to

---

horticulture Small-scale crop cultivation characterized by the use of simple technology and the absence of irrigation.

shifting cultivation (swidden cultivation, slash-and-burn method) A form of plant cultivation in which seeds are planted in fertile soil prepared by cutting and burning the natural growth; relatively short periods of cultivation are followed by longer fallow periods.

FIGURE 7.11 An Indian boy from Venezuela assists his family in slash-and-burn agriculture by setting fire to an old garden. The ash from the fire will restore the soil's fertility for the next growing season.

lie fallow. In such cases the forests may be replaced by grasslands or the soil nutrients may be depleted, which results in poverty for the farmers.

The crops grown by horticulturalists can be divided into three categories: perennial (those items that can be used year after year), annual seed (seed that has to planted yearly), and root. Perennial crops include bananas and plantains, figs, dates, and coconuts; the major seed crops (which tend to be high in protein) are wheat, barley, corn, oats, sorghum, rice, and millet; and the main root crops (which tend to be high in starch and carbohydrates) are yams, arrowroots, taro, manioc, and potatoes. Experienced horticulturalists know to rotate the crops in their fields so as not to plant the same thing in the same place year after year. Because seed crops require more nutrients than root crops, seed cultivators need to allow longer periods of time between plantings. In some cases these delays can have consequences for settlement patterns. That is, if seed cultivators need a longer time to rejuvenate their fields,

MEXICO

Lacandon Maya People of Chiapas

GUATEMALA

they may be less likely to live in permanent settlements than are root cultivators. However, even though swidden cultivation involves the shifting of fields, it does not necessarily follow that the cultivators also periodically shift their homes.

At first glance it appears that slash-and-burn cultivation makes poor use of the land. Because most land must be left fallow at any given time, the system of slash and burn cannot support the high population densities that can be sustained by intensive agriculture. Although there are inherent limitations to the technique, slash-and-burn horticulturalists are often extremely adept at maximizing their resources. Some slash-and-burn farmers produce abundant harvests of tropical forest products and do so without destroying the land. To illustrate, R. Jon McGee (1990) showed that the Lacandon Maya of Chiapas, Mexico, grow more than forty different crops throughout their cleared fields (*milpas*). By spreading many crops over a milpa, the Lacandon are imitating both the diversity and the dispersal patterns found in the natural primary forest. Their tiered approach to farming mirrors the layers found in the tropical forest. The Lacandon farmer is able to take advantage of different environmental niches within the same cleared area of the milpa by planting at different levels. For example, corn, beans, squash, and tomatoes are intercropped at ground level. Well above the surface crops are the bananas and oranges, and root crops such as manioc and sweet potatoes are cultivated below the ground's surface. McGee points out that this form of slash-and-burn horticulture is quite efficient because the typical Lacandon Mayan family can feed itself while working fewer than half the days in a year. In regions with vast areas of unused land, slash-and-burn horticulture can be a reasonably efficient method of food production.

The governments of many developing countries, however, are interested in transforming traditional economies (such as those based on slash-and-burn agriculture) into world market economies, thereby attracting foreign capital, providing wage-paying jobs for local people, and raising a country's gross national product. These government officials in parts of Africa, Asia, and South America argue that by restricting (or prohibiting altogether) slash-and-burn horticulture, overall productivity will be increased, people will eat better and be healthier, and the export economy will be expanded. However, a major problem in these efforts to transform traditional horticulture practices has been that government officials often have different value assumptions from the local farmers whose culture they are trying to change. To illustrate, rural horticulturalists in Honduras were asked to shift from subsistence production—growing enough food to feed their family—to the production of chili peppers for the export market. The farmers did not support this initiative because, in their minds, chili peppers did not feed their families. It did not make sense to them to stop producing subsistence crops that fed their families and instead produce cash crops to make money with which they could buy food to feed their families. Outsiders looking on may want to consider what is culturally valued in terms of production per unit of land and the labor used in the process; sometimes what outsiders value or believe is progress is not desired by those residing in the community.

In another example, coastal Miskito Indians of Nicaragua have been farming for centuries while facing hurricanes and droughts. But now they are facing climate change and are no longer able to predict the seasons, so they do not know when to plant. Traditional signs found in nature—white cranes, flowering avocado plants, silver fish, and flashes of lightning—no longer tell them when the rainy season is coming. Because of the unpredictability of the rains coupled with not knowing when to sow their seeds and tubers, their farm production is decreasing. Already among the poorest and most marginalized groups in Nicaragua, they are now on the front lines of a new threat from extreme weather events such as the seasonal hurricanes.

There are success stories of interesting adaptations to cultural and environmental pressures. One example is from Miguel Pinedo-Vasquez (Levine 2008), who spent a decade working among people who live along the Amazon River. He observed how a family had carved out a farm in a patch of jungle that had once been logged; the land is now feeding a family and generating an income. The farmers had carefully handpicked seeds and observed which ones did better in this rapidly changing environment, where the tides change twice daily and flood the area where they grow their crops. The farmers learned that if they planted in November, the seedlings had a chance to mature while the tides were at their seasonal lowest. Through trial and error the farmers have successfully planted cassava, lemon trees, and chili peppers. They found a natural way of dealing with climate change. This new knowledge of subsistence production will be helpful for those cultivating along the various tributaries of the Amazon River.

Today we find horticulture practiced among front and backyard gardeners and those who have transformed their yards into edible landscapes (Figure 7.12). Relying primarily on one's own labor to plant and

harvest for home consumption is providing families with fresh, homegrown produce. Horticulture still exists as a subsistence strategy in South and Central America as well as certain areas of Central Africa, Southeast Asia, and Melanesia. It continues to work well where people have access to land on which to raise crops and livestock for primarily home consumption.

Pastoralism

Like horticulture, *pastoralism* first appeared in the neolithic period. This subsistence pattern is sometimes referred to as *animal husbandry* and involves herding, breeding, consuming, and using domesticated herd animals such as camels, cattle, goats, horses, llamas, reindeer, sheep, and yaks. Pastoralism is practiced in areas with arable lands for good pasture as well as areas of the world that cannot support agriculture because of inadequate terrain, soils, or rainfall. However, these more vulnerable environments may provide sufficient vegetation to support livestock, provided the animals are able to graze over a large enough area. Thus, pastoralism is associated with geographic mobility because herds must be moved periodically to exploit seasonal pastures and water sources (Sutton and Anderson 2009).

Anthropologists differentiate between two types of movement patterns among pastoralists: transhumance and nomadism. A third form of pastoralism found in industrial societies is known as sedentary ranching and dairy farming. *Transhumance* is the seasonal movement of livestock between upland and lowland pastures.

---

pastoralism A food-getting strategy based on animal husbandry; found in regions of the world that are generally unsuited for agriculture.

transhumance The movement pattern of pastoralists in which some of the men move livestock seasonally.

FIGURE 7.12 Today we find family, friends and volunteers planting gardens in front and backyards as well as in vacant lots transforming the land into edible landscapes and community gardens.

Garry Wade/Taxi/Getty Images

Among some pastoral groups there is a base location where the elders, women, children, and lactating animals reside and a herding camp for adolescent boys and young adult men to raise the nonlactating animals. This division of labor and residence helps to lessen the pressures placed on available pasturelands. *Nomadism* is the migration of whole villages relocating when new pastures are needed for the animals. As Rada and Neville Dyson-Hudson (1980) pointed out, however, the enormous variations even within societies render the distinction between transhumance and nomadism somewhat sterile. For example, following seven Karamojong herds over a two-year period, the Dyson-Hudsons found that "each herd owner moved in a totally different orbit, with one remaining sedentary for a full year and one grazing his herd over 500 square miles" (1980: 18).

Even though anthropologists tend to lump all pastoralists into a single subsistence strategy, pastoralism is not a unified phenomenon. For example, there are wide variations in the ways animals are herded. The principal herd animals are cattle in eastern and southern Africa, camels in North Africa and the Arabian Peninsula, yaks in the Himalayan region, and various mixed herds (including goats, sheep, and cattle) in a number of places in Europe, Asia, Africa, South America, and North America. Reindeer are important for today's Sami people (Lapp) in northern Scandinavia as well for others groups in the sub-Arctic areas of eastern Europe and Siberia. The Sami use the reindeer for meat, whereas the Dukha people of northern Mongolia milk and ride their reindeer much as other Mongolians do who raise horses. In addition to variations in the types of animals, other social and environmental factors influence the cultural patterns of pastoral people, including the availability of water and pasturage, the presence of diseases, the location and timing of markets, government restrictions, and the demands of other food-getting strategies (such as cultivation) that the pastoralists may practice.

A general characteristic of nomadic pastoralists is that they take advantage of seasonal variations in pasturage so as to maximize the food supply of their herds. The Kazaks of Eurasia, for example, keep their livestock at lower elevations during the winter, move to the foothills in the spring, and migrate to the high mountain pastures during the summer. Such seasonal movement provides optimal pasturage and avoids climatic extremes that could negatively affect the livestock (Figure 7.13). Moving their animals at different times of the year avoids overgrazing and enables pastoralists to raise considerably more livestock than they could if they chose not to migrate.

The consensus among anthropologists is that pure pastoralists—that is, those who get all of their food from livestock—are either extremely rare or nonexistent. Because livestock alone cannot meet all the nutritional needs of a population, most pastoralists need some plants and grains to supplement their diets. Many pastoralists, therefore, either combine the keeping of livestock with some form of cultivation or maintain regular trade relations with neighboring agriculturalists. Moreover the literature is filled with examples of nomadic pastoralists who produce crafts for sale or trade, occasionally work for the government, or drive trucks. Thus, although many pastoralists have long engaged in nonpastoral activities, they have always considered animal husbandry as their identity and their livelihood.

It is clear that in pastoral societies livestock play a vital economic role not only as a food source but also in other ways. Melville Herskovits (1924), an anthropologist who worked among east African pastoralists, found that cattle served three purposes, from which he derived the term *cattle complex*. First, cattle were an economic venture with a utilitarian purpose. Cattle were a source of food; their milk, blood, and meat were shared and sold; their dung was used for fertilizer, house building, and fuel; their urine was used as an antiseptic; their bones were used for tools and artifacts; their skins were used for clothing and shelter; and their strength provided a means of transportation or traction. Second, cattle had a social function, played a symbolic role and were important status symbols: Large herds conveyed status to families or enabled sons to secure a wife (or wives). Livestock often influence the social relationships among people in pastoral societies. For example, an exchange of livestock between the families of the bride and the

Gina Corrigan/Robert Harding Picture Library Ltd/Alamy

FIGURE 7.13 The summer migration of Kazaks Altay Mountains northeast Xinjiang China Asia avoids overgrazing and enables pastoralists to raise considerably more livestock than they could if they chose not to migrate.

nomadism The movement pattern of pastoralists involving the periodic migration of human populations in search of food or pasture for livestock.

groom is required in many pastoral societies before a marriage is legitimized. In the event of an assault or a homicide, in some societies livestock is given to compensate the victim's family as a way of restoring normal social relations. The sacrifice of livestock at the grave sites of ancestor-gods is a way in which people keep in touch with their deities. Third, farmers were attached to their cattle; cattle were valued and adorned. These and other social uses of livestock remind us that domesticated animals in pastoral societies not only serve as the major food source but also are intimately connected to other parts of the culture, such as the systems of marriage, social control, and religion.

The Maasai of East Africa The Maasai culture of Kenya and Tanzania is an excellent example of a pastoral society. As one of a number of cultures within the east African cattle complex (e.g., the Turkana, Jie, Samburu, among others), the Maasai have experienced enormous sociocultural changes in the last forty years. Occupying an area of about 62 square miles of savanna in southern Kenya and northern Tanzania, the Maasai, who number approximately four hundred thousand people, traditionally lived mainly from their abundant herds of cattle, goats, and sheep. Like many other pastoralists in the region, the Maasai got most of their sustenance in the form of milk and blood from their cows, consuming meat only on rare ritual occasions. This high-protein diet was occasionally supplemented with grains and honey obtained through trade with neighboring peoples.

Over the past century and a half, the Maasai have gained the reputation, among Africans and Europeans alike, of being quintessential cattle keepers. According to their creation myth, Ngai (God) gave all the cattle on earth to the Maasai, and they have used this myth to justify raiding cattle from neighboring peoples. If Ngai did indeed give all the cattle to the Maasai, then it logically follows that any non-Maasai in possession of cattle obtained their livestock unlawfully. Maasai have long felt that cattle raids were not stealing but rather reclaiming their God-given property. It is little wonder that cattle are the major source of wealth among the

Maasai, in much the same way that cash is a major concern of Westerners. Cattle serve both economic purposes (milk and blood for food, dung for building houses, and bone for tools) and noneconomic purposes (*stock friendship*, marriage payments, and ceremonial sacrifices).

British colonial administrators often claimed that the Maasai, with their unending quest to expand the size of their herds, were being ecologically destructive. Although no pastoral societies live in complete harmony with their environments, the Maasai over the centuries have developed a functional system for managing their environmental resources for the benefit of their domesticated herds. Traditional Maasai transhumance patterns followed those of the wildlife (i.e., wildebeest, zebras) with whom their herds competed for grass and water. During the dry season (June through October), the Maasai, and the abundant wildlife of east Africa, congregated at permanent water sources such as rivers and lakes; during the wet season (November through May), both dispersed in search of temporary pastures and water.

The Maasai have traditionally combined their detailed knowledge of the environment (climatic cycles, vegetation, permanent water sources, and the presence of mosquitoes and tsetse flies) with a willingness to remain mobile, flexible, and cooperative. During the dry season, when both wildlife and Maasai pastoralists congregate at the permanent sources of water, a council of elders creates a queuing schedule to ensure that all of the animals have access to the water in an orderly fashion. The Maasai reserve a pasture close to the permanent watering areas for young, sick, and lactating animals that cannot travel to more distant pastures. Moreover, because "rainy seasons" sometimes fail to produce adequate water, the Maasai have established a system of "drought insurance," whereby water sources and pastures that never dry up are not used during normal times. When a drought occurs, these reserves are opened up as emergency sources of food and water for their cattle.

The Maasai, however, have not only managed but have also actually transformed their environment for the benefit of their livestock in important ways. First, owing to their military prowess, the Maasai were able to prevent the permanent settlement of farmers on the grasslands, thereby preserving the savanna for open grazing. And second, they engaged in the controversial practice of controlled burning of the grasslands for two reasons: first, to destroy the breeding grounds of the tsetse fly, which causes trypanosomiasis ("sleeping sickness," affecting both people and cattle) and second, to stimulate the growth of new, more nutritious grasses. In other words, burning is believed to provide Maasai cattle with better pasturage as well as protect them from disease. Thus, for centuries the Maasai system of cattle keeping has worked effectively for all parties concerned: the Maasai, the abundant wildlife, and the environment itself.

---

stock friendship A gift of livestock from one man to another to strengthen their friendship.

✳ The Maasai are nomadic cattle herders and, like other pastoralist tribes, consume the milk and blood of their cattle as part of long-standing cultural traditions. Just as important, cattle are a form of wealth, and a young man seeking to marry must pay a bride-price in cattle to the family of his intended wife. No cattle, no marriage. A prolonged drought severely affected the cattle population in east Africa, and many young men migrated to the already overpopulated cities in search of employment. In some cases families sent sons to the cities to obtain a college education rather than continue to raise cattle in already desperate conditions.

A development consultant from Oxfam International was asked to advise on ways to help the Maasai deal with the drought and its effects on their cattle. The consultant was not a Maasai pastoralist. He had been raised in Nairobi and studied agriculture economics at the University of Kenya. His recommendation, based on the poverty and malnutrition that he saw in some of the more remote pastoral areas, was to encourage dairy ranching, which would enable families not only to feed their families but also to generate income from the sale of milk. The consultant put together a development package whereby pastoralists could secure low-interest loans to construct a barn and milking parlor that would support five cows and one bull. He recommended a small herd size for each family to minimize the grazing lands needed per animal, reasoning that fewer animals would fare better during the drought.

Word traveled fast after the consultant's recommendations were given to the local ministry of agriculture officials. The Maasai were up in arms. What would five cows do for them? How would they not only feed their families but also marry off their sons? If the consultant had taken a course in cultural anthropology, he might have learned that in this culture cattle are a form of wealth as well as a source of food and that the number of animals a family owns is more important than the fitness of each individual cow. Furthermore the suggestion of going into debt to build a barn and milking parlor made no sense to migrating cattle herders.

With the arrival of colonial governments in the late nineteenth century, however, the Maasai found it increasingly difficult to practice their traditional patterns of pastoralism. Beginning in the twentieth century, the Maasai lost some of their best dry-season pastures and water supplies to colonial settlers. Since the 1950s large portions of the Maasai traditional grazing lands have been appropriated as official game reserves (for encouraging tourism), from which the Maasai and their herds have been excluded. The Maasai are being forced into marginal areas or onto smaller and smaller parcels of land, which resemble cattle ranches.

Sandwiched between the fenced fields of cultivators, the Maasai are confined to small landholdings. Gone are the days of moving their herds over vast areas of land. They are becoming permanently settled, investing money in the land (drilling wells), sending their children to school, and engaging in the previously unthinkable practice of selling their livestock for cash.

In the twenty-first century, Maasai herders, still dressed in their traditional red togas, drive pickup trucks, talk on cell phones, and belong to nongovernmental organizations. Many of their traditional houses are now permanent; some women are growing crops; and in some cases the Maasai are keeping chickens, not a traditional herding animal. Today the Maasai are becoming integrated into the modern global economy. Some Maasai who live near game reserves are tapping into tourist dollars by selling beaded leather goods, opening up their compounds for "home tours," and performing traditional Maasai dances for Europeans in zebra-striped minivans (Figure 7.14). But westernization can push only so far before a proud people begin

FIGURE 7.14 Maasai pastoralists in Kenya's Maasai Mara National Reserve now host tourists as a means of added income. Children on a family safari visit a Maasai *manyatta*, or village, just outside the reserve to learn and observe some of the cultural traditions.

to push back. Believing that they have been evicted from their ancestral land, large groups of Maasai are protesting by driving their herds onto nearby farmland. Maasai are being told by the Kenya government to return to their ranches and accept the fact that their free-roaming life as pastoralists is rapidly coming to an end (Lacey 2004).

The Modern Pastoralist A modern form of pastoralism is practiced by cattle and sheep ranchers in western North America, Australia, New Zealand, Argentina, and a few other areas of the world. These ranchers do not identify themselves as subsistence pastoralists, but rather as businessmen who produce milk or beef for national and international markets. To facilitate their form of pastoralism they use mechanized equipment such as trucks and even airplanes and helicopters. These "business ranchers" are risk takers. They know that their livelihoods may be jeopardized by theft, diseases, or other natural disasters or that the size of their herds may double in a few years and make them rich. Whether a traditional pastoralist or a business rancher, both share a disdain for farmers and fences.

The latest craze among a few North American entrepreneurial pastoralists, not driven by cattle ownership and concentrate animal-feeding operations where cattle are fattened up on corn before they are slaughtered for consumption, involves goat herders with their rent-a-goat programs. In the spirit of going green and being environmentally friendly goat herders are renting out their flock to help groom large tracks of pasture grass around airports. San Francisco airport used 250 to 300 goats as part of its annual organic weed abatement program, according to Schuler, a spokes person for the airport (Ramachanran 2012). Schuler explained that on the property is the San Francisco garter snake and the California red-legged frog, and they would be endangered should chemicals or heavy machinery be used to clean up the land. Similar goat programs were started at O'Hare airport in Chicago and Atlanta's in Georgia serving as a way to keep scrub brush down. Small-scale pastoralists are trying to identify ways in which they can stay in business and in this case multipurpose their goats for not only meat and milk, but now also for petrol-free grounds maintenance.

Intensive Agriculture

Intensive agriculture (intensive cultivation), a more recent phenomenon than horticulture, is the most prevalent subsistence pattern. It relies on large-scale

---

intensive agriculture A form of commodity production that requires intensive working of the land with plows and draft animals and the use of techniques of soil and water control.

---

production practices that result in much more food being produced per acre than with other subsistence patterns and thus supports larger populations. The development of intensive farming methods began about five thousand years ago as the human population grew beyond the environment's carrying capacity using horticulture and pastoralism.

Intensive agriculture is characterized by the use of the plow, draft animals, or machinery to pull the plow, fertilizers, irrigation, and other technological innovations that make intensive cultivation much more productive than horticulture. More important, the system is designed with the production of a surplus in mind, and as a consequence of increased productivity there is an increase in the human carrying capacity. A single farmer using a horse-drawn plow, for example, not only can put a larger area of land under production but also, because the plow digs deeper than the hoe or digging stick, unleashes more nutrients from the soil and thereby increases the yield per acre. Applying animal fertilizers (the excrement of the draft animals) enables land to be used year after year rather than having to remain fallow to restore its fertility naturally. Irrigation of fields that do not receive sufficient or consistent rainfall is another innovation contributing to increased production from intensive agriculture. Moreover, the invention of the wheel was a benefit to the intensive farmer by providing transportation, and making the water-raising wheel and large pottery storage vessels for surplus crops possible. Thus, by making use of technology, the intensive cultivator has access to a much greater supply of energy than is available to the horticulturalist (See the discussion of Leslie White in Chapter 4). What sets agriculture apart from horticulture, however, is the surplus from the harvest that may be sold on a market to generate an income and profit for the farming household.

Today, intensive agriculture is the primary food production pattern in all developed nations except those that are too arid or too cold for any form of farming. Over the last century, large-scale agricultural techniques spread rapidly throughout the world with the introduction of farm machinery, seed varieties, and commercially produced fertilizers, pesticides, and herbicides. This essentially resulted in the industrialization of farming in the richer nations, which will be discussed. There is a price for this greater productivity, however, because intensive agriculture requires a large investment of both labor and capital. First, in terms of labor, agriculturalists must devote hours of hard work to prepare the land. In hilly areas the land must be terraced and maintained, and irrigation systems may be developed that involve drilling wells, digging trenches, and building dikes (Figure 7.15). All of these activities increase the land's productivity enormously but are extremely labor intensive. Second, intensive agriculture, as compared to

© David Austen/Stock, Boston

FIGURE 7.15 Terraced farming in Indonesia and elsewhere is labor intensive. Yet commitment to the raised beds on steep terrains enables farmers to cultivate in mountainous regions.

horticulture, requires a much higher investment of capital in plows (which must be maintained), mechanical pumps (which can break down), draft animals (which can become sick and die), and farm inputs such as fuel, fertilizers, seeds, and other needs.

Also closely associated with intensive agriculture, is both higher levels of productivity and more settled communities. In fact, not until early horticultural societies had developed more intensive forms of agriculture could civilizations exist (that is, urban societies). In other words, a fully reliable system of food production, brought about by intensive agriculture, is a necessary, if not sufficient, condition for the rise of civilization. Surplus crops produced by farmers were sold in village markets. Some of these market centers increased in population over time and became towns and eventually cities.

As farming became more intensive, the specialization of labor became more complex. Under a system of intensive agriculture, some people were liberated to engage in activities other than food production. Many new kinds of occupations emerged, such as merchants, craftsmen, professional soldiers, priests, rulers, and bureaucrats. Thus, the intensification of agriculture did not cause, but rather enabled, the development of a more complex division of labor that became differentially valued. Societies became more stratified as a result (that is, marked by greater class differences), political and religious hierarchies were established to manage the economic surpluses and mediate among the different socioeconomic classes, and eventually state systems of government (complete with bureaucracies, written records, taxation, a military, and public works projects) were established. Although the relationship between intensive agriculture and a stratified society is

not necessarily a causal one, these structural changes would not have occurred without the development of a reliable system of food production that could sustain a larger population. Intensive agricultural production provided both the opportunity and the commodities and forever changed the course of history in many parts of the world.

Peasantry

With the intensification of agriculture and the rise of civilization came the development of the *peasantry*. Peasant farmers differ from American Indian horticulturalists, Polynesian fishing people, or east African herders in that they are not isolated or self-sufficient societies. Instead peasants are tied to the larger unit (the city or state)—politically, religiously, and economically. More specifically, peasants are subject to the laws and controls of the state, are influenced by the urban-based religious hierarchies, and exchange their farm surpluses for goods produced in other parts of the state. Peasants usually make up a large percentage of the total population and provide most of the dietary needs of the city dwellers.

The intimate relationship peasants have with the cities and the state was succinctly stated by George Foster (1967: 7), who called peasants "a peripheral but essential part of civilizations, producing the food that makes possible urban life, supporting the specialized classes of political and religious rulers and educated elite." Foster's statement is important because it reminds us that the relationship between the peasants and the state is hardly egalitarian. The peasants almost always occupy the lowest stratum of society. Although they supply the rest of the society with its food, peasants have low social status, little political power, and meager material wealth. The more powerful city dwellers, through the use of force or military power, often extract both labor and products from the peasants in the form of taxation, rent, or tribute.

Industrial Agriculture

As we have seen, the domestication of plants and animals around ten thousand years ago expanded people's food-getting capacity exponentially from what it had been when they relied on hunting and gathering alone. Similarly the intensification of agriculture brought about by the invention of the plow, irrigation, and fertilizing techniques had revolutionary consequences for food production. A third major revolution in our

peasantry Rural peoples, usually on the lowest rung of society's ladder, who provide urban inhabitants with farm products but have little access to wealth or political power.

capacity to feed ourselves occurred several hundred years ago with the industrial revolution. *Industrialization* in food production relies on technological sources of energy rather than human or animal energy. Water and wind power (harnessed by waterwheels and windmills) were used in the early stages of the industrial period, but today industrial agriculture uses motorized equipment such as tractors and combines (powered by fossil fuels and biodiesel). The science of biochemistry has been applied to modern agriculture to produce fertilizers, pesticides, herbicides, and high-yielding seed varieties, all of which increase agricultural yields of food and nonfood commodities (for example, cotton and tobacco).

Farmers operating in industrialized societies today have a wealth of new technology at their disposal to increase productivity. Like most other professionals, industrial farmers now use the Internet for acquiring a wide range of agricultural information—from equipment sales to pesticide use to marketing opportunities. Moreover new systems of gathering weather information are helping farmers with crop management. Rather than individual farmers having to take weather measurements in their own orchards, fields, and vineyards, precise local information is now available on rainfall, temperature, humidity, and soil water content that comes directly to the farmer's own desktop computer. With such information at their fingertips, farmers are able to assess their risk and react quickly to protect their crops and inform their buyers or consumers as to how their crops are responding.

With industrial farming becoming increasingly competitive, a small but growing number of farmers in North America are attempting to gain a competitive edge by using the latest information technology. For example, some farmers equip their grain-harvesting combines with transmitters that allow a GPS satellite to track their exact position in their fields at any given time (Friedman 1999a). The sophisticated technology now available enables farmers to keep records on how much they harvest from each acre of land as well as the precise crop variety, water level, and fertilizer that will produce the highest possible yield for each parcel of land. This high-tech farm management is good for the environment because it uses fertilizer more economically, and it is good for the farmer because it increases the overall yield per unit of land.

Since the late eighteenth century, industrialized societies have experienced some noticeable changes. Before the industrial revolution, farming was carried out primarily for subsistence; farmers produced crops for their own consumption rather than for sale. In the twenty-first century, farming is largely commercialized in that the overwhelming majority of agricultural commodities (wheat, corn, soybean, tobacco, cotton, and flowers) is sold by producers to non-producers for some form of currency. Moreover, industrial agriculture requires complex systems of market exchange because of its highly specialized nature, the high yields produced, and the distance some crops travel before they are eaten or manufactured into something edible.

Within the past several decades, industrial agriculture has witnessed even more changes with the dramatic expansion of agribusiness—large-scale agricultural enterprises involving the latest technology and a sizable salaried workforce. Rather than raise a wide variety of food items for household subsistence, most industrial farmers engage in monoculture, the production of a single commodity on vast acreage (Figure 7.16). Some Canadian, US, South American, Asian, and African farmers have become experts at producing single commodities such as corn, soybeans, wheat, tea, coffee, pineapples, and bananas With the income earned from the sale of the monoculture commodities, industrial farmers purchase food commodities for their households. A consequence of the rise of agribusiness is the demise of small-scale farms that relied mainly on family labor. As the number of family farms decrease, corporate farms displace farmers in most regions of the world where agriculture and small-scale farmers coexisted. The need for farm laborers—be they displaced farmers or immigrant farm workers—to keep the "new" industrial farm working at optimum efficiency, is on the rise. These laborers generally are not family members but rather

© SambaPhoto/Eduardo Barcelos/Getty Images

industrialization A process resulting in the economic change from home production of goods to large-scale mechanized factory production.

FIGURE 7.16 Industrialized agricultural production requires heavy machinery and multiple pieces of farm equipment for the annual corn harvest, a process that is no longer a family enterprise on some farms.

hired laborers who are paid low wages that often keep them in poverty. Numerous examples from the last forty years abound noting the shift away from owner-operated farms and toward transnational corporations. Where we find large-scale export agriculture we tend to find transnational corporations controlling the farms and the farming enterprise. Many plantations, for example, are owned by multinational corporations such as Dole Food Company and Chiquita Brands International. In fact, today Kenya is one of the leading exporters of roses to Europe, whereas Colombia and Ecuador are the leading exporters of bananas to the United States. The net effect of industrial agriculture has been the loss of food sovereignty and the flow of wealth from poorer nations in the Southern Hemisphere to rich ones in the Northern Hemisphere.

Although industrial agriculture has produced farms of enormous size and productivity, these changes have come at a high cost. The machinery and technology needed to run modern-day agribusiness are expensive. Fuel costs to run the machinery are high. With the wide diversity of foods in modern North American diets, which are frequently eaten out of season or year round (oranges from California, Florida, and Israel; cheeses from New York, France, Ireland, and Wisconsin; corn from the Midwest; avocados from California and Chile; and coffee from Colombia and Kenya), additional expenses are incurred for processing, transporting, and marketing. The average food product purchased at a US supermarket has traveled nearly 1,500 miles before a consumer takes it home.

Industrial agriculture has been responsible for considerable environmental degradation. For example, in various parts of the world, the water tables are lower, the ecology of surface water (lakes and rivers) has changed, water fauna have been destroyed by pesticides, aquifers are polluted by pesticides, soil is salinized from over-irrigation, and the air is polluted from crop spraying. Moreover large-scale commercial fishing has decimated fish stocks throughout the world, and commercial animal operations such as hog farms in North Carolina have given us what are euphemistically called "swine lagoons" (man-made reservoirs filled with hog feces and urine), which can breach when hurricanes hit, dumping their contents into local rivers and making their way out to sea. And, as if this were not enough, the twenty-first century is witnessing a proliferation of genetically modified seeds for corn, soybeans, canola, and cotton by agricultural and pharmaceutical corporations to increase yields and control inputs (such as fertilizers and chemical pesticides). The long-term use of these seeds has potentially harmful effects on both human health and traditional seed varieties (Shiva 2000; J. Smith 2003). The litany of the negative effects of agriculture is almost endless. In fact, Jared Diamond (1987) has described agriculture as "the worst mistake in the history of the human race."

Resistance to Industrial Agriculture: An Applied Perspective

Gradually the developed world is becoming more concerned with agriculture and the food system, the environment, and personal health. In some regions of the United States, Canada and Europe, the number of small-scale farmers and farmers markets has actually been increasing. Their success comes as a result of communities wanting to know where their food comes from and providing support for a local food system. Community projects are strengthening ties between the consumer and food and food producers (Goodall 2005). In fact the International Slow Food Movement that Carlos Petrini established in 1989 in Italy now has more than a hundred thousand members from 153 countries who want to help preserve traditional ways of farming, protect heritage animals, and promote native seed varieties along with traditional recipes (www.slowfood.com). These shifting interests in food and food production help smaller farmers hold onto their land and their way of life.

In the past decade there has been a growing awareness of issues and ideas for getting involved in small-scale agriculture, organic agriculture, and other alternatives to industrial agriculture. For example, well-known musicians such as Bruce Springsteen invite cash donations at each concert to provide local assistance to food pantries and nonprofit organizations that are helping people improve their daily lives. There have been any number of films that draw our attention to what we eat, how much we eat, and what it does to our environment, as well as what we can do about it (films such as *Hunger for Profit, Global Gardener, Reinventing the World, Fast Food Nation, Super Size Me, The Real Dirt on John, Global Banquet, King Corn, Deconstructing Supper, Food Inc., Future of Food,* and *Bag It,* to name a few). There are many ways to get involved. Some project ideas that are ongoing that you may be interested in exploring are discussed herein.

Community Gardens

Community gardens in the United States are on the rise. As a way to become more food secure community members are establishing gardens in vacant lots. Food sharing, exchange of recipe,s and planting information are taking place among all peoples, regardless of socioeconomic standing. Community gardens are also on college campuses too. There are ways to get involved with local agricultural extension agents to work with existing partners to help start a community garden in your own community.

Farmers' Markets

Farmers' markets and other forms of direct marketing help small-scale farmers to market their fresh farm products to the public, hospitals, schools, restaurants, and other establishments. Direct marketing minimizes how far the food must travel and pays farmers a fuller dollar because not as many people get a share along the way (Figure 7.17). You can start or be part of and support the small farmers in your community by helping out at farmers markets and U-picks, or by creating CSA arrangementss and fresh-producing buy clubs, among other activities.

Back-to-the-Land-Movement

The Back-to-the-Land Movement also known as the "Back to the landers" is a desire by some to be able to get back to the land to grow their own food for subsistence and to live a life close to nature and in some cases off the grid. Since the 1960s the movement has had its appeal in the United States and in Europe. Some farmers are renting or leasing out their lands to those who cannot afford to buy land. Some aging farmers, who are willing to assist a younger generation to farm and keep the land in production, are getting involved in these arrangements.

Worldwide Opportunities on Organic Farms

A web site of registered Worldwide Opportunities on Organic Farms (WWOOF) farms lists more than a hundred countries where one can learn about organic farming outside of the United States (http://www.wwoof.org/). It is clearly a hands-on learning experience. However, do your home work on this experience; not all farm experiences are equal and none are vacations where you will be sunning yourself in the vineyards of Italy or the olive groves of Greece.

Fishery Projects

Coastal fishery projects are on the rise. With increased awareness of declining species government agencies are developing projects to monitor catch levels. Further research needs to examine the impact these new regulations are having on coastal fishing communities. The Applied Perspective highlighted in this chapter is from the research conducted by Andreatta (one of the authors). Her work with community-supported fisheries (CSFs) has galvanized coastal interest in small-scale fisheries and direct marketing from a prepaid subscription program, from Maine to Florida, Vancouver to Baja California, and coastal regions in between including Nova Scotia, and the Gulf of Mexico. In addition there has been a huge growth in the farm-raised fish industry. More research with an applied perspective on wild caught small-scale artisanal, traditional (heritage) fishing and that of farm-raised, is needed.

Pastoral Projects

National and International development agencies are working on projects to help with pasture management for livestock in regions of the world where climate change has contributed to protracted dry spells. Winrock (http://www.winrock.org/) invites volunteers to help in their educational and outreach projects. Global Livestock—CRSP is one of nine CRSP programs developed under Title XII of the International Development and Food Assistance Act of 1975, which is currently housed at the University of California Davis campus (http://glcrsp.ucdavis.edu/contact/), has projects in which you can assist with pasture management, through the Wallace Center. Other projects are out there; surf the Web and you will find projects in Kenya, Tanzania, Peru, India, Mongolia, and elsewhere.

Gary Retherford/Photo Researchers, Inc.

FIGURE 7.17 Farmers markets and other forms of direct marketing help small-scale farmers to sell their fresh farm products to the public, hospitals, schools, and restaurants. Direct marketing minimizes how far the food must travel and pays farmers a fuller dollar because not as many people handle the product by the time it reaches the consumer.

itical Thinking Questions

As the world's population continues to increase and extreme climatic events are experienced are traditional subsistence strategies sustainable?

2. Why is it that issues of food insecurity and food deserts are more likely to make the papers in the industrialized nations than and in the less develop nations?

Online Study Resources

CourseMate

Access chapter-specific learning tools including learning objectives, practice quizzes, videos, flash cards, glossaries, web links, and more in your Cultural Anthropology CourseMate. Login to http://www.cengagebrain.com to access the resources your instructor has assigned and to purchase materials.

Summary

1. If any culture is to survive, it must develop strategies and technologies for procuring or producing food from its environment. Although they are not mutually exclusive, five major food-procurement categories are recognized by cultural anthropologists: foraging (hunting and gathering), horticulture, pastoralism, intensive agriculture, and industrial agriculture.

2. Though lacking high levels of technology, many small-scale societies have made good subsistence adaptations to their natural environments—hence their long-time survival.

3. The success of various food-getting strategies depends on the interaction between a society's technology and its environment. Although different environments present different limitations and possibilities, it is generally recognized that environments influence rather than determine food-getting practices. The level of technology that any society has at its disposal is a critical factor in adapting to and using the environment.

4. Carrying capacity is the maximum number of people a particular society can support, given the available resources. If a culture exceeds its carrying capacity, permanent damage to the environment usually results.

5. Hunting and gathering, the oldest form of food getting, relies on procuring foods that are naturally available in the environment. Approximately ten thousand years ago, people for the first time began to domesticate plants and animals.

6. Compared to societies with other food-getting practices, hunting-and-gathering societies tend to have low-density populations, are nomadic or semi-nomadic, live in small social groups, and occupy remote, marginally useful areas of the world.

7. Horticulture, a form of small-scale plant cultivation that relies on simple technology, produces low yields with little or no surpluses. He often uses the slash-and-burn metho tion, which involves clearing the land and then planting seeds in the fertile Most horticulturalists plant multiple va seeds to ensure that there is enough fo households.

8. Pastoralism, keeping domesticated livestoc main source of food, is usually practiced in of the world that are unable to support any of cultivation. Pastoralism most often involve a nomadic or semi-nomadic way of life, small family-based communities, scarce food and oth resources, and regular contact with cultivators way of supplementing the diet.

9. Intensive agriculture, a more recent phenomeno than horticulture, uses technology such as irrigation, fertilizers, and mechanized equipment to produce high crop yields capable of supporting large populations. Unlike horticulture, intensive agriculture is usually associated with permanent settlements, cities, high levels of labor specialization, and the production of a surplus to be sold or traded at a market.

10. Industrial agriculture, which began several centuries ago, uses vastly more powerful sources of energy than had ever been used previously. It relies on high levels of technology (such as tractors and combines), inputs, high-yielding seeds, a mobile labor force, and a complex system of markets.

11. Resistance to industrial agriculture comes in many forms, including that of farmers scaling back, farming on smaller pieces of land and with fewer inputs as well as the public's involvement in shopping directly for fresh farm products at farmers markets, or through a CSA or getting involved in home gardening.

Key Terms

carrying capacity	hunting and gathering	nomadism	slash-and-burn method
food desert	industrialization	optimal foraging theory	stock friendship
foraging	intensive agriculture	pastoralism	swidden cultivation
freegan	locavore	peasantry	transhumance
horticulture	neolithic revolution	shifting cultivation	

Employees work on the assembly line of the Ford Ranger truck at Ford truck manufacturing plant located in Rayong province in Japan. The second-largest U.S. automaker plans to launch eight new products over the next five years.

Economics

Wanting to enter the lucrative Japanese sports market, a US producer of golfing equipment decided to explore the possibilities of a joint venture with a Japanese firm. Three representatives from each company met in San Francisco to discuss the details of such a joint venture between their companies. After the six men introduced themselves, they sat down on opposite sides of a long conference table. To demonstrate their sincerity for getting down to business, the three Americans took off their jackets, rolled up their sleeves, and loosened their ties. Then one of the Americans said to his counterpart across the table, "Since we will be working together for the next several days, we should really get to know each other. My name is Harold; what's your name?" The talks were concluded before the end of the first day, and the joint venture never did take place.

In a well-intentioned, but misguided, attempt to convey their interest in working hard on the project, the Americans made two serious cultural business blunders. First, by removing their jackets and rolling up their sleeves, they were using a typical form of nonverbal communication in the United States that conveys a desire to work hard and reach a mutually satisfactory agreement. The Japanese, unfortunately, who are much more formal in their behavior and their dress, interpreted the gesture as inappropriate and un-businesslike. The second blunder was Harold's suggestion that the two negotiating teams get on a first-name basis. Although Harold was simply trying to facilitate their working relationships, he was not aware that business relationships in Japan tend to be based on rigid status distinctions. Thus, in the eyes of the Japanese businessmen, being on a first-name basis was unacceptably informal and egalitarian. ◼

WHAT WE WILL LEARN

- How do anthropologists study economic systems cross-culturally?

- How do people use culture and produce resources to help them survive in their environment?

- How are resources such as land and property allocated in different cultures?

- How has globalization influenced change in various parts of the world?

- How might an applied anthropologist incorporate economic anthropology into their projects?

In the preceding example, the US and the Japanese businessmen were negotiating and interpreting within their own cultural understandings. The Americans wanting to be friendly only offended their potential Japanese business partners. Likewise the Japanese businessmen misinterpreted the Americans behavior and actions through their cultural lens. The business deal failed not because of a poor business plan, but for lack of cultural awareness on both sides— something that easily could have been avoided at the bargaining table (see Chapter 6 for nonverbal communication through body language and culturally sensitive nuances of the spoken language.

Economics and Economic Anthropology

When we hear the word *economics*, many images come to mind. We usually think of such things as money, supply and demand curves, lending and borrowing money at some agreed-on interest rate, factories with production

Sukree Sukplang/Reuters

schedules, labor negotiations, stocks and bonds, foreign exchange, and gross domestic product. Although economics textbooks include all of these subjects, they are not integral parts of all economic systems. Traditionally small-scale cultures had limited or no access to standardized currencies, stock markets, or factories and were not linked to a market economy. Nevertheless all societies (whether small-scale or highly complex) face a common challenge: All have at their disposal a limited amount of vital resources, such as water, land, livestock, machines, food, and labor. This simple fact requires all societies to plan carefully how to allocate scarce resources, produce needed commodities, distribute their products to all people, and develop efficient consumption patterns for their products to ensure the best adaptations to their environment for their survival. In other words, every society, if it is to survive, must develop systems of production, distribution, and consumption.

Studying economics enables anthropologists and other social scientists to study cultural adaptation from another perspective. An examination of economics teaches us how people use their time, money, and social skills to obtain resources. It is from this general understanding that we can then say all societies have an economy and engage in human activities that have economic implications. A society's economic system may include the ideas, institutions, and actions that a people (culture group) engage in to obtain the resources they need to survive, desire to own, or want to share with others. With this general approach to economics, we can say that all societies, be they industrial or nonindustrial, have an economic system.

Anthropology contributes to the study of economics by offering a perspective that looks beyond impersonal monetized transactions to the culturally varied ways in which people acquire resources. The anthropological approach emphasizes the cultural and social context in which people act, and the importance of social and kinship relationships in shaping economic behavior. For example, in the United States a teenager is more likely to babysit for free for a younger sibling than for a neighbor's child. In other regions of the world, such as Africa or Asia, children might take care of not only siblings but also other children, never thinking they would

be paid for their efforts, that is, just how things are done in their community. Anthropologists have noted that the norm in all societies, including our own, is for nonmonetized forms of economic exchange involving relatives and socially close individuals. Social relationships influence the form of the exchange and depends on how close people are and on the desired outcome—and of course depending on cultural traditions.

The science of *economics* focuses on how production, distribution, and consumption occur in the industrialized world. However, the subdiscipline of *economic anthropology* studies production, distribution, and consumption comparatively in all societies of the world, industrialized and non-industrialized alike. The relationship between the formal science of economics and the subspecialty of economic anthropology has not always been a harmonious one. Formal economics has its philosophical roots in the study of Western, industrialized economies. As a result, much of *formal economic theory* is based on assumptions derived from observing Western, industrialized societies. For example, economic theory is predicated on the assumption that the value of a particular commodity will increase as it becomes scarcer (the notion of supply and demand) or that when people are exchanging goods and services, they naturally strive to maximize their material well-being and their profits. As we will see in this chapter, these basic assumptions are not found in all the cultures of the world.

Economists use their theories (based on these assumptions) to predict how people will make certain choices when producing or consuming commodities. Owners of a manufacturing plant, for example, are constantly faced with choices. Do they continue to manufacture only blue jeans, or do they expand their product line to include casual clothes? Do they move some or all of their manufacturing facilities to China, or do they keep them in North Carolina? Should they give their workers more health benefits or longer paid vacations? Should they spend more of their profits on advertising, or pass on the earnings to the workers? Should they invest more capital on new technology and go green, or should they invest more on salaries for the labor force? Western economists assume that all of these questions will be answered in a rational way so as to maximize the company's profits and provide for their shareholders. Similarly Western economists assume that individuals as well as corporations are motivated by the desire to maximize their material well-being.

economics The academic discipline that studies systems of production, distribution, and consumption, typically in the industrialized world.

economic anthropology A branch of the discipline of anthropology that looks at systems of production, distribution, and consumption, wherever they may be found, but most often in the nonindustrialized world.

formal economic theory Assumptions about economic behavior based on the experience of Western, industrialized economies.

Cross-Cultural Examination of Economic Systems

Despite the substantial differences among economic systems throughout the world—as well as the different theories used to analyze them—it is possible to examine economic systems cross-culturally along three key dimensions:

1. *Regulation of resources:* How land, water, and other natural resources are controlled and allocated
2. *Production:* How material resources are converted into usable commodities
3. *Exchange:* How commodities and services, once produced, are distributed among members of the society

The Allocation of Natural Resources

Every society has access to certain natural resources in its territorial environment, including land, animals, water, minerals, trees, and plants. Even though the nature and amount of these resources vary widely from one group to another, every society has developed a set of rules governing the *allocation of resources* and how they can be used. For example, all groups have determined systematic ways for allocating land among their members. Hunter-gatherers must determine who can hunt animals and collect plants from which areas. Pastoralists need to have some orderly pattern for deciding access to pastureland and watering places. Horticulturalists and agriculturalists must work out ways of acquiring, maintaining, and passing on rights to their farmland.

In our own society, where things are bought and sold in markets, most natural resources are privately owned. Pieces of land are surveyed, precise maps are drawn, and title deeds are granted to those who purchase a piece of property. Small pieces of land generally are held by individuals, and larger pieces of property are held collectively, either by governments (as in the case of roads, public buildings, and parks) or by private corporations on behalf of their shareholders.

To be certain, there are limitations on private property ownership in the United States. To illustrate, certain vital resources such as public utilities are either strongly regulated or owned outright by some agency of government, rights of eminent domain (taking of the property) enable the government to force owners to sell their land for essential public projects, and zoning laws set limits on how property owners may use their land. Nevertheless the system of resource allocation found in the United States is based on the general principle of private ownership, whereby an individual or a group of individuals has total or near total rights to a piece of property and consequently can do with it as they see fit.

In other regions of the world, and in particular where a society bases its subsistence strategy on

hunting and gathering, pastoralism, or horticulture, resource allocation is handled differently. The concept of private ownership of land and other natural resources most likely does not factor into their approach to resource allocation. Let us briefly examine how each of these types of societies handles the question of access to land.

Hunters and Gatherers

In most hunting-and-gathering societies, land is not owned in the Western sense of the term, either individually or collectively. Hunters and gatherers have compelling reasons to maintain flexible or open borders. First, because hunters in most cases must follow the migratory patterns of animals, it makes little sense for people to tie themselves exclusively to a single piece of land. Second, claiming and defending a particular territory requires time, energy, and technology that many hunting-and-gathering peoples either do not have or choose not to expend. Third, territoriality can lead to conflict and warfare between those who claim property rights and those who would violate those claims. Thus, for food-foraging and food-collecting societies, having flexible territorial boundaries (or none at all) is the most adaptive strategy. As a general rule, a food-foraging society has open or flexible boundaries if animals are mobile and food and water supplies are unpredictable (Figure 8.1). Conversely, food collectors are more likely to live in semi-permanent settlements, with smaller groups venturing out to obtain vital resources such as food and water (Sutton and Anderson 2009).

Even though traditional hunter-gatherers rarely have private ownership of land, there is some variation in the amount of communal control. At one extreme are the Inuit of Canada and the Hadza of Tanzania, two groups that had no real concept of trespassing whatsoever. Only three decades ago, they could go where they wanted, when they wanted, and were generally welcomed by other members of the society. The traditional Ju/'hoansi of the Kalahari region recognized the association of certain territories with particular tribal bands. Members of one Ju/'hoansi band could track a wounded animal into a neighbor's territory or use the watering holes of any neighboring territory provided he or she asked permission, which was always granted. This type of reciprocity, cooperation, and permissive use rights increased the chances of survival of all Ju/'hoansi peoples. Today, however, the Ju/'hoansi way of life has been changed by modern development and economics, and government regulations that forbid

allocation of resources A society's regulation and control of such resources as land, water, and their by-products.

FIGURE 8.1 Having flexible territorial boundaries for some hunters and gatherers is an adaptive strategy for their survival. Here Ju/'hoansi hunter-gatherers stop to pick wild fruit from a bush.

FIGURE 8.2 For pastoralists to maintain their way of life, they must have access to two vital resources for their livestock: water and pasture. Turkana women and girls are responsible for watering livestock, which is unusual among pastoral societies.

them to hunt in their former territories. Major shifts, therefore, have taken place in their economic system where they have moved from depending on reciprocity and sharing gathered and hunted foods to depending on market exchange and resulting in the accumulation of material items. Such transformations have changed their social and political systems as well (Marshall 1991; Yellen 1990).

Pastoralists

Like hunters and gatherers, nomadic or semi-nomadic pastoralists require extensive territory. For pastoralists to maintain their way of life, they must have access to two vital resources for their livestock: water and pasture. Depending on the local environment, the availability of these two resources may vary widely. In marginal environments where pasture and water are at a premium, pastoralists need to range over wide territories. In more environmentally friendly regions of the world where grasses and water are more abundant, one is likely to find greater control over land and its resources (Figure 8.2). In any event, pastoral groups must work out arrangements among themselves and with non-pastoralists to gain access to certain pastureland for their livestock.

Variations can be found, but corporate (that is, nonindividual) control of pastures is the general rule among pastoral peoples. At one extreme there are pastoral societies whose entire territory is considered to belong to the society as a whole. In such societies (best represented by East African groups such as the Gabra, Herrero, Turkana, Jie, and Samburu), there are no fixed divisions of land that are used by different segments of the society. At the other extreme we find societies in which the rights to use certain pastures are divided among certain segments of the society. These pastoral societies are most often found in the Eurasian steppes and in the Middle East. And in some pastoral societies the use of wells or natural watering sources is controlled, to some degree, by individuals or groups to the exclusion of others. However, as Anatoly Khazanov (1994) reminds us, the variations found in how pastoral societies allocate land and resources depend on a number of factors, including environmental variables (such as climate and rainfall), types of animals herded, the size of the population relative to the land, and the relationship of the pastoralists to the wider society. To avoid overgrazing and conflict, pastoralists may have to enter into agreements with other pastoralist families to share certain areas, or they may have to form contractual arrangements with sedentary cultivators to graze their animals on recently harvested fields.

Preserving Andean Fiber Textiles through Biodiversity

High in the Andean highlands of Peru, somewhere 13,000 feet above sea level, roam alpacas and vicuñas. These camelids live at an elevation where not much can grow, the air is thin, and water is scarce. As part of the camel family these animals have adapted to the Andean range for centuries. Indigenous families, be they descendants of Inca or Aymara people, raise alpaca for their fleece and meat, and use their droppings as fertilizers for their crops. Vicuñas are often found among the alpacas, but their fleece is less valuable. Alpaca wool is extremely soft and used to make blankets, sweaters, hats, shawls, and rugs. At one time the fleece, wool, and meat would have been traded among the Incan and Aymara trading partners. Today the fleece can be found transformed into sweaters and scarves as far away as New York City. Yet the alpaca and their owners are facing new struggles.

Climate change is contributing to a deterioration of water sources and the loss of pasture for livestock. The challenges animals are facing also extend into households; families face lower incomes from a declining market value of alpaca as a result of the poorer quality of wool and little diversity of food. To combat some of the increasing economic and environmental uncertainties, alpaca farmers began to breed selectively, choosing only white alpaca. The white fleece absorbed dye better and their thinking was this would help them in their fiber sales to textile companies. However, this breeding practice added to the vulnerability of the alpaca, making their genetic make up less diverse and less adaptive to climate change. Researchers have shown that the loss of genetic diversity has resulted in a lowering of the genetic quality of the alpaca herds. This has lessened the quality of the fiber to be used in textiles and has made the farmers more vulnerable to external markets.

Other changes have taken place in the preparation of the fleece and marketing. For example, relying on outsiders or intermediaries for sheering the alpaca fleece quality has been comingled, that is to say all the wool that is shorn (removed) from the alpaca is not of an even quality or of similar hue. When everything is tossed together—a mixing of colors and quality—then the value of the fiber is reduced. Middlemen have stepped in, buying the fleece from the alpaca farmer, rather than the farmer having to make all the arrangements to get the fleece to the market. In the end though, the farmer takes a cut by selling to these middleman, earning less than if they had sold it directly to the textile companies. However,

Suzanne Porter/Alamy

today this is how business is conducted, and it does free up the farmer and family not to have to travel down the mountains to these markets.

Edwards (2012), a writer for Heifer International, reports the organization is currently working on an alpaca biodiversity project to improve the quality of the alpaca. They are working with 4,333 alpaca-raising families in twenty-two small-farming communities to reduce their vulnerability to climate change, external markets, and food insecurity. To make this project a success, researchers apply cultural understandings to this breeding and marketing project. They recognize that while breeding diversity back into the herd helps to make them more genetically resilient and resistant to climate change, there is also a new business opportunity for alpaca farmers—that is in breeding and selling of quality stock. Specializing in strong breeding stock and selling these alpaca to other alpaca farmers is one way improve the quality of the animals quickly and help the overall industry.

Returning to fiber quality and color uniformity through genetic diversity is only part of the solution. Developing new artisan markets that value the natural colors as well as more labor intensive animal and fiber care, will help the economy of the Andean alpaca farmer. The improved quality of the fleece and the natural colors has begun to pay off, and fleece and textiles now command a higher price from merchants and tourists. The combined shift toward smaller, local markets that value natural colors over dyed fibers is leading to a resurgence in breeding practices where there is a variety of natural colors among the alpaca and may in the end contribute to economic security for awhile longer among the Andean farmers.

The pastoral Fulani of northern Nigeria, for example, maintain special contacts with sedentary horticulturalists for rights of access to water and pastures. In contemporary times some nomadic Fulani pastoralists from northern Nigeria are migrating into the southwest and becoming more sedentary, trends also seen among other pastoral groups in Kenya, Tanzania, Niger, and the Sudan. For the Fulani, such a change has had a

significant impact on their culture, their economic system, their way of life, and their relationships with their new neighbors. In fact, there are conflicts with host communities, some of whom are horticulturalists. According to Uwem Ekpo, Akin Omotayo, and Morenike Dipeolu (2008:1), "the change from nomadic lifestyle to full sedentary lifestyle is generating changes in their living conditions, food habits, nutrition and health." These changes have negative consequences for child nutrition and health. Ekpo, Omotayo, and Dipeolu (2008) report that malnutrition is rising because of changing eating habits and inequitable distribution of food within families. Their research reveals that the settled Fulani have an increasing need for a cash income to purchase food and to meet the new day-to-day expenses of a sedentary lifestyle. By selling their cattle and dairy products for cash, they deprive themselves of dairy products in their diet. They now consume modern foods such as rice, cassava, yams, wheat, bread, soft drinks, and canned and processed foods.

As we discussed in Chapter 7, climate change is having a serious impact on pastoralists globally, putting both animals and their caretakers and owners at risk. Long dry spells have made it difficult for pastoralists to find forage for their animals, putting both of their survival at risk. Droughts and floods are affecting the Midwest in the United States; 2012 was the hottest year on record. What pastoralism will be like for future pastoralists in these changing climes is anyone's guess.

Horticulturalists

In contrast to hunter-gatherers and most pastoralists, horticulturalists tend to live on land that is communally controlled, usually by an extended kinship group. Individual nuclear or polygynous families may be granted the use of land by the extended family for growing crops, but the rights are limited. For example, small family units usually retain their land rights for as long as they work the land and remain in good standing with the larger family. Because they do not own the land, however, they cannot dispose of it by selling it. They simply use it at the will of the larger group. Such a method of land allocation makes sense, given their farming technology. Because horticulturalists often are shifting cultivators (see Chapter 7), there would be no advantage to having claims of ownership over land that cannot be used permanently.

The Samoans of Polynesia provide a good example of this communal type of land tenure. Under their traditional system, any piece of land belongs to the extended family that clears and plants it. Individual members of that extended family work the land under the authority of a *matai*, an elected family member who holds the title to the land on behalf of the entire group. The

matai's authority over the land depends on meeting his or her responsibility to care for his extended family. If he does not fulfill his obligations, the family can remove his title. Any individual of the extended family group has undisputed rights to use the land provided he or she lives on the family land and serves and pays allegiance to the matai (O'Meara 1990).

Intensive Agriculturalists

In North America, and in most other parts of the industrialized world, resources such as land are allocated according to the principle of private individual ownership (Figure 8.3). Most English-speaking people have no difficulty understanding the concept of private ownership. When we say we "own" a piece of land, the term means that we have absolute and exclusive rights to it. We are able to sell it, give it away, rent it, or trade it for another piece of property, if we so choose. The association between private individual land ownership and intensive agriculture is at least partially the result of the possibility of the same person using and taking care of the land year after year, thereby giving the land a permanent and continuous value such that it is in condition to be farmed year after year.

This concept of individual *property rights* is so entrenched in our thinking and our culture that we sometimes fail to realize that many other cultures do not share that principle with us. This cultural myopia led some early anthropologists to ask the wrong types of questions when they first encountered certain non-Western peoples. To illustrate, when studying a small group of East African horticulturalists who also

property rights The Western concept of individual ownership (an idea unknown to some non-Western cultures) in which rights and obligations to land, livestock, or material possessions reside with the individual rather than a wider group.

FIGURE 8.3 Property lines are often demarcated using some sort of fencing to indicate private ownership of where one's property boundary begins and ends.

kept cattle, some early anthropologists, using their own set of linguistic categories, asked what to them seemed like a perfectly logical question: "Who owns that brown cow over there?" In actual fact, no one "owned" the cow in our sense of the term because no single individual had 100 percent rights to the beast. Instead a number of people may have had limited rights and obligations to the brown cow. The man we see with the cow at the moment may have rights to milk the cow on Tuesdays and Thursdays, but someone else has rights to milk it on Mondays and Wednesdays. The cow is actually controlled by the larger kinship group (the lineage or extended family); the individual merely has limited rights to use the cow. This fundamental difference in property allocation is reflected in the local East African language of Swahili, which contains no word that is comparable to the English word *own*. The closest Swahili speakers can come linguistically to conveying the notion of ownership is to use the word *nina*, which means literally "I am with."

FIGURE 8.4 Worn tires are recycled, repurposed and kept out of the landfill by being refashioned into sandals.

Production

The initial step in meeting the material needs of any society is to establish a system of allocating the right to use resources to certain people. In few situations, however, can people use resources in exactly the form in which they are found in nature. Animals must be butchered; grains must be ground and cooked; metal ores must be mined, smelted, combined with other chemical elements, and crafted before becoming tools or automobiles; stones must be shaped before they can be put into the wall of a house or part of a monument. This process of obtaining goods from the natural environment and transforming them into usable objects is what economists call *production*. In today's "green" times, production also includes the transformation of one item refashioned into another. For example, water and soda bottles may be converted into articles of clothing such as polar fleece, old tires are ground up and used in road fill or sandals, and scrap metals may become corrugated metal sheets for house siding or roofing. As people recycle more items (paper, glass, plastics, metals, and cardboard), fewer products enter the crowded landfills (Figure 8.4).

All humans must meet certain fundamental material needs (such as food, water, and shelter), but how these needs are satisfied varies enormously from society to society. Some groups, such as the Siriono of

eastern Bolivia, meet most of their material needs with goods procured from hunting and gathering and not from manufactured products. The Kwakiutl, Sahlish, and Haida, who live on North America's northwest coast, depend on shellfish and salmon and meet their needs from the sea. Others, such as the Maasai and Samburu of East Africa, get their meat, milk, hides, and other animal by-products from the their livestock. Still others, such as people of the United States, Canada, and certain western European nations, go well beyond meeting their basic physical needs through a complex system of technology and industrialization. How do we explain such diverse systems of production? Why do cultures inhabiting apparently similar environments develop substantially different systems of production?

The answers to these questions can be partially expressed in economic terms. For example, why any society produces the things it does is determined, to some extent, by economic factors such as the accessibility of certain resources, the technology available for processing the resources, and the abundance of energy supplies. This is only part of the explanation, however, because cultural values also play a role in determining production. To illustrate, the Hadza—hunter-gatherers of Tanzania—are aware of the horticultural and pastoral practices of their neighbors but choose not to engage in either because of cultural preference and

---

production The process whereby goods are obtained from the natural environment and altered to become consumable goods for society.

their traditional identification as hunter-gatherers. Also most societies fail to exploit all of the resources at their disposal. Some societies living alongside bodies of water have strong prohibitions against eating fish. The Hindus in India, despite an abundance of cattle, refuse to eat beef on religious grounds. The Inuit, even though they often experience food shortages, maintain taboos against eating certain types of food that may be readily available. And, of course, people in the United States would never dream of routinely eating the flesh of horses, dogs, cats, guinea pigs, or rats, although these animals are a rich source of protein.

The apparent failure by some societies to exploit all available resources may not stem from irrationality or arbitrariness. As some cultural ecologists and cultural materialists have shown convincingly (see Chapter 4), often there are good reasons for certain economic behaviors that at first glance might appear irrational. The sacred cow in Hindu India is a case in point. Even though the Indian population needs more protein in their diet, the Hindu religion prohibits slaughtering cows and eating beef. This taboo has resulted in large numbers of half-starved cows cluttering the Indian landscape, disrupting traffic, and stealing food from marketplaces. But, as Marvin Harris demonstrated (1977, 1979a), the taboo makes good economic sense because it prevents the use of cows for less cost-effective purposes. To raise cows as a source of food would be an expensive proposition, given India's economic and ecological conditions. Instead cows are used as draft animals and for the products they provide, such as milk, fertilizer, and fuel (dung). The religious taboo, according to Harris, rather than being irrational, serves to effectively regulate the system of production by having a positive effect on the carrying capacity of the land (Figure 8.5).

Units of Production

Like other parts of culture, the way people go about producing is not haphazard or random but rather is systematic, organized, and patterned. Every society organizes its members into some type of productive unit comprised of people with specific tasks to perform. In industrialized societies the productive unit is the private company that exists for the purpose of producing goods or services. These private firms range from small, individually owned operations to gigantic transnational corporations. Whatever the size and complexity, however, these private companies are made up of employees performing specific roles, all of which are needed to produce the goods and services that are then sold for a profit. The employees do not consume the products of the firm, but instead receive salaries, which they use to purchase the goods and services they need.

Production in the Household

In most nonindustrialized societies, the basic unit of production is the household. In these small-scale societies, most, if not all, of the goods and services consumed are produced by the members of the household. This example holds true for small-scale farmers in Western and non-Western cultures, where farming households rely on family labor to produce farm products. The household may be made up of a nuclear family (parents and children) or a more elaborate family structure containing married siblings, multiple wives, and more than two generations. Although household members are most often kin, they can also include nonrelatives. Moreover some members may not actually live in the household but contribute to its economic well-being while living and working elsewhere. For example, some members of the household may migrate internally or externally to another country to find work or jobs that pay more than they might have earned in their own communities. We see examples of Algerians working in France and England, and eastern Europeans working in western Europe. We also find seasonal immigrant workers from Mexico and the Caribbean working in agricultural areas of the United States and Canada. Such family members generally send remittances back home to help provide for the household.

In a typical horticultural society, household members produce most of what they consume; their work includes planting, tending, and harvesting the crops; building houses; preparing and consuming food; procuring firewood and other fuels from the environment; making their own tools; tending some livestock; making their own clothes; and producing various containers for storing and cooking foods. When a particular task is too complex to be carried out

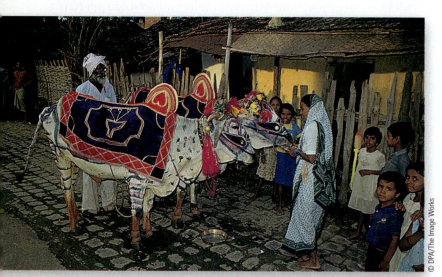

© DPA/The Image Works

FIGURE 8.5 Among Hindus in India, the cow is sacred and never killed for food. This is an example of how a religiously based food prohibition can be economically rational as well.

by a single household, larger groups of family members or neighbors usually join together to help complete the task. The Miskito Indians of the Nicaragua coast call this form of communal labor sharing *pana-pana* ("hand go and hand come") and use it to prepare their horticultural fields and repair the roofs on their houses.

Even though both the business firm and the household are units of production, there are significant structural differences between them. Whereas the business firm is primarily—if not exclusively—just a unit of production, the household performs a number of overlapping functions. When two male kinsmen who are part of the same household work side by side threshing wheat, it is likely that they play other roles together. For example, one man, because of his advanced age, may be a religious specialist; the other man, because of his leadership skills, may play an important political role in the extended family; and both men may enjoy spending their leisure time together drinking beer and telling stories. Thus, this productive unit of the household is the same group that shares religious, political, and social activities.

A second structural difference between the business firm and the household is that the household is far more self-sufficient. In most cases the members of the household in small-scale societies can satisfy their own material needs without having to go outside the group. In contrast, people employed in a business firm as wage workers rely on a large number of people for their material well-being, including the butcher, the television repairperson, the barber, the schoolteacher, the auto mechanic, and all of the thousands of people who make all of the things with which people surround themselves.

A third difference is that a business firm concentrates exclusively on its economic function and is therefore a more productive unit than the household. Because the family household is more than just a productive unit and must also be concerned with the emotional, social, psychological, and spiritual needs of its members, it is likely to use some of its resources in economically nonproductive ways. Consequently the family-based household is less likely than the business firm to use highly productive, progressive, or innovative methods.

In this context, we should recognize that the highly productive methods of technology used in modern businesses have some drawbacks. For example, computer technology and the Internet enable us to communicate and process information infinitely faster than we could twenty years ago. Nevertheless this same office technology is contributing to making workers less productive. According to a study on multitasking in the office (Wood 2010), 28 percent of an office worker's time is lost to interruptions and recovery time from taking telephone calls, reading blogs, using e-mail, surfing the net, and tweeting. Taking into account the size of the US office workforce (more than 65 million people) and other data, researchers calculate that interruptions cost the United States about $900 billion per year.

CROSS-CULTURAL MISCUE

While managing a project in Mexico City, you notice that one of your employees is particularly intelligent, successful, and diligent. Thinking he would make a great addition to the home office in Chicago, you offer him a job. Although your employee would receive a promotion, a large salary increase, and a company car if he moves to Chicago, he declines your offer. You simply can not understand why he refuses the offer when it would be so beneficial to his career.

Many highly successful people in Mexico (and parts of Central and South America) do not make career decisions based primarily on their own self-interest, as is often the case north of the Rio Grande. In Mexico people tend to first consider the needs of their family or company before considering their own self-interest. Receiving a promotion and higher salary would not be the most compelling reasons to take a new position. Rather your employee would think primarily about the interests of extended family members, many of whom probably would not want him to move. Then the employee would consider the interests of the local company, which probably needs him to continue working in Mexico City. What is best for the individual is not always the prime factor in a job decision.

Division of Labor

One important aspect of the process of production is the allocation of tasks to be performed—that is, deciding which types of people will perform which categories of work. Every society, whether large or small, distinguishes, to some degree, between the work that is appropriate for men and women and for adults and children. Even though many societies have considerably more complex *divisions of labor*, all societies make distinctions on the basis of gender and age.

To begin with there is an important to distinction in paid and unpaid work. Curiously those, and genuinely it is women, who work at home are often classified as unemployed or inactive if the work they are involved in is not remunerated—paid labor. Cleaning, cooking, shopping, doing laundry, caring for children, and a sundry of many other things that make a home run smoothly is not a job that contributes to the household income, unless one was a paid domestic (maid). In Table 8.1, there is a higher percentage of economically inactive women in North Africa, the Middle East, and South Asia where there is a higher control over women's activities. For example, in rural Afghanistan

divisions of labor The assignment of day-to-day tasks to the various members of a society.

TABLE 8.1

Regional Distribution of Female and Male Working-Age Populations, 2009

	Employed		Unemployed		Inactive	
	Men	**Women**	**Men**	**Women**	**Men**	**Women**
Sub-Saharan Africa	74.8	57.1	6.3	5.5	18.8	37.4
North Africa	69.9	23.1	6.6	4.3	18.8	72.6
Middle East	69.5	21.6	5.8	3.8	23.6	74.6
Latin America and Caribbean	74.3	46.5	5.5	5.2	24.7	48.3
South Asia	77.7	32.8	3.9	2.1	20.3	65.1
Southeast Asia and the Pacific	77.5	54	4.5	3.4	18.4	42.6
East Asia	75.4	64	4	2.5	18	33.5
Central and southeastern Europe (non-EU) and CIS	61.7	45.6	7.3	5	20.6	49.4
Developed Economies and EU	63	48.3	5.6	4.6	31.4	47.1
World	72.8	48	4.9	3.6	22.3	48.4

CIS, Commonwealth of Independent States; EU, European Union.

SOURCE: author created with stats from: International Labor Office Geneva, March 2010. Regional Distribution of Female and Male Working-age Populations by Main Economic Status, 2009: 11–14.

women are generally forbidden to work outside their home let alone be allowed to walk outside unescorted by a mail relative. And, in many other cultures we see further gender specialization in the work they carry out.

Gender Specialization

Although some roles (jobs) are played by both women and men throughout the world, many others are associated with one gender or the other, as you will read in Chapter 11. Women generally tend crops, gather wild foods, care for children, prepare food, clean house, fetch water, and collect cooking fuel. Men, on the other hand, hunt, build houses, clear land for cultivation, herd large animals, fish, trap animals, and serve as political functionaries. There are exceptions to these broad generalizations about what constitutes men's and women's work, however. In some parts of traditional Africa, for example, women carry much heavier loads than men, work long hours in the fields, build houses, and even serve as warriors. And among the northwest coast peoples, such as the Tlingit, it is the women who collect shellfish, thereby getting assigned to the task. In Tlingit culture a man who collects shellfish is considered lazy because it is believed that men should be out hunting or fishing and not taking the easy way out by collecting shellfish.

Men and women are often assigned roles for various social, political, or historical reasons. When these factors are inadequately

understood, they can appear to be quite arbitrary. For example, although sewing clothes for the family is thought of as women's work in North America (most men have never operated a sewing machine or made a purchase in a fabric store), among the Ecuadorian men and traditional Hopi of Arizona, it is the men who are the spinners, weavers, and tailors (Figure 8.6). Also among the Hopi it is the women who are the potters

FIGURE 8.6 Cultures determine which tasks are for men and which are for women. An Ecuadorian man works at a sewing machine, a job usually associated with women in the United States.

and not the men; however, in US culture both men and women can become potters. Moreover, in our own society, women have been virtually excluded from a number of occupations (such as jockey and Major League Baseball umpire), even though men have no particular biological advantage over women in performing these jobs.

Sometimes the division of labor by gender is so rigid that both men and women remain ignorant of the occupational skills of the opposite sex. This point is well illustrated by the traditional Mixe Indians of Mexico, where men traditionally grew corn and women processed it for eating. According to Ralph Beals, Harry Hoijer, and Alan Beals (1977), this division of labor between men and women was complementary and created a mutual dependency between men and women. For example, men's work was in the field, planting, raising, and harvesting maize. Men received no training in processing maize, however, so if they wanted to eat tortillas, they had to rely on women's work, which was equally complicated and time-consuming. Mixe women removed the maize from the cob and boiled it with the proper amount of lime for a sufficient time for the kernel to soften. Then the women ground it into dough using a flat stone slab and shaped it into a flat cake—the tortilla, which was then cooked on a flat griddle. A Mixe woman with a family of five spent about six hours a day making tortillas. Given the time demands of making tortillas, it would have been challenging for a Mixe woman to harvest the maize, just as it would have been impossible for her husband to make tortillas. Thus, their shared responsibilities helped to feed the family.

Age Specialization

In much the same way that societies divide labor on the basis of gender, they also allocate tasks according to age. Often children do not perform certain tasks because they lack the knowledge and physical strength that are needed. In our own society, where formal education routinely lasts through the late teens (and often beyond), young people generally do not engage in much productive work, especially because most of them are not raised in families that depend on what they produce from the land or on their efforts at hunting and gathering. By way of contrast, children in less industrialized societies, who do not require a formal education to provide for their families, usually become involved in work activities at a considerably younger age. In traditional times, children in the United States and elsewhere were expected to do household chores, help with subsistence farming, and tend flocks of animals; their survival depended on the entire group's effort.

Today children in many parts of the developing world participate in the market economy, and as a result an increasing number of children aged fourteen and younger are engaged in wage employment or commercial activity. Poverty is the reason for much of the use of child labor, with children working to help their families, particularly during times of crisis. Children find work, sometime in hazardous conditions and at low pay in agriculture, in industry, possibly in sweatshops, and in the service industry. Child labor by young girls decreased considerably (by 15 million, or 15 percent), yet it increased among boys (by 8 million, or 7 percent), reflecting the challenging economic times people around the world are facing. According to the United Nations, India has become the world capital for child labor, employing more than 55 million children aged 5 to 14, primarily in the garment industry.

Numerous examples of using child laborers are found in Asia and Africa. To illustrate, children in Kenya are working in light industry, mines (salt and soapstone), plantation agriculture (tea, coffee, sugar, and pineapple), and service areas such as street vendors, domestic servants, scavengers, and bus conductors. Some of the worst forms of child labor worldwide involve slavery, trafficking in children, debt bondage, forcible recruitment for warfare, and prostitution (Figure 8.7). In addition child laborers are also found in South America. For example, in Brazil children living in *favelas* (shanty or slum shacked villages) with their families may find themselves living alongside garbage dumps. Hundreds of families who live in and near the dump awaiting the daily arrival of the truck from the city's refuse. Children collect plastics, glass, and other items for home use or sale. The little bit sold helps to put food on the table.

Unlike child labor in traditional societies, which is required by the family's subsistence pattern, child labor in the twenty-first century has some serious negative consequences. Young child workers today are exposed to dangerous substances (pesticides, asbestos, and mercury), work under dangerous conditions (in mines or factories), and are often expected to exert enormous effort for long hours. The extent to which child labor exists in any society depends largely on its level of affluence and the availability of educational opportunities and future employment for children.

By way of contrast, the transition from being employed to being retired in the United States and China is considerably more abrupt. When most workers reach the age of retirement, they receive a plaque or a certificate and cease their productive activity. When workers in the United States and China retire, they usually suffer a noticeable loss of prestige and self-esteem. Some retirees may even begin a second career at the time of their retirement. Adults in the United States today sometimes work well into their sixties and seventies because of financial need or by choice, whereas in China government regulations

FIGURE 8.7 Child workers in the developing world are often subject to unsafe conditions. (*Right*) Workers sewing Mango jeans in garment factory in city of Shenzhen, China. This Kenyan man (*left*) is walking with a backpack sprayer used to spray pesticides in a coffee plantation without any protective clothing or safety equipment.

require professional men and women working for government institutions and companies to retire at the ages of sixty and fifty-five, respectively. The trend in China has been for blue-collar workers to retire at even younger ages, with women retiring at fifty and men at fifty-five. Many employees of state-owned enterprises are allowed to retire in their forties or fifties to create openings for the younger generation. This early retirement is causing a social security burden for the government, which has to support a growing number of retirees who live into their seventies on average. The proportion of elderly people is growing faster in China than in any major country, with the number of retirees projected to double between 2005 and 2015, when it will reach 200 million. By the mid-twenty-first century, 430 million people—about a third of China's population—will be retired. However, if China raised the retirement age, with a rapidly aging society, it could worsen the unemployment situation; fewer people would be relinquishing their jobs to younger members of the workforce.

Labor Specialization

Labor specialization—another term for *division of labor*—is an important descriptive characteristic of any society. At one extreme, subsistence societies with low population densities and simple technologies are likely to have a division of labor based on little more than gender and age. Most men in these societies engage in essentially the same activities and the same holds true for most women. If specialists do exist, they are usually part-timers engaged in political leadership, ceremonial activities, or specialized tool making. At the other extreme are industrialized societies, where most people are engaged in specialized occupations, such as computer programmer, television repairperson, kindergarten teacher, janitor, accountant, or orthopedic surgeon. One need only consult the Yellow Pages of the phone directory to get an idea of the vast diversity of specialized occupations in our own society. These two extremes should be viewed as opposite poles on a continuum of the division of labor, between which all societies of the world may be placed.

One of the major consequences of the transition from hunting and gathering to plant and animal domestication (the Neolithic revolution) has been the increased specialization of labor in the world. Because intensive agriculture produces food for larger populations than hunting and gathering, some people were freed up from the tasks of food production. Simple horticulture evolved into more complex forms of cultivation, which eventually led to the rise of civilizations (urban society).

With each advance in food-producing capacity came an increase in the complexity of labor specialization. This more complex division of labor is significant because more specialization of tasks provided a new basis for social solidarity. According to French sociologist Emile Durkheim (1933), in highly specialized societies in which people engage in complementary roles, social solidarity arises from their mutual dependence on one another. That is, teachers need to be on good terms with a butcher, a carpenter, and an auto

labor specialization See division of labor.

mechanic because teachers are so specialized that they cannot procure meat on their own, build a wood deck, or fix a faulty carburetor. Durkheim calls the social solidarity resulting from this labor specialization and mutual interdependence *organic solidarity*. Societies with minimal division of labor also possess a form of solidarity, but of a different type. This type, which Durkheim calls *mechanical solidarity*, is based on common interests, social homogeneity, strict conformity, kinship, mutual affection, and tradition.

Distribution of Goods and Services

Once goods have been produced or procured from the environment, they need to get into people's hands. Although people often consume some of the commodities they produce, surpluses often remain (and remember not all goods consumed are edible; they are consumed by virtue of being used). Systems of exchange are essential for every economy because they allow people to dispose of their surpluses and, at the same time, maximize the diversity of the goods and services consumed. As Karl Polanyi (1957) explains, goods and services are allocated in all societies according to three different modes of distribution: reciprocity, redistribution, and market exchange.

In the United States, most commodities are distributed according to a free-market exchange system based on the principle of "capacity to pay." People receive money for their labor and then use that money to purchase the goods and services they need or want. In theory, at least, if people have the money, they can purchase a loaf of bread; if they do not, they can not. Although this is the prevailing type, we can see examples of the other two modes operating in the United States as well. The principle of reciprocity operates, for example, when friends and relatives exchange gifts on birthdays, holidays, and other special occasions. We can see the principle of redistribution at work when people hand over a certain portion of their personal income to the government for taxes, which are then redistributed to public school systems, road maintenance, and other social services. Even though more than one mode of distribution can operate in any given society at the same time, usually only one mode predominates. Let us examine each of these three modes of distribution in greater detail.

Reciprocity

Reciprocity is the exchange of goods and services of roughly equal value between two parties without the use of money. Economic anthropologists generally recognize three types of reciprocity, depending on the degree of closeness of the parties involved in the exchange: generalized reciprocity, balanced reciprocity, and negative reciprocity (Sahlins 1972).

Generalized Reciprocity

Generalized reciprocity, which is usually played out among family members or close friends, carries with it the highest level of moral obligation. It involves giving a gift without any expectation of immediate return. Generalized reciprocity is perhaps best illustrated by the giving that takes place between parents and children in our own society. Parents usually give their children as much as they can while their children are growing up: food, toys, educational advantages, a room of their own, and the like. In fact, providing goods and services for children often continues after the children become adults. For example, parents may provide babysitting services, pay school fees for their grandchildren, or subsidize a vacation for their adult children.

In most cases parents provide for their children materially without expecting that their children will repay them at any time in the future. Because of the intimate bonds between parents and children, parents usually provide for their children out of a sense of love, obligation, and social responsibility. In reality, this sense of love and obligation typically becomes a two-way street because children usually come to the assistance of their elderly parents when the parents become too old to care for themselves. Thus, even in this most generalized form of reciprocity, the exchange of goods and services often balances out over the long run.

Even though generalized reciprocity is found in our own society, it is not the predominant form of exchange, as it is in smaller-scale societies, where the primary unit of economic organization is the family and where material resources may be uncertain. An exchange system based primarily on generalized reciprocity is common among hunters and gatherers because it contributes to their survival.

---

organic solidarity A type of social integration based on mutual interdependence, found in societies with a relatively elaborate division of labor.

mechanical solidarity A type of social integration based on mutuality of interests, found in societies with little division of labor.

reciprocity A mode of distribution characterized by the exchange of goods and services of approximately equal value between parties.

generalized reciprocity The practice of giving a gift without expecting a gift in return; creates a moral obligation.

© Washburn/Anthro-Photo

FIGURE 8.8 In hunting-and-gathering societies, such as the Ju/'hoansi of the Kalahari region, men butcher animals that they will later share along kinship lines and based on need.

For example, in most hunting-and-gathering societies, when a large animal such as a bushbuck is killed, the hunter keeps enough meat for his own immediate family and distributes the rest to his more distant relatives (Figure 8.8). In warmer regions where there is no means of refrigeration or other way of preserving meat, it makes little sense for the hunter to hoard all of the meat himself because it would spoil before it could be eaten. Instead, sharing with others is the expected norm. And, of course, given the uncertainty of hunting, sharing your kill today entitles you to share someone else's kill tomorrow. This form of sharing ensures that no member of the group goes hungry. Whether you are an Inuit or a Ju/'hoansi, reciprocity of hunted and gathered foods also means that if you contribute during the year, you may then take during leaner or harder times. Such an economic strategy sustains all family members by providing a fairly steady supply of meat despite the inconsistent success of most individual hunters. In such societies generosity is perhaps the highest ideal, and hoarding and stinginess are considered extremely antisocial.

We should not think of generalized reciprocity as being motivated totally by altruism. For all people who live at a subsistence level, maintaining reciprocal exchange relationships is vital to their economic self-interest. At subsistence levels, a person is more dependent on others for her or his material security. In the absence of worker's compensation, unemployment insurance, and bank loans, people must rely on others when their crops fail or they become too sick to hunt. Subsistence farmers, for example, might not

survive without occasional help from their relatives, friends, and neighbors. A farmer may need extra seeds for planting, help with fixing a roof, or extra cash to pay for a child's school fees. The best way of ensuring that these needs will be met is to respond quickly and unselfishly to the requests of others for similar types of assistance.

Although we do not always recognize it, reciprocal gift giving in our own society takes a number of different forms. Either consciously or unconsciously, we often give gifts with the expectation of getting something in return. We may expect gratitude, acceptance, friendship, or obligation rather than a material item. For example, why do we send wedding invitations to our friends? Is it solely for the sake of sharing with them the joy of the ceremony? When we give our brother a birthday present, would we not be hurt or disappointed if he did not reciprocate on our birthday? And do Western industrialized nations give millions of dollars in foreign aid to less industrialized nations totally out of a sense of altruism and generosity? Or are the donor nations looking for something in return, such as access to natural resources, political cooperation, or prestige? Thus, it appears that in all societies, including our own, gifts almost always come with strings attached.

After having lived in Kandoka village in Papua New Guinea on several different occasions, anthropologist David Counts (1995: 95-98) learned important lessons about life in a society that practices reciprocity:

> First, in a society where food is shared or gifted as part of social life, you may not buy it with money. … [Second,] never refuse a gift, and never fail to return a gift. If you cannot use it, you can always give it to someone else. … [Third,] where reciprocity is the rule and gifts are the idiom, you cannot demand a gift, just as you cannot refuse a request.

Balanced Reciprocity

Balanced reciprocity is a form of exchange involving the expectation that goods and services of equivalent value will be returned within a specified period of time. In contrast to generalized reciprocity, balanced reciprocity involves more formal relationships, greater social distance, and a strong obligation to repay the original gift. The repayment in balanced reciprocity does not have to be immediate; as Marcel Mauss (1954) suggested, any attempt to repay the debt too quickly can be seen as an unwillingness to be obligated to one's trading partner.

A major economic reason for balanced reciprocity is to exchange surplus goods and services for those that are in short supply. Shortfalls and surpluses can result from different levels of technology,

---

balanced reciprocity The practice of giving a gift with the expectation that a similar gift will be given in the opposite direction after a limited period of time.

FIGURE 8.9 Women spread flowers on graves in honor of deceased family members for "Dia de los Muertos".

collected from the forest at an agreed-on location near the village of their trading partners. They return at a later time to receive the commodities (usually salt, beads, and tools) left in exchange. By avoiding social contact, both the Semang and their exchange partners eliminate the risk of jeopardizing the relationship by haggling or arguing over equivalencies (Service 1966).

Negative Reciprocity

Negative reciprocity is a form of exchange between equals in which the parties attempt to take advantage of one another. It is based on the principle of trying to get something for nothing or to get the better end of the deal. Involving the most impersonal (possibly even hostile) social relations, negative reciprocity can take the form of hard bargaining, cheating, or out-and-out theft. In this form of reciprocity, the sense of altruism and social obligation is at its lowest, and the desire for personal gain is the greatest. Because negative reciprocity is incompatible with close, harmonious relations, it is most often practiced between strangers and enemies.

environmental variations, or different production capacities. But whatever the cause, balanced reciprocity enables both parties in the exchange to maximize their consumption.

In Oaxaca, Mexico, balanced reciprocity is illustrated with the exchange of both goods and services (Figure 8.9). According to social custom, a man is expected to sponsor at least one fiesta celebrating a major saint's day. Such events, involving elaborate food, beverages, and entertainment, almost always are beyond the capability of a man to provide by himself. Consequently the man solicits the help of his relatives, friends, and neighbors, thereby mortgaging his future surpluses. Those who help out expect to be repaid in equivalent amounts when they sponsor a similar fiesta.

Redistribution

Another principle of exchange is *redistribution*, whereby goods are given to a central authority and then given back to the people in a new pattern. The process of redistribution involves two distinct stages: an inward flow of goods and services to a social center, followed by an outward dispersal of these goods and services back to society. Although redistribution is found in some form in all societies, it is most common in societies that have political hierarchies.

Redistribution can take a number of different forms. In its simplest form, redistribution operates within large families, where family members give their agricultural surpluses to a family head, who in turn stores them and reallocates them back to the individual family members as needed. Among pastoral societies where livestock are shared within the

The Semang In some cases of balanced reciprocity, people go to considerable lengths to maintain the relationship. For example, the Semang of the Malay Peninsula engage in a form of *silent trade*, whereby they studiously avoid any face-to-face contact with their trading partners. The Semang leave their products

silent trade A form of trading found in some small-scale societies in which the trading partners have no face-to-face contact.

negative reciprocity A form of economic exchange between individuals who try to take advantage of each other.

redistribution A mode of distribution in which goods and services are given by members of a group to a central authority (such as a chief) and then distributed back to the donors, usually in the form of a feast.

tribe, livestock are raised and used for bridewealth exchanges, where the groom's family pays the bride's family in cattle for her hand in marriage. In complex societies with state systems of government, such as our own, taxation is a form of redistribution. That is, we give a certain percentage of our earnings to the government in exchange for certain goods and services, such as roads, education, and public health projects. The giving of gifts to charitable organizations (such as the Salvation Army or Goodwill) is also a form of redistribution because benefits are usually given to the poor and homeless.

Bridewealth

There are social institutions that allocate material goods according to the principles of redistribution and reciprocity. Because some of these social institutions perform functions other than economic ones, we often overlook their economic or distributive functions. One such social institution (discussed in detail in Chapter 9) is *bridewealth*, which involves the transfer of valuable commodities (often livestock) from the groom's extended family to the bride's extended family as a precondition for marriage.

Even though bridewealth performs some noneconomic or social functions—such as legalizing marriages, legitimizing children, creating bonds between two groups of relatives, and reducing divorce—it is also a mechanism for maintaining the roughly equitable distribution of goods within a society. Because extended families are the giving and receiving groups and are made up of a relatively equal number of men and women, the practice of bridewealth ensures that all people have access to the valued commodities. That is, no extended family is likely to have a monopoly on the goods because each group must pay out a certain number of cows when marrying off a son while receiving a roughly equivalent number of cows when marrying off a daughter. Even though the amounts paid may differ depending on the social status of the bride's family, all families have access to some of the material goods of the society.

Chiefly Redistribution (Tribute)

In some societies that do not have a standardized currency, tribal chiefs are given a portion of food and other material goods by their constituents. The chiefs then give back most of these food items to the people in the form of a feast. This system of *chiefly redistribution* or—also known as *tribute*—serves several important social functions at once. In addition to dispensing goods within a society, it affirms both the political power of the chief and the value of solidarity among the people.

A good illustration of chiefly redistribution can be seen in the traditional Nyoro of Uganda (Taylor 1962). Even though most goods and services were dispersed within the family or local village, some chiefly redistribution followed feudal lines. The rank and file often gave gifts of beer, grain, labor, and livestock to the king and to various levels of chiefs. The king and chiefs in return gave gifts to their trusted followers and servants. These gifts might have included livestock, slaves, or pieces of land. Among the Nyoro, the major criterion for redistribution was, by and large, loyalty to the political hierarchy. Consequently the king and the chiefs had no particular incentive to make an equitable redistribution or to see that the commoners received something roughly equivalent to what they had donated.

Equitable distribution is rarely found in most situations in which tribute is given. Instead the chiefs, headmen, and other high-status people invariably come out ahead. For example, among the Fijian Islanders of Moala, somewhat larger quantities and higher quality goods usually went to the chiefs and people of high status; leaders among the Hottentots in southern Africa often took the best portions of meat at the communal feasts; and according to Jesuit accounts, important Huron chiefs in North America always took the large share of furs at ritual redistributions. As Laura Betzig (1988: 49) describes it, the redistributor "seems inclined to skim the fat off the top."

Big Men/Feast-Givers

In less centralized societies that do not have formal chiefs, goods are redistributed by economic entrepreneurs whom anthropologists call *big men*. Unlike chiefs, who usually inherit their leadership roles, big men are self-made leaders who are able to convince their relatives and neighbors to contribute surplus goods for communitywide feasting. Big men are found widely throughout Melanesia and New Guinea. By using verbal coercion and setting an example of diligence, they persuade their followers to contribute excess food to provide lavish feasts for the followers of other big men. The status of a local big man—and of his followers—increases in direct proportion to the size of the feast, his generosity, and his hospitality. Big men of the South Pacific distinguish themselves from ordinary men by their verbal persuasiveness, generosity, eloquence, diligence, and physical fitness. Unlike chiefs, who are usually not producers themselves, big

---

bridewealth The transfer of goods from the groom's lineage to the bride's lineage to legitimize marriage.

chiefly redistribution or tribute The practice in which goods (usually food) are given to a chief as a visible symbol of people's allegiance, and then the chief gives the items back to the people (usually in the form of a feast).

men work hard to produce surpluses and encourage their followers to do so as well, all for the sake of giving it away. In fact, because generosity is the essence of being a big man, many big men often consume less food than ordinary people to save it for the feasts (Figure 8.10).

The many studies on big men during the first half of the twentieth century described exclusively males playing these roles. However a growing body of evidence suggests that there are also *big women* in Melanesia. Anthropologist Maria Lepowsky (1990) found that on the island of Vanatinai (in southeastern Papua New Guinea) there are *giagia* (singular *gia*), a gender-neutral term that simply means "giver." These giagia, who are both men and women, are successful in accumulating and then redistributing ceremonial goods and in hosting mortuary feasts for their kin and neighbors. In some parts of the Pacific, such as the Trobriand Islands, women have their own sphere of exchange of goods and products (yams and skirts) that they have produced by their own labor. But on Vanatinai, Lepowsky (1990: 37) found that "women and men exchange valuables with

exchange partners of both sexes and compete with each other to obtain the same types of valuables. … He or she accumulates ceremonial valuables and other goods in order to give them away in acts of public generosity." Under this system it is possible for a woman to be more prominent and influential than her husband, owing to her greater ability to acquire and redistribute valuable goods. Although there are, in fact, more big men than big women in Vanatinai, there are some women who are far more active and successful at exchanging goods than most men.

Potlatch

Still another customary practice that serves as a mechanism of redistribution is the *potlatch* found among certain American Indians of the northwest coast (Jonaitis 1991). Perhaps the best-known example of the potlatch was found among the Kwakiutl Indians of British Columbia, for whom social ranking was of great importance (Rohner and Rohner 1970). Potlatches were ceremonies in which chiefs or prominent men publicly announced certain hereditary rights, privileges, and high social status within their communities. Such claims were always accompanied by elaborate feasting and gift giving provided by the person giving the potlatch. In fact, at a potlatch, the host would either give away or destroy all of his personal possessions, which could include such articles as food, boats, blankets, pots, fish oil, elaborately engraved copper shields, and various manufactured goods.

The number of guests present and the magnitude of the personal property given away were measures of the host's prestige. The more the host could give away, the stronger was his claim to high social status. In a sense the gifts given at a potlatch served as payment to the guests for being witnesses to the host's generosity. In addition to providing a way of allocating social status,

FIGURE 8.10 Big men, such as Onka from Papua New Guinea, play a major role in the redistribution of goods within their societies.

big men or big women Self-made leaders, found widely in Melanesia and New Guinea, who gain prominence by convincing their followers to contribute excess food to provide lavish feasts for the followers of other big men or big women.

potlatch A competitive giveaway found among American Indians from the northwest coast that serves as a mechanism for both achieving social status and distributing goods.

the potlatch was an important mechanism for dispersing material goods because each time a person was a guest at a potlatch, he or she returned home with goods. The potlatch was a multifaceted ceremonial activity that also served important sociopolitical functions. According to Kenneth Tollefson (1995), potlatches, as practiced by the northwest coast Tlingit, were occasions for clans to gather for the purposes of installing new clan leaders, verifying clan titles to certain resources, bestowing clan titles, resolving interclan disputes, establishing and reaffirming alliances, and maintaining regional stability (Figure 8.11).

FIGURE 8.11 A Tlingit dancer in Alaska poses in traditional ceremonial attire in 1898 during a potlatch ceremony, which serves as a mechanism for both allocating social status and distributing goods.

market exchange A mode of distribution in which goods and services are bought and sold and their value is determined by the principle of supply and demand.

standardized currency (money) A medium of exchange that has a well-defined and understood value.

Potlatches were widely held during the nineteenth century until missionaries convinced the Canadian government that potlatches were demonic and satanic. As a result, the Canadian government banned potlatches in 1885. In the late nineteenth century, the US government placed a similar ban on potlatches. Potlatches continued to be held despite the bans, but on a much smaller scale and in secrecy away from non-native eyes. The bans on the potlatch were eventually lifted in the United States in 1934 and in Canada in 1951. Potlatches are still held today but, of course, the types of gifts are more contemporary and may include useful household items, native art, and cash (Leung 2007).

In this section we have looked at several redistribution systems found in the non-Western world. All of these economic institutions do, in fact, serve as mechanisms for the redistribution of goods and services throughout the societies in which they are practiced. But they also serve as ways of allocating social status and prestige. Moreover many of these systems of redistribution play important ceremonial, political, and integrative roles within the society. That these so-called economic institutions play important societal roles other than economic distribution should serve as a reminder that various domains of culture are interrelated, not separate and isolated.

Market Exchange

The third major mode of distribution is *market exchange*, whereby goods and services are bought and sold, often through the use of a standardized currency. In market exchange systems, the value of any particular good or service is determined by the market principle of supply and demand. Market exchange tends to be less personal than exchanges based on reciprocity or redistribution, which often involve ties of kinship, friendship, or political relationships. In this respect, market exchanges are predominantly economic in nature because people are more interested in maximizing their profits than in maintaining a long-term relationship or demonstrating their political allegiance to a chief or leader.

Market exchange systems are most likely to be found in sedentary societies that produce appreciable surpluses and have a complex division of labor. Societies with simple technologies, such as hunters and gatherers, are likely to have either no surpluses or such small ones that they can be disposed of quite simply by reciprocity or redistribution. More labor specialization in a society also contributes to a market exchange system because an `increase in the division of labor brings with it a proliferation of specialized commodities and an increased dependence on market exchange.

Standardized Currency

A common trait of market economies is the use of *standardized currency (money)* for the exchange of goods and services. *Money* can be defined as a generally accepted medium of exchange that also measures the value of a particular item. Money is significant for a number of reasons. First, the use of money to purchase items is a more flexible system than direct exchange of one item for another; as the range of goods increases, it becomes more difficult to find another person who has exactly what you want and wants something that you have to give. Second, money is divisible to the extent that its various forms and values are multiples of each other. Third, money comes in conveniently small sizes, which allows it to be transported from one transaction to another; in other words, a bag of coins is easier to deal with than a herd of camels. And fourth, money serves as a form of deferred payment in that it represents a promise to pay in the future with similar value. The anthropological literature suggests that money is most often found in societies that have high levels of economic development, which coincide with a complex use of technology and an accumulation of material items.

Market economies do not always involve money, however. In some small-scale societies, for example, market exchanges may be based on *barter*, the exchange of one good or service for another without using a standardized form of currency. In a bartering situation, a metal smith may exchange a plow blade for several bushels of wheat, or an artist and a migrant laborer may swap a piece of sculpture for three days of labor. Even in the highly complex market economy found in the United States, we find bartering institutions that facilitate the wholesale bartering of goods and services between large corporations. By turning over part of its surplus to a bartering corporation, a company that manufactures office furniture can exchange its surplus furniture for items it may need, such as air conditioners, automobile tires, or computers. In the United States and Canada, an increasing number of people (such as artists, therapists, and other freelance suppliers) are creating an underground economy by using bartering as a way to supplement their incomes during tough economic times.

The major prerequisite of a market exchange is not whether the exchange is based on currency or barter but rather that the value (or price) of any good or service is determined by the market principle of supply and demand. That is, we can consider an exchange to be based on the market principle when a pig can be exchanged for ten bushels of corn when pigs are scarce but bring only four bushels of corn when pigs are plentiful.

Variety of Markets

The extent to which markets are responsible for the distribution of goods and services in any given society varies widely throughout the world. The market economy of the United States, with its vast network of commercial interests and consumer products, is one extreme. There is virtually nothing that cannot be bought or sold in our highly complex markets. In some of our markets (such as supermarkets, shops, and retail stores), buyers and sellers interact with one another in close proximity to the goods. But other types of markets in the United States are highly impersonal, with no interaction between the buyers and sellers. For example, stock, bond, and commodities markets are all conducted electronically (through brokers), with buyers and sellers having no face-to-face contact. Beginning in the late 1990s, an increasing number of goods and services (everything from books, CDs, and household items from Amazon.com to personal banking with Bank of America) have been marketed over the Internet.

At the opposite extreme are certain small-scale economies that have little labor specialization, small surpluses, and a limited range of goods and services exchanged

CROSS-CULTURAL MISCUE

❋ Stella and Vern decided to take the family to Mexico for a vacation and for their children to experience another culture. The children had taken Spanish in school, and Stella and Vern spoke some Spanish, but was it enough to get around? There were many cultural experiences that caught the family unprepared. For example, forgetting shops closed during siesta hour also meant not being able to fill up the car when it was running out of gas. Learning about Mexico's standard currency, the *peso*, also provided the family with humor. One peso is not the same as one US dollar. Not understanding the standard currency not just because it looked different, (Mexico has pretty colored pesos for the different values), but because the exchange rate meant knowing how to convert between the two systems and where to place a decimal point. Stella was amusing when she offered the equivalent of US $20 in pesos for a single postcard instead of 20 Mexican pesos, which was worth about $1.57. She heard the number and mentally miscalculated. Rather than paying the appropriate amount in pesos Stella had heard incorrectly and made the wrong mathematical conversion. It caused a lot of chuckles for the family and the shopkeeper who could have sold an expensive postcard to Stella, but no harm was done. She knew her Spanish, but she did need to work on her quick math skills. From then on she used a conversion chart she made for her wallet for quick reference. She made similar conversion charts for each country she visited in the future, making shopping all that much more fun and interesting for her and shopkeepers.

---

barter The direct exchange of commodities between people that does not involve standardized currency.

in markets. In horticultural societies in South America, such as in Colombia, most of the material needs of a household are met by the productive activities of its members. Whatever surpluses exist are brought to market for sale or exchange, and the profits are used to purchase other goods or needed services or to pay taxes. In such societies the actual location of the market is important because many social functions are performed there in addition to the economic exchange of goods and services. In west Africa the market is a place where buyers and sellers meet to exchange their surplus goods, but it may also be the place where a man goes to meet his friend, settle a dispute, watch dancing, hear music, pay respects to an important chief, have a marriage negotiated, catch up on the latest news, or see distant relatives (Figure 8.12).

Many societies today find themselves in a transition between these two fundamentally different types of market economies. Some cultural anthropologists (Chambers and Chambers 2001) are examining are rethinking their research agendas to explore these times of transition in market economies. Of interest is exploring the dynamics of culture change by asking questions such as: How will societies change when individualistic market rationality (individuals wanting more and not less of a good) replaces the values of sharing, personal relationships, and community well-being? Is it possible to hang onto one's traditional core of community values when technologies, including global satellites, cell phones, and the World Wide Web, are used to exchange goods and services? To what extent do people in small-scale societies choose to participate in the global economy? Should a member of the family migrate to another country to seek gainful employment? How might this influence others from the same community to migrate along with the successful individual? And, what cultural changes might occur over time as a result of these new international economic ties? These and other questions concerning the impact of global markets on local communities are being posed with increased frequency by anthropologists all over the world. These questions are provocative because they question the sustainability of natural resource extraction, the distribution of goods, services as well as the shift in where there are employment opportunities.

Informal Economy This worldwide transition from small-scale to global markets raises the distinction between formal and informal market economies. Informal market economies include legal but unregulated producers of goods and services that, for a variety of reasons, escape government control and regulation (taxation, public monitoring, and auditing). The informal economy should not be confused with the underground economy, however, which involves illegal activities such as prostitution, drug dealing, human trafficking, and racketeering. Informal economies include some self-employed individuals as well as those employed in homes and at factories operating "under the radar." Workers do not claim income on personal tax forms, nor do employers file employment records.

Working conditions, earnings, and safety standards in the informal economic sector are almost always far inferior to those in the formal sector. There is a wide variety of informal economic activities, including house cleaning, garment work done in homes, construction work, gardening, selling crafts or fruit and vegetables on street corners (petty retailing), begging, child care, independent taxi driving, home catering, hair cutting, and other microenterprises.

Economists have recognized these informal economic activities for years, but because they are difficult to track, they are challenging to study. In some parts of the developing world, the informal economy has generated more economic activity than the formal economy. The presence of informal activity has been obvious for decades in many of the megacities of Africa, southern Asia, and South America—where millions of people struggle to survive by hawking single pieces of fruit on the street.

Erik-Jan Ouwerkerk/Redux

FIGURE 8.12 Women in Burkina Faso are selling vegetables at an open air market. Each one has a little surplus to sell, but may spend the entire day visiting with others while selling.

Cruise Liners and the Environment: When do the environment and its local inhabitants matter more than profit?

✳ Cruise liners have been taking tourists to the northwest coast to visit Glacier Bay and the surrounding regions in Alaska and Canada for decades. The main attractions for tourists are to see glaciers and wild life and enjoy the Tlingit villages, a First Nation tribe that has shared the region along with other First Nation Tribes such as the Haida and Tshimshin for centuries. Cruise liners along with other large ships call into the major ports bringing with them food and supplies for commerce for the residents. For the Tlingit, a good portion of their annual income is derived from their economic interactions with tourists. For example, the Tlingit base their livelihood on the crafts and other souvenir items they sell as well as on the sale of fresh-caught fish.

Over the years, cruise ships have increased in size, where some are transporting 5,000 to 7,000 travelers—a moving city—at any one time (Eilperin 2012). The ships have to transport sufficient fuel for most of the journey to carry everyone, the crew, and everyone's belongings. The upshot of the frequent visits to the region on these large ships is the amount of pollutants that is emitted. Experts from the US Environmental Protection Agency (EPA) comment that the amount of sulfur dioxide produced is equal to that of 13.1 million cars and as much soot as from 1.06 million cars. The EPA has recognized that these air pollutants contribute to respiratory illnesses and lung disease and affect air quality as far away as North Dakota. Beginning in November 2012, the various cruise liners that travel within 320 km (198 miles) up the Alaska and Canadian coast to view the orcas and glaciers have to burn cleaner fuel.

In 2007, under President George W. Bush's administration, emissions of sulfur dioxide were limited. Three years later the International Maritime Organization adopted the joint US-Canadian proposal to create an "Emissions Control Area" within the 320 km shoreline. Eilperin (2012) reports similar acts were taken in the 1990s for ships cruising the Baltic and North Seas. Large ships traveling in the region will had to reduce the sulfur content of their fuel from 2.7 to 1 percent by the end of 2012 and further reduce it another 0.1 percent by 2015.

The environmental and health benefits to the region will be substantial. According to the EPA, the new rule will have an impact on the environment similar to removing 12.7 million cars off the road per day and eliminating the soot and sulfur dioxide

from 900,000 cars. Removing these emissions will help save between 12,000 and 31,000 premature deaths as a result of environmental factors each year by 2030.

Large ships and the cruise liners are weighing the costs of the new rule requiring the use of cleaner fuels against payoffs to the environment. They fear that if fuel prices rise they will have to raise their prices or cut back in some way to control costs. However, if the emissions are not reduced they will cut the health benefits to the residents. Some companies are considering traveling outside of the 320-km mark as a solution to avoid having to complying with the new regulations.

Questions for Further Thought

1. As an applied cultural anthropologist what economic conversation would you be engaged in with local residents, should you be hired as a consultant to work on a community-based environment and health project with the Tlingit?

2. Who is responsible for protecting a natural environment, the local inhabitants, government, or another entity?

3. Can the cruise industry market a "green line" to help the environment, help the local communities, and provide some profit to their shareholders?

For example, street vendors make up a large part of the informal economy in Central America, where they are often found on busy city street corners (Figure 8.13). According to Danillo Valladares (2010), women in Guatemala are playing an increasing large role in the informal economy working as domestics, street vendors, and in-home seamstresses. Working in the informal sector enables women to provide additional income for their families, in part because their own positions do not pay well enough and their husbands also may not

FIGURE 8.13 In the village of Chichicastenango, Guatemala these local women are selling a wide variety of fresh foods items.

bring in enough money. "According to the third regional report on the labor market in Central America and the Dominican Republic produced by the International Labour Organization (ILO) and the Central American Integration System (SICA), 64 percent of women in the labor force in the region work in the informal sector, compared to 50 percent of men in the workforce" (Valladares 2010). Female vendors would love to be employed in jobs that pay a regular wage, social security, and other benefits, but such jobs are not available for everyone, especially for those who lack formal education and skills for the higher paying positions.

Market Economies Societies with well-developed market economies have always struggled with the question of whether to rely on market forces or the government to regulate the economy. Free markets and government regulation are entirely different forces that can determine what goods and services will be available and, consequently, what the population will consume. Historically the United States, perhaps as much as any country in the world, has relied on the free-enterprise (free-market) system for economic decision making. By and large the US economy is based on the principle that prices are set by market forces as buyers and sellers vie with one another in a changing balance of supply and demand. Motivated by what Western economists call enlightened self-interest, people make decisions to produce goods and services on the basis of the public's

desire or willingness to purchase them. On the other hand, a number of other countries during the twentieth century opted for state-controlled economies in which the government (not impersonal market forces) determined what goods and services would be produced and what they would cost. One example was the Soviet Union. Its collapse in the 1980s, however, exposed many of the liabilities of relying too heavily on government bureaucracies for making basic economic decisions. To avoid the pitfalls of relying on either one of these strategies exclusively, every market economy is a blend of both government control and free markets. Even in its heyday, the Soviet economy also relied heavily on free markets, particularly with domestic farm products; and at different times, the US economy has experimented with varying levels of governmental control. The controversy arises when societies attempt to determine just what that blend should be.

Supporters of the free-market-economy approach point to the collapse of the Soviet Union as a vindication of the free-market system. They also cite a number of inefficient enterprises, such as the US Postal Service and Amtrak, to support their argument. Calling for a minimum of government regulation, they claim that the forces of the free market are most likely to produce the highest quality of goods and services.

Supporters of government regulation, however, argue that an uncontrolled free-market economy is not in the public interest for three reasons. First, they claim that free markets are not likely to make products that cost less but do not produce high profits. Because building low-income housing is not likely to generate large profits, for example, builders operating in a free-market economy will choose to build middle- and upper-class housing instead. If governments do not intervene to either build or subsidize low-income housing, the poor will have even fewer places to live. Second, capitalistic, free-market economies lead to increased social stratification—where the rich get richer and the poor get poorer. And third, critics argue that unregulated market economies can lead to a number of negative tendencies, including price gouging by monopolistic companies, misrepresentation of corporate profits to shareholders, disregard for dangerous working conditions (including sweatshops that overwork and underpay adults and children), harm to consumers because of faulty products, and predatory lending practices that can create problems for the entire world economic system, as we saw in the

2009 housing crisis. Although most people prefer some economic regulation, what the balance should be continues to be debated throughout North America and other free-market economies.

Globalization of World Economies

Since the end of the Cold War in the late 1980s, world markets have experienced dramatic changes. This process, known as *globalization*, essentially involves the spread of free-market economies to all parts of the world. The basic idea behind globalization is that economies will be healthier and growth will occur more rapidly if we allow market forces to rule and if we open up all economies to free trade and competition. This involves lowering tariff barriers (or eliminating them altogether), deregulating the economy, and privatizing services formerly provided by governments. The world's economies are becoming so intricately interconnected that, with BMWs made in South Carolina and Nike running shoes made in Taiwan, it is often difficult to determine the nationality of brands.

With the disintegration of the former Soviet Union in the late 1980s, followed by the rapid rise of China on the global market scene, the world has witnessed a stunning proliferation of free trade, opening up of markets, and heightened competition. The European Union (EU), North American Free Trade Agreement (NAFTA), and Central American Free Trade Agreement (CAFTA) are good examples of this process of globalization. And with the advent of e-commerce, anyone with a good product, a computer, a telephone, access to the Internet, a web site, and a UPS account has the potential to become a successful entrepreneur. The global revolution has encouraged the participation of large numbers of new players in the markets. It is now possible to enter the world marketplace one day, with a small capital outlay, and become a global competitor by the next afternoon.

Not only has trade become globalized, but so has the process of manufacturing. For much of the twentieth century, most countries, including the United States and Canada, had relatively self-contained systems of production. Goods were manufactured domestically (in country) by local laborers and then sold either at home or abroad. But by the 1970s, wages and the general prosperity of workers in the industrialized world had increased significantly. As a way of

reducing production costs, many multinational corporations moved their production operations to less-developed countries where labor costs a fraction of what it does at home. For example, a worker in Chile or Honduras might receive a weekly salary comparable to several hours' pay for a worker doing the same job in Toronto or Atlanta. Moreover the overwhelming majority of offshore laborers, particularly in the area of light assembly, are women—because they are more docile, have more dexterous fingers, and are paid less than their male counterparts. Although a growing number of multinational corporations regard this "labor outsourcing" as good business, many workers at home (and their unions) complain that domestic workers are losing their livelihood.

Since 2000, the world has witnessed the outsourcing of not just light manufacturing jobs but white-collar jobs as well. Accounting firms in the United States, for example, have been sending electronically the tax information of their clients to certified public accountants (CPAs) in Bangalore, India, which, for a fraction of the cost, fill out the tax forms (Figure 8.14). The Internet revolution now makes it possible to send large amounts of information all over the world at almost no cost. The development of software applications such as TurboTax, e-mail, and Microsoft Office provides the workforce with platforms that can be used anywhere in the world.

FIGURE 8.14 The Internet revolution now makes it possible to send large amounts of information all over the world at almost no cost. International call centers such as this one in Bangalore, India, increasingly answer many of our information technology and computing service calls.

globalization The worldwide process, dating back to the fall of the Berlin Wall, that involves a revolution in information technology, a dramatic opening of markets, and the privatization of social services.

Perhaps the best example of person-to-person outsourcing is in the medical professions. Staggering health care costs in the United States are sending patients overseas for medical procedures. Less than a decade ago patients from Tennessee or Maryland traveled to Duke Medical Center, Johns Hopkins University, or the Mayo Clinic for major medical procedures. Today, however, a half million people each year receive new hips or bypass surgery in India, Thailand, and Singapore. Although some of these medical globetrotters are well-off seekers of liposuction or breast enhancements, most are among the ranks of the uninsured or underinsured looking for affordable heart surgery or major dental work. A comparison of medical costs in the United States, Thailand, and India makes it clear why so many US citizens are choosing to go abroad for major medical procedures. For example, heart valve replacement, which costs between $159,000 and $230,000 in the United States, costs $10,500 in Thailand and $9,500 in India. Or a hip replacement, costing between $44,000 and $63,000 at home, can be obtained in Thailand for $10,000 and in India for $8,500. Even though we often think of India as a developing country, the medical expertise of the physicians and the medical care in general are comparable to those in the United States (Garloch 2006).

Views on Globalization

The process of globalization (the rapid movement of goods, capital, labor, technology, and ideas) has been met with mixed reactions. Although most developed nations tend to benefit, some people view the trend positively as an endless source of possibilities and cheap goods, and others see it negatively as leading to decreased job security and employment stability.

For many Western policy makers, globalization is seen as a new planetary reality linking Wall Street with the streets of the poorest sections of Manila, Nairobi, and Buenos Aires. Some pundits see globalization as the savior of humankind, whereas others see it as a boon to the rich and a curse for the poor. These two opposing views have pitted policy makers, economists, and individuals against one another. Proponents of globalization are quick to point out that the revolutions in technology, open markets, and information flow have stimulated production, consumerism, and rapid communication. They see McDonald's, Citicorp, and Microsoft creating a dynamic new world in which the boats of the poor (as well as the wealthy) are being lifted by the rising tide of global economics. Yet many other people, particularly those in poorer countries along with the anthropologists who study them, blame these same forces for joblessness, the economic collapse in Southeast Asia in the late 1990s, the United States in 2008, and the EU in 2010. Political corruption, environmental degradation, reductions in public services,

poor enforcement of international labor standards, and a growing gap between the rich and the poor are also seen as by-products of the a global free market economy. They believe that large global businesses, in their relentless quest for maximizing profits, are benefiting most from this unregulated (or minimally regulated) free trade, while at the same time demonstrating little concern about the human and environmental costs of globalization. British Petroleum (BP) illustrates the dangers of maximizing profits at the expense of workers' safety and the health of the environment as well as all the people who make a living on and around the Louisiana coast. BP's quest for oil, a commodity that people around the world are dependent on, led to a huge human and environmental catastrophe in April 2010, when one of its oil-drilling platforms exploded and millions of gallons of crude oil gushed into the waters of the Gulf of Mexico (see Chapter 7). In agreement with the US government in 2011 BP set up a $20 billion trust for losses and expenses incurred by this disaster. More than two years after the spill in 2012, BP plead guilty to 14 criminal charges and paid out 4.5 billion dollars in fines and other expenses (*New York Times* 2012). Yet what the final payout will be and will it cover the true cost of all that was lost remains to be seen. Sometimes money is not the answer and cannot make amends, no matter how large the sum. At the time we are writing these revisions, the victims of a natural disaster, Sandy, the hurricane that hit the northeast during the fall of 2012, families went without electricity and water for several months after the event. It is anticipated this natural disaster will cost billions of dollars. But who pays for this? What happens in other natural disasters? Does it make a difference in who pays when it is nature versus a corporation is behind it?

Globalization is perceived in different ways depending on one's viewpoint. The pro-corporation perspective is widely held in the United States, showing deference toward big business while glossing over the negative consequences of globalization on labor, the poor, and the environment. Another viewpoint holds that more government oversight is needed to ensure stability for the workers, whereas a third viewpoint attempts to blend social justice with environmental awareness in the approach to economic development and globalization.

In the view of high-level government officials, hedge fund administrators, heads of multinational corporations, and many others, globalization fosters big business, which provides jobs and opportunities for a country and its people. But what is the cost of this job growth and development? Consider working environments such as sweatshops that produce blue jeans or sneakers, what is the cost of this kind of globalization and its impact on the environment and human health? What effect has Walmart had in countries that produce for this international company and in local

AN APPLIED PERSPECTIVE

Helping Clean Up a Problem: A local charity recycles hotel soaps to kill germs around the world

Developing projects out of nothing or being a clever entrepreneur is part of the allure when thinking about applied anthropology and economic development. Project ideas may come out of nowhere or they may be stimulated by the simplest question and its timing. For example, when we think about recycling we often think about where that plastic water bottle goes. Does it end up in a fleece jacket or in the landfill? Others think about a different kind of recycling that refashions something into some other usable product, rather than giving something a new use before being tossed into the landfill.

A highly paid business executive was on one of his many business trips. On one occasion, he questioned: What happened to all those little bottles of shampoo and lotion and bars of soap that I leave behind? Do they just get tossed out when I check out? These questions have since changed his life and that of his business partner's. They both thought those 1 million bars of hotel soap being dumped in landfills every day in the United States could be put to better use.

The former business executive, Shawn Seipler, is now an executive director who along with his business partner, are co-founders of a non-profit called Clean the World (http://cleantheworld.org/) "In less than three years his vision has grown from a soap-recycling project based in a friend's garage to an international charity that has distributed 9.5 million bars of recycled soap in 45 countries, including the U.S." (Santich 2012). However, knowing the US culture, they knew there would be resistance to the product, even though semi-used bars would undergo sterilization. Nevertheless the business partners were undeterred and they researched and found studies saying that millions of children worldwide could be saved each year if they simply used soap and water to wash their hands, thus cutting down on the spread of infectious diseases. They even found one study that pointed out that the top two killers of children younger than 5—acute respiratory illness and diarrheal disease—could be cut by 60 percent if kids had regular access to soap.

Yet, how to get hotels and foundations (donors) on board remained an obstacle. Hotels were reluctant to sign on to this program because Clean the World wanted a small fee of 65 cents per room per month to fund this venture, which would kill germs around the world and at the same time free landfills from deposits of hotel soap. The two partners invested thousands of dollars of their own money, and despite nearing bankruptcy, they stuck with their vision.

Visiting Haiti in October 2009, they took with them some of their recycled bars of soap. The partners claimed that "children clamored for the small unwrapped bars of soap like they were gold" (Santich 2012). It so happened that on January 12, 2010, there was a 7.0 earthquake outside the Haitian capital of Port-au-Prince where an estimated 316,000 died and more than 1 million were left homeless. The partners were in a perfect position to offer a solution for survivors who would be threatened with outbreaks of cholera and other socially transferable diseases without proper sanitation. (See http://www.globalsoap.org/)

The Washington Post/Getty Images

"The CBS Evening News" ran a story on Clean the World's soap contribution, and soon after, Walt Disney World with its 28,000 hotel and time-share rooms, signed on to the project.

Applied medical anthropologists work on many kinds of health-related projects, including those of sanitation and access to potable water. Teaming up with a medical anthropologists early on in the project design phase or for the post-quake Haitian crisis would have helped the partners identify local collaborators in the host countries, as well as work with stateside hotel management staff. The potential for saving children's lives with access to recycled soap and clean water are ideal outreach projects for the Peace Corp and UNICEF, provided these organizations have access to the soap. You have to hand it to these partners for trying to clean up such a big problem with a small bar of soap.

Questions for Further Thought

1. In thinking about applied anthropology, how might an applied anthropologist contribute to this project?

2. What challenges would communities face in accessing the soap?

3. What ethical considerations do the partners and anthropologists need to be mindful of if they are interested in expanding their project or remaining in certain countries for the long term?

and international towns that host a Walmart store (Fishman 2006)? Some employees of big stores and factories that make television sets, computers, and T-shirts might reply that globalization has impoverished rather than enriched them, that just because one receives a paycheck may not mean that one can survive on that paycheck.

In the case of agriculture, perhaps the most damaging specific government action against the farmers of the developing world is the US government's continuing practice of paying subsidies to US farmers. To see how subsidies to US farmers hurt poor farmers in the developing world, let us look at the single crop of cotton, grown in both the United States and a number of poor African countries. Cotton is produced in the United States at a cost of roughly $0.68 per pound as compared to only $0.35 per pound in the west African country of Benin. In a totally open world market system, the farmer from Benin would be able to sell his cotton at the world market price of $0.50 per pound, whereas the US farmer would have to sell his crop at a loss. But if Congress subsidizes US farmers by giving them (from tax revenues) $0.40 for each pound of cotton grown, then the wealthy US farmer sells his cotton on the world market at a loss, but still making a profit through government subsidies. These subsidies encourage farmers to grow as much cotton as possible so as to receive the largest possible subsidies. But as the subsidized US cotton finds its way into the world marketplace, the increased supplies force the world price of cotton down. Subsidized US farmers can tolerate these lower prices for cotton, but the unsubsidized African farmer (who probably works for less than a dollar a day and whose government depends on cotton exports to fund public services such as health and education) has no such cushion. If the African farmer is forced to sell his crops at below his production costs, he loses his means of livelihood. Thus, US subsidies mean that the world's highest priced producers of cotton increase their share of the world's cotton market (more than 40 percent) and in the process, drive the low-priced producers of cotton out of business. According to World Bank estimates, the end of US farm subsidies would bring in approximately $250 million to the cotton-producing countries of west and central Africa (Prestowitz 2003). This type of unlevel playing field creates support for food and product sovereignty, whereby nations produce their annual harvest for consumption.

For the past several decades, Western policy makers have claimed that greater global economic integration would reduce poverty and economic inequality throughout the world. Because deregulated economies tend to grow faster, they argued, all countries would benefit—rich and poor alike. Yet the facts show a different picture. The true interconnectedness of the global market was never more apparent than in the fall of 2009, when Wall Street banks and the US auto industry teetered on the edge of bankruptcy. Repercussions were felt by members of the EU, China, and elsewhere. In May 2010, the nation of Greece was headed toward bankruptcy. The possibility of a nation brought to its knees for global debt contributed to a new fear for other EU nations, who in the end helped to bail Greece out of its financial crisis. Failure to address this persistent and widening inequality between the haves and the have-nots will breed more instability, violence, and terrorism, thereby posing a major threat to democracies around the world.

The process of globalization over the past several decades has indeed produced a mixed bag of benefits and drawbacks. Although some people have benefited from global deregulation, many others have not fared so well. Some have argued that globalization is at a turning point, and world leaders need to address the many social inequities in the world economy. Even the wealthy countries, threatened by global terrorism, are beginning to rethink the future of open markets with little regulation. Among the issues that need to be considered are (1) improving international governance, (2) providing a level playing field for poorer countries, and (3) enforcing international labor and environmental standards more effectively. New questions arise as to how societies will be able to develop economic strategies collectively so that they incorporate issues at the local, state, and regional levels, at the same time as those at the international level. Currently nations and even some corporations are trying to develop sustainable, long-term economic strategies that blend the local and global economies of societies so that the right balance is achieved to benefit all both now and in the future.

Applied anthropologists can play a vital role when given the opportunity to participate in international business. Understanding globalization from a cross-cultural, ethnographic perspective, being sensitive to gender issues in the workplace, and recognizing environmental and social inequities are only a few areas in which an applied social scientist could jump in and make a difference. Whether a person works in the private sector, public sector, or is self-employed, it is likely he or she will find himself or herself managing overseas employees, marketing products to foreign markets, dealing with overseas suppliers, and engaging in international and cross-cultural negotiations. Having an understanding of other cultures is more important than ever before. The formula is pretty straightforward: The more we know about the cultures of our overseas employees, partners, clients, customers, suppliers, and colleagues, the more likely we will be to meet our professional objectives. And of course, the opposite is also true: If we fail to understand cultural differences in the global economy, we are likely to shoot ourselves in the foot, as illustrated in many of the cross-cultural miscues described throughout this book.

Summary

1. The study of economic anthropology involves the study of all economic systems.

2. Economic anthropology involves examining how resources are allocated, converted into usable commodities, and distributed.

3. Whereas property rights to land are strongly protected in the United States, in most hunting-and-gathering societies land is not owned either individually or collectively. The extent to which people have free access to land in pastoral societies depends on local environmental conditions, with free access to land found in environments where water and grazing lands are scarce. Land rights are more rigidly controlled among horticulturalists and agriculturalists than among hunter-gatherers and pastoralists.

4. People in some parts of the world do not share most North Americans' notion of property ownership. Instead of owning something in our sense of the word, people have limited rights and obligations to a particular object, resource, or piece of land.

5. Every society, to one degree or another, allocates tasks according to gender. Because the same type of activity (such as weaving) may be associated with either gender in different cultures, the division of labor by gender is sometimes seen as arbitrary.

6. The amount of specialization (division of labor) varies from society to society. Based on the extent of division of labor, French sociologist Durkheim distinguished between two different types of societies: those based on mechanical solidarity and those based on organic solidarity. According to Durkheim, societies with a minimum of labor specialization are held together by mechanical solidarity, which is based on a commonality of interests, whereas highly specialized societies are held together by organic solidarity, which is based on mutual interdependence.

7. Goods and services are distributed according to three different modes: reciprocity, redistribution, and market exchange. Reciprocity is the exchange of goods and services of roughly equal value between two trading partners; redistribution, found most commonly in societies with political bureaucracies, is a form of exchange whereby goods and services are given to a central authority and then reallocated to the people according to a new pattern; and market exchange systems involve the use of standardized currencies to buy and sell goods and services.

8. Economic anthropologists generally recognize three types of reciprocity depending on the degree of closeness of the parties: Generalized reciprocity involves giving a gift without any expectation of immediate return; balanced reciprocity involves the exchange of goods and services with the expectation that equivalent value will be returned within a specific period of time; and negative reciprocity involves the exchange of goods and services between equals in which one or both parties try to gain an advantage over the other.

9. Whereas reciprocity is essentially the exchange of goods and services between two partners, redistribution involves a social center from which goods are distributed. The potlatch ceremony among the American Indians of the northwest coast is an example of redistribution.

10. Market exchange, based on standardized currencies, tends to be less personal than either reciprocity or redistribution because people in such an exchange are interested primarily in maximizing their profits. As a general rule, the higher the degree of labor specialization in a society, the more complex the system of market exchange.

11. There are differing views on globalization: those who see globalization as increasing opportunities worldwide and others who think globalization has negative effects on people and the environment. Although globalization has stimulated world trade, it has also increased the gap between the haves and the have-nots. Societies with market economies have to decide to what extent they will allow free markets or the government to control the economy.

Key Terms

allocation of resources	division of labor	market exchange	reciprocity
balanced reciprocity	economic anthropology	mechanical solidarity	redistribution
barter	economics	negative reciprocity	silent trade
big men	formal economic theory	organic solidarity	standardized currency (money)
big women	generalized reciprocity	potlatch	tribute
bridewealth	globalization	production	
chiefly redistribution	labor specialization	property rights	

Critical Thinking Questions

1. Although most people prefer some economic regulation, what should the balance be in North America and other free-market economies?

2. How can applied anthropologists get more involved in economic planning for communities?

3. What would be an applied anthropologist's role in economic development and what should applied anthropologists be mindful of when contributing to economic development plans, their implementation or evaluation?

Online Study Resources

CourseMate

Access chapter-specific learning tools including learning objectives, practice quizzes, videos, flash cards, glossaries, web links, and more in your Cultural Anthropology CourseMate. Login to www.cengagebrain.com to access the resources your instructor has assigned and to purchase materials.

The concepts of marriage and family are changing as gay and lesbian couples marry and have children.

Marriage and the Family

Mark Smith, twenty-eight, and Michael Jones, thirty-two from New York City have been partners for three years and felt ready to tie the knot. They were married on August 2012 with eighty-seven of their closest family members and friends sharing in their ceremony. They exchanged personal vows and white gold rings. They and their guests exchanged heartfelt toasts and everyone enjoyed feasting and dancing. As the evening was winding down and guests were feeling the effects of merriment several friends and family members approached them casually asking: Are you going to have kids? Are you going to have kids right away? How many kids do you want? Adoption and surrogacy were in the cards for them.

Mark and Michael realized they are living in a new era. With more states now recognizing same-sex marriage, especially after the 2012 election, it is increasingly possible for same-sex families (gay and lesbian) to adopt children. Mark remembers his father's brother was gay and was in a committed relationship for forty-seven years. His uncle always wanted to have children, he recalls, but back when they were younger it was not possible for same-sex partners to adopt and raise a family.

Mark and Michael were moved by their friends and families' understanding of love, marriage, and family. Rachel Swarns (2012) contends that today's same-sex newlyweds are feeling the pressure to fill the cradle much like their heterosexual counterparts (straight people). In the gay community, Swarns writes "it is another welcome sign of their increasing inclusion in the American mainstream. But for others, who hear the persistent questions at the office, dinner parties and family get-togethers, the matter can be far more complicated." As with other married couples considering adoption, surrogacy, or involved in family planning, similar questions arise, such as when to have children? can they afford them? how many? These are only a few of the logistical and financial questions facing all couples wanting to expand their family.

Our cultural understanding of family is continuing to evolve and popular culture is helping in this process. TV sitcoms such as "Modern Family" provide viewers with a cultural context and the language for the *new modern* family. Today, and in some states in the United States a child can live under the same roof with his or her two dads or two moms. And for Mark and Michael, time will tell when they are ready to make the decision to expand their family. ■

Juanmonino/E+/Getty Images

WHAT WE WILL LEARN

■ What do anthropologists mean by the term *family*, and is the family found in all cultures?

■ What functions do family and marriage systems perform?

■ Who can marry whom?

■ What economic considerations are associated with marriage in the world's contemporary societies?

■ How have modern family structures changed?

■ What role is biotechnology playing in the structures of marriage and family?

In all known societies people recognize a certain number of relatives who make up the basic social group generally called the family. This is not to imply, however, that all societies view the family in the same way. In fact humans have developed a wide variety of family types. To many middle-class North Americans, the family includes a husband and a wife and their children. To an East African herdsman, the family includes hundreds of kin related through both blood and marriage. Among the Hopi, the family is made up of a woman and her husband and their unmarried sons and married daughters, along with the daughters' husbands and children.

Many young couples today face new challenges in the globalized and biotech world in which they find themselves. Pressure to get an education, then a job is delaying marriage for some young couples. Marrying later in life has contributed to a range of fertility problems for some men and women. In other instances couples elect to have smaller families or are forced to have only one child. Sex selection becomes important for some families when faced with having only one child or smaller families. Biotechnology is providing new avenues for applied anthropologists specializing in marriage and family planning. Our notions of family and marriage are changing from same-sex couples having children to orphaned children raising younger brothers and sisters. This chapter examines the variety of family types found throughout the world and the process of marriage that leads to the formation of families.

obligations between them. Marriage usually involves an explicit contract or understanding and is entered into with the assumption that it will be permanent.

It is critical to point out that our definition of marriage uses the term *partners* rather than *wives* and *husbands*. Although many Westerners assume that marriage takes place only between men and women, others recognize marriages of men to men and women to women as being legitimate. In parts of west Africa, a successful woman merchant, who may already be married to a man, may take a wife to help with the domestic duties while she is at work (Amadiume 1987). Moreover, among the Nandi of Kenya, a woman can marry a woman (female husband) when the female bride's father has only daughters and no male heirs. Under such conditions the female husband arranges for a male consort to father children biologically for her bride. And historically among the Cheyennes of the Great Plains, warriors were permitted to take male transvestites as second wives (Hoebel 1960).

Until recently same-sex couples could not legally marry anywhere in the world (Figure 9.1). In a limited number of countries, however, same-sex marriage has been legalized and thus protected under the law in the same way as heterosexual unions. The Netherlands was the first country to legalize same-sex marriage in April 2001, followed by Belgium, three Canadian provinces (British Columbia, Ontario, and Quebec), Spain, South Africa, Norway, and Sweden (see Table 9.1). In the United States, the residents of Connecticut, Iowa, Maine, Maryland, Massachusetts,

Marriage and the Family

Even though we use the terms *family* and *marriage* routinely, their meanings are ambiguous. Because social scientists and laypeople alike use these terms indiscriminately, it will be helpful to define them in more detail. *A family* is a social unit characterized by economic cooperation, the management of reproduction and child rearing, and common residence. It includes both male and/or female adults who maintain a socially approved sexual relationship. Family members, both adults and children, recognize certain rights and obligations toward one another. *Marriage* can be defined as a series of customs formalizing the relationship between adult partners within the family. Marriage is a socially approved union between two or more adult partners that regulates the sexual and economic rights and

FIGURE 9.1 Newly wed gay lesbian couple celebrate one of the first same sex weddings in England.

Roger Bamber/Alamy

TABLE 9.1

Legalization of Same-Sex Marriage

Country	Year Enacted
Netherlands	2001
Belgium	2003
United States (Massachusetts in 2004; Connecticut in 2008; Iowa, Maine, and Vermont in 2009; New Hampshire and the District of Columbia in 2010, New York in 2011, Washington in 2012, and Maryland in 2013	2004–2013
Canada	2005
Spain	2005
South Africa	2006
Norway	2009
Sweden	2009
Argentina	2010
Iceland	2010
Portugal	2010
Denmark	2012

New Hampshire, New York, Vermont, Washington, and the District of Columbia may be legally married in same-sex unions, whereas most other states have banned same-sex marriage either through legislation ("defense of marriage" acts) or amendments to state constitutions. Clearly, the meaning and legality of same-sex marriage will be fought out in courts and legislatures in the years to come.

In 2012, the president of the United States, Barak H. Obama, campaigned for a second term and while doing so declared his support for the legalization of same-sex marriage. The administration of the past president, George W. Bush, had called for the banning of gay marriage, seeing it as a threat to civilization. In reaction to the previous administration, the American Anthropological Association (AAA; 2006), the world's largest organization of anthropologists, weighed in on this controversial issue by releasing the following statement:

> The results of more than a century of anthropological research on households, kinship relationships, and families, across cultures and through time, provide no support whatsoever for the view that either civilization or viable social orders depend upon marriage as an exclusively heterosexual institution. Rather, anthropological research supports the conclusion that a vast array of family types, including families built upon same-sex

partnerships, can contribute to stable and humane societies. (Passed on February 26, 2004, and posted on the AAA website: www.aaanet.org)

Sexual Union

Like any term, the definition of marriage often must be qualified. Marriage, according to our definition, is a socially legitimate sexual union. When two adults marry, it is implied that they are having a sexual relationship or that the society permits them to have one, if they desire it. Although this is generally true, we should bear in mind that this social legitimacy is not absolute; there may be specified periods during which sexual relations with one's spouse are taboo. To illustrate, in many societies, sexual relations between spouses must be suspended during periods of menstruation and pregnancy. After a child is born, women in many societies are expected to observe a *postpartum sex taboo*, lasting in some cases until the child is weaned, which can be as long as several years. As William Stephens (1963: 10) suggested, "There may be other sex taboos in honor of special occasions: before a hunting trip, before and after a war expedition, when the crops are harvested, or during various times of religious significance." Given this wide range of occasions when sex with one's spouse is prohibited, it is possible that in some societies, husbands and wives are prevented from having sexual relations for a significant segment of their married lives.

Permanence

A second qualification to our definition involves the permanence of the marital union. Often, as part of the marriage vows recited in Western weddings, spouses pledge to live together in matrimony "until death do us part." Even though it is difficult to ascertain a person's precise intentions or expectations when entering a marriage, an abundance of data suggest that the permanence of marriage varies widely, and in no societies do all marriages last until death. For example, recent statistics indicate that nearly one of every two marriages in the United States ends in divorce. Impermanent marriages can also be found in smaller-scale societies. Dorothea Leighton and Clyde Kluckhohn (1948: 83) reported that they often encountered Navajo men who had "six or seven different wives in succession." In short, when it comes to the permanence of marriage, there is always a discrepancy between ideal expectations and actual behavior.

---

postpartum sex taboo The rule that a husband and wife must abstain from any sexual activity for a period of time after the birth of a child.

Common Residence

A qualifying statement must also be added about the notion that family members share a common residence. Although family members usually do live together, there are some obvious definitional problems. If we define "sharing a common residence" as living under the same roof, a long list of exceptions can be cited. In Western society, dependent children sometimes live away from home at boarding schools and universities. Additionally, in this age of high-speed transportation and communication, it is possible for a married couple to live and work in two different cities and see each other only on weekends. This trend historically is found on a more global scale in African societies listed in George Murdock's "Ethnographic Atlas" (1967) and are characterized by wives and their children living in separate houses from the husbands. In some non-Western societies, adolescent boys live with their peers apart from their families; and in some cases, such as the Nyakyusa, adolescent boys have not only their own houses but also their own villages. In each of these examples, family membership and participation are not dependent on living under the same roof (Wilson 1960).

Thus, as we are beginning to see, the terms *marriage* and *family* are not easy to define. For years anthropologists have attempted to arrive at definitions of these terms that will cover all known societies. Anthropologists have often debated whether families and the institution of marriage are universals, but increasingly there are challenges for this interpretation. For example, some Sumburu women of Kenya, who are nomadic pastoralists, created their own independent village with the guidance of Rebecca Lolosoli, the village of Umoja Uaso (Wax 2005). Umoja Uaso is devoid of any men (Hansen 2012). The women who are part of the village have been thrown out of their families' villages because they had been raped by British soldiers and thus were considered tainted and spoiled. After twenty years the women of Umoja live together with only their children who were born there, doing the tasks of both men and women in their village (see Chapter 11 for further details).

Marriage and the Family: Functions

The functionalist school of anthropologists, represented by Bronislaw Malinowski and Alfred Radcliffe-Brown (Chapter 4), sought to understand how the parts of a culture contributed to the well-being of the society. Following some of the early functionalist research, we can better understand how the formation of families through marriage serves several important functions for the societies in which they operate. One function is to create fairly stable relationships between men and women that regulate sexual mating and reproduction. Because humans are continually sexually receptive and (in the absence of contraceptives) heterosexual intercourse often leads to reproduction, it is imperative that societies create and maintain unions that will regulate mating, reproduction, and child rearing in a socially approved manner.

A second social function of marriage is to provide a mechanism for regulating the sexual division of labor that exists to some extent in all societies. For reasons that are both biological and cultural, men in all societies perform some tasks and women perform others. To maximize the chances of survival, it is important for a society to arrange the exchange of goods and services between men and women. Hetereosexual and same-sex marriage usually brings about domestic relationships that facilitate the exchange of these goods and services.

Third, marriage creates family relationships that can provide for the material, educational, and emotional

CROSS-CULTURAL MISCUE

❋ Marriage in every society contains certain structural stresses and strains between partners. This holds true for spouses who share a common cultural background, but it is even more challenging in so-called "mixed marriages," where the partners were raised in different cultures or subcultures. Anthropologist Edward T. Hall, an expert in nonverbal forms of communication, tells the story of a mixed marriage in the United States in which the wife was so concerned about marital problems that she consulted a psychiatrist. Her husband, raised in a reserved family in New England, was taught to keep a tight rein on his emotions and to respect the privacy of others. His wife, by way of contrast, was raised in a large, boisterous Italian American family, where the family members were warm, loud, emotional, volatile, demonstrative, and physical. Coming from two such different family backgrounds, each with its own way of expressing caring and emotions, this husband and wife faced some serious communication problems arising from different expectations. According to Edward and Mildred Hall (2009: 23):

> When the husband came home after a hard day at the office, dragging his feet and longing for peace and quiet, his wife would rush to him and smother him. Clasping his hands, rubbing his brow, crooning over his weary head, she never let him alone. But when the wife was upset or anxious about her day, the husband's response was to withdraw completely and leave her alone. No comforting, no affectionate embrace, no attention—just solitude. The woman became convinced her husband didn't love her, and, in desperation, she consulted a psychiatrist. Their problem wasn't basically psychological but cultural.

needs of children. Unlike most other animal species, human children depend on adults for the first decade or more of their lives for their nourishment, shelter, and protection. Moreover, human children require adults to provide the many years of cultural learning they need to develop into fully functioning members of the society. Even though it is possible for children to be reared largely outside a family unit (as is done on the kibbutzim of Israel), in most societies, marriage creates a set of family relationships that provide the material, educational, and emotional support children need for their maturation.

Young Children Raising a Family

In some families young children have stepped in to the picture to become young adults raising their younger brothers and sisters. In many African countries such as Nigeria, South Africa, Tanzania, Kenya, Uganda, and Ethiopia, each with more than a million children orphaned as a result of parents dying from AIDS (Figure 9.2). It is estimated that nearly 16 million children have been orphaned by AIDS, with more than 14 million residing in sub-Saharan Africa! The statistics are alarming in and of themselves and raise important questions about the continuity of their culture. For example, how will these children learn their cultural traditions? Who will show them how to farm, raise their livestock, or conduct the appropriate rites of passage? With the loss of elders, parents, and grandparents, so much of culture is lost for the children.

Organizations, such as UNICEF, SOS Children's Villages, AIDS Orphans and Street Children, and the Global Fund to Fight AIDS Tuberculosis, and Malaria, are raising funds and awareness to reduce the vulnerability of children orphaned as a result of AIDS. Such organizations also provide health care (antiviral treatment for HIV and AIDS) in addition to a safe environment for the children to grow into adults. However, education and informal means for imparting knowledge of local cultural traditions for specific villages and communities in the regions hardest hit by AIDS will be critical for the future generations and the children's own

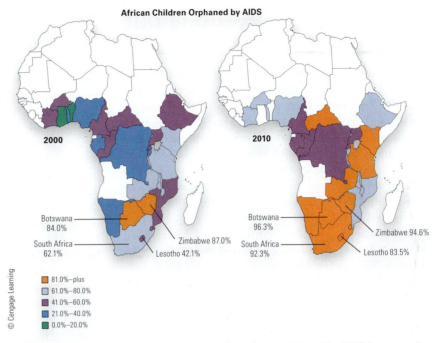

African Children Orphaned by AIDS

2000

Botswana 84.0%

South Africa 62.1%

Zimbabwe 87.0%

Lesotho 42.1%

2010

Botswana 96.3%

South Africa 92.3%

Zimbabwe 94.6%

Lesotho 83.5%

© Cengage Learning

- 81.0%–plus
- 61.0%–80.0%
- 41.0%–60.0%
- 21.0%–40.0%
- 0.0%–20.0%

FIGURE 9.2 More than 14 million children have been orphaned by AIDS in sub-Saharan Africa.

cultural survival (Figure 9.3). Applied anthropologists with specializations in local language and culture, the environment, livestock management, ethnomedicine, and so on can play an important role in assisting these children orphaned as a result of AIDS.

Amanda Koster/Corbis

FIGURE 9.3 These Kenyan school children have been orphaned as a result of AIDs as have more than 14 million children in sub-Saharan Africa.

Mate Selection: Who Is out of Bounds?

Every society known to anthropology has established for itself rules that regulate mating (sexual intercourse). The most common form of prohibition is mating with certain types of kin who are defined by the society as being inappropriate sexual partners. The prohibition on mating with certain categories of relatives is known as the *incest taboo*. Following the lead of Robin Fox (1967), we distinguish between sexual relations and marriage. Incest taboos (prohibitions against having sexual relations) are different from rules that prohibit marrying certain kinsmen. Although incest taboos and rules prohibiting marrying certain kin often coincide with each other (that is, those who are forbidden to have sex are also forbidden to marry), it cannot be assumed that they always coincide.

The most universal form of incest taboo involves mating between members of the immediate (nuclear) family—that is, mothers and sons, fathers and daughters, and brothers and sisters—although there are several notable yet limited exceptions. For political, religious, or economic reasons, members of the royal families among the ancient Egyptians, Incas, and Hawaiians were permitted to mate with and marry their siblings, although this practice did not extend to the ordinary members of those societies. The incest taboo invariably extends beyond the scope of the immediate or nuclear family, however. In some, but not all, states in the United States, people are forbidden by law from mating with their first cousins. In some non-Western societies, the incest taboo may extend to large numbers of people on one side of the family but not on the other. And in still other societies, a man is permitted (even encouraged) to mate with and marry the daughter of his mother's brother (a first cousin) but is strictly prohibited from doing so with the daughter of his mother's sister (also a first cousin). Thus, although it seems clear that every society has incest taboos, the relatives that make up the incestuous group vary from one society to another. Given that incest taboos are universally found throughout the world, anthropologists have long been interested in explaining their origins and persistence. A number of possible explanations have been suggested.

Inbreeding Theory

A popular theory that attempts to explain the existence of the incest taboo focuses on the potentially harmful effects of inbreeding on the family. This inbreeding theory, proposed well before the introduction of the science of genetics, holds that mating between close kin, who are likely to carry the same harmful recessive genes, tends to produce a higher incidence of genetic defects (which result in an increased susceptibility to disease and higher mortality rates). There is, however, little solid genetic evidence to support this view. What we do know is that outbreeding, which occurs in human populations that have strong incest taboos, has positive genetic consequences. According to Bernard Campbell (1979), the benefits of outbreeding include increases in genetic variation, a reduction in lethal recessive traits, improved health, and lower rates of mortality. This inbreeding theory has, no doubt, led to numerous state laws prohibiting cousin marriage in the United States. It should be noted, however, that there is hardly consensus on this issue among state legislatures because thirty states have laws against cousin marriage whereas twenty do not. Moreover no European nations prohibit cousin marriage. Martin Ottenheimer (1996) argues that this confusion is the result of a long-standing nineteenth-century myth that cousin marriage would threaten the civilized world. Ottenheimer notes that there is no compelling scientific evidence to support legislation forbidding cousin marriage.

Family Disruption Theory

Whereas the inbreeding theory focuses on the biological consequences of incest, a second theory centers on its negative social consequences. This theory, which is most closely linked with Bronislaw Malinowski (1927), holds that mating between a mother and son, father and daughter, or brother and sister would create such intense jealousies within the nuclear family that the family would not be able to function as a unit of economic cooperation and socialization. For example, if adolescents were permitted to satisfy their sexual urges within the nuclear family unit, fathers and sons and mothers and daughters would be competing with one another, and consequently normal family role relationships would be seriously disrupted. The incest taboo, according to this theory, originated as a mechanism to repress the desire to satisfy one's sexual urges within the nuclear family.

In addition to causing disruption among nuclear family members through sexual competition, incest creates the social problem of *role ambiguity*. For example, if a child is born from the union of a mother and her son, the child's father will also be the child's half-brother, the child's mother will also be the child's grandmother, and the child's half-sister will also be the child's aunt. These are just some of the bizarre role combinations created by such an incestuous union. Because different family roles, such as brother and father, carry with them vastly different rights, obligations, and behavioral expectations, the child will have great difficulty deciding how to behave toward immediate family members. Does the child treat the male who biologically fathered him or

---

incest taboo The prohibition of sexual intimacy between people defined as close relatives.

role ambiguity Confusion about how one is expected to behave.

her as a father or as a brother? How does the child deal with the woman from whose womb he or she sprung—as a mother or as a grandmother? Thus, the incest taboo can be viewed as a mechanism that prevents this type of role ambiguity or confusion.

Theory of Expanding Social Alliances

Incest avoidance can also be explained in terms of positive social advantages for societies that practice it. By forcing people to marry out of their immediate family, the incest taboo functions to create a wider network of interfamily alliances, thereby enhancing cooperation, social cohesion, and survival. Each time one of your close relatives mates with a person from another family, it creates a new set of relationships with people toward whom your family is less likely to become hostile. This theory, first set forth by Edward Tylor (1889) and later developed by Claude Lévi-Strauss (1969), holds that it makes little sense to mate with someone from one's own group with whom one already has good relations. Instead there is more to be gained, both biologically and socially, by expanding one's networks outward. Not only does mating outside one's own group create a more peaceful society by increasing one's allies, but it also creates a larger gene pool, which has a greater survival advantage than a smaller gene pool.

The extent to which wider social alliances are created by requiring people to mate and marry outside the family is illustrated by a study of Rani Khera, a village in northern India. In a survey of the village population (Lewis 1955), it was found that the 226 married women residing in the village had come from approximately two hundred separate villages and that roughly the same number of village daughters married out. Thus, the village of Rani Khera was linked through marriage to hundreds of other northern Indian villages through village exagamy. In fact this pattern of mating and marrying outside one's own village (created out of a desire to avoid incest) is an important factor integrating Indian society.

Mate Selection: Whom Should You Marry?

As we have seen, every society defines a set of kin with whom a person is to avoid marriage and sexual intimacy. In no society is it permissible to mate with one's parents or siblings (that is, within the nuclear family), and in most cases the restricted group of kin is considerably wider. Beyond this notion of incest, people in all societies are faced with rules either restricting their choice of marriage partners or strongly encouraging the selection of certain people as highly desirable mates. These are known as rules of *exogamy* (marrying outside of a

certain group) and *endogamy* (marrying within a certain group) (Figure 9.4).

Rules of Exogamy

Because of the universality of the incest taboo, all societies have rules about marrying outside a certain group of kin. These are known as rules of exogamy. In societies such as the United States and Canada, the exogamous group extends only slightly beyond the nuclear family. It is considered either illegal or inadvisable to marry one's first cousin and, in some cases, one's second cousin, but beyond that one can marry other more distant relatives and encounter only mild disapproval. In societies that are based on unilineal descent groups, however, the exogamous group is usually the lineage, which can include hundreds of people, or even the

FIGURE 9.4 At one time in the United States, interracial marriage was illegal. Although these laws no longer exist, the overwhelming majority of blacks and whites in the United States continue to practice endogamy.

exogamy A rule requiring marriage outside of one's own social or kinship group.

endogamy A rule requiring marriage within a specified social or kinship group.

clan, which can include thousands of people who are unmarriageable. Thus, when viewed cross-culturally, rules of exogamy based on kinship do not appear to be based on the closeness of blood ties.

Rules of Endogamy

In contrast to exogamy, which requires marriage outside one's own group, the rule of endogamy requires a person to select a mate from within one's own group. Hindu castes in traditional India are strongly endogamous, believing that to marry below one's caste would result in serious ritual pollution. Caste endogamy is also found in a somewhat less rigid form among the Rwanda and Banyankole of eastern central Africa. In addition to being applied to caste, endogamy may be applied to other social units, such as to the village or local community, as was the case among the Incas of Peru, or to racial groups, as was practiced in the Republic of South Africa for much of the twentieth century.

Even though there are no strongly sanctioned legal rules of endogamy in the United States, there is a certain amount of marrying within one's own group based on class, ethnicity, religion, and race. This general de facto endogamy found in the United States results from the fact that people do not have frequent social contacts with people from different backgrounds. Upper-middle-class children, for example, tend to grow up in the suburbs, take golf and tennis lessons at the country club, and attend schools designed to prepare students for college. By contrast, many lower-class children grow up in urban housing projects, play basketball in public playgrounds, and attend schools with low expectations for college attendance. This general social segregation by class, coupled with parental and peer pressure to "marry your own kind," results in a high level of endogamy in complex Western societies such as the United States.

Arranged Marriages

In Western societies, with their strong emphasis on individualism, mate selection is largely a decision made jointly by the prospective bride and groom. Aimed at satisfying the emotional and sexual needs of the individual, the choice of mates in Western society is based on such factors as physical attractiveness, emotional compatibility, and romantic love. Even though absolute freedom of choice is constrained by such factors as social class, ethnicity, religion, and race, individuals in most contemporary Western societies are free to marry anyone they please.

In many societies, however, the interests of the families are so strong that marriages are *arranged marriages*. Negotiations are handled by family members of the prospective bride and groom, and for all practical purposes, the decision of whom one will marry is made primarily by one's parents or other influential relatives. In certain cultures, such as parts of traditional Japan, India, and China, future marriage partners are betrothed while they are still children. In one extreme example—the Tiwi of North Australia—females are betrothed or promised as future wives before they are born (Hart and Pilling 1960; Robinson 1997). Because the Tiwi believe that females are liable to become impregnated by spirits at any time, the only sensible precaution against unmarried mothers is to betroth female babies before birth or as soon as they are born.

All such cases of arranged marriage, wherever they may be found, are based on the cultural assumption that because marriage is a union of two kin groups rather than merely two individuals, it is far too significant an institution to be based on something as frivolous as physical attractiveness or romantic love.

Arranged marriages are often found in societies that have elaborate social hierarchies; perhaps the best example is Hindu India (Figure 9.5). Indeed

FIGURE 9.5 Arranged marriages are often found in societies that have elaborate social hierarchies; perhaps the best example is Hindu India.

---

arranged marriages A marriage in which the selection of the spouse is outside the control of the bride and groom.

maintaining the caste system in India depends largely on a system of arranged marriages. Indian arranged marriages are further reinforced by other traditional Indian values and beliefs. Fathers, it was traditionally held, sinned if they failed to marry off their daughters before puberty. Both parents in India shared the common belief that they were responsible for any sin the daughter might commit because of a late marriage. For centuries Hindu society has viewed females as lustful beings who tempt males with their sexual favors. Thus, a girl had to be married at an early age to protect both herself and the men who might become sinners. And, if girls were to become brides before reaching adolescence, they could hardly be trusted to select their own husbands.

Prompted by this belief, in certain parts of India girls marry at a young age. Although the average age at marriage for females in India has been rising modestly over the past thirty years, the practice of child marriage is still widespread. According to the *Population Reference Bureau: The World's Women and Girls 2011 Data Sheet*, 47 percent of India's women aged twenty to twenty-four were married before the legal age of eighteen, with an even higher rate (56 percent) in rural areas. Even though the Indian government passed a law in 1978 setting the minimum age of marriage for females at eighteen, the law has been largely unenforced owing to cultural conservatism and the sheer size of the Indian population.

According to Anahita Mukherhi (2011), "This is higher than the average for South Central Asia (45%), of which India is a part. The average for Africa as a continent works out to 34%. Most African countries fare better than India, including Ghana, Sudan and Nigeria. While Pakistan's score works out to 24%, even Afghanistan, with a pathetic score of 43%, does a better job than India when it comes to curbing child marriage."

Anthropologist Serena Nanda (1992) reminds us that arranging marriages in India is serious business and should not be taken frivolously. In addition to making certain that a mate is selected from one's own caste, parents must be careful to arrange marriages for their children that take into consideration such factors as level of education, physical attractiveness, compatibility with future in-laws, and level of maturity. Requiring seriousness, hard work, and patience, an arranged marriage may take years to bring about, as one of Nanda's Indian informants explains: "This is too serious a business. If a mistake is made we have not only ruined the life of our son or daughter, but we have spoiled the reputation of our family as well. And, that will make it much harder for their brothers and sisters to get married" (1992: 142).

Indian couples were once introduced by family members who spent months, even years, researching potential partners. Today these matchmaking kinsmen are being rendered obsolete by an explosion of matrimonial websites. Would-be brides and grooms from India (as well as Indians living abroad) can go to websites with URLs such as Asianmatches.com, Suitablematch.com, and Matrimonials.com, where they can search for the ideal partner according to language, religion, caste, level of education, occupation, and even height, complexion, or astrological sign. By participating in these electronic matchmaking services, Indian young people are essentially agreeing with the traditional notion of arranged marriages but asking for (and getting) more input into the process. These new high-speed matrimonial websites greatly expand the pool of potential candidates, increase the amount of information that is available for prescreening, and allow the bride and groom more time to make up their minds. Traditional Indian parents are willing to move from the traditional arranged marriage to what might be called "assisted marriage" largely because they are more efficient and are likely to lead to what both parents and children want: strong, long-lasting marriages between compatible partners and compatible families. In fact many parents today are searching these matrimonial websites themselves on behalf of their unmarried sons and daughters.

Even though mate selection in North America generally is a matter of individual choice, many singles are not opposed to seeking help. Whereas Indians use the Internet to find potential marriage partners, the matchmaking services used by North Americans focus on dating, romance, and finding the right relationship, with marriage as a more distant goal. The number of websites devoted to matchmaking has exploded in the last five years. For example, a simple search for the term *matchmaking* in January 2013 resulted in 19 million "hits" on Google. Online dating services, which have millions of subscribers and generate hundreds of millions of dollars in revenue each year, are no longer for the socially inept. Rather, they have become a normal part of the singles scene for people of all ages. The top five online matchmaking services are: Match.com, Zoosks.com. eHarmony.com, Chemistry.com, and PerfectMatch.com.

Dating in the United States also has changed with the times. Whether it be from busy and overly complicated lives and schedules, people find that their life partner is not always their high-school sweetheart, a sorority or fraternity member, someone from church, work, or a pick-up from the bar scene. Some adults seeking love and romance are using a type of matchmaking service known as speed dating to find Mr. or Ms. Right. Speed dating are organized venues where people can meet a lot of eligible singles in one evening. Events are controlled with rules and time, people have an opportunity to meet and greet for a few minutes and then move onto another person. At the end of the event, people share their real identify or not and give out their contact information only to those they may be interested in for a longer meeting.

Many matchmaking services, including speed dating, specialize in a variety of demographics, such as nationality (Russia, China, Colombia), ethnicity (Latino, African American), religion (Catholic, Jewish, Hindu, Muslim), sexual orientation (gay, lesbian, straight), or lifestyle preference (vegetarians, Harley-Davidson enthusiasts, farmers, pet lovers, yoga practitioners, or singles with sexually transmitted diseases). There are even matchmaking services today that specialize in helping subscribers find their political soul mates. For example, Conservativematch.com and Singlerepublican.com are custom made for those "red state"–types looking for love; whereas Democraticsingles.com is where "blue state"–singles can go to find a politically compatible partner. Yet, several blogs also come up when searching for these online dating sites as warnings. These matchmaking site services also provide opportunities for husbands and wives to seek out extramarital relations. Straying partners generally get caught, which often puts an end to their marriages.

Matchmaking services in the twenty-first century are not just for the common folks. Singles who are trying to manage their fast-track careers often have special needs that require special services. To illustrate, Wall Street has its own "romantic headhunter," Janis Spindel, who for a fee of $100,000 offers wealthy male clients a dozen dates over the course of a year. Although client confidentiality makes it impossible to verify the statistics, Spindel claims to be America's top matchmaker brokering nearly one thousand marriages among her upper-class clients (Kim 2011). Such matchmaking at the elite level is found all over the world. A simple Google search reveals quite a bit on alternative dating and marriage practices.

All of these recent matchmaking services—both electronic and more personal—are noticeably different from the traditional forms of matchmaking, which were largely in the hands of family members. Nevertheless these new mechanisms for arranging marriages fit in nicely with the pressures of the modern world. Young people, particularly those trying to manage their careers, simply do not have the time or are not interested in cruising singles bars in hopes of finding Mr. or Ms. Right.

In some countries, matchmaking, or at least facilitating marriage for young adults, is becoming the business of the government. For example, Singapore is concerned about its low birthrate, which was at 1.2 in 2011 and well below the replacement level of 2.0 for the country. They attribute the trend of the best-educated professionals postponing marriage until their careers are established. The government of Singapore has been sponsoring love seminars at several of its technical institutes as well as supporting popular rap music to spark a national campaign to encourage baby making (Mukherhi 2012). Singapore is well known for its many public programs of social engineering, including campaigns to discourage being rude, littering, speaking improper English, and chewing gum. Encouraging matchmaking websites, such as singaporelovelinks.com as the premier dating site for young couples, is the government's latest attempt at societal improvement, designed to boost the birthrate by encouraging young professionals to date, fall in love, marry, and have children earlier in their careers than is the case today. It remains to be seen whether this latest attempt to boost the birthrate in Singapore will be any more successful than previous failed government-sponsored programs of wine tastings, tea dances, cooking classes, cruises, and screenings of romantic movies.

Preferential Cousin Marriages

A somewhat less coercive influence on mate selection than arranged marriages is found in societies that specify a preference for choosing certain categories of relatives as marriage partners. A common form of preferred marriage is *preferential cousin marriage*, which is practiced in one form or another in most of the major regions of the world. Some kinship systems distinguish between two different types of first cousins: cross cousins and parallel cousins. This distinction rests on the gender of the parents of the cousin. *Cross cousins* are children of siblings of the opposite sex—that is, one's mother's brothers' children and one's father's sisters' children. *Parallel cousins*, on the other hand, are children of siblings of the same sex (the children of one's mother's sisters and one's father's brothers). In societies that make such a distinction, parallel cousins, who are considered family members, are called "brother" and "sister" and thus are excluded as potential marriage partners. However, because one's cross cousins are not thought of as family members, they are considered by some societies as not just permissible marriage partners but actually preferred ones.

The most common form of preferential cousin marriage is between cross cousins because such a union strengthens and maintains the ties between kin

---

preferential cousin marriage A preferred form of marriage between either parallel or cross cousins.

cross cousins Children of one's mother's brother or father's sister.

Parallel cousins Children of one's mother's sister or father's brother.

A Crisis of Births: Family Making in Italy

❋ Some parts of the world are experiencing a crisis of over-population. Worldwide the figures calculate fertility rates at 3.1 births per women, yet globally they range from 1 to 7. Some campaigns attempting to reduce their national population explosion have taken on aggressive family-planning policies such as those which limit the number of children per household (China) or use coercive measure to reduce births through sterilization (India).

Western Europe, however, is experiencing a crisis of under-population and doing so without family planning initiatives. Demographers and politicians worried about nationalism along with social and economic issues drew media attention for some time on the region's low fertility rates. Anthropologist Elizabeth Krause conducted her fieldwork in central Italy during the height of the media blitz that encouraged families to become larger. In her ethnographic account Krause (2005) explores the phenomenon of making smaller families and the implication it has on society, politics and culture in "A Crisis of Births: Population and Family-Making in Italy." What Krause discovers is that the small family has become a symbol of the postwar era for the upwardly mobile and modern Italians where the average Italian family now has one child. However, this low birthrate which is 1.4, is less than the 2 children per household necessary for population stability, has become a national problem that demographers, politicians, and policymakers want to fix because it is below replacement for society (Krause 2005).

When Krause presented her work in the 2005 monograph, she drew on World Health Organization 2001 fertility rates. She noted that Spain's fertility rate was at 1.1, Italy's at 1.2, and Germany, Sweden and Greece were around 1.4. These rates do not meet replacement rates needed to maintain the respective national populations. Hence, the red flags flying among the demographers and politicians for these European countries.

Krause relied on ethnographic methods, such as interviewing, gathering oral histories, and participation observation; she also conducted archival and media research while she lived in an industrial-agricultural province of Tuscany for two years with her husband and her five-year-old daughter. She had a number of questions guiding her research, but one underlying theme she explored was what contributed to Italy's declining fertility rate? In her research she wanted be understand "what happens when a whole society's pattern of making families changes dramatically" (Krause 2005: xiii)?

During the course of her two years she worked in a family-operated workshop for a sweater factory, sewing on buttons. In this capacity, getting involved in the community, meeting locals as a local, she was able to get a real appreciation of the life of working-class families and family making from different social and economic classes. It is from this ethnographic experience that she was able to articulate how economics and family

Environmental Images/Universal Images/Age fotostock

influence gender roles, division of labor, the concept of work, immigration, racism, nationalism, as well as emotions, feelings, expectations, and ultimately family making. History played a critical role in her experience because the older generation of Italians have a different perspective on family and family size than that of the younger generations. She found that low fertility is much about struggles over male and female relations. It is about men and women carving out new identities in what it means to be Italian, European, and modern.

From an applied perspective Krause's research findings could contribute to demographers and politicians' approaches to future family-planning initiatives and create family policies to mitigate the low birthrate. She points out, "Family-making is not merely about reproducing babies, but also about producing the material goods and wages, as well as the care and nurturing, that make for a viable family" (Krause 2005:67). Demographers and politicians who fear immigrants will reproduce at a more rapid rate and alter the old social and class structures of Italian society are clearly missing the contemporary Italian cultural context (that of smaller families) that figures prominently into current family-making beliefs and practices. Incidentally since Krause's monograph was published, the fertility rate for Sweden has increased to 1.9, Spain is now at 1.5, Germany remains at 1.4, and Italy increased to 1.4. (www.google.com/publicdata for each country).

Questions for Discussion

1. Why is Italy experiencing a low birth rate?
2. How does the trend of people going from having large families to having small families play out at different levels of society?
3. What would be necessary to construct an effective pro-family campaign?

groups established by the marriages that took place in the preceding generation. That is, in the system of cross-cousin marriage, a man originally marries a woman from an unrelated family, and then their son marries his mother's brother's daughter (cross cousin) in the next generation. Because a man's wife and his son's wife come from the same family, the ties between the two families tend to be solidified. In this respect cross-cousin marriage functions to maintain ties between groups in much the same way that exogamy does. The major difference is that exogamy encourages the formation of ties with a large number of kinship groups, whereas preferential cross-cousin marriage solidifies the relationship between a more limited number of kin groups over a number of generations.

A much less common form of cousin marriage is between parallel cousins, the children of one's mother's sister or father's brother (Murphy and Kasdan 1959). Found among some Arabic-speaking societies of the Middle East and North Africa, it involves the marriage of a man to his father's brother's daughter. Because parallel cousins belong to the same group, such a practice can prevent the fragmentation of family property and facilitate arranged marriages.

The Levirate and Sororate

Individual choice also tends to be limited by another form of mate selection that requires a person to marry the husband or wife of deceased kin. The *levirate* is the custom whereby a widow is expected to marry the brother (or some close male relative) of her dead husband. Usually any children fathered by the woman's new husband are considered to belong legally to the dead brother rather than to the actual father. Such a custom serves as a form of social security for the widow and her children and preserves the rights of the husband's family to her future children. The levirate, practiced in a wide variety of societies in Oceania, Asia, Africa, and India, is closely associated with placing high value on having male heirs. African men and ancient Hebrews, for example, prized sons so that a man's lineage would not die out. In such cases men were under great pressure to marry their dead brothers' widows.

The levirate is found in patrilineal societies (those societies made up of a man, his sons, and the sons' wives and children) in which the bride marries into her husband's family and essentially severs her ties with her

---

levirate The practice of a man marrying the widow of his deceased brother.

sororate The practice of a woman marrying the husband of her deceased sister.

---

original family. Under such an arrangement, the levirate functions to look after the interests of the woman in the event that she becomes a widow. The solution is for her to become the bride of one of the male relatives of her husband. But in more recent times, particularly in India, widows are not always supported by their dead husband's families. It has been estimated (Damon 2007) that 44 million widows in India live in abject poverty because their husband's families have chosen not to support them. These widows cannot return to their natal families because they severed those ties when they married. Thus, facing a type of "social death," these Indian widows are at the mercy of inadequate support provided by either the government or local Hindu temples.

The *sororate*, which comes into play when a wife dies, is the practice of a widower marrying the sister (or some close female relative) of his deceased wife. If the deceased spouse has no sibling, the family of the deceased is under a general obligation to supply some equivalent relative as a substitute. For example, in societies that practice the sororate, a widower may receive as a substitute wife the daughter of his deceased wife's brother.

The Role of Romantic Love and Courtship

With all of the previously mentioned requirements and restrictions for selecting a spouse found throughout the world (exogamy, endogamy, arranged marriages, preferential cross-cousin marriage, the levirate, and the sororate), there seems to be little room left for basing a marriage on romantic love. To be certain romantic love has been a major prerequisite for marriage in Western cultures for generations. Western social historians could hardly disagree with the lyrics of the song from the play *Our Town* made popular by Frank Sinatra: "Love and marriage, love and marriage, go together like a horse and carriage." Although the song is an accurate representation of the role of romantic love in Western marriage, we cannot assume (particularly in light of the previous discussion) that this connection is universal (Figure 9.6).

Unfortunately, early anthropologists who have examined those many marital systems *not* based on romantic love have left us with the impression that the notion of romantic love does not exist in non-Western cultures. Confronted by the many variations of arranged marriage in their fieldwork, and assuming (erroneously) that romantic love was an exclusively Western phenomenon, most nineteenth- and twentieth-century anthropologists tended to overlook romantic love in the non-Western world because it

redsnapper/Alamy

FIGURE 9.6 Romantic love has been a major prerequisite for marriage in Western cultures for generations, maybe this cycling couple will one day marry to one another.

was not supposed to exist. In fact the "conventional wisdom" among most social scientists until quite recently was that romantic love was a luxury that only affluent societies had the time and energy to engage in. However, cross-cultural research by W. R. Jankowiak and E. F. Fischer (1992) found clear ethnographic evidence for the existence of the idea of romantic love in 147 of the 166 cultures studied. And, in the remaining 19 cultures, the absence of explicit ethnographic evidence was more the result of anthropological oversight (researchers never asked the appropriate questions) than the absence of romantic love. The findings of this cross-cultural study are clear: Even though many non-Western people do not base a marriage on romantic love, they certainly have the notion of romantic love, and they actually practice it with their pre- and postmarital lovers and even their own spouses.

So far we have seen how young people throughout the world face cultural prescriptions about whom they should or should not marry. Even in highly restrictive societies, however, the number of possible spouses is enormous. The critical question all cultures must answer is: To what extent do the two young people *themselves* decide whom they shall marry? The ethnographic possibilities range from permissive societies that allow sexual experimentation, "dating," and courtship by early adolescents to societies in which the groom does not see the face of his bride until after the official wedding ceremony.

The Trobriand Islanders of Papua New Guinea are on the permissive end of the continuum. According to Annette Weiner (1988: 66–71), Trobriand boys and girls begin playing erotic games with one another when they are seven or eight years old. By the early to mid-teens, they begin experimenting with sexual partners with no expectation of any committed relationship on the part of either party. Adolescents are free to pursue these liaisons because they do not sleep in their parents' house but rather with their peers in boys' houses or girls' houses. Even though adolescents do engage in some productive work, they are largely left to pursue freely their own relationships and adventures. Girls are every bit as assertive and proactive as boys in their acceptance or rejection of lovers. Thus, traditional Trobriand courtship practices and experimenting with heterosexual relationships are not that different from the types of "virtual courtships" young adults in the United States and Canada engage in today through such web sites as Facebook, Twitter, Linked in, Pinterest, and MySpace.

At the opposite end of the continuum, where any contact between unmarried men and women is forbidden, is Saudi Arabia, perhaps the most socially conservative Islamic country in the world. Until young adults marry, they are expected to live in their parental home, which is segregated by gender, with males living in one part of the house and women in another. The males in a typical Saudi household do everything in their power to protect the reputations of their unmarried sisters by rigidly enforcing the prohibition against any type of social contact between unmarried people. If they fail to protect their sisters and daughters from heterosexual contact from outside the family, the honor of the entire family will be jeopardized. Thus, marriages are arranged between men and women who often have never seen, or spoken to, one another. There should be no social contact between the prospective bride and groom even during the months between the signing of the marriage contract and the wedding ceremony. As with any set of cultural practices anywhere in the world, however, the extent to which *all* young adults adhere to these rigid standards of no social contact is not 100 percent.

Trobriand culture and Saudi Arabian culture are clearly two examples at the extreme ends of the spectrum. In actual fact most young people in the world today live in cultures that fall somewhere between these two extremes. Moreover many of these cultures, owing to modern communication and transportation technology, are experiencing rapid sociocultural change. For example, as was pointed out in the final section of Chapter 6, cell phones and text messaging now permit both men and women to circumvent the traditional prohibitions against premarital social interaction.

Number of Spouses

In much the same way that societies have rules regulating whom one may or may not marry, they have rules specifying how many mates a person may or should have. Cultural anthropologists have identified three major types of marriage based on the number of spouses permitted: *monogamy* (the marriage of one man to one woman at a time), *polygyny* (the marriage of a man to two or more women at the same time), and *polyandry* (the marriage of a woman to two or more men at the same time).

Monogamy

The practice of having only one spouse at a time is so widespread and rigidly adhered to in the United States and Canada that most people have great difficulty imagining any other marital alternative. We are so accustomed to thinking of marriage as an exclusive relationship between two spouses that, for most North Americans, sharing a spouse is unthinkable. Any person who chooses to take more than one marriage partner at a time is in direct violation of conventional norms, most religious standards, and the law.

So ingrained is this concept of monogamy in Western society that we often associate it with the highest standards of civilization, while associating plural marriage with social backwardness and depravity. Interestingly, many societies that practice monogamy circumvent the notion of lifelong partnerships by either permitting extramarital affairs (provided they are conducted discreetly) or practicing *serial monogamy* (taking a number of different spouses one after another rather than at the same time). In fact serial monogamy is common in the United States, Canada, and much of western Europe.

Polygyny

Even though monogamy is widely practiced in the Western world, the overwhelming majority of world cultures do not share our values about the inherent virtue of monogamy. Polygyny was practiced widely in traditional India and China and remains a preferred form of marriage throughout Asia, Africa, and the Middle East. There is also evidence to support the idea that polygyny played a significant role in our own Western background by virtue of the numerous references to polygyny in the Old Testament of the Bible. Many Westerners, steeped in a tradition of monogamy, interpret the existence of polygyny as having its basis in the male sex drive. Because they presume that men have a stronger sex drive than women, polygyny is seen as a mechanism for men to satisfy themselves at the expense of women. This interpretation is flawed on a number of counts. First, there is little hard evidence to suggest that the sex drive is innately stronger for men than for women. Moreover, if men were interested in increasing their sexual options, it is not likely that they would choose multiple wives as a way of solving the problem. Instead they would resort to multiple extramarital liaisons, which would be far less complicated than taking on the responsibilities of multiple wives (Figure 9.7).

To suggest that approximately 70 percent of the world's *cultures* practice polygyny is not to say that 70 percent of the world's *population* practices polygyny. Many cultures that practice polygyny are small-scale societies with small populations. Moreover, even in polygynous societies, the majority of men at any given time still have only one wife. Even in societies where polygyny is most intensively practiced, we would not expect to find more than 35 percent of the men actually having two or more wives. Polygyny in these societies

monogamy The marital practice of having only one spouse at a time.

polygyny The marriage of a man to two or more women at the same time.

polyandry The marriage of a woman to two or more men at the same time.

serial monogamy The practice of having a succession of marriage partners, but only one at a time.

FIGURE 9.7 Polygyny is practiced in many parts of the world. A member of Malaysia's 'Ikhwan' Polygamy Club poses for a family photograph during Maulidur Rasul gathering in Rawang outside Kuala Lumpur with his two of his three wives and five of his six children.

is the *preferred* or *ideal,* not the usual, form of marriage. It is something for which men strive but only some attain. Just as the ideal of becoming a multimillionaire is usually not realized in the United States, so too in polygynous societies only a minority of men actually has more than one wife at a time. There are a number of reasons most men in polygynous societies never acquire more than one wife. First, marriage in many polygynous societies requires the approval (and financial support) of large numbers of kinsmen, and this support is not always easy to obtain. Second, in some polygynous societies it is considered inappropriate for men of low rank to seek additional wives, thereby restricting a certain segment of the males in the society to monogamy. And third, being the head of a polygynous household, which invariably carries high prestige, is hard work. The management of two or more wives and their children within a household requires strong administrative skills, particularly if relations between the wives are not congenial. A study of polygyny among the Zulu of South Africa (Möller and Welch 1990) indicates that Zulu men tend to opt for monogamy over polygyny for two additional reasons: They are under increasing pressure to accept the socially dominant values of South African whites, and the dominant white Christian churches have opposed polygyny militantly. In short, most men in polygynous societies, for a variety of reasons, do not have the inclination, family power base, or social skills needed to achieve the high status of a polygynist.

Sex Ratio in Polygynous Societies

For polygyny to work, a society must solve the practical problem of the sex ratio. In most human populations, the number of men and women is roughly equal. The question therefore arises: Where do the excess women who are needed to support a system of polygyny come from? It is theoretically possible that the sex ratio could swing in favor of females if males were killed off in warfare, if women were captured from other societies, or if the society practiced male infanticide. All of these quite radical solutions may account for a small part of the excess of women needed for a polygynous marriage system in some societies. More commonly this numerical discrepancy is alleviated simply by postponing the age at which men can marry. That is, if females can marry from age fourteen on and males are prohibited from marrying until age twenty-six, the marriage pool always has a surplus of marriageable women.

Advantages of Polygyny

Having two or more wives in a polygynous society is usually a mark of prestige or high status. In highly stratified kingdoms, polygyny is one of the privileges of royalty and aristocrats, as was the case with the late King Sobhuza of Swaziland, who, it was estimated, had more than a hundred wives. In societies that are stratified more on age than on political structure, such as the Azande of the Sudan and the Kikuyu of Kenya, polygyny is a symbol of prestige for older men. Whether a man is an aristocrat or a commoner, however, having multiple wives means wealth, power, and high status for both the polygynous husband and the wives and children (Deng 2009). That is, a man's status increases when he takes additional wives, and a woman's status increases when her husband takes additional wives. For this reason women in some African societies actually urge their husbands to take more wives. Clearly these African women do not want to be married to a nobody.

Sometimes a man takes multiple wives because the society views them as economic and political assets. Each wife not only contributes to the household's goods and services but also produces more children, who are valuable economic and political resources. The Siuai of the Solomon Islands provide an excellent example of how having multiple wives can be an economic advantage for the polygynous husband. Pigs are perhaps the most prized possession of Siuai adults. According to Douglas Oliver (1955: 348), "To shout at a person 'you have no pigs' is to offer him an insult." Women are particularly valuable in the raising of pigs because the more wives a man has, the more hands are available to work in the garden, the more pig food can be produced, and consequently the more pigs can be raised. Because polygynous households average more pigs than monogamous ones, it is not unusual for some men to take additional wives for the sake of enlarging their gardens and pig herds.

The old anthropological literature (written before the 1970s) gave the impression that women in polygynous societies generally favored polygyny over monogamy. However such a conclusion was to some extent the result of male bias because the majority of ethnographers for the first half of the twentieth century were men. Nevertheless there is evidence to suggest that polygyny remains popular among women in many parts of the world (Kilbride 1997; Mulder 1992; Shahd 2005). It is also true that men in polygynous societies view the practice even more positively than women. Opposition to polygyny usually comes from younger, better-educated women, who prefer monogamy (or remaining single) to polygyny.

Competition among Wives

Despite the advantages just discussed, living in a polygynous household has drawbacks. Even though men desire multiple wives, they recognize the potential pitfalls. The major problem is jealousy among the wives, who often compete for the husband's attention, sexual favors, and household resources. In fact, in some African societies, the word for *co-wife* is derived from the root word for *jealousy.*

Even though competition among wives in polygynous societies can threaten domestic tranquility, there are ways to minimize the friction. First, wives will be less jealous if they have a hand in selecting subsequent wives. Some societies practice a form of polygyny called *sororal polygyny*, in which a man marries sisters or other female relatives. It is possible that sisters may be less likely to feel jealous of one another when they become wives. Second, wives in many polygynous societies are given their own separate living quarters. As Paul Bohannan and Philip Curtin (1988) remind us, because women may have more difficulty sharing their kitchens than their husbands, jealousy can be minimized by giving each wife her own personal space. Third, dissension is lessened if the rights and obligations among the wives are clearly understood. Fourth, potential conflict among wives can be reduced by establishing a hierarchy among the wives. Because the senior wife often exerts considerable authority over more junior wives, she can run a fairly smooth household by adjudicating the various complaints of the other wives.

Not only can the jealousies among wives be regulated, but some ethnographic reports from polygynous societies also reveal considerable harmony and cooperation among the wives. Sometimes co-wives become companions and allies because they are all "outsiders" to the husband's kin group.

Polygyny in the United States

Although North America is adamantly monogamous, the practice of having more than one wife at a time does exist, particularly in Utah. Although the Church of Jesus Christ of Latter-Day Saints outlawed polygyny in 1890, the practice persists on a small scale by those who have left the church and started their own religions. Officially polygyny is prohibited by both the church and the state of Utah, but because it is considered relatively benign, it is generally not prosecuted. Although accurate statistics are unavailable, it is estimated that as many as thirty thousand people practice polygyny in the United States. Some practice polygyny today because of its deep-seated religious significance. Others practice it because it provides a desirable lifestyle choice. Some of the polygynist homesteads in this subculture are quite elaborate. The *Charlotte Observer* (Williams 1998) showed a picture of one such home: a 35,000-square-foot structure with thirty-seven bathrooms and thirty-one bedrooms, that housed a wealthy Mormon fundamentalist, his ten wives, and twenty-eight children! (Figure 9.8)

Viewed from a global perspective, polygyny is one of many legitimate forms of marriage. There is nothing inherently immoral or exploitative about the practice of having more than one wife at a time. However polygyny, as practiced in the United States, has come under fire recently because of certain *abuses* to the practice. As long as consenting adults choose to live in a polygynous relationship, authorities tended to look the other way. But in some communities—such as Hildale,

FIGURE 9.8 Polygyny is practiced in many parts of the world, including the United States. Tom Greene, a twenty-first-century polygynist from Utah, with his five wives and some of his twenty-nine children.

Utah, and Colorado City, Arizona—young girls barely in their teens are being coerced to marry men more than twice their age. Moreover, since the year 2000, more than four hundred teenage boys have been cast out of their families and their communities, largely as a way of reducing competition for wives. These "lost boys," some as young as thirteen, experience severe emotional and psychological trauma because they are relegated by their elders to homelessness without any education or the support of their families. Rather than targeting polygyny per se as a marriage practice, law enforcement officials in Utah and Arizona are going after the adults of these communities, focusing on sexual abuse, child neglect, child endangerment, welfare fraud, and tax evasion (Kelly 2005; Madigan 2005).

Polyandry

Polyandry, the mirror image of polygyny, is the marriage of a woman to two or more men at the same time. A much rarer form of plural marriage than polygyny, polyandry is found in fewer than 1 percent of the societies of the world, most notably in Tibet, Nepal, and India. Polyandry may be fraternal (where the husbands are brothers) or nonfraternal. Perhaps the best-known case of polyandry is found among the Toda of southern India, who practice the fraternal variety. When a woman marries a man, she also becomes the wife of all of his brothers, including even those who have not yet been born. Marriage privileges rotate among the brothers. Even though all of the brothers live together with the wife in a single household, there is little competition or sexual jealousy. Whenever a brother is with the wife, he places his cloak and staff at the door as a sign not to disturb him. When the wife becomes pregnant, paternity is not necessarily ascribed to the biological father (genitor) but is determined by a ceremony that establishes a social father (pater), usually the oldest brother. After the birth of two or three children, however, other brothers are chosen as the social fathers for all children born to the woman thereafter.

Toda society is characterized by a shortage of females brought about by the traditional practice of female infanticide, and this shortage of women may be one of the reasons for the existence of polyandry among the Toda. Because of the influence of both the Indian government and Christian missionaries, however, female infanticide has largely disappeared today, the male-to-female sex ratio has become essentially balanced, and polyandry among the Toda is, for all practical purposes, a thing of the past.

In addition to explaining the existence of polyandry by a shortage of women, there are certain economic factors to consider. According to William Stephens (1963), senior husbands among the wealthier families on the Marquesas Islands recruited junior husbands as a way of augmenting the manpower of the household. It has also been suggested that Tibetan serfs practice polyandry as a solution to the problem of land shortage (Goldstein 1987). To prevent their land from being divided up among their sons, brothers keep the family land intact by marrying the same woman. By marrying one woman, two or more brothers are able to preserve the family resources; that is, if all of the sons split up to form their own monogamous households, the family would multiply and the family land would rapidly be fragmented. In a monogamous situation, the only way to prevent this fragmentation of family land is to practice primogeniture (all land is inherited by the oldest son only). Such a system, though keeping the land intact, does so at the expense of creating many landless male offspring. In contrast, the practice of fraternal polyandry does not split up the family land but rather maintains a steady ratio of land to people.

Economic Considerations of Marriage

Most societies view marriage as a binding contract between at least the principal partners, and in many cases between their respective families. Such a contract includes the transfer of certain rights between the parties involved—rights of sexual access, legal rights to children, and rights of the spouses to each other's economic goods and services. Often the transfer of rights is accompanied by the transfer of some type of economic

consideration. These transactions, which may take place either before or after the marriage, can be divided into four categories: bridewealth, bride service, dowry, and reciprocal exchange.

Bridewealth

Bridewealth is the compensation given upon marriage by the family of the groom to the family of the bride. Where it is practiced, societies give substantial bridewealth payment as a normal part of the marriage process. The bridewealth exchange serves to ratify the marriage between the two families. Although bridewealth is practiced in most regions of the world, it is perhaps most widely found in Africa, where some societies require a substantial payment of bridewealth whereas for others the practice is that of offering a token bridewealth or *bride service* (providing labor, rather than goods, to the bride's family).

Bridewealth is paid in a wide variety of currencies, but in almost all cases the commodity used for payment is highly valued in the society. For example, reindeer are given as bridewealth by the reindeer-herding Chukchee, horses by the equestrian Cheyenne of the Central Plains, sheep by the Navajo, and cattle by the pastoral Maasai, Samburu, and Nuer of eastern Africa (Figure 9.9). In other societies, marriage payments

© Arco Images/GmbH/Alamy

FIGURE 9.9 Among the Maasai of Kenya and Tanzania, cows are used as the medium of exchange in marriage transactions.

---

bridewealth The transfer of goods from the groom's lineage to the bride's lineage to legitimize marriage.

bride service Work or service performed for the bride's family by the groom for a specified period of time either before or after the marriage.

take the form of blankets (Kwakiutl), pigs (Alor), mats (Fiji), shell money (Kurtachi), spears (Somali), loincloths (Toda), and even the plumes of the bird of paradise (Siane).

Just as the commodities used in bridewealth transactions vary considerably, so does the amount of the transaction. To illustrate, an indigenous Nandi of Kenya can obtain a bride with no more than a promise to transfer one animal to the bride's father. A suitor from the Jie tribe of Uganda, on the other hand, normally transfers fifty head of cattle and one hundred head of small stock (sheep and goats) to the bride's family before the marriage becomes official. Large amounts of bridewealth, as found among the Jie, are significant for two reasons. First, the economic stakes are so high that the bride and groom are under enormous pressure to make the marriage work. And second, large bridewealth payments tend to make the system of negotiations between the two families more flexible and consequently more cordial. When the bridewealth is low, the addition or subtraction of one item becomes highly critical and is likely to create hard feelings between the two families.

Not only do bridewealth payments vary among different cultures, but variations also exist within a single cultural group. In a study of bridewealth payments among the Kipsigis of western Kenya, Monique Mulder (1988) found that intragroup variations depended on three key factors. First, high bridewealth is given for brides who mature early and are plump because such women are thought to have greater reproductive success. Second, lower bridewealth is given for women who have given birth previously. And third, women whose natal homes are far away from their marital homes command higher bridewealth because they spend less time in their own mother's household and therefore are more available for domestic chores in their husband's household.

The meaning of bridewealth has been widely debated by scholars and non-scholars for much of the twentieth century. Early Christian missionaries, viewing bridewealth as a form of wife purchase, argued that it was denigrating to women and repugnant to the Christian ideal of marriage. Many colonial administrators, taking a more legalistic view, saw bridewealth as a symbol of the inferior legal status of women in traditional societies. Both of these negative interpretations of bridewealth led to vigorous yet unsuccessful attempts to stamp out the practice.

Less concerned with moral and legal issues, cultural anthropologists saw bridewealth as a rational and comprehensible part of traditional systems of marriage. Rejecting the interpretation that bridewealth was equivalent to wife purchase, anthropologists tended to examine how the institution operated within the total cultural context of which it was a part.

These functionalist anthropologists (see Chapter 4) identified some important *functions* that the institution of bridewealth performed for the well-being of the society. For example, bridewealth was seen as security or insurance for the good treatment of the wife, as a mechanism to stabilize marriage by reducing the possibility of divorce, as a form of compensation to the bride's lineage for the loss of her economic potential and her childbearing capacity, as a symbol of the union between two large groups of kin, as a mechanism to legitimize traditional marriages in much the same way that a marriage license legitimizes Western marriages, and as the transference of rights over children from the mother's family to the father's family.

Although a much-needed corrective to the previous interpretations of bridewealth as wife purchase, the anthropological interpretation overlooked the real economic significance of bridewealth. It was not until the end of the colonial period that Robert Gray (1960) reminded social scientists that it also was legitimate to view bridewealth as an integral part of the local exchange system. It is now generally held that a comprehensive understanding of the practice of bridewealth is impossible without recognizing its economic as well as its noneconomic functions.

Since the mid-twentieth century, bridewealth has become "monetized" (that is, money is becoming the typical medium of exchange). The transition from subsistence-based to cash-based economies has profoundly affected traditional bridewealth practices. Traditionally bridewealth was an exchange of (often valuable) commodities from the groom's lineage to the bride's lineage. Because traditional bridewealth solidifies long-term ties between two entire lineages, the bride and groom did not benefit directly from the exchange. However, when bridewealth becomes tied to money that can be earned by the individual prospective groom, the close interdependence of family members (and their sanctioning of the marriage) becomes much less important. Today a growing number of wage earners in societies that practiced traditional bridewealth are becoming independent of their kinship group when it comes time to get married.

The monetization of bridewealth in Oceania is particularly well described in a volume called *The Business of Marriage* (Marksbury 1993). Contributing authors show how people from the Fiji Islands and Papua New Guinea are viewing marriage increasingly as a financial transaction. This commercialization of bridewealth is having important consequences for the entire marital process. According to Marksbury (1993), people are postponing marriage until a later age, marriage payments are being used for personal fulfillment rather than redistributed among a wide range of kin, men are incurring serious debts in their attempts to meet their payments, marriages are becoming less stable, and traditional husband-wife roles are changing.

Increasingly because of climate change young girls of poor rural families, and in particular girls younger than eighteen years of age, are being married off to lessen the burden on their families. These early marriages are referred to as "child-drought brides" and are found in Africa, India, the Philippines, and other parts of the world. It is reported that in Kenya, families were selling their daughters into marriage, sometimes for as little as $168.00. Marrying their young daughters allowed the families to no longer feed, clothe, and educate them; it was the parent's attempt to ease their economic burden brought on by drought. Yet marrying young puts the adolescent girls at greater risk for exposure to HIV and AIDS, at-risk pregnancies, spending more time caring for the household (gathering wood and water and collecting food or food aid) and less time in getting an education. Plan International (2011) a child-centered community development organization (http://plan-international.org/) recommends action. Their aim is to create a variety of programs and policies with the emphasis placed on the impact climate change will have on the reproductive health of adolescent girls such as in Kenya and elsewhere in the world where child-drought brides are pressured into marrying at a young age.

Bride Service

In societies with considerable material wealth, marriage considerations take the form of bridewealth paid in various commodities. But because many small-scale societies cannot accumulate capital goods, men often give their labor to the bride's family instead of material goods in exchange for wives. In some cases, bride service is practiced to the exclusion of property transfer; in other cases it is a temporary condition, and the transfer of some property is expected at a later date. When a man marries under a system of bride service, he often moves in with his bride's family, works or hunts for them, and serves a probationary period of several weeks to several years. This custom is similar to that practiced by Jacob of the Old Testament (Genesis, Chapter 29), who served his mother's brother (Laban) for his wives, Leah and her sister, Rachel.

Bride service is likely to be found in nomadic foraging societies such as the traditional Ju/'hoansi of southwestern Africa. According to Janice Stockard (2002: 28–29), Ju/'hoansi men select husbands for their daughters based largely, but not exclusively, on the hunting skills of the prospective groom. Suitors must demonstrate considerable hunting expertise before they are eligible to marry because the father-in-law will depend on the daughter's husband to provide him with adequate supplies of meat through a prolonged period of bride service.

Dowry

In contrast to bridewealth, a *dowry* is goods or money transferred in the opposite direction, from the bride's family to the groom or to the groom's family as a precondition for a marriage. The dowry is always provided by the bride or the bride's family, but the recipient of the goods varies from one culture to another. In some societies the dowry was given to the groom, who then had varying rights to dispose of it. In rural Ireland the dowry was given to the father of the groom in compensation for land, which the groom's father subsequently bequeathed to the bride and groom. The dowry was then used, wholly or in part, by the groom's father to pay the dowry of the groom's sister.

More often than not, the dowry was not given to the husband but was something that the bride brought with her into the marriage. In traditional society in Cyprus, the dowry often consisted of a house or other valuable property. If the husband mistreated his wife or if the marriage ended in divorce, the woman was entitled to take the dowry with her. The dowry in this sense, much like bridewealth, functioned to stabilize the marriage by providing a strong economic incentive not to break up.

In certain European countries, where it is still practiced to some extent today, substantial dowry payments have been used as a means of upward mobility—that is, as a way to marry a daughter into a higher-status family. Around the beginning of the twentieth century, a number of daughters of wealthy US industrialists entered into mutually beneficial marriage alliances with European nobles who had fallen on hard economic times. The US heiresses brought a substantial dowry to the marriage in exchange for a title.

In India, gift-giving as a precondition marriage has escalated to the extreme. If the in-laws and husbands are not satisfied with the amount received by the bride's family she is harassed and physically abused, in some case until death, which is known as dowry deaths. Dowry deaths are the deaths of women who are murdered or driven to suicide by continuous harassment or physical abuse by their husbands and in-laws as a means to increase the amount of a bride's dowry her family must pay. In India, dowry death is considered one of the many acts of violence against women. These young brides may commit suicide by poisoning and hanging to avoid burdening their families. In more extreme cases the husband or his family may set the bride on

---

dowry Goods or money transferred from the bride's family to the groom or the groom's family to legalize or legitimize a marriage.

Climate Change Preparing for Resettlement for Environmental Refugees

❀ Climate change is no longer disputed; however, its impact on the earth and the world's population varies considerably. Some populations will feel the impact of coastal shores or island nations disappearing as sea level rise; for others, rains will continue to fall less frequently lessening available pasture for livestock or reduce yields from crops traditional to the zone; and still others will experience loss of their traditional way of life resulting from prolonged and profound climatic changes. Technological fixes, policy changes, or economic development strategies no longer will be sufficient adaptive measures to combat these dramatic changes to the environment resulting from climate change. National and international planning discussions are for a more dire response, that of relocation of entire communities and nations—environmental refugees.

The United Nations Intergovernmental Panel on Climate Change estimates a temperature increase between two and four degrees in this century. This degree of warming would result in changes to water availability, ecosystems, pasture availability, agricultural productivity, disaster risk, and rising sea levels (Sherbinin et al. 2011). In time, such environmental transformations make a region uninhabitable or unsustainable for small or large populations to exist as they had been as urban or rural societies. Climate-related resettlement is already underway among small island nations such as the Pacific Islands and

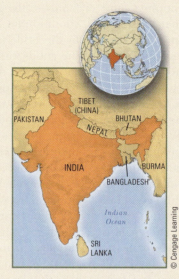

others will occur in the future. For example, crop conditions and pasture lands for climatic zones are changing in Southeast Asia and throughout Africa. These southern hemispheric climatic zones are not able to produce the yields they once generated, creating protracted food shortages. People can no longer produce sufficient food for themselves or their animals because of soil erosion, drought, desertification, deforestation, and other environmental transformation related to changing climatic conditions. Additional changes are found in coastal regions of the world where rising sea waters are causing permanent loss of shorelines, communities, megacities, and roadways. People are being forced from their way of life because of extreme weather-related events. The increasing frequency and intensity of storms, the impact of flooding, cyclone, hurricanes (and other wind and rain events), droughts, and related crop damage are forcing people to leave their communities and villages, and in some cases, climate change is putting further pressure on already taxed or exasperated environmental conditions.

Preparing the migration and adaptation actions for major population displacements requires the attention of scientists, policy makers, anthropologists, public health specialists, economists, community members, and many others working together. According to Janos Bogardi, director of the Institute for Environment and Human Security at the United Nations in Bonn,

fire, which is known as bride burning. Bride burning is the groom's family's response for not getting a large enough dowry from her parents.

Since 1961, dowries have been banned in India under various acts, such as the Dowry Prohibition Act (1961); its revised version of 1983 has been passed as a way to decrease the incidence of dowry deaths. Since passing of the Protection of Women from Domestic Violence Act in 2005 women can put a stop to harassment for dowry extortion. Nevertheless next to rape, dowry deaths remain one of the top acts of violence against women in India (Figure 9.10). Bedi (2012) reports that in 2010 there were 8,391 dowry death cases documented across India. A decade early there were 6,695 cases reported, but by 2007 had reached to 8,093 dowry deaths. For 2010 it means a bride was burned every ninety minutes.

FIGURE 9.10 Next to rape, dowry deaths remain one of the top acts of violence against women in India. For 2010 it means a bride was burned every 90 minutes.

Germany, environmental deterioration currently displaces up to 10 million people a year, and is estimated to increase to 50 million by 2020 and 150 million by 2050 (SAAW 2007).

Past research on disaster recovery by Oliver-Smith, development initiatives for forced displacement migrants or resettled refugees by Scudder (1995); Cernea (1995) as well as the United Nations, US Agency for International Development, Canadian International Development Agency, and many other government and nongovernment agencies will aid in planning for environmental relocations in particular regions of the world currently experiencing the accumulated effects from climate change. Given the nature of this work, migration and adaptation projects require careful planning, cultural sensitivity, and multiple levels of training. Policies may be put in place to facilitate a migration process; however, adequate funds also need to be in place for those communities that lack resources to relocate to drier grounds. Social scientists can contribute thoughtful planning and capacity building to minimize the impact the relocation process will have on communities and families who are forced into relocating as an adaptive measure to climate change. Care needs to be taken to avoid resettling communities in areas where there are preexisting ethnic antagonisms or marginalizing people in where they are relocated. Maintaining family structure and cultural cohesiveness is critical to the planning efforts.

Migration is not new, and food foragers and pastoralists have for millennium relocated when resources in an area are depleted. Today, planning for environmental migration takes on new challenges and impediments for easy transitions. No longer is the migratory path one of a few miles to another resource patch, but rather the planning is for internal migration for communities to seek higher ground or leave one country for another where culture, language, religion, customs, ecosystems, food traditions, employment opportunities, and individual rights are different.

Imagine being a wetland rice farmer now being shown how to raise tuber crops in the highlands. As can be imagined, spatial relocation requires more than just bringing along one's material possessions. Such environmentally resettled peoples face a loss of employment, land, shelter, access to common resources, and a future of economic and political marginalization, increased morbidity and mortality, food insecurity, and negative cultural and psychological impacts. Given these possibilities, a more successful approach to resettlement would be one that included economically feasible reconstruction of productive activities (that is, jobs and education), with sufficient opportunities for generating an income and restoring livelihoods, maintaining family structure, and ensuring adequate cultural integration with hosts communities and countries.

Nevertheless even with the best social and cultural safeguards in place, the complexity of resettlement may confound good planning. For example, large dams and banana plantations may create jobs that are more quickly exploited by outsiders than those who are resettled. Worse yet, there may be unanticipated health consequences related to the migration process and resettlement (that is, malaria outbreaks and tuberculosis upsurges). Although improving livelihoods is possible and may even lead to higher levels of prosperity post-resettlement, such benefits may be offset by health, cultural, and social costs. Follow-up studies will determine if long-term successes have been achieved by working with second and subsequent generations.

Questions for Discussion

1. Why will technological fixes no longer work in some coastal regions or low laying island communities?

2. What precautions should be taken when planning for environmental relocation and resettlement strategies? What are the implications for families and their culture?

3. What are some of the impacts climate change is having on certain populations in the world?

Divorce

Just as all cultures have established a variety of ways of legitimizing marriages, they also have many ways of dealing with separation and *divorce*, the formal dissolution of a marriage. Divorce arrangements found in the many cultures of the world vary widely according to the reasons for divorce and how easy or difficult it may be to get divorced. Although marriages break down in all societies, some societies are reluctant to officially sanction divorce, and some may even forbid it. Some societies have no official mechanism for legally dissolving a marriage, whereas some organizations, such as the Roman Catholic Church, prohibit divorce outright. By way of contrast, a Hopi woman from Arizona could divorce her husband quite easily by simply putting his belongings outside the door.

As a general rule, divorce rates are lower in societies that have strong kinship and large bridewealth payments, which represent compensation for a woman's limited procreative power, which is essentially a payment for her to bare children. The larger the bridewealth payment, the more complete the transfer of rights over children from the bride's lineage to the groom's lineage. If a marriage is subsequently dissolved, the bridewealth payment would have to be returned to the groom's lineage, which could be a problem if it has already been allocated to a wide range of the bride's kin. Thus relatively large bridewealth payments, coupled with wide lineage involvement, promote greater marriage stability. By way of contrast,

divorce The legal and formal dissolution of a marriage.

in foraging societies, such as the Ju/'hoansi and the Inuit, divorce is quite easily accomplished. In such nomadic or semi-nomadic societies, because material wealth is limited, marriage payments are either small or nonexistent. Moreover foraging societies generally lack large, formal social groups beyond the nuclear family that could complicate divorce proceedings.

In the industrialized world, the incidence of divorce has increased dramatically over the last hundred years, and most industrialized nations have legal procedures for dissolving marriages. To illustrate, the United States, which has one of the highest divorce rates in the world, experienced a tenfold increase in the rate of divorce between 1890 and 1980. Divorce rates rose precipitously from 1950 to 1980, but the rate has been steadily receding since 1980 (see Table 9.2). A number of factors have been cited for the initial dramatic rise of divorce in the United States. First, industrialization and urbanization modified the functions of the family. When the basic unit of production changed from family to factory, the economic ties holding the family together were weakened. And as people had more disposable income, the notion of recreation and leisure time changed from family-based activities to attendance at paid events, such as movies and concerts. Second, the rise of individualism and the pursuit of personal happiness have led some people to spend less time with family members and made some less willing to make sacrifices for the good of the family. Third, the emphasis Western culture puts on romantic love as the basis for marriage makes marriages vulnerable when sexual passion subsides. Fourth, much less stigma is attached to divorce today than a century ago. In the 1950s, a divorced couple was looked at with pity, if not contempt, for not being able to "save their marriage," whereas in

FIGURE 9.11 Like many marriages in Western society, the marriage of Katie Holmes and Tom Cruise ended in divorce after five years of marriage.

contemporary US society, less than half of all marriages end in divorce. And fifth, divorce in the United States today is relatively easy to obtain. No longer must a spouse prove infidelity or physical abuse. Rather, today in most states a wife or husband seeking to end a marriage needs to claim only that the marriage has "failed" or that there are "irreconcilable differences." As one law professor has commented, "It is easier to walk away from a marriage than from a commitment to purchase a new car" (quoted in Etzioni 1993) (Figure 9.11).

Marriage: Continuity and Change

As with any aspect of culture, marriage practices and customs change over time. In some cultures, and at certain times in their histories, changes are rapid and far reaching, whereas at other times these customary practices remain fairly stable. In the United States, for example, marital practices (at least in the Christian tradition) have not undergone widespread changes. In the 1940s, men were expected to propose matrimony, the father of the bride usually "gave her away," the ceremony was officiated by a religious functionary or someone licensed by the state, the bride's family was responsible for the major expenses of a wedding, brides wore white dresses, and the newlyweds typically took time after the ceremony for a honeymoon. Many of these practices are still followed today although they have been modified to fit the times. For example, on TLC tv show "Is This the Dress?" some brides have been known to wear bridal gowns that are ivory, champagne, red, black, and

TABLE 9.2

Divorce Rates in the United States, 1950–2010

Year	Divorces per 1,000 Population
1950	2.6
1960	2.2
1970	3.5
1980	5.2
1990	4.7
2000	4.2
2010	3.6*

*Provisional

SOURCE: US Department of Health and Human Services 2013; the National Center for Health Statistics 2013 (www.cdc.gov).

even multicolored. Some brides choose to walk down the isle with their life partner and greet each of their families at the end of the isle as a symbol of families uniting rather than that of the bride being given away.

In contemporary Japanese society, however, changes in wedding practices have occurred both dramatically and rapidly. Until just several decades ago, the overwhelming majority of Japanese were married according to the traditional Shinto wedding ceremony conducted at a religious shrine by a Shinto priest and attended by only the close family members of the bride and groom. The wedding couple was purified and drank rice wine (*sake*), and only the groom read the words of commitment. The couple, dressed in the traditional *kimono*, gave symbolic offerings to the *kamt* (Shinto spirit gods who took the form of wind, trees, rivers, and fertility). Most Japanese weddings today, however, are conducted in Western-style hotels, the bride wears a white wedding gown and the groom is clad in a tuxedo, and the ceremony is officiated by an English-speaking American or European wearing white vestments and a gold cross. The so-called "ministers" or "pastors" are not required to have any seminary education whatsoever, and in fact most are teachers, disc jockeys, or part-time actors looking to make some extra money. Even though fewer than 2 percent of all Japanese are practicing Christians, it has been estimated that these Christian/Western-style ceremonies account for three of every four Japanese marriages conducted today (Brooke 2005b).

Family Structure

Cultural anthropologists have identified two fundamentally different types of family structure: the nuclear family and the extended family. The *nuclear family* is based on marital ties, and the *extended family*, a much larger social unit, is based on blood ties among three or more generations of kin.

The Nuclear Family

Consisting of husband and wife or partners, and their children, the nuclear family is a two-generation family formed around the marital union. Even though the nuclear family to some degree is part of a larger family structure, it remains an autonomous and independent unit (Figure 9.12). That is, the everyday needs of economic support, child care, and social interaction are met within the nuclear family itself rather than by a wider set of relatives. In societies based on the nuclear family, it is customary for married couples to live apart from both sets of parents (neolocal residence). The married couple is also not particularly obliged or expected to care for their aging parents in their own home. Generally parents are not actively involved in mate selection for their children, in no way legitimize the marriages of their children, and have no control

Courtesy of Gary Ferraro

FIGURE 9.12 Consisting of husband and wife or partners, and their children, the nuclear family is a two-generation autonomous and independent unit.

over whether their children remain married. The nuclear family is most likely to be found in societies with the greatest amount of geographic mobility. This certainly is the case in the United States and Canada, which currently have both considerable geographic mobility and the ideal of the nuclear family.

During much of our early history, the extended family—tied to the land and working on the family farm—was the rule rather than the exception. Today, however, the family farm—housing parents, grandparents, aunts, uncles, cousins, and siblings—is a thing of the past. Now, in response to the forces of industrialization, most adults move to locations where they can find suitable employment. Because one's profession largely determines where one will live, adults in the United States and Canada often live considerable distances from their parents or other extended family members.

nuclear family The most basic family unit, composed of wife, husband, and children.

extended family The family that includes in one household relatives in addition to a nuclear family.

In addition to being found in such highly industrialized societies as our own, the nuclear family is found in certain societies located at the other end of the technological spectrum. In certain foraging societies residing in environments where resources are meager (such as the Inuit of northern Canada and the traditional Shoshone of Utah and Nevada), the nuclear family is the basic food-collecting unit. These nuclear families remain highly independent foraging groups that fend for themselves. Even though they cannot expect help from the outside in an emergency, they have developed a family structure that is well adapted to a highly mobile life. Thus, both US society and some small-scale food-collecting societies have adopted the nuclear family pattern because of their need to maintain a high degree of geographic mobility.

Although the independent nuclear family was the ideal in the United States for much of the twentieth century, significant changes have occurred in recent years. According to recent census data, only one in five households consists of the nuclear family (two parents and one or more children), a sharp decline from previous decades. The remaining 80 percent of the US households in the twenty-first century are made up of married couples without children, single adults, single parents, unmarried couples, roommates, extended family members, or adult siblings. There are three explanations for the recent decline of the nuclear family in the United States. First, as more and more women complete higher education and enter the job market, they are more likely to delay marrying and having children. Second, the increasing cost of maintaining the ideal middle-class household that includes the parents, children, a three- or four-bedroom house, a golden retriever, and an SUV or two has caused some couples to opt for remaining childless altogether. Third, the divorce rate in the United States has contributed to the increase in non-nuclear families in recent decades.

The Extended Family

Extended families consist of two or more nuclear families that are linked by blood ties. Most commonly this takes the form of a married couple living with one or more of their married children in a single household or homestead and under the authority of a family head. Such extended families, which are based on parent-child linkages, can be either patrilineal (a man, his sons, and the sons' wives and children) or matrilineal (a woman, her daughters, and her daughters' husbands and children). It is also possible for extended families to be linked through sibling ties, consisting of two or

FIGURE 9.13 Extended families consist of two or more nuclear families that are linked by blood ties. Most commonly this takes the form of a married couple living with one or more of their married children in a single household or through sibling ties, consisting of two or more married brothers and their wives and children.

Julie Keen/Shutterstock.com

more married brothers and their wives and children (Figure 9.13).

When a couple marries in a society with extended families, the newlyweds are not expected to establish a separate and distinct family unit. Instead, for example, the young couple may take up residence in the homestead of the husband's father, and the husband continues to work for his father, who also runs the household. Moreover most of the personal property in the household is not owned by the newlyweds but is controlled by the husband's father. In the event that the extended family is large, it may be headed by two or more powerful male elders who run the family in much the same way that a board of directors runs a corporation. Eventually the father (or other male elders) will die or retire and allow younger men to assume positions of leadership and power within the extended family. Unlike the nuclear family, which lasts only one generation, the extended family is a continuous unit that can last an indefinite number of generations. As old people die off, they are replaced through the birth of new members.

In extended family systems, marriage is viewed more as bringing a daughter into the family than acquiring a wife. In other words, a man's obligations of obedience to his father and loyalty to his male kin are far more important than his relationship to his wife. When a woman marries into an extended family, she most often comes under the control of her mother-in-law, who allocates chores and supervises her domestic activities.

In some extended family systems, the conjugal relationship is suppressed to such an extent that contact

❋ Tony Manza, a high-level sales executive with a Canadian office furniture company, was in Kuwait trying to land a large contract with the Kuwaiti government. Having received an introduction from a mutual friend, Manza made an appointment with Mr. Mansour, the chief purchasing agent for the government. In his preparation for the trip, Manza had been told to expect to engage in a good deal of small talk before actually getting down to business. So Manza and Mansour chatted about the weather, golf, and Manza's flight from Toronto. Then, quite surprisingly, Mansour inquired about Manza's seventy-year-old father. Without giving it much thought, Manza responded by saying that his father was doing fine, but that the last time he had seen him four months ago in the nursing home, he had lost some weight. From that point onward, Mansour's attitude changed abruptly from warm and gracious to cool and aloof. Manza never did get the contract he was after.

Although Manza thought he was giving Mansour a straightforward answer, his response from Mansour's perspective made Manza an undesirable business partner. Coming from a society that places high value on family relationships, Mansour considered putting one's own father into a nursing home (to be cared for by total strangers) to be inhumane. If Manza could not be relied on to take care of his own father, he surely could not be trusted to fulfill his obligations in a business relationship.

between husband and wife is kept to a minimum. Among the Rajputs of northern India, for example, spouses are not allowed to talk to each other in the presence of family elders. Public displays of affection between spouses are considered reprehensible; in fact, a husband is not permitted to show open concern for his wife's welfare. Some societies take such severe measures to subordinate the husband-wife relationship because it is feared that a man's feelings for his wife could interfere with his obligations to his own blood relatives.

Modern-Day Family Structure

Most Western social thinkers over the past century have been in general agreement concerning the long-term effects of urbanization and modernization on the family. They see a progressive nuclearization of the family in the face of modernization. In fact, the concept of family is changing with increased acceptance of same-sex marriage and same-sex couples adopting children on the rise. Yet, that is only one modification in the modern family.

The challenging economic times from 2009 to the present has made it more difficult for young adults, especially those who are recent college graduates to find employment that allows them to start out on their own. Anyone, not earning above $11,490 is said to be living

at the poverty level in the United States and for a family of five the figure is $27,570 (US Department of Health and Human Services 2013). Moving in with relatives, especially parents, has helped fuel the largest increase in the number of Americans living in multigenerational households (composed of two or more generations) in modern history. It has provided a financial lifeline for many households. A study conducted by the Kochhar and Coh (2011) from the Pew Research Center report that from 2007 to 2009, multigenerational households spiked from 46.5 million to 51.4 million, or 16.7 percent of all households are multigenerational. Among the unemployed in 2009, the poverty rate was 17.5 percent for those living in multigenerational households, compared with 30.3 percent for those living in other households. In this case, relying on kinship ties helped multigenerational households cope with challenging economic times better.

A number of factors are responsible for this rise in the number of multigenerational households, including the high unemployment rate between 2008 and 2009, the high cost of housing, the rising cost of living, growing expenses for child and elder care, and the 1996 welfare reform law requiring teenage mothers to live with a responsible adult to receive welfare benefits. But there are more positive explanations as well. Traditionally, African American families have maintained extended kinship ties to support family (Stack 1975; Sharff 1981). Immigrant families also have family traditions for staying together while they acculturate in the United States. Navaro (2006 :1) states "Multigenerational living, especially those in which grandparents care for their grandchildren, have long been common in Asian and Hispanic countries, and the arrangement is popular among immigrants from those nations. Also driving the trend are … active baby boomers who want to be involved in the lives of their offspring and who see little appeal in flying off to a Sun Belt retirement in isolation." With the intensification of these negative and positive forces, we are likely to see the multigenerational household trend continue into the next US Census. Table 9.3 provides additional data on the changing nature of family life in the United States between 1970 and the last available US Census of 2010.

TABLE 9.3

US Family Structure (1970–2010)

	1970	2000	2010
Nuclear family	40.3	23.5	20.2
Married without children	30.3	28.1	28.2
Singles	17.0	31.9	33.6
Other family types	10.6	16.5	18.0

SOURCE: US census data for 1970, 2000, and 2010.

The global economic decline since late 2009 is being felt everywhere including participating countries in the European Union. Spain for example has been struggling along with Greece and Portugal. In Spain, the unemployment rate was at 25 percent when families had to rethink household finances and where aged relatives were to be placed at home or in elder homes. Nearly 10,000 aged relatives had been living in private old age homes before the economic decline forced them to return to live with their families (Tremlett and Roberts 2012).

The decline of the traditional family (that is, the two-parent household) in the United States (as viewed in Table 9.3) has resulted from the legitimization of a number of nontraditional, alternative family patterns. One such nontraditional form that has been on the rise in the past half-century is families made up of unwed single mothers and their children. While raising children as an unwed mother in the United States is not easy, it is not a lifestyle choice that is reviled by the rest of society, nor does the government discriminate against it. In Korea, however, there are few unwed mothers raising their children because they are so thoroughly ostracized by their society. According to one commentator (Sang-Hun 2009: 6), unwed mothers are ostracized "to such an extent that Koreans often describe things as outrageous by comparing them to 'an unmarried woman seeking an excuse to give birth.'" This social stigma puts enormous pressure on unwed pregnant women in Korea to either have an abortion or give the child up for adoption. To illustrate, 96 percent of all unwed pregnant Korean women end their pregnancies in abortion, and the great majority of those children who are born (the remaining 4 percent) are given up for adoption. In contrast, only 1 percent of unwed mothers in the United States give up their newborn infants for adoption (Sang-Hun 2009: 6). Thus, we can see that families headed by unwed mothers are legitimate and relatively widespread in the United States, but the same certainly is not true in contemporary Korea.

Summary

1. Because of the vast ethnographic variations found in the world, the terms *family* and *marriage* are not easy to define. Recognizing the difficulties inherent in such definitions, anthropologists define *family* as a social unit whose members cooperate economically, manage reproduction and child rearing, and most often live together. Marriage, the process by which families are formed, is a socially approved union between adult partners.

2. The formation of families through the process of marriage serves important social functions by reducing competition for spouses, regulating the sexual division of labor, and meeting the material, educational, and emotional needs of children.

3. Every culture has a set of rules (incest taboos) regulating which categories of kin are inappropriate partners for sexual intercourse. The explanations for this universal incest taboo include the inbreeding theory, the family disruption theory, and the theory of expanding social alliances.

4. Cultures restrict the choice of marriage partners by such practices as exogamy, endogamy, arranged marriages, preferential cousin marriage, the levirate, and the sororate.

5. In many cultures romantic love is not a major criterion for selecting a spouse. Courtship practices found throughout the world vary widely from being virtually nonexistent at one extreme to permissive at the other.

6. All societies have rules governing the number of spouses a person can have. Societies tend to emphasize monogamy (one spouse at a time), polygyny (a man marrying more than one wife at a time), or polyandry (a woman marrying more than one husband at a time).

7. In many societies marriages involve the transfer of some type of economic consideration in exchange for rights of sexual access, legal rights over children, and rights to each other's property. These economic considerations involve such practices as bridewealth, bride service, dowry, and reciprocal exchange.

8. Just as all societies have customary ways of establishing marriages, they also have ways of dissolving them. As a rule, divorce rates are lower in societies that have strong kinship groups and systems of bridewealth.

9. Cultural anthropologists distinguish between two types of family structure: the nuclear family, comprising the wife, husband, and children; and the extended family, a much larger social unit, comprising relatives from three or more generations.

Key Terms

arranged marriage

bride service

bridewealth

cross cousins

divorce

dowry

endogamy

exogamy

extended family

incest taboo

levirate

monogamy

nuclear family

parallel cousins

polyandry

polygyny

postpartum sex taboo

preferential cousin
  marriage

role ambiguity

serial monogamy

sororate

Critical Thinking Questions

1. Evaluate the effects of globalization and migration on marriage and family practices in patrilineal and matrilineal societies. What should outsiders consider about marriage and family when working cross-culturally on health-related projects?

2. As climate change increases, so will the number of environmental refugees; what strategies and precautions can be taken in development planning to maintain family structure and cultural traditions for displaced persons?

3. Increasingly biotechnology is being used for reproductive health and gender selection purposes. In what ways is biotechnology reshaping marriage practices and family structure?

Online Study Resources

CourseMate

Access chapter-specific learning tools including learning objectives, practice quizzes, videos, flash cards, glossaries, web links, and more in your Cultural Anthropology CourseMate. Login to www.cengagebrain.com to access the resources your instructor has assigned and to purchase materials.

An extended family in the United States comes together for a family reunion.

Kinship and Descent

Kathryn Skye, an organizational consultant for an international firm based in Washington, D.C., had been flying to Mexico City every month for the past year to help her Mexican client develop a more effective payroll system. On one of these three-day visits, Kathryn had scheduled to meet with some of the key Mexican employees working on the project. On the first day of the scheduled meetings, Kathryn was informed that all of the employees would be leaving work at 2:00 P.M. because it was a *fiesta* day. Kathryn was furious because she had come all the way from Washington to have half of her first workday cut short. She became even more agitated because her Mexican colleagues just could not understand why she was so upset.

Clearly Kathryn did not understand the basic value difference between people living in Washington and Mexico City. Unlike Washingtonians, Mexicans place a high value on fiestas because they provide a chance to socialize with, and reinforce their ties to, friends and relatives. Moreover work for its own sake is not as highly valued in Mexico as it is north of the Rio Grande. In other words, whereas most Washingtonians "live to work," most Mexicans tend to "work to live." This is not to say that Mexicans are lazy and do not work hard. Rather they do not define themselves by how much work they can accomplish. Work among Mexicans is more balanced with other aspects of their lives, particularly their need to constantly maintain and strengthen their relationships with their kinfolk. So, as we can see from this situation, things as seemingly unrelated as working hours and attitudes about maintaining strong kinship ties can actually affect the job performance of a payroll consultant in Washington, D.C. ■

WHAT WE WILL LEARN

- What do anthropologists mean by the term *kinship*?

- Why have cultural anthropologists spent so much time studying kinship?

- What are the various functions of descent groups?

- What are the different ways in which cultures categorize kin?

- Why is it important to know something about the kinship systems in other cultures?

- How do matrilineal and patrilineal systems of kinship differ?

- How have the reproductive technologies of the twenty-first century confused our understanding of how people are related to one another?

It has been said many times that humans are social animals. Even though other species display certain social features (such as baboons living in permanent troops), what sets humans apart from the rest of the animal world is the complexity of their social organization. People live in groups to a much greater degree than any other species. Individuals play specific social roles, have different statuses, and form patterned relationships with other group members. Human social groups are formed on the basis of factors such as occupation, kinship, social class, gender, ethnic affiliation, education, and religion.

For much of the twentieth century cultural anthropologists have spent a disproportionate amount of time and energy describing kinship systems. Not only have they devoted more time to studying kinship systems than any other single topic, but they have spent more time on kinship systems than have other social scientists. The reason cultural anthropologists spend so much

FIGURE 10.1 Cultural anthropologists generally have studied societies in which kinship activities play a very important role. This family from Beijing, China includes three generations.

time on what Bronislaw Malinowski called "kinship algebra" is related to the type of societies they have traditionally studied.

Cultural anthropologists, although interested in all societies of the world, have in actual practice concentrated on studying small-scale societies where kinship relations tend to be all-encompassing. In highly urbanized, technological societies, such as those studied most often by sociologists, fewer social relationships are based on kinship. In the United States, for example, social relationships that are essentially political, economic, recreational, or religious are usually not played out with kin. But even in the United States, where kinship ties are sometimes overshadowed by nonkinship ties, kin relations are usually more long term, intense, and emotionally laden than are relations with non-kin. By way of contrast, in small-scale, non-Western, preliterate, and technologically simple societies, kinship is at the heart of the social structure. Whom a person marries, where he or she lives, and from whom a person inherits property and status all depend on the person's place within the kinship system. In such societies, it might not be an exaggeration to say that kinship relations are tantamount to social relations (Figure 10.1).

Whether we are considering small- or large-scale societies, kinship systems are important because they help people adapt to interpersonal and environmental challenges. Kinship systems are adaptive because they provide a plan for aligning people and resources in strategic

ways. They set limits on sexual activity and on who can marry whom, they establish the parameters of economic cooperation between men and women, and they provide a basis for proper child rearing. Moreover kinship systems often provide a mechanism for sharing certain pieces of property (such as land or cattle) that cannot be divided without being destroyed. Beyond the limits of the immediate family unit, kinship systems extend one's relationship to a much wider group of people. To illustrate, membership in a small, local group of kin enables an individual to draw on more distant kinsmen for protection or economic support during difficult times. Also, when small family groups are confronted with large-scale projects, they often recruit cooperative labor from among already existing groups of extended kinsmen.

Kinship Defined

Kinship refers to the relationships—found in all societies—that are based on blood or marriage. Those people to whom we are related through birth or blood are our *consanguineal relatives*; those to whom we are related through marriage are our *affinal relatives*. Each society has a well-understood system of defining relationships between these different types of relatives. Every society, in other words, defines the nature of kinship interaction by determining which kin are more socially important than others, the terms used to classify various types of kin, and the expected forms of behavior between them. Although the systems vary significantly from one society to another, one thing is certain: Relationships based on blood and marriage are culturally recognized by all societies.

All kinship systems are founded on biological connections. Family and kinship groups would not exist if men and women did not mate and have children. However kinship systems involve more than biological relationships. Each society classifies its kin according to a set of cultural rules that may or may not account for biological factors. For example, according to our own kinship system, we refer to both our father's brother and our father's sister's husband as uncles even though the former is a blood relative and the latter is not. In many societies a man refers to his father's brother and his mother's brother (both blood relatives) by different terms and is expected to behave differently toward the two. This distinction between the biological and cultural dimensions of kinship can be seen in US society when we refer to our adopted children as sons and daughters (with all of the rights and obligations that biological children have) even though they have no genetic connection. Thus, as we can see, the way that different societies sort and categorize kinship relationships is as much a matter of culture as it is a matter of biology.

All kinship systems, wherever they may be found, serve two important functions for the well-being of the total society. First, by its *vertical function of kinship*, a kinship system

consanguineal relatives One's biological or blood relatives.

affinal relatives Kinship ties formed through marriage (that is, in-laws).

vertical function of kinship The ways in which all kinship systems tend to provide social continuity by binding together different generations.

provides social continuity by binding together successive generations. Kinship systems are most directly involved with passing on education, tradition, property, and political office from one generation to the next. Second, kinship systems tend to solidify or tie together a society horizontally (that is, across a single generation) through the process of marriage. Because kinship systems define the local kin groups outside of which people must take a spouse, groups are forced to enter into alliances with other kinship groups, thereby creating solidarity within a much larger society. This *horizontal function of kinship* was perhaps best illustrated by the late King Sobhuza II of Swaziland, who solidified his entire kingdom (composed of approximately a half-million people) by taking a wife from virtually every nonroyal lineage in the country.

The term *fictive kinship* is used for people who are not related by either blood or marriage. Fictive kinship can take a number of different forms. For example, the process of adoption creates a set of relationships between the adoptive parents and child that have all of the expectations of relationships based on descent or marriage. Often close friends of the family are referred to as aunt or uncle, even though they have no biological or marital relationship. College fraternities and sororities and some churches use kinship terminology (such as brothers and sisters) to refer to their members. And of course, the godparent–godchild relationship, which carries with it all sorts of kinship obligations, often involves people who do not share blood or marriage connections. These examples should remind us that it is possible to have kinship-like relationships (complete with well-understood rights and obligations) without having an actual biological or marital connection.

In the United States the *biological* meaning of kinship is powerful (Figure 10.2). This is particularly true when determining legal parenthood. For example, surrogate mothers who have borne children for wealthy women have had some success in the courts in reclaiming those children purely on the basis of being the biological mother. And biological fathers who have abandoned their families have returned to claim custody of their children solely on the basis of biological paternity. In some parts of the world, however, the *social* component of kinship is given far more weight than in the United States. For the Zumbagua of highland Ecuador, parenthood is not established solely and automatically on the basis of either giving birth or impregnating a woman. Rather it involves a relationship that must be *achieved* over a relatively long period of time. According to Mary Weismantel (1995: 698):

> Among the Zumbagua, if the biological father's role ends after conception, or if the mother's role

Courtesy of Gary Ferraro

FIGURE 10.2 Parenthood as defined by this Western family is very different from the Zumbaguan definition of parenthood.

ends shortly after birth, these biological parents have a very weak claim to parenthood should they re-enter the child's life at a later time. Thus, the Zumbagua notion of parenthood involves *working* at nurturing the child over a number of years; mere conception or childbirth alone does not, in and of itself, give a man or a woman the right to claim parenthood of a child.

Thus, the Zumbagua of Ecuador place a higher priority on social parenthood that is earned than is found in mainstream US society, which places a higher value on genetically based parenthood. This, of course, has important implications for the process of adoption in these two cultures. Rather than automatically designating parenthood on the basis of biological connections, Zumbaguan culture insists that claims to parenthood are created by the adult nurturing and caring

© Cengage Learning

---

horizontal function of kinship The ways in which all kinship systems, by requiring people to marry outside their own small kinship group, function to integrate the total society through marriage bonds between otherwise unrelated kin groups.

fictive kinship Relationships among individuals who recognize kinship obligations even though the relationships are not based on either consanguineal or affinal ties.

for the child over a long period of time. In fact the Zumbaguan notion of nurturing is taken quite literally, defined as actually *feeding or sharing food with* the child. In a sense, food is what binds parents to children because, according to Weismantel (1995: 695), "Those who eat together in the same household share the same flesh."

In Zumbaguan society, social parenthood is given higher priority than biological parenthood. There are additional ethnographic examples in which kinship is socially constructed rather than universally defined. For example, some aboriginal cultures in South America believe in "partible paternity"—the notion that a child can have more than one biological father. In other words, it is believed that all men who have sex with a woman during her pregnancy actually contribute to the formation of the fetus. When the baby is born, the mother names the men whom she identifies as fathers, who then are expected to assume social responsibility for the child. Even though this concept of partible paternity flies in the face of our scientific understanding of conception, recent studies have shown that defining fatherhood as a multiple phenomenon actually is beneficial for children. For example, among the Bari people of Venezuela, children with two or more official fathers had an 80 percent chance of reaching adulthood, as compared to only 64 percent for those with one father (Beckerman and Valentine 2002). In societies such as the Bari, a strong case can be made for a pregnant woman taking lovers so that her child will have more than one male provider. The Bari notion of multiple fatherhood is significant because it illustrates how, as in the Zumbaguan case, kinship categories such as father or parent are defined differently in various cultures.

EGO The person in kinship diagrams from whose point of view the relationships are traced.

Using Kinship Diagrams

Although kinship systems are found in every society, the definitions of the relationships between kin vary widely from one group to another. In different societies people with the same biological connection may be defined differently, labeled differently, and expected to behave differently toward one another. And, as we shall see, societies can choose from a vast array of possibilities. Before sorting out the complexities of different kinship systems, we will introduce some symbols that cultural anthropologists use in analyzing kinship systems.

As a way of simplifying kinship systems, anthropologists use kinship diagrams rather than relying on verbal explanations alone. In this standardized notational system, all kinship diagrams are viewed from a central point of reference (called *EGO*), the person from whose point of view we are tracing the relationship. All kinship diagrams use the symbols shown in Figure 10.3.

Starting with our point of reference (EGO), we can construct a hypothetical family diagram, as in Figure 10.4. We refer to all of the people in the diagram with the following symbols:

1. Father's sister (FZ)
2. Father's sister's husband (FZH)
3. Father's brother's wife (FBW)
4. Father's brother (FB)
5. Father (F)
6. Mother (M)
7. Mother's sister's husband (MZH)
8. Mother's sister (MZ)
9. Mother's brother (MB)
10. Mother's brother's wife (MBW)
11. Father's sister's son (FZS)
12. Father's sister's daughter (FZD)

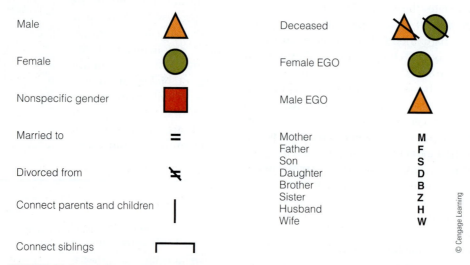

FIGURE 10.3 Kinship diagram symbols (*Note:* symbols with the same numbers below them are referred to in the same way by EGO).

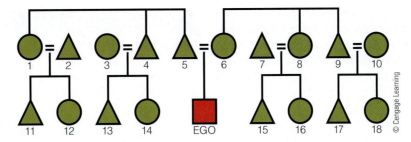

FIGURE 10.4 Generic kinship diagram.

13. Father's brother's son (FBS)

14. Father's brother's daughter (FBD)

15. Mother's sister's son (MZS)

16. Mother's sister's daughter (MZD)

17. Mother's brother's son (MBS)

18. Mother's brother's daughter (MBD)

Principles of Kinship Classification

No kinship system in the world uses a different term of reference for every single relative. Instead all kinship systems group relatives into certain categories, refer to them by the same term, and expect people to behave toward them in a similar fashion. How a particular society categorizes relatives depends on which principles of classification it uses. Various kinship systems use different principles to group certain relatives together while separating others, as discussed in the following subsections.

Generation

In some kinship systems—our own being a good example—distinctions between kin depend on generation. Mothers, fathers, and their siblings are always found in the first ascending generation, immediately above EGO; sons, daughters, nieces, and nephews are always one generation below EGO in the first descending generation; grandmothers and grandfathers are always two generations above EGO; and so forth. Although this seems like the natural thing to do, some societies have kinship systems that do not confine a kin category to a single generation. It is possible, for example, to find the same kin category in three or four different generations. The Haida of British Columbia use the same kinship term to refer to one's father's sister, father's sister's daughter, and the daughter of the father's sister's daughter.

Sex or Gender

Some kinship systems group certain kin together because of common gender (Collier and Yanagisako 1987). In our English system, kin categories such as brother, father,

father's brother, son, and grandfather are always males; sister, mother, mother's sister, daughter, and grandmother are always females. The one area where we do not distinguish on the basis of gender is at the cousin level (but, then, the consistent application of a particular principle is not required). Even though this principle of gender operates at most levels of our own system, it is hardly universally applicable. Some societies allow for the possibility of both males and females occupying a single kin category.

Lineality versus Collaterality

Lineality refers to kin related in a single line, such as son, father, grandfather. *Collaterality*, on the other hand, refers to kin related through a linking relative, such as the relationship between EGO and his or her parents' siblings. Whereas the principle of lineality distinguishes between father and father's brother, the principle of collaterality does not. That is, in some societies, EGO uses the term *father* to refer to both his or her father and his or her father's brother; similarly, EGO's mother and her sisters may be referred to by the single term *mother*.

Consanguineal versus Affinal Kin

Some societies make distinctions in kinship categories based on whether people are related by blood (consanguineal kin) or through marriage (affinal kin). Our own kinship system uses this principle of classification at some levels but not at others. To illustrate, we distinguish between sons and sons-in-law and between sisters and sisters-in-law. But in EGO's parents' generation, we fail to distinguish between mother's brother (a blood relative) and mother's sister's husband (an affinal relative), both of whom we call *uncle*.

Relative Age

In certain kinship systems, relative age is a criterion for separating different types of relatives. In such societies a man uses one kinship term for younger brother

---

lineality Kin relationships traced through a single line, such as son, father, and grandfather.

collaterality Kin relationships traced through a linking relative.

and another term for older brother. These different terms based on relative age carry with them different behavioral expectations. Often a man is expected to act toward his older brother with deference and respect while behaving much more informally toward his younger brother.

Sex of the Connecting Relative

Some societies distinguish between different categories of kin based on the sex of the connecting (or intervening) relative. To illustrate (see Figure 10.2), a mother's brother's daughter (18) and a mother's sister's daughter (16), who are both called *cousins* in our system, are given two different kinship terms. Similarly a father's brother's daughter (14) and a father's sister's daughter (12) are given different kinship terms. One category of cousins (12 and 18) is called *cross cousins*, and the other (14 and 16) is called *parallel cousins*. According to this principle, these first cousins are considered to be different by virtue of the sex of their parents.

Social Condition

Distinctions among kin categories can also be made based on a person's general life condition. According to this criterion, different kinship terms are used for a married brother and a bachelor brother or for a living aunt and one who is deceased.

Side of the Family

A final principle has to do with using different kin terms for EGO's mother's side of the family and EGO's father's side of the family. The kinship system used in the United States makes no such distinction; we have aunts, uncles, cousins, and grandparents on both sides of our family. In societies that use this principle of classification, different terms are used to refer to a mother's brother and a father's brother.

---

kinship systems Those relationships found in all societies that are based on blood or marriage.

descent A person's kinship connections traced back through a number of generations.

unilineal descent Tracing descent through a single line (such as matrilineal or patrilineal) as compared to both sides (bilateral descent).

matrilineal descent groups A form of descent in which people trace their primary kin connections through their mothers.

patrilineal descent groups A form of descent in which people trace their primary kin relationships through their fathers.

cognatic descent A form of descent traced through both females and males.

CROSS-CULTURAL MISCUE

Geraldine Brooks (1990) relates an incident of intercultural misunderstanding that occurred in Saudi Arabia between a North American woman and her local Saudi landlord. The woman, the wife of a US Marine chaplain stationed in Saudi Arabia, was at home when the landlord arrived with several workmen to make repairs. On entering, the landlord passed the US woman but never spoke to her or even acknowledged her presence. The wife thought that the landlord's behavior was extremely rude. Actually, according to Saudi culture, the landlord was treating her with the utmost respect. He did not want to invade her privacy by speaking to her without her husband being present. Thus, according to his own culture, the landlord was treating her in the most appropriate way to ensure both her privacy and to uphold her husband's honor.

The Formation of Descent Groups

As we have seen, kinship systems play an important role in helping people sort out how they should behave toward various relatives. In anthropological terms *kinship systems* encompass all of the blood and marriage relationships that help people distinguish among different categories of kin, create rights and obligations among kin, and serve as the basis for the formation of certain types of kin groups.

Anthropologists also use the narrower term *descent* to refer to the rules a culture uses to establish affiliations with one's parents. These rules of descent often provide the basis for the formation of social groups. These social groups, or descent groups, are collections of relatives (usually descendants of a common ancestor) who live out their lives in close proximity to one another. In fact, in those societies that have descent groups, the group plays a central role in the lives of its members.

Rules of descent may be divided into two distinct types. The first is *unilineal descent*, whereby people trace their ancestry through either the mother's line or the father's line, but not both. Unilineal groups that trace their descent through the mother's line are called *matrilineal descent groups*, those tracing their descent through the father's line are called *patrilineal descent groups*. The second type of descent is known as *cognatic* (or *multilineal*) *descent*, which is traced through both females and males and includes double descent, ambilineal descent, and bilateral descent. Because descent is traced in mainstream North America according to the bilateral principle, many Westerners have difficulty understanding unilineal kinship systems.

Unilineal Descent Groups

Approximately 60 percent of all kinship systems found in the world are based on the unilineal principle. Unilineal descent groups are particularly adaptive because they are clear-cut, unambiguous social units. Because a person becomes a member of a unilineal descent group by birth, there is no confusion about who is a group member and who is not. For societies that rely on kinship groups to perform most of their social functions (such as marriage, dispute settlement, and religious ceremonies), unilineal descent groups, with their clear-cut membership, provide a social organization with unambiguous roles and statuses. It is clear to which group one belongs, so a person has no questions about her or his rights of inheritance, prestige, and social roles.

Anthropologists distinguish between two different types of kinship groups that are based on the unilineal principle, lineages and clans. A *lineage* is a unilineal descent group of up to approximately ten generations deep. Its members can trace their ancestry back (step by step) to a common founder. When descent is traced through the male line, the groups are known as *patrilineages*; when it is traced through the female line, they are known as *matrilineages*. The other type of unilineal descent group is the clan. A *clan* is a group of kin, usually comprising ten or more generations, whose members believe they are all related to a common ancestor but are unable to trace that genealogical connection step by step.

When clans and lineages are found together, the clan is usually made up of a number of different lineages. In some societies, clans are close-knit groups, much like lineages, whose members have a high degree of interaction with one another. More commonly, however, clan members are widely dispersed geographically and rarely get together for clanwide activities. Unlike lineages, which serve as corporate, functioning groups, clans tend to be larger and more loosely structured categories with which people identify. Often clans are associated with animals or plants (that is, totems) that provide a focal point for group identity.

Patrilineal Descent Groups

Of the two types of unilineal descent groups, patrilineal descent is by far more common. Patrilineal descent groups are found on all of the major continents and in a wide range of societies, including certain food-collecting Native American groups, some East African farmers and pastoralists, the Nagas of India, the Kapauku Papuans of the New Guinea Highlands, and the traditional Chinese. In societies with patrilineal descent groups, a person is related through the father, father's father, and so forth. In other words, a man,

FIGURE 10.5 This Kikuyu family of Kenya has a patrilineal descent system.

his own children, his brother's children (but not his sister's children), and his son's children (but not his daughter's children) are all members of the same descent group (Figure 10.5). Females must marry outside their own patrilineages, and the children a woman bears belong to the husband's lineage rather than to her own. The principle of patrilineal descent is illustrated in Figure 10.6.

We will use traditional China to illustrate patrilineal descent because China is by far the largest patrilineal society in the world. It is important to emphasize here that we are talking about *traditional* China for approximately a hundred years prior to the Communist takeover in 1949. During this period the Chinese family, at least ideally, was made up of the patrilineage, comprising a man, his wife or wives, his sons, daughters-in-law, grandchildren, and great-grandchildren. When a son reached marriageable age, the extended family provided a wife for him. In most cases the wives came from other unrelated families, but sometimes Chinese couples adopted unrelated infant girls for the express purpose of providing a future bride for one of the sons, a practice known as *simpua*. A family with many sons became large by producing many children. The residence pattern was patrilocal, in which the wives lived with and became part of the husband's lineage and produced children for it. The extended family typically occupied a set of buildings forming a single estate. As in any patrilineal society, inheritance passed from the father to his son(s) and grandson(s).

---

lineage A unilineal descent group whose members can trace their line of descent back to a common ancestor.

clan Unilineal descent groups, usually comprising ten or more generations, consisting of members who claim a common ancestry even though they cannot trace step by step their exact connection to that ancestor.

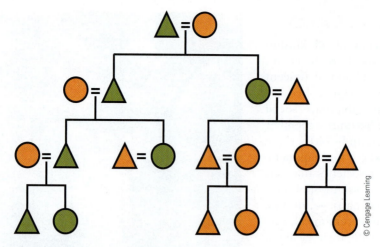

FIGURE 10.6 Patrilineal descent: In a patrilineal descent system, a person is connected to relatives of both sexes related through males only. Sons and daughters belong to their father's descent group, as do the fathers' sons' children but not the father's daughters' children.

CONTEMPORARY ISSUES

Does the gender of the anthropologist influence his or her findings?

✿ Until the 1970s, with the exception of some fairly well-known female anthropologists, such as Margaret Mead and Ruth Benedict, most ethnographers were men. Over the past four decades, however, an increasing number of women have entered the field, and in fact, the membership of the American Anthropological Association (AAA) is presently between 55 and 60 percent women. Nevertheless, many of our previous ethnographic accounts of cultural phenomena have had a distinctively male bias. Nowhere has this been more evident than in the descriptive accounts of patrilineal kinship systems found throughout the world.

A case in point is the patrilineal family groups found in traditional China. To be certain, patrilineal families *are* male-focused. Men are born into a patrilineage and remain in that group for the rest of their lives. A man's sisters leave his patrilineage to take up residence with their husbands, and his own wife has left her father's homestead to take up residence with his family. When young women marry, they sever their ties with their father's family, literally, with a ritual slamming of the door. The bride can return for visits to her natal lineage for as long as her mother is alive, but the frequency of such visits varies with geographic proximity. Women in traditional China are raised in one family and then, on marriage, are expected to transfer both their residence and their allegiance to the families of their husbands. By way of contrast, men's lives in patrilineal societies have continuity, security, and predictability.

Early ethnographic accounts of Chinese patrilineages have almost exclusively looked at the family from the male perspective, and by default, have assumed that both men and women view the "family" in essentially equivalent terms. But, according to Margery Wolf (1972), the most meaningful family for a Chinese woman is neither her father's patrilineage, which she will eventually leave, nor her husband's patrilineage, into which she will marry. Instead, it is what Wolf refers to as the "uterine family," composed of her mother and her mother's children. After the woman marries and takes up residence with her husband's lineage, her allegiances slowly transfer from the uterine family headed by her mother to a uterine family of her own, which includes her own children. The uterine family lacks the continuity of a patrilineage because it lasts only as long as the mother is alive. Although the uterine family has no official ideology, formal structure, or public recognition, it is nevertheless a real family in terms of feelings and behaviors.

The uterine family does not exist solely within the context of the husband's larger patrilineage. Women, who are strangers and outsiders in their husbands' lineages, also form strong alliances in the village with other women, who, by definition, are also outsiders. Much of women's work is conducted outside of the family compound. Thus, while washing clothes at the river, a woman is able to make alliances with other women (both within and outside her husband's patrilineage), which she can draw on to advance the interests of her own uterine family. A woman who has exercised good judgment and has nurtured productive allegiances over the years is able to exert considerable influence over her husband and his patrilineage.

Wolf's work on women and the family in rural Taiwan serves as a useful corrective to our understanding of the Chinese patrilineal family. It also is a reminder to anthropologists, as well as to other social scientists, that the gender and perspective of the investigator may contribute to a skewed picture of reality. Moreover, it justifies Franz Boas's insistence (see Chapter 4) many decades ago that anthropology needs both men and women ethnographers to construct the most complete description of another culture.

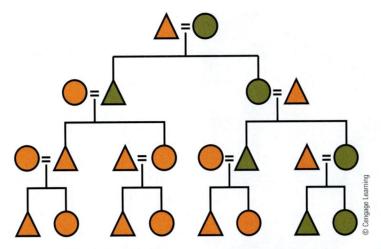

FIGURE 10.7 Matrilineal descent: In a matrilineal descent system, a person is connected to kin of both sexes related through females only. Sons and daughters belong to their mother's descent group, as do the mother's daughters' children but not the mother's sons' children.

In the United States and much of western Europe, parents are expected to give priority to the needs of their children. But in the traditional Chinese family, the reverse is true: It is the children who have the major obligation to the family. Children must show deference, respect, and obedience to their parents for as long as the parents are alive. Children are obligated to provide for the comfort of their aging parents and, even after their death, must attend to the parents' spiritual needs through ceremonies of ancestor worship. And sons are under constant pressure to perpetuate their father's lineage by producing sons of their own. The male members of the families are responsible for maintaining the ancestral tablets, kept in the family shrine and on which all the names of the family are carefully recorded. A man takes seriously the place of his name in the family tablets as a way of connecting himself to his ancestors and his descendants.

Matrilineal Descent Groups

In a matrilineal kinship system, a person belongs to the mother's group. A matrilineal descent group comprises a woman, her siblings, her own children, her sisters' children, and her daughters' children. Matrilineal descent groups make up about 15 percent of the unilineal descent groups found among contemporary societies. They are found in a number of areas of the world, including some Native Americans (such as Navajo, Cherokee, and Iroquois), the Truk and Trobriand Islanders of the Pacific, and the Bemba, Ashanti, and Yao of Africa.

It is important not to confuse matrilineal descent with *matriarchy*, a situation known only in myth, in which the women in a society have greater authority and decision-making prerogatives than the men. In most cases where matrilineal descent is practiced, men retain the lion's share of the power and authority. Men hold the political offices, and it is men, not women, who control property. In matrilineal societies both property and political office pass from one man to another, but through a woman. To illustrate, whereas in a patrilineal society a man passes his property and hereditary political office to his own son, in a matrilineal society property and office pass from a man to his sister's son. In fact, in a matrilineal society, the most important male relationship a man has is with his sister's son (or mother's brother). The principle of matrilineal descent is illustrated in Figure 10.7.

A good example of a matrilineal society is the Zuni people of New Mexico, one of the best-described and most typical groups among the western Pueblos (Figure 10.8). The Zuni are divided into thirteen matrilineal clans, each of which comprises several lineages. The clan, not the lineage, is the exogamous group. The household, which is the essential economic unit, is occupied by a woman or group of women (made up of the grandmother, her sisters, and their daughters) who are descended through females. Because the Zuni practice matrilocal residence, husbands live with their wives and their wives' matrilineal kin. The women are the permanent residents of the house and are bound together by their joint care of all the sacred objects in the house. Just as wives are viewed as strangers or outsiders in the traditional Chinese extended family, so are the husbands in the Zuni family.

Wives have no practical connection to their husbands' families. Husbands, however, need to divide their energy and allegiances between their wife's matrilineage and that of their mothers and sisters. When important ceremonial activities need to be conducted, it is the married brothers (presently married and living with the matrilineages of their wives) who return to perform them at their mother's house. Even though husbands contribute to the economic well-being of their

matriarchy A system of governance whereby women rule over men or are empowered to make decisions over men.

FIGURE 10.8 This Zuni grandmother and granddaughter from New Mexico practice matrilineal descent.

and the ceremonial needs of their sisters and mothers, it is not surprising that marriages are fairly fragile. According to ethnographic accounts, Zuni men tend to desire marriage more than women because if a man should divorce or never marry at all, he would be forced to live at home with his female kin, a living arrangement that most Zuni men would consider undignified at best. In Zuni society, men are more willing to become husbands than women are to become wives. Women in Zuni society always have a desirable home, but men do not (Benedict 1934; Eggan 1950).

The Corporate Nature of Unilineal Descent Groups

One feature of all unilineal descent groups—whether we are talking about lineages or clans—is that they clearly define who is a member and who is not. These collective kinship groups also endure over time. Even though individual members are born into the group and leave it by dying, the unilineal descent group itself continues on. Because of their unambiguous membership and continuity, unilineal descent groups are good examples of corporate entities that play a powerful and multifaceted role in the lives of the individual

wives' matrilineal household, they play no role in the ritual or ceremonial activities of the household because this role is performed by the brothers and uncles of the wife's matrilineage. Thus, men perform economic roles for their wives but ritual roles for their own matrilineages. And, in fact, the ritual roles in everyday Zuni life are more important than how many material possessions a man can accumulate. The important Zuni man of high prestige is not the wealthiest in a material sense but rather the one who performs many ceremonial roles with his family's religious fetishes.

Because Zuni men are divided between serving the economic interests of their wives

TABLE 10.1

Comparison of Patrilineal and Matrilineal Descent Groups

	Patrilineal Descent	Matrilineal Descent
Percentage of unilineal descent groups	85 percent	15 percent
Line of descent	Children follow father's line	Children follow mother's line
Role of women	Give birth to husband's kin; minimal role in own group	Central role in own group by bearing their own descendants
Male child's authority figure	Biological father	Mother's brother
Male authority/ status	Strong in marital household	Weak in marital household but strong in sister's
Strength of marital union	Strong (divorce rare)	Relatively weak (divorce more common)
Geographic distribution	Native Americans, traditional Chinese, sub-Saharan Africa, India, New Guinea	Some Native Americans, southeast Africa, Trobriand Islands, Ashanti of West Africa

members. We can cite six indicators of the corporate nature of unilineal descent groups:

1. Unilineal groups such as lineages often shape a person's identity. When a stranger asks the simple question "Who are you?" lineage members are likely to respond, "I am a member of such and such a lineage," rather than "I am John Smith." Lineage members, in other words, see themselves first and foremost as members of the kinship group rather than as individuals.

2. Unilineal descent groups regulate marriage. Because unilineal descent groups are exogamous, the incest taboo is extended to all group members, which may involve thousands of people. Moreover in most unilineal descent groups, large numbers of kin on both the bride's and the groom's side of the family must give their approval before the marriage can take place.

3. Property (such as land and livestock) is usually regulated by the descent group, rather than controlled by the individual. The group allocates specific pieces of property to individual members for their use but only because they are kin members in good standing. This control of economic resources by the descent group requires the group to help young adults get established economically, pay bridewealth (see Chapter 9), and support group members during times of crisis.

4. Unilineal descent groups function politically to the extent that lineage elders have the right to settle disputes within their lineage (albeit usually without the power to impose a settlement) and may act as intermediaries in disputes with opposing descent groups.

5. Unilineal descent groups often have their own set of religious deities, and in many cases those deities are deceased family members. When a respected lineage or clan elder dies, he is not buried and forgotten but often is elevated to the status of "ancestor-god." Because it is believed that these deceased ancestors can both protect and curse the living group members, living elders periodically perform religious or supernatural ceremonies to appease the ever-vigilant ancestor-deities.

6. Even the criminal justice system in societies with unilineal descent groups has a strong corporate focus. For example, if a member of lineage (a) assaults a member of lineage (q), the entire lineage (q) will seek compensation from or revenge on lineage (a). The assaulter would not be held solely accountable for her or his individual actions, but rather the group (the lineage or clan) would be culpable.

The corporate nature of unilineal descent groups is no better illustrated than in the strong bonds of obligations that exist among members. The kinship group provides a firm base of security and protection for its individual members. If crops fail, an individual can always turn to her or his unilineal descent group members for assistance; in the event of any threat from outsiders, a person may expect support and protection from members of her or his own descent group. The strength of these bonds of obligation depends on the closeness of the ties. Mutual assistance is likely to be taken seriously among lineage members, less so among clan members.

Multilineal Descent Groups

Approximately 40 percent of the world's societies have kinship systems that are not based on the unilineal principle. These multilineal descent groups are classified into three basic types: double descent, ambilineal descent, and bilateral descent.

Double Descent

Some societies practice a form of *double descent* (or double unilineal descent), whereby kinship is traced both matrilineally and patrilineally. In such societies an individual belongs to both the mother's and the father's lineages. Descent under such a system is matrilineal for some purposes and patrilineal for others. For example, movable property such as small livestock or agricultural produce may be inherited from the mother's side of the family, whereas nonmovable property such as land may be inherited from the father's side. Double descent is rare; only about 5 percent of the world's cultures practice it.

Ambilineal Descent

In societies that practice *ambilineal descent*, parents have a choice of affiliating their children with either kinship group. Compared with unilineal systems, which restrict one's membership to either the mother's or the father's group, ambilineal systems are more flexible because they allow for individual choice concerning group affiliation.

Bilateral Descent

In societies (such as mainstream US society) that practice *bilateral descent*, a person is related equally to both the mother's and the father's sides of the family. A bilateral system tends to be symmetrical to the extent that what happens on one side of the kinship diagram also

---

double descent A system of descent in which individuals receive some rights and obligations from the father's side of the family and others from the mother's side.

ambilineal descent A form of descent in which a person chooses to affiliate with a kin group through either the male or the female line.

bilateral descent A type of kinship system in which individuals emphasize both their mother's kin and their father's kin relatively equally.

happens on the other side. In other words, the grandparents, aunts, uncles, and cousins are treated equally on both sides of the family.

The kinship group recognized in a bilateral system is known as the *kindred*—a group of closely related relatives connected through both parents to one living relative (or to EGO). Unlike unilineal descent, which forms discrete, mutually exclusive groups, bilateral systems give rise to a situation in which no two individuals (except siblings) have the same kindred. The kindred is not a group at all but rather a network of relatives. It has no founding ancestor, precise boundaries, or continuity over time. In short, because kindreds are not corporate groups, they cannot perform the same functions—such as joint ownership of property, common economic activities, regulation of marriage, or mutual assistance—as unilineal groups. An individual can mobilize some members of his or her kindred to perform some of these tasks, but the kindred does not function as a corporate entity.

This type of loosely structured network of relatives (kindred) works particularly well in a society like our own that highly values individuality, personal independence, and geographic mobility. Although the kindred in bilateral societies establishes a fairly wide set of relationships with mutual obligations, those ties are rather loosely defined and amorphous. The looseness of the ties thus allows for greater autonomy from the demands of kinsmen. In other words, the typical North American can be more economically and geographically mobile if fewer people can make kinship demands on his or her time and resources.

Bilateral descent is also adaptive for small-scale foraging societies, such as the Ju/'hoansi of Botswana and Namibia, but for different reasons than found in economically complex societies. In small-scale societies that are geographically mobile and have scarce resources, bilateral descent enables people to make claims on a large set of kinsmen who may be dispersed over a wide area. This is adaptive because kinsmen may be asked for help, particularly in hard times.

---

kindred All of the relatives a person recognizes in a bilateral kinship system.

patrilocal residence A residence pattern in which the married couple lives with or near the relatives of the husband's father.

matrilocal residence A residence pattern in which the married couple lives with or near the relatives of the wife.

avunculocal residence A residence pattern in which the married couple lives with or near the husband's mother's brother.

ambilocal (bilocal) residence A residence pattern in which the married couple may choose to live with either the relatives of the wife or the relatives of the husband.

neolocal residence A residence pattern in which the married couple has its own place of residence apart from the relatives of either spouse.

Residence Patterns: Where Do Wives and Husbands Live?

In the same way that all societies establish rules of affiliation with parents (descent), they also set guidelines regarding where married couples will live. When two people marry in North American society, it is customary for the couple to take up residence in a place of their own, apart from the relatives of either spouse. This residence pattern is known as *neolocal residence* (that is, a new place). As natural as this may seem to us, by global standards it is an atypical residence pattern, practiced in only about 5 percent of the world's societies. The remaining societies prescribe that newlyweds will live in the same household with or close to relatives of the wife or the husband.

Most residence patterns fall into one of five types (percentages are based on tabulations from George Murdock's "Ethnographic Atlas" [1967]):

- *Patrilocal residence.* The married couple lives with or near the relatives of the husband's father (69 percent of societies).

- *Matrilocal residence.* The married couple lives with or near the relatives of the wife (13 percent of societies).

- *Avunculocal residence.* The married couple lives with or near the husband's mother's brother (4 percent of societies).

- *Ambilocal (bilocal) residence.* The married couple has a choice of living with either the relatives of the wife or the relatives of the husband (9 percent of societies).

- *Neolocal residence.* The married couple establishes an independent place of residence away from the relatives of either spouse (5 percent of societies).

To a significant degree, residence patterns are linked to the types of kinship systems found in any society. For example, there is a reasonably close correlation between patrilocal residence and patrilineal descent (tracing one's important relatives through the father's side) and between matrilocal residence and matrilineal descent (tracing one's important relatives through the mother's side). To be certain, residence patterns do not *determine* kinship ideology, but social interaction between important categories of kin can be facilitated if those kin live in close proximity to one another.

It should be kept in mind that these five residence patterns, like most other aspects of culture, are ideal types. Consequently, how people actually behave—in this case, where they reside—does not always conform precisely to these ideals. Sometimes normative patterns of residence are altered or interrupted by events such as famines or epidemics that force newlyweds to live in areas that will maximize their chances for survival or their economic security. To illustrate, during the Depression years of the 1930s, the normal neolocal pattern of residence in the United States was disrupted when many young married adults moved in to live with one set of parents to save money.

Different Systems of Classification

Every society has a coherent system of labeling various types of kin. In any given system, certain categories of kin are grouped together under a single category, whereas others are separated into distinct categories. In our own society, we group together under the general heading of "aunt" our mother's sisters, father's sisters, mother's brothers' wives, and father's brothers' wives. Similarly, we lump together under the heading of "uncle" our father's brothers, mother's brothers, father's sisters' husbands, and mother's sisters' husbands. In contrast, other societies might have separate terms for all eight of these categories of kin. Whatever system of classification is used, however, cultural anthropologists have found them to be both internally logical and consistently applied. Even though individual societies may have their own variations, six basic classification systems have been identified: Eskimo, Hawaiian, Iroquois, Omaha, Crow, and Sudanese. We will describe two of these classification systems—the Eskimo (which serves as the basis for our own kinship system) and the Iroquois—in greater detail.

Eskimo System

Found in approximately one-tenth of the world's societies, the *Eskimo (Inuit) system* of kinship classification is associated with bilateral descent (see Figure 10.9). The major feature of this system is that it emphasizes the nuclear family by using separate terms (such as mother, father, sister, brother) that are not used outside the nuclear family. Beyond the nuclear family, many other relatives (such as aunts, uncles, and cousins) are lumped together. This emphasis on the nuclear family is related to the fact that societies using the Eskimo system lack large descent groups such as lineages and clans. Moreover the Eskimo system is most likely to be found in societies (such as the United States and certain food-collecting societies) in which economic conditions favor an independent nuclear family.

Iroquois System

In the *Iroquois system*, EGO's father and father's brother are called by the same term, and EGO's mother's brother is called by a different term (see Figure 10.10). Likewise EGO's mother and mother's sister are lumped together under one term, and a different term is used for EGO's father's sister. Thus, a basic distinction of classification is made between the sex of one's parents' siblings (that is, mother's brothers and sisters and father's brothers and sisters). Within EGO's own generation, EGO's own siblings are given the same term as the parallel cousins (children of one's mother's sister or father's brother), and different terms are used for cross cousins (children of one's mother's brother or father's sister). Thus, the terminological distinction made between cross and parallel cousins is logical, given the distinction made between the siblings of EGO's parents. The Iroquois system emphasizes the importance of unilineal descent groups by distinguishing between members of one's own lineage and members of other lineages.

We have shown how two of the six kinship systems (Eskimo and Iroquois) divide kinsmen into different categories. It is not necessary to specify in similar detail how all six of the common types of kinship systems are structured. What is important, however, is to grasp the

---

Eskimo (Inuit) system The kinship system most commonly found in the United States; it is associated with bilateral descent. Usually a mother, father, and their children live together.

Iroquois system A kinship system associated with unilineal descent in which the father and father's brother are called by the same term, as are the mother and the mother's sister.

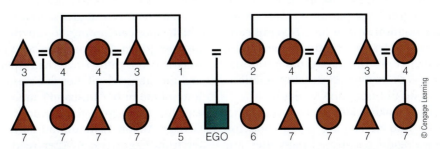

FIGURE 10.9 Eskimo kinship system (*Note:* symbols with the same numbers below them are referred to in the same way by EGO).

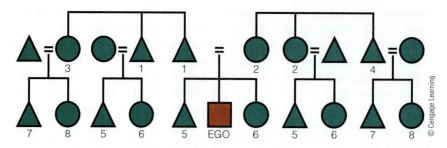

FIGURE 10.10 Iroquois kinship system (*Note:* symbols with the same numbers below them are referred to in the same way by EGO).

notion that different societies divide up the kinship pie in different ways. As a general rule, those kinsmen in any system who are given similar labels are expected to be treated in equivalent ways, whereas those having different labels are not. The particular form any given system takes is neither better nor worse than any other; they are simply different. However different they are, though, every kinship system is internally logical and consistently adhered to.

Kinship and the Modern World

The Broadway play *Six Degrees of Separation* written by John Guare, is based on the stunning premise that everyone has a potential connection to any other person in the world by simply tracing their relationship through six other people. Although this is an interesting theory, it has been difficult, if not impossible, to test the theory owing to a lack of information—*until recently*. With the explosion in information technology in the past two decades we now have data bases that enable us to explore how we are connected to others. For example, in 2011 researchers at Facebook analyzed 69 billion connections and found that 99.6 percent of Facebook users are connected by five degrees (six steps) and that 92 percent are connected by only four degrees of separation (five steps). Thus, the original theory of "six degrees of separation" actually *overstated* the number of links between typical pairs of Facebook users by about 1.3 degrees of separation. Such a powerful piece of information technology is significant not only because it enables us to connect personally to vast networks of people who share our interests, but it also enables us to locate and develop relationships with relatives we did not know we had.

But in addition to making kinship connections in the present, we are also developing power tools for accessing our genealogical histories. Unless they are born into a family that has kept careful records of its

history, most people have little knowledge of their ancestors beyond three or four generations. However, within the last fifteen years it is now possible for people to reconstruct their genealogies many generations into the past. The Internet now has a number of online sites that enable people to find information about long-forgotten family members. The site with the largest family database in the world is Ancestry.com, which for a fee of several hundred dollars provides access to more than 11 billion digitized records on immigration, births, marriages, and deaths. Moreover the database includes more than four hundred historical newspapers as well as thousands of family histories and biographies from the United States, Canada, and Great Britain dating back to the mid-1500s. All of these documents have been scanned into this company's database, allowing subscribers to find information on a particular relative by using "optimal name recognition" technology. So, if you are interested in reconstructing your family connections or would like to learn more about your bizarre great-great-great-uncle Harry, the technology now exists to enable you to do so with relative ease and fairly inexpensively.

Sometimes amateur sleuths and aspiring family genealogists, using these vast data bases, stumble on some eye-popping kinship connections. If they dig deeply enough, just about any of the more than two million subscribers to Ancestry.com will discover a kinship connection to some convicted felon, pirate, or unsavory scoundrel. But there are also many findings that are uplifting. One such story involved a young woman by the name of Josie Jones, who, in January 2012, was midway through her senior year at Hamilton College, a small co-ed liberal arts school in Clinton, New York, which was celebrating its 200th anniversary. Josie's mother, Jody Clark Jones, an avid family historian and Ancestry.com subscriber, had spent weeks researching the ancestry of her husband, Stephen Calhoun Jones. One of her husband's more interesting relatives was his great-great-great grandfather, the Reverend George Albion Calhoun, an early 19th-century minister from Connecticut. After reading a number of his published sermons and his obituary, she learned that the Reverend Calhoun was the *very first* graduate from Hamilton College in the class of 1814. Because the first graduating class had only two graduates, and because "Calhoun" came alphabetically before the surname of the other graduate, then it was reasonable to consider George Albion Calhoun to be Hamilton College's first graduate.

What made this story all the more coincidental was that the Jones family had no known connection to Hamilton College. No family members, to their knowledge, had ever attended the school, and in fact, Josie had no interest in applying until she was invited by the Hamilton women's lacrosse coach to visit the school her senior year in high school. She fell in love with the college on this initial trip, subsequently applied, was accepted, and had a highly successful academic and athletic career there. So you can imagine her surprise when she returned from Christmas holidays to complete her final semester at Hamilton (as it was celebrating its 200th anniversary) knowing that she was the great-great-great-great granddaughter of Hamilton's *very first* alumnus.

In this chapter, we have examined the basic features of kinship systems in a number of different forms. By necessity our discussion has been simplified. Kinship systems and relationships are never as neat and tidy in real life as they are in theory. Exceptions to the rules and aberrant forms of individual behavior can be found in any system. Moreover kinship systems are constantly experiencing changes through contact with external forces such as industrializing economies, colonization and decolonization, missionary intrusions, and cultural diffusion in general.

Of all aspects of human societies, kinship systems represent the most intimate, intense, and long-lasting set of social relationships a person will experience. Based as they are on birth and marriage, they create social ties that are often close and emotional. Kinship groups often involve strong bonds of obligation, security for their members, and moral coercion to adhere to social norms. We cannot assume, however, that these well-integrated kinship groups remain unchanged in the face of external pressures such as urban migration, poverty, unemployment, and a host of other hardships.

Anthropologist Nancy Scheper-Hughes (1989) documented how one essential feature of all kinship systems, the mother–infant bond, has been altered among poor women living in a shantytown in Brazil (Figure 10.11). Conducting fieldwork in the sugar plantation area of northeast Brazil, Scheper-Hughes described this area's vast array of social problems. Life expectancy is only about forty years, largely because of high infant mortality. Children are at high risk of death as a result of inadequate child care, poor diet, and lack of access to breastfeeding. Single mothers are the norm in this shantytown. Wages for these single mothers are extremely low, sometimes less than a dollar a day. Mother–infant contact is minimal because mothers cannot take their babies to work, nor can mothers carry their babies to the river where they wash clothes because of the danger of parasitic

CROSS-CULTURAL MISCUE

❋ Medical anthropologist Geri-Ann Galanti (1991), tells of a tragic incident that resulted from a US physician working in Saudi Arabia failing to understand the culture of one of his patients. An eighteen-year-old Bedouin girl from a remote village was brought in to the hospital with a gunshot wound in the pelvis. When the doctors took X-rays to determine the extent of the girl's injury, they discovered, much to their surprise, that she was pregnant. Because Bedouin girls receive no sex education, the girl was unaware that she was pregnant.

Three doctors were involved in the case: a US neurosurgeon who had worked in the region for several years, a European gynecologist who had worked in the Middle East for a decade, and a young internist from the United States who had just arrived in the area. They all realized that the girl's pregnancy presented a real problem because tribal custom punishes out-of-wedlock pregnancies with death.

To save the girl's life, the physicians decided to send the girl to Europe for a secret abortion, telling her parents that her gunshot wound needed special treatment available only in Europe. The young US physician was hesitant to make such a recommendation, but the other two doctors, more experienced in Middle Eastern cultures, convinced him of the seriousness of the situation. They explained that a pregnant unmarried girl was a terrible slur on the reputation of the men of the family, who were responsible for her protection. Her pregnancy was a sure sign that they had not done their job. The only way that the family could restore its honor would be to put the girl to death.

The young American reluctantly agreed not to tell the parents, but at the last minute changed his mind because he could not be deceitful. He told the girl's father as she was being wheeled to the airplane. The father immediately grabbed the girl off the stretcher, rushed her to his car, and drove away. Several weeks later the hospital staff learned that the girl had been killed by her family. The family's honor had been restored, but the ethnocentric internist had a nervous breakdown and returned to the United States.

Nancy Scheper-Hughes

FIGURE 10.11 Anthropologist Nancy Scheper-Hughes has studied the effects of poverty on the mother-infant bond in northern Brazil.

infections. Consequently, infants spend a good deal of their early lives in the care of older siblings who are reluctant babysitters, or they are simply left alone at home.

Following an outbreak of infant deaths in the shantytown in 1965, Scheper-Hughes observed an apparent indifference on the part of the mothers toward the death of their infants. After nearly a quarter of a century of conducting research in this shantytown, Scheper-Hughes has come to see that what appears to be indifference on the part of the mothers is the result of their living with continuously high infant mortality in conditions of hunger, poverty, powerlessness, and economic exploitation. Under such conditions, infant deaths have come to be expected. As a psychological coping strategy, mothers do not allow themselves to become emotionally attached to their infants until they are reasonably certain their children will survive. Thus, Scheper-Hughes provides a poignant case study of what can happen to kinship systems—and to the mother–infant bond that is at the heart of such systems—in the face of radical change, abject poverty, and powerlessness.

Changes in kinship behavior and values—such as those described by Scheper Hughes among poor Brazilian women—also occur in more complex societies such as our own, albeit for different reasons. Some social scientists have suggested that people living in

western societies with thriving market-driven economies have essentially outsourced many of their traditional kinship roles and obligations to professional service providers for a fee. We now employ wedding planners to design and execute a wedding celebration that had in previous times been the job of parents and close relatives; nannies now care for small children while the parents both go off to work; "love coaches" advise their clients (many of whom are online daters) how to write a profile that will attract the kind of people they want to meet; etiquette counselors are hired to teach children how to behave in polite society because parents do not have time in their day to do it themselves; the highly emotional and exhausting work of caring for one's aging parents is now being done by a rapidly growing industry of elder-care providers; and perhaps the most dramatic form of outsourcing of kinship roles is surrogate motherhood, whereby a woman, "rents her womb for a fee" by carrying and delivering a child for another couple or person. All of these twenty-first–century social services, and many others too numerous to include here, are examples of how roles traditionally performed by kinsmen are now being handled by professionals who, to one degree or another, are giving not only their time and expertise to their clients, but also the emotional energy required for doing their jobs well. Whatever the causes of this trend of outsourcing kinship roles and obligation, we must conclude that the nature and emotional content of kinship interaction in the United States and other industrialized nations is changing rapidly and in some dramatically new ways.

The study of kinship has always presented a challenge to students of anthropology because of the numerous ways by which different cultures reckon kinship. Even the study of a single system requires an ease with working at different levels of abstraction. The task of understanding our own kinship system in recent years has been made all the more difficult by such complex phenomena as transnational adoptions, gay and lesbian families, and new *reproductive technologies* at our disposal, such as sperm banks, artificial insemination, in vitro fertilization (test tube babies), and surrogate motherhood. For example, we now have the technology to create an embryo in a laboratory by combining a husband's sperm with an egg from a woman other than his wife, and then implanting the embryo into the uterus of a surrogate mother who will carry the baby for nine months. When the baby is born, the original sperm-donating husband and his wife will raise the child as their own. The question arises: Who is the mother? Is it the woman who donated the egg (the genetic mother)? Is it the woman who carried the child and gave birth (the gestational mother)? Or is it the woman who will raise the child (nurturing/social mother)? A number of difficult court cases have dealt with disputes involving

reproductive technologies Recent developments, such as in vitro fertilization, surrogate motherhood, and sperm banks, that make the reckoning of kin relationships more complex.

The Ethnography of Homeless Youths in the United States

It has been estimated by federally sponsored research that at least 1.6 million youths in the United States either run away from home or are kicked out of their homes every year. Although most runaways eventually return home, a sizable percentage of young people never return home. Instead they separate themselves permanently from their parents and families and adopt a risky lifestyle of homelessness, vagrancy, and delinquency. This world of homeless youths often operates below the radar of societal institutions that might provide them with needed social services.

Perhaps the best measure of homeless youths in the United States is the number of contacts that federally financed outreach programs make with runaway youths. The number of contacts rose from 550,000 in 2002 to 761,000 in 2008 (Urbina 2009). Since 2008, when the negative effects of the current economic downturn became severe, the number of homeless youths has increased significantly. A double-digit unemployment rate, home foreclosures, short supplies of low-cost housing, and the rising cost of food and fuel have all put many US families under enormous pressure. Sadly, this financial stress has led to a surge in the number of youth runaways.

In an effort to learn more about their hardships and adventures, anthropologist Marni Finkelstein (2005) conducted ethnographic research among a group of these nomadic street youths in the East Village of New York City. Finkelstein defined her subject group as people under the age of twenty-one who have separated themselves (either voluntarily or not) from their families and who do not live in homeless shelters. Previous studies of homeless youths used their family backgrounds as the major explanatory variable of their behavior. In contrast, Finkelstein's more emic approach (see Chapter 1) studied the world of these homeless youths by observing and interviewing them about their own experiences on the streets. Allowing her informants to use their own words, Finkelstein described the process of leaving home, developing functional social networks, finding sources of food and cash, and coping with the often violent and hostile world of the street.

Finkelstein uncovered a number of useful features of the culture of street kids. First, contrary to popular stereotypes, the homeless youths who congregated in the East Village did not come from wealthy homes in suburban New York and were not playing the role of street kids for the summer because it was a cool thing to do; rather these were kids from the South and the West Coast, and in many cases they had been on the streets for a number of years. Second, the lifestyle of these homeless youths was nomadic. They tended to glorify mobility while rejecting the notions of boundaries, territories, and conventional definitions of sedentary communities. Not unlike European Roma (gypsies), the street kids romanticized their nomadism as a natural part of their life journey, in which they were free from the constraints of established society. Third, street kids had extensive networks of friends and companions, many of whom took on the character of fictive kin. These family-like relationships—which took the place of the real family relationships they had left behind—were important mechanisms for socializing the newly homeless to life on the street and giving them access to resources, opportunities, and psychological support.

Finkelstein's unique study of traveling street youths has important implications for improving social services and healthcare resources. For example, an important finding from this study was that these homeless youths did not take advantage of conventional social service agencies because the agencies were too restrictive and invaded their privacy. These young runaways were not likely to sleep at youth shelters, preferring instead to sleep on the street and use "drop-in" centers that provide some basic services without asking many questions. Given this lifestyle preference, Finkelstein suggests that social service providers become more proactive by going where street kids congregate (such as known parks) to provide information and basic services. Another suggestion derived from the study is that social service providers "find a balance between not coming on too strong because of street kids' mistrust of adults, and not being too relaxed because of perceptions that adults don't care about them" (Finkelstein 2005: 134). And finally, Finkelstein learned that service providers tried to entice the street kids to use their services by offering food and condoms, commodities that were fairly easy to come by. What the homeless youths wanted most was to have their hygiene needs met, such as access to hot showers, clean socks, toothpaste, and tampons. If social service providers can follow the recommendations that emerged from this ethnographic study, perhaps these highly mobile street youths will make more use of the available services.

Questions for Further Thought

1. In what way(s) was Finkelstein's study of homeless youths in the East Village of New York City different from other studies?
2. How would some of the findings from the study be useful for law enforcement officials in New York City?
3. What do these homeless youths have in common with European Roma (gypsies)?

children conceived through various reproductive technologies. These new technologies have created challenges for our legal system, our ethical and moral standards, and our basic vocabulary of kinship.

These legal and ethical problems are becoming even more acute in recent years because of the commercialization and globalization of the new reproductive technologies. A rapidly increasing number of couples from the developed world are contracting with women in countries like India who gestate for a living. The high cost of acquiring a child through the process of maternal surrogacy in the United States is driving many childless couples to seek a surrogate mother in India (Figure 10.12). Whereas the process of surrogate motherhood in the United States can cost an estimated $70,000, it usually costs about $14,000 in India, about half of which is payment to the surrogate mother. A study conducted in 2008 valued the surrogate motherhood industry in India at about half a billion dollars annually (Roy 2011).

Viewed in purely economic terms, this seems to be a pretty good arrangement. Couples who choose international surrogacy receive a child with at least half their own genes, and usually for less than it costs to have a nine-month pregnancy and delivery in the United States. At the other end of the contractual relationships, the third-world surrogate mother will earn the equivalent of a decade of local wages and will experience minimal guilt for giving up the baby because (genetically) the child is not really hers.

The commercialization of making babies (particularly across international borders) raises troubling ethical and legal questions. For example, what obligations does a couple have to the birth mother after the child is born? What control during the nine-month pregnancy period should the contracting parents have over the birth mother? And what happens if the child is born

Bettmann/Corbis

FIGURE 10.12 Newly arrived immigrants were processed at Ellis Island in New York City, the initial point of entry into the United States during the first half of the 20th century. Recent developments in information technology now enable us to search immigrant records to learn more about our family histories.

with serious birth defects? And, as Ellen Goodman (2008: 13) points out, how different is this whole process from buying and selling babies (that is, trafficking in newborns)? Quite apart from how one might answer these ethical questions, one thing is certain: The availability of these new reproductive technologies is making it increasingly difficult to define what we mean by kinship connections.

Summary

1. Although kinship relations are more important in some societies than others, kinship is the single most important aspect of social structure in all societies. Kinship is based on both consanguineal (blood) relationships and affinal (marriage) relationships. Most societies recognize some type of fictive kinship, whereby kinship terms and obligations are applied to people who have no biological connection.

2. A fundamental feature of all kinship systems is that they group relatives into certain categories, call them by the same name, and expect people to behave toward these relatives in similar ways. How a particular culture categorizes its relatives varies according to different principles of classification. These principles are based on criteria such as generation, gender, lineality, consanguineality, relative age, sex of the connecting relative, social condition, and side of the family.

3. Many societies have sets of rules, called *rules of descent*, that affiliate people with different sets of kin. Patrilineal descent affiliates a person with the kin group of the father, matrilineal descent affiliates a person with the kin group of the mother, and ambilineal descent permits an individual to affiliate with either the mother's or the father's kin group.

4. Patrilineal descent groups, which are more common than matrilineal, are found in most areas of the world. In a patrilineal system, a man's children belong to his lineage, as do the children of his son, but not the children of his daughter. Women marry outside their own lineage.

5. In matrilineal systems, a woman's children are affiliated with her lineage, not her husband's. Because the mother's brother is the social father of the woman's children, the relations between husband and wife in a matrilineal system tend to be more fragile than in patrilineal societies.

6. In societies that trace their descent unilineally (through a single line), people identify themselves with a particular lineage (a set of kin who can trace their ancestry back through known links) and clans (a group claiming descent but unable to trace all of the genealogical links).

7. Bilateral descent, which is found predominantly among foraging and industrialized societies, traces one's important relatives on both the mother's and the father's sides of the family equally. Bilateral systems, which are symmetrical, result in the formation of kindreds, which are more like loose kinship networks than permanent corporate functioning groups.

8. All societies have guidelines regarding where a married couple should live after they marry. Residence patterns fall into five different categories. The couple can live with or near the relatives of the husband's father (patrilocal), the wife's relatives (matrilocal), the husband's mother's brother (avunculocal), the relatives of either the wife or the husband (ambilocal), or the husband and wife can form a completely new residence of their own (neolocal).

9. There are six primary types of kinship systems based on how the society distinguishes different categories of relatives: Eskimo, Hawaiian, Iroquois, Omaha, Crow, and Sudanese.

10. Reproductive technologies (such as in vitro fertilization and surrogate motherhood) that have become available in recent decades raise legal, ethical, and definitional questions about the nature of kinship.

Key Terms

affinal relatives
ambilineal descent
ambilocal residence
avunculocal residence
bilateral descent
clan
cognatic descent
collaterality

consanguineal relatives
descent
double descent
EGO
Eskimo (Inuit) system
fictive kinship
horizontal function of kinship

Iroquois system
kindred
kinship systems
lineage
lineality
matriarchy
matrilineal descent groups

matrilocal residence
neolocal residence
patrilineal descent groups
patrilocal residence
reproductive technologies
unilineal descent
vertical function of kinship

Critical Thinking Questions

1. Surrogate motherhood raises a number of complex legal and ethical issues. What position on this issue would you expect the following people to take?
   ■ A World Bank official interested in reducing poverty levels worldwide
   ■ A Roman Catholic bishop
   ■ A women's rights advocate in the United States

2. If you were asked to construct a network of all of your living relatives (on both sides of your family), how would you go about doing it?

3. Why has the study of kinship been so important for cultural anthropologists for the past 150 years? Select any three relatively high ranking officials in the federal government in Washington and explain how they could do their jobs better if they knew more about kinship systems.

Online Study Resources

CourseMate

Access chapter-specific learning tools including learning objectives, practice quizzes, videos, flash cards, glossaries, web links, and more in your Cultural Anthropology CourseMate. Login to http://www.cengagebrain.com to access the resources your instructor has assigned and to purchase materials.

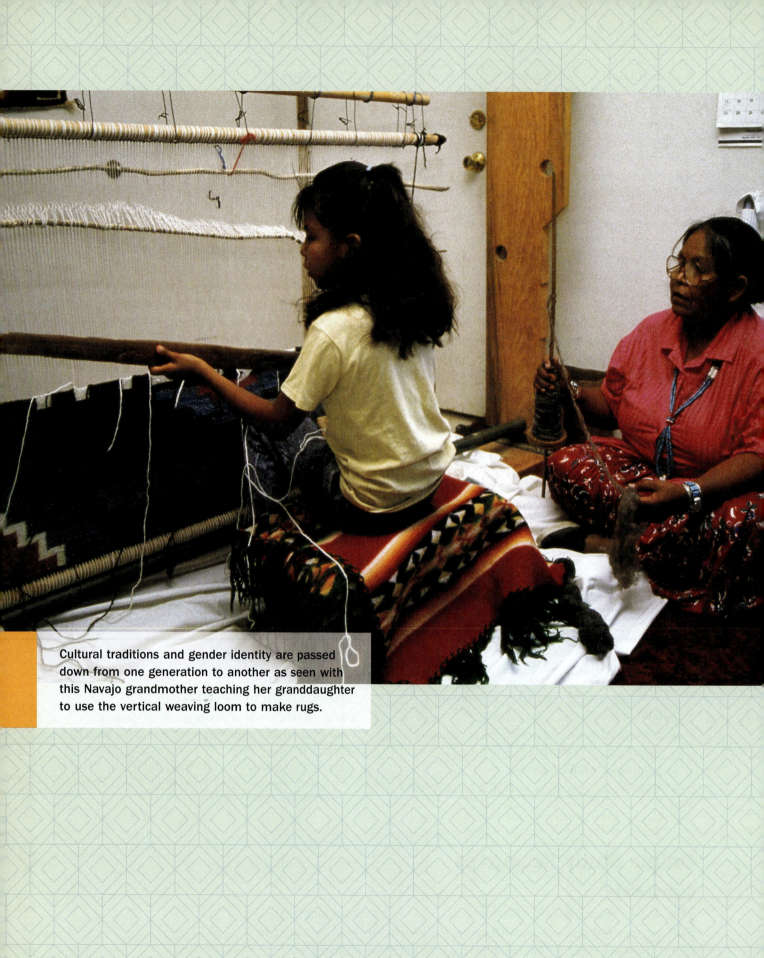

Cultural traditions and gender identity are passed down from one generation to another as seen with this Navajo grandmother teaching her granddaughter to use the vertical weaving loom to make rugs.

Sex and Gender

As a senior Spanish major at the University of Toronto, Melissa Post was rooming with Maria, a foreign student from Ecuador, with whom she had become good friends. Melissa had noticed that whenever Maria greeted her other female friends from Ecuador, they kissed each other on the check. Because Melissa was feeling good about her relationship with Maria, she decided that the next time they ran into each other outside their apartment, she would greet Maria with a kiss on the cheek. So, several days later Melissa met Maria unexpectedly at a campus coffee house and greeted her roommate with an enthusiastic kiss on the cheek. Much to Melissa's surprise, Maria seemed startled and somewhat put off by the greeting. Had Melissa done something inappropriate? How might she have misinterpreted intragender communication?

Melissa's intentions were good, but her execution was incorrect. Although it looked to Melissa like good female friends from Ecuador kiss each other on the cheek, in actuality they are "kissing the air" and just brushing their cheeks together. What had startled Maria was not the gesture itself, but rather that she actually felt Melissa's lips on her cheek. This scenario illustrates the importance of knowing not only something about intragender communication in another culture, but also some of the fine points of how that communication is conveyed between members of the same gender. ■

WHAT WE WILL LEARN

■ What is the difference in meaning between the terms *sex* and *gender*?

■ How do gender roles and gender relations vary across cultures?

■ How does a subsistence strategy influence gender roles and gender relations?

■ How does male dominance or gender equality affect a society?

■ How can cross-cultural understandings of sex and gender be better applied in development projects?

Understanding sex and gender as a specialization within anthropology can play an important role in applied anthropology and applying anthropological concepts to real-world contemporary issues. For example, having an understanding of the principal ways in which a gendered approach to social inquiry can be applied to the design, implementation, monitoring, and evaluation of development projects is of considerable importance, especially when unequal rights between men and women are present in a culture. As you can well imagine, combining gender perspectives and participatory practices that include both men and women, with other forms of technical expertise can be extremely useful in development work. However, to begin the task we will use this chapter to introduce some terms and concepts related to sex, gender, and sexuality to provide a context for how they may be used in an applied perspective.

Sex Is Biological and Gender Is Cultural

One need not be a particularly keen observer of humanity to recognize that men and women differ physically in important ways. What is the reason for these physical differences, and how are they expressed within a culture? And how do these differences affect men and women across different cultures? Within anthropology we draw on both biology and cultural traditions to explain the differences between men and women (Mascia-Lees and Black 2000). From a biological perspective we can examine the physical differences through an evolutionary framework. Evolutionary theories fall into four categories: male strength, male aggression, male bonding, and women's child-bearing hypotheses. Biology and evolutionary theory help to explain why men on average are taller and have considerably greater body mass than women as well as the differences between men's and women's sex organs, breast size, hormone levels, body hair, and muscle-to-fat ratios (Brettell and Sargent 2005). Some men have greater physical strength because of their larger hearts and lungs and greater muscle mass. At the most basic level, biology informs us that sex is where men and women differ genetically, with women having two X chromosomes and men having both an X and a Y chromosome. Unlike humans, some animals (such as mice and pigeons) manifest no visible sexual differences between males and females. Because of the significant physiological differences in humans, however, we are *sexually dimorphic*.

In rare instances the X and Y chromosomes have incomplete separations and the result is hermaphroditism, where an individual has both male and female sexual characteristics. One of the more controversial examples is the eighteen-year-old female runner from South Africa who won the gold medal in the 800-meter event in the 2009 World Championships in Athletics. Her sex was questioned, and extensive laboratory tests have confirmed that she has both male and female sex organs but a female identity. Now what is at stake is not just the gold medal, but her identity as a woman. What is brought into question is what it means to be male and female from a physical and cultural perspective.

Most researchers can agree on the physiological (genetically based) differences between men and women, but there is considerably less agreement on the extent to which these differences actually cause differences in behavior or in the way men and women are treated in society (Brettell and Sargent 2005). These lines of questioning focus on a society's practices that contribute to how men and women are socialized into culturally appropriate roles and behavior.

Gender Is Cultural

As in so many other aspects of behavior, the nature—nurture debate is relevant in the area of behavioral differences between men and women. In other words, do men and women behave differently because of their genetic predisposition or because of their culture? During the twentieth century, ethnographers showed that the definition of femaleness and maleness varies widely from society to society. Because of significant cultural variability in behaviors and attitudes between the sexes, most anthropologists now prefer to speak of *gender differences* rather than *sex differences* (Mascia-Lees and Black 2000). The term *sex* refers to the biological or genetic differences between males and females. *Gender* refers to "the socially constructed roles, behaviors, activities and attributes that a given society considers appropriate for men and women" (World Health Organization 2009) (Figure 11.1).

Although the use of the term *gender* acknowledges the role that culture plays, it is not always possible to determine the extent to which culture or biology determines behavioral or attitudinal differences between the sexes. What we can say, however, is that biological differences influence (or set broad limits on)

© Louise Gubb/The Image Works

FIGURE 11.1 Young children learn by observing and copying their parents. A Ju/'hoansi from the Kalahari, South Africa, is teaching his son to hunt with a bow and arrow, which is predominantly men's work.

---

sexually dimorphic The physiological difference in form between men and women.

sex The biological or genetic differences between males and females.

gender The roles, behaviors, and attributes a society considers appropriate for members of the two sexes.

social definitions of maleness and femaleness to varying degrees. To illustrate, the fact that only women can give birth provides a basis for a particular set of attitudes and behaviors for women, and this results in some cultures socializing women to be nurturing and have life-giving qualities. Likewise, because of their greater body mass, men in some cultures are encouraged to be courageous, aggressive, and war-like. Nevertheless, as we will see, many different social definitions of *masculinity* and *femininity* can be found throughout the world.

Margaret Mead's (1935) classic study of sex and temperament in three New Guinea cultures illustrates the range of gender variation found among the Arapesh, Mundugumor, and Tchambuli. Mead found that among the Arapesh, both men and women were cooperative, nonaggressive, and responsive to the needs of others—all traits that most Westerners would consider to be feminine. In contrast, both genders among the Mundugumor were expected to be fierce, ruthless, and aggressive.

Among the Tchambuli, there was a complete reversal of the male—female temperaments considered usual in our own society; that is, females were the dominant, impersonal partners who were aggressive food providers, whereas males were less responsible, more emotionally dependent, more preoccupied with art, and spent more time styling their hair and gossiping about the opposite sex. Mead argued that if those temperaments that we regard as traditionally feminine (that is, nurturing, maternal, and passive) can be held as a masculine ideal in one group and can be frowned on for both sexes in another, then we no longer have a basis for saying that masculinity and femininity are biologically based. Although Mead's work has been criticized in recent years for its subjectivity, it nevertheless demonstrates the enormous variability in gender roles across cultures.

Cross-cultural studies further complicate our understanding of gender. Mainstream US culture recognizes two genders, male and female, which marginalizes other gender alternatives, such as transgender and androgynous individuals. People who are uncomfortable with anything other than two genders tend to explain anything else away as being abnormal or even curable. However, some cultures not only accommodate the ambiguities of these gender alternatives but see them as legitimate or, in some cases, powerful. Third-gender individuals, or transgenders, are well established in Native American literature, particularly in the Plains between the Great Lakes and California. According to Charles Callender and Lee Kochems (1983), at least 113 Native American groups provided a third gender as a legitimate social alternative. Also known as Two-Spirits, these are both females and males who adopt some of the roles and traits of the opposite gender. To illustrate, the Lakota of the northern Plains

CROSS-CULTURAL MISCUE

A US businessman was headed to the Middle East to negotiate a business deal for his company. He was a friendly, outgoing kind of guy and was known as the "closer" for his ability to get deals signed for the company. This was his first trip overseas. He was excited and felt on his game. After a fourteen-hour flight he arrived in Saudi Arabia, where at the hotel he received his schedule for the next couple of days. The following day he was to meet with his host, who he hoped would become an international business partner, if he could seal the deal. He arrived at the office a bit early and was offered a small cup of coffee, followed by a second and a third because his host was tied up with another meeting. When the host greeted him and invited him into his office, he offered the American yet another cup of coffee that he accepted, but with his left hand. When another cup was offered he declined; he had had his fill of coffee. While getting comfortable and not wanting to jump right into business, the American proceeded to ask his host about his wife and daughters. The businessman sat relaxed with his leg crossed, showing the sole of his shoe. In no time, the tenor of the business meeting had completely changed and no deal was made.

In Oman, it is improper to receive things with one's left hand, one should not bare the sole of their shoe, and between acquaintances one should not ask about the other's wife and daughters. Had this businessman had an anthropology course, he might have studied cross-cultural etiquette and gender rules before he departed, and not lost the deal for his company.

region had transgendered men called *winkte*, who possessed both masculine and feminine spirits; the Zuni of the southwestern United States recognized as fully legitimate members of society a third gender that they called *We'wha*; and the Cheyenne had a similar transgender category called *hemanah* (literally meaning "half-woman, half-man"), who often accompanied war expeditions in ceremonial roles as noncombatants. In all of these cases, people became transgendered through spiritual calling, individual inclination, or parental selection—where parents were involved in selecting their child's sexual orientation.

Another interesting example is the male/female Hijra in Hindu India. The notion of a combined male/female

masculinity The social definition of maleness, which varies from society to society.

femininity The social definition of femaleness, which varies from culture to culture.

role is a major theme in Hindu art, religion, and mythology. For example, androgynous people and impersonators of the opposite sex are found widely in Hindu mythology among both humans and their deities. These same themes are played out in parts of contemporary India. For example, Serena Nanda (1990) describes a festival that takes place in Tamil Nadu in south India, in which the Hijras are transformed. During the festival the Hijras identify with Krishna, who is a deity that changes form from male to female. The Hijras become the wives and then the widows of Koothandavar, a male deity. As part of the festival the Hijras make their wedding vows to Koothandavar dressed as women. A priest performs the traditional ceremony and ties on the wedding necklace. The following day the deity is a carried to the burial ground where all the Hijras who have "married" him remove their wedding necklaces and mourn as widows by crying, beating their breasts, and removing the flowers from their hair. With the Hijras dressed in their finest clothes and jewelry, the ritual reaffirms their identification with Krishna.

The Hijras of Hindu India are significant because they provide an example of a society that tolerates a wider definition of gender than is found in our own society. The Hijras, who undergo an emasculation rite, present themselves as being "like women," or female impersonators. In fact their "emasculation rite," involving voluntary castration, indicates their high level of commitment to this special gender category. The Hijras do not function sexually as men, claim to have no sexual feelings for women, dress in women's clothing, wear women's hairstyles, and even walk and carry themselves as women do. Clearly the Hijras are neither male nor female in the conventional sense of the terms. But rather than being viewed as social deviants who should be discouraged, the Hijras are seen as a special, even sacred, gender group (Figure 11.2).

human sexuality The sexual practices of humans, usually varying from culture to culture.

FIGURE 11.2 This Hijra man, who presents himself as being "like a woman," is an example of the socially constructed basis for sexuality.

Human Sexuality

As we have said, anthropologists pride themselves on being holistic in their approach to understanding a people's culture. As such, anthropology has a long history of documenting the sexual practices of Western and non-Western peoples. From this early work on *human sexuality*, which was formally recognized as an area of study in 1961 when the American Anthropological Association (AAA) held a session on the topic at its national meetings, anthropologists have been amassing data on sexual practices and incorporating these practices into their ethnographic accounts.

Over many decades anthropologists and other social scientists (including sociologists and psychologists) have broadened their understanding of human sexuality and provided multicultural perspectives. In addition, social scientists have been amassing information on gender inequality, especially for women. As a result of these collective efforts, the quantity of information gathered, and sensitive interest in the subject matter, many universities have created separate departments, programs, and majors that focus on women and gender studies, which also include courses on human sexuality.

There is wide interest in human sexuality. Culture teaches us what kind of sexual feelings and practices are normal and natural in one's society and go so far as to prescribe which ones are deviant, inappropriate, and unlawful. To be sure, gathering ethnographic information on human sexuality is a delicate subject. First, because sexual activity in all societies is a private matter, it remains off limits to anthropological observation. Second, when anthropologists have interviewed people about sexuality, they tend to confine their questions to more objective matters such as number of sexual partners, frequency of sexual intercourse, and acceptance of premarital sexual activity. Anthropologists today look back at findings from research on human sexuality conducted before the 1970s and recognize a strong male bias because most anthropologists were males who had access to predominantly male informants. Fortunately times have changed; in more recent ethnographic studies, both sexes are portrayed with greater representation and a more balanced picture of human sexuality.

Within the past four decades, anthropologists studying human sexuality have become more interested in explaining why there is such diversity in gender roles across cultures. Perhaps the most fundamental generalization that has emerged is that human sexuality varies widely from culture to culture. In other words, we find enormous variations throughout the world in the sexual behaviors permitted or encouraged before marriage, outside marriage, and within marriage. This cross-cultural variation in human sexuality raises interesting theoretical and methodological questions, especially for how one may go about organizing fieldwork or developing applied health-related projects to address the transmission of HIV and AIDS.

Although no society fails to regulate sexual conduct, some societies are permissive whereas others are more restrictive. Some cultures have serious sanctions against premarital sex, and others treat it much more casually. Of course for the anthropologist this begs the question of why cultures have these polar opposite attitudes toward premarital sex and experimentation. Is there a functional or utilitarian reason for controlling or not controlling sexual behavior? Perhaps something inherent in a culture determines how one individual or group controls the sexual actions of another. Before embarking on one's research topic or applied project, anthropologists must be sensitive to the conduct of a particular culture. A few examples will help to illustrate the variation.

Among the more sexually restrictive cultures were the traditional Cheyenne Indians of the American Plains, whose women were legendary for their chastity. When adolescent Cheyenne girls began to attract the attention of suitors, they were constantly chaperoned by aunts to ensure total abstinence from sexual behavior. The courting process was long and not particularly intense, often lasting five years before the couple could marry. Adolescent boys and girls had little or no contact, and young men were taught to suppress their sexual impulses, a Cheyenne value that they took with them into marriage. Premarital and extramarital sex were extremely rare among the Cheyenne, and when they occurred, they led to powerful social sanctions (Hoebel 1960).

Another society with limited sexual expression is the Dani of New Guinea. Whereas the Cheyenne were socialized to avoid intimate sexual displays from early childhood and deviants were punished, the Dani appear to be uninterested in sexual behavior. According to Karl Heider (2006), the Dani do not have sexual relations during the first two years of marriage and they adhere to a four- to six-year period of postpartum sexual abstinence; that is, husband and wife abstain from any sexual activity for four to six years after the birth of a child. Although all societies prescribe abstinence after the birth of a child, usually for several weeks or several months, in some societies, however, it lasts until the child is weaned, which may take several years. Not only do the Dani practice these long periods of abstinence, but they appear to have no other sexual outlets, such as *extramarital sexual activity* or homosexuality. Nor do Dani adults seem to be bothered by these periods of abstinence because the Dani people learn that low sexual expressiveness is a cultural norm.

At the other extreme from such groups as the Cheyenne and the Dani are societies in which people are expected to have a great deal of sexual experience before marriage. Among such Oceanian societies as the Trobriand Islanders, the Tikopia, and the Mangaians of Polynesia, premarital sex is not only permitted but encouraged; indeed it is viewed as a necessary preparatory step for marriage. Young boys and girls in these societies receive sex education at an early age and are given permission to experiment during their adolescent years. Premarital lovers are encouraged, and in some societies in the Pacific, trial marriages are actually permitted.

The Mangaians of central Polynesia provide an interesting case of a society that distinguishes between the public and private domains. This society is characterized by near total segregation of men and women in their public lives. Around the age of four or five, boys and girls are separated into gender-defined groups that will identify them for the rest of their lives. Brothers and sisters, husbands and wives, old men and old women, and female and male lovers have little social contact in their

extramarital sexual activity Sexual activity outside marriage.

everyday lives. Nevertheless, in their private lives, away from the public eye, men and women engage in sexual behavior that is both frequent and intense. Sexual intercourse is a principal concern for both Mangaian men and women, a concern that is backed up by a detailed knowledge of the technical and biological aspects of sex. According to ethnographer Donald Marshall (1971: 110), "The average Mangaian youth has fully as detailed knowledge—perhaps more—of the gross anatomy of the penis and the vagina as does a European physician."

Like the Mangaians, the Ju/'hoansi of southwestern Africa believe that sexual activity is a natural, and indeed essential, part of life. Ju/'hoansi adolescents are permitted to engage in both *heterosexual* and *homosexual* play, and discreet extramarital sexual activity is condoned. Conversations among women about their sexual exploits are commonplace, as is sexually explicit joking between men and women. According to Marjorie Shostak (1983: 31), sexual activity is considered essential for good mental and physical health. As one female informant put it, "If a girl grows up without learning to enjoy sex, her mind doesn't develop normally ... and if a woman doesn't have sex her thoughts get ruined and she is always angry."

Sexual behavior in the United States and Canada tends to be on the more permissive end of the continuum. As Edward Laumann and colleagues noted (1994), young people are becoming sexually active at an earlier age; the percentage of sexually active young people is increasing; and among those who are sexually active, sex is becoming more frequent. These authors also report that the way in which people conduct their lives is shaped by many factors and may have profound consequences for their health and quality of life. In a later book, Edward Laumann and Robert Michael (2001) presented a wide range of information on the consequences of sexual experiences, ranging from physical and emotional satisfaction with sex partners and general life satisfaction to the challenges of unwanted pregnancy and sexually transmitted diseases.

The range of openness and restrictiveness among societies in terms of heterosexual relationships to some degree also holds true for same-sex relationships. Some people in societies based on Judeo-Christian-Islamic beliefs, however, consider homosexuality a violation of natural law. Societies that incorporate this religious thinking into their political process have laws that criminalize homosexual conduct or limit certain rights between same-sex couples.

Homosexuality

In societies that are more supportive of same-sex activity, there is a wide range of socially acceptable behavior,

and this variability makes it difficult to determine how prevalent the actual practice of homosexuality is in different societies. In more open societies, which are generally tolerant of same-sex relationships, homosexuals tend to be fairly open about their behavior. In societies where homosexual activity is stigmatized or punished, most homosexuals do not manifest their sexual orientation as openly. Yet the incidence of homosexual activities in both restrictive and open societies may be the same; the only difference is the extent to which it is freely discussed and lived.

When examining variations in male or female homosexuality, anthropologists distinguish between *sexual preference* and *sexual activity*. It is possible to engage in homosexual activity while maintaining a heterosexual preference, and conversely it is possible to live in a heterosexual marriage and have homosexual preferences. Patrick Gray and Linda Wolfe (1988) describe three culturally distinct patterns of male homosexuality: in mainstream United States, the Azande of the Sudan, and the Sambia of New Guinea.

In the United States, the cultural definition of male and female homosexuality does not distinguish between preference and activity. Rather it is assumed that a man or woman who engages voluntarily in homosexual activity does so because of a dominant same-sex preference. The normative view of homosexuality in the United States today remains generally negative. This is most clearly illustrated in the ongoing debates over legally recognizing same-sex marriages, gay men and lesbian women serving in the military, and same-sex adults adopting children.

Although there is increasing tolerance of homosexuality in the United States, not all countries share this attitude. For example, since 2009 the government in Uganda is attempting to make homosexuality illegal. In fact, if a revised bill (as of December 2012) becomes law, a man or woman convicted for having gay sex could be imprisoned or even put to death. This bill is problematic for humanitarian reasons: it violates human rights and it is discriminatory and also disenfranchises people from seeking out health care. People who test positive for HIV could be executed, which in effect bans organizations from working on HIV and AIDS prevention or testing anyone for the disease (Figure 11.3). As of 2011 seventy-five countries criminalized same-sex behavior, and it is punishable by death in eight countries including Iran, Iraq, Sudan, Saudi Arabia, and Yemen. In many African and Asian nations, Oceania, and most of the English-speaking Caribbean islands including Jamaica, Antigua, Barbuda, Barbados, Dominica, and Guyana, same-sex behavior is criminalized but is not punishable by death. Jamaica has one of the toughest punishments; those found guilty of having same-sex relations can be jailed for ten years.

Interestingly, among the precolonial Azande of the Sudan, the cultural definition of male homosexuality made an explicit distinction between sexual

---

heterosexual Having a sexual attraction to people of the opposite sex.

homosexual Having a sexual attraction to people of the same sex.

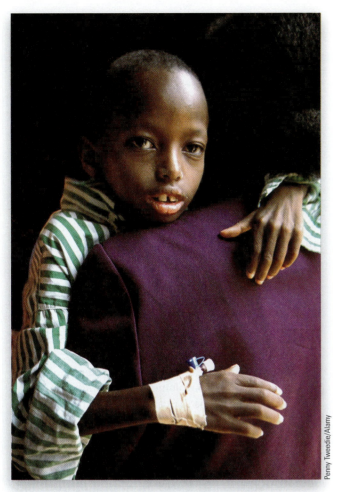

Penny Tweedie/Alamy

FIGURE 11.3 This Rwandan child is dying of HIV/AIDS, for his mother was raped by a Hutu man carrying the virus.

preference and sexual activity. Owing to a shortage of marriageable women, young Azande men sought sexual satisfaction, for a limited time period, through homosexual activity. Unmarried men serving in organized military units often married boys between the ages of twelve and twenty. The husband paid bride-wealth to the boy's father and was expected to have the same relationship with his in-laws that he would have had if he had married their daughter. These younger "male wives" performed domestic household chores for their husbands and also served as sexual partners. When the husband was old enough to take a female wife of his own, however, the marriage to the "boy-wife" ended, and he too was free to marry a woman.

Thus, here was an accepted institutional arrangement for men (albeit a minority of men) to engage in limited homosexual activity while retaining their basic heterosexual preference. Men who took temporary boy-wives were not defined by the wider Azande society as feminine or morally shameful because, after all, they were military men performing a definite masculine role. Instead, in the words of Gray and Wolfe (1988), such male homosexual behavior "was a poor

substitute for heterosexual behavior, an unfortunate necessity due to the shortage of women."

The actual practice of homosexuality can change significantly and rapidly depending on contemporary sociopolitical developments. To illustrate, before the US invasion of Iraq in 2003, Iraqi society had tacitly accepted the lifestyles of gay men and women. Since then, however, the rise of religious fundamentalism in Iraq has led to considerable vilification and persecution of gays and lesbians, particularly in Baghdad, where sexual freedom once flourished. According to Reuter's (Gaff 2012), "Since the start of this year, death squads have been targeting two separate groups—gay men, and those who dress in a distinctive, Western-influenced style called 'emo,' which some Iraqis mistakenly associate with homosexuality."

When living in countries that have greater sexual freedom, gays, lesbians, and bisexuals from the Middle East practice their homosexuality more openly and without fear of reprisals. For example, the large Muslim population in Berlin has the opportunity to attend an event called Gayhane, a monthly dance club event for Arab and Turkish gays and lesbians (Kulish 2008). This event allows gays and lesbians from the Middle East to merge their cultural and sexual identities. These immigrants may still face discrimination in Berlin for both their ethnicity and their sexual orientation, but at least they are not being put to death "in the worse, most severe way" for their homosexual lifestyles.

So we are left with the big question: Why do some countries have sexual freedom and others do not? At the simplest level, one can say it is because of culture. However, we need to broaden this notion of culture to include religion and politics. For example, in some societies it is their interpretation of their religion or belief system that governs their sexual behaviors. In societies that link their belief system with their political system, it is possible to establish laws governing sexual behavior and sexuality. Nevertheless, there is no clear pattern to answer why it is culturally permissible to engage in homosexual acts in one country and it is unlawful in another, and the degree to which a crime of engaging in a homosexual act is punished.

Gender Roles

As mentioned in Chapters 7 and 8, all societies make some distinctions between what men are expected to do and what women are expected to do. In some societies *gender roles* are rigidly defined, but in others the roles of men and women overlap considerably.

gender roles Expected ways of behaving based on a society's definition of masculinity and femininity.

For instance, gender roles include the kinds of work assigned to men and women, the familial roles that people play, the leadership positions assigned to men and women in the home and outside of the home, and the roles men and women are assigned in ritual practices. Yet, despite the near-universality of the division of labor by gender, cultures of the world share some general patterns in the ways in which they divide tasks between women and men. To illustrate, in most cases men engage in warfare, trap and kill large animals, work with hard substances such as wood and stone, clear land, build houses, and fish at sea. Women, on the other hand, are more likely to tend crops, gather wild fruits and plants, trap and kill small animals (including fish in lakes and streams), prepare food, care for children, collect firewood, clean house, launder clothing, and carry water. In addition, a number of tasks are performed by both men and women. These include tending small domesticated animals, making utilitarian products (pottery, baskets, and the like), milking animals, planting and harvesting crops, and collecting shellfish. (See Table 11.1)

Some roles (such as hunting for men and child care for women) are closely associated with gender. Although George Murdock (1967) classifies hunting as an exclusively male activity in a majority of societies that practice hunting and gathering, he notes that in societies in which both males and females hunt, "males do appreciably more than females." In more contemporary ethnographies of hunter-gatherers, researchers frequently describe the role of men as the hunters of large game, but both men and women might be the hunters of small game, such as with the Ju/'hoansi of the Kalahari. On the other side of the equation, child care is an overwhelmingly female activity, although in some cases men make substantial contributions, such as among the Navajo of the US Southwest. In addition, women tend to devote far more time to maintaining the household and providing food, shelter, clothing, and the necessary tools for survival than do men. In many such hunting-and-gathering societies, men's work and women's work are complementary, though not always valued equally. Such is the case in contemporary societies, as you will see when we discuss subsistence strategies in relation to gender roles (Figure 11.4).

TABLE 11.1

Labor by Gender (Worldwide Trends)

Generally Male Tasks

- Hunting large animals
- Fishing at sea or some distance from home base as a primary task
- Tending large animal herds
- Mining, smelting, and metalworking
- Conducting and engaging in warfare
- Building boats
- Working wood and stone
- Clearing and preparing the land for crops
- Making musical instruments
- Making nets and ropes

Generally Male and Female Tasks

- Hunting small animals
- Fishing as a secondary task
- Tending small animals
- Planting and harvesting crops
- Building houses
- Making certain craft items
- Trading in the local market

Generally Female Tasks

- Caring for children
- Collecting fuel and water
- Preparing food
- Gathering wild plants, fruits, and nuts
- Making clothes
- Maintaining the household

© Agustus Buteral/ABStudio/Getty Images

FIGURE 11.4 Men's and women's work is complementary, although not always equal in how it is valued or in the amount of time devoted to maintaining the household, providing food, shelter, clothing, and the necessary tools for survival. This father, engaged in child care and doing the weekly errands, is just one example of changing gender roles in the United States.

Gender and Subsistence

Chapters 7 and 8 introduced the modes of subsistence: hunting and gathering, horticulture, pastoralism, intensive agriculture, and industrial agriculture. These modes relate to the way each subsistence strategy defines gender roles, with hunting-and-gathering societies tending to have greater gender equity and be more egalitarian in their gender relations. Of course, there are exceptions, such as when a society decides it is culturally appropriate for one or the other gender's status to be elevated for the group's survival. Horticultural, pastoral, and agricultural societies tend to have greater gender inequality relative to the ownership and control of subsistence resources, specifically access to land, water, and trees. Among such societies there is a greater tendency for male dominance. As mentioned previously, cultures are influenced by other cultures through borrowing, diffusion, and globalization, which influences gender ideologies of culture constructs. For example, industrial societies that are now supported by industrial agriculture have retained the ideology that males dominate political and economic life even though there has been an increase in economic and political opportunities for women. In countries such as Argentina, Chile, India, Gabon, Germany, Liberia, Nicaragua, and Pakistan, which are known for their agricultural exports, there have even been female heads of state.

In many hunting-and-gathering societies, women and men's interdependent contributions to their households are reflected in equal social relations and social status. Among some societies, however, male dominance is more apparent. We can compare two hunting-and-gathering societies: the Ju/'hoansi of southern African and the Inuit of the North American Artic. Both these small, nomadic societies were traditionally organized around kinship ties to the father's and the mother's sides (bilateral kinship ties). Economic roles were defined according to gender, but there were some flexibility and overlap. The productive labor of both women and men was essential for survival and was socially recognized. It is the complementary social and economic activities of both genders that have contributed to their survival over the millennium. The absence of formal political structures and leaders has also contributed to gender symmetry within settlements.

In horticultural societies, control over the distribution of produce and goods influences gender status. In societies that are generally egalitarian, women exert their rights to make decisions concerning economic activities. In horticultural economies, women perform most of the farm work, including planting and tending crops and harvesting. In addition, women gather a wide assortment of fruits, nuts, and tubers and are responsible for domestic tasks and child care. Men's subsistence roles include preparing the farm fields and garden plots as well as hunting and fishing to supplement the basic plant diet. Trading with other native peoples for luxury and utilitarian items is also the work of men. Both women's and men's work is highly valued and socially recognized. This is particularly true of horticulturalists in the tropical rain-forest areas in the Amazon Basin and on mountain slopes in South and Central America as well as areas with low population density in Central Africa, Southeast Asia, and Melanesia.

Anthropologists who study pastoral societies, especially in Africa, have found that they tend to have strong patriarchal social and political organization in which men control access to the lands and herds. Men own the animals, particularly cattle, which are the basis of both subsistence and ideology. The people think of themselves as pastoralists with male pursuits, male interests, and male norms. For example, to be a Maasai (cattle herders of Kenya and Tanzania) is to be a pastoralist. Maasai men, therefore, fit this ideal, but Maasai women are marginalized because they are not herders. If women share in the identity of the Maasai, it is as wives of men and mothers of sons, whom they socialize into the male-centered ideal (Figure 11.5).

Ton Koene/age fotostock/Getty images

FIGURE 11.5 Women and children can milk the livestock in Ngoiroro, Kenya, a village of 200 inhabitants belonging to the Massai Tribe. The Massai live very close to nature and their animals.

Umoja Uaso: A Women's Village in Kenya

England maintained military training facilities in its former colony, Kenya, for more than five decades. One of the training facilities was located in northern Kenya in the Sumburu region, which is home to the Sumburu, Massai, Rendile, and Turkana peoples, all of whom are pastoralists. The presence of the military in this region resulted in high instances of rape. Women from these villages filed more than six hundred official claims against the British soldiers; but their voices were not heard and a three-year internal investigation by the Royal Military Police cleared the soldiers of any wrong doing. The women, the victims, had been shamed, outcast by their communities and families, and many were forced into exile for being raped.

In response a small group of women established their own village, which as a shelter for women to seek refuge. One such example is the village of Umoja Uaso Women's Village that began in 1990. Umoja means unity in Swahili. Under the leadership of Rebecca Lolosoli, who has served as its matriarch, the women live by self-imposed rules of respect. Umoja Village is a village for only women and the children born (boys and girls) to the women since the village was established.

Without men in the village, the women share equally in the daily routines. For example, women do the tasks of both men and women. The women construct their houses, collect water and firewood, and care for the children, all of which was women's work. They also raise their livestock (goats and cattle), which was traditionally men's work. Now though, they are free to make their own decisions, including how much and which part of the animal they want to eat after they have slaughtered it. They are no longer given just the intestines and unsavory parts to eat as in traditional Sumburu society.

Drought is common in northern Kenya, making it difficult to maintain the lifestyle accustomed to Sumburu pastoralists. Being able to overcome adversity, stigma, and shame, the fifteen

founding women of Umoja became entrepreneurs and created a new beginning for the affected Sumburu women. They created beaded necklaces and other handicraft items for the tourist market, raising money for themselves and their families. They modified their village to include a camping site, a cultural center, and a gift shop to accommodate tourists who stop when visiting the Samburu National Reserve.

Gradually as the village became more successful, they found themselves facing increasing harassment by men in neighboring communities who believe women's independence is not appropriate. Traditionally Sumburu women are subordinate to men; they are the property of their husbands and could never expect an education or have their own money to buy their own things. Women are married off at young ages and could be one of several wives of their husband because polygyny is practiced. The wives and children would be completely dependent on their husbands for their basic needs and survival.

Villages such as Umoja Uaso allow women to be independent, self-sufficient, and provide their children, both boys and girls, with an education. Lolosoli and others are educating the women and the next generation on abandoning the cultural practice of female genital mutilation (FGM) and the forced marriage of girls at young ages. Lolosoli believes that if you educate the children differently, in time things may change and pave the way for a more equitable existence and the abandonment of FGM.

Word spread to other women about the village of only women. In 2005 Emily Wax wrote "They became so respected that troubled women, some beaten, some trying to get divorced, started showing up in this little village in northern Kenya." And word traveled far. Lolosoli was invited to the United Nations in New York to attend a conference on gender empowerment. According to Wax (2005), "'That's when the very ugly jealous behaviors started,' Lolosoli said, adding that her life was threatened by local men right before her trip to New York. 'They just said, frankly, that

Similar pastoralist cultural traditions are found among the Gabra, Sumburu, Turkana, Pokat of Kenya, and the Dinka of Sudan. In these groups women are similarly marginalized. Among pastoral groups in eastern Africa and the Horn, young girls are socialized to be helpers to their mothers, who are subordinate to their husbands. Within pastoral groups, girls are thought to be the weaker sex and taught to obey,

respect, and submit to men. Men achieve their status by taking care of the livestock and protecting the community. Pastoral women and girls continue to be subjected to gender discrimination because they are not viewed as "real" pastoralists. Moreover, their health status and social status are adversely affected because they are not able to fully participate in their communities. Women and girls have limited access to health care they wanted to kill me' Lolosoli said." For Sumburu men, Lolosoli is considered a troublemaker. A chief of a neighboring village stated, "she is questioning our very culture, this seems to be the thing in these modern times. Troublemaking ladies like Rebecca" (Wax 2005). Since then, Lolosoli has gone on to be named one of the "100 Women Changers by Women in the World" in 2011 and The Daily Beast named her one of "The World's 150 Fearless Women" also in 2011 (Ross 2012).

In the past two decades the Umoja village has become a safe haven for women where they can begin a new life. They escape shame, beatings, rape, FGM, and forced marriages (sometimes when the girls are just thirteen years of age). Today the village consists of about forty-eight women and a few children. The village size goes up and down as women come to live or leave to live elsewhere. Over the years Umoja women have been successful with the sale of their beaded art and most of Umoja's annual income comes from selling their beaded art in Santa Fe, New Mexico at the Santa Fe Folk Art Festival.

In July 2012, Lolosoli was sponsored by Vital Voice Global Leadership Network (www.vitalvoices.org), an organization supporting women's leadership, to travel to the Santa Fe Folk Art Festival to sell the women's art. On returning she deposited the earnings in the Umoja bank account. With all of their successes, the women of Umoja Uaso Women's Village cannot escape violence. Vital Voices reported that on August 18, 2012, men armed with a gun came to Umoja, scaring the women and children. Lolosoli was attacked and beaten by her estranged husband before he demanded she turn over the earnings from the sale of their art. Lolosoli went to the local authorities, but the police claimed that her attack was a domestic dispute and they would not intervene but her husband would be warned not to enter the Umoja village is all they would promise to do.

Since the event, Lolosoli has not returned to Umoja. Vital Voices is working with partners in Nairobi, Kenya, members of the Advocacy Project, and the United States to assist Lolosoli and the village women and to monitor threats to their safety. The US State Department Africa Bureau, the US Embassy in Nairobi, and the Office of Global Women's Issues at the US State Department also are keeping abreast of this situation.

This example brings up a number of issues for women, including domestic violence, gender inequality, sexual violence, the spread of HIV and AIDS, the positive and negative impacts of the gender empowerment process, the influence of global feminism,

the rejection of FGM, the prosecution of rape, and of course the profound impact of culture change. Even though Umoja Uaso Women's Village is successful in getting women to take charge of their own lives, they could not be immediately free of their larger cultural traditions. Their successes went against the cultural traditions of the Sumburu people. Their families, and especially the men of their culture, believe these women did not know their place, even after they had been exiled. The Umoja women were not meant to succeed and be more prosperous and independent of their husbands.

In its twenty-two years of existence, Umoja has inspired change for those who call it home, for the villages surrounding it, and for the men and women of Kenya and elsewhere around the world. Sara Ross (2012) asked Lolosoli what made her build Umoja? Lolosoli responded,

"We founded Umoja because of the problems faced by the women in Samburu. They had no rights, no food, money for the hospital or even to take their children to school. At the same time, women were just dying like animals and no one was taking care of them or talking about it. That was what made us come together to help each other, make the lives of our women better and make them understand that they too are human beings."

And when asked by Ross (2012), "Today is International Women's Day, what is your message to women around the world?" Lolosoli replied,

"Women should not be scared to stand up [for] their rights. Women should know that they have to be strong, network and help each other create awareness and teach other women about their rights because there are women, who are still behind. We have to work together so that our countries will develop and care for the women because women are the source and light of the world."

Questions for Further Thought

1. Why is Rebecca Lolosoli a hero among some local Kenya women and a troublemaker for the Sumburu men?

2. Why are international organizations geared to provide women with leadership skills and other forms of education important to empowering women?

3. What are the downsides of outside feminist influences on local cultures?

and education, high mortality rates, low life expectancies, and insufficient medical information and access to family planning and reproductive health care and other public services.

Agrarian states are complex societies with centralized political systems that maintain some degree of control over local areas within the state. Their economies are based on intensive farming and the

production of a surplus that is sold for profit or cash, which is used to support a ruling elite. Generally such complex societies segment the population into classes that occupy different positions in society with different occupations and different standards of living. Frequently such societies are (or were) characterized by male dominance in gender relations. As in other types of societies, however, the degree of male dominance varies widely. Contributing factors to the variation in male dominance are economics, politics, and history as well as kinship and marriage patterns and family structure. Historical examples of agrarian states are found throughout the world, such as the feudal system in Europe, the slave systems of the Maya of Central America, and the Inca of South America. There are also many contemporary examples because most nations are involved in some sort of food production for local and global consumption. However, more recent shifts in the political economy of agricultural production are keeping some male farmers at home while female partners or spouses are employed off the farm. The off-farm earnings may provide needed income for the farm, access to health insurance, and cash when everyone is waiting for the harvest to get to market. In other contexts farmers are being displaced from their land and likewise their agrarian mode of production, which makes both genders more vulnerable to economic uncertainties (Wright 2006).

There are some notable exceptions to the general rule that men engage in roles that demand maximum physical strength. In certain parts of East Africa, women routinely carry enormous loads of firewood on their backs for long distances. Not only is this a normative practice, but among some groups a woman's femininity is directly related to the size of the load she is able to carry. Also, among the foraging Agta of the Philippines, hunting is not exclusively a male activity; women hunt regularly. Both men and women begin to hunt when they have matured and developed sufficient stamina; likewise, they stop hunting when they lose their strength and become less successful (Dahlberg 1981).

It appears that the wide range of variation in gender roles and subsistence activities requires anthropologists to ask the pertinent questions related to culture and subsistence before designing, implementing or evaluating any project. Surveying what are women and men's roles as well as observing what people of all age groups and socioeconomic classes are doing in everyday life are relevant in planned changed initiatives. Experienced field researchers will tell you there is a difference from what people say they do and what they actually do on a day-to-day basis.

Child Rearing for Men and Women

Although exceptions do not invalidate the general rule, some authors (Burton, Brudner, and White 1977; Mascia-Lees and Black 2000) have argued that the division of labor by gender is more the result of constraints women face as a result of childbirth and infant care than of differences in strength. This brings us to another

argument often used to explain this nearly universal type of gender division of labor: Women do the things they do because those tasks are compatible with pregnancy, breast feeding, and child care. Unlike certain male tasks, such as hunting and warfare, women's tasks can be done without jeopardizing their own and their children's safety and without having to stray too far from home. This theory suggests that pregnant women would be at a marked disadvantage in running after game; lactating mothers would need to interrupt their tracking and hunting activities several times a day to nurse their children; and, given the danger involved in hunting, small children accompanying their mothers would not be safe. Judith Brown (1970) was the first to hypothesize that women tend to concentrate on tasks that are compatible with child care (that is, nursing and looking after children). Women's tasks can be interrupted without reducing efficient performance, pose limited threat to the safety of small children, and can be performed in or near the home.

Although this theory is sensible and no doubt can account for some of the division of labor by gender, it also does not tell the whole story. A number of ethnographic studies from around the world since the late 1970s have seriously questioned this connection between female reproductive and child care roles and the division of labor. To illustrate, some researchers (Burton, Brudner, and White 1977) have argued that although pregnancy and breast feeding do limit work roles for women, a woman's economic (work) obligations sometimes take precedence over child care considerations. In other words, a woman may make alternative child-care arrangements to engage in some type of work outside the home. This is done in parts of the preindustrial world, where women leave their small

© Sylvain Grandadam/age fotostock

FIGURE 11.6 This Navajo father spends time with his two children in their traditional Hogan (Navajo mud hut) on a Navajo reservation in Utah.

children in the care of older siblings or other adults, and in the United States, where working mothers leave their infants at professional day care centers. In addition, others (Raphael and Davis 1985) have found that women often purposefully choose supplemental feeding rather than breast feeding for their children because of work considerations.

There are societies where fathers play an active role in child care. For example, according to Ziarat Hossain and colleagues (1999), Navajo fathers invest about 60 percent as much time as mothers do in direct caregiving tasks. The father role has shifted primarily from an economic provider to a more balanced partner, including playing, emotional bonding, and child rearing. Fathers' investment in child care varies tremendously across families depending on cultural values (Lamb 1997).

Focusing on child-rearing practices, anthropological accounts suggest that traditional Navajo women often made family financial decisions and cared for children in the family, whereas maternal uncles taught and disciplined the children (Blanchard 1975; Hamamsy 1957) (Figure 11.6). Mothers are the primary caregivers and are nurturing, dependable, and protective of their infants (Hauswald 1987; Witherspoon 1975). Within the matrilocal and matrilineal family system of the Navajo, maternal grandmothers and aunts are highly involved with infants, too. Such a family system may not encourage fathers to heavily invest in children because the father does not control family assets and his children will leave the family when they marry.

Later research indicates, however, that the father does play an important role in his children's life by disciplining, teaching, playing with, and providing economically for his children (Hauswald 1987). The father provides a strong role model especially for his male

children, and the availability and involvement of other adult family members in child care suggest that Navajo child-rearing takes place within an extended family network system.

Today in the US, the stay-at-home father is not that unusual. Traditionally, in the US the family of the breadwinning father and the stay-at-home mother has long since disappeared. Since the 1960s when more women entered the workforce, opportunities for women as well as their desire to remain employed after having children gradually increased. For some families the stability, work schedule or salary of the employed mother benefitted the family by having her go back to work and have the father remain at home with the children. It is difficult to determine with precision how many fathers are stay-at-home dads because some fathers work from home, have part-time jobs, or are between jobs. The US Census Bureau (2012, based on 2010 data) reports that there are 176,000 stay-at-home dads. According to the Census Bureau (2012), 17 percent of preschool children from married-couple households were cared for by their fathers. With increased use of social networking from home computers, a number of web sites have emerged for stay-at-home fathers. Sites such as Dadstayshome.com and Fatherville.com provide blogging opportunities and supportive information on topics such as time management, how to talk with children to facilitate learning, part-time work that can be done from home, and effective parenting strategies for stay-at-home dads (Figure 11.7). New forms of language and gender communication are found in social media as they help with parenting as well as in everyday life.

FIGURE 11.7 Traditional gender roles are sometimes reversed in the United States in the twenty-first century, as with this women in the military who may have to make alternative child care arrangements in order to work and serve outside of the home, or as in the case of this stay-at-home dad.

Gender and Language

A degree of *sexual asymmetry* is often evident in the forms of language spoken by men and women. Sometimes the linguistic distinctions between men and women are reflected in vocabulary. For example, some languages have pairs of words (called *doublets*) that carry the same meaning, but men use one word and women the other. To illustrate, among the Island Carib of the West Indies, men use the word *kunobu* to mean "rain" and women use the word *kuyu* (Hickerson 1980). Among the Merina in Madagascar, speech patterns associated with men, which are indirect, allusive, and formal, are considered respectable and sophisticated (Keenan 1974). Merina women, on the other hand, are thought to be ignorant of the subtleties of sophisticated speech and consequently are considered inferior. The speech patterns of women in the United States also convey submissiveness and lack of social power through intonation, loudness, and assertiveness. For example, US women tend to have a less forceful style of speaking than men in that they use a greater number of qualifiers (such as "It may be just my opinion, but …"). Also many US women soften the impact of a declarative statement by ending it with a question, such as "Wouldn't you agree?" (Kramer 1974).

These linguistic gender differences in the United States (called *genderlects*) are the subject of a best-selling book by Deborah Tannen (1990), who claims that women and men in the United States have different linguistic styles and communication goals. Women engage in "rapport-talk" and men use "report-talk." Rapport-talk, characteristic of women, seeks to establish connections, negotiate relationships, and reach agreement. Women's speech tends to be cooperative, with women acknowledging one another's contributions and engaging in more active listening. Report-talk, in contrast, is a male mode of discourse that is more competitive. Men's conversations are less social, more individualistic, and aimed at controlling the flow of talk. In cross-sex conversations, men tend to dominate women by talking more, interrupting women more often, and focusing the conversation on topics of their own choice.

Julia Wood (1994) suggested that these basic speech differences between men and women in the United States result, at least in part, from the childhood games that girls and boys play. On one hand, girls tend to play games that are cooperative, collaborative, and inclusive.

There is little incentive to outdo others, and there is a strong inclination to be sensitive to others' feelings. Boys, on the other hand, are expected to assert themselves, establish their leadership, and win. By focusing on outcomes, boys' games encourage participants to solve problems, achieve goals, and generally "make things happen." Because of these differences in childhood games and socialization, Wood finds that women talk for the purpose of building and supplementing rapport with others, but men talk to assert themselves; women use self-disclosure as a way of learning about others, but men tend to avoid self-disclosure; women's discourse strives for equality in social relationships, but men's discourse attempts to establish status and power; women often match their experiences with others for the sake of showing understanding and empathy ("I know how you feel"), but men match experiences for the sake of gaining attention ("I can top that"); and finally women show their support by expressing their understanding, whereas men show their support by giving advice or trying to solve a problem.

These differences in linguistic style between men and women have important implications for everyday interactions. New studies demonstrate that how men and women communicate, even with a mobile phone, shows gender differences that may be cultural. Naomi Baron and her undergraduate research assistant, Elise Campbell (2012: 15), identified gender patterns in a cross-national study of mobile phone use by university students in Sweden, the United States, Italy, Japan and Korea. Their research indicates "females send more and/or longer texts, or are more likely to use texting, than males." To be certain, any number of important applied uses may be derived from the outcomes of this kind of research, especially for future users and developers of technology business, and the marketing of products. For example, Apple anticipates the iPad will go gender neutral in the near future and become the global shopping tool for both men and women.

Gender Stratification

It is generally recognized that the status of women varies from one society to another. In some East African pastoral societies, women are in a clearly subordinate position in their social relationships with men. In other societies, such as the Ju/'hoansi, the relationships between the genders are more egalitarian. Social scientists generally agree that *gender stratification* exists to some degree in all societies, but there is considerably less agreement about how one measures the relative status of men and women because gender stratification involves a number of different components that may vary independently of one another. It is now recognized that there are many important indicators of women's status, including economics, political power, prestige,

---

sexual asymmetry The universal tendency of women to be in a subordinate position in their social relationships with men.

genderlects Linguistic differences in the way in which men and women may speak within their culture.

gender stratification The hierarchical ranking of members of a society according to gender.

autonomy, and ideological dimensions. To illustrate, when considering the relative status of women in any society, one needs to look at the roles women play, the value society places on their contributions, their legal rights, whether and to what degree they are expected to be deferential to men, their economic independence, and the degree to which they decide on the major events of their lives such as marriage, profession, and child bearing, among other factors.

The multidimensional nature of women's status was illustrated by Martin Whyte's (1978) comparative study of ninety-three societies, which identified fifty-two status dimensions found in the anthropological litera-ture. Interestingly all of these status dimensions varied independently of one another. In other words, no single cluster or complex of variables of women's status varied consistently from culture to culture. To illustrate, women in certain West African societies, because of their influence in the marketplace, may have an appre-ciable amount of economic independence, but they nevertheless remain subordinate to their husbands in most other respects. Thus, determining the status of women is difficult because it is not a one-dimensional phenomenon.

Another difficulty in ascertaining the status of women is that it is not static. In some societies the relative status of men and women fluctuates along with political changes. For example, during the reign of the shah of Iran in the 1960s and 1970s, women's roles kept pace with modernization. Increasingly Iranian women abandoned the rules of *purdah* (domestic seclusion and veiling), obtained higher education, and gained entry to traditionally male professions. With the return of religious and cultural fundamentalism after the Shah was deposed in 1979, women were forced to resume traditional female roles and dress by order of the Ayatollah. In fact, their life and death depended on their adherence to the new order.

Since the US invasion of Afghanistan in 2001, gradual changes have also been occurring for Afghan women. In the past decade there have been strides to improve the situation for women in Afghanistan, yet the majority still live in poverty and only 15 percent can read and write. Yet in 2012 a new code of conduct was authorized, which is considered a step backward for women because it requires women not to go in public without a male guardian. Women's

FIGURE 11.8 Burkas and veils remain common attire for women in rural and urban areas of Afghanistan. These women receive cold relief supplies to help them in the severe winter in northern Afghanistan.

groups in and outside of Afghanistan have complained this is a major setback for improving the living condi-tions for women. There is still a need for greater access to education and health care for Afghan women. Organizations such as Revolutionary Association of the Women in Afghanistan (RAWA), Afghanistan Women Council (AWC), Women for Afghan Women (WAW), and the Afghan Women's Writing Project are just a few of the organizations working toward addressing basic human rights for Afghan girls and women and fighting against gender-based violence. These organi-zations work to enable women to be represented in all areas of life: political, social, cultural, and economic (Figure 11.8).

Yet another complicating factor in determining the status of women can occur even before birth. Hindu society in northern India is among the most highly stratified along gender lines of any society in the world. India as a whole, and particularly northern India, has enormously skewed sex ratios as a result of the widespread neglect of girls in terms of health care and nutrition (Khanna 2010). In this part of the world, sons are more highly valued than daughters. Sex ratios have become even more unbalanced in recent years with the widespread use of ultrasound equipment to determine sex prenatally. The termination of female fetuses has increased so rapidly in the last several decades that the female population of some rural

purdah The Hindu or Muslim system of sex segregation, which keeps women in seclusion or requires clothing that conceals them completely.

Son Preference: New Reproductive Technologies and Family Building Strategies in India

Sometimes ethnographic fieldwork takes an anthropologist into delicate or contentious situations. One example of this is the research conducted by applied anthropologist Sunil Khanna (2010) in northern India and who was born in New Delhi. Khanna's research focused on son preference and daughter neglect in a small village established by Haryana Jat migrants. From his experience, Khanna wanted to better understand why some families (and physicians) used reproductive technology, specifically ultrasound, to identify the sex of a fetus and seek selective abortions of female fetuses. He reports on his research experience in *Fetal/Fatal Knowledge: New Reproductive Technologies and Family Planning Strategies in India* (2010).

By taking an ethnographic approach, Khanna relied on unstructured interviews and participant observation to collect data in Shahargaon, an agrarian village community that was undergoing increased modernization and urbanization, which affected the peasant community's social and cultural characteristics. However, to better understand gender inequality Khanna hired two Jat women as research assistants to aid in collecting sensitive data on reproductive histories. Over time he, too, was able to ask questions on "household income, conception, contraception, pregnancy, childbirth, abortion, decision-making processes about family-building strategies in their households" (Khanna 2010: 11). Although sons were no longer needed in agriculture, son preference intensified because they added prestige and status to the family by becoming economic and political assets. "Sons received better education, health care and opportunities for growth in life" (Khanna 2010: 69). Daughters were viewed as economic liabilities because families had to save for their wedding dowries and daughters would move away to the husband's family (*patrilocality*). The ideal family is two sons and a daughter. A Jat family with no sons was seen as economically and politically weak. Sons take advantage of paid employment and provide for the family and the community. Daughters were not offered these jobs and women were excluded from participating in the economic sector for fear of their safety and reputation. Women still had to be accompanied by a male family member in public, thus, reducing their chances of respectfully gainful employment.

The Indian government has policies aimed at slowing down population growth and is involved in media campaigns and in creating population control slogans advocating the benefits of a small family. In the late 1990s the government revised its national policy to promote reproductive health. A decade later the government's efforts to control population growth expanded to include "improving health care infrastructure, making contraceptive methods easily available and promoting integrated service delivery for reproductive and child health care" (Khanna 2010: 60). Since the 1990s, Shahargaon residents have had access to free contraceptives and family planning services at a state-funded Primary Health Clinic (PHC), a clinic that offers prenatal and postnatal care services (Khanna 2010: 61).

New reproductive technologies, specifically the use of ultrasound and amniocentesis, designed for measuring human growth and developmental abnormalities, have been used to determine fetus sex. In fact, billboards and newspaper advertisements promoted the benefits of using ultrasound as a means of avoiding the birth of unwanted daughters. Yet, not all of the local physicians at the medical clinics supported this selective use of the reproductive technology. Nevertheless, the recent trends indicate the total population of the village is increasing, but at a slower rate and the sex ratio continues to favor males at an alarming rate. Khanna collected demographic data in Shahargaon in 1993, 1999, and 2003 and found a steady decline in the number of females to the number of males, during which time the overall population for the village increased 17 percent, (from 782 in 1993 to 938 in 2003). However, the sex ratio of children (0–6 years) indicated a decline in the number of girls from 710 in 1993 to 597 per 1,000 boys in 2003 (Khanna 2010:70). Clearly families are making cultural choices about the use of reproductive technologies with respect to family building and son preference.

Questions for Further Thought

1. Why does a son preference exist?
2. Why are new reproductive technologies so popular?
3. What role does government play in prenatal sex selection and selective abortions?

---

villages has been reduced by nearly 25 percent. And even for those women who live to adulthood, many face impoverished widowhood or dowry death (as discussed in Chapter 9).

In contrast to the marked status distinctions between the genders found in India, the relationship between men and women in some foraging societies tends to be more egalitarian. For example, Colin Turnbull (1981) reported a good deal of mutual respect between the sexes among the Mbuti Pygmies of Central Africa, particularly among elders of the group. Adult Mbuti call their parents *tata* (elders) without distinguishing by gender. Mbuti men and women see themselves as equals in all respects but one: Women have the enormously important power of giving birth. This equation of womanhood with motherhood, which affords Mbuti women high status, is played out through a number of rituals in their everyday lives. Even their natural habitat (the forest), which is considered both sacred and supreme, is often called *mother*. Moreover Mbuti women choose their own mates, determine their own daily activities, and exercise considerable power as social critics.

In such food-foraging societies, the roles performed by men and women are different, but their relative statuses are not. Sexual equality is not surprising, however, because marked status differences of any type are rare in hunting-and-gathering societies. Because constant migration makes it difficult to accumulate possessions, foraging societies tend to have little private property, and thus sharp status distinctions are minimized for both men and women.

Although it is possible to identify societies where gender distinctions are kept to a minimum, the overwhelming evidence suggests that in many critical areas of life women are subordinate to men. From time to time women in various cultures have wielded considerable power, such as the Iroquois of the US Northeast (George-Kanentiio 2000) and the Hopi of the US Southwest. Some researchers (Gero and Conkey, 1991) have argued that there is ethnographic or archaeological evidence for matriarchy—women's rule or domination over men and it is possible to find societies that the people themselves describe as matriarchies, but while the women have power, they do not rule over men in the same way that men rule over women. For example, among the Minangkabau of West Sumatra, Indonesia, females and males interact more like partners than competitors. The foundation of gender relationships among the Minangkabau is their central philosophical notion of *adat*: People, animals, and wildlife should be nurtured so that society will be strong. This emphasis on nurturing tends to favor cooperation and the maternal in everyday life rather than competition and male dominance. According to Peggy Sanday (2004), women in Minangkabau society on ceremonial occasions are addressed by the term reserved for the mythical queen, and symbolically the maternal is viewed as the spiritual center and the original foundation of the society. Moreover women exert considerable power in everyday social life. Women control land inheritance, husbands reside in their wives' residences, and in the event of divorce, the husband gathers his belongings and leaves. Yet, despite the central role of women in society, this is hardly an example of matriarchy. Rather neither men nor women rule in Minangkabau society because decision making is based on consensus and cooperation.

Despite such examples as the Minangkabau, we find that women, to one degree or another, tend to be excluded from the major centers of economic and political power and control in most societies (Figure 11.9). Moreover the roles women play invariably carry with them fewer prerogatives and lower prestige than male roles. Although to speak of *universal male dominance* would be an oversimplification, the evidence does suggest a general gender asymmetry among most cultures of the world in the allocation of power and influence, particularly in the economic and political spheres.

This gender asymmetry is so pervasive that some anthropologists have attributed it to biological differences between men and women, such as greater size, strength, and physical aggressiveness. Ernestine Friedl (1978), however, argued that men tend to dominate not because of biological traits but rather because they control the distribution of scarce resources. Irrespective of who produces the goods, Friedl contended that the people *controlling* the allocation of resources (usually men) possess the currency needed to create and maintain powerful political alliances and obligations. By using examples from a number of societies, Friedl demonstrated how men dominate in those societies in which women have little or no control over the allocation of scarce resources and, conversely, how women with some control of resources have achieved greater equality.

Gender inequality, however, is not a unified phenomenon; it takes many different forms in different societies. There has always been sexual violence directed against women, during both war and peace time (Brettell and Sargent 2005; Rylko-Bauer, Whiteford, and Farmer 2009). Sometimes the acts of aggression and domination have been individual (rape) and sometimes collective (gang rape). Sometimes these acts have been organized, and other times they have been spontaneous. However, this inequity is not a new phenomenon. The record of sexual violence is at times disguised as prostitution, which remains today a huge and global industry. In postindustrial countries, gender inequity

THAILAND
VIETNAM
PHILIPPINES
BRUNEI
MALAYSIA
SUMATRA
BORNEO
Jakarta
Minangkabau People
INDONESIA
Indian Ocean

© Cengage Learning

---

universal male dominance The notion that men are more powerful and influential than women in all societies.

FIGURE 11.9 Among the Minangkabau of West Sumatra (*left*), decision making between wives and husbands is relatively equal and cooperative. Because of gender ideology, this boy in Rajasthan, India, (*right*) is more likely to receive medical attention than is his sister.

is creating disparities in access to formal education, employment, health care, and finances. We will discuss some of the varieties of these gender disparities next.

Education

Women throughout the world have made progress toward equal educational enrollment, but huge gaps remain. Two-thirds of all the illiterate people in the world today are women. More than 70 percent of women aged twenty-five and older in sub-Saharan Africa, southern Asia, and western Asia are illiterate (UNESCO 2010). There are more illiterate women than men in every major region of the world. Even though world literacy has been on the rise in recent decades, it has risen faster for men than for women, thereby widening the gender gap. In developing countries such as Pakistan, India, Yemen, and Afghanistan, the large literacy gap between men and women is most often related to poverty and access to education. Where there are high levels of poverty coupled with gender discrimination, women and girls are the ones who are marginalized. Recall the international outrage when fifteen-year-old Malala

Yousafzai, a Pakistani girl, was shot in the head by the Taliban because she campaigned for girls' rights to be educated (Boon and Saddiqu 2012). Continued efforts are being made, however, by individuals and nonprofit organizations, to reduce the gender disparities through creating more equitable access education.

Global organizations working toward increasing educational opportunities, such as UNICEF (www.unicef.org/), provide assistance for basic education and gender equality for nations around the world. Many of UNICEF's projects are aimed toward early childhood development and childhood readiness, empowerment, and equal access to education for *all* children—boys and girls, rich and poor. Other organizations such as World Education Ghana (http://ghana.worlded.org), the Kenya Education Fund (http://kenyaeducationfund.org/), and other country-specific voluntary organizations develop programs that combine education with health, economic, social, and civic development in youth education. The initiatives are geared to help break the cycle of poverty. Some of these programs also incorporate education on HIV and AIDS prevention and treatments for the children and their families.

Employment

The percentage of women in the world's workforce has increased in the last several decades, largely because of economic necessity. However, the majority of the world's women, particularly in developing countries, are concentrated in the lowest-paid occupations and receive lower pay and fewer benefits than men. Women are also more likely to work part-time, have less seniority, and occupy positions with little or no upward mobility. Moreover, an increasing number of women in Asia, Africa, and South America are being pushed into the informal economy characterized by the small-scale, self-employed trading of goods and services. Some of the activities associated with the informal economy—such as street vending, beer brewing, and prostitution—are outside the law. All of this has led to the impoverishment of women worldwide, a phenomenon known as the *feminization of poverty*. The United Nations on Women (UN Women 2012) estimates 70 percent of all people living in poverty throughout the world are women, and the inequities are increasing. In some regions, women provide 70 percent of agricultural labor, produce more than 90 percent of the food, and yet are nowhere represented in their government budget deliberations. Overall the number of women living in poverty increased disproportionately to the number of men during the past decade, in part from the growing number of female-headed households (single women). Moreover the increasing feminization of poverty was particularly acute in poorer, developing countries and for minority women living in wealthier, more industrialized nations.

The struggles women face combating poverty, violence, and domestic abuse do not go unrecognized nationally or internationally. Once again, there are many international agencies (US Agency for International Development [USAID], United Nations Development Fund for Women [UNIFEM], and Food and Agriculture Organization [FAO]), nongovernment or private voluntary agencies working toward gender equality and the empowerment of women. Contacting any one of these agencies for voluntary work or possible future employment will take particular skills, sensitivity, and cultural understanding of gender relations in the workplace.

Reproductive Health

A third area in which the world's women have not fared as well as men is in access to health care and for many women it is access to reproductive healthcare. Although most women in the developed world control the number of children they have, in some parts of the world there is pressure to have small families, as in parts of Europe and China (Krause 2005). In other parts of the world there is pressure to have large numbers of children, and women on average have four or five children. In certain countries with particularly high birthrates (such as Niger, Mali, Uganda, Zambia, Burkina Faso, Somalia, Malawi,), the average woman bears more than seven children in her lifetime (CIA Factbook 2012; Holloway 2007; MacFarquhar 1994). Pregnant women in developing countries face risks that include malnutrition and a lack of trained medical personnel to deal with high-risk pregnancies. In fact, it has been estimated that pregnant women in developing countries are eighty to six hundred times more likely to die of complications from pregnancy and birthing than are women in the industrialized world (Holloway 2007).

A related health issue for women is the extent to which gender inequalities make them more vulnerable to HIV and AIDS. Women's economic dependence on men, as well as the threat of violence against wives and girlfriends, makes them less able to protect themselves. In many parts of the world, it is unacceptable for a woman to say no to unwanted or unprotected sex. Adding to the problem is the sex trade industry. Poverty has forced many women in African communities and elsewhere to put themselves at great risk of contracting HIV and AIDS by engaging in the sex trade for financial gain to support their families. In other instances women and girls enter or are forced into unfaithful marriages or other unsafe relationships with men whose sexual behavior has either already made them HIV-positive or puts them at greater risk to contract the disease.

Among societies where polygyny is common there are higher risks for contracting HIV and AIDS. Polygyny in and of itself is not the culprit however; when a man engages in sexual activity unknowingly with a woman who is HIV-positive and subsequently passes on the infection to his other wives, the rate increases. A study conducted in Zambia (Urdang 2001) revealed how vulnerable wives can be to HIV and AIDS and other diseases sexually transmitted by their husbands. Less than one in every four women, according to the study, believed that they could refuse to have sex with their husbands, even if the husband had been unfaithful and was infected. Similarly anthropologist Richard Lee (2007) attributes the low incidence of HIV and AIDS among the Ju/'hoansi of Namibia and Botswana to, among other factors, the traditional high status of women and their relative gender equality. Because the typical Ju/'hoansi wife tends to be relatively empowered, she is more likely to insist that her husband wear a condom and, should he refuse, to not have sex with him. In addition, social customs are so restrictive in some countries that often young women are denied access to information about the dangers of HIV and AIDS and how best to protect themselves.

---

feminization of poverty The trend of women making up the world's poor; refers to the high proportion of female-headed families that live below the poverty line, which may result from the high proportion of women found in occupations with low prestige and income.

Organizations such as the United Nations are actively helping women and children. The Global Strategy for Women's and Children's Health is a program of the United Nations that is directed at improving women's and children's health in the developing world, but much more needs to be done. The World Health Organization (WHO) reports that worldwide people are becoming newly infected with HIV at twice the rate of people who are starting antiretroviral treatment. Every day seven thousand people in the world are newly infected, including one thousand children. The majority of these newly infected people are in Africa. Any applied healthcare program needs a clear understanding of culture, specifically sex, gender, and marriage and family patterns, to play a critical role in reducing these statistics.

Finance

The women of the world are also at a disadvantage in obtaining credit from financial institutions (Waring 1989, 2004). According to World Bank estimates, 90 percent of the more than half billion women living in poverty around the world do not have access to credit. Small loans of $100 would go a long way in helping women to start their own small businesses, which could substantially improve their economic conditions. But both private lenders and aid organizations, by and large, have not made even this level of credit available to women. A notable exception is Grameen Bank in Bangladesh, the world's best-known micro-lender, which for three decades has made small-business loans to the poorest segments of Bangladesh society. The community development bank makes loans to impoverished people without requiring collateral. Since its inception Grameen Bank has distributed USD $11.35 billion in loans and has been repaid USD $10.11 billion, a loan recovery rate of 97 percent. Loans are given primarily to women who use them to turn their operations into viable businesses. Extending this type of credit to impoverished women has proven to be an excellent investment. First, World Bank data show that women repay their loans in 98 percent of the cases, as compared with 60 to 70 percent for men. And second, the World Bank has found that credit given to women has a greater impact on the welfare of the family because women tend to spend their money on better nutrition and education for their children—areas given lower priority by male borrowers. According to Yunus, the founder of Grameen Bank, the main reason for providing loans to women is

that a woman was a "better fighter" against poverty than a man. A woman, he said, went to greater lengths to improve her children's nutrition and health and educate her daughters. Simply put, she used the loans more effectively. In the past few years, the field of development has come to a similar conclusion, with many aid workers asserting that the best way to fight poverty is to strengthen the positions of women and girls. (Bornstein 2012).

Thus, it is clear that women throughout the world continue to carry a heavy burden of inequality. Although they make up half of the world's population, women do approximately two-thirds of the work, earn one-tenth of the world's income, and own less than 1 percent of the world's property. Even in the wake of some political and economic advances, women in many parts of the world are falling further behind their male counterparts. Moreover gender inequality does not necessarily depend on how wealthy a country is. Some developing countries have done much better at narrowing the gender gap than have some wealthy, industrialized nations. In terms of women's participation in politics and jobs, for example, Costa Rica has made considerably better progress than Italy or France, whereas Poland is ahead of Japan.

As part of the Human Development Index (HDI) the United Nations developed an indicator of progress toward equality for women called the Gender Empowerment Measure (GEM), which assesses gender inequality in three main areas: (1) political participation and decision-making power (that is, parliamentary seats), (2) economic participation and decision-making power, and (3) power over economic resources (that is, income). Only 146 countries of the 187 countries for which data have been collected for the HDI have sufficient data reported to determine the Gender Inequality Index measuring the GEM. A score of 1.0 indicates equality between men and women. As is apparent in Table 11.2, Sweden, Netherland, Denmark,

TABLE 11.2

Countries with the Highest and Lowest Ranks on the Gender Inequality Index

Country	Rank
Sweden	1
Netherlands	2
Denmark	3
Switzerland	4
Finland	5
Norway	6
Germany	7
United States	47
Papau New Guinea	140
Afghanistan	141
Democractic Republic of the Congo	142
Mali	143
Niger	144
Chad	145
Yemen	146

SOURCE: *UNDP 2011 Report on Gender Inequality Index and related indicators Gender Empowerment Measure,* http://hdr.undp.org/en/media/HDR_2011_EN_Table4.pdf

Switzerland, Finland, Norway, and Germany indicate they have the scores reflecting the highest degree of gender equality on the Gender Inequality Index, whereas Yemen, Chad, Niger, Mali, Congo, Afghanistan, and Papua New Guinea have the lowest scores. Note that the United States ranked 47 among 146 countries in the world for which there are data.

Gender Ideology

Generalized male dominance is buttressed by a *gender ideology*, which we define as a system of thoughts and values that legitimizes gender roles, statuses, and customary behavior. In religion women are often excluded categorically by gender ideology from holding major leadership roles or participating in certain types of ceremonies. In some African societies, for example, men's physical well-being is thought to be jeopardized by contact with a woman's menstrual discharge. In Bangladesh and in some African cultures, men are associated with the right side and women with the left side, a dichotomy that also denotes purity–pollution, good–bad, and authority—submission. Even in the area of food production, foods procured by men (such as meat from the hunt) are often more highly valued than those procured by women (such as roots, nuts, and berries), even though the latter foods are the major source of nutrition. In many parts of the world such as in Afghanistan, women are treated legally as minors in that they are unable to obtain a driver's license, bank account, passport, or even birth control device without the consent of their husbands or fathers. One particularly effective ideological mechanism for keeping women in a subordinate position is found among the Luo of western Kenya, whose creation myth (no doubt originated and perpetuated by men) blames women for committing the original sins that resulted in the curse of work for men.

In many parts of the world, such as India and China, the devaluation of women starts early in life. The birth of a son is often cause for rejoicing, but the birth of a daughter is met with silence. In some patrilineal societies, boys are more highly valued because they will contribute to the longevity of the lineage, whereas their sisters will produce children for their husband's lineage. Because parents often assume that sons will provide for them in their old age, they are much more likely to give sons preferential treatment for education and careers. However, over time the preference for sons in China and India has created such a lopsided ratio of boys to girls that economists project there may be as many as 30 to 40 million more men than women of marriageable age in both countries by 2020. In societies in which girls are less valued, they are also not likely to be able to support their parents financially later in life because they are often denied access to schooling, medical facilities, and nutritious diets. To be certain, there are some societies that prefer female children (in East Africa and New Guinea), but the dominant trend is toward a preference for male children.

These are just some of the values that legitimize the subordination of women, as reported in the ethnographic literature. Nevertheless we need to ask whether women in societies with such powerful gender ideologies actually buy into the ideologies. In other words, do they accept these ideological justifications for their subjugation? Because so many ethnographic reports were based on male testimony given to male ethnographers, it is likely that women, if their opinions were solicited, would describe themselves quite differently from the way they are portrayed in the ethnographic literature. As early as the 1980s, some ethnographers (Bossen 1984; Errington and Gewertz 1987; Gottlieb 1988; Kirsch 1985; Shostak 1983; Strathern 1984) wrote from the perspective of female informants, demonstrating the distorted interpretations of gender ideology seen only through a male perspective.

An example of this distortion is provided by Thomas Buckley (1993), who showed how our Western view of menstruation and pollution led to a one-sided understanding of the culture of the Yurok Indians of northern California. Early ethnographic accounts of the Yurok suggested that menstruating women were required to seclude themselves as a way of protecting men from the pollution of menstrual blood. Buckley's study of Yurok women, however, gives a different interpretation of female seclusion during menstruation. Yurok women went into seclusion for a ten-day period not because they saw themselves as unclean or polluting, but because they were at the height of their power. Because this was a time of meditation, introspection, and personal growth, they did not want to be distracted by mundane tasks or concerns of the opposite sex. Rather women were taught to be proud of their menstrual cycle and were expected to accumulate spiritual energy by meditating about the mysteries of life. Thus, for Yurok women menstruation was a highly positive part of their lives. As Buckley (1993: 135) describes it, "The blood that flows serves to 'purify' the woman, preparing her for spiritual accomplishment."

Another study that illustrates the complexity of gender ideology was conducted by Sandra Barnes (1990) among Yoruba women in Lagos, Nigeria. Female subordination among the Yoruba can best be described as contextual or situational. That is, women subordinate themselves in some contexts by showing great deference to their husbands, male family elders, employers,

gender ideology A system of thoughts and values that legitimizes gender roles, statuses, and customary behavior.

and public officials, but in other situations (such as market activity) they are independent, assertive, and powerful. Thus, we see a basic paradox in Yoruba society: Although female subordination is clearly the norm, particularly in family affairs, it is widely held that women can, and even should, strive for powerful positions in the world of economics and politics. Barnes explains the apparent paradox in terms of home ownership. Because of their success in the markets, women are able to attain high status through home ownership, and once they become homeowners, they are able to cross over into the realm of politics and public affairs (Figure 11.10).

As mentioned previously, traditional ethnographies tended to be conducted by male anthropologists focusing on male informants, and the perspective of women was often overlooked or misinterpreted. Nowhere is this more evident than in the Middle East, where women are secluded and protected from the wider society. To most Westerners the veil is a symbol of repression, representing extreme restrictions, coercion, immobility, and degradation. In a number of Islamic countries, however, well-educated computer experts and business professionals wear the veil. Many of these women look at the veil not in terms of what it denies them but rather in terms of the demands that it makes on the men in the society. For many Islamic women, educated and uneducated alike, the veil is a symbol of safety, security, protection, privacy, and religious purity that they would not readily choose to abandon.

Studies written from a woman's perspective provide a long-overdue corrective to the male gender bias found in many of our ethnographies. They also remind us that gender issues are far more complex than one might perceive by looking at a society only from a male perspective. Nevertheless these new studies, though providing a richer and more accurate description of reality, should not obscure the fact that in most societies men still enjoy the majority of the power, prestige, and influence.

FIGURE 11.10 Although they assume a subordinate position in their family lives, some African women are able to gain considerable power, authority, and autonomy by virtue of their economic activities, as with this vegetable vendor in Ethiopia.

Exploitation Caused by Gender Ideology

In some parts of the world, gender ideology is so biased toward males that females can suffer dire consequences. The United Nations reports approximately 200 million girls in the world today are "missing." China and India are said to do away with more female infants than the number of girls born in the United States each year. In most countries, including the United States and Canada, women slightly outnumber men (approximately 105 women for every 100 men). But in India and China, where traditionally there has been a strong gender bias against females, the sex ratio strongly favors males. In China, for example, the government reported that the sex ratio had reached 120 boys for every 100 girls, and Lianyungang, China, has the worst infant gender ratio on record with 163 boys born for every 100 girls. This imbalance is caused by poorer nutrition and medical care for females, selective sex abortions, and the underreporting or hiding of female births. Demographers predict that in twenty years China could have 40 million bachelors unable to find a wife. However, despite government efforts to provide incentives for girl babies (such as free tuition for girls and annual pensions for elderly people who have only daughters), there remains a strong cultural preference, for in Chinese culture they area patriarchal society with a patrilineal kinship system that requires male heirs to continue the lineage, which especially true in rural areas where land inheritance is important for male children (Yardley 2005).

A particularly malignant manifestation of *male gender bias* is found elsewhere in the world. Taiwan, South Korea, and northern India are also countries in which unwanted female babies are aborted, killed, or abandoned. This form of killing is known as *female infanticide*, the outright killing of female babies. Sons are much more desirable than daughters because they are considered economic assets. They are needed for farming, they are more likely to be employed for wages, they receive marriage dowry, and because they do not leave home when they marry, they can support parents in their later years.

There are also more subtle forms of female child abuse, such as sustained *nutritional deprivation*, which, though perhaps not fatal, can retard learning, physical development, and social adjustment (Rose 1994). Sunil Khanna (2010) reports that in his home country of India gender bias against girls leads to significant differences in weight-for-age statistics for boys and girls younger than five years of age. Barbara Miller (1993) found considerable evidence in India of this less direct form of gender exploitation. For example, the sex ratio of children being admitted to hospitals is at least two to one in favor of boys, an imbalance caused by the sex-selective child care practices of the parents. Betty Cowan and Jasbir Dhanoa (1983) examined a large sample of *infant mortality* cases in Ludhiana district in northern India and found that girls accounted for 85 percent of all deaths of children between ages seven months and thirty-six months. They also found that the incidence of malnutrition for children between the ages of one and three years was more than three times as high for girls as it was for boys. All of these studies indicate how an extreme gender ideology can lead to a lethal form of gender exploitation.

Another graphic form of gender exploitation is female genital cutting (FGC), also known as female circumcision. Amnesty International estimates that more than 140 million women worldwide have had their childhood or early adolescence interrupted by a traumatic operation in which a girl's genitalia (labia and clitoris) are either partially or completely removed surgically. Although this practice, customary in large parts of Africa and the Middle East, has been condemned by international medical and human rights groups, it is thought that more than three million FGCs are still performed every year, which is equivalent to four procedures performed every minute worldwide. These operations are typically performed with crude and unsterile instruments, without benefit of anesthesia, and with little or no protection against infection. The practice is justified by traditionalists on the grounds of protecting a girl's chastity and thus the family's honor, promoting cleanliness, repressing a girl's sexual desires, and reducing the likelihood of rape. It has long been known, however, that the operation itself poses severe medical risks for women. Moreover a large-scale medical study

(Rosenthal 2006) concluded that FGC raises the likelihood that mothers or their newborns will die during childbirth by 50 percent. There is, in other words, an increasing amount of evidence from many sources that millions of girls worldwide continue to be subjected to pain, psychological trauma, infection, death, and compromises to their reproductive health to an extent that their brothers are not.

Another form of extreme gender bias is *honor killings* of women, which occur in a number of countries of the Middle East as well as in India and Pakistan. The men of a traditional family believe that a woman's purity is most important to the family's reputation. If it is even rumored that a daughter has lost her virginity, the family as a group will be shamed. An unchaste woman is considered worse than a murderer because she affects not a single victim but an entire family. The only way for the family to restore its honor and avoid public humiliation, it is thought, is to kill the daughter. Despite laws against it, honor killings remain widespread because an unchaste woman is seen as a threat to the reputation of the family. Because honor killings are often disguised to look like accidents, and because of the general reluctance in traditional societies to blow the whistle on the killer, it is difficult to determine the number of honor killings that occur each year, but international women's groups estimate nearly 20,000 women are killed each year.

A 2011 Human Rights Commission report in Pakistan has revealed some horrific statistics about women's rights violations throughout the country. At least 943 women were killed in 2011 for damaging their family name; more than 100 from the previous year. During the last five years, at least 9,670 women have been killed in Punjab alone. About 8,040 Pakistani women were killed because of property and other such issues, and about 3,380 women were killed for not bringing dowry with them and asking for their rights (*The Nation* 2010). Whatever the number, however, this particular practice of honor killings places the entire burden of maintaining the family's honor on the woman, rather than punishing the man who also played a part in the loss of the girl's virginity.

---

male gender bias A preference found in some societies for sons rather than daughters.

female infanticide The killing of female children.

nutritional deprivation A form of child abuse involving withholding food; can retard learning, physical development, and social adjustment.

infant mortality Infant death.

honor killings A euphemism referring to a practice found in various Middle Eastern cultures whereby women are killed by their own family members because they are thought to have dishonored the family.

Another inequality-related crime against women is *dowry deaths* in rural India, Pakistan, and Bangladesh (as mentioned in Chapter 9). Following marriage and the required giving of a dowry, the family of the groom often makes demands on the bride's family for more money or goods. Because the bride is living with her husband's family, she is subject to harassment, humiliation, abuse, and even death from beatings, burnings, and suicide for failing to meet the dowry demands of her in-laws. A commonly reported form of dowry death involves a wife being drenched in kerosene and set on fire.

Widespread abuse of women in other cultures is deeply disturbing and shocking, but we should not assume that equally appalling gender-based violence does not occur in our own culture. Both physical violence, in the form of wife battering and homicide and sexual assault against women are pervasive and direct consequences of extreme gender ideology. Sexual and physical violence against women has been, and continues to be, a serious problem in the United States and around the world. For example, rape in India is the most common crime against women, with some of the highest offenses taking place in New Delhi. Lori Heise and colleagues (1999) reported that around the world at least one in three women has been beaten, coerced into sex, or otherwise abused during her lifetime through some form of mental or physical form of sexual harassment. Most violence against women in the United States occurs not in a dark alley but within the home. According to the Domestic Violence Resource Center (2012), nearly one-quarter of all women in the United States (more than 12 million) will be abused by a former or current partner during their lifetime. FBI statistics indicate that 30 percent of female murder victims are killed by their husbands or boyfriends, and 52 percent are killed by current or former intimate partners (Figure 11.11).

Because many women still do not define a sexual assault by their husband as a rape, it is likely that many such assaults go unreported, and consequently these findings must be considered low estimates. With data like these, it is little wonder that Richard Gelles (quoted in Roesch 1984) has suggested that, with the exception of the police and the military, the family is the most violent institution in the United States.

FIGURE 11.11 Physical violence against women by a husband or intimate partner is the result of gender ideology and occurs in our own culture as well as in many other cultures around the world.

dowry deaths The killing of a wife by her in-laws if the wife's parents fail to pay additional dowry.

CROSS-CULTURAL MISCUE

When Marianne first arrived as the new director for the domestic violence center in Kenya she was nervous, a bit reserved, and guarded because it was her first major assignment overseas. Her assistant director, Karen, tried to make her feel welcomed and comfortable, but for Marianne her approach was not working. Karen was genuinely a nice person, but she approached her work with humor and frequently cracked jokes, which irritated Marianne. Marianne thought, this is a crisis center, why the humor, women are hurting. Nevertheless Karen was popular among the other cross-cultural aid workers; her ease with them and the clients made for a comfortable setting. As Marianne gradually grew more confident in her role, she came to appreciate Karen's approach to her work. Marianne also realized she was so focused on getting the job done, always working in a crisis management mode that she forgot about living life and finding the new normal, especially for those women who had been victimized. In time Marianne came to learn to bring humor into her work. She came to realize that appropriate cultural humor can be important in maintaining mental and physical health, social relationships, team unity, and camaraderie.

© Robin Nelson/Photo Edit

Gender in the United States

When we think of traditional gender roles in the United States, two words usually come to mind: *breadwinner* and *housewife*. According to this traditional view, males, who are often characterized as logical, competitive, goal-oriented, and unemotional, were responsible for the economic support and protection of the family. Females, on the other hand, with their warm, caring, and sensitive natures, were expected to restrict themselves to child rearing and domestic activities: preparing meals, cleaning the house, collecting wood and water, working in kitchen gardens, and doing a variety of other tasks that helped to support the household.

This traditional view of gender roles in the United States was valid for only a relatively brief period in our nation's history, however—from roughly 1860 through the 1950s. Kingsley Davis and Wilbert Moore (1988: 73) called the years from 1860 to 1920 the "heyday of the breadwinner system"; they identified 1890 as its peak because less than 3 percent of native-born married women in the United States worked outside the home at that time. Although women may not be called "breadwinners," working is not new to them. Women have always worked both inside and outside the home, especially minority and lower-class women. Before industrialization, pioneer women were fully productive contributors to the rural homestead. With the start of the industrial revolution, minority and lower-class women started working outside the home while still caring for their own homes.

With the rise of industrialization in the late nineteenth century, the nation's economy shifted from agriculture to manufacturing. This rapid industrialization was revolutionary because it tended to separate work life from family life. Unlike work on the family farm, factory work could not be easily combined with child rearing and domestic tasks. As women became more confined to the home, their direct contribution to economic production decreased. As men's and women's spheres were separated, the terms *breadwinner* and *housewife* became entrenched in our vocabulary. Interestingly, we have retained this view of separate spheres for men and women into the twenty-first century even though the forces of change that eroded those separate spheres were under way by the early 1900s. From the 1910s through the early 1920s, young, middle-class women joined the workforce outside the home, and it went largely unnoticed until the Great Depression. Then, with the high rate of unemployment, most people opposed women working because they saw it as women taking jobs from unemployed men.

It is true that men entered the workforce in greater numbers than women during the twentieth century, but we must not assume that women did not also make significant contributions to factory production. This is particularly true of poor and working-class women, minority women, immigrant women, and single mothers. The entry of women into the workforce was facilitated by several factors. First, as industrialization became more complex, more clerical workers were needed, and most of them were women. Second, as infant mortality rates fell, women bore fewer children, thereby increasing the number of years they could work outside the home. Third, many women gravitated toward the textile industry because they were thought to possess greater manual dexterity than men and therefore to be more adept at sewing clothes. Fourth, World War II helped galvanize women's role in the workplace. The government launched a propaganda campaign with the fictional character "Rosie the Riveter." Rosie was considered an ideal female worker: efficient, loyal, patriotic, and pretty (Yellin 2004). Fifth, the rising divorce rate forced many women to support themselves and their children without the financial aid of a spouse. Sixth, the development of infant formula enabled many women to work outside the home without jeopardizing the nutritional needs of their infants. And, finally, periodic economic downturns drove an increasing number of women to join the workforce because two salaries are often needed to make ends meet (Figure 11.12).

Today both men and women are in the paid labor force, with approximately 70 percent of men and 58 percent of women participating. The percentage of women working outside the home has changed dramatically over the past four decades. Table 11.3 illustrates, the number of working women older than sixteen years of age rose from about 43 percent in 1970 to 58 percent in 2011 (US Department of Labor 2012). The figure had been higher in 2000, but the steady unemployment rate nationally, which hovered between 9.0 and 10.0 percent between 2009 and 2011, makes it difficult for people who want work to find employment. It is important to point out that employed married women, particularly those with children, often carry a *double workload* by being both wage employed and primarily responsible for housework and child care.

---

breadwinner A traditional gender role in the United States that views males as being responsible for the economic support and protection of the family.

housewife A traditional gender role in the United States that views females as responsible for child rearing and domestic activities.

double workload The situation in which employed married women, particularly those with children, are both wage employed and primarily responsible for housework and child care.

FIGURE 11.12 Be they in the office, factory, field or in the home, women often multitask. For many families two salaries are often needed to make ends meet.

Another characteristic of the wage sector of the US economy is its high rate of *occupational segregation* along gender lines. Despite decades of legislation aimed at reducing gender discrimination in the workplace, the majority of both men and women continue to work in gender-segregated occupations. The majority of women in the United States work as clerk and secretaries, hairdressers, sales clerks, food service workers, healthcare personnel, and child-care workers, all relatively low-paying jobs. More than 90 percent of nurses, 80 percent

of librarians and elementary and middle school teachers are women. At the other end of the spectrum, women make up only 2 percent of corporate CEOs, 6 percent of partners in private law firms, and 8 percent of state and federal judges (US Department of Labor 2011). In addition men tend to dominate supervisory positions, even in areas where a majority of the workers are women. This occupational segregation is even more pronounced for minority women because gender segregation is aggravated by race. Despite these data illustrating occupational segregation, in the last several decades women have made considerable inroads into some high-status professions such as medicine. According to the American Medical Association (2012), the number of women physicians increased from 447 percent between 1980 and 2010. Women comprise nearly a third of all physicians now and half of the medical students in the United States.

Although an increasing number of women are entering professions that require advanced education, such as law, medicine, and engineering, occupations associated with low prestige and low income still have higher proportions of women. Poverty in the United States has become "feminized" just as it has in other parts of the world. For example, more than half of all female-headed families with children are living below the poverty line—a poverty rate that is approximately four times higher than the poverty rate for two-parent families. The feminization of poverty is particularly acute when we look at minorities. Although the total poverty level for all families headed by single women was 30 percent, when the statistic is broken down a different picture emerges. For example, among white, female-headed families 23 percent live in poverty, yet approximately 42 percent of families headed by African American women and 44 percent of families headed by Hispanic

TABLE 11.3

US Labor Force Participation Rates by Sex 1970–2011

| Year | Labor force participation rates by sex (in percent) | | |
	Both sexes	Men	Women
1970	60.4	79.7	43.3
1975	61.2	77.9	46.3
1980	63.8	77.4	51.5
1985	64.8	76.3	54.5
1990	(b) 66.5	(b) 76.4	57.5
1995	66.6	75.0	58.9
2000	67.1	74.8	59.9
2005	66.0	73.3	59.3
2010	64.7	71.2	58.6
2011	64.1	70.5	58.1

SOURCE: United States Department of Labor.

occupational segregation The separation of different occupations in a society.

women are officially living in poverty (US Census 2012). A number of factors have contributed to the feminization of poverty in the United States in recent decades. These include the continued involvement of women in low-paying jobs; the additional responsibilities for child rearing, which many men do not have; the relative dearth of women in political and policy-making positions; and women's limited access to education, skills training, financial credit, and health care.

As we look back on our discussion of gender stratification in the United States, it seems fairly obvious that in time the gap between men and women will narrow. The cost of gender stratification is high for both men and women, with the perpetuation of inequality in the workplace as well as at home. One can recognize that the culturally constructed male and female roles and statuses in the United States have negative consequences. For example, men in the United States have higher mortality rates than women at all ages and for most of the fifteen leading causes of death. They abuse their bodies with drugs, alcohol, and tobacco more than women. And men engage in certain professions that carry higher risks, such as mining, construction, and deep-sea fishing, In addition, to live up to culturally defined notions of masculinity, many men engage in high-risk (health-reducing) behaviors. The pressure to

be a tough, competitive winner can lead a man to take on more than he can handle, thereby resulting in excessive stress. And when things do not go well, a growing sense of failure can lead to what Terrence Real (2001) calls "covert depression," a form of depression that often goes undiagnosed because it is largely repressed. Adult males in the United States rarely seek help for stress, depression, and other emotional problems because to do so would be to admit weakness.

Women continue to adapt to the changing times in the twenty-first century. They are making choices that influence their home and family life as well as their place in the workforce. For example, US women are marrying later in life, staying in school longer, delaying childbirth, and having fewer children than in previous years. More women are choosing to continue working while also balancing the traditional parenting role. Gender discrimination persists and at its worst is coupled with fighting battles for equal pay for equal work. Although working women still face the demands of a heavy workload balancing family, jobs, and possibly sexual harassment at the workplace, women have made great strides in the workplace. Nevertheless we should see continued efforts for gender equity by both men and women at home *and* in the workplace throughout twenty-first–century US culture.

Summary

1. The word *gender* refers to the way members of the two sexes are perceived, evaluated, and expected to behave. Although biology sets broad limits on definitions of gender, there is a wide range of ideas about what it means to be feminine or masculine, as Mascia-Lees and Black (2000) review in their book *Gender in Anthropology*.

2. There are considerable differences in degrees of permissiveness, but all societies regulate the sexual conduct of their members. Some societies, such as the Cheyenne of the US Plains, are sexually restrictive, whereas others, such as the Mangaians of Polynesia, not only permit but also actually encourage frequent and intense sexual activity between men and women.

3. In general terms, there is considerable uniformity in sex roles throughout the world. Men engage in warfare, clear land, hunt animals, build houses, fish, and work with hard substances; women tend crops, prepare food, collect firewood, clean house, launder clothes, care for children, and carry water.

4. The status of women is multidimensional, involving such aspects as the division of labor, the value placed on women's contributions, economic autonomy, social and political power, legal rights, levels

of deference, and the extent to which women control the everyday events of their lives.

5. Hindu society in northern India is among the most highly stratified along gender lines. At the other extreme, certain hunting-and-gathering societies, such as the Mbuti Pygmies of Central Africa, take the most egalitarian (or least stratified) approach to men and women. Although these represent the two extremes of the status of women in the world, in most critical areas women tend to be subordinate to men in nearly all societies of the world.

6. Gender ideology is used in most societies to justify universal male dominance. Deeply rooted values about the superiority of men, the ritual impurity of women, and the preeminence of men's work are often used to justify the subjugation of women. However, it has been demonstrated in recent years that women do not perceive themselves in the same ways they are portrayed in these (largely male) gender ideologies.

7. In some societies gender ideologies are so extreme that females suffer serious negative consequences, such as female infanticide, female genital cutting, female nutritional deprivation, dowry death, honor killing, rape, and spouse abuse.

8. Although the words *breadwinner* and *housewife* accurately described the middle-class US household around the beginning of the twentieth century, the separate spheres suggested by these two terms have become more myth than reality. In fact, over the past five decades, the number of women in the United States working outside the home has increased dramatically.

9. The economy of the United States is characterized by a high rate of occupational segregation along gender lines. Not only are occupations gender segregated, but women tend to earn considerably less than men. Moreover there has been a trend in recent decades toward the feminization of poverty around the world as a result of unequal access to education and the higher paying skilled jobs.

Key Terms

breadwinner	feminization of poverty	homosexual	nutritional deprivation
double workload	gender	honor killing	occupational segregation
dowry death	gender ideology	housewife	purdah
extramarital sexual activity	genderlects	human sexuality	sex
female infanticide	gender roles	infant mortality	sexual asymmetry
femininity	gender stratification	male gender bias	sexual dimorphism
	heterosexual	masculinity	universal male dominance

Critical Thinking Questions

1. If you were hired by USAID to work on a series of local development projects because of your expertise in sex and gender, what cultural understandings would you want to know before you started on any project?

2. If you were employed at large accounting firm with upper management responsibilities, how might you ensure sexual harassment among your colleagues and disenfranchisement because of gender or sexual orientation were avoided?

3. In many parts of the world, genders are not equal. Should development projects remain gender neutral or perpetuate gender inequality?

Online Study Resources

CourseMate

Access chapter-specific learning tools including learning objectives, practice quizzes, videos, flash cards, glossaries, web links, and more in your Cultural Anthropology CourseMate. Login to www.cengagebrain.com to access the resources your instructor has assigned and to purchase materials.

Both rich and poor people live in their own distinct neighborhoods in Sao Paulo, Brazil, which has a population of nearly 20 million people.

Social Stratification

While spending his junior year studying in Canberra, Australia, Peter Gorman, a political science major from Duke University, had tickets to a concert at a club located miles from his apartment. Normally, he would take a bus, but this evening he was running late and did not want to miss any of the opening set, so he had to take a taxi. He signaled to a cab on the street by raising his right hand, jumped into the backseat, and told the driver where he wanted to go. As the driver began to pull away, however, he turned to Peter and said, "What's wrong, mate? Do you think I have leprosy?" Peter was not sure whether the taxi driver was joking or not.

Even though Peter had been in Australia for several months, he had not yet learned a fundamental trait—that Australian society is highly egalitarian. Egalitarian societies are those in which all members have relatively equal access to social prestige, wealth, and power, and no one exerts dominance over others. Because of Australia's egalitarian worldview, single riders in a taxi are expected to ride up front with the driver. Even high-paid executives and government officials ride up in the front of a limousine with the chauffeur. A single passenger riding alone in the backseat of a taxi makes many Australians uncomfortable because it symbolizes a gap in status and prestige between the passenger and the driver. ■

An important distinguishing characteristic of societies is the degree to which individuals have equal access to wealth, power, and prestige. In every society, people are socially differentiated on the basis of criteria such as physical appearance, ethnicity, profession, family background, gender, ideology, age, or skill in performing certain kinds of economic or political roles. Societies confer a larger share of the rewards (that is, wealth, power, and prestige) on those who possess the most admired characteristics. Scholars generally agree that all complex societies are stratified; that is, these societies make distinctions among certain groups or categories of people that are hierarchically ranked relative to one another. Anthropologists do not find clear-cut social strata in many of the simpler societies of the world, yet even these societies have role and status differences.

Dimensions of Social Inequality

Max Weber (1946) delineated three basic criteria for measuring levels of social inequality: wealth, power, and prestige. First, people are distinguished from one another by the extent to which they have accumulated economic resources, or

WHAT WE WILL LEARN

■ How do anthropologists measure social inequality?

■ How do egalitarian, rank, and stratified societies differ from one another?

■ To what extent do the societies of the world vary in terms of the equitable distribution of power, prestige, and wealth?

■ How do class systems differ from caste systems?

■ What is the distinction between race and ethnicity?

■ What are the different ways of interpreting systems of social stratification?

Florian Kopp/Glow Images

their *wealth.* The forms that wealth may take vary from one society to the next. For the Mexican farmer, wealth resides in the land; for the Samburu of East Africa, a man's wealth is measured by the number of cows he has; and in the United Kingdom, most people equate their wealth with income earned in wages, property, stocks, bonds, equity in a home, or other resources that have a cash value.

The extent of economic inequality varies from society to society. In some societies, such as the Pygmies, there are virtually no differences in wealth. In terms of their material possessions and well-being, all people in egalitarian societies are virtually indistinguishable. By way of contrast, enormous differences in wealth exist in certain capitalistic societies such as the United States and Mexico. The range of wealth in Mexico, for example, runs from the unemployed father in Mexico City who sells his blood to feed his children to the wealthiest man in the world, Carlos Slim Helu, a self-made telecommunications mogul from Mexico, whose total net worth in 2010 (according to the *Forbes* list of wealthiest people in the world) was $73 billion (that's billion, not million!). Just behind Helu in the billionaire sweepstakes are Bill Gates worth $67 billion and Amancio Ortega of Spain worth $57 billion (Figure 12.1). Economists Paul Samuelson and William Nordhaus (1989: 644) captured the magnitude of the economic inequities in the United States: "If we made an income pyramid out of a child's blocks, with each layer portraying $500 of income, the peak would be far higher than Mount Everest, but most people would be within a few feet of the ground."

It is important to note the close correlation between income and level of education, particularly among the wealthier nations of the world. According to the US Census Bureau (2012), average incomes vary widely with different levels of education, from $20, 241 for

FIGURE 12.1 Carlos Slim Helu, who built a telecommunications empire in Mexico topped the Forbes list of the world's wealthiest people in March, 2013 with a net worth of $73 billion, surpassing both Warren Buffet and Bill Gates of the United States.

those with less than a high school diploma to $73, 737 for those with a masters degree (see Table 12.1).

A second dimension of social inequality, according to Weber, is *power,* which he defined as the ability to achieve one's goals and objectives even against the will of others. Power, to be certain, is often closely correlated with wealth because economic success, particularly in Western societies, increases one's chances of gaining power. Nevertheless wealth and power do not always coincide. In certain parts of the world, power can be based on factors other than wealth, such as specialized

wealth The material objects that have value in a society.

power The capacity to produce intended effects for oneself, other people, social situations, or the environment.

TABLE 12.1

Average Annual Incomes by Level of Education in the United States (Amounts in US dollars)

	No High School Diploma	High School Grad	Some College	Associate Degree	Bachelor Degree	Masters Degree
All	20,241	30,627	32,295	39,771	56,665	73,737
Men	23,036	35,468	39,204	47,572	69,479	90,964
Women	15,514	24,304	25,340	33,432	43,589	58,534

SOURCE: *U.S. Census Bureau, 2012 Statistical Abstract,* Education, Table 232. (census.gov/compendia/statab/2012/tables/1250232).

knowledge or eloquence as a speaker. In such cases, the wealth or material possessions of the powerful and the not-so-powerful may not differ significantly.

Where does power reside in the United States? According to our democratic ideology, power is in the hands of the people. We all exercise our power by voting for our political representatives, who see to it that our will is carried out. Although this is how it works in theory, in real life the picture is quite different. Some social scientists (Hellinger and Judd 1991) have suggested that this ideology is no more than a democratic facade that conceals the fact that the real power resides with an unofficial power elite. As early as the 1950s, C. Wright Mills (1956) insisted that power was concentrated in the hands of a power elite comprising corporate, government, and military leaders.

Since then William Domhoff (2009) has arrived at a similar conclusion. The power elite share many of the same values, belong to the same clubs, sit on the same boards of directors, are graduates of the same schools, and even vacation at the same resorts. They are the owners and managers of major corporations, advisors to governments, and members of commissions and agencies. They give large sums of money to the fine arts, contribute heavily to their favorite political candidates, and are often on a first-name basis with the political establishment. According to Mills and Domhoff, the concentration of real power in the hands of an elite in the United States has remained constant for much of the nation's history.

The third dimension of social stratification, according to Weber's formulation, is *prestige*: the social esteem, respect, or admiration that a society confers on people. Because favorable social evaluation is based on the norms and values of a particular group, sources of prestige vary from one culture to another. For example, among certain traditional Native American groups, warriors on horseback held high prestige; in certain age-graded societies, such as the Samburu of Kenya, old men were accorded the highest prestige; and in the United States, high prestige is closely associated with certain professions.

Research indicates that occupations in the United States carry different levels of prestige and that those rankings remained remarkably stable throughout the twentieth century (Coleman and Rainwater 1978; Hodge, Treiman, and Rossi 1966; Nakao and Treas 1990; National Opinion Research Center 1996). That is, the occupations that ranked high in the 1950s continued to rank high at the end of the twentieth century. Not surprisingly, physicians, corporate presidents, scientists, and top-ranking government officials enjoyed high levels of occupational prestige, whereas garbage collectors, day laborers, and janitors were at the low end of the prestige scale. Essentially, four factors separated the occupations at the top from those at the

bottom during the twentieth century. The occupations at the top end offer higher salaries, require more education, offer greater autonomy (less supervision), and require more abstract thinking and less physical labor.

Since the year 2000, there has been some rearranging of occupational prestige in the United States, according to popular opinion surveys. For example, the Harris Poll conducted in July 2009 (harrisinteractive. com, 2009) reported that firefighters, scientists, doctors, nurses, and teachers are among the highest prestige occupations, whereas stock brokers and real estate brokers rank at the bottom. These new findings should come as no surprise given early-twenty-first-century US history. The incredible selflessness of the New York City firefighters on September 11, 2001 (343 of whom lost their lives trying to rescue people from the World Trade Center), certainly explains why firefighters top the list of high-prestige jobs. It is important to note, however, that firefighters, much like teachers and scientists, are now considered the highest prestige jobs despite the fact that they receive modest financial compensation for their noble (and selfless) labors. The lowest level of occupational prestige, according to recent surveys, now includes Wall Street brokers and real estate brokers, whose selfish behavior is generally considered to have led directly to the recession of 2008, the worst economic downturn since the Great Depression of the 1930s.

We should keep in mind that although wealth, power, and prestige are often interrelated, they can also operate independently. Consider that it is possible to possess both power and wealth while having little prestige, as is the case with leaders of organized crime. Some people, such as classical pianists, may be highly esteemed for their musical virtuosity yet have modest wealth and little power or influence over people. And odd as it may seem to Westerners, people in some societies (such as the Kwakiutl of British Columbia) acquire high prestige by actually destroying or giving away all of their personal possessions (see the discussion of the potlatch in Chapter 8).

Types of Societies

Following the lead of Morton Fried (1967), most anthropologists distinguish three types of societies based on levels of social inequality: egalitarian, rank, and stratified societies. Egalitarian societies have few or no groups that have greater access to wealth, power, or prestige; they are usually found among food collectors, have economies based on reciprocity, and have little or no political role specialization. In rank societies certain groups enjoy higher prestige, even though power and

---

prestige Social honor or respect within a society.

wealth are equally distributed; they are usually found among chiefdoms, have economies based on redistribution, and exhibit limited political role specialization. Stratified societies manifest the greatest degree of social inequality in all three forms of social rewards (wealth, power, and prestige). They are found in industrialized societies, have market economies, and are associated with state systems of government. Rather than thinking of these three types of societies as discrete and mutually exclusive, it is more accurate to view them as points on a continuum, ranging from egalitarian societies (the least amount of social inequality) to stratified societies (the greatest degree of social inequality).

Egalitarian Societies

In *egalitarian societies*, which are located at the low end of the inequality continuum, no individual or group has appreciably more wealth, power, or prestige than any other. Of course, even in the most egalitarian societies, personal differences in certain skills are acknowledged. Some people are more skilled than others at hunting, others may be recognized as particularly adept at crafts, and still others may be well known and respected for their skills at settling disputes. Even though certain individuals in an egalitarian society may be highly esteemed, they are not able to transform their special skills into wealth or power. No matter how much or how little respect an individual in an egalitarian society may have, he or she is neither denied the right to practice a certain profession nor subject to the control of others. Moreover, whatever esteem an individual manages to accrue is not transferable to his or her heirs.

In an egalitarian society, the number of high-status positions for which people must compete is not fixed. According to Fried (1967: 33), "There are as many positions of prestige in any given age-sex grade as there are persons capable of filling them." The esteem gained by being a highly skilled dancer is given to as many individuals in the society as there are good dancers. If fifteen people are highly skilled dancers this year, all fifteen will receive high status. If next year there are twenty-four skilled dancers, all twenty-four will be so recognized. Thus the number of high-status positions in an egalitarian society is constantly changing to reflect the number of qualified candidates. In other words, everyone, depending on her

or his personal skill level, has equal access to positions of esteem and respect.

Egalitarian societies are found most readily among geographically mobile food collectors, such as the Ju/'hoansi of the Kalahari region, the Inuit, and the Hadza of Tanzania (Figure 12.2). There are logical reasons unequal access to wealth, power, and prestige would be discouraged among nomadic foragers. First, the nature of a nomadic existence inhibits the accumulation of large quantities of personal possessions. Second, because foragers do not hold claims to territory, individuals can forage in whatever areas they please. If one person wants to exercise control over others, the others can choose to live in some other territory. Finally, food collectors tend to be egalitarian because sharing maximizes their chances for adaptation. When a hunter kills a large animal, he is unlikely to try to keep the entire carcass for himself, given the lack of refrigeration. Rather it makes much more sense for the hunter to share the meat with the expectation that others will share their kills with him. In fact, foraging societies, with economies based on the principle of generalized reciprocity, place a high value on sharing. Generosity in such societies is expected, and attempts to accumulate possessions, power, or prestige are ridiculed.

Rank Societies

Rank societies have unequal access to prestige and status but not unequal access to wealth and power. In rank societies, there is usually a fixed number of high-status positions, which only certain individuals are able to occupy. Other candidates for these positions are

egalitarian societies Societies that recognize few differences in status, wealth, or power.

rank societies Societies in which people have unequal access to prestige and status but not unequal access to wealth and power.

Martin Harvey/Peter Arnold/Getty Images

FIGURE 12.2 Small-scale foraging societies, such as the Ju/'hoansi of Namibia, tend to be egalitarian.

systematically excluded regardless of their personal skills, wisdom, industriousness, or other personal traits. High-prestige positions such as chief—which are largely hereditary—establish a ranking system that distinguishes among various levels of prestige and esteem. In fact kinship plays an important role in rank societies. Because some clans or lineages may be considered aristocratic, their members qualify for certain titles or high-status positions. Other kin groups are rank ordered according to their genealogical proximity to the aristocratic kin groups. Thus, the number of high-status positions in ranked societies is limited, and the major criterion for allocating such positions is genealogical.

Even though the chiefs in a rank society possess great prestige and privilege, they generally do not accumulate great wealth; their basic standard of living is not noticeably different from that of an ordinary person. Chiefs usually receive gifts of tribute from members of other kin groups, but they never keep them for their personal use. Instead, they give them all away through the process of redistribution (see Chapter 8). In many rank societies, chiefs are considered to own the land but not in the Western sense of the term. The chief certainly has no power to keep anyone from using the land. The chief may control land to the extent that he encourages people not to neglect either the land or their obligation to contribute to the chief's tribute. But the chief has no real power or control over the land. He maintains his privileged position as chief not by virtue of his capacity to impose his will on others but because of his generosity.

Examples of rank societies are found in most areas of the world, but most prominently in Oceania and among Native Americans of the northwest coast of North America. In fact, for reasons that are not fully understood, some strikingly similar cultural traits are found both in parts of Polynesia and among Native Americans residing in a narrow coastal region between northern California and southern Alaska. These cultural similarities are particularly noticeable in the area of status ranking. One such group that exemplifies a rank society is the Nootka of British Columbia (Service 1978). Like a number of ethnic groups in the US Northwest, the Nootka, a hunting-and-fishing society, live in an area so abundant in food resources (such as big game, wild edible plants, waterfowl, and fish) that their standard of living is comparable to societies that practice horticulture and animal husbandry.

Stratified Societies

Unlike rank societies, which are unequal only in terms of prestige, *stratified societies* are characterized by considerable inequality in all forms of social rewards (power, wealth, and prestige). The political, economic, and social inequality in stratified societies is both permanent and formally recognized by the members of the

society. Some people—and entire groups of people—have little or no access to the basic resources of the society. Various groups in stratified societies, then, are noticeably different in social position, wealth, lifestyle, access to power, and standard of living. The unequal access to rewards found in stratified societies is generally inheritable from one generation to the next.

Although distinctions in wealth, power, and prestige began to appear in the early neolithic period (approximately 10,000 years ago), the emergence of truly stratified societies is closely associated with the rise of civilization approximately 5,500 years ago. A basic prerequisite for civilization is a population with a high degree of role specialization. As societies become more specialized, the system of social stratification also becomes more complex. Different occupations or economic interest groups do not have the same access to wealth, power, and prestige but rather are ranked relative to one another. As a general rule, the greater the role specialization in a society, the more complex is its system of stratification.

Class versus Caste

Social scientists generally recognize two different types of stratified societies: those based on class and those based on caste. The key to understanding this fundamental distinction is *social mobility*. In *class* systems, a certain amount of upward and downward social mobility exists. In other words, an individual can change his or her social position dramatically within a lifetime. An individual, through diligence, intelligence, and good luck, could go from rags to riches; conversely, a person born to millionaire parents could wind up as a homeless street person (Newman 1988). *Caste* societies, on the other hand, have little or no social mobility. Membership in a caste is determined by birth and lasts throughout one's lifetime. Whereas members of a class society are able to elevate their social position by marrying into a higher class, caste systems are strictly endogamous (allowing marriages only within one's own caste).

Another important distinction is how statuses (positions) within each type of society are allocated. Class systems are associated with an *achieved status*, whereas

---

stratified societies Societies characterized by considerable inequality in all forms of social rewards—that is, power, wealth, and prestige.

social mobility The ability of people to change their social position within the society.

class A ranked group within a stratified society characterized by achieved status and considerable social mobility.

caste A rigid form of social stratification in which membership is determined by birth and social mobility is nonexistent.

achieved status The status an individual acquires during the course of her or his lifetime.

ascribed status The status a person has by virtue of birth.

TABLE 12.2

US Class Structure

Class	Annual Income	Education	Occupation	Approx. Percentage
Privileged Classes				
Capitalist	$1,000,000 +	Prestige universities	CEOs, investors, heirs	1
Upper middle	$100,000 +	Top colleges/postgraduate	Upper managers, professionals	14
Majority Classes				
Middle	$55,000	High school/some college	Lower managers, teachers, civil servants	30
Working class	$35,000	High school	Clerical, sales, factory	30
Lower Classes				
Working poor	$22,000	Some high school	Service jobs, laborers	13
Underclass	$10,000 or less	Some high school	Unemployed	12

SOURCE: Gilbert, Dennis, *The American Class Structure in an Age of Growing Inequality*, Pine Forge Press (Sage Publications): Thousand Oaks, California, 2011.

caste systems are associated with an *ascribed status*. Achieved statuses are those that the individual chooses or at least has some control over. An achieved status is one that a person has attained as a result of her or his personal effort, such as graduating from college, marrying someone, or securing a particular job. In contrast, a person is born into an ascribed status and has no control over it. Statuses based on such criteria as sex, race, and age are examples of ascribed statuses, which are found mainly in caste societies.

It is important to bear in mind that stratified societies cannot all be divided neatly into either class or caste systems. In general, class systems are open to the extent that they are based on achieved statuses and permit considerable social mobility, and caste systems tend to be closed to the extent that they are based on ascribed statuses and allow little or no social mobility, either up or down. Having made these conceptual distinctions, however, we must also realize that in the real world, class and caste systems overlap. In other words, most stratified societies contain elements of both class and caste. Rather than think in either-or terms, we should think in terms of polarities on the ends of a continuum. There are no societies that have either absolute mobility (perfect class systems) or a total lack of mobility (perfect caste systems). Rather all societies found in the world fall somewhere between these two ideal polarities, depending on the amount of social mobility permitted in each.

Class Societies

Even though the boundaries between social strata in a class society are not rigidly drawn, social inequalities nevertheless exist. A social class is a segment of a population whose members share similar lifestyles and levels of wealth, power, and prestige. The United States is a good example of a class society (see Table 12.2). In some areas of the United States, such as coal-mining towns in Appalachia, there may be only two classes: the haves and the have-nots. More often, however, social scientists have identified a number of social classes: capitalist (upper), upper middle, middle, working, working poor, and underclass (Bensman and Vidich 1987; Gilbert 2011; Sullivan and Thompson 1990; Vanneman and Cannon 1987).

The capitalist class in the United States, comprising approximately 1 percent of the population, consists of old wealth (Carnegies, Rockefellers), corporate executives, and owners of lucrative businesses; their incomes derive largely from returns on assets such as stocks, bonds, securities, and real estate. The ownership of the means of production by the capitalist class affords them the power over jobs for the rest of society. In addition, their control of the media largely shapes the nation's consciousness. Because they are the main source of *soft money* contributions to political campaigns, they exert enormous influence over national politics. Primarily because of the rapid development of the postindustrial economy, the number of people in the upper class has increased in recent decades. Moreover the size of their incomes has grown much faster than for any other class. To illustrate, according to the *Forbes* list of the wealthiest people in the world (see Forbes.com), fourteen of the top twenty-five billionaires on the planet in 2013 are

soft money A form of political contribution not covered by federal regulation, which works to the advantage of wealthy candidates and their benefactors.

from the United States with wealth ranging from $67 to $20 billion dollars.

The upper-middle class, comprising about 14 percent of the US population, is made up of business and professional people who have high incomes and considerable amounts of overall wealth. This is the class that is most shaped by education. Nearly all members of the upper-middle class are college educated, and many have postgraduate degrees. These people are professionals (such as doctors and lawyers), own their own businesses, or manage the corporations owned by members of the capitalist class. This class consists of the working rich, whose incomes are generated by executive salaries or fees rather than from income-producing assets. They have secure economic positions, almost always send their children to college, drive new automobiles, and are likely to be active in civic organizations and local politics.

The middle class, constituting approximately 30 percent of the population, is made up of hardworking people of modest income, such as small entrepreneurs, teachers, nurses, civil servants, and lower-level managers. People in this class make a modest income, enjoy relative security (threatened occasionally by rising taxes and inflation), and have the potential for upward social mobility. Though sometimes indistinguishable from the working class, the lower-middle class generally has slightly higher income and more prestige.

Comprising approximately 30 percent of the population, members of the working class hold occupations that tend to be fairly routine and closely supervised and usually require no more than a high school education (blue-collar and some white-collar jobs). Included in this category are factory workers, sales clerks, construction workers, office workers, and appliance repairpersons. Because of their lack of higher education, members of this group tend to have little social mobility. Vulnerable to downturns in the economy, working-class people are subject to layoffs during recessions and justifiably feel threatened by our increasingly globalized economy, in which many jobs are going to workers abroad. The working class, which has a low rate of political participation, is also most vulnerable to the shift to a postindustrial economy with fewer manufacturing jobs and more high-tech positions requiring higher levels of education.

The working poor, about 13 percent of the population, barely earn a living at unskilled, low-paying, unpleasant, and often temporary jobs with little security and frequently no benefits. They tend to be under-educated, and even though some may have completed high school, others are functionally illiterate. They live from paycheck to paycheck, often depend on food stamps, and have little or no savings as a safety net. Members of the working poor are often just a layoff away from living on the streets or in a homeless shelter. Nevertheless the working poor in the United States, despite their lack of rewards, maintain a strong work ethic (Newman 1999).

The underclass occupies the lowest rung of US society. Some have suggested that the underclass actually represents the people who are beneath the class structure, a type of caste-like group that has little or no chance of ever making it to the next rung of the social ladder. The underclass are unemployed (or severely underemployed), are homeless, and often suffer from substance abuse and in some cases mental illness. They are almost always confined to blighted urban areas plagued by violence, gangs, and drugs.

One of the most visible traits of members of the underclass is homelessness (Figure 12.3). It is generally thought that the rise in homelessness in the

Anton Oparin/shutterstock.com

Auremar/Shutterstock.com

FIGURE 12.3 In stratified societies, different groups, ranging from the homeless to the upper class, have different levels of power, prestige, and wealth. In the United States over the past four decades, the gap has widened between those at the top and those at the bottom.

United States is directly related to a wide range of societal factors, such as drug addiction, crime, alcoholism, and mental illness. However, John Quigley, Steven Raphael, and Eugene Smolensky (2001) have found that homelessness is caused largely by the high price of housing in general and the scarcity of low-income housing in particular. Moreover these researchers found that the incidence of homelessness decreased when there were even just modest reductions in the cost of housing and increased availability of affordable rental properties. With the bursting of the real estate bubble and the dramatic rise in unemployment in the United States starting in 2008, the number of homeless people has grown substantially. Most of the newly homeless people are not chronic members of the underclass, but rather working-class people who have lost their jobs and lost their homes through foreclosure.

Is the class system in the United States changing? If we examine the years since World War II, the relationship among the different classes has gone through two distinct periods. According to Dennis Gilbert (2008), the period from 1945 until 1975 was a time of "shared prosperity" in which class differences were shrinking. Since 1975, however, there has been a marked expansion of class disparities. For example, the official poverty rate plunged during the 1960s, but since 1970, the poverty rate has remained fairly constant even as the size of the overall economy has doubled. Since 1975 incomes have grown slowly or not at all at the lower- and middle-class levels, whereas they have soared at the top. Inequalities of wealth (measured by the concentration of wealth held by the top 1 percent of the population) shrank between 1960 and 1975 from 32 percent to 20 percent. Since the mid-1970s, however, the inequalities have grown steadily to more than 43 percent by 2012. The next 4 percent of the wealthiest Americans control an additional 29 percent. Thus, by 2012, 72 percent of the nation's wealth was controlled by the top 5 percent, whereas the remaining 28 percent was controlled by the bottom 95 percent of the population. Although a disproportionate amount of wealth in the United States has always been in the hands of a relatively small privileged minority, we have not experienced as wide a wealth gap since the Great Depression of the 1930s. (Dunn 2012).

Nowhere was the US class structure more dramatically demonstrated than in the aftermath of Hurricane Katrina in New Orleans in September 2005. Almost all the people stranded for days without food and water in the Superdome and the Convention Center were the city's poor because clearly everyone else had driven their Volvos to higher ground (Figure 12.4). Those images, which horrified the rest of the nation and indeed the

© Associated Press

FIGURE 12.4 Many Hurricane Katrina victims waited for days at the New Orleans Superdome for government help because they were stranded in the flooded city.

world, drove home a long-forgotten truth about life in the United States; that is, substantial pockets of poverty persist despite the nation's unsurpassed affluence. According to the US Census Bureau, the number of people living below the poverty line has continued to increase steadily since the turn of the new millennium.

The growing inequity in earnings is most dramatic at the highest levels. The compensation of CEOs in the United States increased 600 percent between 1980 and 2000, whereas earnings at the middle were rising slowly and those at the bottom were actually shrinking. The statistics on executive compensation over the past four decades are stunning. In 2004, half of the CEOs in the United States earned more than 104 times the pay of the average worker, up from 25 times in 1970. CEO compensation was scaled back during 2008 and 2009 as a result of the worst financial downturn since the Great Depression of the 1930s. However, total compensation packages for CEOs (salaries, bonuses, and stock options) came roaring back in 2010 even though the economy remained weak. In 2010, the median top executive compensation increased 27 percent over the previous year—well on its way to prerecession levels. The total annual compensation in 2010 for the top twenty CEOs in the United States ranged from $84.5 million for number one to $16.8 million for number twenty (Krantz and Hansen 2011).

The growing gap in earnings between workers and CEOs was described in personal terms by Eric Dash (2006: 1) in his account of James P. Smith, who, at age twenty-one, took a job as a meat grinder in 1977 at a ConAgra pepperoni plant in Omaha, Nebraska, for $6.40 per hour. Thirty years later Smith was still working at ConAgra for $13.25 per hour, but his $28,000-per-year salary was not even keeping up with Omaha's relatively low cost of living. Smith worried that after three decades of working, he might have to work indefinitely because his meager savings would be insufficient for retirement. Now compare Smith (the meat grinder) with Bruce Rohde, ConAgra's former chairman and CEO, who stepped down in 2005 (Figure 12.5). During his eight years as head of ConAgra, Rohde earned more than $45 million in salary, bonuses, and stock options. This is generous compensation for a corporate leader who in all eight years missed earnings targets, cut nine thousand jobs, underperformed the competition, and oversaw a 28-percent decline in the company's share price. For this less-than-stellar eight-year performance, Rohde was given an additional $20-million severance package.

Not only has money been concentrated increasingly in the hands of the capitalist class in recent decades, but so has political power. In fact money is intimately interconnected with political power and influence. The largest contributors to political campaigns in the United States are, not surprisingly, the wealthiest. The 2012 presidential election broke the $2 billion milestone, with candidates Barrack Obama and Mitt Romney each raising slightly more than a billion dollars. The greatest number of large campaign donations came from the wealthiest segment of the society, from either their personal or corporate resources. Although there were many million-dollar donations given to help the campaigns of both candidates, the undisputed winner of the campaign "give-a-thon" was Los Vegas casino owner Sheldon Adelson and his wife, who gave the

FIGURE 12.5 Bruce Rohde, former CEO and Chairman of ConAgra Corporation, was rewarded generously for eight years of underperforming on the job. Rohde is one of the winners in the ongoing competition for wealth and social status in the United States, which has witnessed a widening gap between the haves and the have-nots.

Romney campaign and other Republican candidates a total of $95 million during the 2012 election season. And of course, there are no limitations on the amount of their own money candidates can spend on their campaigns. Members of the Senate and House have spent millions of their own fortunes to buy their way into political office. Senator Jay Rockefeller of West Virginia and Mayor Michael Bloomberg of New York City immediately come to mind. In 2000 Wall Street multimillionaire Jon Corzine spent $67 million of his own money on getting elected to the Senate from New Jersey.

The capitalist class has played an increasingly prominent role in the political decision-making process through direct financial contributions (either individually or as representatives of corporations) to political campaigns. But they exert vast influence (well beyond their numbers) by other means as well. First, members of the capitalist class are recruited for top-level positions in the federal government, such as cabinet posts and ambassadorships. Second, the capitalist class exerts untold pressure on all levels of government decision making through corporate lobbying efforts. Third, many policy planning groups (such as the Committee for Economic Development and the Business Council) and private foundations (Rockefeller and Ford) are funded and represented by members of the capitalist class. And finally, virtually all mass media (television, newspapers), which have enormous influence on public opinion and public policy, are owned and controlled by the capitalist class.

Not only is life at the top of the US social hierarchy more opulent, prestigious, and influential, but it is also healthier and lasts longer. Even though medical advances over the past half century have increased longevity throughout the entire society, the benefits have disproportionately gone to the upper echelons— namely, those with the greatest income, education, and connections. Class definitely influences people's diet, the understanding of their illnesses, the support they receive from their families, their relationship with medical providers, and even their capacity to afford health insurance. And the health-longevity gap is widening. According to a recent government study (Pear 2008: 14), in 1980–1982 people in the most affluent group lived 2.8 years longer than those in the poorest group. By 2000 the difference in life expectancies between the top and bottom groups had increased to 4.5 years. Thus, the disparities in wealth between rich and poor in the United States have been paralleled by disparities in health and longevity over the past twenty-five years.

Why has inequality, particularly between the top and the middle strata of our society, grown so precipitously over the past four decades? We must point out that income inequality has occurred during this same period in other Western nations as well, but not as dramatically as it has in the United States. A combination of factors has been at work. First, the change from an industrial

CROSS-CULTURAL MISCUE

Tom Young, an up-and-coming executive for a US electronics company, was sent to Japan to work out the details of a joint venture with a Japanese electronics firm. During the first several weeks, Tom felt that the negotiations were proceeding better than he had expected. He found that he had cordial working relationships with the team of Japanese executives, and they had in fact agreed on the major policies and strategies governing the new joint venture. During the third week of negotiations, Tom was present at a meeting held to review their progress. The meeting was chaired by the president of the Japanese firm, Mr. Hayakawa, a man in his mid-forties, who had recently taken over the presidency from his eighty-two-year-old grandfather. The new president, who had been involved in most of the negotiations during the preceding weeks, seemed to Tom to be one of the strongest advocates of the plan that had been developed to date. Also attending the meeting was Hayakawa's grandfather, the recently retired president. After the plans had been discussed in some detail, the past president proceeded to give a long soliloquy about how some of the features of this plan violated the traditional practices on which the company had been founded. Much to Tom's amazement, Hayakawa did nothing to explain or defend the policies and strategies that they had taken weeks to develop. Feeling frustrated, Tom gave a strongly argued defense of the plan. To Tom's further amazement, no one else in the meeting spoke up. The tension in the air was quite heavy, and the meeting adjourned shortly thereafter. Within days the Japanese firm completely terminated the negotiations on the joint venture. How could you help Tom understand this bewildering situation?

The demise of these joint-venture negotiations cannot be explained by the fact that contemporary Japanese firms are inextricably wedded to traditional practices. Present-day Japanese firms have shown an enormous willingness to adopt innovative policies and strategies, which has contributed to their rapid rise in the world economy. Yet, equally high on the Japanese list of cultural priorities is the value placed on respect for elders and saving face. Even though Hayakawa may have disagreed with his grandfather's position, it would have been totally inappropriate for him to have disagreed with his grandfather in a *public* meeting. The Japanese way would have involved private discussions between Hayakawa and his grandfather to try gently to convince the former president of the need for these innovative policies. Tom's impassioned attempt to change the retired president's mind in the public meeting was seen as a serious breach of etiquette, which caused the old man to lose face.

---

to a postindustrial society created a high demand for people with advanced training and education, most of whom are from the upper classes. At the same time many manufacturing jobs, on which the lower classes depend, have been moving abroad. Second, the influence of labor unions, which traditionally fought for higher wages for US workers, has declined in recent decades. Third, current trends in family life (such as higher divorce rates and more people choosing to remain single) have led to more female-headed households, which tend to have lower family incomes. Fourth, the tendency for US corporations to become leaner and meaner through "downsizing" has had its most negative effects on the lower income groups. Fifth, the gap between the haves and the have-nots widened as a result of the substantial tax cuts during the administrations of Ronald Reagan and George W. Bush, which had the effect of helping the wealthy far more than the rest of the population. Sixth, our nation's broken immigration policy encourages more unskilled foreign workers to enter the country, thereby putting downward pressure on the (already low) wages of the US labor force. And finally, the political system failed to keep the minimum wage ahead of inflation (see Noah 2013).

Our national mythology includes the belief that the United States offers a good deal of social mobility. Although it is possible to cite a number of contemporary Americans who have attained great wealth, power, and prestige from modest beginnings, studies of social class in the United States have shown that most people remain in the class into which they are born and marry within that class as well.

In many cases a child's physical and social environment greatly influences his or her career opportunities and identification with a particular class. To illustrate, the son of a school janitor in Philadelphia living in a lower-class neighborhood will spend his formative years playing in crowded public playgrounds, working at the grocery store after school, and generally hanging out with kids from the neighborhood. The son of a bank president, on the other hand, also living in Philadelphia, will attend a fashionable prep school, take tennis lessons at the country club, and drive his own car. When the two youths finish high school, the janitor's son will probably not continue his education, whereas the banker's son will go off to a good college, perhaps go on to law school, and then land a high-paying job. Even though it is possible that the janitor's son could go to Harvard Law School and become upwardly mobile (or that one of the vastly privileged class could become downwardly mobile), such scenarios are not likely.

Members of the same social class share not only similar economic levels but also similar experiences, educational backgrounds, political views, memberships in organizations, occupations, and values. In addition, studies of social class have shown, not surprisingly, that members of a social class tend to associate more often with one another than with people in other classes. In other words, a person's life chances, though not determined, are very much influenced by social class.

"Education Is the Way out of Poverty!" Easier Said than Done?

As we tried to demonstrate with Table 12.1, there is a close correlation between earned income and level of education attained. Simply put, the longer you stay in school, the more money you will make during your working life. If that is the case, then it would seem to be a no-brainer that the best way to reduce the number of people living below the poverty line would be to provide their children with a good education. But recent research is showing that our educational system—which is designed to eliminate class borders—could be instead fortifying them. We have created many "Opportunity" enrichment programs for children from low income families, but nevertheless evidence shows that the gaps between students from poor and rich families are widening rather than narrowing. This holds true for every measure, including standardized test scores, dropout rates, graduation rates, admission to good colleges, and success in higher education.

To be certain, we can find increasing numbers of financially challenged students who are graduating from high schools at or near the top of their classes. Their academic success in high school qualified them for acceptance to a number of competitive colleges and universities. But often when they make the jump to a good to excellent college, even with generous financial aid, they face a number of obstacles that wealthier students do not have to worry about. For example, unlike their wealthier classmates, high-achieving students from low income families

1. Have not had access to all of the cultural or educational experiences that children of the wealthy take for granted such as family vacations abroad, private lessons in piano, tennis, swimming, and so on, trips to museums and concerts, summer camps, and private tutoring in weak subject areas, to mention just some of the more obvious opportunities for out-of-school learning.

2. Often miss the positive influence of two supportive parents at home who are focused on providing everything their children will need to succeed in school, including serving as pro-active advocates for their children when they need special help (rather than deferring to the judgment of school officials).

3. Attended K–12 public schools, which by and large, are much less likely than private schools to provide enriching educational experiences and the skills necessary for success in higher education and later in life in the world of work.

4. Do have to worry about graduating from an excellent college strapped with tens of thousands of dollars in student loan debt, particularly if they are also expected to help support other family members after graduation.

5. Will generally have to combine her or his full-time college schedule with part-time employment to help finance rapidly rising college expenses.

6. Will be expected to adjust to a different and unfamiliar sociocultural environment, different from the one in which they spent their first eighteen years.

Faced with such daunting challenges, it is little wonder that an increasing number of high-achieving, low-income students have lower graduation rates from good-to-excellent colleges and universities in the United States. The children of wealthier families have always had greater success in higher education, but today the success gap is widening. According to Jason DeParle (2012), in the early 1980s there was a 31 percent difference in the share of poor and wealthy students completing college; by 2012, that percentage difference was 45 percentage points. Thus, in much the same way that wealth inequality has been increasing in the United States in the past thirty years, the rich are having greater success in educating their children than are the poor, thereby further increasing class barriers.

Caste Societies

In contrast to class societies, those that are based on caste rank their members according to birth. Membership in castes is unchangeable, people in different castes are segregated from one another, social mobility is virtually nonexistent, and marriage between members of different castes is strictly prohibited. Castes, which are usually associated with specific occupations, are ranked hierarchically.

Caste societies, wherever they may be found, have certain characteristics in common. First, caste membership is directly related to economic issues such as occupation, workloads, and control of valuable resources. The higher castes have a monopoly on high-status occupations, control the allocation of resources to favor themselves, and avoid engaging in difficult or low-status work. In short, the higher castes have more

resources and do less. Second, members of the same caste share the same social status, largely because of their strong sense of caste identity, residential and social segregation from other castes, and uniformity of lifestyles. Third, caste exclusiveness is further enhanced because each caste has its own set of secret rituals, which tend to intensify group awareness. Fourth, the higher castes are generally most interested in maintaining the caste system for the obvious reason that they benefit from it the most.

Hindu Caste System Caste societies can be found in a number of regions of the world, such as among the Rwandans in Central Africa, but the best-known—and certainly the best-described—example of the caste system is in Hindu India. Hinduism's sacred Sanskrit texts rank all people into four categories, called *varnas*, which are associated with certain occupations. Even though local villagers may not always agree about who belongs to which varna, most people accept the varna categories as fundamentally essential elements of their society.

According to a Hindu myth of origin (see Mandelbaum 1970), the four major varnas originated from the body of primeval man. The highest caste, the Brahmins (priests and scholars), came from his mouth; the Kshatriyas (warriors) emanated from his arms; the Vaishyas (tradesmen) came from his thighs; and the Shudras (cultivators and servants) sprang from his feet. Each of these four castes is hierarchically ranked according to its ritual purity. Below these four castes—and technically outside the caste system—is still another category, called the *Untouchables* or, literally, *outcasts.* The Untouchables, who are confined to the lowest and most menial types of work, such as cleaning latrines or leather-working, are considered so impure that members of the four legitimate castes must avoid all contact with them. Today this lowest caste prefers the term *Dalit*, which means literally the *crushed* or *oppressed* people (Figure 12.6).

Ideally, all of Hindu India is hierarchically ranked according to these four basic castes. In practice, however, each of these four categories is further subdivided and stratified. To add to the complexity of the Indian caste system, the order in which these subcastes are ranked varies from one region to another. These local subgroups, known as *jati*, are local family groups that are strictly endogamous. All members of a jati, who share a common social status, are expected to behave in ways appropriate for that jati. A person's jati commands his or her strongest loyalties, serves as a source of social support, and provides the primary basis for personal identity. Thus, the jati is the important social entity in traditional Hindu society. The members of each jati maintain its corporateness in two ways: first, through egalitarian socializing with members of their own jati; and second, by scrupulously avoiding any type of egalitarian socializing (such as marriage or sharing of food) with members of other jati.

Although the prohibitions against social intercourse among castes are rigidly defined, the amount of interdependence among local castes should not be

FIGURE 12.6 The Dalits of India, such as these street cleaners, engage in only the lowest status jobs.

overlooked. This interdependence is largely economic in nature rather than social. Like any society with a complex economy, India has an elaborate division of labor. In fact one of the basic features of caste in traditional India is that each jati is associated with its own occupation that provides goods or services for the rest of the society. Certain lower-caste jati (such as barbers, potters, and leather workers) provide vital services for the upper castes from which they receive food and animal products. For the economy to work, lower castes sell their services to the upper castes in exchange for goods. Thus, despite the extreme social segregation among the castes in India, there is considerable economic interrelatedness, particularly at the village level.

Even though intercaste mobility has always been limited in India, there are increasing instances in recent years of people moving up the caste ladder. The process, known as *Sanskritization*, involves taking on the behaviors, practices, and values associated with the Brahmin caste, such as being a vegetarian, giving large dowries for daughters, and wearing sacred clothing associated with Brahmins. According to Pauline Kolenda (1978), people accomplish this type of upward

varnas Caste groups in Hindu India that are associated with certain occupations.

Dalit The politically correct term for those formerly called *Untouchables* in India.

jati Local subcastes found in Hindu India that are strictly endogamous.

Sanskritization A form of upward social mobility found in contemporary India whereby people born into lower castes can achieve higher status by taking on some of the behaviors and practices of the highest (Brahmin) caste.

mobility by acquiring considerable wealth and education, migrating to other parts of the country, or becoming political activists. The process of Sanskritization is motivated less by the desire to imitate higher caste values and behavioral patterns than it is an expression of dissatisfaction with the lack of social mobility and socioeconomic deprivations of the caste system.

An important tenet of Hindu religious teachings is reincarnation—the notion that at death a person's soul is reborn in an endless sequence of new forms. The caste into which a person is born is considered to be her or his duty and responsibility for that lifetime. Hindu scripture teaches that the good life involves living according to the prescriptions of the person's caste. Members of higher castes must do everything possible to retain their ritual purity by avoiding any intimate interaction with members of lower castes. Correspondingly, members of lower castes must refrain from polluting higher castes. It is taught that those who violate their caste prescription will come back in a lower caste or, if the transgression is sufficiently serious, in a nonhuman form. Hindu scripture is explicit about the consequences of violating prescribed caste behaviors. For example, the Brahmin who steals the gold of another Brahmin will be reincarnated in the next thousand lives as a snake, a spider, or a lizard. That is a powerful sanction! In other words, people believe that their caste status is determined by how they behaved in former lives and that their present behavior determines their caste status in future lives.

European Gypsies (Roma) Numbering between seven and nine million people, the Roma (gypsies) of present-day Europe are a migratory version of Indian Untouchables. Linguistic and genetic evidence indicates that the Roma originated on the Indian subcontinent about a thousand years ago as low-caste Hindus and subsequently migrated westward, through Persia, into the Balkans, and eventually throughout all of Europe. Wherever they arrived in Europe, they were met with hostility and discrimination. In Romania they were enslaved for nearly five hundred years, whereas elsewhere in Europe they were either expelled or subjected to forced labor. It is estimated that during World War II the Nazis murdered several hundred thousand Roma as part of their deliberate program of genocide. Under the Communist regimes of eastern Europe, Roma experienced serious restrictions of cultural freedom. For example, the Romany language and Romany music were banned from public performance in Bulgaria, and in Czechoslovakia Romany women were sterilized as part of a state policy of ethnic cleansing (Figure 12.7).

Up to the present time, the Roma remain an oppressed underclass, often living in squatter settlements, experiencing high levels of unemployment, and being denied adequate educational opportunities for

FIGURE 12.7 A Roma woman plays the accordion for donations at a public memorial park in Berlin, Germany.

their children. However, in an unusual multinational initiative, twelve central and southeastern European countries with significant Roma populations (Albania, Bosnia and Herzegovina, Bulgaria, Croatia, Czech Republic, Hungary, Macedonia, Montenegro, Romania, Serbia, Slovakia, and Spain) have pledged to close the gap in welfare and living conditions between the Roma and non-Roma populations. Started in 2005, the initiative—called "Decade of Roma Inclusion"—provides state funds to improve housing, employment, health, and education among Roma populations. Although the eight participating governments are appropriating sizable funds to provide more and better social services, reports of systematic discrimination against the Roma are still commonplace. For example, in eastern Slovakia the Roma continue to live in deplorable conditions, with four of every five adults suffering the effects of poverty, unemployment, and alcoholism. Large numbers of Roma children continue to attend schools for the mentally retarded irrespective of their ability level. Moreover residents of one Slovakian town (Ostrovany) have erected a seven-foot-high concrete wall separating their homes from a Roma ghetto (Bilefshy 2010). It will be interesting to see whether a multinational (or regional) approach to eliminating a long-standing underclass of people will be successful. Some skeptics have suggested that it may be easier to eliminate poverty among the Roma than to eliminate the centuries of social exclusion they have had to endure.

Racial and Ethnic Stratification

The discipline of anthropology has as its primary goal to study the extraordinary physical and cultural diversity found among the world's population. This vast physical and cultural diversity is also of great interest to the people themselves because human relationships are often shaped by the differences, either real or imagined, between groups of people. To one degree or another, all societies differentiate among their members, and these differences can become the basis for social inequalities. People are often characterized on the basis of their distinctive physical characteristics or their learned cultural traits. Those sharing similar physical traits are often defined as belonging to the same *race*. Those sharing similar cultural characteristics are said to belong to the same *ethnic group*.

Throughout history, and in many parts of the world, racial and ethnic differences have led to inequality, discrimination, antagonism, and in some cases violence. Over the past decades we have read in the newspaper about racial or ethnic conflict in various parts of the world: racial unrest in South Africa, ethnic cleansing in Bosnia, and terrorist attacks on Palestinians and Jews in Israel. Much closer to home, we have seen racial rioting in Los Angeles, ethnic gang wars in our cities, and racial and ethnic profiling in the aftermath of September 11, 2001. So even in the United States—a country constitutionally and legally committed to social equality—racial and ethnic differences still greatly affect relationships between groups and their relative positions in the social hierarchy.

The terms race and ethnicity are sometimes used synonymously in everyday speech, but to anthropologists they have different meanings. Technically a race is an interbreeding population whose members share a greater number of traits with one another than they do with people outside the group. During the first half of the twentieth century, physical anthropologists devoted

considerable effort to dividing the world's populations into racial categories based on shared physical traits. They carefully measured such traits as hair color and texture, eye color and shape, thickness of lips, breadth of the nose, body stature, and skin color, among others. But when the measuring frenzy was over, what did we really have? Depending on who was doing the categorizing, some racial typologies had hundreds of categories (that is, "races") and others had as few as three (Mongoloid, Caucasoid, and Negroid).

Race, then, is no more than a statistical statement about the occurrence of physical traits. When people who share a large number of biological traits intermarry, it is likely (but by no means certain) that they will have offspring who share those traits. When two blond, blue-eyed Norwegians mate and have children, those children are statistically more likely to look like other Norwegians than like Nigerians. Similarly, when we cross two Chihuahuas, the offspring are more likely to look like Chihuahuas than Great Danes. Based on our knowledge of genetics, we know that there are no pure races because recessive traits are not lost but can reappear in future generations. Because different populations have been interbreeding for thousands of years, a continuum of human physical types has resulted.

The widespread use of DNA evidence has been a major reason for the success of such TV shows as *CSI, CSI: Miami, CSI: NY, Burden of Proof,* and *Bones.* Today, however, DNA testing is also being used as an effective mechanism for teaching university students a central concept about race; that is, racial groups or categories, as we normally define them, are not pure, mutually exclusive biological entities, but rather are arbitrary and socially constructed. In a sociology class on "race and ethnic relations" at Penn State University, students are learning in a personal way that they are not quite who they thought they were (Daly 2005). As part of this course taught by Samuel Richard, students are able to have their DNA analyzed. Most students want to have their DNA tested for a variety of reasons. Some want to be able to prove to themselves that they are 100 percent racially pure; others think it might be cool to find traces of some other racial or biological groups; still others hope to find some unexpected racial footprints so they will be able to shock their parents. One black student from Philadelphia was startled to learn that 52 percent of his DNA was associated with Africans and 48 percent with Europeans. Even though this black student is genetically 48 percent white, he was brought up in a black family and neighborhood, has always identified himself as black, and has no intention of altering that identity. This example is significant because it reminded him, as well as others in the class, that race is not a neat and tidy way of compartmentalizing people into one biological category or another.

A major problem with racial classifications is that the schemes differ depending on the traits on which they are

---

race A subgroup of the human population whose members share a greater number of physical traits with one another than they do with members of other subgroups.

ethnic group A group of people who share many of the same cultural features.

based. For example, it would be possible to categorize all of the world's people based on skin color. But if those same people were categorized according to body stature, many people would be assigned to different categories. Each physical trait is biologically determined by distinct genes that vary *independently of one another*. Therefore, having a particular color of hair in no way determines what your eye color will be. All physical anthropologists who have attempted to classify people according to race have arbitrarily selected the traits they have used. For example, instead of using skin color or hair texture, we could classify people according to their earlobe structure (attached or detached earlobes), which is also a genetically determined physical trait. Although no one ever has, we could divide the world's population into two major races: those with attached earlobes and those with detached earlobes. Then, also quite arbitrarily, we could assert that people with attached earlobes (like your author—Ferraro) are clearly more intelligent than those with detached earlobes. Furthermore we could claim that they have a superior character and are more likely to practice good personal hygiene. We could then insist that we do not want people with detached earlobes living in our neighborhoods, going to our schools, or marrying our daughters. Taking such a position, however, would make as much scientific sense as basing it on any other physical characteristic, such as skin color.

As a scientific concept, then, race is not terribly significant because it gives us little insight into human behavior. Nevertheless, because of the way people interpret physical differences, race is important socially. Race relations and stratification based on race are affected by people's beliefs, not necessarily by scientific facts. Because race is socially constructed, racial definitions vary from group to group. For example, North Americans classify people into discrete racial categories such as Caucasoid (white), Negroid (black), and Mongoloid (yellow). In some states in the United States, a person is defined as black, for legal purposes, if one of his or her great-grandparents is black. Brazilians, on the other hand, have at least seven categories of race, all based on gradations of skin color, hair texture, and facial features (Fish 1995). Because a husband and wife may have children who differ considerably on all of these traits, Brazilians acknowledge that two children having the same biological parents can be classified as racially different. Using the Brazilian criteria for determining race, many US blacks would not be considered black in Brazil. Nevertheless no matter how racial categories are defined, the accompanying beliefs about race are socially constructed and can have real social consequences. All too often in human history, groups have separated themselves according to physical differences. They soon decide that physically different people are inferior and then use that belief to exclude, exploit, or brutalize them.

Whereas race involves physical traits, ethnicity involves cultural traits that are passed on from generation to generation. These cultural traits may include religion, dietary practices, language, humor, clothing, cultural heritage, folklore, national origins, and a shared ancestry and social experience. Members of an ethnic group perceive themselves as sharing these (and perhaps other) cultural characteristics. Moreover ethnic group members have a sense of ethnic identity whereby they define themselves and members of their group as "us" and everyone else as "them."

The European Union (EU), an economic, political, and cultural alliance of most western European nations, is an interesting microcosm of modern ethnicity. Initially formed as a union to promote economic growth for its members, the EU is composed of autonomous nation-states with their own unique cultures, histories, languages, and traditions. People identify with their own ethnicity (e.g. French, Spanish, Italian) rather than seeing themselves as generalized Europeans. To be certain, if an Italian woman was blindfolded and dropped off in any other city in western Europe, she would (1) know she was in Europe and (2) have little difficulty finding a meal or a toilet. But in response to a question about developing a European ethnic identity, one Italian scholar responded, "The people here in Italy know and care nothing about Europe. They hate the people in the next village. Europe is nothing" (Byatt 2002: 48). This opinion speaks volumes about the continued influence of ethnicity and ethnic identity, even in a world that is experiencing rapid globalization.

Ethnic groups are more than mere social entities based on shared cultural origins; rather ethnic groups exist because of their shared social experiences over time. To illustrate, during the first several decades of the twentieth century, hundreds of thousands of Italians immigrated to New York City through Ellis Island. Coming, as they did, from all over Italy, they had identified themselves before leaving Italy with their town, village, or city, and with their extended family networks. On arrival in the new world, however, they shared a number of common experiences, including living in the Lower East Side of Manhattan, reading Italian-language newspapers, competing with other groups for jobs and resources, and buying ricotta cheese by the pound rather than in little eight-ounce plastic containers. These shared *experiences* over time forged a new ethnic identity as Italian Americans, an identity that to some degree still exists today.

In some cases certain groups are both racially and ethnically distinct from their neighbors. For example, some Native Americans, such as the Zuni, have distinctive physical features and identify themselves strongly using their native language, political organizations, family networks, and cultural practices. Other groups, such as Greek Americans, may be physically indistinguishable from the majority but form their own distinctive (and usually exclusive) social clubs and social networks.

Race and Ethnicity in the United States

Because individual states in the United States define race differently, attempting to compare the sizes of different racial groups is an exercise in futility. The task is further complicated by people of mixed race, such as Barack Obama, whose mother was a Caucasian from Kansas and father was Kenyan; or far more complicated situations involving citizens whose four grandparents are Italian, Cherokee, Mexican, and Chinese (Figure 12.8). Because the current practice of US census takers is to allow people with multiple ethnic and racial identities to check more than a single box, it is possible for a single person to be counted as "Causasian," "Native American," "Hispanic," and "Asian." This situation is hardly inconsequential because statistics on race and ethnicity are used for many important purposes, such as assessing disparities in health, employment, education, civil rights protection, and determining which underrepresented minority groups qualify for special consideration for state and federally sponsored programs. Although each ten-year census attempts to measure racial representation in the country, the results should (at best) be taken with a grain

FIGURE 12.8 President Barack Obama is the son of a man from Kenya and a Caucasian woman from the United States. What race is he?

of salt because of the myriad problems of both definition and categorization.

Moreover the categories used in census enumerations have changed over time. For examples, according to Sharon Lee (1993), Native Americans have explicitly included Eskimos (that is, Inuits) in some years but not others; Hindus (a religious category) have been included under the heading of Asians in some years but not others; and not since the 1920 census has the term *mulatto* been included under the general heading of black or African American. The fact that categories of classification keep changing from one census to the next makes the tracking of demographic trends across census periods difficult indeed.

For much of the twentieth century, the United States was described as a large melting pot in which people from many cultural backgrounds merged into a homogeneous US nationality. However this image of mass cultural amalgamation does not match reality. Although significant numbers of individuals have broken out of their ethnic patterns, ethnic groups remain. To illustrate, large numbers of Asian Americans (Chinese, Japanese, Vietnamese) live in California; Latinos in Miami, Los Angeles, Chicago, and New York; Arabic-speaking peoples in Detroit; Amish in Pennsylvania and Indiana; and hundreds of different Native American groups throughout North America. In fact the United States has experienced a revival of ethnic consciousness in recent decades, particularly in urban areas. We often hear about ethnic neighborhoods, ethnic foods, and various ethnic studies programs at universities. Thus, the notion of the melting pot appears to be more of a metaphor than a reality. Perhaps we should think of contemporary US society less as a melting pot and more as a salad bowl, in which the individual ethnic groups are mixed together but retain their distinctiveness and identity.

This is not to say, however, that North Americans of mixed race do not often lose their ethnic identity after several generations. To ensure that their children do not lose their cultural identity, some foreign-born North Americans are encouraging their children to participate in cultural study tours of their countries of origin. To illustrate, the Expatriate Youth Summer Formosa Study Tour, subsidized partially by the Taiwanese government, is designed to expose Taiwanese Americans to their Chinese language and culture. But, like cultural study tours sponsored by other ethnic groups, there is an added bonus for parents who wish to preserve their ethnic identity: Many of the young Taiwanese American men and women find romance, and wind up marrying, their fellow tour participants. In fact, according to Francesca Segre (2008: 14), the study tour to Formosa (which has been in existence for forty years) has been nicknamed the "Love Boat." Taiwanese American parents are well aware that the number of Asian American women who marry Asian men dropped from 59 percent in 1994 to 37 percent in 2008. Thus, these Taiwanese American parents are not adverse to engaging in a little indirect matchmaking by encouraging their children to take a ride on the Love Boat.

Not only can ethnic groups maintain their identity within a pluralistic society, but the ethnic landscape is also constantly rearranging itself. New York City, over the past century, reflects this changing ethnic mosaic. The unified ethnic communities of Chinatown, Little Italy, and Germantown (the East 80s) that gave New York City much of its character in the early 1900s, although still in existence, are much less monolithic today. In fact, one of the longest standing ethnic neighborhoods in New York City, Little Italy, is today mostly a memory rather than the functional Italian American neighborhood it once was. In 1950 about half of the 10,000 residents of Little Italy actually identified themselves on the census roles as Italian in origin. By 2010 the proportion of Italian Americans in the same twenty-four-square block area was a mere 5 percent. To be certain, there are still some of the best Italian restaurants and specialty food stores in Little Italy, but most of the residents have long since migrated to other parts of the city or the suburbs of Long Island and New Jersey. As a vivid reminder of how ethnic neighborhoods change over time, a 2009 population survey identified 51 percent of the residents living in Little Italy as "foreign born," with nine out of ten having been born in *Asia* and not a single person having been born in Italy (Roberts 2011).

According to a report titled "The Newest New Yorker 2000" (New York City Department of City Planning 2000), there were seventeen distinct neighborhoods in the city that have a majority of foreign residents. In fact, between the 1990 and 2000 censuses, the number of foreign-born residents in the five boroughs of New York City increased from 2.1 million to 2.9 million, or 38 percent. Unlike the ethnic neighborhoods of the preceding century, those of the twenty-first century are much more multicultural. To illustrate, in the Elmhurst section of Queens it is possible to see a Korean woman having her hair styled by either a Mexican or Jewish Russian hair stylist in the Bollywood Beauty Salon, which is owned by an Indian Muslim. Even the Bensonhurst section of Brooklyn (an Italian American neighborhood, which was the "screen" home of Tony Manero, aka John Travolta, from the 1977 film Saturday Night Fever) is now composed of more than seventy-eight thousand Chinese immigrants as well as sizable Russian and Ukrainian populations (Berger 2005).

At the start of the twenty-first century, the fastest growing ethnic category in the United States is really not an ethnic group at all. Referred to by the catchall term *Hispanics* by the US Census Bureau, this rapidly growing segment of the US population is composed of a number of different subcultural groups that share

CROSS-CULTURAL MISCUE

❀ Several years ago while walking to class with an armload of books, one of your textbook authors, Gary Ferraro, met a group of five students who were also on their way to my class. Four of the students were local, born and raised in North Carolina, whereas the fifth was a foreign student from Nigeria. On meeting, we all greeted one another and proceeded to walk together to class. Almost immediately the Nigerian student turned to me and asked if he could carry my load of books. I refused, but because the Nigerian young man insisted, I relented. As soon as I handed over the books, I noticed that the Nigerian student was receiving some "funny looks" from the North Carolina students. It became immediately apparent to me that we were witnessing a classic example of a cross-cultural misunderstanding.

When we arrived in class, I decided to see if this incident could provide us with some insight into the nature of cross-cultural miscommunication. After describing the incident to the class, I asked the four students from North Carolina to share with us what was behind those negative "nonverbal" looks they were giving their classmate from Nigeria when he took my load of books. As predicted, all four of the students thought that the Nigerian had offered to carry my books in an effort to curry favor with the professor and perhaps get a higher grade in the course than he might deserve. The four US students were clearly put off by what they considered to be a blatant attempt to "suck up" to the professor.

Hearing this explanation, the Nigerian student was shocked that his gesture was so thoroughly misunderstood. He then explained that he offered to carry my books out of a deep sense of respect for my high status as a college professor. Professors in Nigeria enjoy much higher social status than do their counterparts in the United States. It would be considered demeaning for a Nigerian professor to engage in any form of manual labor, including carrying a heavy load of books. The somewhat startled Nigerian student went on to say that he offered to carry my books so I would not "lose face" by engaging in physical labor. Clearly the status system in Nigeria is appreciably different from that found in the United States.

a common language. Some have lived in the United States for generations, but the majority has immigrated from Central and South America more recently. Coming from more than twenty different countries, many prefer to be identified by their former nationality (e.g. Cubans, Mexicans, Guatemalans) rather than as Hispanics. Others prefer the term *Latino*, which we will use to refer to this large and complex group.

However we choose to classify them, collectively they are changing the face of the country and having an enormous impact on the nation's economy, politics, entertainment, and educational systems. The Latino population during the 1990s grew approximately 58 percent (from 22.3 million to 35.3 million) as compared to 13 percent for the overall population. From 2000 to 2010 grew another 43 percent to a total of 50.5 million, as compared to 16 percent for the overall population (US Census 2011). And during the same intercensus period, according to the *Statistical Abstract of the United States* (2006), Latinos replaced African Americans as the largest minority group. With these rates of growth, Latinos will represent one-quarter of the total US population by 2050.

Not only do they have numbers, but many Latinos are also making their mark on all aspects of US culture. Young Americans of all types are dancing to salsa music; listening to recordings Marc Anthony, Enrique Iglesias, and Christina Aguilera; and cheering for their favorite major league baseball players with names such as Martinez, Palmeiro, and Rodriguez. Yet not everyone in the United States has been willing to embrace this rapidly growing Latino presence. As part of the debate on immigration reform in the United States, many local communities are in favor of building a wall on the US-Mexican border, denying the children of undocumented laborers the right to attend school, and enacting strong measures for deporting illegal immigrants.

This backlash is based on myths about the Hispanic population. First, because of the widespread use of Spanish on signs in cities such as Los Angeles and Miami, many people assume that Latinos do not speak English or have no desire to learn it. But the rate of learning English for Latinos is approximately the same as for other immigrant groups, and in fact one-third of Latinos living in Los Angeles speak only English. Second, Latinos are sometimes viewed (erroneously) as not fully participating in the economy. However, Mexicans and Central Americans have a labor force participation rate of 62 percent, which exceeds the Anglo rate and far exceeds that of African Americans. Latinos generally are found doing the jobs that other Americans refuse to do: harvesting crops, making beds, landscaping, and doing construction-related work such as house framing, roofing, and masonry. They have the diligence and enterprise, coupled with strong family ties, that characterized the Irish, Italians, and Poles during the early 1900s. And third, many mainstream Americans view recent migrants as "short-timers" who are interested only in making enough money to return home. But when asked in a national survey if they planned to stay permanently in the United States, more than 90 percent of the legal immigrants said yes (Pachon 1998). To be certain, some immigrants do return home, and others continue to send sizable portions of their income to relatives back home. But, like their European counterparts a century previous, most Latinos plant their roots and commit to becoming citizens.

Race and Intelligence

For much of the history of the United States, racial ideology has been used to justify the privileged positions of Caucasians (those of European ancestry) compared to African Americans and Native Americans. The concept of race, in other words, is used to suggest that non-Caucasians are biologically inferior to Caucasians in terms of ability, character, and particularly intelligence. To be certain, the United States is not alone in using racial ideology to justify exploiting minorities and indigenous populations. We only need to cite Adolf Hitler's notion of the "Aryan Race," South Africa's "Apartheid," or nineteenth-century England's "White Man's Burden" to remind us that exploitation and subjugation based on race are worldwide phenomena. Yet, despite the considerable progress made in race relations in the United States over the past sixty years, substantial numbers of people still believe in the strong correlation between race and intelligence.

Before the 1920s it was generally thought, even among those in the scientific community, that intelligence (innate, God-given mental ability) varied according to race. Immediately following World War I (after 1918), there was a chance for researchers to test the relationship between race and intelligence. As a way of determining who would be selected as officers in the military during the war, all inductees into the US armed forces were given an "intelligence test" based on a format developed in France to diagnose learning problems in French schools. Because millions of test scores were available after the war, it seemed a relatively easy task to compare large numbers of blacks and whites to determine which racial group, in the aggregate, scored higher on these standardized tests. And as conventional wisdom would have predicted, white soldiers scored more than ten percentage points higher than black soldiers. Given the enormous sample size of this study, these data appeared to confirm the intellectual inferiority of black Americans. However, when these data were compared on two variables rather than one (geographic location and race), the results pointed to the exact opposite conclusion. Researchers found that blacks from northern states (which spent much more money on education per student than southern states) scored on average considerably higher than whites from southern states. These findings would suggest that what was being measured on these so-called "intelligence tests" was not some genetically based mental ability or abilities, but rather how well your local schools prepared you to answer the questions on the test. These tests were really achievement tests rather than tests of one's God-given, unchangeable, biologically derived brain force.

Despite these startling findings from the 1920s, intelligence tests have been used routinely in schools for nearly a century to determine which students receive the most enriching education (with the most demanding courses and the most qualified and highly motivated teachers) and which do not. Many professional educators and elected officials still believe that scores on intelligence tests predict success in school and success in adult life. As a result, they claim that schools should reserve the best resources, courses, and teachers for high test performers, because those with low test scores, and with less innate capacity to learn, have much less of a chance to succeed.

The problem with this reasoning, however, is it violates a basic scientific tenet—that is, confusing correlation with causation. It certainly is true that people who score high on intelligence tests also (1) do better in school, (2) are more likely to attend college, and (3) obtain jobs with higher pay in adulthood. This statement makes the correlation between intelligence test scores and these other three variables (that is, all four variables vary together). But one cannot logically conclude from this correlation that these three variables are caused by intelligence score. For those who believe (erroneously) that intelligence tests actually measure a genetically based and immutable intelligence, there is no reason to expect that low test performers will ever be able to boost their achievement in school and beyond.

But after nearly a century of administering intelligence tests to K–12 students in the United States, most researchers do not put much stock in intelligence tests as measures of some innate level of genetic intelligence. Intelligence tests are, however, accurate measures of how well an individual has mastered his or her mainstream cultural knowledge, or at least the cultural knowledge deemed important by those middle- and upper-middle-class psychologists who construct the test questions. Middle- and upper-class children, in other words, who share a cultural background with the authors of the tests, are likely to achieve higher scores than children who do not. To illustrate, an intelligence test question for young children may ask: "What color is a banana: (a) blue, (b) yellow, (c) pink, or (d) brown?" The correct answer seems painfully obvious. "Yellow" would be the correct answer—provided the student is from an upper- or middle-class family. The only bananas they have ever seen are yellow with a blue Chiquita sticker. But if the student comes from a family living below the poverty line, the only bananas he or she would have ever seen would have been brown because they were half rotten by the time they came home from the grocery store. The result of including such a culture-bound question on the test is that the lower-class child loses several points of intelligence and his wealthier classmate gains several points. Yet this is hardly a measure of innate brain power. Rather it simply reflects that these two children learned different cultural content, even though they could have learned it with relatively equal efficiency.

Forms of Intergroup Relations

Some racial and ethnic groups live together in peace and with a high degree of social equality. In most situations, however, racial and ethnic groups tend to experience varying levels of conflict and inequality. How racial and ethnic groups relate to one another can be viewed as a continuum ranging from cooperation to outright hostility. George Simpson and J. Milton Yinger (1985) identified six major forms of interracial and interethnic relations, arranged from most humane to least humane.

1. Pluralism. In this situation two or more groups live in harmony with one another while each retains its own ethnic heritage, pride, and identity. Swiss society—composed of Germans, Swiss Germans, French, and Italians living together peacefully, if not always amicably—is a good example of pluralism.

2. Assimilation. *Assimilation* occurs when a racial or ethnic minority is absorbed into the wider society. The many Asian and Pacific ethnic groups that have peacefully and voluntarily assimilated into Hawaiian society over the past several centuries are an example.

3. Legal protection of minorities. In societies where racial and ethnic groups are hostile toward one another, the government may step in to legally protect the minority group. In Great Britain the Race Relations Act makes it a criminal offense for anyone to express publicly any sentiments that might lead to racial or ethnic hostility. In the United States, three constitutional amendments (the thirteenth, fourteenth, and fifteenth), several civil rights laws, and a number of executive directives have provided legislative and administrative protection to minorities over the past decades.

4. Population transfer. One solution to intergroup conflict is *population transfer*, which involves the physical removal of a minority group to another location. The forced relocation of sixteen thousand Cherokee Indians from North Carolina to Oklahoma in 1838 is a case in point. A more recent example from the United States, though a temporary situation, was the forced relocation of thousands of Japanese Americans into internment camps during World War II. Unfortunately,

---

assimilation The process of the wider society absorbing a racial or ethnic group.

population transfer The physical relocation of a minority group from one area to another.

FIGURE 12.9 Don Cheadle starred in the movie *Hotel Rwanda*, the true-life story of Paul Rusesabagina, a hotel manager who housed more than a thousand Tutsi refugees during their struggle against genocide by the Hutu militia in Rwanda.

this particular form of intergroup relationship has been played out in many different places in the world in recent years. For example, large numbers of ethnic Tutsi from Rwanda fled to Zaire, Tanzania, and Uganda to avoid persecution by the majority Hutu government (Figure 12.9). Often these population transfers cause enormous hardships both for those being moved and for the local people into whose territories they are arriving.

5. Long-term subjugation. In some parts of the world, racial and ethnic minorities have been politically, economically, and socially repressed for indefinite periods of time. Until the changes in the mid-1990s, the repression of blacks under the apartheid system in the Republic of South Africa was an example of the long-term institutionalized (legal) repression of one ethnic and racial group by another. Separate and unequal facilities (schools, restrooms, housing) and strict legalized segregation were government policy in South Africa for much of the twentieth century.

6. Genocide. Sometimes the symbols of race and ethnicity can be so powerful that they cause people to engage in *genocide*: mass annihilation of groups of people. The most notorious example, of course, is Hitler, who during World War II sent more than

six million people (Jews, gypsies, Slavs, homosexuals, and others he considered to be subhuman) to be killed in death camps. More recently, there have been many other examples of genocide from around the world that, though involving fewer deaths, are just as inhumane. To illustrate, Serbian forces under the leadership of President Slobodan Milosevic engaged in what has been euphemistically called "ethnic cleansing," whereby Muslims and Croats were murdered by the thousands. In 1994, in a purposeful attempt at genocide, the Hutu extremists in Rwanda massacred an estimated million Tutsi (Figure 12.9). And, for much of the twenty-first century, hundreds of thousands of people in Darfur have been massacred by the Sudanese government while world leaders debate whether anything should be done because they cannot agree on the meaning of *genocide*. Although widely condemned by most people in the world, genocide is still used by some groups as a way to gain political advantage. It is important to note that these ways of classifying racial and ethnic relations are not mutually exclusive. More than one classification can exist in a society at the same time.

Theories of Stratification

The unequal distribution of wealth, power, and prestige appears to be a fundamental characteristic of most societies, particularly those with complex, highly differentiated economies. Some modern societies—such as the former Soviet Union, the People's Republic of China, and Albania—have attempted (in the past) to become classless by eliminating all vestiges of inequality. But even in these societies, high-ranking government officials have been far more generously rewarded than the workers. The basic question is: Why is inequality a nearly universal trait of social life? The debate among social scientists, which at times has been heated, revolves around two conflicting positions that are based on different philosophical assumptions and have distinct political implications. The more conservative position, the *functional theory*, holds that social stratification exists because it contributes to the overall well-being of a society. The more liberal *conflict theory* argues that society is always changing and in conflict because individuals in the upper stratum use their wealth, power, and prestige to exploit those below them.

The Functionalist Interpretation

By stressing the integrative nature of social systems, functional anthropologists argue that stratification exists because it benefits the society. According to Kingsley Davis and Wilbert Moore (1945), complex

---

genocide The systematic annihilation of entire cultures or racial groups.

functional theory A theory of social stratification that holds that social inequality exists because it is necessary for the maintenance of society.

conflict theory A theory of social stratification that explains social inequality as the result of benefits derived by the upper classes using their power and privilege to exploit those below them.

Diabetes among Mexican Americans

It has been found that noninsulin-dependent diabetes mellitus (NIDDM), a serious health problem in the United States, is now approaching epidemic proportions. According to projections by the Centers for Disease Control and Prevention, one-third of all children born in 2000 are expected to become diabetic in their lifetime. The prediction for Latino children of the same age is even bleaker: one in two. Medical researchers have found that Mexican Americans living in the southwestern United States are two to three times more likely to suffer from diabetes than are non-Hispanic whites. Factors accounting for this higher incidence among Mexican Americans include a genetic predisposition, culture, geography, and a number of variables associated with low socioeconomic status (such as income, access to health facilities, and literacy).

Diabetes is not curable at the present time; it must be managed over the course of the patient's lifetime. To manage diabetes, patients need to take medication in the proper doses, exercise regularly, and adhere to a healthy diet. A major problem in the treatment of NIDDM is that patients often fail to follow through on the recommended treatment behaviors. Noncompliance with prescribed treatment is particularly high among Mexican Americans.

Medical anthropologist Linda Hunt, along with her colleagues Jacqueline Pugh and Miguel Valenzuela, wanted to know more about the factors influencing self-care among Mexican American patients with NIDDM, so they could develop recommendations to improve intervention strategies. Hunt and her colleagues (1995) conducted open-ended interviews with fifty-one Mexican American patients with NIDDM in San Antonio and Laredo, Texas. Their findings showed that none of the patients in the sample followed the recommended treatment exactly. However, it was not because of disinterest or ignorance. Rather they were adapting their self-care behavior to the social realities of their everyday lives, making choices based on two important sociocultural factors: (1) their limited financial resources and (2) their desire to conduct "normal" social relationships. Let us look at each of these factors.

Because all interviewees were low-income patients, their diabetes imposed hardships on them. Many felt too sick to work, thereby reducing their income; the cost of treatment, despite the clinics' sliding fee scales, was a major financial burden; and the cost of changing their diets usually involved substituting more expensive foods (such as fresh fruits and vegetables) for the things that they normally ate. Because of their limited finances, patients would conserve resources not by discontinuing a certain treatment (such as taking medication or testing for blood sugar level) but rather by doing it less often than prescribed.

The second factor that influenced decisions about self-care was a desire on the part of both men and women to "feel normal" by continuing in the same roles they had before they developed diabetes. Because many women play the role of family caregiver, those who have sick relatives at home find it impossible to get out of the house to get the proper exercise. Moreover female patients with diabetes find it difficult to cook food for

their families that they themselves are not allowed to eat. Men find it particularly difficult to change their eating habits because they want to maintain their masculine image, to be able to make their own decisions about what to eat and drink, and to participate in social events such as parties or watching football, which often involve drinking alcohol. Thus, for both men and women, altering one's usual roles and behavior was seen as interfering with a normal social life.

Understanding the social and cultural realities of Mexican Americans, the researchers could recommend improved intervention strategies. Rather than blaming the patients for failed treatments, the researchers appreciated the patients' limited finances and were able to come up with some creative solutions. It was possible to cut the cost of self-treatment without sacrificing quality. For example, Hunt and her colleagues suggested cost-cutting strategies such as establishing safe procedures for reusing syringes, using phone follow-up to replace some of the clinic visits, and formulating ways of reducing the cost of the foods needed for a healthy diet. Other recommendations took into account the need of patients to maintain normal social relationships. To illustrate, people who feel pressure to eat and drink inappropriate things at social events need culturally acceptable strategies for turning down food or decreasing the amount they eat. In some cases the solution was as simple as getting people to use different language when describing food. As Hunt and her colleagues suggested, "the concept of a 'diabetic diet' could be replaced by pointing out that it is really just a 'healthy diet' for everyone."

Hunt's research suggests that clinicians, particularly when working with culturally different patients, need to understand why people make certain choices concerning their self-care treatment. Rather than assuming that ignorance or indifference is the cause of poor outcomes, clinicians need to explore what patients are doing and why they are doing it. Only by entering into a continuing dialogue with culturally different patients can clinicians help them make the most medically appropriate choices for managing their illness.

Questions for Further Thought

1. Why did any of the Mexican American patients in Hunt's study not strictly follow the prescribed self-care behaviors?

2. Can you think of additional reasons it might be more difficult for low-income Mexican Americans to get regular exercise than it would be for upper-middle-class people living in the suburbs?

3. From what you know about proper self-care behavior for diabetes, can you identify other ethnic groups in your area of the country that would have similar difficulties adhering to prescribed forms of self-care?

societies, if they are to survive, depend on the performance of a wide variety of jobs, some of which are more important than others because they require specialized education, talent, and hard work. If people are to make the sacrifices necessary to perform these vital jobs, they must be adequately rewarded. For example, because the skills of a physician are in greater demand by our society than are those of a fast-food restaurant employee, the rewards (money and prestige) are much greater for the physician. Functionalists argue that these differential rewards are necessary if societies are to recruit the best trained and most highly skilled people for these highly valued positions. If physicians and fast-food workers received the same pay and social status, few people would opt to become physicians. Thus, according to the functionalist interpretation, social stratification is necessary or functional for the society because it serves as a mechanism for allocating rewards and motivating the best people to fill the key jobs in the society.

Although the functionalist view seems plausible, it has weaknesses. First, some critics of the functionalist position point out that stratified societies do not always give the greatest rewards to those who fill the most vital positions. Rock singers, baseball players, and movie stars often make many times more money than teachers, pediatricians, and US Supreme Court justices. Second, the functionalists do not recognize the barriers that stratification systems put in the way of certain segments of the society, such as members of low-prestige and low-power groups. Ethnic and racial minorities, women, and the poor do not always have equal opportunities to compete because they are too poor or have the wrong accent, skin color, or gender. Third, the functionalist position tends to make a fundamentally ethnocentric assumption. That is, the functionalists assume that people in all societies are motivated by the desire to maximize their wealth, power, and prestige. In actual fact, however, a number of societies emphasize the equitable distribution of social rewards rather than rewarding individuals for amassing as much as possible for themselves.

The Conflict Theory Interpretation

Whereas the functionalist view starts with the assumption of social order, stability, and integration, conflict theorists assume that the natural tendency of all societies is toward change and conflict. According to this theory, stratification exists because the people who occupy the upper levels of the hierarchy are willing and able to use their wealth, power, and prestige to exploit those below them. The upper strata maintain their dominance through the use of force or the threat of force and by convincing the oppressed of the value of continuing the system. Thus, those at the top use their wealth, power, and prestige to maintain—and perhaps even strengthen—their privileged position.

This conflict theory of social stratification is derived largely from the late-nineteenth-century writings of Karl Marx, who, unlike the functionalists, did not view stratification systems as either desirable or inevitable. Believing that economic forces are the main factors that shape a society, Marx (1909) viewed history as a constant class struggle between the haves and the have-nots. Writing during the latter stages of the industrial revolution in Europe, Marx saw the classic struggle occurring between the *bourgeoisie* (those who owned the means of production) and the *proletariat* (the working class who exchanged their labor for wages).

Because they control the means of production, the small capitalist class exerts significant influence over the larger working class. By controlling such institutions as schools, factories, government, and the media, the bourgeoisie can convince the workers that the existing distribution of power and wealth (that is, the status quo) is preferable and that anyone can be successful if only he or she works hard enough. Thus, according to the classic Marxist view, the capitalists create a false consciousness among the workers by leading them to believe that if they are not successful, it is because they have not worked hard enough rather than because their opportunities for advancement were blocked by the powerful upper class.

As long as the workers accept this ideology legitimizing the status quo, the inequities of the stratification system will continue to exist. Believing that class conflict is inevitable, Marx predicted that eventually the proletariat would recognize both the extent of its own exploitation and its collective power to change it. When the workers develop a class consciousness, he asserted, they will revolt against the existing social order, replace capitalism with communism, and eliminate scarcity, social classes, and inequality.

Functionalists versus Conflict Theorists

Functionalists and conflict theorists—with their radically different interpretations of social inequality—have been locking horns for years. Functionalists hold that systems of stratification exist and are necessary because they benefit the societies of which they are a part. Conflict theorists, on the other hand, claim that

---

bourgeoisie Karl Marx's term for those who own the means of production.

proletariat The term used in the conflict theory of social stratification to describe the working class who exchange their labor for wages.

systems of stratification exist because they help the people at the top (that is, the wealthy and powerful) maintain their privileged position. The functionalist position emphasizes the positive benefits of social stratification for the total society. Conflict theorists draw our attention to negative aspects such as the unjust nature of stratification systems and how that inherent unfairness can lead to rebellions, revolts, and high crime rates.

Although there is truth in both of these interpretations, neither theory can be used exclusively to explain the existence of all types of stratification systems. Functionalists are correct to point out that open class systems, for example, are integrative to the extent that they promote constructive endeavor that is beneficial to the society as a whole. Yet, once established, these class systems often become self-perpetuating, with those at the top striving to maintain their superior positions at the expense of the lower classes. At the same time, the underclasses—through political mobilization, revitalization movements, and even violent revolutions—seek to free themselves from deprivation and exploitation. In short, functional integration is real, but so is conflict.

Not only do the functionalist and conflict theories represent two contrasting interpretations of social inequality, but they also have radically different policy implications for modern society. The functionalist view implies that social stratification systems should be maintained because the best-qualified people, through the competitive process, will be motivated to fill the top positions. In contrast, conflict theory implies that social inequality should be minimized or eliminated because many people in the lower strata never have a chance to develop their full potential. Thus, the functionalist position would want the government to take no action (such as welfare programs or a progressive income tax) that would redistribute wealth, power, or prestige. Conflict theorists would call for exactly the opposite course of action, arguing that eliminating barriers to social mobility would unleash the hidden brilliance of those currently living in the underclasses.

Global Stratification

This chapter has looked at social stratification—that is, how societies are made up of different groups that are ranked relative to one another in terms of wealth, power, and prestige. Not only are people stratified relative to one another within a society, but societies (nation-states) are also stratified relative to one another. In much the same way that we can identify upper-, middle-, and lower-class people within a society, it is also possible today to speak of wealthy and powerful countries and poor and weak countries within the

TABLE 12.3

Per Capital GNI (Reported in 2013, Based on 2011 data)

Ten Richest Nations	Per Capita GNI
Norway	$85,380
Luxembourg	$79,510
Switzerland	$70,350
Denmark	$58,980
Sweden	$49,930
Netherlands	$49,720
Finland	$47,170
United States	$47,140
Austria	$47,710
Belgium	$45,420
Ten Poorest Nations	
Mozambique	$920
Malawi	$850
Sierra Leone	$830
Togo	$790
Central African Republic	$760
Niger	$700
Eritrea	$540
Burundi	$390
Liberia	$330
Congo, Democratic Republic	$310

SOURCE: *World Bank Atlas* (www.siteresources.worldbank.org/ DATASTATISTICS/Resources/GNIPC.pdf).

global system. If the world was not so intimately interconnected (and becoming more so with each passing year), we would be living in a world comprising many countries with simply different levels of wealth and power. But as we have shown in preceding chapters, the nations of the world, however different they may be, are not isolated and insulated from one another. Rather the decisions made in New York or Chicago today are having real effects, both positive and negative, on the status and personal wealth of people in Bangladesh.

Perhaps the most concrete measure of global stratification is based on differential levels of wealth. One of the more common ways of measuring national wealth is by using the *per capita gross national income* (GNI) index (see Table 12.3). This measure is calculated by

---

per capita gross national income A commonly used index of relative wealth among nations calculated by adding the output of goods and services in a country to the incomes of residents and dividing by the total population.

FIGURE 12.10 The average income of people in Norway is roughly 219 times greater than the income of this farmer working on a coffee plantation in Burundi.

adding the output of goods and services in a country to the incomes of residents and dividing by the total population. Of the more than two hundred nation-states in the world today, half have per capita GNI of less than $2,500. The United States has a per capita GNI of more than $47,140, whereas the Democratic Republic of the Congo has a per capita GNI of $310 (Figure 12.10). Thus, the average US citizen earns roughly 152 times more than the average citizen of the Democratic Republic of the Congo. The United States has a per capita GNI of more than $47,000, whereas Liberia has a per capita GNI of $330. Thus, the average US citizen earns roughly 143 times more than the average citizen of Burundi. Looked at somewhat differently, the average US worker in a regulated textile factory earns more than $9.00 per hour as compared to $0.31 in Bangladesh, $0.34 in Indonesia, and $0.76 in Nicaragua. Consequently, factory (sweatshop) workers in poor countries (who may be eleven years old and earning less than $2.00 per day) are working so that people in North America can jog in Nike running shoes and wear the latest fashions from The Gap, Banana Republic, or Old Navy.

These enormous inequities in wealth found throughout the world have important social consequences. First, poor countries have the highest birthrates and the lowest life expectancies. Women in poor countries on average have five children during their lifetime as compared to only two children for women in wealthy nations. With high rates of fertility, the populations of poor countries are growing more rapidly than those of wealthy countries, have higher proportions of young children, and have relatively fewer adults to provide for them. Second, in terms of health, poorer countries have higher infant mortality, more children born underweight, and a lower life expectancy. Whereas virtually 100 percent of people in Switzerland and Luxembourg have access to safe drinking water and functioning sewage systems, only about one in ten Afghans do. And third, wealthy countries have near universal education and most adults are functionally literate, but this is not the case in the poorer countries. Thus, we can see the profound differences (in terms of mortality, health, sanitation, education, and population size) between the rich countries and the poor countries within the global system of the twenty-first century.

Summary

1. Social ranking is an important feature found to one degree or another in all societies. The degree to which societies distribute wealth, power, and prestige on an equitable basis can be used to distinguish among three different types of societies: egalitarian, rank, and stratified.

2. Egalitarian societies are unstratified in that they allocate wealth, power, and prestige fairly equally. In rank societies, which are partially stratified, people have equal access to power and wealth but not to prestige. The most completely stratified societies are those based on classes or castes and that have unequal access to wealth, power, and prestige.

3. Stratified societies, which are associated with the rise of civilization, range from open class societies, which permit high social mobility, to more rigid caste societies, which allow for little or no social mobility. Class societies are associated with achieved status—positions that the individual can choose or at least have some control over. Caste societies, on the other hand, are based on ascribed statuses into which one is born and which cannot change.

4. The United States is often cited as a prime example of a class society with maximum mobility. Although our national credo includes a belief in the possibility of going from rags to riches, most people in the United States remain in the class into which they are born because social environment has an appreciable effect on a person's life chances.

5. For the past several decades, class inequality in the United States has increased, not decreased. The income gap between the upper and lower classes has widened, and there has been an increasing concentration of political power in the hands of the capitalist class.

6. Hindu India is often cited as the most extreme form of caste society in the world. Social boundaries among castes are strictly maintained by caste endogamy and strongly held notions of ritual purity and pollution. The Indian caste system,

which has persisted for two thousand years, has created an ideology enabling the upper castes to maintain a monopoly on wealth, status, and power.

7. Race is a classification of people based on physical traits, whereas ethnicity is a scheme based on cultural characteristics. Although the concept of race is not particularly meaningful from a scientific standpoint, it is important because people's ideas of racial differences have led to powerful systems of stratification and discrimination. Despite the globalization of world economies, ethnic group identity remains strong throughout the world.

8. The exploitation and subjugation of minority populations throughout the world have often been justified by the assumption that racial and ethnic minorities are intellectually inferior to their majority populations. Despite the long-term use of intelligence tests in the United States, there

is no convincing research to suggest that some populations are genetically more intelligent than any others.

9. There are two conflicting interpretations of social stratification. The functionalist theory emphasizes the integrative nature of stratification systems, pointing out how class systems contribute to the overall well-being of a society by encouraging constructive endeavor. Conflict theorists believe that stratification systems exist because the upper classes strive to maintain their superior position at the expense of the lower classes.

10. Just as individuals are stratified within a society, so too are nation-states stratified within the world system. Wealthy countries, which can have hundreds of times more wealth than poor countries, have better systems of education and health care and their citizens have much longer life expectancies.

Key Terms

achieved status
ascribed status
assimilation
bourgeoisie
caste
class
conflict theory

Dalit
egalitarian societies
ethnic group
functionalism/functional theory
genocide
jati

per capita gross national income
population transfer
power
prestige
proletariat
race

rank societies
Sanskritization
social mobility
soft money
stratified societies
varnas
wealth

Critical Thinking questions

1. Over the course of the last four decades socioeconomic inequality has increased significantly. For each of the types of North Americans listed, which would support the Functionalist interpretation of social stratification and which would support the Conflict interpretation and why?
   - A medical doctor
   - A president of a local labor union
   - A stock broker
   - A fire fighter
   - The CEO of a $4 million per year corporation
   - A corporate lobbyist
   - A peanut farmer from rural Georgia

2. Do you think that the trend of growing inequality in the United States over the last forty years is a good thing or a bad thing for the long-term sustainability of the society? What arguments would you use to support your position?

3. Class societies, by definition, allow for a good deal of social mobility. But even in the most "class-like" societies, the amount of social mobility has its limits. Looking at the United States—which clearly allows for social mobility—what barriers to *upward* mobility can you identify for certain segments of the US population? What would it take to eliminate some of these barriers?

Online Study Resources

CourseMate

Access chapter-specific learning tools including learning objectives, practice quizzes, videos, flash cards, glossaries, web links, and more in your Cultural Anthropology CourseMate. Login to www.cengagebrain.com to access the resources your instructor has assigned and to purchase materials.

A Hausa chief from western Nigeria in traditional regalia.

Political Organization and Social Control

Cultural and linguistic misunderstandings can occur whenever people from different cultural backgrounds get together. This happens among ordinary people and heads of state as well as government bureaucrats. In February 2004 at the airport in Portland, Oregon, a delegation of seven members of the Moroccan Parliament were detained for several hours by employees of the Transportation Security Administration (TSA) because of a language mix-up.

The visitors, part of a goodwill tour, were searched and interviewed by FBI agents before they boarded the plane. At the gate, however, one member of the delegation realized that he had left a carry-on bag at a terminal coffee shop. When he returned to retrieve the bag, authorities refused to allow him to board the plane and, in fact, the pilot ordered the other six members off the plane for further questioning and inspection. TSA employees were alarmed when they discovered documents written in Arabic containing several references to 911.

Because the TSA officials could not read Arabic and the Moroccan delegation had no fluency in English, it took a while before the incident was resolved. As it turned out, the group's hosts in Dallas had given them instructions to dial 911 if they needed assistance. Here, then, was an unfortunate incident, caused by a lack of linguistic and cultural knowledge on the parts of both parties that did nothing to foster international understanding between Morocco and the United States. ■

As mentioned in the discussion of cultural universals in Chapters 2, all societies, if they are to remain viable over time, must maintain social order. Every society must develop a set of customs and procedures for making and enforcing decisions, resolving disputes, and regulating the behavior of its members. Every society must make collective decisions about its environment and its relations with other societies and about how to deal with disruptive or destructive behavior on the part of its members. These topics generally are discussed under headings such as political organization, law, power, authority, social control, and conflict resolution. In addition to exploring all of these subjects, this chapter deals with the cultural arrangements by which societies maintain social order, minimize the chances of disruption, and cope with whatever disruptions do occur (Kurtz 2001; Lewellen 2003).

WHAT WE WILL LEARN

■ What are the different types of political organization?

■ What are the various theories concerning why people are willing to surrender a portion of their autonomy to the power and control of the state?

■ In what ways have state systems of government changed over the past four decades?

■ In the absence of kings, presidents, legislatures, and bureaucracies, how is social order maintained in stateless societies?

■ What is the distinction between formal and informal means of social control?

■ What are the causes of war?

■ What role should cultural anthropologists play relative to military organizations?

When most North Americans think of politics or political structure, a number of familiar images come to mind:

- Political leaders such as presidents, governors, mayors, or commissioners
- Complex bureaucracies employing thousands of civil servants
- Legislative bodies ranging from the smallest town council to the US Congress
- Formal judicial institutions that comprise municipal, state, and federal courts
- Law enforcement bodies such as police departments, national guard units, and the armed forces
- Political parties, nominating conventions, and secret-ballot voting

All of these are formal mechanisms that our own society uses for making and enforcing political decisions as well as coordinating and regulating people's behavior. Some small-scale societies in the world have none of these things—no elected officials, legislatures, judges, formal elections, armies, or bureaucracies. We should not conclude from this, however, that such societies do not have some form of political organization, if by political organization we mean a set of customary procedures that accomplish decision making, conflict resolution, and social control.

Types of Political Organization

The term *political organization* refers to the way in which power is distributed within a society so as to control people's behavior and maintain social order. All societies are organized politically, but the degree of specialization and the formal mechanisms vary considerably from one society to another. Societies differ in their political organization based on three important dimensions:

1. The extent to which political institutions are distinct from other aspects of the social structure; for example, in some societies political structures are barely distinguishable from economic, kinship, or religious structures.

2. The extent to which legitimate *authority* is concentrated in specific political roles.

3. The level of *political integration*—that is, the size of the territorial group that comes under the control of the political structure.

These three dimensions are the basis for classifying societies (Service 1978) into four fundamentally different types of political structure: band societies, tribal societies, chiefdoms, and state societies. Although some societies do not fit neatly into a single category, this fourfold scheme can help us understand how different societies administer themselves and maintain social order.

Although our discussions of all four types of political organization are written using the "ethnographic present," we need to remember that there are no pure bands, tribes, or chiefdoms in the world today. Rather these nonstate forms of political organization have had more complex state political systems superimposed on them.

Band Societies

The least complex form of political arrangement is the band, characterized by small and usually nomadic populations of food collectors. Although the size of a band can range from twenty to several hundred individuals, most bands are made up of between thirty and fifty people. The actual size of a particular band is directly related to its food-gathering methods; that is, the more food a band has at its disposal, the larger the number of people it can support. Although bands may be loosely associated with a specific territory, they have little or no concept of individual property ownership and place a high value on sharing, cooperation, and reciprocity. *Band societies* have little role specialization and are highly egalitarian in that few differences in status and wealth can be observed. Because this form of political organization is so closely associated with a foraging technology, it is generally thought to be the oldest form of political organization.

Band societies share four traits:

1. Because bands are composed of a relatively small number of people who are related by blood or marriage, a high value is placed on "getting along" with one another.

2. Band societies have the least amount of political integration; that is, the various bands are independent of one another and are not part of a larger political structure.

3. In band societies political decisions are often embedded in the wider social structure. Because bands are composed of kin, it is difficult to distinguish between purely political decisions and those that we would recognize as family, economic, or religious decisions.

---

authority The power or right to give commands, take action, and make binding decisions.

political integration The process that brings disparate people under the control of a single political system.

band societies The basic social units in many hunting-and-gathering societies, characterized by being kinship based and having no permanent political structure.

4. Leadership roles in band societies tend to be informal. In band societies there are no specialized political roles or leaders with designated authority. Instead leaders in foraging societies are often, but not always, older men respected for their experience, wisdom, good judgment, and knowledge of hunting.

The Ju/'hoansi of the Kalahari exemplify a band society with a headman. Although the position of headman is hereditary, the actual authority of the headman is quite limited. The headman coordinates the movement of his people and usually walks at the head of the group. He chooses the sites of new encampments and has first pick of location for his own house site. But beyond these limited perks of office, the Ju/'hoansi headman receives no other rewards. He is not responsible for organizing hunting parties, making artifacts, or negotiating marriage arrangements. These activities fall to the individual members of the band. The headman is not expected to be a judge of his people. Moreover his material possessions are no greater than any other person's. As Lorna Marshall (1965: 267) so aptly put it when referring to the Ju/'hoansi headman: "He carries his own load and is as thin as the rest."

Tribal Societies

Whereas band societies are usually associated with food collecting, *tribal societies* are found most often among food producers (horticulturalists and pastoralists). Because plant and animal domestication is far more productive than foraging, tribal societies tend to have populations that are larger, denser, and somewhat more sedentary than bands. Tribal societies are similar to band societies in several important respects, however. Both are egalitarian to the extent that there are few marked differences in status, rank, power, and wealth. In addition tribal societies, like bands, have local leaders but no centralized leadership. Leadership in tribal societies is informal and not vested in a centralized authority. A man is recognized as a leader by virtue of certain personality traits such as wisdom, integrity, intelligence, and concern for the welfare of others. Although tribal leaders often play a central role in formulating decisions, they cannot force their will on a group. In the final analysis, decisions are arrived at through group consensus.

The major difference between tribes and bands is that tribal societies have certain *pan-tribal mechanisms* that cut across and integrate all the local segments of the tribe into a larger whole (Figure 13.1). These mechanisms include tribal associations such as clans, age grades, and secret societies. Pan-tribal associations unite the tribe against external threats. These integrating forces are not permanent political fixtures, however. Most often the local units of a tribe operate autonomously. The integrating mechanisms come into play only when an external threat arises. When the threat is eliminated, the local units return to their autonomous state. Even though these pan-tribal mechanisms may be transitory, they nevertheless provide wider political integration in certain situations than would ever be possible in band societies.

In many tribal societies, the kinship unit known as the clan serves as a pan-tribal mechanism of political integration. The clan is defined as a group of kin who consider themselves to be descended from a common ancestor, even though individual clan members cannot trace, step by step, their connection to the clan founder. Clan elders, although they do not hold formal political offices, usually manage the affairs of their clans (settling disputes between clan members, for example) and represent their clans in dealings with other clans.

FIGURE 13.1 Tribal societies, such as the Samburu of Kenya, have certain pan tribal mechanisms, such as clans and age organizations, which serve to integrate the tribe as a whole.

tribal societies Small-scale societies composed of autonomous political units and sharing common linguistic and cultural features.

pan-tribal mechanisms Mechanisms such as clans, age grades, and secret societies found in tribal societies that cut across kinship lines and integrate all the local segments of the tribe into a larger whole.

The pastoral Nuer of the southern Sudan are a good example of a tribal form of political organization (Evans-Pritchard 1940). The Nuer, who number approximately three hundred thousand people, have no centralized government and no government functionaries with coercive authority. Of course there are influential men, but their influence stems more from their personal traits than from the force of elected or inherited office. The Nuer, who are highly egalitarian, do not readily accept authority beyond the elders of the family. Social control among the Nuer is maintained by segmentary lineages in that close kin are expected to come to the assistance of one another against more distantly related people.

The term *tribe* has carried with it a generally negative connotation in the Western world for the past several centuries. During the colonial period of the nineteenth century, the term *tribal*, often equated with "uncivilized," was used to disparage any group with no centralized hierarchical authority. Anthropologists do not associate the term *tribal society* with anything negative. Rather the term is used to describe a group of ethnically homogeneous people capable of coordinating political action, yet lacking a centralized bureaucracy. Awareness of negative stereotyping of tribal societies is important because Westerners often speak of "ancient tribal hatreds" (caused by inherent cultural differences) when, in fact, present-day intertribal hostilities often result from the intervention of other cultures. Negative stereotyping can lead us to misunderstand the nature of contemporary ethnic or tribal conflicts in places such as Somalia, the former Yugoslavia, and Iraq (see Whitehead and Ferguson 1993).

Chiefdoms

As we have seen, in band and tribal societies, local groups are economically and politically autonomous, authority is decentralized, and populations tend to be generally egalitarian. Moreover roles are unspecialized, populations are small, and economies are largely subsistent in nature. But as societies become more complex—with larger and more specialized populations, more sophisticated technology, and growing surpluses—their need for more formal and permanent political structures increases. In such societies, known as *chiefdoms*, political authority is likely to reside with a single individual, acting alone or in conjunction with an advisory council.

Chiefdoms differ from bands and tribes in that chiefdoms integrate a number of local communities in a more formal and permanent way. Unlike bands and tribes, chiefdoms are made up of local communities that differ from one another in rank and status. Based on their genealogical proximity to the chiefs, nobles and commoners hold different levels of prestige and power. Chiefships are often hereditary, and the chief and his or her immediate kin constitute a social and political elite. Rarely are chiefdoms totally unified politically under a single chief; more often they are composed of several political units, each headed by its own chief.

Chiefdoms also differ from tribes and bands in that chiefs are centralized and permanent officials who have higher rank, power, and authority than others in the society. Unlike band or tribal headmen or headwomen, chiefs usually have considerable power, authority, and in some cases, wealth. Internal social disruptions are minimized in a chiefdom because the chief usually has authority to make judgments, punish wrongdoers, and settle disputes. Chiefs usually have the authority to distribute land to loyal subjects, recruit people into military service, and recruit laborers for public works projects.

Chiefs are also intimately related to the economic activities of their subjects through the redistributive system of economics (see Chapters 8). Subjects give food surpluses to the chief (not uncommonly at the chief's insistence), which the chief then redistributes through communal feasts and doles. This system of redistribution through a chief serves the obvious *economic* function of ensuring that no people in the society go hungry. It also serves the important *political* function of providing the people with a mechanism for expressing their loyalty and support for the chief.

Within the past 130 years, a number of societies with no former tradition of chiefs have had chiefships imposed on them by European colonial powers. As the European nations created their colonial empires during the nineteenth century, they created chiefs (or altered the nature of traditional chiefs) to facilitate administering local populations. For example, the British created chiefs for their own administrative convenience among chiefless societies in Nigeria, Kenya, and Australia. These new chiefs—who were given salaries and high-sounding titles such as "Paramount Chief"—were selected primarily on the basis of their willingness to work with the colonial administration rather than any particular popularity among their own people. In some cases these new chiefs were held in contempt by their own people because they were collaborators with the colonial governments, which were often viewed as repressive and coercive.

The precolonial Hawaiian political system of the eighteenth century embodied the features of a typical chiefdom. According to Elman Service (1975), Hawaiian society, covering eight islands, was layered into three basic social strata. At the apex of the social

---

chiefdoms An intermediate form of political organization in which integration is achieved through the office of chiefs.

hierarchy were the *ali'i*, major chiefs believed to be direct descendants of the gods; their close relatives often served as advisors or bureaucrats under them. The second echelon, known as the *konohiki*, included less important chiefs who were often distant relatives of the ali'i. And finally the great majority of people were commoners, known as *maka 'ainana*. The major chiefs and their subordinates wielded considerable power and authority over the general population because of their control over the allocation of water for irrigation, communal labor, dispute settlement, and recruiting men for warfare.

State Societies

The *state system of government* is the most formal and most complex form of political organization. A *state* can be defined as a hierarchical form of political organization that governs many communities within a large geographic area. States collect taxes, recruit labor for armies and civilian public works projects, and have a monopoly on the right to use force. They are large bureaucratic organizations made up of permanent institutions with legislative, administrative, and judicial functions. Whereas bands and tribes have political structures based on kinship, state systems of government organize their power on a supra-kinship basis. That is, a person's membership in a state is based on his or her place of residence and citizenship rather than on kinship affiliation. Over the past several thousand years, state systems of government have taken various forms, including Greek city-states; the far-reaching Roman Empire; certain traditional African states such as Bunyoro, Buganda, and the Swazi; theocratic states such as ancient Egypt; and modern nation-states such as Germany, China, Canada, and the United States (Figure 13.2).

The authority of the state rests on two important foundations. First, the state holds the exclusive right to use force and physical coercion. Any act of violence not expressly permitted by the state is illegal and consequently punishable by the state. Thus, state governments make written laws, administer them through various levels of the bureaucracy, and enforce them through mechanisms such as police forces, armies, and national guards. The state needs to be continuously vigilant against threats both from within and from without to usurp its power through rebellions and revolutions. Second, the state maintains its authority by means of ideology. For the state to maintain its power over the

Haruyoshi Yamaguchi/Bloomberg/Getty Images

FIGURE 13.2 State systems of government are characterized by a high degree of role specialization and hierarchical organization. Many of the specialized political roles are played out in legislative bodies, such as the upper house of Parliament in Tokyo, Japan.

long run, there must be a philosophical understanding among the citizenry that the state has the legitimate right to govern. In the absence of such an ideology, it is often difficult for the state to maintain its authority by means of coercive force alone.

State systems of government, which first appeared about 5,500 years ago, are associated with civilizations (see the definition in Chapters 2). Thus, they are found in societies with complex socioeconomic characteristics. For example, state systems of government are supported by intensive agriculture, which is required to support a large number of bureaucrats who are not producing food. This fully efficient food-production system gives rise to cities, considerable labor specialization, and a complex system of internal distribution and foreign trade. Because the considerable surpluses produced by intensive agriculture are not distributed equally among all segments of the population, state societies are socially stratified. That is, forms of wealth such as land and capital tend to be concentrated in the hands of an elite, who often use their superior wealth and power to control the rest of the population. Moreover the fairly complex laws and regulations needed to control a large and heterogeneous population give rise to the need for

state system of government A bureaucratic, hierarchical form of government composed of various echelons of political specialists.

Are the Poarch Creek a Tribe?

In the early 1970s, anthropologist Anthony Paredes (1992) began his studies of the Poarch Creek, an obscure cultural group of approximately 500 Native Americans residing in southern Alabama. As a student of ethnography and social change, Paredes was interested in studying how the Poarch Creek had managed to maintain their Indian identity in the face of considerable intermarriage with non-Indians and the virtual disappearance of their language and culture. During his initial investigations, in which he used the ethnographic methods of interviewing and participant observation, Paredes learned that since the 1940s the Poarch Creek community had actually been attempting to overcome such long-standing problems as poverty, underemployment, poor education, and poor health. One effective way of addressing these problems was to petition the federal government for official recognition as a Native American tribe. If the Poarch Creek community was successful in its petition, it would be eligible for economic support from a number of government agencies.

Although the Poarch Creek had begun petitioning for federal recognition before Paredes entered the community, Paredes's ethnographic and archival research turned out to have a practical use in addition to its scholarly value. The research was instrumental in the group's eventual successful petition for official recognition. To be successful in its claim, the Poarch Creek community needed to demonstrate that they had maintained a continuous existence as a political unit with viable leadership that had authority over its members. One critical problem was the conspicuous information gap during the late 1800s. There were sufficient historical records of government dealings with the Poarch Creek during the first half of the nineteenth century and ample evidence from more recent times gained through ethnographic interviews with living tribal members. Another challenge facing Paredes was to fill in the historical record of the late-nineteenth and early-twentieth centuries through a combination of archival research and ethnographic and ethnohistorical methods.

In the early 1980s, Paredes was hired by the tribal council to conduct research in the National Archives in Washington, D.C., and the state archives in Montgomery, Alabama. Paredes helped to reconstruct periods of tribal history by gathering bits and pieces of information from various government records, including homestead files, obituaries, court cases, and various types of government correspondence. By locating historical materials, he was able to support, confirm, and amplify much of the data he had gained from interviewing his older tribal informants. In his own words, Paredes

some type of writing, record keeping, and a system of weights and measures.

State systems of government are characterized by a large number of *specialized political roles*. Many people are required to carry out specific tasks such as law enforcement, tax collection, dispute settlement, recruitment of labor, and protection from outside invasions. These political and administrative functionaries are highly specialized and work full-time to the extent that they do not engage in food-producing activities. These permanent political functionaries, like the society itself, are highly stratified or hierarchical. At the apex of the administrative pyramid are those with the greatest power—kings, presidents, prime ministers, governors, and legislators—who enact laws and establish policies. Below them are descending echelons of bureaucrats responsible for the day-to-day administration of the state. As is the case in our own form of government, each level of the bureaucracy is responsible to the level immediately above it.

specialized political roles Specific tasks expected of a person or group, such as law enforcement, tax collection, dispute settlement, recruitment of labor, and protection from outside invasions.

The Rise of State Systems

For the overwhelming majority of their existence, humans have lived in small food-collecting bands characterized by little or no political integration and few, if any, specialized political roles. Not until the Neolithic Revolution (the domestication of plants and animals) approximately ten thousand years ago were socioeconomic forces unleashed that permitted the formation of larger, more complex sociopolitical systems. With the new food-producing technologies arriving with the Neolithic Revolution, populations became larger and more heterogeneous, and as a result political organizations became increasingly complex and centralized. Today state systems of government predominate in the world, whereas small-scale band societies account for a small (and decreasing) percentage of the world's societies. Moreover contemporary small-scale societies are operating under the political authority of nation-states.

Although the rise of state systems of government was clearly a significant development, there is little consensus on why these complex forms of government emerged. By examining both ancient and contemporary societies, anthropologists and social philosophers have attempted to explain why some societies have

(1992: 218) was "able to combine disparate bits of seemingly trivial information with data from ethnographic fieldwork to confirm informants' recollections and cast new light on community organization and leadership in an earlier era."

Thus, what started out as a general scholarly inquiry into the recent history of the Poarch Creek Indians turned out to have important practical implications. The information collected by Paredes was used to buttress the tribe's petition to the Bureau of Indian Affairs (BIA) for official recognition by the federal government. This petition, which met with success in 1984, has had far-reaching benefits for the Poarch Creek community. The Poarch Band of Creek Indians is the only federally recognized Indian tribe in the state of Alabama, operating as a sovereign nation with its own system of government and bylaws. The tribe operates a variety of economic enterprises, which employ hundreds of area residents, both Indian and non-Indian. Poarch Creek Indian Gaming Authority manages three gaming facilities (casinos) in Alabama, all three of which provide generous benefits to their employees.

The Poarch Band of Creek Indians is an active partner in the state of Alabama, contributing to economic, educational, social, and cultural projects benefiting both tribal members and residents of these local communities and neighboring towns. As just one indicator of how far the Poarch Creek Indian Nation has come since being officially recognized by the federal government, in February 2013, tribal leaders publically announced that the tribe had donated (as part of its planned giving campaign) more than $2 million dollars to local public schools in surrounding counties. According to tribal chairman Buford Rolin, "Our Tribal members, our employees and our neighbors send their children to these schools. I can think of no better investment in the future than to make sure budget cuts don't limit our children's opportunities or their dreams in any way" (poarchcreekindians.org). Thus, the scholarly research of one cultural anthropologist, initially aimed at reconstructing the history of the Poarch Creek Indians in Alabama, turned out to have a significant impact on the revitalization of this group of Native Americans.

Questions for Further Thought

1. Why was it important for the Poarch Creek community to receive official recognition?

2. Would recognition have been possible without the anthropological research conducted by Paredes?

3. How would you characterize the applied anthropological role that Paredes played in this case?

---

developed state systems whereas others have not. Explanations for the rise of the state hinge on the question of what induces people to surrender at least a portion of their autonomy to the power and control of the state. Some theories suggest that people purposefully and voluntarily gave up their sovereignty because of the perceived benefits. That is, these theorists reason that the limited loss of autonomy was outweighed by the benefits people derived from their integration into a wider political structure. These benefits included greater protection from hostile outside forces, more effective means of conflict resolution, and the opportunity for increased food production.

The Modern Nation-State

In recent times the word *state* has often been combined with the word *nation* to form the entity called a *nation-state*. Although these two words are often used interchangeably in everyday conversation, they are two quite distinct concepts. On the one hand, a *nation* is a group of people who share a common symbolic identity, culture, history, and often religion. A *state*, on the other hand, is a particular type of political structure distinct from a band, tribal society, or chiefdom. When combined, the term *nation-state* refers to a group of people sharing a common cultural background and unified by a political structure that they all consider legitimate.

Although this is a fairly tidy definition, few of the nearly two hundred so-called nation-states in the world today actually fit the definition. This is largely because few such entities have populations with homogeneous cultural identities. For example, the country of Great Britain, which has existed for centuries, comprises England, Wales, Ireland, and Scotland. We sometimes refer to Great Britain as England, but the Welsh, Irish, and Scots clearly do not regard themselves as English in terms of language, tradition, or ethnicity. The collapse of the Soviet Union gave rise to a dozen new nation-states, including Belarus, Ukraine, Georgia, Azerbaijan, and Moldova. And of course many of the newly independent African nation-states represented in the United Nations since the 1960s have enormous ethnic heterogeneity. To illustrate, the country of Tanzania

---

nation A group of people who share a common identity, history, and culture.

state A particular type of political structure that is hierarchical, bureaucratic, centralized, and has a monopoly on the legitimate use of force to implement its policies.

comprises approximately 120 different ethnic groups, all of which speak languages that are mutually unintelligible. Thus, even after a half-century of living in a nation-state, the people of Tanzania tend to identify themselves more as Maasai, Wazaramo, or Wachagga than as Tanzanians.

A major challenge for some contemporary state governments is that they contain within their boundaries ethnic populations that are seeking statehood or expanded autonomy. A particularly good example is the 12 million Kurds living in southern Turkey, who have been struggling for an independent state since the formation of modern Turkey in 1923. Because the Kurds make up approximately 20 percent of Turkey's population and occupy an area that controls the headwaters of the Tigris and Euphrates rivers, the Turkish government is not the least bit interested in granting the Kurds independence. For decades the Turkish government has used political repression as the major strategy for dealing with what they call the "Kurdish problem." Not only have Kurds been oppressed and denied basic civil liberties, but so have non-Kurdish Turks who speak out in favor of Kurdish independence. And yet the Kurds of Turkey represent only one of many groups that are involved in intrastate conflicts. Others quickly come to mind, including Palestinians in Israel, Chechens in Russia, the Kayapo of Brazil, and the French in Canada.

Gender and the Modern State

Irrespective of whether we are looking at small-scale band societies or large-scale state societies, across the political spectrum women do not as a rule hold important positions of political leadership. To be certain, there are examples of women holding top leadership positions, but these exceptional cases are found in societies in which female leadership roles are not typically extended to other women in the society. To illustrate, over the past several hundred years a number of powerful female heads of European states can be cited, including Isabella I of Spain, Elizabeth I and Victoria of England, and Catherine the Great of Russia. Within the last several decades, on average, about 3 percent of the independent countries in the world have had a woman as head of state. In 2012, of the 179 serving heads of state (either presidents or prime ministers) 14 (or 7 percent) were women. And in terms of membership in parliament, of the 46,056 elected upper and lower house parliamentarians globally, 8,990 (or 19.5 percent) are women (CNN 2012). This is an improvement from where

women were a century ago, but it hardly represents a major victory for women in politics. Moreover even this modest gain in political leadership for women must be qualified. First, often when women attain high office, it is because of their relationship to men. That is, a queen may become the titular head of state by virtue of her marriage to the king, or because her father, the former monarch, had no male heirs. And second, many of the women leaders are not particularly strong advocates of women's issues, such as pay equity, access to certain professions, or protection from abuse. In other words, they tend to be "women in men's clothing," finding that they need to downplay feminist issues to garner support within a male-dominated political system.

In Chapters 11 we saw how, because of extreme male gender bias, certain Asian nations have tens of millions fewer women than men. In fact it is conservatively estimated that 90 million women in Asia are "missing" because parents are encouraged to select sons over daughters through female infanticide, selective abortion of female fetuses, and nutritional and medical deprivation. These tens of millions of excess males in countries like China and India have important implications for international peace and security (Figure 13.3). Large numbers of unmarried men at home, particularly ones that are troublemakers, are expendable, and can be recruited to form huge armies. In the years to come, when China wants to resolve its differences with Taiwan, or India wants to

Alexander Ryabintsev/shutterstock.com

FIGURE 13.3 The existence of millions of excess men in China, brought about by gender bias, may increase that nation's willingness to settle its disagreements through warfare.

end its standoff with Pakistan over Kashmir, having armies composed of so many expendable unmarried males may be a factor in a country's willingness to go to war (Hudson and den Boer 2004).

Changing State Systems of Government

The global historical trend during the last several decades has been toward democracy and away from autocracy. *Democracy* is a political system in which power is exercised, usually through representatives, by the people as a whole. *Autocracy*, in contrast, is a political system that is controlled by an absolute leader and that denies popular participation in the process of governmental decision making. According to Freedom House (www.freedomhouse.org), an organization that tracks political trends throughout the world, by the end of 2005, 122 of the world's 192 governments were electoral democracies, up from 66 countries just eighteen years previously. Even though some of these 122 democracies have questionable human rights records, they do allow the existence of opposition parties and meet at least the minimum standards for holding free elections. Freedom House also assigns each nation of the world to one of three categories: free, partly free, and not free. In the three decades between 1975 and 2005, the number of free countries increased from forty to eighty-nine, the number of partly-free countries increased from fifty-three to fifty-eight, and the number of countries deemed not free declined from sixty-five to forty-five (Figure 13.4).

Despite the trend toward democratization in the last several decades, the year 2006 marked an important setback for global democracies. According to Freedom House (Puddington 2013: 1), global declines in freedom outweighed gains in 2012 for the seventh consecutive year, which is the longest period of decline in the forty years that Freedom House has monitored the state of freedom in the world. As with the world at large, the region of the Middle East and North Africa experienced more declines than gain in recent years. The widespread demonstrations for free elections and accountable governments, which became known as the "Arab Spring," were often fiercely suppressed by repressive governments through arrest, police violence, and in some cases, warfare conducted against their own people. The news for 2012 was particularly negative because the declines (a) have spread throughout the world, (b) affected countries that have military and economic power, (c) included countries that had been showing signs of progress in recent years, and (d) were accompanied by more persecution of dissidents and journalists.

Whereas Freedom House has been monitoring the levels of democracy and autocracy found in the nations of the world for over four decades, the Fund for Peace, a nonprofit organization that works to prevent violence in the world by promoting sustainable security, has developed some sophisticated measures for determining which countries are becoming "failed states." Since 2005 the Fund for Peace has produced the Failed State Index (FSI), a comprehensive ranking of 178 nations based on their levels of stability, the pressures they face, and the likelihood of their becoming dysfunctional political entities (that is, failed states). By drawing on data gathered by satellite imaging and sizeable numbers of social scientists working in each of the 178 countries, the index bases its rankings on the following social, economic, political, and military indicators:

1. To what extent can the government protect its citizens from demographic pressures (such as natural disasters, water scarcity, and malnutrition)?
2. Are states under pressure as a result of the large influx of refugees from neighboring countries?
3. To what extent is there uneven and unjust distribution of resources?
4. To what extent is there violence among various subgroups in the society and what is the government's capacity to provide security?
5. Seeing few opportunities, are substantial numbers of people migrating out of the country?

FIGURE 13.4 The worldwide trend during the last several decades has been toward participatory democracy. Here a South African woman casts her vote in the nation's first post-apartheid election in 1994.

© David Turnley/Corbis

democracy A type of political system that involves popular participation in decision making.

autocracy A form of government that is controlled by a leader who holds absolute power and denies popular participation in decision making.

6. Is the nation-state in economic decline?

7. To what extent is the government effective, representative, and free of corruption?

8. Does the state provide such basic social services as education, health care, potable water, and sanitation?

9. Does the state protect basic political freedoms, human rights, and civil liberties?

10. Does the state have a monopoly on the legitimate use of force?

11. Are there power struggles between various political elites?

12. Is external intervention (United Nations' peacekeepers, foreign assistance) needed because the state is failing to meet its international and domestic obligations?

The FSI is an extremely significant tool for identifying the important variables threatening the stability and sustainability of all nation-states. But the annual rankings published by the Fund for Peace are particularly critical because they show when those threats are pushing a particular country to the brink of failure or dysfunctionality. In other words, the FSI can (a) assist world leaders in assessing political risk and (b) serve as an early warning device for future conflicts. The need for such a critical tool as the FSI is particularly great in our highly interconnected world, where a failed state can have a negative ripple effect on other neighboring nations as well as nations on the other side of the world.

The FSI for 2012 showed that the most endangered states (that is, the most likely to become failed states) were Somalia (at number one), followed (in rank order) by the Democratic Republic of the Congo, Sudan, the new country of South Sudan, Chad, Zimbabwe, Afghanistan, Haiti, Yemen, Iraq, and the Central African Republic. At the opposite end of the index, indicating those stable nations that were least likely to become dysfunctional were Finland (as number one), followed by Sweden, Denmark, Switzerland, Norway, Luxembourg, New Zealand, Ireland, Canada, and Austria. If we compare these best and worst nation states to the rankings of the ten richest and the ten poorest countries in the world (see Table 12.3), we see almost the same cast of characters. This would suggest a strong correlation between high per capita wealth and highly functioning, stable, and sustainable nation states. However, the FSI in 2012 revealed how wealthy and stable countries can experience dramatic reversals from one year to the next. For example, between 2011 and 2012 Japan (the third wealthiest country in the world, and a democracy as well) dropped 13 positions as a result largely of the earthquake and subsequent meltdown of the Daiichi nuclear reactor, which overwhelmed the Japanese government's capacity to respond to the natural disaster. Also, Norway, which had been ranked "the least likely country to become a failed state" for every year since the FSi began, dropped from first to fifth place in 2012 because of the bombing and mass shooting of Norwegian teenagers by Anders Breivik. The worsening of the positions of both Japan and Norway in 2012 dramatically demonstrated how a single traumatic event can negatively impact highly stable and wealthy nation states.

As information technology developed dramatically during the 1990s, proponents of the Internet claimed that it was leading to new forms of democracy. To be certain, the Internet is the most important information technology since the printing press. Theoretically, the Internet makes it possible for anyone with Internet access to have free access to information, for opposition parties to spread their agendas, and for formerly oppressed people to connect with others via e-mail to present a united front against those who would exploit them. In short, the World Wide Web has the *potential* to serve as a powerful tool to fight political repression, racism, and economic exploitation. Yet there is another side to this coin. As effective as the Internet can be in freeing up information and giving a voice to oppressed people, it certainly has its limitations. In reality most oppressed people throughout the world probably do not own a personal computer, nor can they afford a monthly subscription to the Internet. Although the Internet has been touted as a boon to economic development, this development tends to be uneven (Figure 13.5).

Zvet/Shutterstock.com

FIGURE.13.5 To what extent can this impoverished young woman from Nepal rely on the internet to protect herself from a repressive government?

In many cases the rich are using the Internet to get richer while the poor remain poor and powerless.

For the Internet to be a democratizing force, it must be accessible to all people, not just those who can afford the technology. Although the Internet may permit the sending of uncensored information, it can, at the same time, be used by oppressive governments to "create new possibilities for surveillance and sabotage." Not only has the Internet been used by some repressive governments to quell dissent, but it appears that they have been aided and abetted by some pillars of the US free-enterprise system. Eager to curry favor with the government that controls access to Chinese markets, Western technology firms have been helping the Chinese government limit free expression by blocking access to political web sites, snitching on users, and selling filtering equipment.

In those nation-states that have relatively unencumbered access to information, the Internet is significantly influencing the political and electoral processes. Within the last decade, political campaigns have become more sophisticated in taking advantage of what the Internet has to offer. Politicians of the twenty-first century have access to computer-generated mailing lists, enabling them to target issue voters. They can become much more efficient in raising campaign funds by using computer programs to identify potential donors. The Internet is a cost-effective way of disseminating information (and "disinformation") about a candidate as well as recruiting and mobilizing supporters, volunteers, and campaign funds. Moreover a candidate's web site allows for two-way communication with the voter, establishing an avenue for instant feedback on issues. And, with the explosive popularity of such personal networking sites as Facebook, MySpace, and blogs, circulating political information and educating the voting public have become enormously more efficient and participatory. In the past an election could be (and usually was) decided by the number and effectiveness of the TV commercials a candidate could purchase. Such a system clearly worked to the advantage of those candidates who had the most money. With the widespread accessibility of the Internet, however, candidates can get their message across for a fraction of the cost of TV ads.

Variations in Political Structures

In the preceding sections, we have looked at four fundamentally different types of political systems. This fourfold scheme, though recognized by some anthropologists, is not universally accepted. For example, in a classic study of political systems in Africa, Meyer Fortes and E. E. Evans-Pritchard (1940) distinguished between only two types of structures: state systems and *headless societies*. Others (Cohen and Eames 1982)

recognize three major forms of political structure: simple, intermediate, and complex. Such differences in the way various ethnologists have conceptualized political structures should serve as a reminder that all of these schemes are ideal types. That is, not all of the societies in the world fit neatly into one box or another. Instead of discrete categories, in reality there is a continuum with bands (the simplest form) at one extreme and states (the most complex form) at the other. Thus, whether we use two, three, or four major categories of political organization, we should bear in mind that the political systems of the world vary along a continuum on a number of important political dimensions. As we move from bands through tribes and chiefdoms to states, gradations occur in terms of (a) level of political integration, (b) the extent to which political institutions are distinction from family or religious institutions, and (c) the extent to which legitimate authority in concentrated in purely political roles.

Social Control

As the preceding section explained, political structures vary from informal structures such as bands at one extreme to highly complex state systems of government at the other extreme. Whatever form of political organization is found in a society, however, it must inevitably address the issue of *social control*. In other words, every society must ensure that most of the people behave in appropriate ways most of the time. State-like societies, such as our own, have a wide variety of formalized mechanisms to keep people's behavior in line, including written laws, judges, bureaucracies, prisons, execution chambers, and police forces. At the other extreme, small-scale band societies, such as the traditional Inuit or Ju/'hoansi, had no centralized political authority but nevertheless maintain social order among their members quite effectively through informal mechanisms of social control. In fact people deviate from what is considered to be acceptable behavior considerably less in most band societies than in societies that have more formal, elaborate, and complex forms of political organization.

Every society has defined what it considers to be normal, proper, or expected ways of behaving. These expectations, known as *social norms*, serve as behavioral

---

headless societies Societies that have no political leaders such as a presidents, kings, or chiefs.

social control Mechanisms found in all societies that function to encourage people not to violate the social norms.

social norms Expected forms of behavior.

Anthropology in the Courtroom

Although we normally think of cultural anthropologists as being both researchers and university professors, they are, with increasing frequency, venturing outside of academia to apply their cultural insights to real-world situations. One example is cultural anthropologists who serve as expert witnesses in court cases involving disputing parties from different cultural backgrounds. Barbara Joans, head of the anthropology program at Merritt College in Oakland, California, has served as an expert witness on a number of occasions over the past twenty-five years. To illustrate how the insights from cultural anthropology can be applied to court cases, we will look at two cases in which Joans played a prominent role.

The first court case involved a misunderstanding between six Bannock-Shoshoni Native American women from the Fort Hall Reservation and officials of the Social Services Agency in Pocatello, Idaho (Joans 1984). The six Native American women were accused in court of withholding information from the agency and failing to report social service payments they had received. To be eligible for supplemental security income (SSI), the women were required to report all forms of income. Some of the women had received several thousand dollars of rent from a small land-holding. They rented the land in January but were not paid until the following December, at which time they reported the income. The agency maintained that the money should have been reported as soon as the property was rented (January) rather than when the income was received. When agency officials learned

of the unreported income, they stopped the SSI payments to the women and insisted that they return the money already paid to them. The women claimed that they did not understand the instructions, given in English, concerning the reporting of income. The agency claimed that the women knew full well about the regulations and simply chose to ignore them. When the case came to court, the central issue was whether the women understood what was expected of them.

Joans was brought in to help resolve the issue. Because the verbal exchanges between the six women and the agency officials had been conducted in English, she designed a study to determine the extent to which the six Native American women understood the English language. To do this, she constructed a three-tiered English proficiency exam. Level one tested how well the women understood everyday questions, such as Where is the gas station? Are you too hot? How much is the loaf of bread? Level two tested how well the women understood jokes, double entendres, mixed meanings, and puns. The third level consisted of government or bureaucratic language dealing with such subjects as police operations and the workings of the town council.

The findings of the study demonstrated that the women all understood level-one English, only one of the women could follow the conversation using level-two English, and none of the six women understood level-three English. Over the course of three months, Joans had frequent contact with the women in their homes, at the reservation trading post, in the lawyer's office, and in

guidelines that help the society work smoothly. To be certain, social norms are not adhered to perfectly, and in fact there is a certain amount of deviance from them in all societies. But most people in any given society abide by the norms most of the time. Moreover social norms take a number of different forms, ranging from etiquette to formal laws. Some norms are taken more seriously than others. On one hand, all societies have certain social expectations of what is proper, but such behavior is not rigidly enforced. To illustrate, although it is customary in the United States for people to shake hands when being introduced, a person's refusal to shake hands does not constitute a serious violation of social norms. The person who does not follow this rule of etiquette might be considered rude but would not be arrested or executed. On the other hand, some

social norms (such as those against grand larceny or murder) are taken seriously because they are considered absolutely necessary for the survival of the society (Figure 13.6).

Social scientists use the term *deviance* to refer to the violation of social norms. However, it is important to keep in mind that deviance is relative. What people in one culture consider to be deviant is not necessarily considered deviant in other cultures. In other words, it is not the act itself but rather how people define the act that determines whether it is deviant. To illustrate, suicide among middle-class North Americans is considered to be unacceptable under any conditions. In traditional Japan, however, the practice of *hara-kiri*, committing ritual suicide by disembowelment, was considered in traditional times the honorable thing to do for a disgraced nobleman. Thus, whereas ritual suicide was normative for the Japanese nobleman, it is considered deviant for a businessperson in Toronto or Tampa.

All social norms, whether trivial or serious, are sanctioned; that is, societies develop patterned or

---

deviance The violation of a social norm.

sanctions Any means used to enforce compliance with the rules and norms of a society.

her own office. Joans concluded that even though the women and the agency personnel all spoke English, they used the language differently. On the basis of these findings, the judge ruled that, because of the differences in language usage, the women did *not* understand what was expected of them and thus were not responsible for returning the money. The judge added that in the future agency officials had to use a Bannock-Shoshoni interpreter when they went to the reservation to describe program requirements.

Nearly a quarter of a century after helping to resolve the case in Pocatello, Idaho, Joans became an expert witness in a court case involving the accidental cremation by a funeral home of a member of a Plains Indian group in the United States (Joans 2007). The case never went to trial because her anthropological brief was used to successfully negotiate a pretrial settlement. The Native American plaintiffs were suing a funeral home for wrongful cremation of a family member who had lived far from home for the fifty years before his death. The aggrieved family claimed that cremation had prevented their relative from receiving a proper burial and end-of-life ceremony according to their traditional cultural practices. Although the funeral home owners admitted to the mistake and expressed proper remorse, the plaintiffs were so aggrieved that they were seeking a financial judgment that, if successful, would have put the funeral home out of business. The lines had been drawn in what appeared to be an unsolvable legal battle. It was at this point that Joans was asked to serve as a consultant to the court to see whether a fair and just settlement could be reached between both parties.

Joans's anthropological brief was based on a library study of the tribe's traditional and contemporary cultural practices. Her research led to interesting findings that had bearing on the dispute. First, according to tribal traditions, cremation, under unusual circumstances (such as a warrior killed far from home), was neither unknown or explicitly forbidden. Second, there was considerable flexibility in how end-of-life ceremonies were performed, even in the absence of any physical remains whatsoever. And third, it was highly unusual for an important family member not to be seen for fifty years, as was the case with the accidentally cremated relative in the lawsuit. This last finding called into question the sincerity of the plaintiff's claim of "extreme grieving."

After both sides read the anthropological brief, they agreed to settle without going to trial in a way that was fair to both parties. The family was awarded a smaller, but fair, financial settlement for the erroneous cremation, and the funeral home readily admitted the mistake and compensated the family without having to go out of business. Thus, a win-win situation was possible because anthropological data and insights were used to clarify the central issues in a court of law.

Questions for Further Thought

1. The first case discussed revolved around a misunderstanding between the Bannock-Shoshoni and government bureaucrats. Was this misunderstanding the result of cultural differences, class differences, or differences in power?

2. Do you feel it is appropriate for law courts in the United States to take into consideration the cultural values and practices of various subcultural groups such as the Bannock-Shoshoni American Indians? Why or why not?

3. In what other areas of the law can you suggest that applied anthropologists can serve as expert witnesses to provide culturally relevant information for a judge or jury to consider?

institutionalized ways of encouraging people to conform to the norms. These *sanctions* are both positive and negative because people are rewarded for behaving in socially acceptable ways and punished for violating

FIGURE 13.6 (L) and 13.6 (R) All societies control behavior with both positive sanctions (rewards) and negative sanctions (penalties).

the norms. *Positive sanctions* range from a smile of approval to being awarded the Congressional Medal of Honor. *Negative sanctions* include everything from a frown of disapproval to the death penalty.

Social sanctions may also be formal or informal, depending on whether a formal law (legal statute) has been violated. To illustrate, if a woman in a restaurant is talking in a voice that can be easily overheard by people at nearby tables, she will probably receive stares from the other diners. But if she starts yelling at the top of her lungs in the restaurant, she will probably be arrested for disturbing the peace or disorderly conduct. The difference, of course, is that in the first case the woman is not breaking the law, but in the second case she is. Figure 13.7 illustrates a continuum of the formal-informal dimension of social norms and sanctions in US society.

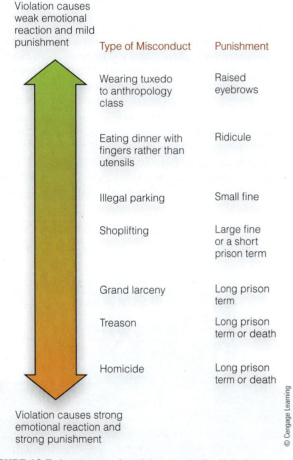

Type of Misconduct	Punishment
Wearing tuxedo to anthropology class	Raised eyebrows
Eating dinner with fingers rather than utensils	Ridicule
Illegal parking	Small fine
Shoplifting	Large fine or a short prison term
Grand larceny	Long prison term
Treason	Long prison term or death
Homicide	Long prison term or death

© Cengage Learning

FIGURE 13.7 Continuum of social norms in the United States. A similar graphic could be constructed for each of the thousands of discrete cultures in the world, although the types of misconducts and the resulting punishments would vary considerably from culture to culture.

positive sanctions Mechanisms of social control for enforcing a society's norms through rewards.

negative sanctions Punishments for violating the norms of a society.

socialization Teaching young people the norms in a society.

Just as the types of social norms found in any society vary, so do the mechanisms used to encourage people to adhere to those norms. For most North Americans, the most obvious forms of social control are the formal or institutionalized ones. When asked why we tend to behave ourselves, we would probably think of formal laws, police forces, courts, and prisons. We do not rob the local convenience store, in other words, because if caught, we are likely to go to prison.

Most of our "proper" behavior is probably caused by less formal, and perhaps less obvious, mechanisms of social control. In band and tribal societies that lack centralized authority, informal mechanisms of social control may be all that exist. It should be emphasized, however, that this distinction between formal and informal mechanisms does not imply that informal means of social control exist only in band and tribal societies. Although societies with complex political organizations (state societies in particular) are best known for written laws and courts, they also rely on an appreciable number of informal mechanisms of social control.

Compared to complex state organizations, bands and tribes have little that appears to be *governmental* in the Western sense of the term. These small-scale political systems have been described as *headless* societies or "tribes without rulers" (Middleton and Tait 1958). In the absence of formal governmental structures, how do these headless societies maintain social order? The following three subsections examine mechanisms of social control that are found (a) universally in all types of societies, from band through state systems; (b) only in small-scale societies such as bands and tribes; and (c) only in complex, heterogeneous, and hierarchical state systems.

Universal Mechanisms Found in All Types of Societies

Socialization

Every society, if it is to survive, must pass on its social rules and norms from one generation to another. It seems obvious that people cannot conform to the social norms unless they learn them. Thus, all societies have some system of *socialization*, which involves teaching the young what the norms are and that they should not be violated. In other words, not only do people live in societies, but societies live in people. People learn their social norms with a certain degree of moral compulsion. We learn, for example, that in North America people wear clothes in public and that we should do so as well. Usually we internalize our social norms so effectively that we would never consider violating them. Some social norms—such as not appearing nude in public—are so thoroughly ingrained in us through socialization that the thought of violating them is distasteful and embarrassing. Other social norms do not have the same level of moral intensity, such as driving within the speed limit or maintaining good oral hygiene. But as a general rule, when people learn the norms of their society, they are at the same time internalizing the moral necessity to obey them.

Public Opinion

One of the most compelling reasons for not violating social norms is *public opinion* or social pressure. In general, people from all parts of the world wish to be accepted by the other members of their society. Most people fear being rejected or criticized by their friends or neighbors. This strong desire to be liked is reflected in comments such as "Don't do that! What will the neighbors think?" Of course, it is impossible to determine how many people are deterred from violating the social norms by fear of negative public opinion. At the same time, we can cite many examples of how societies use social pressure (or what is called "strategic embarrassment") deliberately to keep people in line. Indeed gossip, ostracism, rumor, sarcasm, and derision are powerful corrective measures for reforming social behavior. For example, some city and county governments in the United States print the names of tax delinquents in the local newspaper in an attempt to embarrass them into paying their taxes. In colonial America the stocks and pillory were excellent examples of using public opinion to control people's behavior. Someone who was caught breaking the social norms (such as committing adultery or stealing) was confined to the stocks or pillory, which, not coincidentally, was always located in the center of town. Even though long confinements were physically uncomfortable, the realization that all of a person's friends, relatives, and neighbors would see someone and know of his or her crime was by far the greater punishment.

Supernatural Belief Systems

A powerful mechanism of social control in all types of societies is *supernatural belief systems*—belief in supernatural forces such as gods, witches, and sorcerers. People will refrain from antisocial behavior if they believe that some supernatural (suprahuman) force will punish them for it. Of course it is impossible to determine how many norms are *not* violated because people fear supernatural retribution, but we have to assume that the belief in supernatural sanctions acts as a deterrent to some degree. Nor is it necessary to prove that the gods, for example, will punish the social deviants. If people believe that "god will get them" for doing something wrong, the belief itself is usually enough to discourage the deviant behavior. This is certainly the case in Western religions (Judeo-Christian), which teach about atonement for one's sins, Judgment Day, and heaven and hell, which are the ultimate positive and negative sanctions (Figure 13.8). In small-scale societies there

CROSS-CULTURAL MISCUE

Stephen Gaither, a junior foreign service officer had just arrived at his new assignment as a "cultural attaché" at the US Embassy in Kuwait. Within his first month in Kuwait City, Stephen had scheduled an important meeting with the Kuwaiti Minister of Education to discuss a new program of cultural exchanges between Kuwait and the United States. Stephen's previous telephone conversation with the Minister had led him to believe that the Kuwaiti Minister was eager to work on the cultural exchange project between their two countries. When Stephen and the minister met, things proceeded extremely well, with both men agreeing on most of the issues discussed. At the end of the meeting the two men shook hands, and to emphasize the depth and sincerity of his goodwill, Stephen grasped the Minister's hands with two hands and shook vigorously. For reasons that Stephen never understood, the subsequent meetings with the minister were never as cordial and friendly as that first meeting.

Among middle class men in the United States it is customary to shake hands as a gesture of friendship, as it is also among men in Kuwait. When communicating extreme friendliness, a US man may grasp his friend's right hand with both of his own hands. If, however, a US man gives such an emphatic handshake to a Kuwaiti man, he will be sending and extremely offensive message. In Kuwait, and generally throughout the Islamic world where the right hand is sacred and the left hand is profane, touching someone with your left hand is highly offensive.

are other forms of supernatural belief systems (such as ancestor worship, sorcery, and witchcraft) that are equally effective social mechanisms for controlling people's behavior.

Belief in *witchcraft*, which is common in some small-scale societies, illustrates how people are discouraged from engaging in socially deviant behavior. In many societies in which witchcraft is practiced, people reject the idea that misfortunes are the result of natural causes. If crops fail or large numbers of people die, the usual explanation is that someone has been practicing witchcraft. In societies that believe in witchcraft, a deviant runs the risk of being labeled a witch, and fear of being accused of witchcraft strongly encourages

public opinion What the general public thinks about some issue; when public opinion is brought to bear on an individual, it can influence his or her behavior.

supernatural belief systems A set of beliefs in forces that transcend the natural, observable world.

witchcraft The use of inborn, involuntary, and often unconscious powers to cause harm to other people.

Dmitry Morgan/Shutterstock.com

FIGURE 13.8 Many people in the world, including the members of this Roman Catholic church in Minsk, Belarus, tend to conform to social norms out of a belief in supernatural forces.

conformity. For example, in colonial America, nonconformists, freethinkers, and others who did not conform to expected behavioral norms were driven from their communities for allegedly being witches. Jean La Fontaine (1963: 217) notes the way witchcraft serves as a mechanism of social control among the Bantu-speaking Bagisu of East Africa:

> Witchcraft beliefs act as a form of social control in discouraging behavior that is socially unacceptable. In Bagisu the eccentric is branded a witch.... Children grow up with the realization that the stigma of nonconformity is dangerous; too great a departure from the norms of everyday conduct will attract the suspicion of others and lead to isolation and eventual destruction.

corporate lineages Kinship groups whose members engage in daily activities together.

Mechanisms of Social Control Found in Small-Scale Societies

Corporate Lineages

Corporate lineages (which can number in the hundreds) play an important role in most small-scale societies and are kinship groups whose members often live, work, play, and pray together. Property is controlled by the lineage, people derive their primary identity from the group, and even religion (in the form of ancestor worship) is a lineage matter. Acting like a small corporation, the lineage has a powerful impact on the everyday lives of its members and can exert considerable pressure on people to conform to the social norms.

One means by which a corporate lineage exerts control over its members is economic. All important property, such as land and livestock, is controlled by the elders of the corporate lineage. Often property is allocated on the basis of conformity to societal norms. Those who behave as the society expects them to behave are likely to receive the best plots of land and use of the best livestock. Conversely those who violate social norms are likely to be denied these valuable economic resources.

Corporate lineages, to some degree, also act as mechanisms of social control because of their scale. Corporate lineages serve as localized communities, numbering from several hundred to several thousand relatives. Because members of the lineage have frequent and intense interaction with one another on a daily basis, it is virtually impossible for anyone to maintain her or his anonymity. People's lives are played out in such close proximity to one another that everyone knows what everyone else is doing. To illustrate, a man who wants to engage in socially inappropriate behavior (such as having an extramarital affair) would think twice because it would be difficult, if not impossible, to keep it a secret. By way of contrast, it is considerably easier to have an extramarital affair and remain undetected in a large city. Thus, the small scale of corporate lineage communities tends to inhibit social deviance because it is much more difficult for people to get away with breaking the rules.

The way roles are structured in corporate lineage societies also contributes to social control. In terms of role structure, corporate lineages have what Talcott Parsons and Edward Shils (1952) call "diffuse roles." People play social roles in a number of different domains, such as kinship, economic, political, ritual and religious, and recreational roles. A role is diffuse when it ranges over two or more of these domains. For example, a diffuse role structure occurs when a man's uncle (kinship role) is also his teacher (educational role), his priest (religious role), the local chief (political role), and his hunting partner (economic role). The man has several overlapping roles and plays roles from a number of different domains with the same person.

In contrast, roles in large-scale, complex societies such as our own tend to be segmented or narrowly defined so that single roles are played out with one person at a time. People in corporate lineage societies (with diffuse or overlapping roles) have a built-in incentive not to violate the social norms because to do so would have serious consequences. If the man in the preceding illustration offends his uncle, he is negatively affecting not only his kinship domain but also the educational, economic, political, and religious domains.

Marriage in corporate lineage societies also plays a role in social control. Marriage in such societies is regarded primarily as an alliance between two lineages—that of the bride and that of the groom—and only secondarily as a union between two individuals. In many cases the marriage is legitimized by bridewealth (the transfer of property, often livestock, from the kin group of the groom to the kin group of the bride). When a man wants to get married, he cannot pay the bridewealth himself because he does not have personal control over property. Like the rest of his relatives, he has limited rights and obligations to property such as cattle. If marriage cattle are to be transferred, the prospective groom must convince a number of his kin to give up their limited use of cows. If the prospective groom has a reputation for violating the social norms, it is unlikely that the permission to transfer the cows will be given. Thus, the members of a corporate lineage, through their collective capacity to control marriage, have considerable power to coerce people to behave appropriately.

Song Duels

Just as societies differ in the incidence of crime, they also differ in the way they handle disputes and crimes. One example of a formal mechanism for resolving disputes was found among the Inuit of Canada, Alaska, and Greenland. Because the Inuit had little property because of their nomadic way of life, conflicts rarely arose over violation of property rights. However, disputes often arose between men over the issue of wife stealing. A man would attempt to steal the wife of a more prominent man as a way of elevating his own standing within the community. One common way of punishing wife stealing among the Inuit was to murder the wife stealer. In fact Knud Rasmussen (1927) found that all of the men he studied had been a party to a murder, either as the murderer or as an accessory, and invariably these murders stemmed from allegations of wife stealing. However, there were alternative ways to resolve disputes over wife stealing. One was to challenge the alleged wife stealer to a *song duel*, a derisive song contest, which was fought with song and lyrics rather than with weapons. The plaintiff and defendant, appearing in a public setting, chided each other with abusive songs especially composed for the occasion. The contestant who received the loudest applause

emerged the winner of this "curse by verse" song duel. Interestingly, the resolution of the conflict was based not on a determination of guilt or innocence but on one's verbal dexterity.

Intermediaries

Some societies use *intermediaries* to help resolve serious conflicts. The Nuer of the African Sudan are a case in point (Evans-Pritchard 1940). Even though the Nuer political system is informal and decentralized, one role in the society—the *Leopard-Skin Chief*—is, to a degree, institutionalized. In the absence of any formal system of law courts to punish serious crimes such as murder, the Leopard-Skin Chief serves as a mediator between the victim's family and the family of the murderer. When a homicide occurs, the murderer, fearing the vengeance of the victim's family, takes sanctuary in the home of the Leopard-Skin Chief. In an attempt to prevent an all-out feud, the Leopard-Skin Chief attempts to negotiate a settlement between the two families. His role is to work out an equitable agreement whereby the murderer's family will compensate the victim's family with some form of property settlement (say, forty head of cattle) for the loss of one of its members. These animals will be used as bridewealth for the lineage to obtain a wife for one of its members. It is thought that the sons from such a marriage will fill the void left by the murder victim.

If either side becomes too unyielding, the Leopard-Skin Chief can threaten to curse the offending party. The Leopard-Skin Chief does not decide the case, however. Rather he is only an intermediary, with no authority to determine guilt or force a settlement between the parties. Intervening on behalf of the public interest, he uses his personal and supernatural influence to bring the disputing parties to some type of settlement of their dispute.

Age Organization

In some headless societies, *age organizations* serve as effective means of social control. Societies with age organizations have particular groups of people passing

---

song duel A means of settling disputes over wife stealing among the Inuit, which involves a public contest using derisive songs and lyrics.

intermediaries Mediators of disputes among individuals or families within a society.

Leopard-Skin Chief An intermediary between a murderer's family and the family of the victim, found among the Nuer of the African Sudan.

age organizations A type of social organization found in East Africa and among certain Native American groups, wherein people of roughly the same age pass through different levels of society together; each ascending level, based on age, carries with it increased social status and rigidly defined roles.

High Status

Senior Elders
(Societal advisors)

Intermediate Elders
(More serious
dispute adjudicators)

Junior Elders
(Small dispute
adjudicators)

Senior Warriors
("Officers" in the military)

Junior Warriors
(Foot soldiers in
the military)

Uninitiated
(Non-adults)

Low Status

© Cengage Learning

FIGURE 13.9 The general structure of an age-graded society.

periodically through distinct age categories (see Figure 13.9). This shows the basic distinction between age sets and age grades. An *age set* is a group of people (usually men) initiated during a periodic ceremony and having a strong sense of group identity with one another. An age set lasts from its inception, usually when most members are late adolescents, until its last member has died. Age sets pass (as a group) through successive categories, called *age grades*, such as warriors, elders, or various subdivisions within these grades. Each age grade is associated with a well-understood set of social roles (that is, they perform exclusive functions) and statuses (that is, higher prestige is associated with increasing age). To illustrate this distinction further, an age set is analogous to a group of students who go through college together. The academic grades through which they pass (freshman through senior) are comparable to the age grades. Thus, we can speak of a particular age set occupying the senior warrior grade at a particular moment.

Age organizations control behavior in significant ways. First, because age organizations establish a clear

set of roles and statuses, there is little room for infringing on the authority or domain of others. There is little incentive, in other words, to try to usurp the authority of those above you for the simple reason that if you live long enough, you will eventually have that authority by virtue of your own advanced age. If you do not live long enough, then it really does not matter.

Second, individuals enter the age-set system at the lowest echelon through the process of initiation. These rites of passage are almost always preceded by intense periods of training in the norms and values of the society. This socialization teaches the soon-to-become adults not only the expected behaviors but also the penalties for deviation and why the behaviors should be followed.

Third, the bonds of camaraderie among members of the same age set are usually so strong that age sets tend to take on the characteristics of a corporate group. Age-set members who have experienced their initiation ceremonies together support one another throughout the remainder of their lives in much the same way as do members of the same lineage. Unlike lineages, though, age sets are neither self-perpetuating nor property owning, but they exert the same type of pressure toward conformity as lineages do (Figure 13.10).

Irven DeVore/Anthro-Photo

FIGURE 13.10 The age organization into which these boys in Papua New Guinea are being initiated can serve as an effective mechanism of social control.

---

age set A group of people roughly the same age who pass through various age grades together.

age grades Permanent age categories in a society through which people pass during the course of a lifetime.

Moots: Informal Courts

Found in many African societies, moots are a highly effective mechanism for conflict resolution. *Moots* are informal airings of disputes involving kinsmen and friends of the litigants. These adjudicating bodies are ad hoc, with considerable variation in composition from case to case. Moots generally deal with the resolution of domestic disputes, such as mistreating a spouse, disagreeing about an inheritance, or not paying debts.

Anthropologist James Gibbs (1963) describes in considerable detail the moot system as found among the Kpelle, a Mande-speaking group of rice cultivators in Liberia and Guinea. Gibbs found that moots differ from the more formal court system that is administered by district chiefs in Kpelle society. First, unlike the more formal court system, moots are held in the homes of the complainants rather than in public places. Second, all parties concerned (*council of elders*, litigants, witnesses, and spectators) sit close to one another in a random and mixed fashion. This seating arrangement is in marked contrast to more formalized (Western) courts, which physically separate the plaintiff, the defendant, the judge, and the jury. Third, because the range of relevance in moots is broad, the airing of grievances is more complete than in formal courts of law. Fourth, whereas in formal courts the judge controls the conduct of the proceedings, in moots the investigation is more in the hands of the disputants themselves. Fifth, moots do not attempt to blame one party unilaterally but rather attribute fault in the dispute to both parties. Finally, the sanctions imposed by the moot are not so severe that the losing party has grounds for a new grudge against the other party. The party found to be at fault is assessed a small fine, is expected to give the wronged party a token gift, and is required to make a public apology.

Unlike more formal court systems—including those in our own society—moots do not separate the guilty party from society by incarceration. Just the opposite is true. Moots attempt to *reintegrate* the guilty party back into the community, restore normal social relations between disputing parties, and achieve reconciliation without bitterness and acrimony. The ritualized apology given by the guilty party symbolizes the consensual nature of the resolution and its emphasis on healing the community rather than simply punishing the wrongdoer.

Oaths and Ordeals

Another way of resolving conflicts—particularly when law enforcement agencies (such as governments) are not especially strong—is through religiously sanctioned methods such as oaths and ordeals. An *oath* is a formal declaration to some supernatural power that what you are saying is truthful or that you are innocent. Although they can take many different forms, oaths almost always are accompanied by a ritual act, such as smoking a peace pipe, signing a loyalty document, or swearing on the Bible (as in our courts of law). Because some believe that to swear a false oath could lead to supernatural retribution, oaths can be effective in determining guilt or innocence.

An *ordeal* is a means of determining guilt by submitting the accused to a dangerous test. If the person passes the test, it is believed that a higher supernatural force has determined the party's innocence; if he or she fails, the gods have signaled the party's guilt. In some African societies, an accused person is expected to plunge his hand into a pot of boiling water, lift out a hot stone, and then put his hand into a pot of cold water. The hand is then bandaged and examined the following day. If the hand is blistered, the accused is deemed guilty; if not, his innocence is proclaimed. To Westerners steeped in the principles of the physical sciences, such an approach to determining guilt or innocence seems mystical at best. But there is often more information being gathered than meets the untrained eye. For example, those in charge of conducting the ordeal prepare the accused psychologically to take the proceedings seriously. They explain in considerable detail how the ordeal works; they may put their own hands in the water briefly to show how the innocent are protected from blistering. During these preliminaries to the actual physical ordeal, the person administering the ordeal is looking for nonverbal behaviors of the suspect that may indicate probable guilt: signs of excessive anxiety such as muscle tension, perspiration, or dilation of the pupils. Based on an assessment of these nonverbal signs of anxiety, the ordeal administrator may alter such factors as the length of time the suspect's hand stays in the water, which, in turn, may affect the outcome of the ordeal.

Mechanisms of Social Control in State Societies

Courts and Codified Laws

As previously noted, *all* societies use informal mechanisms of social control to some degree. Western cultures rely heavily on such mechanisms as socialization, public opinion, and supernatural sanctions to encourage people to maintain social order by behaving appropriately. Often, however, these informal mechanisms of social control are not sufficient to maintain

---

moots Informal hearings of disputes for the purpose of resolving conflicts, usually found in small-scale societies.

council of elders A formal control mechanism composed of a group of elders who settle disputes among individuals in a society.

oath A declaration to a god to attest to the truth of what a person says.

ordeal A painful and possibly life-threatening test inflicted on someone suspected of wrongdoing to determine guilt or innocence.

the desired level of conformity to the norms. The violation of social norms often results in disputes among people in the society. When such disputes become violent conflicts (such as theft, assault, or homicide), we call them *crimes*. Because societies face the possibility of violent conflict erupting among their members, they need to develop explicit mechanisms to address and, it is hoped, resolve the conflicts.

Although no society in the world is free from crime, the incidence of crime varies considerably from society to society. It appears that crime is more likely to occur in large, heterogeneous, stratified societies than in small-scale societies. For example, the crime rate in US cities is approximately ten times as high as in rural areas. Several logical arguments support these findings. First, as mentioned in the discussion of corporate lineages, people in small-scale societies have little or no anonymity, which makes getting away with a crime more difficult. Second, because people in small-scale societies know most of the other people, they are more likely to be concerned with negative public opinion. Third, the heterogeneous character of populations in large-scale, complex state societies means that there are many groups with different, and sometimes conflicting, interests. Finally, the fact that large-scale societies are almost always stratified into classes or castes means that the lower strata of the population may feel blocked from upward mobility and consequently may be more likely to want to violate the rights of those in the more privileged strata.

A characteristic of state systems of government is that they possess a monopoly on the use of force. Through a system of codified laws, the state both forbids individuals from using force and determines how it will use force to require citizens to do some things and prevent them from doing others. These laws, which are usually in written form, are established by legislative bodies, interpreted by judicial bodies, and enforced by administrators. When legal prescriptions are violated, the state has the authority, through its courts and law enforcement agencies, to fine, imprison, or even execute the wrongdoer. To suggest that the state has

a monopoly on the use of force does not mean that only the government uses force. State systems of government constantly have to deal with unauthorized uses of force, such as crime (violent disputes between individuals or groups), *rebellion* (attempts to displace the people in power), and *revolution* (attempts to overthrow the entire system of government).

The system of codified laws used to resolve disputes and maintain social order in complex societies is different from other types of social norms. Legal anthropologist E. Adamson Hoebel (1972) identified three basic features of *law*. Although his definition of law goes beyond the type of law found in Western societies, it certainly holds true for that type of law as well.

1. Law involves the legitimate use of physical coercion. Law without the force to punish or deprive is no law at all, although in most cases force is not necessary because the threat of force or compulsion acts as a sufficient deterrent to antisocial behavior (Figure 13.11).
2. Legal systems allocate official authority to privileged people who are able to use coercion legitimately.
3. Law is based on regularity and a certain amount of predictability; that is, because laws build on precedents, new laws are based on old ones.

Legal systems in complex societies have different objectives from systems of conflict resolution found in other societies. The objective of the Nuer Leopard-Skin

crimes Harm to a person or property that society considers illegitimate.

rebellion An attempt within a society to disrupt the status quo and redistribute the power and resources.

revolution An attempt to overthrow the existing form of political organization, the principles of economic production and distribution, and the allocation of social status.

law Cultural rules that regulate human behavior and maintain order.

AP Photos/John Minchillo

FIGURE 13.11 By means of codified laws, state systems of government maintain a monopoly on the use of force. Here an Occupy Wall Street protestor is arrested during a march on Broadway in New York, after police ordered demonstrators to leave their encampment in Zuccotti Park.

Chief and the Kpelle moots, for example, was to compensate the victim and to reestablish harmony among the disputants and consequently peace within the community. Law enforcement and conflict resolution in complex societies, in contrast, tend to emphasize punishment of the wrongdoer, which often takes the form of incarceration or, in some cases, death. In other words, the legal system is not aimed at either compensating the victim or reintegrating the offender back into the community.

This fundamental difference in legal philosophy has played itself out in a number of conflicts around the world. In the tribal violence that has been occurring for the past two decades in northern Uganda, the International Criminal Court at The Hague is indicting rebel leaders to hold them responsible for killing innocent civilians. Local leaders in Uganda, however, want to use age-old rites designed to have the defendants admit publicly to their atrocities, pay a reasonable compensation to the victims, and then make amends with the total community. The traditional solution, based on a powerful capacity to forgive, emphasizes peace, healing between the parties, and reintegration of the wrongdoers back into the community. Although the Ugandan government supports the efforts of the International Court, it has also adopted the traditional notion of forgiveness and healing as one of its strategies to restore peace to the country. Since 2000 an amnesty program has led thousands of rebels to lay down their arms, admit publicly to their misdeeds, and be welcomed back into the society. Using these traditional African philosophies of justice and law in Uganda is similar to the Truth and Reconciliation Commission (headed by Bishop Desmond Tutu [Figure 13.12]) used to heal racial hatred and distrust after decades of the apartheid system in South Africa (Lacey, 2005: 1).

The incompatibility of customary law and Western law presented some legal challenges for newly independent countries beginning in the early 1960s. When Western governments (such as the British, French, Portuguese, Belgians, and Spanish) administered colonies in the nineteenth and twentieth centuries, they invariably imposed their own laws on the local people, which were often at odds with local customary laws. As the colonial period came to an end during the 1960s and 1970s, many newly independent governments needed to develop legal systems based on their own customs and traditions rather than on those of the former colonial powers. For many newly independent governments, this proved to be a formidable task, given their considerable ethnic diversity.

One such former colony was the country of Papua New Guinea, which won its independence in 1975. With a population of 3.5 million, Papua New Guinea was made up of approximately 750 mutually unintelligible languages and at least that many customary

FIGURE 13.12 Archbishop Desmond Tutu served as co-chair of the Truth and Reconciliation Commission, which used traditional African philosophies of law and justice to heal racial hatreds and distrust after decades of segregation in South Africa.

legal systems (Scaglion 1987: 98). The government of this newly independent country was faced with the daunting task of identifying the legal principles of these diverse customary legal systems and reconciling them into a new national legal system. To accomplish this, the parliament established the Law Reform Commission, which sponsored the Customary Law Project (CLP). Headed by legal anthropologist Richard Scaglion of the University of Pittsburgh, the CLP conducted research on local customary law to determine how, and to what extent, it might serve as the basis for a national legal system.

Collecting this database of customary law (made up of hundreds of detailed case studies) made two important practical contributions to the emerging legal system of Papua New Guinea. First, this legal database was immediately useful to lawyers in searching out legal precedents for their ongoing court cases. Second, the database helped to identify, and subsequently alleviate, certain problems arising from a conflict between customary law and the existing national legal system. To illustrate, in the area of family law, polygyny was perfectly permissible under customary law but was strictly forbidden under existing statutory law. Drawing on the legal database of case studies, the Law Reform Commission, in conjunction with the legislative and judicial branches of the government, drafted and passed a family bill that formally recognized the legality of customary marriages and provided for polygyny under certain circumstances.

Warfare

Just as societies have ways of regulating the social relationships of people within their own society, they also have mechanisms for managing external relationships with other groups, be they states, tribes, bands, clans, or lineages. One such mechanism of social control outside one's own group or society is *warfare*, which we can define as systematic, organized, and institutionalized fighting between different groups. People will be less willing to engage in antisocial or aggressive behavior if that behavior might bring about an attack by outside forces. As with most other aspects of culture, there is enormous cultural variability in the extent to which societies use warfare, or other forms of large-scale violence, as a way of resolving conflicts and controlling people's behavior. In some small-scale societies, warfare as we know it is virtually nonexistent; at the other end of the spectrum are societies like the United States, which participated in World War II at a cost of hundreds of thousands of lives and nearly $3 trillion.

It is often stated that warfare has been around as long as there have been people. Although it is probably true that violence has occurred on occasions throughout human prehistory, warfare began during the Neolithic period, starting about ten thousand years ago. Most prehistorians agree that warfare, as we know it, was unknown before the invention of food-production techniques. Before food production, foraging societies had little motivation for engaging in warfare. We can cite four compelling reasons that foraging societies were not warlike: First, they had no centralized governments that could finance and coordinate the relatively large numbers of people needed for military campaigns. Second, the absence of food surpluses precluded prolonged combat. Third, because foraging societies did not control land or territorial boundaries, one of the major motivations of warfare simply did not exist. And fourth, because foraging societies are small in scale (usually composed of exogamous bands), people are not likely to become hostile toward other bands into which their own relatives have married.

CROSS-CULTURAL MISCUE

❁ Even leaders of large nation-states sometimes send unintentional nonverbal messages. As his motorcade passed a group of protesters in Canberra, Australia, in 1992, President George H. W. Bush held up his middle finger and forefinger with the back of his hand toward the protesters. He thought that he was giving the "V for victory" gesture but failed to realize that in Australia that hand gesture is the same as holding up the middle finger in the United States.

With the arrival of food production ten thousand years ago, populations became more sedentary, people began to claim rights over specific pieces of land, and the world experienced its first population explosion. If farmers and pastoralists, by the nature of their means of livelihood, experience significant population growth and land scarcity, they are more likely to resort to warfare as a solution to the problem of resource depletion. They will, in other words, resort to warfare to procure rights to other people's land and scarce resources.

Even though small-scale warfare was a possibility 10,000 years ago, war increased in scale with the rise of civilizations (state societies) 5,500 years ago. The formation of large, hierarchically organized states allowed the creation of significant military organizations. In fact some have argued that state systems of government could not exist without powerful armies to both protect and control their populations. Since the emergence of those early states, the sophistication of military organization and technology has increased steadily over the centuries. During the past century, we have witnessed an incredible escalation in the power of warfare throughout the world. Not only does humankind now possess the technological capacity to totally annihilate itself within a matter of hours, but also warfare during the past century, in part because of that technology, has resulted in the killing of large segments of civilian populations. Modern warfare is likely to produce more civilian than military casualties.

The Causes of War For decades anthropologists and other social scientists have been fascinated with the question What causes war? To address this question, a number of anthropologists over the past thirty years have examined the Yanomamo peoples of the Amazon region of Brazil and Venezuela. The Yanomamo have been of interest to anthropologists because of their institutionalized warfare and their reputation for fierceness. Anthropologist Napoleon

---

warfare Institutionalized, armed conflict between nation-states or other politically distinct groups.

Chagnon attempted to explain their system of warfare on the basis of their headless political structure and their competition for women (1983, 1992). Marvin Harris (1979c, 1984), a cultural materialist (see Chapters 4), offered a materialist explanation—namely, that Yanomamo warfare is the result of shortages of protein. The most recent entry in the debate is anthropologist R. Brian Ferguson (1995), who claims that the Yanomamo go to war over the scarcity of metal tools.

Thus, we have three anthropologists attempting to explain Yanomamo warfare using three different sets of causal factors. Chagnon ascribes Yanomamo warfare to social structure—namely, their headless political structure and the competition for women. Harris and Ferguson suggest that the major reason for going to war is a shortage of either protein or metal tools. That three competent scholars can come up with three different primary causes for Yanomamo warfare illustrates the complexity of trying to understand warfare. In all likelihood, warfare among the Yanomamo is a multidimensional phenomenon, with all three causal factors valid to some degree. Any attempt to explain why the Yanomamo go to war by using any single factor is like trying to explain the motion of an airplane exclusively in terms of the power of its engine while ignoring other factors such as wind speed, altitude, the design and weight of the aircraft, and the skill of the pilot.

If we try to search for the causes of war in general, the task becomes even more daunting. When considering warfare (for all time) in both small-scale societies and modern nation-states, we can identify four general factors that contribute to warfare:

1. *Social problems.* When internal social problems exist, political leaders may turn the society's frustrations toward another group. The outsiders may be portrayed as having more than their share of scarce resources or even as causing the social problems. It matters little whether this blame is justified; what is important is that people are convinced that other groups are the cause of their problems. When that happens, one group can declare war on another. Examples of this factor are when the Yanomamo go to war with neighboring villages over scarce metal tools, and when Adolf Hitler moved his troops into neighboring European countries to acquire more "living room" for the German people.

2. *Perceived threats.* In some cases societies go to war when they think their security or well-being is in jeopardy. The people of North Vietnam during the 1960s were willing to wage war because they felt that their security was threatened by the long-term influence of the French and Americans in the southern part of Vietnam. The Americans, on the other hand, felt, either rightly or wrongly, that Vietnam, and indeed all of Asia, was being threatened by the presence of a godless, Communist regime; if South Vietnam fell to the Communists, it would start a domino effect that would eventually threaten the entire free world.

3. *Political motivations.* Sometimes governments wage war to further their own political objectives. The brief wars (or "military actions") that the United States initiated in Haiti, Grenada, Panama, and Somalia were motivated by the desire to show sufficient power to enforce its political will.

4. *Moral objectives.* It is difficult to think of any war in human history that has been waged without moral urgency. Even when wars are waged primarily for political or economic reasons, those who commit their soldiers to battle justify their actions on some moral grounds. Europeans waged the Crusades against the Islamic infidels because they were convinced that God was on their side. Interestingly, if we read accounts of those same wars written by Islamic historians, it is the European Christians who were the godless bad guys. Both sides justified waging wars for generations on the basis of moral correctness.

It is possible, even likely, that more than one of these factors operate at the same time. To illustrate, the US Congress authorized the use of military action in Iraq in 2003 based on the perceived threat that Saddam Hussein had stockpiles of chemical and biological weapons and intended to sell them to the terrorists who were responsible for the September 11, 2001, attacks. After the weapons of mass destruction and the links to al-Qaeda failed to materialize, the US government argued that its preemptive war in Iraq was justified on political grounds; that is, establishing one democratic regime in the region would cause democracy to spread throughout the Middle East. In addition the government used the moral justification by arguing that Hussein needed to be overthrown because he was an evil dictator responsible for many atrocities perpetrated against his own people. Thus, in this example three of the four factors contributing to warfare (listed previously) have been used at one time or another to justify the war in Iraq.

Summary

1. All societies have political systems to manage public affairs, maintain social order, and resolve conflict. The study of political organization involves topics such as the allocation of political roles, levels of political integration, concentrations of power and authority, mechanisms of social control, and means for resolving conflict.

2. Political anthropologists generally recognize four fundamentally different levels of political organization based on amounts of political integration and specialization of political roles: bands, tribes, chiefdoms, and states.

3. Societies based on bands have the least political integration and role specialization. They are most often found in foraging societies and are associated with low population densities, distribution systems based on reciprocity, and egalitarian social relations.

4. Tribal organizations are most commonly found among horticulturalists and pastoralists. With larger and more sedentary populations than are found in band societies, tribally based societies have certain pan-tribal mechanisms that cut across a number of local segments and integrate them into a larger whole.

5. Chiefdoms have a more formal and permanent political structure than is found in tribal societies. Political authority in chiefdoms rests with a single individual, acting either alone or with the advice of a council. Most chiefdoms, which tend to have quite distinct social ranks, rely on feasting and tribute as a major way of distributing goods.

6. State systems—with the greatest amount of political integration and role specialization—are associated with intensive agriculture, market economies, urbanization, and complex social stratification. States, which first appeared about 5,500 years ago, have a monopoly on the use of force and can make and enforce laws, collect taxes, and recruit labor for military service and public works projects.

7. A major challenge for many state governments today is that they contain within their boundaries distinct ethnic populations that seek independence or greater autonomy, as illustrated by the French in Canada, the Kurds in Turkey, and the Chechens in Russia.

8. As a general rule, women do not hold important positions of political leadership in state systems of government.

9. During the past several decades, there has been a general trend toward democracy and away from autocracy, although that trend has reversed during the period of 2006 to 2012.

10. The "Failed States Index," compiled by the Fund for Peace, can (a) assist world leaders in assessing political risk and (b) serve as an early warning device for future conflicts.

11. In the absence of formal mechanisms of government, many band and tribal societies maintain social control by means of informal mechanisms such as socialization, public opinion, corporate lineages, supernatural sanctions, and age organizations.

12. In addition to using informal means of social control, societies control behavior by more formal mechanisms, with the major goal of maintaining social order and resolving conflicts. These mechanisms include verbal competition, intermediaries, councils of elders, oaths, ordeals, formal court systems, and warfare.

13. A society will go to war when it (a) blames another society for its own social problems, (b) believes that it is threatened, (c) wants to further its own ends, or (d) is defending a moral position.

Key Terms

age grades

age organizations

age set

authority

autocracy

band societies

chiefdoms

pan-tribal mechanisms

corporate lineages

council of elders

crime

democracy

deviance

headless societies

intermediaries

law

Leopard-Skin Chief

moots

nation

negative sanctions

oath

ordeal

pan-tribal mechanisms

political coerciveness

political integration

positive sanctions

public opinion

rebellion

revolution

sanctions

social control

socialization

social norms

song duel

specialized political roles

state

state system of government

supernatural belief systems

tribal societies

warfare

witchcraft

Critical Thinking Questions

1. In the discussion of the rise of state systems of government we mentioned that people were willing to surrender a portion of their autonomy to the state (that is, hierarchical government) for the anticipated benefits of public works projects (roads, water systems, etc.), protection from outside attacks, and effective conflict resolution between the various subgroups within the state. Thus, most people viewed this as a contract between the general public (who paid taxes and gave up some personal autonomy) and the government, which provided social services that the people could not provide on their own.

   In the twenty-first century United States there is a powerful group of legislators who want to restrict the role of government to only the most essential functions. Do you feel that this political philosophy loses sight of this fundamental contract between people and their government? Why or why not?

2. *Deviation* is defined in this chapter as "the violation of a social norm." Do you think there is more social deviation in small-scale societies or in larger, more complex societies? Why or why not?

3. Although the United States is hardly becoming a "failed state," it did rank eighteenth (among the 178 nations of the world). In other words, there were seventeen other countries (including Iceland, Slovenia, and Portugal) that were ranked even less likely than the United States of becoming a failed state. Despite the fact that the United States remains the world's largest economy, how do you explain its relatively low ranking? (Hint: Look at the list of twelve criteria for "failed statehood" on page 325–326.

Online Study Resources

CourseMate

Access chapter-specific learning tools including learning objectives, practice quizzes, videos, flash cards, glossaries, web links, and more in your Cultural Anthropology CourseMate. Login to www.cengagebrain.com to access the resources your instructor has assigned and to purchase materials.

A Hindu religious pilgrim prays in Varanasi, India.

Belief Systems

✻

The city of El Alto, a twin city to Bolivia's capitol of La Paz, has a population of 800,000 residents and is the home of a thriving witches market. The indigenous Aymara people generally believe that the month of August, as winter begins to turn to spring, is when the Pachamama (or Earth Mother) becomes especially hungry and needs to be fed. Merchants at the witches market sell a wide variety of animal products (including llama, dog, cat, pig, and vicuña fetuses), which are sacrificed to the traditional deities to ensure good fortune for the coming year.

Many of the merchants in the witches market are also ritual specialists called *yatiris*, who sell not only the ritual animal parts but also their own services. The yatiris perform elaborate rituals that incorporate dead animals, coca leaves, and locally distilled alcohol. The rituals are concluded after the yatiri sets the sacrificial items on fire and buries the residue as food for Earth Mother. For a cost of between three and ten dollars (depending on the price of ingredients), a yatiri will perform a ritual that will improve his or her client's chances of having good fortune in the year ahead.

Although these ritual animal sacrifices originated with traditional rural farmers seeking plentiful harvests, customers at the witches market in the twenty-first century are looking for success in business, good health, and freedom from misfortune. According to one observer (Romero 2008), a sign on one stall at the El Alto witches market indicates how a traditional supernatural ritual is used today to meet the needs of modern city dwellers in Bolivia. It says simply, "For love, travel, marriage, health, legal problems, making lost things appear, duty inspections, exams at the teacher's college." ■

WHAT WE WILL LEARN

■ What is religion?

■ What different forms does religion take among the societies of the world?

■ What functions does religion perform for the individual and for the society as a whole?

■ What role does religion play in the process of cultural change?

■ How are religions changing in the age of globalization?

Beginning in the nineteenth century, religion was studied from a scientific, rather than just a theological, perspective. For example, in *The Elementary Forms of Religious Life*, French sociologist Émile Durkheim ([1912] 2001) argued that religion enables people to transcend their individual identities and to see themselves as part of a larger collective. Another social scientist, Max Weber, analyzed religion as it relates to economic institutions. In his classic study, *The Protestant Ethic and the Spirit of Capitalism*, Weber (1958) claimed that the Protestant faith supported the rise of capitalism in Western societies. And, of course, Marx, studying religion from a nontheological perspective, linked organized religions with social inequality by suggesting that religion was a tool for oppressing the lower classes.

The scientific study of religion during the nineteenth and twentieth centuries has been interpreted by some as the beginning of the end for organized religion. Yet the analysis of religion by social scientists has not caused people to abandon their religions in great numbers. To be certain, some religious groups in different parts of the world have lost followers, but others have gained

© David Samuel Robbins/Corbis.

adherents in recent decades, particularly fundamentalist groups (both at home and abroad). For example, long before September 11, the world witnessed a rise in Islamic fundamentalism in such places as Saudi Arabia, Iran, and Egypt; the recent governments in Israel have been elected largely by the growing number of Jewish fundamentalists; and the most dramatic growth in church affiliation in the United States in the last several decades has been among various fundamentalist (evangelical) churches, such as the Assembly of God and the Church of God in Christ. Thus, the scientific study of religion has hardly inhibited these particular religious movements, and in fact their "antisciencce" stance on most contemporary issues might suggest that a scientific view of the world has contributed to their growth.

Cultural anthropologists have devoted considerable attention to analyzing religion since they began to make direct field observations of peoples of the world. Although twentieth-century anthropologists have not always agreed on how to interpret different religious systems, all would agree that the many religious practices found throughout the world vary widely from one another as well as from our own. These religious systems involve sacrificing animals to ancestor-gods, using a form of divination called ordeals to determine a person's guilt or innocence, and submitting oneself to extraordinary pain as a way of communicating directly with the deities (Lehmann and Myers 1993).

Defining Religion

The forms of religion vary enormously, but all are alike to the extent that they are founded on a belief in the supernatural. For our purposes in this chapter, we shall define *religion* as a set of beliefs in supernatural beings and forces directed at helping people make sense of the world and solve important problems. Because human beings face important life problems that cannot all be resolved through the application of science and technology alone, they attempt to overcome these human limitations by manipulating supernatural forces.

Anthropologists have long observed that all societies have a recognizable set of beliefs and behaviors that can be called *religious*. According to George Murdock's (1945) widely quoted list of cultural universals, all societies have religious rituals that appease supernatural forces, sets of beliefs concerning what we would call the soul or human spirit, and notions about life after death.

To be sure, nonreligious people can be found in all societies. But when we claim that religion (or a belief in the supernatural) is universal, we are referring to a cultural phenomenon rather than an individual one. For example, we can find individuals in the Western world who do not believe personally in supernatural forces such as deities, ghosts, demons, or spirits. Nevertheless these people are part of a society that has a set of religious beliefs and practices to which many (perhaps a majority) of the population adhere.

Because religion, in whatever form it may be found, is often taken seriously and passionately by its adherents, there is a natural tendency for people to see their own religion as the best while viewing all others as inferior. Westerners often use science, logic, and empirical evidence (for example, through the study of biblical texts) to bolster and justify their own religious practices. Nevertheless science and logic are not adequate to either establish the inherent validity of Western religious beliefs or demonstrate that non-Western religions are false. In other words, no religion is able to demonstrate conclusively that its deities can work more miracles per unit of time than those of other religions, although some certainly try. The central issue for anthropologists is not to determine which religion is better or more correct but rather to identify the various religious beliefs in the world as well as how they function, to what extent they are held, and the degree to which they affect human behavior.

Problems of Defining Religion

Defining religion is difficult because anthropologists disagree on how to distinguish between religious and nonreligious phenomena. In some societies religion is so thoroughly embedded in the total social structure that it is difficult to distinguish religious behavior from economic, political, or kinship behavior. To illustrate, when a Kikuyu elder sacrifices a goat at the grave of an ancestor-god, is he engaging in religious behavior (he is calling for the ancestor-god to intervene in the affairs of the living), economic behavior (the meat of the sacrificed animal is distributed to and eaten by members of the kinship group), or kinship behavior (kin have a chance to express their group solidarity at the ceremonial event)?

Such a ritual sacrifice performs all of these functions at the same time. In highly specialized societies, such as our own, people tend to divide human behavior into what, at least for them, are logical categories: social, economic, political, religious, educational, and recreational, for example. Because many small-scale, less specialized societies do not divide human behavior into the same categories used in Western society, it is often difficult for Westerners to recognize those aspects of human behavior that we think of as religious.

Another difficulty in defining religion and the supernatural is that different societies have different ways of distinguishing between the natural world and

---

religion A set of beliefs in supernatural forces that functions to provide meaning, peace of mind, and a sense of control over unexplainable phenomena.

the supernatural world. In our own society, we reserve the term *supernatural* for phenomena we cannot explain through reason or science. Other societies, however, do not divide the world into either natural or supernatural arenas. For example, the Nyoro of Uganda have a word for *sorcery* that means "to injure another person by the secret use of harmful medicines or techniques" (Beattie 1960: 73). Sorcery in Nyoro society can take different forms. Placing a person's body substances (such as pieces of hair or fingernail clippings) in an animal horn and putting the horn on the roof of the person's house with the intention of causing that person harm is an act of sorcery in Nyoro society, but so is putting poison into an enemy's food or drink.

Given our own Western dichotomy between the natural and the supernatural, we would interpret these two acts as substantially different in nature. We would interpret the first act as an attempt to harm another person by the use of magic. If the intended victim dies, our own Western law courts would never hold the perpetrator culpable, for the simple reason that it could not be proven scientifically that placing the magical substances on the roof was the cause of the death. However, Westerners would view the poisoning as premeditated murder because it could be determined scientifically (that is, through an autopsy) that the poison did cause the person to die. This illustration should remind us that not all societies share our Western definition of the supernatural. It is precisely because of this difference in viewing the natural and supernatural worlds that Westerners have so much difficulty understanding non-Western religions, which they usually label as irrational or contradictory.

Another source of confusion when we try to define religion is our inability to separate supernatural beliefs from other aspects of culture. People often claim to be acting in the name of their religion, but in fact they are using their religion to support or reject other (nonreligious) features of their culture. For example, we often think of such policy issues as opposition to abortion, gay marriage, Darwin's theory of evolution, and stem-cell research as being part of the philosophy of evangelical Christianity. Instead these are social issues that many rural evangelicals in the so-called "red states" tend to support by citing their own interpretations of scripture. But it is certainly possible—and definitely demonstrable—to believe in the central core of evangelical Christianity (e.g., personal conversion and the full authority of the Bible) without rejecting abortion, Darwinian evolution, or gay marriage. In fact evangelical Christianity is making significant headway in various urban ministries throughout the country, from San Francisco to New York City, among well-educated members of the creative class who express just the opposite positions on these social issues. For example, Rev. Timothy J. Keller has been wildly successful at growing his Redeemer Presbyterian Church

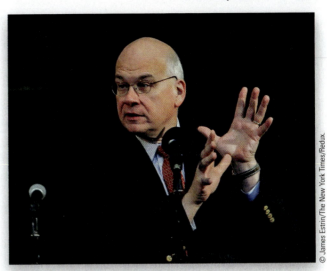

FIGURE 14.1 Evangelist Rev. Timothy J Keller thrives in Manhattan by embracing the city and identifying with its culture.

in Manhattan to five thousand attendees over the last several decades (Figure 14.1). He appeals to all sorts of urban professionals—from designers to university students—because his sermons are literary and intellectual. He replaces the traditional "hellfire and brimstone" with well-reasoned sermons quoting such sources as C. S. Lewis and the liberal newspaper *The Village Voice*. Keller (along with other urban evangelical ministers) has been successful because he understands the difference between the core evangelical (religious) message and a number of contemporary sociocultural issues on which Jesus and the Bible had nothing to say (Luo 2006). Thus there seems to be a growing number of young Christian fundamentalists in the United States who are refusing to put conservative politics at the heart of their Christian ideology.

Religion and Magic

Anthropologists who study supernatural beliefs cross-culturally have long been fascinated by the relationship between religion and magic. Whereas some anthropologists have emphasized the differences between these two phenomena, others have concentrated on their similarities. It is important to examine both the similarities and the differences because, even though religion and magic can be found operating separately, most often are combined. Religion and magic share certain features. Because both are systems of supernatural belief, they are non-rational; that is, they are not susceptible to scientific verification. In other words, whether religious or magical practices actually work cannot be empirically demonstrated. Rather such practices must be accepted as a matter of faith. Moreover both religion and magic are practiced—at least in part—as ways of coping with the anxieties, ambiguities, and frustrations of everyday life.

CONTEMPORARY ISSUES

Religious Freedom in Florida

Sultaana Freeman, a thirty-four-year-old Islamic resident of Winter Park, Florida, had no difficulty getting a Florida driver's license in February 2001 despite having insisted (on religious grounds) that her picture be taken behind a veil. Several months after September 11, however, officials from the Florida Department of Motor Vehicles changed their minds and informed Freeman that to keep her license, she would need a new photo showing her entire face. She subsequently gave up her driver's license and then sued the state to get it reinstated (Canedy 2002; Pristin 2002). Here is a clear case of a conflict between a person's rights to be true to her religion (Islam requires that she shield her face in public) and the government's need to maintain public safety by being able to identify a person in a traffic stop.

The state argued that law enforcement officials need a full-face photo to verify one's identity, which is, after all, why driver's licenses have photos. Admittedly, after September 11, this need for public safety and security took on greater urgency when it was assumed that there was a strong relationship between some religious beliefs and acts of terrorism.

On the other side of the issue, lawyers for Freeman argued that forcing her to have a full-face picture is unreasonable, subjective, and violates her freedom of religion. It was pointed out that Florida statutes do not prohibit a person from being veiled in photos for driver's licenses. Moreover Florida's Religious Restoration Act explicitly states that laws that burden the exercise of religion must have a compelling government purpose. Lawyers for Freeman claimed that the state had no such compelling purpose because their client was open to providing fingerprints, DNA, or other information that could be used to verify her identity. It was patently unfair, they argued, to expect Freeman to have to choose between her religious beliefs and the convenience of having a valid driver's license.

If you were the judge in this civil case, how would you rule?

© Peter Dazeley/Getty Images

On the other hand, magic and religion differ in important respects. First, religion deals with the major issues of human existence, such as the meaning of life, death, and one's spiritual relationship with deities. In contrast, magic is directed toward specific, immediate problems, such as curing an illness, bringing rain, or ensuring safety on a long journey. Second, religion uses prayer and sacrifices to appeal to or petition supernatural powers for assistance. Magicians, on the other hand, believe they can control or manipulate nature or other people by their own efforts. Third, religion by and large tends to be a group activity, whereas magic is more individually oriented. Fourth, whereas religion is usually practiced at a specified time, magic is practiced irregularly in response to specific and immediate problems. Fifth, religion usually involves officially recognized functionaries such as priests, whereas magic is performed by a wide variety of practitioners who may or may not be recognized within the community as having supernatural powers.

Despite these five differences, elements of religion and magic in actual practice are usually found together. In any religion, for example, there is a fine line between praying for God's help and coercing or manipulating a situation to bring about a desired outcome. Also it is not at all unusual for a person to use elements of both religion and magic simultaneously. To illustrate, a soldier about to enter combat may ask for divine protection through prayer while carrying a lucky rabbit's foot (a magical charm). Following the lead of nineteenth-century anthropologist Sir James Frazer, modern-day anthropologists distinguish between two types of magic: imitative magic and contagious magic. *Imitative magic* is based on the principle "what you do is what you get." The religion of voodoo contains some elements of imitative magic. The idea behind a voodoo doll is that by doing harm to the doll (such as sticking it with pins, burning it, or throwing it into the ocean), you will magically harm the person the doll represents. *Contagious magic* is the notion that an object that has been in contact with a person retains a magical connection to that person. The strongest magical connection exists between a person and something that has been a part of his or her body, such as hair, nail clippings, or teeth. Those who practice contagious magic believe that a person can be harmed by evil magicians if they

---

imitative magic A form of magic based on the idea that the procedure performed resembles the desired result; for example, sticking a doll-like image with pins will harm the person the doll represents.

contagious magic A form of magic based on the premise that things, once in contact with a person (such as a lock of hair), continue to influence that person after separation.

can obtain any of these former body parts. In some parts of the world, economic development projects designed to build latrines to improve sanitation have been unsuccessful because people are fearful of defecating in a place where one's feces could be obtained by an evildoer.

Magic involves the manipulation of supernatural forces for the purpose of intervening in a wide range of human activities and natural events. Magic is used ritualistically in some societies to ensure the presence of game animals, to bring rain, to cure or prevent illness, or to protect oneself from misfortune. Magic, however, can also be (and often is) directed to cause evil. In some societies it is believed that certain people called *witches* or *sorcerers* use supernatural powers to bring harm to people. Because these forms of "negative magic" hold such fascination for Westerners, it is instructive to examine them in greater detail.

Sorcery and Witchcraft

Although the terms *witchcraft* and *sorcery* are sometimes used synonymously, cultural anthropologists distinguish between them. According to the traditional anthropological definition, *witchcraft* is an inborn, *involuntary*, and often unconscious capacity to cause harm to other people. That having been said, the discussion later in this chapter on modern urban witchcraft (Wiccans) states that this form of witchcraft is not used for nefarious purposes—thus, the Wiccans do not fall under this traditionally used definition. On the other hand, *sorcery*, which often involves the use of materials, potions, and medicines, is the *deliberate* use of supernatural powers to bring about harm. Some societies have specialized practitioners of sorcery, but in other societies anyone can practice sorcery. Because sorcery involves the use of certain physical substances, the evidence for its existence is easily found. Witchcraft, by contrast, is virtually impossible to prove or disprove because there is no visible evidence of its existence.

Whereas sorcery involves using material substances to cause harm to people, witchcraft, it is thought, relies solely on psychic power (that is, thoughts and emotions). In other words, witches can turn their anger and hatred into evil deeds simply by thinking evil thoughts. How witches are conceptualized varies widely from society to society, but in all cases witches are viewed negatively. Witches are generally seen as being unable to control the human impulses that normal members of society are expected to keep in check. They have insatiable appetites for food, uncontrollable hatred, and perverted sexual desires. The Mandari believe that witches dance on their victims' graves. The Lugbara of Uganda speak of witches who dance naked, which for them is the ultimate social outrage. The Ganda and Nyoro of Uganda believe in witches who eat corpses. Among the Kaguru of Tanzania, witches are believed to walk upside down, devour human flesh, commit incest, and in general fail to recognize the rules and constraints of normal society. In many parts of the world, witches are associated with the night, which separates them from normal people, who go about their business during the daytime. Moreover witches are often associated with certain animals, such as bats, rats, snakes, lizards, or leopards, that are black, dangerous, and nocturnal.

Sorcerers are generally believed to direct their malevolence purposefully against those they dislike, fear, or envy rather than acting randomly or capriciously. In any given society, hostile relations can occur among people who have some relationship to one another— such as outsiders who marry into a local village, rivals for a father's inheritance, wives in a polygynous household, men who are competing for a political office, or even rivals in competitive sports. People are therefore likely to attribute their own personal misfortune to the sorcery of some rival who might gain from harming them. Thus, accusations of sorcery are patterned to the extent that they reflect the conflicts, rivalries, and antagonisms that already exist among the people in any given society.

Although witchcraft and sorcery are usually associated with small-scale societies in the non-Western world, they are also found in highly industrialized parts of the world such as the United States, Canada, and some western European countries. Contemporary Western witches, who use their supernatural powers for humane purposes, call their belief system *Wicca*, a term meaning *witch* derived from Old English. Practiced largely in urban areas, witchcraft, like more orthodox religions, involves worship as a central part of its activities. Although it is possible for both men and women to practice witchcraft, in North American cities most practitioners are women, and Wicca has an unmistakably matriarchal character. Local organizations of witches, called *covens*, are often presided over by high priestesses, symbolic representations of the mother goddess. Some covens consider themselves fertility cults, and some actually involve sexual intercourse as part of their initiation, although this is relatively rare. Although this has attracted a good deal of interest in the news media, the Wiccas emphasize fertility, not sexuality. (Figure 14.2)

---

magic A system of supernatural beliefs that involves the manipulation of supernatural forces for the purpose of intervening in a wide range of human activities and natural events.

witchcraft The practice of an inborn, involuntary, and often unconscious capacity to cause harm to other people.

sorcery The performance of certain magical rites for the purpose of harming other people.

Wicca A modern-day movement of witches and pagans.

covens Local groups of witches that are often presided over by high priestesses.

CROSS-CULTURAL MISCUE

❋ Rod Powell was sent to Hong Kong to set up a new office for his company. He had made arrangements to spend several days with a Chinese colleague to look at office space with a realtor. However, after two full days of looking at a large number of properties, Rod's Chinese colleague has had something negative to say about all of them. Rod became frustrated because he was not sure how long he would have to stay in Hong Kong. How do you explain this situation?

Rod's Chinese colleague was an advocate of Feng Shui, an ancient Chinese philosophy, which calls for finding the most harmonious and auspicious place to live and work. Feng shui dictates how a building should be built to have a smooth flow of positive energy. For example, the front door should face the east, not the west, which is associated with death. There are many such requirements for the physical features of a building if it is to conform to the principles of Feng Shui.

The growth of the practice of Wicca has coincided with the rise of feminism, ecology movements, and movements seeking freedom from authority. Wicca tends to be nondogmatic, nonhierarchical, and nonproselytizing. Its gentle rituals seem to appeal especially to women and are based on the principle "do what you will, but harm no one."

In recent decades, as conventional institutional religions have experienced a gradual decline in membership, there has been increased interest in such esoteric forms of spirituality as the Wiccan movement.

FIGURE 14.2 The Rev. Selena Fox, a Wiccan high priestess of the Circle Sanctuary in Barneveld, Wisconsin.

Although it is difficult to ascertain the precise number of practicing Wiccans today, some recent developments point to its increasing popularity (Figure 14.2). For example, throughout the first decade of the twenty-first century there has been a steady increase in the number of books dealing with the Wiccan movement sold by Amazon.com (more than five thousand), and Yahoo! and Google searches for "Wicca" in 2013 have turned up approximately 14 million hits. In the 1970s various Wiccan groups applied for, and received, tax-exempt status from federal and state governments, thereby conferring on the Wiccans official recognition as a legitimate religion. Since the late 1970s, Wiccans have served as chaplains in prisons, hospices, and the military. Perhaps the most important event validating the Wiccan movement in the United States occurred in 2007, when, after a decade-long court battle, the US Department of Veterans Affairs granted permission for deceased Wiccan soldiers to have their gravestones marked with the symbol of the pentacle (five-pointed star).

Functions of Religion

Anthropological studies of religion are no longer dominated by the search for origins. More recent studies have focused on how religious systems *function* for both the individual and the society as a whole. Because religious systems are so universal, it is generally held that they must meet a number of important needs at both personal and societal levels. Yet, it should be obvious to most religious practitioners that supernatural powers do not always work as effectively as the practitioners think they should. For example, we pray to God for the recovery of a sick friend, but the friend dies nevertheless; a ritual specialist conducts a rain dance, but it still does not rain; or the living relatives sacrifice a goat at the grave site of the ancestor-god but still are not spared the ravages of the drought. Although supernatural beings and forces may not always perform their requested functions (that is, bring about supernatural events), they do perform less obvious functions for both the individual and the society as a whole. These latent functions, as they are called by Robert Merton (1957), fall into two broad categories: social and psychological.

Social Functions of Religion

One of the most popular explanations for the universality of religion is that it performs important functions for the overall well-being of the society of which it is a part. Let us consider three such social functions of religion: social control, conflict resolution, and reinforcement of group solidarity.

Social Control

One important social function of religion is its use as a mechanism of social control. Through both positive and negative sanctions, religion tends to maintain social order by encouraging socially acceptable behavior and discouraging socially inappropriate behavior. Every religion, regardless of the form it takes, is an ethical system that prescribes proper ways of behaving. When social sanctions (rewards and punishments) are backed with supernatural authority, they become more compelling. Biblical texts, for example, are explicit about the consequences of violating the Ten Commandments. Because of their strong belief in ghostly vengeance, the Lugbara of Uganda scrupulously avoid engaging in any antisocial behavior that would provoke the wrath of the ancestor-gods. As mentioned in Chapter 12, Hindus in India believe that violating prescribed caste expectations will jeopardize their progress in future reincarnations.

Religious beliefs and behaviors serve as mechanisms of social control for reasons other than fear of divine retribution. Michael McCullough and Brian Willoughby (2009) have investigated the notion that a sincere belief in religion gives people greater internal control, resistance to temptation, and hence obedience to societal norms. A review of the scholarly research over the past century reveals that devoutly religious people generally are more successful in school, live longer, and have more satisfying marriages. But McCullough and Willoughby were interested in learning whether these findings could be explained by an increase in self-control. They found that brain scan studies reveal that praying, reading holy texts, and meditating (three religious activities) stimulate two parts of the brain associated with self-regulation of attention and emotions. In another study conducted in 2003, people who were subliminally exposed to religious words, like *God* and *Bible*, were slower to recognize words associated with temptation, such as *alcohol* and *pornography*. Although McCullough and Willoughby reviewed research conducted largely on Western and Christian populations, evidence from research conducted in the non-Western world is consistent with their main conclusions that there is a close correlation between religious beliefs and practices, on the one hand, and self-control, conscientiousness, and adherence to social norms on the other.

From an anthropological perspective, it is irrelevant whether supernatural forces really do reward good behavior and punish bad behavior. Rather than concern themselves with whether and to what extent supernatural forces work the way they are thought to, anthropologists are interested in whether and to what extent people actually believe in the power of the supernatural forces. After all, it is *belief* in the power of the supernatural sanctions that determines the level of conformity to socially prescribed behavior.

Conflict Resolution

Another social function of religion is the role it plays in reducing the stress and frustrations that often lead to social conflict. In some societies, for example, natural calamities such as epidemics or famines are attributed to the evil deeds of people in other villages or regions. By concentrating on certain religious rituals designed to protect themselves against outside malevolence, people avoid the potential disruptiveness to their own society that might occur if they took out their frustrations on the evildoers. Moreover disenfranchised and powerless people in stratified societies sometimes use religion as a way of diffusing the anger and hostility that might otherwise be directed against the entire social system. To illustrate, in his study of separatist Christian churches in the Republic of South Africa, Bengt Sundkler (1961) showed how small groups of black South Africans—who until recently were systematically excluded from the power structure by apartheid—created the illusion of power by manipulating their own religious symbols and forming their own unique churches. By providing an alternative power structure, these breakaway Christian churches served to reduce conflict in South Africa by diverting resentment away from the wider power structure.

Sundkler's interpretation of separatist churches in South Africa is similar to Marx's nineteenth-century interpretation of religion as the opiate of the masses. As an economic determinist, Marx claimed that religion, like other institutions, reflects the underlying modes of production in the society. The purpose of religion, according to Marx, was to preserve the economic superstructure that allowed the upper classes (bourgeoisie) to exploit the working classes (proletariat). By focusing people's attention on the eternal bliss awaiting them in heaven, religion diverts their attention from the misery of their lives in the here and now. In other words, religion blinds working people to the fact that they are being exploited by the ruling class. As long as the working class focuses on the afterlife, they are not likely to heed Marx's advice to revolt against their oppressors. Thus, religion is a societal mechanism to reduce conflict between differing economic subgroups.

Reinforcement of Group Solidarity

A third social function of religion is to intensify the group solidarity of those who practice it. Religion enables people to express their common identity in an emotionally charged environment. Powerful social bonds are often created among people who share the experiences of religious beliefs, practices, and rituals.

Because every religion or supernatural belief system has its own unique structural features, those who practice it share in its mysteries, whereas those who do not are excluded. In short, religion strengthens a person's sense of group identity and belonging. And of course, as people come together for common religious experiences, they often engage in other nonreligious activities as well, which further strengthens the sense of social solidarity.

The role of organized religion in creating and maintaining group solidarity is particularly important in immigrant populations. To illustrate, recent Korean immigrants to the United States, even those who are not particularly religious, often join a Korean Christian church as a way of establishing instant social networks with other Korean immigrants. According to Charles Ryu (1992: 162–63):

> In America, whatever the reason, the church has become a major and central anchoring institution for Korean immigrant society. Whereas no other institution supported the Korean immigrants, the church played the role of anything and everything—from social service, to education, to learning the Korean language: a place to gather, to meet other people, for social gratification, you name it. The way we think of church is more than in a religious connotation.... Your identity is tied so closely to the church you go to. I think almost 70 to 80 percent of Korean Americans belong to church.... Living in American society as a minority is a very difficult thing. You are nobody out there, but when you come to church, you are somebody.

Psychological Functions of Religion

In addition to promoting the well-being of the society, religion functions psychologically for the benefit of the individual. Anthropologists have identified two fundamentally different types of psychological functions of religion: a cognitive function, whereby religion provides a cognitive framework for explaining parts of our world that we do not understand, and an emotional function, whereby religion helps to reduce anxiety by prescribing some straightforward ways of coping with stress.

Cognitive Function

In terms of its cognitive and intellectual function, religion is psychologically comforting because it helps us explain the unexplainable. Every society must deal with imponderable questions that have no definitive logical answers: When did life begin? Why do bad things happen to good people? What happens to us when we die? Even in societies like our own—where we have, or think we have, many scientific answers—many questions remain unanswered. A medical pathologist may be able to explain to the parents of a child who has died of malaria that the cause of death was a bite by an infected anopheles mosquito. But that same pathologist cannot explain to the grieving parents why the mosquito bit their child and not the child next door. Religion can provide satisfying answers to such questions because the answers are based on supernatural authority.

Unlike any other life form, humans have a highly developed desire to understand themselves and the world around them. But because human understanding of the universe is so imperfect, religion provides a framework for giving meaning to events and experiences that cannot be explained in any other way. Religion assures its believers that the world is meaningful, that events happen for a reason, that there is order in the universe, and that apparent injustices will eventually be rectified. Humans have difficulty whenever unexplained phenomena contradict their cultural worldview. One of the functions of religion, then, is to enable people to maintain their worldview even when events seem to contradict it.

Emotional Function

The emotional function of religion is to help individuals cope with the anxieties that often accompany illnesses, accidents, deaths, and other misfortunes. Because people never have complete control over the circumstances of their lives, they often turn to religious ritual in an attempt to maximize control through supernatural means. In fact the less control people feel they have over their own lives, the more they are likely to practice religion. The fear of facing a frightening situation can be at least partially overcome by believing that supernatural beings will intervene on one's behalf; a person can reduce shame and guilt by becoming humble and pious in the face of the deities; and during times of bereavement, religion can be a source of emotional strength.

People perform religious rituals as a way of invoking supernatural beings to control the forces over which they feel they have no control. This takes different forms throughout the world. To illustrate, the Trobriand Islanders perform magico-religious rituals for protection before a long voyage; to protect their gardens, men in parts of New Guinea put leaves across their fences, believing that the leaves will paralyze the arms and legs of any thief who raids the garden; and in Nairobi, Kenya, some professional football teams reportedly hire their own ritual specialists to bewitch their opponents. In addition to providing greater peace of mind, such religious practices may actually have a positive *indirect* effect on the events they are intended to influence. For example, even if their witchcraft does not work, football players are likely to play more confidently if they believe they have a supernatural advantage. This ability to act with confidence is a major psychological function of religion.

Anthropology and Medicine

For the past several decades, medical anthropology in the United States has been the most rapidly growing area of applied anthropology (see Chapter 1). Medical anthropologists have helped develop systems of medical knowledge and patient care by turning their cross-cultural lens on doctor-patient relationships, the integration of alternative and mainstream medical practices, and the interaction of social, environmental, and biological factors influencing health and sickness. For half a century, research in medical anthropology has demonstrated that, when medical caregivers are working with culturally different patients, culture is a critical variable in the diagnosis and treatment of illnesses. In other words, the effective treatment of immigrant patients in Chicago or Toronto must take into account the patients' (culturally constructed) *beliefs and customary practices* about their bodies, their bodily processes, and the nature and causes of illness. These findings are now being taken seriously by the Western medical establishment. Hospitals, medical clinics, and the doctors and nurses who treat culturally different patients are now using these cross-cultural data to modify some of their standard operating procedures.

Some hospitals and clinics operating in US cities that have significant immigrant populations have been taking into account (from day one) the supernatural beliefs that people bring with them to a medical setting. To illustrate, a hospital in Brooklyn, New York, postponed the official opening of a new clinic for Chinese immigrants by twenty-four hours. Although the clinic was set to open on April 24, 2006, hospital officials were informed that, according to the Chinese belief in numerology, the number 24 is considered "unlucky." By simply waiting until April 25 (a more auspicious date), officials ensured that most of their Chinese patients would feel more positive about visiting the clinic. Clearly a clinic will not be able to serve its Chinese patients if those patients are reluctant to use the clinic because they fear it is a place of ill fortune (Confessore 2006).

In addition to the date of the official opening, clinic officials must be sensitive to other traditional Chinese beliefs to reduce patient anxiety, which can retard or even prevent recovery from illnesses. For example, because Chinese associate the color white with death, the clinic designers took the culturally appropriate measure of painting the walls shades of pink and yellow. Moreover chefs in the hospital's kitchens have learned to make rice porridge, a widely favored Chinese "comfort food." Had this hospital opened a clinic for immigrants from the Middle East rather than China, they would have applied anthropological insights by facing their patients' beds east (toward Mecca), so they could pray comfortably five times a day as their faith requires; by ensuring that male doctors do not examine female patients; and by not touching patients with their left hands.

Some readers might object to these modifications as pandering to immigrant patients. After all, these ethnocentric observers would argue, if "those people" choose to get sick in the United States, they darn well better expect to do things our way! But such short-sighted super-patriotism misses the point. The primary mission of healthcare professionals is to restore health to those who are ill as quickly and efficiently as possible. It has been demonstrated, time and again, by medical anthropologists that unless health professionals both understand and take into account the supernatural beliefs of all their patients, whatever medical strategies are employed will be less than fully successful. It makes no sense, from a medical perspective, to try to argue your patients out of their beliefs and accept yours. It simply is not going to happen. Medical practitioners are finally beginning to accept a basic truth taught by medical anthropologists—that understanding and accommodating the supernatural beliefs of culturally different patients are absolutely essential for providing them with the best possible health care.

Questions for Further Thought

1. Do Westerners associate any number(s) with bad luck?
2. Can you think of any other ethnic groups in the United States or Canada whose cultural or religious beliefs conflict with conventional Western medical practices?
3. Can you identify a particular chapter-opening scenario in this book that could have been avoided if the professional staff had been more culturally competent?

Although most North Americans think of themselves as highly scientific, on many occasions we too use supernatural forces to ensure that our activities will have a successful outcome. For example, anthropologist George Gmelch (1994b: 352) described how professional baseball players use ritual to try to influence the outcome of a game (Figure 14.3):

To control uncertainty Chicago White Sox shortstop Ozzie Guillen doesn't wash his underclothes after a good game. The Boston Red Sox's Wade Boggs eats chicken before every game (that's 162 meals of chicken per year). Ex–San Francisco Giant pitcher Ron Bryant added a new stick of bubble gum to the collection in his bulging back pocket after each game he won. Jim Ohms, my teammate on the Daytona Beach Islanders in 1966, used to put another penny in the pouch of his supporter after each win. Clanging against the hard plastic genital cup, the pennies made an audible sound as the pitcher ran the bases toward the end of a winning season.

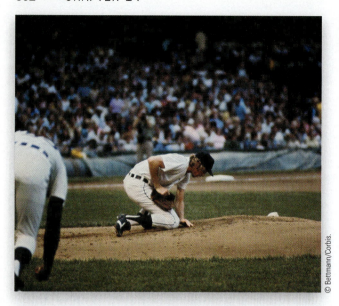

FIGURE 14.3 Mark "The Bird" Fidrych, a pitcher for the Detroit Tigers, practiced ritualistic magic before each game by patting and talking to the pitcher's mound.

In some cases Western governments use non-Western spiritual practices when it is politically expedient to do so. In 1998 the Transit Authority of Portland, Oregon, proudly unveiled its light rail system, featuring the Washington Park Station, which, at 260 feet below ground, was the deepest subway station in the United States. However, members of local Asian communities in Portland were appalled because the tunnel ran under a cemetery, which, they claimed, disturbed the spirits of the dead and created a dangerous situation for the train riders. In fact the Asian groups attributed several aboveground traffic accidents to the angry spirits of the dead. In response to these real concerns of the Asian community, transit authority officials brought in a group of Lao Buddhist monks who performed rituals to appease the dead spirits. Even though transit officials were ribbed for allowing these Eastern rituals to be performed in the subway tunnel, they did ease the minds of local Asians and restored their confidence in the local transit system (D'Antoni and Heard 1998).

cult In the early anthropological literature, a nonjudgmental term that refers to a religious group that has its own set of beliefs, practices, and rituals. In popular discourse, a pejorative term referring to an antisocial group of religious extremists whose goal is mass suicide.

individualistic cults The least complex type of religious organization in which each person is his or her own religious specialist.

Types of Religious Organization

Like other aspects of culture, religion takes a wide variety of forms throughout the world. To bring some measure of order to this vast diversity, it is helpful to develop a typology of religious systems based on certain common features. One commonly used system of classification, suggested by Anthony Wallace, is based on the level of specialization of the religious personnel who conduct the rituals and ceremonies. Wallace (1966) identified four principal types of religious organization based on what he calls cults. Wallace uses the term *cult* in a general sense to refer to forms of religion that have their own set of beliefs, rituals, and goals. This analytical and nonjudgmental use of the term *cult* should not be confused with the more popular, and pejorative, definition used to refer to an antisocial religious group that brainwashes its members before leading them to mass suicide. The four types of religious organization Wallace identified are individualistic cults, shamanistic cults, communal cults, and ecclesiastical cults. According to Wallace's typology, these cults form a scale. Societies with ecclesiastical cults also contain communal, shamanistic, and individualistic cults; those with a communal form also contain shamanistic and individualistic cults; and those with shamanistic cults also contain individualistic cults. Although it is likely that societies with only individualistic cults could have existed in earlier times, there are no contemporary examples of such religious systems.

Wallace's four types correspond roughly to different levels of socioeconomic organization. In a general way, individualistic and shamanistic cults are usually associated with food-foraging societies, communal cults are usually found in horticultural and pastoral societies, and ecclesiastical cults are characteristic of more complex industrialized economies. However, this association between types of religious organization and socioeconomic types is only approximate at best because there are some notable exceptions. For example, certain US Plains Indians and some aboriginal Australians had communal forms of religion even though they were hunter-gatherers and lived in bands. See Table 14.1 for a summary of the characteristics of the four types of religious organizations.

Individualistic Cults

Individualistic cults have no religious specialists and are the most basic type of religious structure, according to Wallace's classification. Each person has a relationship with one or more supernatural beings whenever he

TABLE 14.1

Characteristics of the Four Types of Religious Organizations

Type	Role Specialization	Subsistence Pattern	Example
Individualistic	No role specialization	Food foraging	Crow vision quest
Shamanistic	Part-time specialization	Food foraging, pastoralism, and horticulture	Tungus shamanism
Communal	Groups perform rites for community	Horticulture and pastoralism	Totemistic rituals
Ecclesiastical	Full-time specialization in hierarchy	Industrialism	Christianity and Buddhism

SOURCE: Adapted from Anthony F. C. Wallace, *Religion: An Anthropological View* (New York: Random House, 1966).

or she has a need for control or protection. Because individualistic cults do not make distinctions between specialists and laypersons, all people are their own specialists, or as Harris and Johnson put it, these cults are "a do-it-yourself religion" (Harris and Johnson 2003: 266). Even though no known societies rely exclusively on individualistic cults, some small-scale band societies practice this type of organization as a predominant mode.

The *vision quest*, a ritual found among traditional Plains Indian cultures, is an excellent example of the rituals practiced by an individualistic cult. During traditional times it was expected that, through visions, people would establish a special relationship with a spirit that would provide them with knowledge, power, and protection. Sometimes these visions came to people in dreams or when they were by themselves. More often, however, the individual had to purposefully seek out the visions through such means as fasting, mutilating their bodies, smoking hallucinogenic substances, and spending time alone in an isolated place.

A person would go on a vision quest if he or she wanted to gain special power to excel as a warrior, to restore one's honor after being tormented by a bully or jilted by a lover, or to acquire knowledge about a future course of action. For example, a Crow warrior would go to a place that was thought to be frequented by supernatural spirits. There he would strip off his clothes, smoke, and abstain from drinking and eating. He might even chop off part of a finger or engage in other types of self-inflicted torture for the sake of getting the spirits' attention. Crow visions took a variety of forms but usually had several elements in common. First, the visions usually came in the form of a spirit animal, such as a bison, eagle, or snake. Second, the vision seeker gained some special knowledge or power. Third, the vision often appeared on the fourth day of the quest, four being a sacred number for the Crow. Finally, the animal spirit adopted the quester by functioning as his or her own protector spirit.

Shamanistic Cults

In addition to having individualistic cults, all contemporary societies operate at the shamanistic level. Shamanistic societies are found in arctic and subarctic regions, Siberia, Tibet, Mongolia, parts of Southeast Asia, and widely throughout the South American rain forests. *Shamans* are part-time religious specialists who are thought to have supernatural powers by virtue of birth, training, or inspiration. They use these powers for healing, divining, and telling fortunes during times of stress, usually in exchange for gifts or fees. *Shamanistic cults* represent the simplest form of religious division of labor because, as Anthony Wallace (1966: 86) reminds us, "The shaman in his religious role is a specialist; and his clients in their relation to him are laymen." The term *shaman*, derived from the Tungus-speaking peoples of Siberia (Service 1978), encompasses many different types of specialists found throughout the world, including medicine men and women, diviners, spiritualists, palm readers, and magicians (Figure 14.4).

Shamans are generally believed to have access to supernatural spirits that they contact on behalf of their clients. The reputation of a particular shaman often rests on the power of the shaman's "spirit helpers" (usually the spirits of powerful, agile, and cunning animals) and her or his ability to contact them at will. Shamans contact their spirits while in an altered state of consciousness brought on by smoking, taking drugs,

vision quest A ritual found in some Plains Indian cultures wherein, through visions, people establish special relationships with spirits who provide them with knowledge, power, and protection.

shamans A part-time religious specialist who is thought to have supernatural powers by virtue of birth, training, or inspiration.

shamanistic cults A type of religious organization in which part-time religious specialists called *shamans* intervene with the deities on behalf of their clients.

FIGURE 14.4 Piaroa Indian shaman Miguel Ochoa is pictured here with medicinal plants gathered from the jungle village of Aska aja, near Puerto Ayacucho, Venezuela.

drumming rhythmically, chanting, or dancing monotonously. Once in a trance, the shaman, possessed with a spirit helper, becomes a medium or spokesperson for that spirit. While possessed, the shaman may perspire, breathe heavily, take on a different voice, and generally lose control over his or her own body. Even though Westerners often view shamans as con artists, in their own societies they are seen as a combination of holy person, doctor, and social worker. In many respects traditional shamans in non-Western societies are not appreciably different from professional channelers in the United States, who speak on behalf of spirits for their paying clients.

In shamanistic societies it is believed that everyday occurrences are intimately connected to events in the spirit world. The shaman's role is to enter an altered state of consciousness, allow his or her soul to travel to the spirit world, seek out the causes of earthly problems, and then coerce, beg, or fight with the spirits to intervene on behalf of the living. Inuit shamanism provides a good example of how shamans are thought to work. Most Inuit believe that water mammals are controlled by an underwater female spirit who occasionally withholds animals when Inuit hunters behave immorally. One of the most challenging tests for an Inuit shaman is to travel to the watery underworld to convince the spirit to release the seals and walruses so they can be hunted again.

How an individual actually becomes a shaman varies from society to society. In many societies shamans achieve their power through a series of initiations or ordeals imposed by the spirits of the underworld. Even after acquiring shamanistic power by doing battle with the spirits, a shaman may lose those hard-won powers through subsequent unsuccessful battles with the spirits. In some societies it is possible to become a shaman by having a particularly vivid or powerful vision in which spirits enter the body. In other societies one can become a shaman by serving as an apprentice under a practicing shaman. Among the Tungus of Siberia, mentally unstable people who often experience bouts of hysteria are the most likely candidates for shamanism because hysterical people are thought to be the closest to the spirit world (Service 1978). In societies that regularly use hallucinogenic drugs, almost any person can achieve the altered state of consciousness needed for the practice of shamanism. For example, Michael Harner (1973) reports that among the Jivaro Indians of the Ecuadorian Amazon, who use hallucinogens widely and have a strong desire to contact the supernatural world, about one in four men is a shaman.

As practiced by the Reindeer Tungus of Siberia, shamans are people who have the power to control various spirits, can prevent those spirits from causing harm, and, on occasion, can serve as a medium for those spirits (Service 1978). Tungus shamans—who can be either men or women—use special paraphernalia, such as elaborate costumes, a brass mirror, and a tambourine. The rhythmic beating of a tambourine is used to induce a trance in a shaman and to produce a receptive state of consciousness on the part of onlookers. A shaman, possessed by rhythmic drumming, journeys into the spirit world to perform certain functions for individual clients or for the group as a whole. These functions may include determining the cause of a person's illness, finding a lost object, conferring special powers in a conflict, or predicting future events. Shamanism among the Tungus does not involve the power to cure a particular illness but rather only determines the cause of the malady. In this respect the shaman is a medical diagnostician rather than a healer.

Communal Cults

Communal cults—which involve a more elaborate set of beliefs and rituals—operate at a still higher level of organizational complexity. Groups of ordinary people

communal cults A type of religious organization in which groups of ordinary people conduct religious ceremonies for the well-being of the total community.

(organized around clans, lineages, age groups, or secret societies) conduct religious rites and ceremonies on behalf of the larger community. These rites, which are performed only occasionally or periodically by non-specialists, are considered to be absolutely vital to the well-being of both individuals and the society as a whole. Even though these ceremonies may include specialists such as shamans, orators, or magicians, the primary responsibility for the success of the ceremonies lies with the non-specialists, who return to their everyday activities at the conclusion of the ceremony. Examples of communal cults are the ancestral ceremonies among the traditional Chinese, puberty rites found in sub-Saharan African societies, and totemic rituals practiced by aboriginal peoples of Australia.

Communal rituals fall into two broad categories: rites of passage, which celebrate the transition of a person from one social status to another, and rites of solidarity, which are public rituals that foster group identity and group goals and have explicit and immediate objectives, such as calling on supernatural beings or forces to increase fertility or prevent misfortune. Let us look at these two types of communal cults in greater detail.

Rites of Passage

Rites of passage are ceremonies that mark a change in a person's social position. These ritualistic ceremonies, which have religious significance, help both individuals and the society deal with important life changes, such as birth, puberty, marriage, and death. Rites of passage are more than ways of recognizing certain transitions in a person's life, however. When a person marries, for example, he or she not only takes on a new status but also creates an entire complex of new relationships. Rites of passage, then, are important public rituals that recognize a wider set of altered social relationships (Figure 14.5).

According to Arnold Van Gennep (1960), all rites of passage, in whatever culture they may be found, have three distinct ritual phases: separation, transition, and incorporation. The first phase, separation, is characterized by the stripping away of the old status. In puberty rites, for example, childhood is ritually or symbolically killed by pricking the initiate's navel with a spear. In the second phase, the individual is in a transitional stage, cut off from the old status but not yet integrated into the new status. Because this transition stage is associated with danger and ambiguity, the individual often endures certain unpleasant ordeals while he or she is removed from normal, everyday life for a certain period of time. The third and final phase involves the ritual incorporation of the individual into the new status. Ethnographic data from all over the world have supported Van Gennep's claim that all rites of passage involve these three phases.

These three ritual phases are well demonstrated in the rites of adulthood practiced by the Kikuyu of

FIGURE 14.5 Black clothing, black ostrich feathers and the intricate white patterns on the face of this Maasai young man signify his recent circumcision, a rite of passage marking his change in status from boy to man.

Kenya, who initiate both girls and boys (Middleton and Kershaw 1965). The Kikuyu, like other traditional East African societies, practice initiation ceremonies as a way of ensuring that children will become morally and socially responsible adults. Despite some regional variations, the Kikuyu initiation rite includes certain rituals that conform to Van Gennep's threefold scheme.

Kikuyu initiation into adulthood involves a physical operation—circumcision for males and clitoridectomy for females. Days before the physical operation, the initiates go through rituals designed to separate them from society and their old status and place them in close relationship to god. First, the initiates are adopted by an elder man and his wife; this event symbolically separates them from their own parents. Second, the initiates spend the night before the circumcision singing and dancing in an effort to solicit the guidance and protection of the ancestor-gods. Third, the initiates have their heads shaved and anointed, symbolizing the loss of the old status. And finally, they are sprayed with a mixture of honey, milk, and medicine by their

rites of passage Ceremonies that celebrate the transition of a person from one social status to another.

adoptive parents in another separation ritual, which John Middleton and Greet Kershaw (1965) call the ceremony of parting.

As Van Gennep's theory suggests, the second (transition) phase of the Kikuyu initiation ceremony is a marginal phase filled with danger and ambiguity. The initiates undergo the dramatic and traumatic circumcision or clitoridectomy as a vivid symbolization of their soon-to-be assumed responsibility as adults. Both male and female initiates are physically and emotionally supported during the operation by their sponsors, who cover them with cloaks as soon as the operation is completed. Afterward the initiates spend four to nine days in seclusion in temporary huts (*kiganda*), where they are expected to recover from the operation and reflect on their impending status as adults.

The third and final phase of Kikuyu initiation rituals involves the incorporation of the initiate (with his or her new status) back into the society as a whole. At the end of the seclusion period, the new male adults have ceremonial plants put into the large loops in their earlobes (a form of body mutilation practiced during childhood), symbolizing their newly acquired status as adult men. This phase of incorporation (or reintegration) involves other rituals as well. The men symbolically put an end to their transition stage by burning their kiganda; their heads are again shaved; they return home to be anointed by their parents, who soon thereafter engage in ritual intercourse; they ritually discard their initiation clothing; and they are given warrior paraphernalia. Once these incorporation rituals have been completed, the young people become full adults with all of the rights and responsibilities that go along with their new status.

Rites of Solidarity

The other type of communal cult is directed toward the welfare of the community rather than the individual. These *rites of solidarity* permit a wider social participation in the shared concerns of the community than is found in societies with predominantly shamanistic cults. A good example of a cult that fosters group solidarity is the ancestral cult, found widely throughout the world. Ancestral cults are based on the assumption that, after death, a person's soul continues to interact with and affect the lives of her or his living descendants. In other words, when people die, they are not buried and forgotten but rather are elevated to the status of ancestorghost or ancestor-god. Because these ghosts, who are viewed as the official guardians of the social and moral order, have supernatural powers, the living descendants

---

rites of solidarity Ceremonies performed for the sake of enhancing social integration among groups of people.

CROSS-CULTURAL MISCUE

Several weeks after the great tsunami disaster in December 2004, a female talk-show cohost on US television made the following comment: "I was on my honeymoon in the Maldives islands several weeks before the tsunami hit. I thank God for sparing me from that terrible disaster." Such a proclamation of faith in God is generally seen in the United States as perfectly legitimate, a devout, faith-based statement of her gratitude to God's infinite mercy. Who could possibly take issue with such a statement? Well, for starters we could cite all those tens of millions of people in the world who do not interpret every aspect of their lives as being directed by the purposeful hand of God. They would view the statement by this TV cohost as arrogant and self-serving because it was dismissive of the 170,000-plus people who died in the tsunami and who God, by implication, did not deem sufficiently worthy of being spared from that terrible disaster. This cross-cultural miscue is not meant to suggest that the TV cohost should not have made what, for her, was a sincere statement of faith. However, she should have been aware of how her statement might be heard in other parts of the world by good, religious, well-meaning people like herself who just happen to have a different view of how God works in their everyday lives.

---

practice certain communal rituals designed to induce the ancestor-ghosts to protect them, favor them, or at least not harm them.

Like many of their neighboring cultures in northern Ghana, the Sisala believe their ancestor-ghosts are the guardians of the moral order. All members of Sisala lineages are subject to the authority of the lineage elders. Because the elders are the most important living members of the group, they are responsible for overseeing the interests and harmony of the entire group. Though responsible for group morality, the elders have no direct authority to punish violators. The Sisala believe that the primary activity of the ancestor-ghosts is to punish living lineage members who violate behavioral norms. To be specific, ancestor-ghosts are thought to take vengeance on any living members who steal from their lineage mates, fight with their kin, or generally fail to meet their family duties and responsibilities. Eugene Mendonsa (1985: 218–19) described a specific case that graphically illustrates the power of ancestral cults among the Sisala:

At Tuorojang in Tumu there was a young man named Cedu. He caught a goat that was for the ancestor of his house (*did*), and killed it to sell the meat. When the day came for the sacrifice, the elders searched for the goat so they could kill it at the *lele* shrine. They could not find it, and asked to know who might have caught the goat. They could not decide who had taken the goat, so they caught another and used it for the sacrifice instead. During the sacrifice, the elders begged the ancestors to forgive them for not sacrificing the proper goat. The elders asked the ancestors to find and punish the thief. After the sacrifice, when all the elders had gone to their various houses, they heard that Cedu had died. They summoned a diviner to determine the cause of death, and found that Cedu had been the thief. The ancestors had killed him because he was the person who stole the goat that belonged to the ancestors.

This case illustrates the Sisala belief in the power of the ancestor-ghosts to protect the moral order. When a breach of the normative order occurs, the elders conduct a communal ritual petitioning the ghosts to punish the wrongdoer. As with other aspects of religion, the anthropologist is not concerned with whether the diviner was correct in determining that Cedu died because he had stolen the goat. Instead the anthropologist is interested in the communal ritual and its immediate social effects: It restored social harmony within the lineage and served as a warning to others who might be thinking of stealing from their lineage members.

Ecclesiastical Cults

The most complex form of religious organization, according to Wallace, is the *ecclesiastical cult*, which is found in societies with state systems of government. There are examples of ecclesiastical cults in societies that have a pantheon of several high gods (such as traditional Aztecs, Incas, Greeks, and Egyptians) and in those with essentially monotheistic religions (such as Buddhism, Christianity, Islam, and Judaism). Ecclesiastical cults are characterized by full-time professional clergy, who are formally elected or appointed and devote all or most of their time to performing priestly functions. Unlike shamans who conduct rituals during times of crisis or when their services are needed, these full-time priests conduct rituals that occur at regular intervals. (For a list of the sizes of the major ecclesiastical religions in the world today, see Table 14.2.)

TABLE 14.2

Number and Percent of Adherents of Major World Religions

Religion (percent)	Number of Adherents (millions)
Christianity (33)	2,100
Islam (21)	1,500
No religious preference (16)	1,100
Hindu (14)	900
Chinese traditional (6)	394
Buddhism (6)	376
Primal-indigenous/African traditional (6)	400
Sihks	23
Judaism	14
Bahai	7
Jainism	4.2

SOURCE: National and World Religion Statistics, 2013, (www.adherents.com/Religions_By_Adherents.html).

In addition, these priests are part of a hierarchical or bureaucratic organization under the control of a centralized church or temple. Often, but not always, these clerical bureaucracies are either controlled by the central government or closely associated with it. In many ecclesiastical cults, the prevailing myths and beliefs are used to support the supremacy of the ruling class. In fact, it is not unusual for the priests to be part of that ruling class. Because of this close association between the priesthood and politico-economic institutions, women have not traditionally played active roles as priests. This is another important difference between priests and shamans, because at least as many women as men are practicing shamanism throughout the world. Even in modern, complex societies, women are particularly active as mystics, channelers, palm readers, astrologers, and clairvoyants.

In societies with ecclesiastical cults, there is a clearly understood distinction between laypersons and priests. Laypersons are primarily responsible for supporting the church through their labor and their financial contributions. Priests are responsible for conducting religious rituals on behalf of the lay population, either individually or in groups. Whereas the priests serve as active ritual managers, the lay population participates in rituals in a generally passive fashion (Figure 14.6).

ecclesiastical cult Highly complex religious organizations in which full-time clergy are employed.

Marcia Chambers/dbimages/Alamy

FIGURE 14.6 This Anglican priest from Quebec City, Canada is a full-time religious specialist who works within a hierarchical religious organization.

Although ecclesiastical cults have enormous control over people's lives, they have not wiped out other forms of religion. Inuits, many of whom have converted to Christianity, for example, may continue to consult a shaman when ill; Africans from Tanzania often continue to worship their ancestors despite being practicing Roman Catholics; and in our own society many people have no difficulty consulting a palmist, psychic, or astrologer even though they follow one of the large, worldwide, monotheistic religions.

We certainly do not need to go far from home to see examples of ecclesiastical organizations. The United States has hundreds of religious denominations and approximately a quarter of a million separate congregations. Most people in the United States think they understand the nature of religious institutions around them, but there are probably more misconceptions and stereotypes about religion than about any other area of US life. Most people would be surprised to learn that church membership in the United States has grown, not declined, steadily over the last several

hundred years. According to Roger Finke and Rodney Stark (2005: 23), only 17 percent of the population in 1776 claimed church membership; by the start of the Civil War, the number had grown to 37 percent; by the mid-1920s, it had leaped to 58 percent; and by the early 1990s, 69 percent claimed church affiliation. According to a Gallup poll conducted in 2003, 65 percent of adults in the United States claimed to be a member of a church or synagogue (Newport 2004). Even though most Americans think of themselves as living in a secular society, religion is highly valued in the United States, particularly in comparison with other Western, industrialized nations.

An extensive survey published in 2010 by the Pew Forum on Religion & Public Life details religious affiliation in the United States and explores the shifts that are taking place in the US religious landscape. Based on a sample of more than 35,000 Americans aged 18 and older, the survey concludes that religious affiliation in the United States is both diverse and extremely fluid. See Table 14.3 for the religious affiliations of those questioned in the survey.

According to a 2004 Gallup poll, 61 percent of American questioned said that religion is important in their lives (Newport 2004). Four years later in 2008, the Gallup poll asked Americans a similar question ("Is religion an important part of your daily life?"), to which nearly two of every three respondents (65 percent) answered yes. Although these percentages are aggregate responses, some interesting patterns emerged for subgroups within the US population. For example, religion becomes more important to Americans as they get older, blacks are the subgroup for whom religion is

TABLE 14.3

Religious Affiliation in the United States

Religion	Percent
Evangelical Protestant	26.3
Catholic	23.9
Mainline Protestant	18.1
Unaffiliated	16.1
Historical black churches	6.9
Mormon	1.7
Jewish	1.7
Jehovah Witnesses	0.7
Buddhist	0.7
Muslim	0.6
Hindu	0.4
Other world religions	0.3
Other faiths	1.2

SOURCE: Pew Forum on Religion & Public Life, "U.S. Religious Landscape Survey," 2010 (http://religions.pewforum.org/affiliations).

most important, religion is more important to conservatives and Republicans than to liberals and Democrats, women are more religious than men, and people with lower levels of formal education tend to be more religious than those with higher levels. We should also note that religiosity (the importance of religion) varies significantly with state and geographic region. According to the 2008 Gallup poll, the southern states of Mississippi, Alabama, South Carolina, Tennessee, Louisiana, and Arkansas are the most religious states in the nation (with average scores of 78 to 85 percent), whereas the New England states of Vermont, New Hampshire, Maine, and Massachusetts are the least religious (with average scores of 42 to 48 percent).

However, any way we break it down, religion is perhaps the single most important factor driving beliefs, attitudes, and behaviors in the United States. Religion plays a powerful role in establishing our views on family, politics, and education. To understand the United States, it is absolutely essential that we first understand its complex mosaic of religious beliefs.

Even though people in the United States self-report that they are highly religious, the amount of knowledge and understanding they possess about religion is less than confidence inspiring. According to the Pew Forum on Religion and Public Life, a 2010 survey of 3,412 Americans, large numbers of Americans are uninformed about the tenets, practices, history, and leading figures of major faith traditions, including their own. To illustrate, 45 percent of Catholics did not know that their church teaches that the bread and wine used in Communion do not merely symbolize but *actually* become the body and blood of Christ; and more than half of Protestants interviewed (53 percent) could not correctly identify Martin Luther as the person whose writings and actions inspired the Protestant Reformation, which made their religion a separate branch of Christianity. Moreover, Americans had even less knowledge of other major world religions. Fewer than half of Americans (47 percent) knew that the Dalai Lama was Buddhist and only 27 percent of those questioned knew that Indonesia was the largest Muslim country in the world. On average, Americans correctly answered 16 of the 32 religious knowledge questions on the survey. Surprisingly, those who scored highest were atheists and agnostics with an average of 20.9 correct answers. Jews and Mormons were close behind, averaging 20.5 and 20.3 correct answers, respectively. Protestants on average

FIGURE 14.7 The Islamic religion is one of the fastest growing organized religions in the United States—and not just in urban areas—as illustrated by the Islamic Center of Greater Toledo located in a cornfield in the heartland of America.

answered 16 questions correctly and Catholics as a whole answered 14.7.

Since the elimination of national quotas by the Immigration Act of 1965, the United States has become, without question, the most religiously diverse country in the world. In addition to the many Native American religions, Christian denominations, and branches of Judaism, the United States is now the home of Muslims, Buddhists, Hindus, Bahais, Sikhs, Scientologists, and Rastafarians—among others. The religious landscape has become increasingly diversified over the past four decades, and this diversity is not confined to major urban areas such as New York, Chicago, Detroit, and Los Angeles. Makeshift Hindu temples and Muslim mosques are springing up in such unlikely places as Pawtucket, Rhode Island; Salt Lake City, Utah; and Raleigh, North Carolina. Diana Eck (2002) reminds us that the US Navy now has Islamic chaplains and Los Angeles is the home of more than three hundred Buddhist temples (Figure 14.7).

Religion: Continuity and Change

By examining the various functions of religion, we can see that religion is a conservative force in a society. In a general sense religions support the status quo by keeping people in line through supernatural sanctions, relieving social conflict, and providing explanations for unfortunate events. Moreover some of the major world religions, through both philosophical convictions and political interpretations, have tended to retard social change. To illustrate, orthodox Hindu beliefs, based on the notion that one's present condition in life is determined by deeds in past lives, have had the effect of making people so fatalistic that they accept their present situations as unchangeable. Such a worldview is not likely to bring about major revolutions or even minor initiatives for change. Likewise, on a number of issues facing the world's population, Catholicism has taken highly conservative policy positions. For example, the 1968 papal decree by Pope Paul VI opposing all forms of artificial birth control makes it difficult for developing nations to bring their population growth under control. Conservative Muslims have taken a strong stand against the introduction of new values and behaviors, particularly from the Western World.

Religion, however, has also played a major role in global social change over the past several decades. For example, the Catholic Church, allied with the Solidarity Movement, played a pivotal role in bringing about the downfall of the Communist government in Poland in 1989. By burning themselves alive on the streets of Saigon during the 1960s, Buddhist priests in Vietnam played a powerful role in stimulating antiwar sentiments in the United States, which eventually led to the withdrawal of US troops. In South America during the 1970s and 1980s, a militant form of Catholicism known as *liberation theology* merged Catholic theology with activism for social justice for the poor. Catholic priests and nuns, often without the support or approval of their own church authorities, engaged in various projects designed to help the poor raise themselves up from the lowest echelons of society. Because these liberation theologians were often at odds with government and church officials, many lost their lives through their activism.

---

liberation theology A form of Catholicism found throughout South and Central America in which priests and nuns are actively involved in programs that promote social justice for the poor.

nativistic movements A religious force for social change found among Native Americans.

cargo cults Revitalization movements in Melanesia intended to bring new life and purpose into a society.

separatist Christian churches Small-scale churches that break away from the dominant church to gain greater political, economic, social, and religious autonomy.

mahdist movements Revitalization movements in the Muslim world.

millenarian movements Social movements by repressed groups of people who are looking forward to better times in the future.

revitalization movements Religious movements designed to bring about a new way of life within a society.

Closer to home, black churches in the United States, with their strong theme of struggle against bondage and oppression, have long played a role in social change. Well before the civil rights movement of the 1960s, black churches were headquarters and rallying places for protestors and community activists. Before the abolition of slavery, churches served as stations on the Underground Railroad, which helped slaves travel undetected from the south to the north. Moreover the black Muslim movement in the United States, with its strict dietary prohibitions and behavior codes, has been a force for social change by fostering the idea of autonomous black communities. Thus, for the past 150 years, blacks have used the moral authority of their churches and mosques to push for racial justice and social change.

Under certain circumstances religion can play an important role in transforming a society. At times certain societies have experienced such high levels of stress and strain that the conservative functions of religion could not hold them together. Instead new religions or sects sprang up to create a new social order. Different terms have been used in the literature to describe these new religious forces for social change, including *nativistic movements* among Native Americans, *cargo cults* in Melanesia, *separatist Christian churches* in southern Africa, *mahdist movements* in the Muslim world, and *millenarian movements* in Christian areas of the world.

All of these religious movements, with their aim of breathing new life and purpose into the society, are called *revitalization movements* by Anthony Wallace (1966). The common thread running through them is that they tend to arise during times of cultural stress brought about by rapid change, foreign domination, and perceived deprivation. Because these three conditions are often, but not always, associated with colonialism, many revitalization movements have appeared in societies that have been under colonial domination.

Despite considerable differences in the details surrounding various revitalization movements, Wallace suggests that most follow a fairly uniform process. Starting from a state of equilibrium (in which change occurs, though slowly, and individual stress levels are tolerable), a society is pushed off balance by forces such as conquest and social domination. These conditions lower the self-esteem of an increasing number of individuals and place them under intolerable stress. People become disillusioned and the culture becomes disorganized (with higher crime rates and a general increase in antisocial behavior, for example). When the social fabric deteriorates sufficiently, revitalization movements are likely to appear in an effort to bring about a more satisfying society. Some movements call for a return to the better days of the past; others seek to establish a completely new social order.

Revitalization movements have been found in many parts of the world, but nowhere have they been more widespread and better documented than among

Native American groups. The tragic suffering of Native Americans since their earliest contact with Europeans resulted in a number of revitalization movements, including the movement among the Seneca Indians headed by Handsome Lake, several versions of the Ghost Dance, and the Peyote cults found among the Plains Indians. In recent decades these religious revitalization movements have been replaced by more secular political efforts to reclaim Indian lands, resources, and dignity through legal action, political activism, and civil disobedience.

One of the earliest Native American revitalization movements was started by Handsome Lake (Deardorff 1951; Parker 1913). By the year 1800 the Seneca Indians of New York State had fallen on hard times. They had lost much of their land to whites, who held them in contempt because they were on the losing side of the French and Indian War. The Seneca were confined to reservations, and their numbers were severely reduced by European diseases such as measles and smallpox. Once a proud nation of warriors, hunters, and traders, the Seneca were defeated, dehumanized, and demoralized by the start of the nineteenth century. Alcoholism became rampant, and conflicts and accusations of witchcraft increased.

From this state of cultural disorganization came a prophet—Handsome Lake—who was visited by God in a vision and told to stop drinking and start a new revitalizing religion. The deity warned that the Seneca would suffer a great catastrophe (such as fire, destruction, and death) if they did not mend their ways. Most of the prescriptions set down by Handsome Lake constituted a new set of moral principles and rules of behavior. Followers of the new religious movement were expected to stay sober, be peaceful, and lead pure and upright lives.

Handsome Lake instituted other important cultural changes as well. For example, he urged his followers to adopt European agricultural practices involving both men and women working in the fields. In the Seneca family, he emphasized the priority of the conjugal unit of man and wife over the matrilineage. Divorce, which had been common in traditional Seneca society, was no longer permitted. Thus, Handsome Lake's revitalization movement led to far-reaching cultural changes. The Seneca became models of sobriety, their family structure was altered, they initiated new farming practices, and they changed the traditional division of labor between men and women.

Globalization of World Religions

In much the same way that markets have been globalizing over the past decade, the revolution in information and communication has had far-reaching effects on the various ecclesiastical religions of the world. For much of the twentieth century, most North Americans who identified with a particular religion followed a fairly straightforward set of religious beliefs and practices. People practiced Islam, Christianity, Buddhism, or Judaism, and it was relatively easy to predict what set of beliefs they held. Today, however, many people are practicing a hodgepodge of beliefs. It has been reported (Lamont-Brown 1999) that as many as 40 million people in Japan are now practicing "new religions," which involve blending the two major religions in Japan (Buddhism and Shintoism) with elements of Confucianism, shamanism, animism, ancestor worship, Protestantism, and Catholicism. Traditional world religions, and even denominations of Christian religions, are cross-pollinating at a rapid rate. As Lisa Miller (1999: B1) noted:

> Jews flirt with Hinduism, Catholics study Taoism, and Methodists discuss whether to make the Passover seder an official part of worship. Rabbi Zalman Schachter-Shalomi, a prominent Jewish scholar, is also a Sufi sheik, and James Ishmael Ford, a Unitarian minister in Arizona, is a Zen sensei, or master. The melding of Judaism with Buddhism has become so commonplace that marketers who sell spiritual books, videotapes, and lecture series have a name for it: "JewBu."

It is difficult to tell whether this cross-fertilization of religious beliefs and practices will be a short-term phenomenon or a more permanent condition of the world's ecclesiastical religions. In any event, it is a fairly serious dilemma for many leaders of world religions, who see this intermingling as a threat to their identity. However, the process of globalization will no doubt continue well into the future, thereby throwing culturally and religiously different peoples together, whether we like it or not. If living in close proximity to people of different faiths actually threatens one's religious identity, the likely response will be to build walls around religious communities and systematically exclude non-believers. There are some people of faith, however, who are embracing living in close proximity to newly arrived immigrant groups that practice different religions from their own. The small French town of Bussy Saint-Georges, which had a population of 500 people three decades ago, was declared to be a "new city" by the French government in 1985. Since then, this new planned city has grown to 25,000 and includes hundreds of new apartment buildings, single-family homes, parks, shopping centers, and parks. Located less than 20 miles from Paris, Bussy Saint-Georges is now the home of many immigrants from the former French colonies and elsewhere, who have brought a wide variety of religious beliefs and practices with them. Because the city's mayor saw this influx of new religions more as an opportunity than a threat, the town is building on the edge of the city an "Esplanade of the Religions," an integrated campus of religious buildings including a synagogue, a mosque, a Loatian Buddhist pagoda, and a Taiwanese Buddhist temple. Although the actual religious buildings are not yet completed, the leaders of these local religious communities are optimistic that the Esplanade will be a laboratory for interfaith cohabitation and dialogue. In fact, the United Nations Educational, Scientific, and Cultural Organization (UNCESCO) has already referred to Bussy Saint Georges as a city of interfaith dialogue.

Another major change in the mosaic of world religions is that—owing to decades of Christian proselytizing—the geographic distribution and centers of power in some world religions such as Christianity are actually changing. Over the past half-century, Christianity has experienced a major shift in power and influence from the long-established churches of Europe and North America to the so-called "Global South" (Africa, South America, and south Asia). For decades, European Christian churches have been losing membership and have faced considerable difficulties recruiting priests. This is particularly true of Roman Catholicism, which is the world's largest Christian denomination. Catholic Church membership in the developing world, however, has been booming during this same period. For example, although there are 277 million Catholics presently living in Europe (24 percent), there are 483 million living in Latin America 41 percent), 177 million living in Africa (15 percent), and 138 million living in south Asia (12 percent). This demographic shift in the last sixty years is particularly problematic because although most Catholics live outside of Europe, the Church itself has been run like a European mini-state. Moreover, until the election of Pope Francis of Argentina in 2013, there had never been in the history of the Church a non-European Pope. This is because of the fact that even though Europe is home to less than a quarter of all Catholics, 62 percent of the Cardinals, who actually elect the Pope, are from Europe. With the major demographic center of gravity of Catholicism shifting from Europe to the "Global South," there is an ongoing debate among Roman Catholics as to whether the Pope should represent those parts of the world where most Catholics resident or where the spiritual vision of the Church originated and developed over most of its history (Figure 14.8) (Donadio and Povoledo 2013).

Along with the blending of religious beliefs, in the age of globalization certain religious ideas and practices are working their way into the secular world of international business. For tens of generations, Indians from all segments of society have sought guidance from mystics and astrologers who claim to predict the future by analyzing numbers or studying the alignments of the stars and planets. Today there is growing evidence that these traditional supernatural practices are being used in the offices of multinational corporations to

GABRIEL BOUYS/Staff/AFP/Getty Images

FIGURE 14.8 The late Cardinal Bernardin Gantin (1922–2008) represented a part of the world (Benin) in which the number of people practicing Catholicism is growing rapidly.

help make decisions concerning strategic planning, mergers, and hiring. Some Indian mystics are specialists in *vaastu* (similar to the Chinese belief in feng shui), which seeks to ensure good fortune by means of proper interior design. It is not at all uncommon for Indian high-tech corporations to hire such mystic specialists to review architectural plans before the construction of new corporate facilities. Film producers in Bollywood (India's counterpart to Hollywood) often seek the advice of numerologists, who claim that one's destiny is largely determined by numbers and their configurations, before making a final decision on a film's title or date of release. A person's astrological sign may even be a factor in whether he or she is hired. The line between science and supernatural beliefs is becoming increasingly blurred (Lakshmi 2004).

In some countries the nonreligious changes occurring in the global economy are bringing about fundamental changes in their own traditional religious practices. To illustrate, although Indians have practiced yoga for centuries, many middle-class Indians, whose twenty-first-century jobs are putting increased pressure on their time, feel that the practice of traditional yoga is too complex and time-consuming. Today followers of Swami Ramdev practice a form of "yoga lite" with 12,000 of their closest friends in Jawaharlal Nehru Stadium in New Delhi, India. By concentrating on breath control, which is only one aspect of traditional yoga, the Swami claims that practitioners of his "yoga made easy" will remain healthy in mind and body. This is an appealing message for people caught up in the pressures of the modern global economy (Kumar 2005).

We have heard a good deal in recent years about the outsourcing of manufacturing and high-tech jobs from Canada and the United States to India. Less known, however, is that because of a shortage of priests in North America, local Catholic parishes are sending Mass Intentions (requests for masses said for a sick relative, the remembrance of deceased kin, or a prayer offering for a newborn) to India. Catholic priests in India (who have more time than North American priests and need the money) are now conducting the masses on behalf of North American Catholics after receiving the requests via e-mail (Rai 2004). Thus, here is a dramatic illustration of how, in this age of globalization, we are outsourcing not only jobs to India but also our religious rituals.

Religious Change in the Twenty-First Century: The Rise of Fundamentalism

Much has been written in the last several decades about a worldwide shift toward religious fundamentalism. In the 1990s Benjamin Barber (1996) posited that globalism (modernism) and tribalism (antimodernism) would be the two major, and diametrically opposed, forces competing with each other in the twenty-first century. He referred to globalism by the term *McWorld*, which encompasses expanding world markets, global integration, homogenizing world cultures, and faith in science and technology on steroids. At the opposite polarity, Barber spoke of "Jihad," an antimodern force that sees an ideological struggle among cultures, tribes, and religions. Whereas McWorld seeks global integration, Jihad seeks to focus on the local community and the preservation of traditional customs, values, and religions. Barber's formulation of the polarizing forces of McWorld versus Jihad is similar to that developed several years later by Thomas Friedman (1999a), who spoke of "the Lexus and the olive tree."

Religious fundamentalists (that is, those jihadists interested in protecting the olive trees in their own backyards) feel threatened by an increasingly modern, scientific, secular world. They want to separate themselves from twenty-first-century modernists, whose original religious principles, they believe, have been corrupted through neglect and compromise. The use of the Islamic term *jihad* (meaning struggle) or the reference to olive trees (native to the Middle East) should in no way suggest that religious fundamentalism includes only Islamic fundamentalism. In fact religious fundamentalism includes any group that purposefully chooses to separate itself from the larger religious group from which it arose. Such groups seek to separate themselves from both foreign religions and compromised versions of their own religion. Thus, we see Islamic fundamentalists who, rejecting foreign and modern ideas, advocate a return to Islamic culture, strict principles based on Islamic law (sharia), a literal interpretation of the *Qu'ran*, and close fellowship among Muslims. Likewise Christian fundamentalists, wanting to return to a previous and less-corrupted form of their own religion, insist on interpreting scripture as infallible, historically accurate, and literally true. Moreover, like any other form of religious fundamentalism, Judaic fundamentalists see themselves as distinct from the corruptions of the modern world and hold their own sacred scriptures as divinely inspired, infallible, and unchangeable. What all fundamentalist groups have in common is that they all draw *most* of their converts from among members of their own religion—a religion that, the fundamentalists claim, has strayed from its original principles and practices.

Christian Fundamentalism

The rise of fundamentalism among Christian churches in the United States, despite conventional wisdom, is *not* a phenomenon associated with globalization over the past several decades, but actually has been progressing in an evolutionary fashion over the past several centuries. If we look at just the sixty-year period between 1940 and 2000, we see a dramatic decline in "market share" (that is, relative membership) among the mainline denominations (United Methodists, Episcopal, Presbyterian) and a concomitant increase among the evangelical churches. To illustrate, during this six-decade period, the United Methodist Church lost 56 percent of its membership, the Presbyterian Church (United States) lost 60 percent, and the Episcopalians lost 51 percent; during the same period the Southern Baptists gained 37 percent, the Church of God in Christ gained 1,292 percent, and the Pentecostal Assemblies of the World gained a whopping 2,375 percent (Finke and Stark 2005: 246).

Not only have fundamentalist Christian churches grown dramatically in the United States in the last century, but fundamentalist religions (and their faith-based agendas) are also playing an increasingly important role in the political affairs of the United States. George W. Bush won the presidential election of 2004—one of the closest and most contentious in recent history—primarily because the Republican Party was able to mobilize its Christian religious base in the southern and midwestern states. In the aftermath of the 2004 election, most political observers pointed to a cultural divide (or, perhaps more aptly, a "religious divide") in the United States to explain the election results. The issues that swung the election in favor of Bush were those issues of *personal* morality held most stridently by fundamentalist Christian religious groups. These issues included opposition to abortion rights, same-sex marriage, and embryonic stem-cell research. But in addition to these hot-button issues, the issue of presidential leadership was framed in religious terminology. When speaking to voters in the heartland, President Bush made statements such as "I carry the word of God," "I pray to be as good a messenger of His will as possible," and "I trust God speaks through me" (Suskind 2004: 51). Clearly he was communicating to his religious supporters that (a) he knew what the will of God was and (b) God's will was being carried out through the president's domestic and foreign policies. For many voters in the Republican base, who judged the worth of both candidates on such criteria as character, certainty, fortitude, confidence, and proximity to God, there was no question which candidate was the stronger leader. In much the same way that an evangelical preacher would never question Holy Scripture, a true political leader would never deviate from the course (even in the face of evidence suggesting that things were not going well), provided, of course, that the policy was seen as having divine backing. According to this way of thinking, any candidate who questioned the validity of the war in Iraq (or the war in Vietnam a generation earlier) would be the spitting image of Doubting Thomas. Such a candidate would be denounced as both faithless and unpatriotic, and consequently a poor leader during trying times. Thus, the presidential election of 2004 was described as "the most important election of our lifetime" largely because, for the first time in recent history, religious ideas played a central role in determining the outcome (Figure 14.9).

Since the 2004 presidential election the power of the socially conservative religious fundamentalists has grown, particularly in the US House of Representatives and in state legislatures, to such an extent that it has greatly influenced legislation on such issues as abortion rights, family planning, immigration reform, environmental policy, foreign policy, and gun control, among others.

Islamic Fundamentalism and Religious Nationalism

An extremely significant trend in global religion today is *religious nationalism*. This movement, which can be found in countries that represent a number of different religious traditions, rejects the idea that religion

© Rolin Riggs/The New York Times/Redux.

FIGURE 14.9 The merging of religion and nationalism does not occur only in Middle Eastern countries. On July 4, 2006, this Statue of Liberation Through Christ was consecrated at a fundamentalist church in Memphis, Tennessee to demonstrate the congregation's belief that Christianity is the foundation of American society.

and government should be separate. Instead religious nationalism calls for an absolute merging of traditional religious beliefs with government institutions and leaders. With the collapse of the former Soviet Union and the Communist bloc, many nations are beginning to reject the secular solutions that were so prevalent during the Cold War years. They are increasingly embracing a fundamentalist religious state that does not tolerate non-believers.

Nowhere is religious nationalism more evident than in the Middle East. Islamic nationalism—perhaps the most visible form of religious nationalism—combines fundamentalist religious orthodoxy with contemporary political institutions. The alignment of Islam with contemporary political Arab nationalism stems from the 1967 Arab–Israeli war. Israel's thorough humiliation of Syria, Egypt, and Jordan in just five days left many Arabs feeling that something was wrong in the

---

religious nationalism A trend toward merging traditional religious principles with the workings of government.

When Religious Values Conflict with Individual Values: A Cross-Cultural Example

In September of 2012, a series of violent protests broke out in about twenty Islamic countries against a US-made video appearing on the Internet, which mocked the Prophet Muhammad. Outraged by the film's hateful message and its accessibility on the Internet, demonstrators took to the streets in many Islamic cities demanding a public apology from President Barack Obama. Moreover, demonstrators expected the US government to punish the filmmaker for religious blasphemy. President Obama did make public statements condemning the film as well as the violent demonstrations, which led to the death of the U.S. Ambassador to Libya. But President Obama failed to ban the film or seek punishment for the makers of the film on legal (constitutional) grounds, which protects freedom of expression.

This incident—a classic example of conflicting cultural values—illustrates the seemingly irresolvable problems that can occur in international diplomacy. This was not a clash between good and evil, but rather a clash between two worthy, yet incompatible, value systems, one found widely in the Islamic world and one found in the United States and other secular or democratic societies. Ironically, both contrasting values are described in terms of the concept of "freedom." Placing emphasis on individual rights, the US Constitution explicitly guarantees freedom of speech and expression to its individual citizens, even when that speech may be offensive or hateful. But people in the Islamic world believe (every bit as strongly as Americans believe in freedom of speech) that communities and societies have the right to be *free* from having their cultural and religious values and beliefs denigrated and insulted. Many Islamic societies impose strong sanctions against their own members for denigrating or blaspheming against not only their own religion of Islam, but also for insulting the prophets of either of the other two Abrahamic religions (Christianity and Judaism).

President Obama made a public statement disapproving the offensive message of the film, but he emphasized that this film did not represent the views of most Americans and was certainly not the official view of the US government. And because the filmmaker had the constitutionally protected right to freely express his views about the Islamic religion, he (nor anyone else in the government) had the power to punish the filmmaker for expressing his offensive views. Such a standoff between these two incompatible cultural values illustrates the complexities faced by international statesmen and diplomats when trying to deal with both friendly and unfriendly populations throughout the world.

Arab world. From the late 1960s onward, many Arabs have restructured their sense of nationalism within the religious framework of Islam. Their religion has become a vibrant source of national identity as well as an alternative solution to their political, economic, and military problems. In the early 1980s, Islamic nationalism experienced some significant victories over the non-Arab, non-Islamic world. For example, Hezbollah forced the United States from Beirut, the Israelis were driven out of Lebanon, and Russia finally limped out of Afghanistan. As Islamic nationalism flexed its muscles, it sent a clear message to others both in the Arab world and beyond: Islam is a powerful force and can be mobilized to challenge what it sees as foreign influence and oppression.

In the late 1970s, the pro-American shah of Iran was overthrown in the fundamentalist Islamic revolution headed by Ayatollah Khomeini. That revolution, condemning the United States as the "great Satan," spread throughout other parts of the Islamic world. This form of religious nationalism rejects the individual freedom of expression and political choice so highly valued in the West. Islamic nationalism also represents a rejection of the often-exploitive government and economic systems (such as capitalism and democracy) that Middle Eastern peoples have endured over the decades.

Many Middle Eastern government leaders have succumbed to Western influence because cooperating with Europe and the United States has made them personally wealthy. To their rank-and-file citizens, the royal families in countries such as Saudi Arabia and Kuwait appear to be pawns of the West. In these countries religious nationalism (the merging of Arab political identity with the Islamic religion) goes beyond fighting the infidels abroad; it also extends to their own leaders at home—a type of domestic jihad. Indeed the number of terrorist attacks in Saudi Arabia (directed at the ruling royal family and their Western allies) has increased dramatically in recent years.

In its more extreme form, religious nationalism, which takes on the character of a religious war, can pose a real threat to the rest of the world. Secular nationalistic movements, such as those found in Western democracies, have goals and objectives with imposed time limits. For example, secular nationalists promise their followers that if they do certain things now, they will live for a long time in a peaceful world. Religious nationalism, on the other hand, promises its followers endless rewards; for example, if you martyr yourself in the struggle against the infidels, you will immediately enter paradise and stay there forever. That, needless to say, poses some real challenges for those defined as infidels.

Religious Change and Technology

Although religious evangelists have used the radio to convert non-believers to Christianity, it was not until the 1970s that television greatly increased their ability to gain converts, raise funds, and spread their influence. In fact television was such a powerful medium that many televangelists became superstars, with their own broadcasting empires, news exposure, and political influence. Evangelists such as Jerry Falwell, Billy Graham, Oral Roberts, Pat Robertson, and Robert Schuller recruited by promising personal salvation, material success, and physical health. Their messages resonated particularly well with those who were poor, undereducated, underemployed, sick, elderly, or those who were fearful of crime, changing sexual values, and anything foreign. Through their on-air fundraising many televangelists built multimillion-dollar media empires.

As we have seen in previous chapters, the information technology revolution in general and the Internet in particular are having enormous effects on our economic, social, and political lives. How will information technology affect our religious lives? Although it is too early to answer this question definitively, today's religious organizations have their own web sites and chat rooms. It is now possible to spread your own religious ideas cheaply, instantaneously, and all over the world. In much the same way that radio and television extended the reach of religious ideas, the Internet has enabled religion to expand beyond the walls of a church. Are we headed for a new type of "churchless religion" in which cyber-churches and virtual congregations replace the face-to-face interaction found in traditional churches, mosques, synagogues, and temples?

As with so many aspects of life today, the Internet brings together people who share common religious traditions. Chapter 9 described the proliferation of web sites devoted to dating (and matchmaking) and those specifically designed for particular demographic groups, including Indians, Russians, Chinese, and Latinos, among others. There are matchmaking web sites designed for particular religions as well. For example, Jewish singles can log onto Jdate.com, Christians can visit Christiansingles.com, and Eharmony.com appeals to those of a more "new age" religious persuasion. There is even a boutique web site called Dharmadate .net, designed for the approximately five million Buddhists living in the United States.

Summary

1. Although people in all cultures have supernatural beliefs, these beliefs take widely varying forms from society to society. It is difficult to define supernatural belief systems cross-culturally because different societies have their own ways of distinguishing between the natural and the supernatural.

2. The anthropological study of religion does not attempt to determine which religions are better than others or which gods can perform the most miracles per unit of time. Rather cultural anthropologists concentrate on describing the various systems of religious belief, how they function, and the degree to which they influence human behavior.

3. Religion differs from magic in that it deals with big issues such as life, death, and god, whereas magic deals with more immediate and specific problems. Whereas religion asks for help through prayer, magic is a direct attempt to control and manipulate supernatural forces.

4. Witchcraft and sorcery are two supernatural belief systems that cause harm to people. Whereas sorcery involves the deliberate use of certain material substances to cause people misfortune, witchcraft is an inborn and generally involuntary capacity to work evil.

5. Religion performs certain social functions. It enhances the overall well-being of the society by serving as a mechanism of social control, helping to reduce the stress and frustrations that often lead to social conflict, and intensifying group solidarity.

6. Religion also performs certain psychological functions, such as providing emotional comfort by helping to explain the unexplainable and helping a person cope with the stress and anxiety that often accompany illness or misfortune.

7. Following the scheme suggested by Wallace, the four distinctive types of religious organization are individualistic cults, shamanistic cults, communal cults, and ecclesiastical cults. These types correspond roughly with increasing levels of socioeconomic complexity; individualistic cults are associated with food-foraging societies and ecclesiastical cults with highly industrialized societies.

8. The most basic type of religious organization is the individualistic cult, characterized by an absence of religious specialists. The vision quest of certain Native American cultures is an example of an individualistic cult's religious practices.

9. Shamanistic cults involve the least complex religious division of labor. Shamans are part-time

religious specialists who, it is believed, help or cure their clients by intervening with supernatural powers while in an altered state of consciousness.

10. In communal cults ordinary people conduct religious ceremonies for the well-being of the community. Examples of communal cult ceremonies are the rites of passage (such as circumcision ceremonies) found widely throughout sub-Saharan Africa and the ancestral cults that foster group solidarity among members of a kinship group.

11. Ecclesiastical cults, which are found in societies with state systems of government, are characterized by full-time professional clergy who are usually organized into a hierarchy.

12. Revitalization movements—religious movements aimed at bringing new life and energy into a society—usually occur when societies are experiencing rapid cultural change, foreign domination, or perceived deprivation. Revitalization movements have taken a number of different forms, including nativistic movements, cargo cults, and millenarian movements.

13. Religion has played an important role in global social change through liberation theology (whereby Catholic priests and nuns work for social reform and justice for the poor) and religious nationalism (whereby religious beliefs are merged with government institutions).

14. A significant trend in global religion today is the rise of religious fundamentalism and religious nationalism. Found most prominently in the Islamic world, religious nationalism aims to merge traditional religious beliefs with contemporary political institutions.

Key Terms

cargo cults
communal cults
contagious magic
covens
cult
ecclesiastical cults
imitative magic

individualistic cults
liberation theology
magic
mahdist movements
millenarian movements
nativistic movements
religion

religious nationalism
revitalization movements
rites of passage
rites of solidarity
separatist Christian churches
shaman

shamanistic cults
sorcery
vision quest
Wicca
Witchcraft

Critical Thinking Questions

1. What are the differences and similarities between Christian fundamentalism and Islamic fundamentalism?

2. Arnold Van Gennep suggested that all rites of passage have three distinct phases. Can you identify these phases in certain rites of passage that people in your native culture typically go through?

3. How do you explain or interpret the findings of the Pew Forum on Religion and Public Life (2010) that atheists and agnostics comprise the group in the United States with the greatest amount of knowledge about all religions?

Online Study Resources

CourseMate

Access chapter-specific learning tools including learning objectives, practice quizzes, videos, flash cards, glossaries, web links, and more in your Cultural Anthropology CourseMate. Login to www.cengagebrain.com to access the resources your instructor has assigned and to purchase materials.

This totem pole in Ketchikan, Alaska represents an important art form among many Native American groups from the northwestern coast of North America.

Art

❋

Who would have thought that music could be the motivating force behind the social and economic revitalization of an urban community with more than five thousand people? Carlinhos Brown, a singer, songwriter, and percussionist, was born and raised in the Candyall neighborhood of Salvador, Brazil (Santos 2009). Candyall (pronounced *kahn djee all*) was a blighted neighborhood with a high rate of unemployment, unpaved streets, low-average income, deteriorating homes, and sewage running in the streets. After becoming one of Brazil's best-known musicians, Brown wanted to use his reputation and his relative affluence to pull his old neighborhood up from poverty and despair. In 1994 he started by building a music school in Candyall for local children who had dreams of success but little opportunity to learn music or develop skills. While the school has graduated a sizable number of successful musicians over the years, Brown has leveraged that success by encouraging local residents to join a community-based civic association aimed at rejuvenating the neighborhood. Over the past decade the community organization has built and renovated more than 250 homes and has convinced the city to build a local health clinic, install proper sewer lines, and supply a public source of water. In short, Carlinhos Brown has used his music, his reputation, and his personal resources to restore neighborhood pride and dignity and to make Candyall a cool place to live. ■

WHAT WE WILL LEARN

■ How do anthropologists define the arts?

■ What are the various functions of art in society?

■ How do all forms of art reflect other aspects of a culture?

■ How is art changing in the age of globalization?

Artistic expression is one of the most distinctive human characteristics. No group of people known to cultural anthropologists spends all of its time in the utilitarian pursuit of meeting basic survival needs. In other words, people do not hunt, grow crops, make tools, and build houses purely for the sake of sustaining themselves and others. After their survival needs are met, all cultures, even technologically simple ones, decorate their storage containers, paint their houses, embroider their clothing, and add aesthetically pleasing designs to their tools. They compose songs, tell riddles, dance creatively, paint pictures, make films, and carve masks. All of these endeavors reflect the human urge for self-expression and aesthetic pleasure. It would be hard to imagine a society without art, music, dance, and poetry. As the study of cultural anthropology reminds us, artistic expression is found in every society, and aesthetic pleasure is felt by people everywhere (Coote and Shelton 1992).

PhotoviewPlus/Getty Images

What Is Art?

For centuries, people from a variety of disciplines—including philosophers, anthropologists, politicians, art historians, and professional artists themselves—have proposed definitions of *art*. George Mills (1957: 17) suggested that "definitions (of art) vary with the purposes of the definers." To illustrate, the artist might define art in terms of the creative process, the politician's definition would emphasize the communicative aspects of art that could mobilize public opinion, the art historian or knowledgeable collector would focus on the emotional response art produces, and the cultural anthropologist might define art in terms of the role or function it plays in religious ceremonies. Nevertheless, despite these diverse definitions, any definition of art, if it is to have any cross-cultural comparability, must include five basic elements:

1. The artistic process should be creative, playful, and enjoyable and need not be concerned with the practicality or usefulness of the object being produced.

2. From the perspective of the consumer, art should produce some type of emotional response, either positive or negative.

3. Art should be *transformational*. An event from nature, such as a cheetah running at full speed, may be aesthetically pleasing in that it evokes a strong emotional response, but it is not art. It becomes art only when someone transforms the image into a painting, dance, song, or poem.

4. Art should communicate information by being representational. In other words, once the object of art is transformed, it should make a symbolic statement about what is being portrayed.

5. Art implies that the artist has developed a certain level of technical skill not shared equally by all people in a society. Some people have more highly developed skills than others because of the interplay of individual interests and opportunities with genetically based acuities (Figure 15.1).

Centuries of debate by reasonable people have failed to produce a universally agreed-on definition of art. Although we will not presume to establish a universal definition, it will be useful, for the purposes of this chapter, to suggest a working definition based on the five elements just listed. Thus, art is both the process and the products of applying certain skills to any

transformational The quality of an artistic process that converts an image into a work of art.

© Paa Joe, Ghana, Africa late 20th to early 21st century. Lion-shaped coffin, 2001. Mint Museum, Charlotte, NC.

FIGURE 15.1 This lion-shaped coffin (constructed of wood, enamel, raffia, and fabric) is the creation of Ghanaian artist Paa Joe.

activity that transforms matter, sound, or motion into a form that is deemed aesthetically meaningful by people in a society.

By using these five features, we can include a wide variety of artistic activities in our definition of art. In all societies people apply imagination, creativity, and technical skills to transform matter, sound, and movement into works of art. The various types of artistic expression include the graphic or plastic arts—such as painting, carving, weaving, basket making, and sculpting out of clay, metal, or glass; the creative manipulation of sounds and words in such artistic forms as music, poetry, and folklore; and the application of skill and creativity to body movement that gives rise to dance. It should be pointed out that these three neatly defined categories of artistic expression sometimes include forms that are not familiar to Westerners. To Westerners the graphic and plastic arts include such media as painting and sculpture, but in the non-Western world people may also include the Nubians' elaborate body decoration (Faris 1972), Navajo sand-painting (Witherspoon 1977), and the Inuits' body tattooing (Birket-Smith 1959). Moreover some activities that in our own society have no particular artistic content may be elevated to an art form in other societies. The Japanese tea ceremony is an excellent case in point.

It is also possible for these different types or modes of art to be combined in creative ways. In 2005 the Columbia (South Carolina) City Ballet staged a beautifully choreographed performance titled *Off the Wall and*

Onto the Stage: Dancing the Art of Jonathan Green (Figure 15.2). In this brilliantly conceived marriage of painting with music and dance, each dance selection either started or ended with a painting by African American painter Jonathan Green, whose colorful paintings portray life among the Gullah people of coastal South Carolina. The Gullah people portrayed in Green's paintings, complete with meticulously replicated costumes, came alive on stage through the medium of ballet and modern dance. Thus, through a combination of the art forms of painting, dance, and music, audiences were able to experience a more complete image of the Gullah people and their rich cultural traditions.

Every society has a set of standards that distinguish between good art and bad art or between more and less satisfying aesthetic experiences. In some societies, such as our own, what constitutes good art is determined largely by a professional art establishment made up of art critics, museum and conservatory personnel, professors of art, and others who generally make their living in the arts. Other societies may not have professional art establishments, and their artistic standards tend to be more democratic in that they are maintained by the general public. Thus, the decoration on a vase, the rhythm of a song, the communicative power of a dance, and the imagery of a painting are subject to the evaluation of artists and non-artists alike.

Differences in Art Forms

Many Western people view art from other, less complex societies, as being "primitive" because it does not adhere to our culture's notion of what constitutes good art. Western art is displayed in museums and galleries with the name of the artist prominently featured. When we visit exhibitions of Native American, African, or Polynesian art in Western museums, however, the artist is not even identified by name. Instead the viewer is given a rather elaborate description of where the piece comes from, the materials and techniques used to make it, the function it performs, how it might reflect other aspects of the local culture, and the name of the Western collector who purchased it. According to Sally Price (2001), this practice of identifying the collector rather than the artist is a not-so-subtle way of saying that the value of the art object is determined more by who bought it than by who made it.

This practice of treating art objects in small-scale societies as ethnographic artifacts rather than works of art made by individual artists with actual names is changing, albeit slowly. The Denver Art Museum, under the leadership of Curator of Native Arts, Nancy Blomberg, is making a dedicated effort to display native art that is attributed to the original artist. This is a radical departure from traditional museum practice, which scholars and curators hope will become routine museum practice in the not-too-distant future. Few (if any) art scholars and curators would argue that native artists should be kept in anonymity because their artistry is inferior to Western art. Rather the process of identifying native artists is a long and arduous process requiring enormous amounts of time, energy, and research. Even the Denver Museum, which is taking the lead in artistic attribution research, can only attach names to fewer than 15 percent of the art objects on display. But as more and more museums throughout the world begin to engage in this attribution research, art researchers will be able to build on each other's work, thereby speeding up the process of identifying artistic authorship. With the many financial and staffing challenges facing museums today, this process of identifying native artists will not be completed overnight. But it appears that the traditional practice of keeping native artists anonymous is slowly being reversed (Dobrzynski 2011).

Despite attempts by art historians to perpetuate the use of the term *primitive*, we do not use it in this book because of its misleading connotations of both inferiority and evolutionary sequencing. Instead we use the term *small-scale* to describe egalitarian societies that have small populations, simple technologies, and little specialization of labor.

Painting by Jonathan Green from the collection of Brian and Kristen Hummel. Photo: Tim Stamm

FIGURE 15.2 This painting, *Sea Swing*, was one of many by artist Jonathan Green that was combined with dance and music by the Columbia (SC) City Ballet in the 2005 performance entitled "Off the Wall and Onto the Stage."

Having disposed of the term *primitive*, we can now proceed to look at some of the major differences in art forms between small-scale and complex societies (this discussion is developed in much fuller detail by Richard Anderson [2003]). One difference stems from the lifestyles and settlement patterns found in these logically opposite types of societies. Because small-scale societies tend to be foragers, pastoralists, or shifting cultivators with nomadic or semi-nomadic residence patterns, the art found in these societies must be highly portable. It is not reasonable to expect people who are often on the move to develop an art tradition comprising large works of art, such as larger-than-life sculptures or large painted canvases. Instead art in small-scale societies is limited to forms that people leave behind on rock walls or cliffs or forms that they can take with them easily, such as performing arts (song, dance, and storytelling); body decoration, such as jewelry, body painting, tattooing, and scarification; and artistic decorations on practical artifacts such as weapons, clothing, and food containers.

Frank Tozier/Alamy

FIGURE 15.3 In complex societies artistic standards are defined by full time specialists such as art curators, brokers, critics, and scholars, many of whom are associated with such museums as the Art Institute in Chicago.

The second significant difference between the art of small-scale societies and complex societies stems from their different levels of social differentiation (that is, labor specialization). As societies began to develop increasingly more specialized roles following the Neolithic Revolution (about ten thousand years ago), some segments of the population were freed from the everyday pursuits of providing food. The subsequent rise of civilizations was accompanied by the emergence of full-time specialists, such as philosophers, intellectuals, literati, and aesthetic critics, whose energies were directed, among other things, at distinguishing between good art and bad art. The standards of aesthetic judgment have become much more explicit and elaborately defined by specialists in more complex societies. To be certain, small-scale societies have aesthetic standards, but they are less elaborate, more implicit, and more widely diffused throughout the entire population.

A third major contrast arises from differences in the division of labor. As a general rule, as societies become more specialized, they also become more highly stratified into classes with different levels of power, prestige, and wealth (Figure 15.3). The aesthetic critics responsible for establishing artistic standards in complex societies are invariably members of the upper classes or are employed by them. Thus, art in complex societies becomes associated with the elite. Not only are those who set the standards often members of the elite, but art in complex societies often is owned and controlled by the upper classes. Moreover, in some complex societies, art both glorifies and serves the interests of the

upper classes. In contrast, because small-scale societies are more egalitarian, art tends to be more democratic in that all people have roughly equal access to it.

Random Acts of Culture

This notion that in complex societies, unlike more small-scale societies, the upper classes have greater control over, and access to, art is particularly evident in the United States. If the directors of museums, symphonies, opera companies, or ballet companies want to raise money, they are not likely to go canvassing in working-class or lower-class neighborhoods. Moreover, it is the upper and upper middle classes that are most likely to be season ticket holders for such performance, not the lower classes or even middle classes. This inequality of access to the arts in the United States was demonstrated several years ago by a popular phenomenon known as "random acts of culture," whereby professional opera companies would put on impromptu performances in crowded shopping malls or train stations. On one such occasion at the Reading Terminal Market in Philadelphia on January 8, 2011, a man standing at the cheese steak stand began singing the "Toreador Song" from the opera *Carmen*, was then joined by two other members of the Philadelphia Opera company who were dressed in ordinary casual clothes, and within minutes they were joined by the company's thirty-member chorus who were singing, dancing, and toasting the crowd with whatever drink containers they had in their hand. The stunned audience, who thought they were just doing some shopping, laughed, cried, and captured much of the event on their cell phones. When the music ended, several employees of the opera company held up signs which read "You have just experienced a Random Act of Culture." The event had such a powerful emotional impact because most of the shoppers (who had probably never attended a live opera performance before) were stunned at the enormous amount of singing talent they heard, and interacted, in a personal way, with world-class performers who typically entertained people from a world different from their own. Because this was a planned event, the entire performance was caught on video, which immediately went viral on You Tube.

In addition to these three fundamental differences, art in small-scale societies is often embedded to a greater degree in other aspects of the culture. Although we can observe connections between art and, say, religion in our own society, in small-scale societies art permeates many other areas of culture. In fact, because art is such an integral part of the *total* culture, many small-scale societies do not even have a word for art. That is, because art pervades all aspects of peoples' lives, they do not think of art as something separate and distinct. One such example, sandpainting as practiced in Navajo culture, is as much religion, myth, and healing as it is art. According to Dorothy Lee (1993: 13), Navajo sandpaintings (Figure 15.4) are created as part of a ceremony that

> brings into harmony with the universal order one who finds himself in discord with it.... Every line and shape and color, every relationship of form, is

the visible manifestation of myth, ritual and religious belief. The making of the painting is accompanied with a series of sacred songs sung over a sick person.... When the ceremonial is over, the painting is over too; it is destroyed; it has fulfilled its function.

Because art in small-scale societies is embedded in most other areas of the culture, one is likely to see artistic expressions throughout many realms of peoples' everyday lives. This is not the case in more highly differentiated and stratified societies, which have institutions such as museums and private galleries where art is viewed, appreciated, understood, discussed, and in some cases, bought and sold. Most people who pay admission to an art museum in North America are doing so to view the artistic exhibits, learn more about them, and experience the feelings they engender. Likewise, when people enter a private art gallery, they are interested not only in seeing and experiencing the works shown but also in possibly purchasing the works of art. In other words, in most complex societies people go to places that are essentially single-purpose venues (such as museums, galleries, theaters, and opera houses) to see, experience, or trade in artistic objects.

A rare (and interesting) exception to the general rule of separating art from other aspects of life in complex societies is the Crest Hardware store in Brooklyn, New York (Porter 2008). Since 1994 the hardware store has sponsored the annual Crest Hardware Art Show, which displays the works of more than a hundred local artists alongside its usual items such as nails, drill bits, and extension cords. Many of the works of art (on sale for $20 to $9,800) are related to hardware, such as a classically painted portrait of George Washington with a giant C-clamp on his head.

In some parts of the world, it is possible to see how the political system of a society is reflected in its art. Anthropologist Christopher Steiner (1990) has shown how one form of artistic expression—body decoration—reflects the different political structures in Melanesia and Polynesia. As mentioned in chapter 8, a prominent form of political leadership in Melanesia is big men. In the absence of permanent political offices or hierarchies, big men earn their authority by working hard to attract a large number of followers. Because big men can lose their followers, the system of political leadership in Melanesia is very fluid, always subject to change. In Polynesia, on the other hand, leadership is based on centralized chiefdoms with permanent (usually hereditary) authority. The differences in

FIGURE 15.4 The art form of sand painting among the Navajo of New Mexico is intimately connected with their traditional systems of healing and religion.

Paul Chesley/ Getty Images

the political structures of these societies are reflected in their forms of bodily adornment. Melanesians decorate their bodies with paints—a temporary medium that can be washed off or lost in much the same way that a big man can lose his high status if he loses the support of his followers. In contrast, Polynesians use tattoos, a permanent form of body art, reflecting their more centralized and permanent nature of political authority. Thus, to distinguish themselves from commoners, Polynesian chiefs use tattoos, a particularly appropriate form of body decoration that reflects both the high status and the permanency of their hereditary offices.

The Functions of Art

To gain a fuller understanding of art, we must move beyond our working definition to examine the roles art plays for both people and societies. The fact that artistic expression is found in every known society suggests that it functions in some important ways in human societies. The various functions of art can be divided into two basic types: how artistic elements function for the psychological well-being of the individual and how they function for the well-being and continuity of the society as a whole.

Emotional Gratification for the Individual

Quite apart from whatever benefits art may have for the total society, it is generally agreed that art is a source of personal gratification for both the artist and the viewer. It would be hard to imagine a world in which people engaged only in pursuits that met their basic survival needs. Although people devote most of their time and energy to meeting those needs, it is equally true that all people derive some enjoyment from art because it provides at least a temporary break from those practical (and often stressful) pursuits. After the crops are harvested, the African horticulturalist has time to dance, tell stories, and derive pleasure from making or viewing pieces of art. Likewise, as a diversion from their workaday lives, many Westerners seek gratification by attending a play, a concert, or a museum. No doubt, it was this personal gratification derived from art that prompted Richard Selzer (1979: 196) to comment: "art … is necessary only in that without it life would be unbearable."

The psychologically beneficial functions of art can be examined from two perspectives: that of the artist and that of the beholder. For the artist the creative process releases emotional energy in a concrete or visible way—that is, by painting, sculpting, writing a play, or performing an interpretive dance. Artists, at least

CROSS-CULTURAL MISCUE

George Burgess, an art major at a Canadian university, invited Kamau, his Kenyan roommate, to his family home in Toronto for the Christmas holidays. While in the downtown area, George suggested that they go to the local art museum to see a new exhibition of abstract expressionists from the 1940s. Looking at an abstract painting by Jackson Pollock, Kamau asked George what it meant. George threw up his hands and said cheerfully, "That is the beauty of abstract art; it can mean anything you want it to mean." In a puzzled tone, Kamau inquired, "Then why did he make it?" George could not understand why Kamau did not appreciate this classic piece of abstract expressionism.

George did not realize that different cultures have different ideas about what art is and what function it should perform. Art in Kenya, and in many parts of Africa, is much more public in nature than it is in North America. African artists tend to emphasize both conveying a message to the audience and demonstrating the function of the piece of art for the life of the community. In contrast, the Western artistic tradition that George was studying at the university places much more importance on the individual expressiveness and creativity of the artist. This cross-cultural misunderstanding occurred because Kamau failed to appreciate the highly individualistic nature of the artist in Western society, and George failed to understand the African tradition of the artist explicitly communicating to the audience.

in the Western world, are viewed as living with a creative tension that, when released, results in a work of art. This release of creative energy also brings pleasure to the artist to the extent that she or he derives satisfaction from both the mastery of techniques and the product itself.

From the perspective of the viewer, art can evoke pleasurable emotional responses. For example, works of art can portray events, people, or deities that conjure up positive emotions. The symbols used in a work of art can arouse a positive emotional response. The viewer can receive pleasure by being dazzled by the artist's virtuosity. These pleasurable responses can contribute to the mental well-being of art viewers by providing a necessary balance with the stresses in their everyday lives.

However, it is also possible for art to have the opposite effect by eliciting negative emotions. The artistic process, if not successful from the artist's point of view, can result in increased frustrations and tension. Moreover any art form is capable of eliciting disturbing or even painful emotions that can lead to psychological discomfort for the viewer.

Social Integration

In addition to whatever positive roles it may play for the individual, art functions to sustain the longevity of the society in which it is found. As functionalist anthropologists remind us, art is connected to other parts of the social system. One need only walk into a church, synagogue, or temple to see the relationship between art and religion. Moreover art has been used in many societies to evoke positive sentiments for systems of government and individual political leaders. In this section we will explore some of the ways in which art contributes to the maintenance and longevity of a society.

Through various symbols, art communicates a good deal about the values, beliefs, and ideologies of the culture of which it is a part. The art forms found in any given society reflect the major cultural themes and concerns of the society. To illustrate, prominent breasts on females are a major theme in much of the wood sculpture from West Africa. This dominant theme reflects a important social value in those West African societies: the social importance of having children. Somewhat closer to our own cultural traditions, much of the art in Renaissance Europe reflected religious themes central to Christianity. Thus, certain forms of graphic arts function to help integrate the society by making the dominant cultural themes, values, and beliefs more visible. By expressing these cultural themes in a tangible way, art ultimately functions to strengthen people's identification with their culture by reinforcing those cultural themes.

The intimate interconnectedness of art and religious life is well illustrated in Bali (Indonesia), a culture with a long and rich tradition of dance and music. The large number of ceremonies that occur annually on the Bali-Hindu calendar involve elaborate displays and performances designed to attract the gods and please the people. Various life cycle events such as births and funerals are celebrated by special orchestras with music and dance. Some musical instruments, thought to be the gift of the gods, are considered so sacred that they can only be displayed, not actually played. According to one Balinese expert, "Music and dance are spiritual musts. The arts are an invitation for the gods to come down and join the people. There is a very physical contact with the unseen, with the ancestors … that makes the people in the village very happy" (Charle 1999: 28).

Art helps to strengthen and reinforce both social bonds and cultural themes. For example, cultural values are passed on from generation to generation using the media of song and dance. As part of the intense education in African bush schools, various forms of dance are used to teach proper adult attitudes and behaviors to those preparing for initiation. The role of music in education is well illustrated by Bert, Ernie, Kermit, and the other characters of *Sesame Street*, who sing about values such as cooperation, acceptable forms of conflict resolution, the fun of learning, and race relations. Music also can be used to solidify a group of people. Any history of warfare is woefully incomplete without some mention of the role that martial music played to rally the people against the common enemy.

Sometimes art can be a social integrator in a community by bridging differences among subgroups based on race, class, or ethnicity. Since 1984 the city of Philadelphia has sponsored the Mural Arts Program, which has brought neighborhood residents together to plan and paint more than 2,800 architectural-scale murals on the sides of buildings. But these murals are more than art. They represent neighborhood identity, civic pride, and involvement in the community. And they help bridge racial, ethnic, and class divisions (Hurdle 2008).

To illustrate how the Mural Arts Program works, we can look at the Grays Ferry neighborhood, which in the 1990s was the scene of a racial protest march precipitated by the beating of a black family by a group of whites. With racial tensions running high, the director of the Mural Arts Program suggested that the community create a mural with the theme of racial harmony. Even though many people, both black and white, were skeptical at first, after several community planning sessions, the doubts and suspicions were replaced by a desire to cooperate on the project. The mural, titled "Peace Wall," depicts overlapping hands of varying skin tones on a sky-blue background. The planning and execution of the mural provided an opportunity for people of different backgrounds to get to know one another better and to form a sense of community (Figure 15.5). Once "Peace Wall" was completed, residents took on other community projects such as trash collection and street repair. Thus, as illustrated by the Philadelphia Mural Arts Program, large-scale art projects requiring cooperation can knit people together into the fabric of a unified community.

Social Control

A popular perception of artists and their works in the Western world is that they are visionary, nonconformist, and often anti-establishment. Although this is often true in contemporary Western societies, much art found in other societies (and indeed in our own Western tradition in past centuries) functions to reinforce the existing sociocultural system. For example, art can help instill important cultural values in younger generations, coerce people to behave in socially appropriate ways, and buttress the inequalities of the stratification system in a society. We will briefly examine several ways that the arts can contribute to the status quo.

Section A-23 Jack Ramsdale for Mural Arts Program

FIGURE 15.5 The "peace Wall," created by the Mural Arts Program of Philadelphia, is an example of how art can help a community bridge cultural differences among its members.

Through the medium of these pieces of art, the spirits were thought to be able to intervene in the affairs of the living. Specifically, the masks played an important role in the administration of justice. When a dispute arose or a crime was committed, the case was brought before a council of wise and influential men who reviewed the facts and arrived at a tentative decision. This decision was then confirmed (and given supernatural force) by one of the judges who wore the death mask, thus concealing his own identity. Therefore, in addition to whatever other functions these artistically carved masks played among the Mano, they served as mechanisms of social control within the criminal justice system.

Art also plays an important role in controlling behavior in more complex societies. In highly stratified societies, state governments sponsor art to instill obedience and maintain the status quo. In some early civilizations, for example, state-sponsored monumental architecture—such as pyramids, ziggurats, and cathedrals—was a visual representation of the astonishing power of both the gods and the rulers. Most people living in these state societies would think twice before breaking either secular or religious rules when faced with the awesome power and authority represented in these magnificent works of art.

Particularly in modern times, the state may use art to control (or at least influence) people's behavior in more subtle ways. For example, in present-day China, the music played on state-controlled radio is purposefully chosen to soothe rather than to provoke. In keeping with its desire to build a "harmonious society," Chinese authorities play only light and upbeat music, with such themes as romance, diligence, and "it's not so bad being poor but happy." You will hear no angry rap music, protest songs, or heavy rock tunes on state-monopolized radio in China today. For the Chinese, the purpose of music is to lull the masses into passivity, rather than to arouse any negative or inharmonious sentiments (French 2007).

Preserving or Challenging the Status Quo

By serving as a symbol for social status, art contributes to the preservation of the status quo. To one degree or another, all societies make distinctions

First, art can serve as a mechanism of social control. Art historians generally recognize that art has a strong religious base, but they have been less cognizant of the role art plays in other cultural domains. A notable exception is Roy Sieber (1962), an art historian who has demonstrated how wooden masks serve as agents of social control in several tribal groups in northeastern Liberia. It was generally believed by the Mano, for example, that the god-spirit mask embodied the spiritual forces that actually control human behavior. The death of a high-status man was marked by a wooden death mask carved in his honor. A crude portrait of the deceased, the death mask was thought to be the ultimate resting place of the man's spirit.

between different levels of power and prestige. As societies become more highly specialized, systems of stratification become more complex, and the gap widens between the haves and the have-nots. Power is expressed in different ways throughout the world, including the use of physical force, control over political decisions, and accumulation of valuable resources. One particularly convincing way to display one's power is symbolically through the control of valuable items in the society. The accumulation of such practical objects as tools would not be a particularly good symbol of high prestige because everyone has some and because one hardly needs an overabundance of everyday practical objects to meet one's own needs. The accumulation of art objects, however, is much more likely to serve as a symbol of high prestige because art objects are unique, not commonly found throughout the society, and often priceless (Figure 15.6).

Art is associated with status symbols in many societies that have ranked populations. For example, virtually all the art in ancient Egyptian civilizations was the personal property of the pharaohs. The high status of the hereditary king of the Ashanti of present-day Ghana is symbolized by a wide variety of artistic objects, the most important of which is the Golden Stool. In the Western world, many public art galleries are filled with impressive personal collections donated by powerful, high-status members of society (Getty, Hirshhorn, and Rockefeller, among others).

Art is a force for preserving the status quo, but it is also often used in the opposite way—as a vehicle of protest, resistance, and even revolution. A number of artists have attempted, through their own artistic media, to raise the consciousness of their oppressed countrymen to bring about changes in the political and social structure. For example, Marjorie Agosin (1987) documented the case of the Chilean *arpilleristas*, who told the story of political oppression on scraps of cloth. These courageous artists were considered such a threat to the established government that they were eventually banned in their own country. In Chile during the Augusto Pinochet regime, local artists painted murals under the cover of night depicting scenes of government oppression, only to have them removed by the military police the next morning.

Perhaps one of the most influential forms of art used for social change has come to be known as *liberation theater* started in the 1960s by Augusto Boal in Peru. Boal believed that effective political theater (used to bring about change) should not focus on plot, dialogue, or quality of acting, but rather on the *involvement of the audience* in the creation and the performance of the play itself. Boal developed the now-legendary method called the *liberation theater workshop*. With the help of experienced theater people Boal worked with oppressed people from local communities who were exposed to a series of experiential techniques and the language of theater, which includes elements such as body movement. Participants were then invited to write their own scenarios portraying oppression in their own lives, which are then acted out by professional actors. Only the oppressive scenario is acted out, not its resolution. After seeing the scenario played out, participants are asked to offer possible resolutions to the scenarios, and if they wish, they may play it out themselves by taking over the role from the actor. Thus, through the medium of theater, Boal trained locally oppressed people to assume the protagonist role, offer solutions to the situation, and discuss strategies for change. As Boal (1979: 122) himself wrote, "The theater is not revolutionary in itself, but it is surely a rehearsal for the revolution."

For more current, and dramatic, examples of how various art forms have been used to challenge the status quo, we have only to turn to the revolutions going on in the Middle East known as the "Arab Spring." Fed up with corrupt governments, widespread injustice, growing economic inequality, and little freedom of expression, people have taken to the streets in Tunisia, Egypt, Libya, Bahrain, and Syria since 2010. Dictators have been overthrown, government toppled, and

© Bettmann/Corbis

FIGURE 15.6 A painting by Renoir sells for over $4 million at an art auction at Christie's in London. Because works of Western art can command very high prices, they serve as visible symbols of social status for the upper classes.

liberation theater Theatrical production that uses high levels of audience participation and is aimed at bringing about social change.

in some cases civil wars have raged. But what all of these recent revolutions have in common is that artists, particularly musicians and graphic artists, have played a key role in mobilizing popular support.

Before the Arab Spring, heavy metal bands kept a low profile in all Islamic countries, playing their music largely on the Internet rather than in live public concerts. Most of the hard rock and rave musicians, who were considered by the government to be satanic, lived in fear of the secret police. Playing popular music in public was certainly a risky business for most pop singers, particularly if the lyrics were in Arabic.

But this veil of timidity and caution was shattered by an unlikely, little known rapper in Tunisia by the name of Hamada Ben Amor, aka El Général, a twenty-one-year-old musician who lived in Tunis with his parents. Several months before the revolution broke out in Tunisia, El Général uploaded on to Facebook his in-your-face rap creation titled "President, Your Country," with lyrics that captured the mood of the country:

> My president, your country is dead/
> People eat garbage/
> Look at what is happening/
> Misery everywhere/
> Nowhere to sleep/
> I'm speaking for the people who suffer/
> Ground under feet.

This single musical event was the shot heard around the Middle East. Within hours the song was being listened to by people all across North Africa. It was broadcast by the Tunisian TV network and al Jazeera. And although El Général's MySpace page and cell phone were shut down almost immediately by a nervous dictatorship, this musical act of defiance was seen by many observers as the start of the revolt in Tunisia and indeed the entire Arab Spring itself. Such is the power of music to bring about a radical and dramatic shift in the status quo (Morgan 2011).

Graphic and Plastic Arts

Graphic and plastic arts include a number of forms of expression and a wide variety of skills. Although the Western notion of *graphic arts* and *plastic arts* usually refers to painting, sculpture, print making, and architecture; the anthropological definition also includes such art forms as weaving, embroidery, tailoring, jewelry making, and tattooing and other forms of body

---

graphic arts Forms of art that include painting and drawing on various surfaces.

plastic arts Artistic expression that involves molding certain forms, such as sculpture.

---

decoration. In some societies one form of art, such as wood carving, may be highly developed, and others, such as painting or metal-working, may be nonexistent.

The analysis of these art forms is further complicated because different cultures use different materials and technologies depending, in part, on what materials are available locally. Whereas American Indians of the northwest coast of the United States are well known for their carvings of wood, other cultures use horn, bone, ivory, or soapstone. In some small-scale societies, the nature of people's ceramic art is determined by the availability of locally found clays. Often the level of technology influences whether a culture uses metals such as gold, silver, and bronze in its art traditions.

Not only do different art traditions draw on different materials, techniques, and media, but the nature of the creative process can also vary cross-culturally. To illustrate, in the Western tradition, the practice of commissioning a piece of art is quite common. For a fee, portrait artists use their creative talents to paint realistic (and usually flattering) likenesses of their prominent clients. However, it is not likely that a client could commission an Inuit artist to carve a walrus from a piece of ivory. According to the Inuit notion of the creative process, that would be much too willful, even heavy handed. Whereas the Western artist is solely responsible for painting the canvas or molding the clay in a total act of will, the Inuit carver never forces the ivory into any uncharacteristic shapes. The Inuit artist does not create but rather helps to liberate what is already in the piece of ivory. Edmund Carpenter (1973: 59) describes the Inuit's notion of the role of the artist:

> As the carver holds the unworked ivory lightly in his hand, turning it this way and that, he whispers, "Who are you! Who hides there!" And then: "Ah, Seal!" He rarely sets out to carve, say, a seal, but picks up the ivory, examines it to find its hidden form and, if that's not immediately apparent, carves aimlessly until he sees it, humming or chanting as he works. Then he brings it out: seal, hidden, emerges. It was always there: he did not create it, he released it; he helped it step forth.

Of all the various forms of art in the world, the graphic and plastic arts have received the greatest amount of attention from cultural anthropologists. This is understandable because until recently the analysis of the plastic and graphic arts was the most manageable. Until the recent development of such data-gathering technology as sound recorders, motion pictures, and camcorders, analyzing music and dance was difficult. The graphic and plastic arts, however, produced objects that are tangible and can be removed from their cultural contexts, displayed in museums, and compared with relative ease. Moreover a painting or a sculpture has a permanence of form not found in music, dance, or drama.

Music

We often hear the expression "music is the universal language." By this people mean that even if two people do not speak each other's language, they can at least appreciate music together. But like so many popular sayings, this one is only partially true. Although all people do have the same physiological mechanisms for hearing, what a person actually hears is influenced by his or her culture. Westerners tend to miss much of the richness of Javanese and Sri Lankan music because they have not been conditioned to hear it. Whenever we encounter a piece of non-Western music, we hear it (process it) in terms of our own culturally influenced set of musical categories involving scale, melody, pitch, harmony, and rhythm. And because those categories are defined differently from culture to culture, the appreciation of music across cultures is not always ensured. To illustrate this point, Mark Slobin and Jeff Titon (1984: 1) tell a story about a famous Asian musician who attended a symphony concert in Europe during the mid-nineteenth century:

> Although he was a virtuoso musician in his own country, he had never heard a performance of western music. The story goes that after the concert he was asked how he liked it. "Very well," he replied. Not satisfied with this answer, his host asked (through an interpreter) what part he liked best. "The first part," he said. "Oh, you enjoyed the first movement?" "No, before that!" To the stranger, the best part of the performance was the tuning up period.

Ethnomusicology

The cross-cultural study of music is known as *ethnomusicology*, a relatively new field that involves the cooperative efforts of both anthropologists and musicologists (Nettl and Bohlman 1991). Ethnomusicology has made rapid progress as a result of developments in high-quality recording equipment needed for basic data gathering. Slobin and Titon (1984) identified four major concerns of ethnomusicology:

1. *Ideas about music.* How does a culture distinguish between music and non-music? What functions does music play for the society? Is music viewed as beneficial or harmful to the society? What constitutes beautiful music? On what occasions should music be played?

2. *Social structure of music.* What are the social relationships between musicians? How does a society distinguish between various musicians on the basis

of such criteria as age, gender, race, ethnicity, and education?

3. *Characteristics of the music itself.* How does the style of music in different cultures vary (scale, melody, harmony, timing)? What different musical genres are found in a society (lullaby, sea chantey, hard rock, and so on)? What is the nature of musical texts (words)? How is music composed? How is music learned and transmitted?

4. *Material culture of music.* What musical instruments are used in a culture? Who makes the musical instruments, and how are they distributed? How are musical tastes reflected in the instruments used?

As these areas of interest indicate, ethnomusicology is concerned with both the structure and techniques of music and the interconnections between music and other parts of the culture (Figure 15.7). Yet, during the course of cross-cultural studies of music, ethnomusicologists have been torn between two approaches. At one extreme, they have searched for musical universals—elements found in all musical traditions. At the opposite extreme, they have been interested in demonstrating the considerable diversity found throughout the world. Bruno Nettl (1980: 3) describes this tension: "In the heart of the ethnomusicologist there are two strings: one that attests to the universal character of music, to the fact that music is indeed something that all cultures have or appear to have … and one responsive to the enormous variety of existing cultures."

Christine Osborne/Corbis

FIGURE 15.7 Ethnomusicologists are interested in studying both the music of this gamelan orchestra in Bali, Indonesia as well as how the music reflects the wider culture of which it is a part.

ethnomusicology The study of the relationship between music and other aspects of culture.

Where Is the Line Between Art and Body Parts?

The Maori of New Zealand, like many peoples from the Pacific Islands, considered full-body tattooing a high art form. When Maori warriors were killed in battle, their tattooed heads were often preserved in mummified form as a way of keeping their spirits alive. During the nineteenth century, Europeans traveled to exotic parts of the world, collected these artistically decorated heads, housed them in European museums, and considered them to be part of the European art heritage. The New Zealand government, however, for years has pressed European cultural ministries to return these Maori heads (and other human remains) so they can receive proper burial.

Courtesy of Museum de Rouen

In 2007 the mayor of the French city of Rouen signed an agreement with the New Zealand ambassador to France to return one such Maori head, which had been in its local museum since 1895. The National Ministry of Culture, however, blocked the agreement by claiming that (a) the head belonged to France, (b) the mayor had no authority to sign such an agreement, (c) mayor violated a 2002 French law stating that French art is "inalienable," and (d) the return of the head would set an unfortunate precedent that could lead to the return of other artistic body parts in the future.

The mayor of Rouen, acting on behalf of the people of his city, claimed that he signed the agreement to atone for France's participation in the trafficking of human body parts during the nineteenth century. He insists that the tattooed head is a body part, not a cultural artifact, and therefore should be returned to its place of origin as specified in France's bioethics law. The head, the mayor claims, "belongs to the heritage of humanity, not in storage somewhere in a museum" (Sciolino 2007: 4).

Despite the fact that French courts declared that the city of Rouen lacked the jurisdiction or authority to return the tattooed head, the head was in fact returned to the Maoris of New Zealand in May 2011. The Maori, with the help of the New Zealand government, are seeking the return of about 500 other tattooed heads that are presently in museums and personal collections around the world. While this debate continues, where do you stand on this contemporary issue in the art world?

All ethnomusicologists—whether their background is in music or cultural anthropology—are interested in the study of music in its cultural context. Alan Lomax and his colleagues (1968) conducted one of the most extensive studies of the relationship between music and other parts of culture. Specifically, they found some broad correlations between various aspects of music and a culture's level of subsistence. Foraging societies were found to have types of music, song, and dance that were fundamentally different from those of more complex producers. By dividing a worldwide sample of cultures into five different levels of subsistence complexity, Lomax found some significant correlations. For example, differences emerged between egalitarian, small-scale societies with simple subsistence economies and large-scale, stratified societies with complex systems of production (see Table 15.1).

TABLE 15.1

Comparison of Music between Egalitarian and Stratified Societies

Egalitarian Societies and Simple Economics	Stratified Societies and Complex Economics
Repetitious texts	Nonrepetitious texts
Slurred articulation	Precise articulation
Little solo singing	Solo singing
Wide melodic intervals	Narrow melodic intervals
Nonelaborate songs (no embellishments)	Elaborate songs (embellishments)
Few instruments	Large number of instruments
Singing in unison	Singing in simultaneous intervals

Dance

Dance has been defined as purposeful and intentionally rhythmical nonverbal body movements that are culturally patterned and have aesthetic value (Hanna 1979: 19).

Although dance is found in all known societies, the forms it takes, the functions it fulfills, and the meanings attached to it vary widely from society to society. In some societies dance involves considerable energy and body movement, whereas in other societies it is much more restrained and subtle. Because the human body is capable of a wide variety of postures and movements, which body parts are active and which postures are assumed

---

dance Intentional, rhythmic, nonverbal body movements that are culturally patterned and have aesthetic value.

differ from one dance tradition to another. In some African societies (such as the Ubakala of Nigeria) drums are a necessary part of dance, whereas in others (such as the Zulu) they are not. Dancing alone is the expected form in some societies, but in others it is customary for groups to dance in circles, lines, or other formations. Yet, whatever form dance takes in any culture, it remains a persuasive form of communication that blends body movements with both emotions and cognition. As Judith Hanna (2005: 11) reminds us, "Both dance and verbal language have vocabulary (locomotion and gestures in dance), grammar (ways one movement can follow another), and semantics (including symbolic devices and spheres for encoding feelings and ideas)."

Moreover the relative value of dance as an art form varies widely from one society to another. To illustrate, the government of the small country of Cuba supports dance in a number of visible ways, making Cuba one of the great dance nations of the world. For example, Cuba is the venue for a number of important international dance festivals, and in fact many world-class dancers come to Cuba to study dance. The professional dancers of the Ballet Nacional de Cuba enjoy high status at home and international acclaim when performing abroad. And free dance education is available to any child from kindergarten through university. Now compare this high level of public promotion of all forms of dance in Cuba with the situation just ninety miles to the north in the United States (Figure 15.8). The overwhelming majority of adults in the United States have never attended a fully staged ballet, a contemporary dance performance, or even a ballroom dance competition. Despite the fact that the physical conditioning required of professional dancers often exceeds that of other professional athletes, dance in the United States is generally thought of as a female, or an effeminate, profession. And despite the recent popularity of reality-based dance shows on TV (*Dancing with the Stars* and *So You Think You Can Dance*), government officials (from the courts to the National Endowment for the Arts) expend an enormous amount of time and energy trying to determine whether certain dance forms are too sexual, involve too much nudity or semi-nudity, or encourage inappropriately close contact between partners (Hanna 2005).

Functions of Dance

As with other forms of artistic expression, the functions of dance are culturally variable. Dance is likely to function in different ways both between and within societies. Dance often performs several functions simultaneously within a society, but some functions are more prominent than others. To illustrate, dance can function psychologically by helping people cope more effectively with tensions and aggressive feelings; politically by expressing political values and attitudes, showing allegiance to political leaders, and controlling behavior; religiously by various methods of communicating with supernatural forces; socially by articulating and reinforcing relationships among members of the society; and educationally by passing on cultural traditions, values, and beliefs from one generation to the next.

Dance and Other Aspects of a Culture

Lomax and his colleagues (1968) demonstrated quite graphically how dance is connected to other aspects of a culture. Specifically, their research shows how dance reflects and reinforces work patterns. By examining more than two hundred films, they were able to find a number of similarities between work styles and dance styles. The Netsilik Eskimos (Inuit) provide an interesting—and not atypical—example. For the Netsilik, dancing consists of solo performances that take place during the winter in a large communal igloo. Lomax describes the dance in considerable detail:

One after another, the greatest hunters stand up before the group, a large flat drum covered with sealskin in the left hand, a short, club-like drumstick in the other. Over to the side sit a cluster of women chanting away as the hunter drums, sings, and dances. The performer remains in place

FIGURE 15.8 Dancers from the world-renowned Cuban National Ballet rehearse at the Kennedy Center in Washington, DC. As an art form, ballet is taken much more seriously in Cuba than in the United States.

The Washington Post/Getty Images

holding the wide stance used by these Eskimos when they walk through ice and snow or stand in the icy waters fishing. Each stroke of the short drumstick goes diagonally down and across to hit the lower edge of the drum and turn the drumhead. On the backstroke it strikes the other edge, reversing the motion, which is then carried through by a twist of the left forearm. The power and solidity of the action is emphasized by the downward drive of the body into slightly bent knees on the downstroke and the force of [the] trunk rising as the knees straighten to give full support to the arm on the upstroke. The dance consists largely of these repeated swift and strong diagonal right arm movements down across the body. (1968: 226–27)

Many of the postures and motions in Netsilik dance are the ones that are necessary for successful seal hunting in an Arctic environment. The Netsilik seal hunter may wait patiently and silently for hours over a hole in the ice before a seal appears. When it does, the hunter's harpoon flies instantly and powerfully in a single stroke diagonally across the chest. Thus, the stylistic movements found in Netsilik dance are essentially identical to those used in their everyday hunting activities. The qualities of a good hunter—speed, strength, accuracy, and endurance—are portrayed and glorified in dance. In other words, as part of their leisure activity, hunters, through the medium of dance, redramatize the essentials of the everyday subsistence activities that are so crucial for their survival.

Another example of the merging of dance with other aspects of a culture is *capoeira*, a combination of dance, acrobatics, and martial arts that originated in the state of Bahia in Brazil (Figure 15.9). In the Brazilian city of Salvador, for example, capoeira is as popular a pastime among youngsters as basketball is for their inner-city counterparts in New York, Philadelphia, and Chicago. This high-energy activity, which for Bahians is as much a way of life as a recreational sport, has been described as "a fight like a dance [and] a dance like a fight" (Samuels 2001). Two capoeira "players" perform spectacular high kicks, spins, cartwheels, and back flips, coming within inches of each other's rapidly moving appendages and other body parts. Those players who fail to keep their heads up, their eyes open, and their concentration focused on what they are doing are likely to have their heads pounded by someone else's rapidly and powerfully moving foot or hand. This stunningly frenetic

movement is often accompanied by singing and chanting by capoeira group members, and by music from drums, tambourines, and a traditional stringed instrument called a *berimbau.*

It is generally believed that capoeira originated with the African slaves brought to Bahia by the Portuguese in the 1500s. Because these slaves were forbidden to fight or defend themselves, they developed capoeira as a surreptitious martial art disguised as a dance form (Figure 15.9). Always a group activity, capoeira is about dialogue, camaraderie, and bringing people together. And because it teaches discipline, self-esteem, and personal control, capoeira has been a source of self-confidence and inspiration for those descendants of slaves who continue to face poverty, violence, and discrimination in the twenty-first century.

Capoeira as an art form has received considerable attention in North America and indeed throughout the world. For example, the world-renowned group DanceBrazil, based in New York City and headed by choreographer Jelon Vieira, combines capoeira with

capoeira A combination of dance, martial arts, and acrobatics that originated among African slaves brought to Brazil in the sixteenth century.

FIGURE 15.9 Capoeira, a form of dance combined with acrobatics and martial arts, is a popular pastime in the Brazilian state of Bahia.

CROSS-CULTURAL MISCUE

❀ While participating in a junior-year-abroad program at a private college in Machida, Japan, Daniel French, who grew up in Toledo Ohio, was invited by a small group of his Japanese classmates for dinner. Midway through the dinner the conversation turned to the topic of grandparents and older people in general. Wanting to make an impression on his classmates (and demonstrate his fun-loving nature and knowledge of the art of joke-telling) Daniel decided to contribute a joke:

> There was an old man in my hometown of Toledo, Ohio who was approached by a very attractive 30 year old woman and asked "Hey, Mister, would you like some super sex?" The man thought about it for a moment and answered, "I think I'll take the soup."

Daniel was surprised and disappointed that—despite his delivery and excellent sense of comedic timing—none of his classmates laughed at the punch line. Was it because their English was not sufficiently proficient to distinguish between "super sex" and "soup or sex," or was there another explanation for Daniel's failure to communicate?

Although it is true that no known cultures lack a sense of humor, it is equally true that what is considered funny varies considerably from culture to culture. Humor tends to be so culture-specific that it serves as a window for understanding the culture of the joke teller. In other words it tells a good deal about what is valued, and what is not valued, in a particular culture. Daniel's joke reflected the generally negative stereotypes that most American have concerning the elderly. Coming from a culture that values youth over age and experience, Daniel, and many Americans assume that older people have no interest in sex, are hard of hearing, or are so mentally diminished that they do not know the difference between soup and sex. Even though Americans like to joke about getting old, people from Japan and many parts of Asia, Africa, and South America have the highest regard for the elderly. Thus, what Daniel failed to realize was that any attempt to be funny at the expense of old people would not only be not humorous, but also offensive.

So, here is yet one more reason you should stay awake in anthropology class. Knowing something about the *art of humor*, wherever it may be found, requires that you know as much as possible about the cultural values, beliefs, and assumptions of the people telling the joke. Knowledge of other cultures is absolutely essential if we are to understand (a) why people in other cultures are laughing, (b) what type of joke is appropriate in that culture, (c) what social situations are appropriate for a particular type of humor, and (d) when someone in another culture is laughing *with you* or *at you*.

---

modern dance and the samba (Kourlas 2010). It has played to appreciative audiences at Lincoln Center in New York and the Kennedy Center in Washington, D.C. And, capoeira is gaining fame in mainstream popular culture as well as other cultures worldwide. As Lauren Miller (2006: 28) reminds us, the dance form has appeared in films such as *Lethal Weapon* and *Cat Woman* and in commercials for Dockers and the Mazda Protégé.

Film: A Recent Art Form

When Americans think of film as an art form, instinctively they imagine US filmmaking legends such as Steven Spielberg, Robert Altman, and Francis Ford Coppola. However, many countries in all parts of the world have long and rich traditions of filmmaking as an art form. For example, Ingmar Bergman in Sweden, Sergei Eisenstein in Russia, and Akira Kurosawa in Japan all made world-class films during the twentieth century. The continent of Africa (from Cape Verde to Cape Horn) possesses a rich tradition of filmmaking; since 1981 it has supported its own annual international film festival in Mogadishu, Somalia, exclusively for African films. The latest territory to receive critical acclaim for filmmaking is Nunavut, the new homeland of the Inuit people carved out of the landmass of Canada in 1999 (see Chapter 7). Up until this century, the only connection between the Inuit people and filmmaking was Robert Flaherty's documentary *Nanook of the North*, a silent film about the Inuit, made in 1922. Eight decades later an Inuit filmmaker named Zacharias Kunuk, using all Inuit actors and crew, made a feature-length film in the native language of the Inuit (Inuktitut). The film, *Atanarjuat: The Fast Runner*, while providing ethnographic insights into traditional Inuit culture, is more than just another documentary about a vanishing way of life. Based on an ancient Inuit folk epic, *Atanarjuat* uses Inuit actors to tell a powerful and compelling story in the ancient words of their traditional language. Shot over a period of six months, the film portrays the movement of the seasons, which so thoroughly influence Inuit daily life. Capturing on camera a number of different hues of black and white, Kunuk manages to reveal complex psychological motives behind the actions of his mythical characters, whose story up until now had always been conveyed in oral tradition. *Atanarjuat* won the "best first feature film" award at the Cannes International Film Festival in 2001, just two years after the founding of the Inuit self-governing territory.

While Hollywood studios have been making big-budget films for decades, filmmakers in Mumbai, India (colloquially known as "Bollywood"), have made far more films than Hollywood over the decades and have won the hearts and minds of a much larger audience (Figure 15.10). Bollywood films are devoured not only by a potential audience of a billion people at home, but also by the millions of Indians living in the United States, the United Kingdom, Europe, the Middle East, and elsewhere. These films have been dubbed into other languages, including French, Russian, and Mandarin Chinese. They are watched by Iraqis and Iranians, Dominicans and Haitians, and even Pakistanis. In short, they provide the primary form of entertainment for probably half of the world's population.

The popularity of Bollywood films rests on their story lines, which have been called "pre-cynical" (Mehta 2004). Unlike their Hollywood counterparts, which tend to be edgy and ambiguous when dealing with such topics as love, family, and patriotism, Indian films are melodramatic and always celebrate true love, courage, devotion to country, and, above all, motherhood. Moreover every Bollywood film is a musical that lasts as long as three and a half hours, with as many as a dozen "big production" song-and-dance numbers. Even though many Americans have heard of these Indian-made films, few have actually seen one, unless they happen to be Indians living in the United States. For most Americans these films are too corny, illogical, and Pollyanna-like for the coffeehouse crowd and certainly too sedate for US men, who prefer to watch things being blown up. Even though Indian films are popular among the several million Indian Americans living in the United States, it remains to be seen whether Bollywood will make as much of an inroad into mainstream US cinema as Indian engineers and computer scientists have made into Western technology industries.

Art: Continuity and Change

Like all other aspects of culture, the various forms of expressive arts (graphic and plastic arts, music, dance, and film) are subject to both internal and external forces of change. Anyone who has ever taken a course on the history of twentieth-century US art, for example, knows that unique schools of painting (with their own distinctive styles, materials, and themes) emerge, become prominent, and eventually die out and become part of history. To illustrate, the Ashcan School (Edward Hopper and Arthur Davies) of 1908–1918 featured scenes of urban realism; the 1920s and 1930s witnessed the Art Deco style, characterized by straight lines and slender forms; abstract expressionists during the 1940s, such as Jackson Pollock and Willem de Kooning, emphasized spontaneous personal expression over more conventional artistic values; minimalism, popular in the 1950s, emphasized pure, simple, and reduced forms; and finally the pop art of Andy Warhol and Roy Lichtenstein used images from mass media, advertising, and popular culture in ironic ways. In the early centuries of US art, painting styles and approaches were relatively stable, often lasting a number of decades. In the absence of high-speed transportation and communication technology, different artistic traditions were not able to diffuse rapidly. The late twentieth century, however, witnessed many more changes than had occurred in the two preceding centuries.

Rapid and dramatic changes occurred in the art world even before the term *globalization* became fashionable. Nowhere is this truer than in the area of glass sculptural art during the last half-century. In the early 1960s advances in small-furnace technology—along with the pioneering efforts of Harvey Littleton in the United States and Erwin Eisch in Germany—brought the art of glassmaking out of the factory and into the artist's studio. In a little more than four decades, many new techniques of glass blowing, casting, constructing, and lamp-working diffused rapidly throughout the world. US artist Dale Chihuly traveled to Venice in 1969, Venetian master Lino Tagliapietra traveled to the Pilchuck Glass School in Seattle, and the influential Czech glass artists Stanislav Lebenski and Jaraslava Brychtova traveled all over the world. This frenzy of cross-fertilization since the 1960s has produced a worldwide art movement that now numbers more than five thousand studio glass artists.

FIGURE 15.10 Far more people see films made in Bollywood (india) than in Hollywood (California).

Dreampictures/Getty

APPLIED PERSPECTIVE

Anthropologist-Turned-Detective Finds Stolen African Statues

❋ In 1985 Monica Udvardy, a cultural anthropologist from the University of Kentucky, was conducting field research among the Mijikenda people on the Kenya coast. During the course of her research, Udvardy took a photograph of a local man standing in front of two traditional wooden statues (known as *vigango*) erected to appease the ancestor-spirits and to honor and protect his two deceased brothers. When Udvardy returned several months later to give the man a copy of the photo, he told her that the two statues in the photo had been stolen and asked for her help in trying to locate them. Before leaving Kenya, Udvardy searched curio shops in some of the tourist-oriented towns in hopes of finding the purloined statues, but she never did locate them.

Then, fourteen years later in 1999, while attending the African Studies Association meetings in Philadelphia, Udvardy was startled to see one of the missing statues in a slide presentation given by Linda Giles on some of the artifacts from the Museum at Illinois State University. Udvardy, with the collaboration of Giles, then began to research how the statue made its long journey from the coast of Kenya to the museum in Illinois. In the process of their sleuthing, the two scholars tracked down 294 other vigango in nineteen museums in the United States, among which was the second stolen statue from the 1985 photograph.

It was determined that most of these 294 vigango were brought into the United States by a single art dealer from Los Angeles, who claims to have purchased the statues legitimately from tourist shops in Mombasa, Kenya. He sold these statues to private collectors and to museums for as much as $5,000 each. The most generous interpretation of the art dealer's behavior is that he was unaware of the cultural and religious significance of these vigango, which, he claims, he bought and sold as nothing more than works of art. But no self-respecting Mijikenda adult would ever erect a statue to the spirits in honor of dead relatives and then sell it for money. This would be as absurd as a person in the United States ripping the headstone from the grave of her or his deceased mother and selling it to get a little extra cash. Anyone who understands the cultural significance of vigango in Mijikendo society would immediately realize that such a statue in a tourist shop in Mombasa would have had to be stolen.

In February 2006 the National Museums of Kenya requested that museum officials in Illinois return the vigango to the original family owners in eastern Kenya. Because the original photograph, coupled with Udvardy's investigations, provided solid evidence that the statue had been stolen, museum officials agreed to return the supernatural statue to its rightful owners. Hampton University Museum in Virginia, where the second stolen statue in the photograph resided, also agreed to return the stolen vigango.

In June 2007 a repatriation ceremony was held by the National Museums of Kenya at the ancestral home of the family that had lost the statues twenty-two years previously. This ceremony marked the first time in history that stolen artifacts were returned from the United States. The media attention surrounding this event raised global awareness of the theft of vigango and other cultural property from non-Western countries. The rest of the world is finally beginning to understand the devastating impact that global trafficking of African artifacts has on local communities. In fact, art dealers in the United States have voluntarily returned an additional nine vigango to Kenya. Here, then, is another example of how original anthropological fieldwork, along with years of sleuthing and investigating, led to the solution of a real-life societal problem—namely, the return of stolen sacred objects to their rightful owners (Lacey 2006; Udvardy and Giles 2008).

Questions for Further Thought

1. Is it rare for stolen artifacts to become part of a museum's permanent collection, or is it fairly common?

2. Should those museums that have *vigango* as part of their holdings return them to the Mijikenda people of East Africa?

3. Does the government of Kenya have a responsibility to prevent the sale and exportation of vigango and similar spiritual artifacts?

The growth of the glass art movement over the last four decades is noteworthy not only for its scale and global distribution, but also because of its prominence in the art world and in the marketplace. To illustrate, single pieces of glass art (which would fit on an ordinary end table in one's living room) by contemporary artists such as Lino Tagliapietra or William Morris sell for $60,000 and upward. Larger pieces by these same artists (such as Chihuly chandeliers or Morris's life-sized pieces from his "Man Adorned" series) retail for between $300,000 and $800,000 each.

The possibilities in the twenty-first century for quick and widespread cultural diffusion, and the accompanying cross-fertilization of artistic traditions, are increasing. Art exhibits today travel around the world rather than remaining in galleries or museums for centuries on end as they did in the past. Similarly, in the area of music, both rock stars and symphony orchestras go on world tours, performing in front of audiences all over the globe. It is not unusual today for Celine Dion to perform in South Africa, the Chicago Symphony to perform in Bangkok, or Lady Antebellum to perform in Copenhagen. And, it is not just Western music that is being exported and diffused to other parts of the world; there is considerable flow in the opposite direction. In recent decades we have seen recording artist Paul Simon collaborate with Ladysmith Black Mambazo, a singing group from South Africa, and Sting record fusion music with Cheb Mami from Algeria. Perhaps an even less likely collaboration is between Jaz Coleman, lead singer for the British rock group Killing Joke, and Maori singer and poet Hinewehi Mohi. According to anthropologist Renata Rosaldo, "Cultural artifacts flow between unlikely places, and nothing is sacred, permanent, or sealed off" (Jenkins 2001: 89).

Nowhere in the art world has this "flow between unlikely places" been more startling than in the recent merging of Muslim American culture in the United States with the genre of hip-hop music. One such rap band from Chicago, MPAC, uses typical rapper dress (baggy pants and oversized T-shirts), hip-hop beats and instrumentation, and even the assertively confident strutting around the stage so characteristic of contemporary hip-hoppers. But their lyrics are strictly religious, focusing on the forgiveness of sins, proclamations of faith, and "there is no god but God." Curse words (or any off-color language) are absent, female concert-goers almost all wear head scarves, and soft drinks are sold, not alcohol. Thus, Muslim Americans, through the medium of music, are developing creative ways of adapting to life in the United States, fusing with other cultures and traditions, and showing potential converts that Islam can be both empowering and cool (Abdo 2004).

Also, we are beginning to see how a particular society adopts new art forms from other parts of the world and infuses them with its own traditional cultural content. *Indian Idol*, like its US counterpart, involves a talent competition between unknown Indian singers of Western pop music. A new and popular TV show produced in Abu Dhabi, United Arab Emirates (UAE), uses the same glamorous sets and big-budget productions, but rather than scantily clad singers competing with Western love ballads, the contestants compete in an elaborate style of Bedouin poetry popular among the Gulf States but virtually unknown in the rest of the Arab world (Fattah 2007). Not only has the success of the show (titled *Poets of Millions*) spawned similar shows in other Islamic countries such as Egypt and Lebanon, but it is catapulting the UAE to cultural leadership in the Arab world. No longer is the UAE considered to be an ultraconservative, oil-wealthy country with no popular culture of its own. In the twenty-first century the UAE is transforming its traditional art forms and dialects into forms that can be understood and appreciated in other parts of the Arab world and beyond. And interestingly, this repackaging of traditional art from the UAE for both internal and external consumption is occurring in a country that is planning to spend $10 billion to build and operate branches of the Guggenheim and the Louvre museums.

Not only are artists from around the world collaborating with one another as well as borrowing and blending their artistic traditions, but art is also even finding its way into diplomatic relations between twenty-first-century nation-states. Madeleine Albright, the first female US Secretary of State, serving from 1997 to 2001 in the Bill Clinton administration, was well known for her jewelry collection of broaches and pins, which clearly had communicative value and were judiciously used as implements of foreign policy (Figure 15.11). In 2009 a show of several hundred pieces of her jewelry opened at the Museum of Arts and Design in New York City. The title of the show, "Read My Pins," is a clever paraphrasing of the statement "Read my lips," made famous by former President George H. W. Bush.

The book published for the Albright show is filled with compelling (and often humorous) stories about the role her broaches played in global politics. Although fully aware that jewelry is hardly the most powerful tool at the disposal of a secretary of state, Albright believed that jewelry, like any work of art, is symbolic, and thus, "the right symbol at the correct time can add warmth or needed edge to a relationship" (Albright 2009: 20).

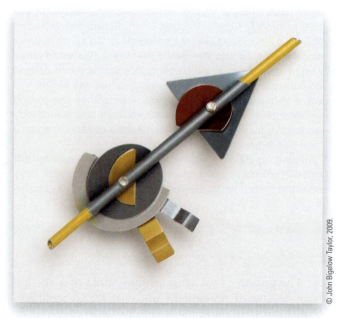

FIGURE 15.11 Former Secretary of State Madeleine Albright wore this "interceptor missile pin when she met with Russian Foreign Minister Igor Ivanov to renegotiate the antiballistic missile treat between Russia and the United States.

The relationship between the United States and Russia during the 1990s provides the backdrop for a dramatic case in point. On one of her trips to Russia, Albright met with President Vladimir Putin wearing her three-monkey broach representing "Hear no evil, speak no evil, see no evil." This was her not-so-subtle way of communicating to Putin that he "saw no evil" in the way that Russian troops were brutally putting down the rebellion in Chechnya. Another contentious issue was the renegotiation of the antiballistic missile treaty. The United States and Russia were miles apart on any agreement. When Albright met her Russian counterpart, Foreign Minister Igor Ivanov, she wore a pin in the shape of an interceptor missile. The foreign minister asked whether it was a U.S. interceptor missile. "Yes," she responded, "and as you can see, we know how to make them very small. So you better be ready to negotiate" (Albright 2009: 110).

Summary

1. Although there is no universal definition of *art*, for purposes of this chapter we define *art* as the process and products of applying certain skills to any activity that transforms matter, sound, or motion into a form that is deemed aesthetically meaningful to people in a society. The creative process of making art should be enjoyable, produce an emotional response, be transformational, convey a message, and involve a certain level of skill on the part of the artist.

2. The forms of artistic expression discussed in this chapter are the graphic and plastic arts (such as painting, sculpting, and weaving), music, dance, and film.

3. Rather than using the term *primitive* to refer to certain types of art, we use *small-scale*, which refers to essentially egalitarian societies that have small populations, simple technology, no written language, and little labor specialization. In contrast to the art found in small-scale societies, the art of more complex societies is more permanent, has more elaborate and explicit standards of evaluation, and is associated with the elite.

4. Art contributes to the well-being of both the individual and the society. For the individual, art provides emotional gratification to both the artist and the beholder. From a social perspective, various forms of art strengthen and reinforce both social bonds and cultural themes, promote social control, and serve as a symbol of high status, particularly in complex societies.

5. Ethnomusicologist Alan Lomax suggests that the music traditions found in small-scale societies differ from those of more complex societies in that the former are characterized by more repetitive texts, slurred articulation, little solo singing, nonembellished songs, few instruments, and singing in unison.

6. Like other forms of art, dance has many different forms and functions. Moreover dance is intimately connected to other aspects of culture, as illustrated by Brazilian capoeira, a dance form with ties to religion, martial arts, and social commentary.

7. Like all other aspects of culture, forms and styles of art change over time. Despite the Internet and the information technology revolution (which has accelerated the sharing of art across cultures), cultures do not appear to be surrendering their unique forms of artistic expression.

Key Terms

capoeira	ethnomusicology	liberation theater	transformational
dance	graphic arts	plastic arts	

Critical thinking Questions

1. The Contemporary Issues box in this chapter involved the Maori of New Zealand seeking the repatriation of a tattooed head belonging to one of their ancestors from a museum in Rouen, France. There have been, and continue to be, thousands of works of art (not necessarily body parts) belonging to various cultural groups throughout the world that were taken over the course of the last several centuries and remain the property of most Western museums. Because these pieces of art belong to the cultural heritage of the peoples who made them, these Western museums are constantly being petitioned (or sued) to return these art objects to their original owners. Do you think these works of traditional art should be returned or should they remain in the Western museums? Support your answer.

2. The second Cross-Cultural Miscue box in the chapter demonstrated how humor does not translate well from one culture to another. Can you give any (other) specific examples of how and why a joke you might tell to a member of another culture might really "bomb" badly? Be specific about the joke and which culture was involved. Be sure to explain *why* the joke bombed.

3. Take several minutes to experience (via YouTube) a "random act of culture" that took place at the Reading Terminal Market in Philadelphia on January 8, 2011.

[(http://search.yahoo.com/search;_ylt=AgGnqqnvpgLd7X1nq.bfHxebvZx4?p=Toreador+song+AND+Reading+Terminal+Market&toggle=1&cop=mss&ei=UTF-8&fr=yfp-t-900-77)]

What feelings did you have when watching this video? Why do you think the Philadelphia Opera Company staged this impromptu opera? What does this random act of culture have to do with social integration?

Online Study Resources

CourseMate

Access chapter-specific learning tools including learning objectives, practice quizzes, videos, flash cards, glossaries, web links, and more in your Cultural Anthropology CourseMate. Login to www.cengagebrain.com to access the resources your instructor has assigned and to purchase materials.

Women in Tamil Nadu, India are making bricks the traditional way in front of wind turbines used for generating electricity.

Global Challenges and the Role of Applied Anthropology

A CLOSING LETTER TO STUDENTS

Congratulations on working your way through this textbook! We opened Chapter 1 with a letter to you explaining the nature of the book's "Applied Perspective" and what you might hope to gain from it. We said that this not only is a comprehensive textbook introducing you to the field of cultural anthropology, but it is also designed to show you how the research findings, theories, methods, and insights of cultural anthropology can be useful in your everyday personal and professional lives. The real-life relevance of cultural anthropology has been highlighted in three special features (identified by the SWAP logo) found throughout the text: (a) real (not hypothetical) chapter-opening scenarios, (b) boxed "Applied Perspective" case studies, and (c) boxed "Cross-Cultural Miscue," or negative, case studies.

Now that you have had nearly a semester to familiarize yourself with both the comprehensiveness and relevance of cultural anthropology, we want to conclude the book with this capstone chapter. This final chapter will focus on three major concerns. First, we will examine the present-day world order and how it has emerged over the course of the past 500 years. Second, we will identify some of the major global challenges of the twenty-first century for all peoples of the world, including (but not limited to) climate change; overurbanization in Africa, Asia, and Latin America; environmental degradation; the spread of world health pandemics; the rise of militant religious fundamentalism; and the widening gap between the rich and the poor. And finally we will explore how cultural anthropologists are contributing to the resolution of many of these global challenges.

As we have seen, anthropological insights can be helpful (and in many cases essential) in solving social problems. Basic cultural information certainly is useful to help us avoid breakdowns in communication when interacting with people from different cultural or subcultural backgrounds, both at home and abroad. In addition, cross-cultural competency can be valuable in meeting your professional objectives, whether you choose a career in medicine, business, education, law,

© Joerg Boething/Peter Arnold, Inc.

WHAT WE WILL LEARN

- What roles did the periods of colonization and post-colonization play in shaping the world order of the twenty-first century?

- Has the period of colonization really ended?

- What is meant by the term *globalization*?

- What are some of the major post–World War II trends that anthropologists study?

- What contributions have anthropologists made to the solution of such global challenges as income inequity, human justice violations, and climate change?

- Have economic development programs always helped the people they are intended to benefit?

- What is multiculturalism, and why is it the world's best hope for the future?

architecture, counseling, public administration, criminal justice, marketing, or just about any other area we could imagine. And as we shall see in this chapter, anthropologists are helping to solve many of the global challenges of the twenty-first century. Anthropologists are making a difference by drawing on the same data, insights, methods, and theories that you have been studying this semester!

The purpose of this letter is to make sure that you have fully understood how important cultural anthropology can be to the future of your personal lives, your neighborhoods, your towns, your states, your nation, and the planet itself. Not only is it important for you to appreciate the importance of cultural anthropology, but you should also know it well enough to be able to communicate it to your parents and friends (who still may be wondering why you are not taking only courses in business management and finance) and also to your future employers, no matter what field you actually enter. ■

The Growth of the Modern World Order: Colonialism and Globalization

As we have seen throughout this book, culture is an ever-changing, dynamic phenomenon. This holds true both for the general outlines of world cultures over time and for the thousands of distinct cultures that exist throughout the world today. Cultures change internally by means of inventions and innovations, and they change from outside forces through the process of cultural diffusion. Cultures change in response to changing technologies, economies, demographics, natural environments, values, and ideologies. Although it is true that no cultures stay frozen in time for long periods, the *pace* of change varies from one society to another and from one historical period to another.

Colonialism

Since the rise of state systems of government (approximately 5,000 years ago), state societies in China, Peru, Mexico, North Africa, and the Middle East have solidified their power by conquering neighboring peoples and incorporating them into their expanding societies. Within the last five centuries, European societies have expanded their territories and influence throughout the world even more thoroughly than previous state governments. European countries created global empires by not only expanding their own territorial borders but also increasing their control over societies in distant lands and continents.

---

colonialism The political, economic, and sociocultural domination of a territory and its people by a foreign nation.

European *colonialism* over the past 500 years was really the beginning of our globalized world—that is, the creation of a worldwide system of interconnected nation-states and commercial enterprises. Prior to 1500 C.E. the world was composed of relatively insulated and isolated nation-states. But with the age of exploration came opportunities for Europeans to expand their economic and cultural influence to all corners of the earth. Technological advances in navigation, ship building, cartography, and warfare enabled European explorers, merchants, missionaries, and armed forces to venture all over the globe. A number of motives have been suggested for European expansion throughout the world. Some explorers were motivated by the desire for adventure and the discovery of water routes to the exotic lands of China and the Far East. Others, no doubt, were motivated by a sincere desire to spread Christianity to other parts of the world. But the major motivation for European expansion was the desire to obtain wealth and a more comfortable and secure way of life, which wealth was thought to ensure.

European powers, especially Britain, France, Portugal, Spain, Belgium, and Holland, solidified their influence worldwide through the process of colonization. To one degree or another, colonization by European countries was imperialistic—that is, involved empire-building through state expansion of both territories and commerce. European colonies were of three types depending on their basic purpose. In the first type, some European countries acquired colonies primarily for the sake of exploiting their local economic resources (such as copper and diamonds) needed to drive the industrial revolution and gaining cheap labor and markets for their finished products. To one degree or another, all European colonies were created and maintained for economic reasons. A second type of European colony was acquired to gain maritime areas and thereby control trade. For example, the Dutch settled Cape Town, South Africa, in the nineteenth century as a restocking area and safe haven for the long trade voyages between Holland and the Far East. And third, some Europeans established settlement colonies where groups of Europeans permanently resided; built comfortable farms, (cash crop) plantations, and other businesses on appropriated land; and used local people as inexpensive labor. In all three types of colonies, European powers exercised total, or near total, control over the political, commercial, and social systems of the colonial territories. The extent to which these state societies coerced the conquered peoples to give up their indigenous cultures varied from culture to culture and through time.

European colonization during the nineteenth century involved the actual possession and administration of foreign territories by European governments. This period had perhaps the most influence on our present world order. Many of the European colonial powers (Britain, France, Spain, Portugal, Belgium, and the Netherlands) amassed great wealth and political power as a direct result of obtaining, controlling, and exploiting their colonial territories. In fact, these acquisitions of wealth and influence during the nineteenth century created the world economic order of the twentieth century. And most of these former European colonial powers—even though they granted independence to most of their colonies decades ago—have retained their economic and political influence into the twenty-first century (Figure 16.1).

Although colonization proved exceedingly beneficial for the economic and political ascension of the European colonial powers, the indigenous populations paid a high price.

- Many colonies were conquered by military force, including violence and slaughter if people resisted colonial rule.

- During the earlier stages of colonization (the seventeenth and eighteenth centuries), native African people were sold like chattel in the trans-Atlantic slave trade.

- Natural resources, which belonged to indigenous peoples, were simply taken from the colonies for the benefit of European industrialization.

- The best land was often appropriated for European settlers, and many indigenous peoples were thrown off their ancestral (and often sacred) lands.

- Landless people, who could no longer support themselves by farming or keeping livestock, were hired for meager wages to work on plantations or in factories. In some colonies unpaid work (*corvee labor*) was demanded of native populations for months or even years at a time to build roads, bridges, and other public works projects.

FIGURE 16.1 Until the 1960s the British ruled a number of colonies in sub-Saharan Africa, including Kenya. Here the Governor of Kenya (in white) speaks with British appointed chiefs in 1952.

© Time & Life Pictures/Getty Images

- Many indigenous peoples were stripped of their traditional livelihoods, forced to work for low wages to produce commodities desired by European colonialists, and then taxed to help pay for the colonial system that was exploiting them.

- This exploitation of natural and human resources led to a permanently stratified social structure, with European settlers and colonial administrators at the top and indigenous peoples at the bottom.

When many colonies won their political independence in the aftermath of World War II (1939–1945), the local populations were severely undereducated and undercapitalized. At the time the former colonies were euphemistically referred to as "newly independent but underdeveloped nation-states." In the years from 1960

corvee labor A system of required labor practiced during the colonial period.

onward, these nation-states have remained among the poorest nations in the world, while the economic gap between the former colonies and the former colonizers has become increasingly wide. To illustrate, based on calculations from the International Monetary Fund (IMF), the World Bank, and the *CIA World Factbook*, of the forty poorest countries in the world in 2010, 84 percent were former African colonies of Britain, Belgium, France, Portugal, and Italy. The other 16 percent of the world's poorest countries, although not in sub-Saharan Africa, had, in one way or another, a colonial experience in their histories. The relative wealth of one of the first colonial powers (Belgium) and its largest colony (The Democratic Republic of the Congo, originally known as the Belgium Congo) makes an equally dramatic statement about the general gap in wealth and power between the *colonizers* and the *colonized*. In 2013, the country of Belgium had a per capita gross national income (GNI) of $45,420 whereas The Democratic Republic of the Congo has a per capita GNI of $310, and (ironically) the former colony is seventy-seven times larger in square miles than its former colonizer! Moreover, the end of colonial rule brought a host of other serious problems, including severe poverty, high rates of unemployment, substance abuse, political corruption, rapid population growth, underfunded educational systems, human rights abuses, environmental degradation, rapid urbanization, violent civil wars, inadequate housing, exploitation by multinational corporations, staggering medical pandemics, and foreign assistance programs that resulted in little economic development while ensuring that the former colonies became permanent debtor nations. Although colonial rule is now a thing of the past, many nation-states of the twenty-first century remain seriously scarred by their colonial histories.

Neocolonialism (Multinational Corporations)

Although the period of colonialism had all but ended by the turn of the millennium, turning over the reins of government to the local people has not necessarily resulted in complete autonomy for the

less-developed countries (LDCs). Through the process known as *neocolonialism*, the wealthy (former colonial) nations continue to exercise considerable political, economic, financial, and military power over the LDCs. By virtue of their economic dominance, the industrialized nations control the international markets of the commodities they buy from LDCs, such as Ghanaian cocoa, Bolivian tin, and Kenyan coffee. The wealthier nations also lend capital to the LDCs, which has the effect of turning them into perpetual debtors. Debt can be a major form of control, with the creditors calling the shots. Moreover, with the debtor nations obliged to make large interest payments, they never have enough surplus capital to invest in building their own economic infrastructure.

The wide gap between rich and poor nations is also maintained by the increasing power and influence in recent years of *multinational corporations*. In some cases multinational corporations directly exploit LDCs, as with the Firestone Rubber Company in Liberia or the United Fruit Company in Central America. More often, however, multinational corporations tend to exploit LDCs simply by doing business as usual. These multinational corporations have assets and power that far exceed those of most governments of the developing world. To illustrate, the hundred largest multinational corporations control approximately one-third of the world's assets. Specifically, the revenue generated by Walmart (United States) is roughly equivalent to the gross national product (GNP) of Belgium; British Petroleum's (United Kingdom) revenues are the size of Denmark's GNP; and Mitsubishi (Japan) generates revenues roughly the size of Israel's GNP. No matter how they make their profits, though, one thing is certain: Most of the corporate profits go back to the home country rather than staying in the developing nation. This perpetuates the nineteenth- and twentieth-century conditions of economic dependence and exploitation of colonies by wealthy nations (Figure 16.2).

When a multinational corporation decides to open a plant in another country, you can be certain that it will exert considerable influence over the government of that country. For example, during the summer of 2002, India and Pakistan, both having nuclear capabilities, were on the brink of war over the issue of Kashmir. The two countries threatened to attack each other as the leaders of the United States and western Europe tried to bring them back from the brink. In the end, the hostilities between India and Pakistan cooled because of pressure exerted by the information technology (IT) industry—not the US government (which has more military firepower than the next fifteen most powerful nations combined). The global revolution in IT (satellites, the Internet, and so on) since the early 1990s has had an enormous effect on the Indian economy, whose IT industry now brings in $60 billion per year. Taking advantage of the large tech-savvy

---

less-developed countries (LDCs) Countries that have a relatively low gross national product and low annual family income.

neocolonialism The process of developed nations continuing to exert economic, political, and military influence over less-developed countries, even though the official period of colonization ended in the 1960s.

multinational corporations Large corporations that have economic operations in a number of different countries throughout the world; their resources may be greater than the gross national product of independent nations.

FIGURE 16.2 These Vietnamese Buddhist monks walk past a huge inflatable Pepsi can in Ho Chi Minh City. Many multinational corporations, such as Pepsico, have more assets than the countries in which they operate, which gives them enormous control over those governments and their economies.

CROSS-CULTURAL MISCUE

❋ Randy Lombardi from Pittsburgh, recently appointed to manage his firm's office in Singapore, was anxious to do well in his first overseas assignment. Shortly after his arrival, he called his first staff meeting to outline the objectives for the coming fiscal year. He had already met with his senior staff members individually and was feeling quite confident about the prospects for having a good first year. Toward the end of the staff meeting, Randy, in his characteristic upbeat fashion, told his employees that he looked forward to working with them and that he anticipated that this would be their best year ever. To emphasize his optimism for the coming year, Randy punctuated his verbal remarks by slapping his fist against his palm. The reaction was instantaneous: Most people laughed, giggled, or looked embarrassed. He felt that the point of his dramatic climax was lost amid the laughter.

Here is another example of how certain nonverbal actions—in this case, the pounding of a fist into one's palm—have different meanings in a foreign country than in the United States. In Singapore, as well as in several other Southeast Asian countries, such a gesture is a sexual insult, comparable in the United States to extending the middle finger. This is just another example of the importance of understanding cultural differences (in this instance, the meaning of nonverbal gestures) when living and working in another cultural during this "age of globalization."

Indian population, many of the world's largest companies (including American Express, Sony, Reebok, and General Electric) have located their back rooms and research facilities in India. If you lose your luggage anywhere in the world, it will likely be tracked down by an Indian techie in Bangalore (India's Silicon Valley). Accounting, inventory control, payroll, billing, and credit card approval (among other functions) for many of the world's largest corporations are electronically managed by highly skilled Indian engineers, computer scientists, and information technicians. With India so intimately involved in the IT lifeblood of so many global corporations, the possibility of India going to war threatened to seriously disrupt the world's economy. In the final analysis, it was powerful international corporations that convinced the Indian government to disengage with the Pakistanis under the threat of taking their IT business elsewhere.

The Recent Intensification of Globalization

By far the most significant recent worldwide trend is the rapid cross-national integration known as *globalization*, a term that has become one of the most overused and poorly understood words in the English language. For centuries interconnections among countries and cultures have had far-reaching implications for cultural change through diffusion. But when the Berlin Wall came down in 1989, the world began to change in dramatic ways (Figure 16.3). Economic forces, such as deregulation, privatization, and the lowering of tariffs, were unleashed that have had profound effects on all cultures of the world. It is now generally assumed that the well-being of *all* peoples of the world will be maximized if economic systems concentrate on four basic concerns: (1) continual economic growth (as

globalization The worldwide process, dating back to the 1989 fall of the Berlin Wall, that includes a revolution in information technology, a dramatic opening of markets, and the privatization of government services.

Regis Bossu/Corbis

FIGURE 16.3 The fall of the Berlin Wall in 1989 marks the symbolic beginning of our present period of globalization characterized by a radical expansion of free market economies, privatization, and information technology.

measured by gross national product), (2) the continued lowering of trade barriers between nations, (3) the reduction of government control of free markets, and (4) privatization (that is, shifting governmental functions and resources to the private sector).

These worldwide economic trends have been greatly facilitated by the simultaneous revolution in information technology (that is, fiber-optics, satellite communication, and the Internet). People are now able to communicate with one another instantaneously. To illustrate how dramatic the IT revolution has been, during the mid-1980s, grandparents in Pennsylvania had to wait several weeks to see a photograph of their new grandchild born in Istanbul. Today a photo of the new baby can be taken on one's cell phone in Istanbul and sent via e-mail or text message to the grandparents on the other side of the globe in seconds. In short, these revolutionary developments in IT greatly facilitate the exchange of ideas across national and cultural boundaries.

Previous chapters pointed out examples of the recent acceleration of globalization. Anyone who is even vaguely aware of current events knows about the outsourcing of not only manufacturing jobs but also more highly skilled jobs in accounting, software development,

and even human organ replacement. In Chapter 14, we described how even religious rituals are being outsourced from Catholic parishes in the United States to Catholic priests in India. There is certainly no shortage of examples of this growing global interconnectedness:

- Coca-Cola sells more of its product in Japan than it sells in the United States, even though Japan has only half the population of the United States.
- Foreign-owned firms operating in the United States employ more than 5 million workers, approximately one in ten manufacturing jobs.
- Internet users worldwide increased approximately 545 percent between 2000 and 2010.
- Direct foreign investments in the United States have increased from $66 billion in 1990 to $328 billion in 2008, an increase of nearly 500 percent. And, in the opposite direction, US direct investment abroad has grown from $430 billion in 1990 to $2.3 trillion in 2006, an increase of 540 percent.
- Major league baseball and football teams in the US schedule some of their preseason games in Europe and Japan.
- Many high-skilled jobs, formerly performed in the United States, are now being performed abroad, such as a CPA in Bangalore, India filling out state and federal income tax forms for someone in San Francisco; a mathematician in Mumbai, India, tutoring a high school student in Cleveland via e-mail; or a Western-trained Thai surgeon in Bangkok performing a heart valve operation on a New Yorker.
- More than half of US franchise operators (for example, Dunkin' Donuts or Kentucky Fried Chicken) are in markets outside the United States.
- The environmental organization Greenpeace, founded in Vancouver in the early 1970s, now has offices in more than thirty countries.

These and other facts and figures suggest the dimensions of this movement toward greater global integration, but we often do not fully comprehend how intimately we ourselves are connected to the rest of the world. Barbara Garson (2001) gives us a glimpse into the international money marketplace by tracing a small sum of money she personally invested in Chase Manhattan Bank as it travels around the globe. Along the way she interviews people whose lives are affected by this initial bank deposit. She learned that Chase loaned some of her money to Caltex, a US petrochemical company, to build an oil refinery in Thailand. The Thai government's initial opposition to the oil refinery was overcome when Caltex spent some of Garson's money for campaign contributions to US politicians who lobbied the Thai government to relent on its opposition. Another part of Carson's deposit was used to bribe a Thai government official. Once the opposition was eliminated, still more of Garson's money was used to build the refinery, which, in fact, as government officials had originally argued, damaged the environment and displaced both local fishermen and farmers. Eventually, because of an economic downturn, the refinery was shut down, thereby putting a number of Thai oil workers out of work. By tracing both the flow of money and its impact on the lives of real people around the world, Garson demonstrates how her own small investment in a US bank account had enormous and immediate implications for people on the other side of the world.

The globalization phenomenon itself is a dynamic process because markets for both labor and products do not stay the same for long periods of time. To illustrate, during the 1980s and part of the 1990s, large numbers of highly trained engineers and technicians from India took jobs in the United States, particularly in the high-tech center of Silicon Valley. During this time Indian engineers had a comfortable living in California suburbs and began the process of Americanization. During the mid- to late-1990s, however, with India developing high-tech industries of its own, many of the Indians living in the United States returned to India, took even higher-paying jobs with Indian high-tech firms, and reestablished their California-style neighborhoods in cities such as Bangalore. Moreover an increasing number of US graduates from US universities are now choosing to take their first job in India's software, IT, and business-process outsourcing industries, rather than stay in their own country. Thus, the so-called "brain drain," which saw vast numbers of highly trained Indians emigrating to the United States in the 1980s, has been reversed a mere two decades later.

The long-term effects of globalization on the cultures of the world have yet to be fully realized. Some early scholars (Jameson 1990; Robertson 1992) suggested that globalization will eventually lead to the formation of a single global culture. They argue that the rapid flow of money, commodities, and information to every corner of the world, if allowed to continue unchecked, will tend to eradicate cultural differences. In recent years, however, an alternative view has emerged to suggest that globalization, rather than totally changing cultures, can stimulate local cultures to redefine themselves in the face of these external forces. In other words, local cultures, though eventually changing some features, will reaffirm much of their uniqueness while entering into a dialogue with global forces (Figure 16.4).

It is certainly true that some languages and cultures are becoming virtually extinct, but at the same time other cultures and ethnic groups are

CROSS-CULTURAL MISCUE

Kevin Higgins had served as the manager of a large US timber company located in a rather remote rain forest in a South American country. Since it began its logging operations in the 1950s, a major problem facing the company has been the recruitment of labor. The only nearby source of labor was the sparsely populated local Indian groups. Kevin's company has been in direct competition for laborers with a German company operating in the same region. In an attempt to attract the required number of laborers, Kevin's company has invested heavily in new housing and offered considerably higher wages than the German company, as well as a guaranteed forty-hour workweek. Yet the majority of the available workers continued to work for the German company, despite its substandard housing and a minimum hourly wage.

Kevin finally brought in several US anthropologists who had worked among the local Indians. As it turned out, the answer to Kevin's labor recruitment problem was quite simple, but it required looking at the values of the Indian labor force rather than simply building facilities that would appeal to the typical US laborer. The anthropologists told Kevin that, for the local Indian labor pool, flexibility of time was of greater significance than housing or high wages. Under the German system, which paid an hourly wage rather than a forty-hour-per-week salary (as with Kevin's company), local laborers could take time off for their festivals and ceremonies without fear of losing their jobs. The solution to Kevin's labor recruitment problem required the relatively simple task of changing to a more flexible hourly wage system rather than a weekly salary system.

© Richard Allerby-Pratt/Arabian Eye/Redux

FIGURE 16.4 Young men in baseball caps gathering at a Starbucks in Dubai, United Arab Emirates, illustrate the concepts of both globalization and cultural diffusion.

experiencing a resurgence. It is important to recognize that states, formed by merging a number of ethnic entities together, also have the tendency to eventually come apart. The best contemporary example of this is the Soviet Union, established in 1945 from fifteen constituent republics (Armenian, Azerbaijan, Belarusian, Estonian, Georgian, Kazakhstan, Kyrgyzstan, Latvian, Lithuanian, Moldovan, Russian, Tajikistan, Turkmenistan, Ukrainian, and Uzbekistan). When this strongly centralized federal union collapsed in 1991, all fifteen republics, with their own distinctive languages and cultures, became independent nations. Also during the 1990s, Czechoslovakia split into the Czech and Slovak Republics, and the francophone province of Quebec came close to declaring its independence from the rest of Canada. Today this tendency for pluralistic societies to fragment can be seen among the Kurds in Turkey and Iraq, the Basques in Spain, the Tibetans in China, and, according to statements made in 2009 by Texas Governor Rick Perry, Texans in the United States.

Thus, it seems unreasonable to expect that the world, through the process of globalization, is moving relentlessly toward a single, benevolent, culturally homogeneous nation-state. News media every day report cultural differences throughout the world, with each group operating from its own unique cultural heritage and narrowly shared values and interests. The overwhelming power of any single nation-state—whether we are talking about the United States, China, India, or the European Union—is insufficient to change the rest of the world into its own likeness. At the turn of the millennium, the United States was unquestionably the most influential power (politically, economically, militarily, and culturally) on earth, and yet its attempt to spread its influence to the rest of the world in recent decades has not been particularly successful. Its attempts to open trade relations with other nations, to spread democracy throughout the world, and to diffuse its popular culture into every corner of the earth have met with considerable resistance. For example, even though some Austrians may appreciate the convenience of being able to drink a tall latte at a Starbucks in Vienna, they have no interest in becoming culturally indistinguishable from the residents of Seattle.

Global Challenges and the Role of Applied Cultural Anthropology

As we have tried to show throughout this text, the discipline of anthropology looks at humans, wherever they may be found, from earliest prehistory up to the present. Because of the enormous time frame it has

carved out for itself, anthropology is able to observe both long-term and short-term sociocultural trends. To illustrate, because archaeologists have looked at cultural development over the last several million years, they have been able to identify some major cultural trends or transformations, such as the Neolithic Revolution, the rise of urban societies, and the industrial revolution. Cultural anthropologists, who focus on contemporary cultures and societies of the world, are constantly looking at more recent and, by definition, more short-term sociocultural trends and developments. These include post–World War II trends such as world immigration patterns; the rise of religious fundamentalism; rapid urbanization in Africa, Asia, and Latin America; the spread of world health pandemics such as AIDS; environmental degradation; and the widening gap between the rich and the poor throughout the world.

Because anthropologists have identified these recent trends, they are often asked to predict where these trends will lead humankind in the future and what effects they will have on the human condition. Anthropologists, like the members of any other profession, have no special powers of prediction. They cannot tell us, with any degree of certainty, what the global cultural mosaic will look like at the end of the twenty-first century. What anthropologists *are* able to do, however, is document the recent trends and changes, and then predict how things might be in the future, *provided these changes continue on their present course.* How the world actually looks ninety years from now will depend on natural phenomena, such as earthquakes, over which humans have little control, as well as on purposeful actions taken by people and their governments. In any event, it is impossible to predict how either will affect current sociocultural trends. The best anthropologists can do is to describe the recent trends so as to enable reasonable people in the future to reinforce the beneficial trends and take action to slow down or reverse the more deleterious trends.

The former colonies are not alone in facing the many daunting challenges mentioned previously. To one degree or another, these are *global problems* for all nations, rich and poor alike. We are not suggesting that people from affluent nations are suffering the consequences of these global problems as much as people from poor nations do, but wealthy nations have a real stake in helping to ameliorate these pressing issues. Unless some of the more egregious inequities and injustices between rich and poor nations are addressed, the affluent nations will continue to grapple with political instability, global pandemics, and military interventions. The problems that face former colonies and other poor nations are global issues that cannot be ignored by any nation because they affect the sustainability of humankind.

The world of the new millennium poses a number of major challenges. These include, but are not limited to, global health problems, the widening gap between poor and wealthy nations (and between poor and wealthy people *within* these nations), demographic shifts both between and within nation-states, environmental destruction, the depletion of the world's natural resources, the need for cleaner and more sustainable sources of energy, children's need for quality education and health care, and the injustices inflicted on the world's indigenous peoples and other vulnerable populations. In one way or another all of these global issues are both interrelated and have their origins in nineteenth- and twentieth-century industrialization and colonialism. For the remainder of this final chapter, we want to look at three of these major global challenges in some detail: (1) sustainable economic development in the developing world, (2) the cultural survival of indigenous populations, and (3) global environmental challenges. We will describe each of these global problem areas in its contemporary context and then discuss how anthropologists have addressed (and are addressing) these challenges in their research and policy recommendations.

In keeping with the theme of this textbook, we want to reiterate that cultural anthropologists bring a good deal to the table in addressing today's global challenges. First, because cultural anthropologists rely so heavily on direct research (participant-observation) at the grassroots level, they are in the best position to observe the impact of global changes on people's lives. In other words, unlike economists, anthropologists are studying the real consequences of colonialism, industrialization, and rapid globalization on real people rather than focusing on such impersonal "leading indicators" as GNP and demographic shifts. Second, because anthropologists take a holistic approach, they tend to look for those interconnections between the parts of local societies that other specialists (such as agronomists, development planners, and other social scientists) might miss. Third, because anthropologists work from a comparative and cross-cultural perspective, it is likely that they will be aware of how similar peoples in different parts of the world are dealing with these global challenges. And finally, *applied* cultural anthropologists in particular, owing to their collaborative orientation, make excellent members of interdisciplinary development teams.

Sustainable Economic Development for Marginalized Peoples

Today's countries can be roughly divided into two broad categories: the haves and the have-nots. This dichotomy is sometimes characterized as the industrialized versus the nonindustrialized worlds, or the developed versus the developing worlds. There is considerable disagreement about the reasons for these differences, but no one can deny the vast differences in material wealth between the richest nations (such as Norway, Switzerland, the United States, and Sweden) and the poorest nations (such as Liberia, Burundi, Niger, and the Democratic Republic of the Congo). As pointed out in Chapter 12, the income of the average American is 152 times greater than the income of the average person in the Democratic Republic of the Congo. Enormous disparities can also be seen in noneconomic measures. To illustrate, the life expectancy is seventy-seven years in Norway but only forty-seven years in Burkina Faso. The infant mortality rate in Mali is 168 per one thousand live births, whereas in Finland it is only 6 (Figure 16.5).

How did the contemporary world become so uneven in terms of economic development? Social scientists have offered differing interpretations, but they usually boil down to one of two competing theories. One broad theory explains these vast differences in economic development in terms of the inherent

FIGURE 16.5 Whereas **168** of every thousand children in Mali die in infancy, only **6** of every thousand infants die in Finland and **12** of every thousand die in the United States.

Xavier Rossi/Getty Images

sociocultural differences between the rich and the poor. Often called *modernization theory*, this model is based on a dichotomy of traditional versus modern that serves not only as an attempted description of reality but also as a planning strategy for bringing about economic development in less-developed nations. The modern nations are associated with high levels of technology, industrialization, scientific rationality, formal education, efficient bureaucratic governments, strong market economies, punctuality, religious pluralism, low birth and death rates, upward mobility based on merit, rapid change, plans for the future, and a decline in the extended family. Traditional nations, on the other hand, have fewer of these characteristics. Modernization theory posits that for developing nations to become developed, they must engage in activities that will make them more like the developed nations. In short, they need to become more modern by taking on more of the "modern" characteristics listed previously. The process of economic development occurs through the mechanism of foreign aid from the wealthy nations to the less developed nations.

The modernization theory of economic development suffers from several ethnocentric assumptions. First, modernization theorists assume that all people in the world ought to gladly embrace all of the economic, cultural, and social changes inherent in "becoming modern." Second, they clearly overestimate the extent to which some non-Western people resist modernization, in large part because they ignore the many creative adaptations these people have made for centuries. Third, and perhaps most important, proponents of modernization theory assume that traditional people will be better off if they become modern. Because becoming modern is progressive, it is widely held that it must be beneficial. Modernization theorists assume that the advantages of becoming modern—such as higher incomes and standards of living—are universally beneficial. Even though becoming modern also involves giving up one's traditional culture, modernization theorists see it as a small price to pay in exchange for the obvious benefits.

The other major theory to explain the disparities between rich and poor has been called the *world systems theory*. According to this theory, the rich and poor nations of the world are not fundamentally different because of innate cultural features but rather because of how they have operated within the world system. The wealthy countries of the world have achieved high levels of development by exploiting other regions, plundering their natural resources, using their people as cheap sources of labor, and dominating their markets. In 1884 at the Conference of Berlin, European powers carved up the entire continent of Africa. The French took large parts of West Africa; the British controlled Nigeria, the Gold Coast, Kenya, Uganda, and the Rhodesias; the Portuguese got Angola and Mozambique; and the tiny country of Belgium took control of the mineral-rich Congo, an area seventy-seven times larger than itself. These nineteenth-century industrializing nations of Europe set up plantations and mining operations in their colonies, exploited cheap African labor, exported some of their own excess people to the colonies, and then sold many of their finished products back to the Africans they claimed to be helping.

Whereas Europeans actually took political control over their colonies, the United States chose to establish commercial influence through its corporations, mostly in Central and South America. Whether we are talking about corporate imperialism or outright colonialism, however, the consequences were the same: The exploitation of people and resources by the dominant powers impeded the economic growth of the subordinate nations. Thus, according to the world systems theory, economic development is not the result of an enlightened or progressive population but instead occurs when one group purposefully increases its own wealth at the expense of others.

The present debate in development anthropology revolves around the question of whether rising incomes and standards of living always have a positive effect on all parties concerned. Modernization theorists answer this question affirmatively, but a number of studies over the past several decades have strongly suggested that economic growth and development do not always improve people's lives. Some have even suggested that economic progress (as defined by rising wages, increased GNP, and so on) actually has lowered the quality of life for many non-Western people (Bodley 2007, 2008). Despite the best intentions of international development agencies, multimillion-dollar foreign aid projects have often resulted in greater poverty, longer working hours, overpopulation, poorer health, more social pathology, and environmental degradation.

Contrary to conventional thinking, many of the anticipated benefits of economic development have turned out to be illusory or downright detrimental. Attempts to engage non-Western people in programs of planned economic development often result in an increase in the incidence of disease for four reasons. First, many of the more modern lifestyles that people adopt bring new diseases associated with the industrialized world. For example, as early as the

---

modernization theory The idea that differences in economic development may be explained by inherent sociocultural differences between the rich and the poor.

world systems theory The idea that differences in economic development may be explained by the exploitation of the poor by the rich nations of the world.

1970s Charles Hughes and John Hunter (1972) and Ian Prior (1971) found that rapid cultural change was followed by dramatic increases in the incidence of diseases such as diabetes, heart disease, obesity, hypertension, gout, and high blood pressure in areas where these conditions previously had been unknown. Second, the incidence of certain bacterial or parasitic diseases increases precipitously in areas experiencing rapid cultural change. To illustrate, the construction of dams and irrigation systems in the Sudan as part of the Azande development scheme created ideal breeding conditions for the snail larva that causes schistosomiasis, one of Africa's most deadly diseases. Third, environmental degradation caused by drilling for oil and gas, mining, and industrial pollution present a host of health threats to people in developing nations. As Alicia Fentiman (2009) has suggested, Nigerian fishing people in the Niger Delta face contaminated drinking water, skin disorders from bathing in oil-polluted water, and respiratory diseases from oil flairs as a direct result of oil drilling by the Shell Oil Company. And fourth, health problems in the developing world are further aggravated by the rapid urbanization that often accompanies economic development. People crowding into cities looking for employment have more exposure to contagious diseases, which are made even worse by poor nutrition and unsanitary living conditions.

Programs of economic development often lead to changes in people's dietary habits. In some cases these dietary changes are voluntary to the extent that some new foods, associated with powerful outsiders, are status symbols. But more often than not, diets change because of circumstances associated with the objectives of economic development that are beyond the control of the local people. For example, in an attempt to grow more cash crops (which help to raise wages and bring in foreign exchange capital), non-Western people often divert time and energy from growing their normal subsistence crops. The result is that they spend much of their hard-earned cash on foods that are both costly and nutritionally inferior to feed their families.

This was the case among Brazilian farmers who made the transition from growing food crops to growing sisal, a cash crop used in the production of rope (Gross and Underwood 1971). Although the farmers spent most of their income on food, they could not provide adequate nutrition for their families. The study showed that the children of sisal workers were particularly at risk because most of the food went to the adults so they could maintain the strength needed for their strenuous work. These children of sisal workers, owing to their caloric deficiencies, experienced slower growth rates in their physical development. In addition to physical retardation, improper nourishment can lead directly to a reduced mental capacity and a lowered resistance to infection.

Not only do people who are caught up in economic development often eat less food, but they also eat food that is worse for them than their traditional diets. Often these foods, purchased rather than homegrown, are low in minerals, vitamins, fiber, and protein but high in sugar, sodium, and saturated fats. The lack of vitamins and minerals leads to an increased incidence of nutritionally related diseases, and the lack of protein may cause kwashiorkor (protein malnutrition), the leading cause of death in Africa and other parts of the developing world. The marked increase in sugar consumption by non-Western people has led to both a rapid and dramatic deterioration of dental health (Bodley 2008) and an alarmingly high rate of obesity among the world's poor (Figure 16.6).

Economic development programs have had deleterious effects on sizable segments of the target populations. Not only is health negatively affected, but other unfortunate (and usually unanticipated) consequences also occur. The natural environment is often degraded, families break down, social problems increase, and support systems disintegrate. In most

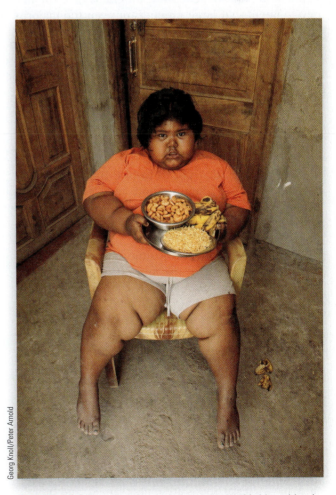

Georg Knoll/Peter Arnold

FIGURE 16.6 Obesity is becoming a major worldwide epidemic, even among the relatively poor peoples of the world. This Serbian man reminds us that obesity is no longer a medical problem exclusively among affluent Westerners.

cases economic development brings with it higher productivity, lower prices for goods and services, and a rising standard of living; however, higher productivity eventually may lead to fewer jobs as a result of automation or outsourcing. Automobiles in developing countries get better and more affordable, but as cars become more desirable, the roads become jammed with traffic, air pollution increases, and people waste more time stuck in traffic. Economic development brings higher living standards, but stress, anxiety, and clinical depression become more prevalent. E-mail is cheap and fast, but users must deal with hundreds of spam messages each day. Cell phones are convenient, but cell-phone owners are virtually never out of contact with the office. SUVs may be cool and macho, but they cause more traffic fatalities, increase a nation's dependency on Middle East oil, and are the newest twenty-first-century symbol of the principle of "power without responsibility." Biotechnology may increase people's life expectancy, but it also may leave them dependent on costly synthetic drugs.

To be certain, there are segments of non-Western populations that benefit from programs of economic development, but large numbers or even the majority wind up worse off than they would have been if the development efforts had never begun. To point out these negative consequences, however, is not to suggest that we should abandon foreign assistance programs or stop trying to increase people's access to material resources. The negative results occur most often when development programs are introduced without the full participation and understanding of the people they are designed to help. They are, in other words, "top-down" programs that fail to involve the local people in planning and administration and, perhaps more wrong-headed, fail to ask the appropriate questions about the cultures of the people who are the prospective beneficiaries of the program.

Specifically, what sociocultural information can anthropologists provide to assist economic development efforts? For example, if a development agency wants to resettle a group of nomadic cattle herders onto farmland so that they can become agriculturalists, the agency will need to know the answers to a number of *cultural* questions to assess (a) how best to meet the program's objectives or (b) whether they should attempt the project at all. To illustrate, the following questions about nomadic pastoralists—routinely asked by anthropologists—are but a few of the many that need answers:

- How are resources shared and distributed in the community?
- What material goods are highly valued, and how are they related to other nonmaterial aspects of the culture?

- How is labor divided according to age and gender?
- Do household tasks change according to the season of the year?
- What is the composition of the family (the basic economic unit)?
- Are there significant differences in family composition throughout the society?
- How stratified (in terms of wealth, power, and prestige) is the society?
- How is decision-making power distributed? Are some groups or individuals systematically excluded from positions of power?

If we take seriously the notion of the systemic nature of culture, then we must assume that a change in one part of the system is likely to bring about changes in other parts. It is only when development planners understand the nature of those parts, and how they are interrelated, that they can anticipate what some of the negative consequences may be and thus take steps to mitigate or avoid them. And because cultural anthropologists are the ones *on the ground* studying the cultures of those local populations targeted for sustainable development projects, it is only logical that anthropologists be intimately involved in the design, administration, and evaluation of sustainable development projects.

The literature on development anthropology is filled with examples of *good* development projects and *bad* ones or—put another way—those that have been largely beneficial to local people and those that have caused more harm than good. As a general rule, good programs of sustainable economic development are those that are initiated from within the country and culture(s) rather than imposed by some well-meaning, but often short-sighted, international development agency such as the World Bank or the United States Agency for International Development (USAID). One recent sustainable economic development program was started by the not-for-profit organization called PhytoTrade Africa, established in 2002 as a trade association for natural products (that is, products derived from indigenous plants and used in the food, drink, and cosmetic industries) in southern Africa (Cox 2008). As a membership organization, PhytoTrade Africa represents private-sector businesses, development agencies, and individuals for the purpose of alleviating poverty, protecting biodiversity, and developing economically successful industries that are ethical, environmentally friendly, and sustainable. The organization accomplishes its goals in three key ways: by identifying and developing new products, by developing world markets for these new products, and by nurturing the local African harvesters and producers.

One of the major products PhytoTrade has identified and is bringing to world markets is the harvestable fruit of the baobab tree, which grows naturally and abundantly throughout southern and eastern Africa (Figure 16.7). PhytoTrade partners with local fruit distribution companies (such as the Baobab Fruit Company of Senegal) that agree to purchase their fruit only from those local suppliers who meet their health and processing standards. Thus, local individuals and families harvest the baobab fruit and sell it for a fair market price to local or regional distribution companies.

The fruit of the baobab tree is becoming a popular food product because it has a number of desirable features. Traditionally, it was used as a highly nutritious and tasty snack for children; a dietary supplement for pregnant women; medicine to relieve stomachaches, fevers, and malaria; and, when hydrated, a refreshingly tangy drink similar to lemonade. It is exceptionally nutritious, containing high levels of antioxidants, essential minerals such as calcium, potassium, iron, and magnesium, and twice as much vitamin C as an orange. In a study by the United Nations, a solution of water and baobab powder was found to be a more effective remedy for dehydration in children than the standard remedies used by the World Health Organization. Today baobab fruit powder (which is just one form of the product) is being used in a wide variety of food and drink products sold internationally, including smoothies, juices, breakfast cereals, cereal bars, snacks, ice cream, yogurt, jams, sauces, marinades, specialty teas, and health supplements.

Why do anthropologists and development experts consider this a good economic development project? Let us count the ways:

- The baobab fruit industry in southern Africa is an excellent example of "economic development from within." Rather than an already established industry imported from the developed world, this new source of jobs and income is based on a traditional product grown in their own backyards, and, as a result, much of the profits stay with the local people.

- The baobab trees in Africa today are plentiful, large, mature, and, perhaps most important, extremely resilient. With trunk circumferences greater than sixty feet and heights reaching ninety feet, the baobab tree (which has a life expectancy of more than 500 years) is highly resilient to climate change, disease, and deforestation. As a result, the baobab fruit harvesters do not have to worry about possible crop failures.

- The development of a baobab fruit industry requires little or no capital investment on the part of the local harvesters, who are the primary beneficiaries of the entire enterprise.

- Becoming a harvester requires no special set of skills. Anyone with two hands and a large sack can harvest the plentiful fruit of the baobab tree.

- Because PhytoTrade sets a fair market price for the fruit, local harvesters always receive a fair and reasonable price for their product. In 2008, women in Tanzania (who normally earned less than eighty dollars per year) earned twelve to thirty dollars per day. They could save money in bank accounts and contribute to the economic well-being of their households. Moreover they were learning valuable skills on running a small business.

- An industry based on local baobab fruit is sustainable because the major product (unlike extractive products like coal, petroleum, and minerals) is a renewable resource.

FIGURE 16.7 Phyto Trade Africa is a company that is starting local sustainable industries using the fruit from baobob trees such as this one in Tanzania.

© Johnny Johnson/Getty Images

APPLIED PERSPECTIVE

A Cultural Anthropologist Revitalizes the Small Town of Star, North Carolina

Anthropologists often work in rural communities studying social changes brought on by economic development and cultural forces of change. Globalization has created dramatic economic and social shifts not only around the world but also in rural areas and small towns in the United States. The central region of North Carolina has been profoundly affected by globalization because of the relocation of manufacturing jobs (primarily in textiles and furniture) to other countries, especially during the last several decades.

Rhonda McCanless

For years rural areas in North Carolina, and indeed throughout the country, have experienced the loss of farms, corporate downsizing, a shift to service-sector employment, and the substitution of mega-chain stores for small, main-street businesses. Moreover factory closings have led to the loss of not only vibrant small-town main streets but also community identity, community leadership, and, in many cases, social cohesion. In 2006, Central Park NC, a rural sustainable development not-for-profit organization directed by anthropologist Nancy Gottovi, took over a former sock factory in the small town of Star, North Carolina (population 803). In 2003, the sock company had relocated its manufacturing operations to Central America and Mexico, thereby eliminating more than a thousand jobs. Because many small businesses had been supported by the town's largest employer, the closing of the factory led to the closing of most small businesses, abandoned buildings, and a shuttered-up downtown.

Gottovi was interested in how the former factory building could be used to create a new "economic engine" for the town while at the same time providing opportunities for the community's leaders to craft a new identity that was not based solely on textile manufacturing. As an anthropologist, Gottovi wondered whether a community-based approach to development could meet the needs of individuals, workers, and businesses as well as the greater needs of the whole community. For example, the large factory environment with its multiple shifts of diverse workers had provided a common "public" space for members of the community to come together. Conversations "around the water

- Unlike many Western high-tech industries, baobab fruit harvesting is ecologically friendly. In fact, because the industry uses the fruit of the tree rather than the tree itself, it is likely that more trees will be planted as the industry matures.
- There is now a new and rapidly expanding world market for products made with baobab fruit. Thanks to a petition submitted by PhytoTrade, the European Union in 2008 approved baobab products as a novel food import, thereby opening up the entire European market.

All of these features make the new African baobab fruit industry a highly successful effort at sustainable economic development. It avoids harmful consequences such as environmental degradation, increased incidence of disease, human rights abuses, and exploitation of the people it intends to help. But most important, it is a homegrown development project, using local resources and giving the target population a real stake in creating and maintaining profitable employment. Because the major product of the development project (fruit from baobab trees) has played both economic and spiritual roles in the traditional culture, local harvesters protect their sacred baobab trees as well as earn a good livelihood from them. From an anthropological perspective, this project is culturally sensitive because local people are using their own resources, labor, and work procedures to earn a reasonable income. And, as a bonus, it is enabling the African harvesters and entrepreneurs to provide a highly nutritious food product to the rest of the world.

Cultural Survival of Indigenous Peoples

In recent years, cultural anthropologists have become increasingly concerned with a particular type of cultural change—namely, the rapid disappearance of cooler" informed a wide cross-section of community members about births, deaths, and other individual and family life events. When the factory was closed, there were few such opportunities for adults to maintain social networks, other than in churches, which are often segregated socially and by ethnicity.

Traditional economic development professionals tend to focus on what is commonly called the "big buffalo hunt": recruiting large manufacturing industries to rural areas to provide as many jobs as possible in as short a time as possible. However, this has proven to be a risky strategy for small communities that do not have the economic diversity and size to absorb the ebb and flow of plant closings. Increased globalization means that industries are more footloose than ever; they are likely to move their operations according to the "bottom line" at a faraway corporate headquarters. The loss of several hundred jobs overnight can be devastating to a small town, as the residents of Star discovered in 2003.

Another critical issue for Gottovi was how to stop the "hollowing out" of rural small towns such as Star through the loss of its most talented young people who leave in search of better economic and social opportunities. Gottovi's group focused on ways to build links between high school and post-secondary education, particularly in sustainable energy, creative arts, and local food production, as a relatively inexpensive way of capturing and maintaining creativity and innovation in the community.

In 2006, Gottovi and her colleagues opened STARworks Center for Creative Enterprises in the abandoned factory building. STARworks provides training in glass blowing, ceramics, and sustainable energy, which includes biodiesel production from waste vegetable oil collected from restaurants, geothermal heating and cooling of homes, and a small-scale, sustainable, and organic community supported agriculture program. Not only has STARworks been successful in providing a place for young rural people to engage in innovative, creative work in the small town, but it also provides social opportunities for area residents—particularly youth—to combat the rampant boredom that often drives talented young people to urban areas. Creative types have traditionally felt isolated in small towns, yet STARworks has been able to attract people from all over the United States and the world to come to Star to work in its programs and businesses.

Gottovi's STARworks is one example of making a transition from an export-based manufacturing economy to one that is more "consumption" based. Cultural facilities and programs such as STARworks bolster the local economy. By bringing in new artists and other creative entrepreneurs, such centers spur new local spending, including revitalization of main streets and low-income housing for artists' spaces, and attract tourism. They also provide indirect opportunities and skills, including grant writing and other capital investment abilities, new ideas, and new local leadership. Anthropologists have often studied the interaction between the local and the global to avoid disassociating economic issues from local meaning. The STARworks case study is an example of how a local culture, with the help of anthropological insights, is redefining itself in response to external forces of globalization.

Questions for Further Thought

1. What is meant by "Think globally, but act locally?"

2. What should STARworks do to continue to attract the young "creative class" to relocate and work in Star, North Carolina?

3. After four years of operation, STARworks has "incubate" businesses focusing on clay processing for potters, furnace construction for glass blowers, biodiesel fuel production, and organic vegetable growing. What other business enterprises should STARworks include in its economic development project in the abandoned sock factory?

---

indigenous populations of the world. An *indigenous population* is a group of people who (a) are the original inhabitants of a region; (b) identify with a specific, small-scale cultural heritage; and (c) have no significant role in the government (Bodley 2008: 4). Classic examples of indigenous peoples are the hundreds of small-scale cultures in Asia, Africa, and the Americas that came under the influence of colonial powers during the past several centuries.

Many anthropologists are concerned about the survival of these indigenous peoples not because they are the subject of much anthropological research, but because their disappearance is a basic human rights issue. A growing number of cultural anthropologists feel strongly that indigenous populations over the past several centuries have been negatively affected by the onslaught of civilization. Cultural patterns—and in some cases the people themselves—have been eradicated as a direct result of civilization's pursuit of "progress" and economic development.

The industrial revolution in nineteenth-century Europe was "revolutionary" to the extent that it led to explosions in both population and consumerism, which in turn had drastically negative effects on indigenous peoples. The technological efficiency of the industrial revolution resulted in a quantum leap in population growth. At the same time that populations were expanding in the industrializing world, there was

---

indigenous population People who are the original inhabitants of a region, identify with a specific cultural heritage, and play no significant role in government.

a corresponding growth in consumerism. If economies were to grow and prosper, production had to be kept high, which could be accomplished only if people purchased and consumed the products of industry. To meet the needs of a growing population with ever-increasing desires to consume, people needed to control and exploit natural resources wherever they might be found.

A major motivation for the colonization of the non-Western world was economic, in that the natural resources found in Asia and Africa were needed to fuel European factories. The so-called scramble for Africa, which began when European leaders set national boundaries in Africa at the Conference of Berlin in 1884, was thought to be a "civilized" and "gentlemanly" way of dividing up the continent's natural resources among the industrializing nations of Europe. Unfortunately, the rights of indigenous populations were not protected. In many cases, lands and resources needed by the indigenous peoples were simply appropriated for use by the colonial powers. Landless populations were forced to become laborers, dependent on whatever wages the colonialists wished to pay. Native resistance to this systematic exploitation was usually met with force. In some cases, large segments of the population were killed directly or died from European diseases. In less severe situations, indigenous peoples were economically exploited, systematically kept at the lowest echelons of the society, and forced to give up their land and traditional identities.

A number of anthropologists, historians, and journalists have documented specific examples of the demise of indigenous populations over the course of the past 150 years. In fact, one anthropologist, John Bodley (2007, 2008), has devoted much of his career reminding us how the spread of civilization and industrialization has resulted in the creation of millions of "victims of progress" throughout the non-Western world. These tragic consequences, all done in the name of civilization, economic development, and progress, have included everything from the annihilation of the entire population of Tasmania in the nineteenth century to the introduction of measles and influenza to the indigenous peoples of the Amazon when the government built roads through the Brazilian frontier.

Anthropologists believe that the most dramatic examples of the degradation of indigenous peoples have come from the area of the Brazilian Amazon, where Indians are being swept away by the relentless movement of resettlement and economic development. To illustrate, during the 1960s an Indian village in Brazil was attacked by a gang of gunslingers allegedly hired by a large Brazilian corporation that wanted the Indians off the land. Shelton Davis (1977) described the Massacre at

FIGURE 16.8 In 2007, this leader of a group of Yanomamo Indians from the Amazon region presented to German Chancellor Merkel a letter urging Germany to sign Convention No. 169 concerning protecting the rights of indigenous and tribal peoples living in independent countries.

Parallel Eleven, in which hired hit men attempted to wipe out the village and its inhabitants by throwing dynamite from a low-flying airplane. During the 1970s the threats to indigenous peoples, though not quite so blatantly genocidal, were no less devastating. By building roads through the Amazonian frontier, the Brazilian government introduced diseases such as influenza and measles to the indigenous peoples of the region. By the beginning of the 1990s, tens of thousands of gold prospectors had invaded the territory of the Yanomamo (Figure 16.8), extracting millions of dollars' worth

of gold from the land and leaving the Yanomamo ravaged by disease (Brooke 1990).

The twenty-first century has presented additional challenges to the cultural survival of indigenous peoples. To illustrate, the Tikuna community in western Brazil (close to the border with Colombia and Peru) has become an important link in drug trafficking. Some young indigenous Tikuna men, working as drug "mules," use their knowledge of the rivers and dense rain forest to carry cocaine into Brazil's substantial drug market. Unfortunately, not only are a growing number of Tikuna men working in the illicit drug trade, but many have also become addicted to both cocaine and alcohol. In addition to facing unemployment, disease, poor health care, substance abuse, and the destruction of their natural environment, contemporary Tikunas are struggling to keep some vestiges of their traditional culture (Barrionuevo 2008).

But we need not go to the far corners of the earth to find tragic examples of the exploitation of indigenous peoples. The litany of atrocities committed against Native Americans in the name of progress and manifest destiny dates back to the earliest European settlements. The massacre of the Pequot in Connecticut in 1637 and the massacre of the Sioux at Wounded Knee in 1890 are just two examples from US history. More recent examples of the demise, or potential demise, of indigenous cultures in the United States are far less violent but devastating nevertheless. To illustrate, a small tribe of 125 Native Americans currently are threatened with having their last remaining ancestral land flooded by a proposed expansion of the Shasta Dam in northern California. The Winnemem Wintu Indian tribe is no stranger to having their lands swallowed up in the name of water conservation. When the Shasta Dam was constructed in the 1930s, the tribe lost its ancestral lands along the McCloud River to the reservoir. Some 183 corpses were exhumed from their traditional graveyard and reburied, while tribal members watched their homes being destroyed. The plan now is to elevate the height of the dam by 18 feet, thereby inundating most of the remaining twenty sacred tribal sites. If even one site is destroyed, the symbolic circle of connection between it and the remaining nineteen sites will be broken, which would make the practice of Winnemem religion difficult at best and deprive the tribe of one of its major mechanisms for maintaining its tribal identity. The project, if approved, is scheduled to begin in 2010. One enterprising Winnemem, an ardent opponent of the proposed dam expansion, is making and selling T-shirts with the inscription "Homeland Security: Fighting Terrorism Since 1492" (Murphy 2004).

Not only do cultural anthropologists document the demise of indigenous peoples, but many also use their specialized knowledge to help these endangered cultures survive against the homogenizing effects of globalization. In one of the most urgent forms of applied anthropology, a number of cultural anthropologists in recent years have contributed to the efforts of Cultural Survival, Inc., a nonprofit organization based in Cambridge, Massachusetts, that supports projects on five continents designed to help indigenous peoples survive the changes brought about by contact with industrial societies. In partnership with indigenous peoples, Cultural Survival advocates for native communities whose rights, cultures, and dignity are threatened by (a) strengthening their languages and cultures, (b) educating their communities about their rights, and (c) fighting marginalization, discrimination, and exploitation.

Founded in 1972 by Harvard anthropologist David Maybury-Lewis, Cultural Survival works to guarantee the land and resource rights of tribal peoples while supporting economic development projects run by the peoples themselves. As part of their work with Cultural Survival, cultural anthropologists have conducted research on vital cultural issues, served as cultural brokers between the indigenous peoples and government officials, and published literature informing the public about the urgency of these survival issues. To help support its work, Cultural Survival has maintained, for more than three decades, the premier databank for anthropological and social scientific information on the indigenous peoples of the world. This vast collection of literature is available free of charge from the Cultural Survival web site (www.cultural-survival.org). *Cultural Survival Quarterly*, the organization's major publication, is an award-winning periodical specializing in articles written by anthropologists and non-anthropologists, with a number of pieces written by indigenous peoples themselves. A periodic newsletter, *Cultural Survival Voices*, is circulated to more than 350 indigenous organizations worldwide, providing them with the practical information they need to protect their cultures and native territories.

At any given time Cultural Survival has a number of ongoing projects around the world. One such project entails working with Panama's largest indigenous group, the Ngobe, whose homeland is being threatened by a hydroelectric dam (Lutz 2007, 2008). Numbering about 170,000 people, the Ngobe, who occupy a remote area in western Panama, have traditionally supported themselves by subsistence agriculture and fishing. In the last several years, however, a US construction company, in partnership with the Panamanian government, has started building a major hydroelectric dam on the river that runs through the Ngobe homeland. It has been estimated that the new dam will swallow up the homes and lands of more than a thousand people. Other Ngobe, who will not lose their land, will become even more isolated by losing their transportation routes. Moreover, the dam will disrupt the migration of several fish species that make up a significant portion of the Ngobe diet.

Even though a new hydroelectric dam will provide a much-needed supply of "clean" energy, the Ngobe case has become a human rights battleground largely because of the heavy-handed way the US company and the government of Panama have treated the Ngobe people. Many of the Ngobe, under enormous pressure to sell their lands to the government, put their thumbprints on sales contracts that they could not read and did not understand. In other cases, people's homes were destroyed and their lands confiscated in the absence of even bogus contracts. When the local people staged a peaceful protest against the dam project in January 2008, government police in riot gear attacked the protesters with clubs; by the end of the day they had arrested fifty-four people, including thirteen children and two infants. After this incident the construction site was cordoned off to any outsiders who sought to meet with the Ngobe.

Organizations such as Cultural Survival—and its local Panamanian partner, the Alliance for Conservation and Development (ACD)—are intensifying their efforts to block the dam project until these blatant human rights injustices have been resolved. The ACD has been pressing the government to legally justify its condoning off of Ngobe property. It is also conducting workshops for indigenous peoples on their legal rights as Panamanian citizens and, more practically, on how to file legal complaints with their government. Cultural Survival has sponsored former Peace Corps volunteers to return to Ngobe communities to document human rights violations. Moreover, it has sponsored the visit of anthropologist Philip Young of the University of Oregon to document Ngobe cultural and land tenure customs.

In addition to these in-country efforts, Cultural Survival worked on a larger legal project to stop the dam and protect Ngobe human rights. With the help of a group of US law students, Cultural Survival submitted a petition to the Inter-American Commission on Human Rights, an intergovernmental group that has the authority to ask the Panamanian government to stop the dam project. However, the dam was completed over the protests of the Ngobe people, environmentalists, and human rights advocates in Panama, and despite precautionary measures taken by the Inter-American Commission on Human Rights. In early June 2011, the construction company began filling the reservoir, which flooded the homes of the Ngobe who had refused to negotiate a settlement with the company. Recently the Ngobe people and the various opponents of the dam had cause to celebrate when Panama's National Public Service Authority (ASEP) decided to prevent AES Corporation from building a second dam on the Changuinola River.

Climate Change and Applied Anthropology

The third, and final, global challenge of the twenty-first century that we will consider in this chapter is climate change. As recently as the start of this millennium, there was an ongoing debate among scientists, politicians, and pundits about whether or not climate change was real, and if it was, whether it was caused by civilization or was simply part of a natural cyclical pattern of climatic variations. That debate has largely been resolved. With the exception of some hard-line deniers, most responsible voices in the world accept climate change caused by global warming as a fact. Three questions remain: (1) How serious a problem is it? (2) What are the consequences of climate change likely to be? (3) What can be done to avoid the damaging, perhaps cataclysmic, effects on our natural environment?

Established by the United Nations Environment Programme and the World Meteorological Organization, the Intergovernmental Panel on Climate Change (IPCC) is the premier organization for the assessment of climate change. The IPCC is a scientific body made up of leading scientists from around the world who voluntarily contribute their work. The IPCC reviews and evaluates the most recent scientific data to provide the world with a clear view on the current state of climate change and its potential environmental and socioeconomic consequences. The differing viewpoints that exist within the scientific community are reflected in the IPCC reports. Moreover, the IPCC is candid about which of its findings are in dispute and which are not. Among those findings on which virtually all of the contributing scientists agree are the following (Emanuel 2009: 183–84):

▪ The levels of greenhouse gases, including carbon dioxide, methane, ozone, and nitrous oxide, are rising as a result of burning fossil fuels. The amount of carbon dioxide in the atmosphere has increased approximately 35 percent since the start of the industrial period.

- The earth's average surface temperature has increased by 1.2 degrees Fahrenheit during the past century, with much of the increase occurring after 1975.

- The warmest year (in terms of average temperature) since temperatures have been instrumentally recorded (the past hundred years) was 2005.

- As a direct result of the melting of polar ice caps, sea levels have risen 2.7 inches over the past forty years.

- The annual mean amount of arctic sea ice has decreased by 15 to 20 percent since satellite measurements began in 1978.

This is what the world's climate scientists agree on. Even more alarming are the findings on which *most* scientists agree, but on which there is *some* disagreement.

- Most of the increase in average temperature is caused by variable solar output, volcanic eruptions, man-made aerosols, and greenhouse gases.

- The dramatic increase in average temperature over the past three decades is the result primarily of rising levels of greenhouse gases.

- Unless levels of greenhouse gases are reduced, global average temperatures will increase between 2.5 and 9.0 degrees over the next century.

- As a result of the continued melting of the arctic ice caps, sea levels will rise between 6 and 16 inches over the next century.

- The incidence, intensity, and duration of floods and droughts will increase in the future.

As a professional group, cultural anthropologists have known for years that climate change is a reality and not merely the opinion of paranoid physical scientists. Unlike economists, political scientists, politicians, and policy makers, cultural anthropologists study and live with those populations all over the globe that are the first to experience the negative consequences of climate change. These are the small-scale, nonindustrialized societies that live in the marginal areas of the world as pastoralists, hunters, fishermen, and subsistence farmers. Because these people live so close to the earth, they have acquired a wealth of knowledge about their immediate environment and, as a result, are sensitive to minute changes in animal behavior, water temperatures, amount of rainfall, planting cycles, climate, and soil conditions. In fact,

these people's accumulated knowledge about their ecology has been largely responsible for their being able to make the cultural changes needed to successfully adapt to their changing environments over the past millennia. Even today Inuit hunters know when to move their hunting grounds further north so that their snowmobiles do not fall through the ice. Anthropologists are able to show how people have altered their lifestyles to accommodate the changing environment. Unfortunately, the poor, nonindustrialized, marginalized peoples of the world—those who have been the subject of most studies by cultural anthropologists—are serving today as the barometers of climate change.

Not only are the people in small-scale societies the first to suffer the consequences of global warming, but they are the most vulnerable because many live in marginal areas. The Republic of Kiribati, located in the central Pacific, provides an excellent example of how vulnerable some small-scale societies are to climate change. With a total population of approximately 98,000, Kiribati became independent from Britain in 1979 and became a member of the United Nations in 1999. Because the island nation straddles both the equator and the 180th meridian, it has the distinction of being the only nation in the world that is in all four hemispheres. Although some consider Kiribati an idyllic paradise, it is one of the poorest nations in the world (Beck and Blair 2008).

Kiribati may become the first nation to fall victim to global warming. It comprises thirty-three coral atolls that are less than 1,000 feet across and barely above sea level. In 1999 two small, uninhabited Kiribati islets disappeared underwater as a result of rising sea levels. Rising ocean tides are causing two additional problems. First, the people are rapidly becoming unable to grow their basic tuber crop because the pits in which the crops grow are being inundated with sea water. And second, continual flooding by high tides is making the freshwater supply too brackish to drink. Today the people of Kiribati are among about a million people worldwide living on coral islands, who are losing their livelihoods and cultures as their land is being consumed by the rising sea levels.

People from low-lying Pacific Island nations are not the only ones vulnerable to climate change. The million people presently living in the Bolivian city of El Alto (a neighboring city to La Paz, which

© Cengage Learning

APPLIED PERSPECTIVE

Climate Change Adaptation through Micro-insurance in Ethiopia

Farmers in every part of the world face different types of climate variability, including seasonal droughts, periods of excess rainfall and flooding, intense storms, and longer patterns of desertification. This is particularly true for the past half-century, which has witnessed an intensification of all of these climatic challenges for small-scale farmers. Large-scale agriculture, supported by technology and enormous resources, are less vulnerable to drought and other climate-related changes. Most small-scale farmers, wherever they may be located, have developed a variety of protective responses, including crop diversification, planting drought-resistant crops, finding alternative sources of income, and using traditional social networks such as family or neighborhood in times of need. In the United States and other more affluent countries, farmers have also come to rely on financial mechanisms such as insurance and loans to help buffer against losses. Because scientists expect that climate change will increase the risks for many small-scale farmers, many development organizations are considering strategies such as crop micro-insurance to help farmers in developing countries survive more frequent droughts.

Environmental anthropologist Nicole Peterson, was part of a multidisciplinary research team (comprised of economists, sociologists, ecologists, and political scientists) that were interested in knowing if crop insurance would help smallholder farmers in Ethiopia adapt to increasing climate variations and the risks of drought. Before the development agency would establish and fund a crop insurance program in Ethiopia, it needed to know whether it would be a cost-effective mechanism for providing security against the risks of drought.

By using such anthropological field methods as surveys, interviews, focus groups, and economic games, Peterson focused her concerns on two major research tasks. First, she assessed the heterogeneity of local farmers and their differential interests in crop insurance. Peterson and her research team found that farmers vary along several dimensions, including wealth, age, education, and religion. Differences in landholding are also important, because some farmers own irrigated land in addition to rain-fed fields, they are less susceptible to the ravages of drought. Moreover, some young men are landless and work as laborers for other farmers. Another important segment of the Ethiopian farm population is comprised of female heads of household, comprising about 30 percent of the farming households. Single, female farmers were disadvantaged by lack of available labor; they often leased their land to young landless farmers in exchange for less than half of the value of the harvest.

The second research task Peterson set for herself was to assess what risks farmers actually faced and how they have coped with these risks in the past. Although all Ethiopian farmers faced the risk of drought, economic differences and labor availability led to differences in how farmers responded to it. Wealthier farmers owned more irrigated land, which they viewed as a form of insurance against drought. They were also more likely to own herd animals such as goats and sheep, which can be sold to supplement reduced incomes. Poorer farmers on the whole had only rain-fed land, and fewer herd animals. They also had less money saved, and less available credit. One popular coping strategy against loss of crops through drought is the government sponsored food-for-work program. This program enabled poor farmers to be eligible for food during periods of crop failure in exchange for labor on local public works projects such as roads, terrace building, and tree planting.

The findings from this anthropological research led to a number of useful outcomes. First, the insurance program that was eventually designed for the farmers was based on their preferences and design suggestions stemming from the interviews and

is the highest capitol city in the world) are threatened by too little water rather than too much water (Figure 16.9). Each year the people of El Alto can see their once-majestic glaciers, a source of water and electrical power, shrinking. A World Bank report recently concluded that El Alto's glacier (called Illimani), and many other lower-altitude glaciers throughout the Andes, could totally disappear in the next several decades, thereby eliminating their water supply. As of 2010 the demands for water in El Alto have already exceeded the supply, and the problem is getting more acute because some of the water is being sold off to the wealthier residents of La Paz. With a lack of drinking water as well as water for irrigation and power generation, the people of El Alto could become the first urban casualty of climate change (Hicks, Fabricant, and Revilla 2010; Rosenthal 2009).

As we can see from the cases of low-level Kiribati and high-altitude El Alto, millions of people are already being negatively affected by climate change. If climate change continues on its present course,

focus groups. Increased attention was given to female-headed households, landless farmers, and other kinds of diversity within the farm population. In addition, there was greater attention given to differences in wealth among the farmers, and to differences in soil types, as suggested by the farmers. Another major outcome of the project has been to show that climate change and strategies such as crop insurance are not simply technical problems and solutions, but also have social, political, and economic components. This view was integrated into the project from the beginning. Peterson's research demonstrated that farmer ideas, preferences, social interactions, and cultures are central to successful adaptation to climate change.

This research is significant because it brings cultural insights to policy debates on climate change, thereby demonstrating that climate change is not just a technical problem which must be addressed, but a sociocultural one as well. Peterson's use of the anthropological techniques of focus groups, surveys, and interviews provided the interdisciplinary research team with information about farmers and others that would otherwise not have been available. Interviews and focus groups were particularly useful in getting a sense of the bigger picture, like the issues facing farmers and their current strategies for coping with drought. These data gathering techniques also provided more detail than could ever be derived from a survey. In other words, the farmers themselves talked about their experiences, the stories they had heard, as well as their feelings and fears. Data from these methods was also used to inform other aspects of the project. For example, experimental games were designed that mimicked insurance contracts based on what farmers said. Previous discussions and survey data were used to create a realistic and culturally appropriate exercise that participants found entertaining and educational.

As an anthropologist, Peterson brought a holistic perspective to this development project. Rather than seeing climate change or crop insurance from a primarily technical perspective, her data broadened the focus to other aspects of farming, risk, and everyday lives in Ethiopia. This led to her focus on both (a) existing coping strategies and (b) local needs and desires. Though more difficult, she also worked to situate Ethiopian farmers within a global set of economic, political, and social relationships by studying links between farmers, markets, development organizations, governments, nongovernmental organizations, and development policies. As an applied anthropologist committed to the traditional notion of holism, Peterson was committed to exploring the ways this crop insurance project intersected (or might have intersected) with a variety of processes, both positively and negatively. She took seriously the ways that development projects can create problems, unintentionally, or at least fail to solve existing ones. Like most anthropologists who are conducting face-to-face participant-observation research in local communities, she understood that the "development process" is deeply political and cultural, in that politics and cultures can set the agenda, thereby ignoring local voices. For this reason, she strongly advocated for plans that start with the community members and their desires, rather than from the boardrooms of international development agencies. Keeping an anthropological focus on the local can keep well-intended development projects from missing key aspects of the situation and can also work to give control of livelihoods back to local people. Similarly, anthropologists often emphasize diversity and heterogeneity, rather than assuming everyone shares the same needs and desires. In Ethiopia, this led to increased attention to female heads of household, landless men, and other differences among farmers. This focus on diversity keeps projects from missing people and their experiences, and from creating development projects that benefit only a few.

Questions for Further Thought

1. The research reported on in this case study poses the question: Will crop insurance help Ethiopian farmers deal with drought? Why is it particularly important for a study of this nature to be interdisciplinary in its approach?

2. How did the anthropologist (Peterson) in this case study contribute a holistic view to this research project? Be specific.

3. What specific data-gathering techniques did Peterson use in this multidisciplinary research project? Why did she not use participant observation, cultural anthropology's most widely used technique?

most scientists agree that many more millions will suffer, some so severely that their societies will cease to exist. One of the cruelest ironies, of course, is that most of these vulnerable populations who are the first to experience the negative consequences of climate change are trying to adapt to problems not of their own making. Climate change has been caused primarily by the industrialized world's (Europe, Japan, Russia, the United States, India, and China) burning of fossil fuels, which produce the globe-warming gases. Although scientists and politicians have been debating the causes of global warming and their effects on human existence in the future, cultural anthropologists have been documenting the real changes occurring *on the ground*

among the most vulnerable peoples and cultures. Irrespective of what decisions are made at world climate conferences (such as the 2009 meeting in Copenhagen, Denmark), anthropological data on these most immediately affected communities will be vital for policy makers who work to avoid the more deleterious effects of climate change or at least ameliorate them after they have occurred.

But cultural anthropologists are doing more than just documenting the effects of climate change on the physical environment and the lives of those people most immediately affected. The challenges facing these vulnerable peoples of the world should serve as a wake-up call to those in the developed world who will

FIGURE 16.9 This housing area (foreground) in El Alto, Bolivia, overlooks the capitol city of La Paz. Both cities have been experiencing water shortages in recent years, largely due to retreating glaciers.

me. If burning gas is contributing to climate change, one woman said matter-of-factly, then we should use our generators less. The others nodded in agreement…. Kiribati uses the fourth-smallest amount of oil of any country in the world and both produces and uses the sixth lowest amount of electricity. Yet, when these women learned that their actions, however insignificant, might contribute to climate change and affect others around the world, their first reaction was to reduce their own consumption.

Conclusion

If, as we suggested previously in this chapter, the many cultures of the world are not becoming a single homogeneous megaculture, then what is the most sensible foreign policy strategy for interacting with other peoples of the world? Rather than deliberately trying to eradicate cultural differences, a more workable approach is some type of *multiculturalism*—that is, an official policy that recognizes the worth and integrity of different cultures at home and abroad. Such an approach, which has been operating effectively in Switzerland and Canada for generations, requires the basic anthropological understanding that culturally different people are not inherently perverse or immoral. Rather it is possible to live together in peaceful coexistence, provided we understand the logic of culturally different peoples and are willing to negotiate with them in good faith and without exploitation.

At the least, multiculturalism requires an awareness that people from other cultures, who do not share our cultural assumptions, probably do not sympathize with some of our behaviors, ideas, and values. For example, living in a culture that highly prizes individualism, most middle-class North Americans see themselves as strong, competitive, assertive, and independent achievers. People with a more collective value orientation, in contrast, view North Americans in far less flattering terms as self-absorbed, greedy materialists with hardly a shred of altruism. Many Americans are proud that they are sufficiently motivated by the value they place on individualism to achieve power, fame, and financial security by working seventy hours per week to be able to afford payments on their $75,000 Cadillac Escalade SUV. Many Swedes, however, look at the values and behavior of a thirty-something lawyer from Chicago, for example, as being selfish and dismissive of others. Working seventy hours per week translates, for them,

be facing these same difficulties down the road. Island states like Kiribati may be underwater in a few decades, but so could much of Florida and all of Manhattan just decades after that. Ethnographic accounts of the human costs of climate change will, no doubt, serve as a dramatic incentive for leaders in the industrialized world to reassess some of their basic assumptions about climate change, their role in causing it, and their responsibility in fixing it. And it will expose the industrialized world to cultures that have radically different worldviews. To illustrate, many people in the industrialized world place a high value on consuming unlimited amounts of energy, allowing markets to solve all problems, and thinking that a system of "cap and trade" will really control the amount of greenhouse gases escaping into the atmosphere. By way of contrast, the people in Kiribati and El Alto have a worldview that values respect for the earth and a solemn responsibility to protect the natural environment for future generations. This alternative way of looking at the world is poignantly related by Casey Beck and Austin Blair (2008):

> On my first night (in Kiribati) a group of middle aged women threw a botaki (party) for me. Every guest at the botaki is expected to give a speech. When it was my turn, I told the women that I was there to learn about Kiribati culture in the face of climate change. I explained climate change to them, and their immediate reaction shocked

multiculturalism A public policy philosophy that recognizes the legitimacy and equality of all cultures represented in a society.

Want to Work in an International Economic Development Program?

❋ It would be extraordinarily rare to find an advertised job description (for any nonacademic position), which includes the statement: "BA in cultural anthropology required." There are, however, a significant number of anthropology majors who take jobs, and indeed follow careers, in which the insights, knowledge, theories, methods, and skill sets derived from studying cultural anthropology play a critical role. In today's global environment, any job (either at home or abroad) that requires working with people from different cultural backgrounds could be better accomplished with a background in academic anthropology at the bachelor, master, or doctorate level.

One such career field in which anthropological skills and knowledge are useful is in the area of sustainable economic development programs funded by international aid organizations such as the World Bank or the US Agency for International Development. These aid organizations, through the competitive grants process, contract with private sector firms or nongovernmental organizations that design and carry out specific projects in such areas as health, education, infrastructure development, and democratic institution building. Your textbook authors were able to conduct an interview with a high-ranking human resources officer from one of the more prominent companies that has received many contacts to design and administer sustainable economic development programs in the areas of education, democratic transitions, and stabilization in post-conflict environments. At the time of the interview, the company had a field presence in twenty-five different countries, including Afghanistan, Honduras, Yemen, Tajikistan, Malawi, and Colombia. We interviewed Kathryn Erskine, a personnel expert whose job consists largely, but not exclusively, of recruiting the best development experts (from the United States and other parts of the world as well) to serve in senior staff positions. Here are some of her responses to our questions:

Question 1: *Do you hire many people with MAs and PhDs in anthropology?*

Kathryn Erskine: For full-time positions, I hire many with MAs, perhaps even 1 in 15 or so. I hire fewer full-time staff with PhDs, although those with PhDs often serve as short-term consultants on particular projects.

Question 2: *What are the skill sets you are looking for in your overseas program personnel?*

Kathryn Erskine: We work a lot in conflict and post-conflict countries, so I want to make sure that our hires can manage the stress of working in a non-permissive environment where security is at times compromised. Also, a lot of our work takes place at the community level, with a very light expat footprint, so I want to make sure our employees know how to work well with local staff. For example, they need to have a participatory management style, be good listeners, and know how to build the capacity of their host country staff. At a minimum, I want to see that they have prior work experience in the region and, if possible, in-country experience. Relevant foreign language experience is often, but not always, required.

Question 3: *What skill sets do you think anthropologists bring to the table?*

Kathryn Erskine: Anthropologists tend to be calm and patient with their local staff and with the communities in which they work. Often, the desire to quickly meet goals and objectives leads to sacrifices in work quality and difficult relationships with local staff, but anthropologists are able to find a balance amongst these things. Anthropologists are also strong mentors and trainers, as they look at the context in which their employees work and use that lens to make the project successful. Finally, they are more comfortable living in environments that are usually much different from the environment in which they grew up, and they often speak the local language. This decreases stress and leads to higher work satisfaction.

Question 4: *Do you look for those skills/capacities associated with successful living/working abroad in radically different cultures (for example, developing a broad/holistic perspective, perceptual acuity, valuing intercultural teamwork/collaboration)?*

Kathryn Erskine: Absolutely. I would never hire someone who has only worked in Paris and send them to Yemen or Afghanistan, for example. One of the bullets on our "Required Skills" section is "experience living in a non-permissive or conflict environment." And during the interview process, questions are always asked about the candidate's level of understanding of the culture, their comfort living in difficult environments, and how they manage stress in challenging environments. Anthropologists often have a deep appreciation and knowledge about where they are working and how best to succeed there, and because of this appreciation and knowledge, they are more comfortable.

Question 5: *When filling overseas positions, how important is knowledge about the culture(s) and language(s) found in the project areas?*

Kathryn Erskine: A typical project has 3 expats and 100 local staff, so the imbalance of the cultures is heavily weighted toward the culture in which we are working. In this context, cultural sensitivity is critical to the success of a project. No matter how skilled expats might be technically, if they do not understand, respect and trust the culture in which they are working, the project will be a failure (personal communication).

(Continued)

Want to Work in an International Economic Development Program? (*Continued*)

What should we take away from this interview? Essentially, this human resources expert, Kathryn Erskine, who has an MA in Latin American Studies from American University, reminds us that you do not need to have a BA, MA, or even a PhD in anthropology to be an effective economic development program officer. What you do need, however, are the cross-cultural sensitivities, skills, and understandings that one can develop in a number of different ways, but can acquire more effectively through the formal study of anthropology than through any other discipline in academia.

Questions for Further Thought

1. In which US city do you think a company (like the one that employs Kathryn Erskine) is located? Why?
2. Other than technical competencies, what skill sets are most sought after when recruiting expatriate program officers for international development projects?
3. What are some ways (other than taking courses in anthropology) for becoming qualified to serve as a foreign development officer abroad? Be specific.

into less time spent with one's family and fewer social activities, which leads to a more balanced life and a healthier society. Moreover, working so hard to be able to afford a luxury like a Cadillac Escalade SUV is considered antisocial because driving this luxurious cousin of the military assault vehicle increases the cost of gasoline for everyone, destroys the environment quicker than a more conventional automobile, and essentially makes the statement that my vehicle, although keeping me and my children safe in the event of an accident, could kill you and your children. So, here are two radically different perceptions of the same behavior, one by Americans and one by Swedes. We are not arguing here that Americans need to give up their individualism or the high value some of them place on seventy-hour workweeks. Nor are we suggesting that Americans should agree with the typically Swedish interpretation. What is important, however, is that we learn to recognize the perceptions of other people, try to understand the reasons behind those perceptions, and acknowledge their right to have their perceptions.

The reason that most anthropologists since the nineteenth century have insisted on looking at the rationality of another culture within its proper cultural context is that it will enable us to better understand that culture. And when we reach this greater understanding, we will be in a position to interact with people more rationally, humanely, and collaboratively. The rationale behind a multicultural approach to dealing with the rest of the world is that it can lead to win-win

situations, whereby global solutions are likely to be more sustainable.

Multiculturalism remains the best hope for enabling all people to have the security, prosperity, and freedom they desire and deserve. And yet multiculturalism should not be seen as a totally selfless and altruistic philosophy. Rather it should be considered a win-win opportunity. Kishore Mahbubani (2005: 203–4) poignantly captures the value of multiculturalism in this parable:

> There was a farmer who grew award-winning corn. Each year he entered his corn in a state fair, where it won a blue ribbon. One year, a newspaper reporter interviewed him and learned something interesting about how he grew it. The reporter discovered that the farmer shared his seed corn with his neighbors. "How can you afford to share your best seed corn with your neighbors when they are entering corn in competition with yours each year?" the reporter asked. "Why sir," said the farmer, "didn't you know? The wind picks up pollen from the ripening corn and swirls it from field to field. If my neighbors grow inferior corn, cross-pollination will steadily degrade the quality of my corn. If I am to grow good corn, I must help my neighbors grow good corn."

Here is the point of this simple tale: The only way we can be safe and prosperous is if we enable our neighbors to be safe and prosperous as well.

Summary

1. Whereas previous states in China, India, and Mexico expanded their borders by conquering adjacent lands, European countries (especially Britain, France, Portugal, Spain, Belgium, and Holland) created global empires by both extending their territorial borders and increasing their control over societies in distant lands through technological advances in navigation, ship building, cartography, and warfare.

2. European colonization during the nineteenth century (involving the actual possession and administration of foreign territories) was perhaps the strongest influence on our present world order. Although colonization proved exceedingly beneficial for the economic and political growth of the European colonial powers, the indigenous populations paid a high price.

3. After many colonies won their political independence following World War II, the local populations were severely undereducated and undercapitalized. Many of these former colonies have remained among the poorest nations in the world. By a process known as *neocolonialism*, the wealthy nations continue to exercise considerable political, economic, financial, and military power over their former colonies.

4. The most significant recent trend is the rapid cross-national integration known as globalization, which involves the lowering of trade barriers and the rapid expansion of world markets, privatization, regional alliances, and information technology.

5. It is unreasonable to expect that the world, through the process of globalization, is moving relentlessly toward a single, benevolent, culturally homogeneous nation-state. Although some languages and cultures are becoming virtually extinct, other cultures and ethnic groups are experiencing a resurgence.

6. The basic trends of the post–World War II era that concern anthropologists are world immigration patterns; the rise of religious fundamentalism; rapid urbanization in Africa, Asia, and Latin America; the spread of world health pandemics such as AIDS; environmental degradation; and the widening gap between the rich and the poor throughout the world.

7. A major concern of anthropology in the last half-century has been sustainable economic development for the poor and marginalized peoples of the world. Because anthropologists study the alleged beneficiaries of economic development projects in a face-to-face way, they are in the best position to ascertain whether the projects are actually helping the local populations.

8. Development anthropologists look at the gap between the haves and the have-nots in terms of either *modernization theory* (the poor must strive to attain the cultural characteristics of the non-poor) or *world systems theory* (the exploitation of the poor by the rich is the main cause of the widening income gap).

9. Many of the anticipated benefits of economic development (rising incomes and GNPs) have turned out to be illusory or downright detrimental in terms of health, environmental degradation, dietary quality, family breakdown, and increasing social pathology.

10. Cultural anthropologists, through such organizations as Cultural Survival, work to help indigenous populations survive the onslaught of civilization and "economic progress."

11. A relatively new branch of applied cultural anthropology is environmental anthropology (described in Chapters 1 and 3), which focuses on the relationships among people, their culture, and their physical environment.

12. With the world and all of its five-thousand-plus cultural groups becoming increasingly interconnected, all nations must become more multicultural; that is, they must become more adept at understanding and dealing with people from different cultural traditions. If the world is to successfully meet the challenges of this century, people can no longer afford to have an us-versus-them mentality, because resolving our problems depends on cross-cultural understanding. And there is no academic discipline better equipped to provide cross-cultural understanding than anthropology.

Key Terms

colonialism

corvee labor

globalization

indigenous populations

less-developed countries (LDCs)

modernization theory

multiculturalism

multinational corporations

neocolonialism

world systems theory

Critical Thinking Questions

1. What examples of globalization can you cite (other than those given in this chapter), which affect the way that all people live their lives today that did not exist twenty-five years ago? Be specific.

2. Despite the preponderance of evidence that global warming is at least partially caused by human factors, the topic of global climate change is hotly debated in the United States. Why is there so much controversy over this topic?

3. This chapter has suggested that the world in the twenty-first century faces a number of challenges including global health pandemics, the widening gap between the have and the have-nots, environmental destruction, human rights violations, and the need for quality education and health care, to mention just some. Do you feel that your society (whichever one it is) has a moral obligation to contribute to the solution of these problems? What specifically can you do as an individual to help toward solving some of these problems?

Online Study Resources

CourseMate

Access chapter-specific learning tools including learning objectives, practice quizzes, videos, flash cards, glossaries, web links, and more in your Cultural Anthropology CourseMate. Login to www.cengagebrain.com to access the resources your instructor has assigned and to purchase materials.

Glossary

acculturation A specific form of cultural diffusion in which a subordinate culture adopts many of the cultural traits of a more powerful culture.

achieved status The status an individual acquires during the course of her or his lifetime.

adaptive nature of culture The implication that culture is the major way human populations adapt or relate to their specific habitat to survive and reproduce.

affinal relatives Kinship ties formed through marriage (that is, in-laws).

age grades Permanent age categories in a society through which people pass during the course of a lifetime.

age set A group of people roughly the same age who pass through various age grades together.

allocation of resources A society's regulation and control of such resources as land, water, and their by-products.

ambilineal descent A form of descent in which a person chooses to affiliate with a kin group through either the male or the female line.

ambilocal residence A residence pattern in which a married couple may choose to live with either the relatives of the wife or the relatives of the husband.

American historicism Headed by Franz Boas, a school of anthropology prominent in the first part of the twentieth century that insisted on the collection of ethnographic data (through direct fieldwork) before making cross-cultural generalizations.

analyzing data One of five stages of fieldwork in which the cultural anthropologist determines the meaning of data collected in the field.

ancestor worship The worship of deceased relatives; these souls are considered supernatural beings and fully functioning members of a descent group.

animatism The belief in a generalized, impersonal power over which people have some measure of control.

animism The belief that spiritual beings exist and that spirits also reside in plants, inanimate objects, and natural phenomena.

anthropological linguistics The scientific study of human communication within its sociocultural context.

applied anthropology The application of anthropological knowledge, theory, and methods to the solution of specific societal problems.

arbitrary nature of language The meanings attached to words in any language are not based on a logical or rational system but rather are arbitrary.

archaeology The subfield of anthropology that focuses on the study of prehistoric and historic cultures through the excavation of material remains.

arranged marriage A marriage in which the selection of the spouse is outside the control of the bride and groom.

artifact A type of material remain (found by archaeologists) that has been made or modified by humans, such as tools and arrowheads.

ascribed status The status a person has by virtue of birth.

assimilation The process of absorbing a racial or ethnic group into the wider society.

attitudinal data Information collected in a fieldwork situation that describes what a person thinks, believes, or feels.

authority The power or right to give commands, take action, and make binding decisions.

autocracy A form of government that is controlled by a leader who holds absolute power and denies popular participation in decision making.

avunculocal residence A residence pattern in which a married couple lives with or near the husband's mother's brother.

balanced reciprocity The practice of giving a gift with the expectation that a similar gift will be given in the opposite direction either immediately or after a limited period of time.

band societies The basic social units in many hunting-and-gathering societies; characterized by being kinship based and having no permanent political structure.

barbarism The middle of three basic stages of a nineteenth-century theory developed by Lewis Henry Morgan holding that all cultures evolve from simple to complex systems: savagery, barbarism, and civilization.

barter The direct exchange of commodities between people that does not involve standardized currency.

behavioral data Information collected in a fieldwork situation that describes what a person does.

bicultural perspective The capacity to think and perceive in the categories of one's own culture as well as in the categories of a second culture.

big men or **big women** Self-made leaders, found widely in Melanesia and New Guinea, who gain prominence by convincing their followers to contribute excess food to provide lavish feasts for the followers of other big men or big women.

bilateral descent A type of kinship system in which individuals emphasize both their mother's kin and their father's kin relatively equally.

binary oppositions A mode of thinking found in all cultures, according to Claude Lévi-Strauss, based on opposites, such as old–young, hot–cold, and left–right.

bound morpheme A morpheme that can convey meaning only when combined with another morpheme.

bourgeoisie Karl Marx's term for those who own the means of production.

breadwinner A traditional gender role in the United States that views males as being responsible for the economic support and protection of the family.

bride service Work or service performed for the bride's family by the groom for a specified period of time either before or after the marriage.

bridewealth Goods transferred from the groom's lineage to the bride's lineage to legitimize marriage.

capoeira A combination of dance, martial arts, and acrobatics that originated among African slaves brought to Brazil in the sixteenth century.

cargo cults Revitalization movements in Melanesia intended to bring new life and purpose to a society.

carrying capacity The maximum number of people a given society can support, given the available resources.

caste A rigid form of social stratification in which membership is determined by birth and social mobility is nonexistent.

census taking The collection of demographic data about the culture being studied.

chiefdoms An intermediate form of political organization in which integration is achieved through the office of chiefs.

chiefly redistribution or **tribute** The practice in which goods (usually food) are given to a chief as a visible symbol of people's allegiance, and then the chief gives the items back to the people (usually in the form of a feast).

civilization A term used by anthropologists to describe any society that has cities.

clans Unilineal descent groups, usually comprising more than ten generations, consisting of members who claim a common ancestry even though they cannot trace their exact connection back to that ancestor.

class A ranked group within a stratified society characterized by achieved status and considerable social mobility.

closed system of communication Communication in which the user cannot create new sounds or words by combining two or more existing sounds or words.

code switching The practice of adapting one's language depending on the social situation.

coercive theory of state formation The argument that the state came into existence as a direct result of warfare.

cognatic descent A form of descent traced through both females and males.

collaterality Kin relationships traced through a linking relative.

collecting data The stage of fieldwork that involves selecting data-gathering techniques and gathering information pertinent to the hypothesis being studied.

colonialism The political, economic, and sociocultural domination of a territory and its people by a foreign nation.

communal cults A type of religious organization in which groups of ordinary people conduct religious ceremonies for the well-being of the total community.

conflict theory A theory of social stratification that holds that social inequality is the result of benefits derived by the upper classes that use their power and privilege to exploit those below them.

consanguineal relatives One's biological or blood relatives.

contagious magic A form of magic based on the premise that things, once in contact with a person (such as a lock of hair), continue to influence that person after separation.

corporate lineages Kinship groups whose members engage in daily activities together.

corvee labor A system of required labor practiced during the colonial period.

council of elders A formal control mechanism composed of a group of elders who settle disputes among individuals in a society.

covens Local groups of witches that are often presided over by high priestesses.

crime Harm to a person or property that is considered illegitimate by society.

cross cousins Children of one's mother's brother or father's sister.

cult In the early anthropological literature, a nonjudgmental term that refers to a religious group that has its own set of beliefs, practices, and rituals. In popular discourse, a pejorative term referring to an antisocial group of religious extremists whose goal is mass suicide.

cultural anthropology The scientific study of cultural similarities and differences wherever and in whatever form they may be found.

cultural diffusion The spreading of a cultural trait (that is, a material object, idea, or behavior pattern) from one society to another.

cultural ecology An approach to anthropology that assumes that people who reside in similar environments are likely to develop similar technologies, social structures, and political institutions.

cultural emphasis of language The idea that the vocabulary in any language tends to emphasize words that are adaptively important in that culture.

cultural linguistics The study of the relationship between language and culture.

cultural materialism A contemporary orientation in anthropology holding that cultural systems are most influenced by such material things as natural resources and technology.

cultural relativism The idea that cultural traits are best understood when viewed within the cultural context of which they are a part.

cultural resource management A form of applied archaeology that involves identifying, evaluating, and sometimes excavating sites before roads, dams, and buildings are constructed.

cultural universals Those general cultural traits found in all societies of the world.

culture shock A psychological disorientation experienced when attempting to operate in a radically different cultural environment.

Dalit The politically correct term for those formerly called *Untouchables* in India.

dance Intentional, rhythmic, nonverbal body movements that are culturally patterned and have aesthetic value.

deductive approach The act or process of reasoning from general propositions to specific cases, used by the cultural anthropologists of the late nineteenth and early twentieth centuries.

degradation ceremonies Deliberate and formal societal mechanisms designed to publicly humiliate someone who has broken a social norm.

democracy A type of political system that involves popular participation in decision making.

Dengue fever An infectious tropical disease caused by the dengue virus that is transmitted by the mosquito *Aedes aegypti*. Dengue fever also is known as breakbone fever. Symptoms include a high fever, headache, muscle and joint pains, and a skin rash.

descent A person's kinship connections traced back through a number of generations.

descriptive linguistics The branch of anthropological linguistics that studies how languages are structured.

deviance The violation of a social norm.

diachronic analysis The analysis of data through time, rather than at a single point in time.

dialects Regional or class variations of a language that are sufficiently similar to be mutually intelligible.

diffusionism The spreading of a cultural trait (that is, material object, idea, or behavior pattern) from one society to another.

diglossia The situation in which two forms of the same language are spoken by people in the same language community at different times and places.

displacement The ability to talk about things that are remote in time and space.

division of labor The assignment of day-to-day tasks to the various members of a society.

divorce The legal and formal dissolution of a marriage.

document analysis Examination of data such as personal diaries, newspapers, colonial records, and so on.

double descent A system of descent in which individuals receive some rights and obligations from the father's side of the family and others from the mother's side.

double workload The situation in which employed married women, particularly those who have children, are both wage employed and primarily responsible for housework and child care.

doublespeak The use of euphemisms to confuse or deceive.

dowry Goods or money transferred from the bride's family to the groom or the groom's family to legalize or legitimize a marriage.

dowry death The killing of a wife by her in-laws if the wife's parents fail to pay additional dowry.

dysfunction Stress or imbalance caused by cultural traits within a cultural system.

ecclesiastical cults Highly complex religious organizations in which full-time clergy are employed.

ecofacts Physical remains—found by archaeologists—that were used by humans but not made or reworked by them (for example, seeds and bones).

economic anthropology A branch of anthropology that looks at systems of production, distribution, and consumption, wherever they may be found, but most often in the nonindustrialized world.

economics The academic discipline that studies systems of production, distribution, and consumption, typically in the industrialized world.

egalitarian societies Societies that recognize few differences in status, wealth, or power.

EGO The person in kinship diagrams from whose point of view the relationships are traced.

emic approach A perspective in ethnography that uses the concepts and categories that are relevant and meaningful to the culture under analysis.

enculturation The process by which human infants learn their culture.

endogamy A rule requiring marriage within a specified social or kinship group.

epidemiology The study of the occurrence, distribution, and control of disease in populations.

Eskimo (Inuit) system The kinship system most commonly found in the United States; associated with bilateral descent. Usually a mother, father, and their children live together.

ethnic group A group of people who share many of the same cultural features.

ethnocentrism The practice of viewing the customs of other societies in terms of one's own.

ethnographic fieldwork Research carried out by cultural anthropologists among living peoples in other societies and among subcultures of our own society.

ethnographic mapping A data-gathering tool that locates where the people being studied live, where they keep their livestock, where public buildings are located, and so on, to determine how that culture interacts with its environment.

ethnography A strategy of anthropological research, and an anthropological description of a particular contemporary culture by means of direct fieldwork.

ethnolinguistics The branch of anthropological linguistics that studies the relationship between language and culture.

ethnology The comparative study of cultural differences and similarities.

ethnomusicology The study of the relationship between music and other aspects of culture.

ethnoscience A theoretical school popular in the 1950s and 1960s that tries to understand a culture from the point of view of the people being studied.

etic approach A perspective in ethnography that uses the concepts and categories of the anthropologist's culture to describe another culture.

event analysis Photographic documentation of events such as weddings, funerals, and festivals in the culture under investigation.

evolutionism The nineteenth-century school of cultural anthropology, represented by Tylor and Morgan, that attempted to explain variations in world cultures by the single deductive theory that they all pass through a series of evolutionary stages.

exogamy A rule requiring marriage outside of one's own social or kinship group.

extended family The family that includes in one household relatives in addition to a nuclear family.

extramarital sexual activity Sexual activity outside marriage.

features Archaeological remains that have been made or modified by people and cannot easily be carried away, such as house foundations, fireplaces, and postholes.

female infanticide The killing of female infants.

femininity The social definition of femaleness, which varies from culture to culture.

feminist anthropology A theoretical approach that seeks to describe and explain cultural life from the perspective of women.

feminization of poverty The trend of women making up the world's poor; refers to the high proportion of female-headed families that live below the poverty line, which may result from the high proportion of women found in occupations associated with low prestige and income.

fictive kinship Relationships among individuals who recognize kinship obligations even though the relationships are not based on either consanguineal or affinal ties.

fieldnotes The daily descriptive notes recorded by an anthropologist during or after observing a specific phenomenon or activity.

fieldwork The practice in which an anthropologist is immersed in the daily life of a culture to collect data and test cultural hypotheses.

folklore Unwritten verbal arts that can take a variety of forms, such as myths, legends, proverbs, jokes, and folktales.

folktales Stories from the past that are instructive, entertaining, and largely secular.

food foraging A form of subsistence that relies on using animal and plant resources found in the natural environment (also called hunting and gathering).

foraging (hunting and gathering) A form of subsistence that relies on using animal and plant resources found in the natural environment.

formal economic theory Assumptions about economic behavior based on the experience of Western, industrialized economies.

formalism A school of economic anthropology that argues that the broad ideas of formal economic theory can serve as analytical tools to study any economic system.

free morpheme A morpheme that can convey meaning while standing alone without being attached to other morphemes.

French structuralism A theoretical orientation holding that cultures are the product of unconscious processes of the human mind.

functional unity A principle of functionalism stating that a culture is an integrated whole consisting of a number of interrelated parts.

functionalism/functional theory A theory of social stratification that holds that social inequality exists because it is necessary for the maintenance of society.

gender The roles, behaviors, and attributes a society considers appropriate for members of the two sexes.

gender ideology A system of thoughts and values that legitimizes sex roles, statuses, and customary behavior.

gender roles Expected ways of behaving based on a society's definition of masculinity and femininity.

gender stratification The hierarchical ranking of members of a society according to gender.

genderlects Linguistic differences in the ways in which men and women speak within their culture.

genealogical method A technique of collecting data in which the anthropologist writes down all the kin of an informant.

generalized reciprocity The practice of giving a gift without expecting a gift in return; creates a moral obligation.

genetics The study of inherited physical traits.

genocide The systematic annihilation of entire cultures or racial groups.

ghost invocation The practice of a living person (typically an elder) calling forth the wrath of ancestor-gods against an alleged sinner.

ghostly vengeance The punishment of sinners by ancestor-gods or ancestor-ghosts.

globalization The worldwide process, dating back to the 1989 fall of the Berlin Wall, that involves a revolution in information technology, a dramatic opening of markets, and the privatization of social services.

glottochronology The historical linguistic technique of determining the approximate date that two languages diverged by analyzing similarities and differences in their vocabularies.

grammar The systematic rules by which sounds are combined in a language to enable users to send and receive meaningful utterances.

graphic arts Forms of art that include painting and drawing on various surfaces.

headless societies Societies that have no political leaders, such as presidents, kings, or chiefs.

heterosexual Having a sexual attraction to people of the opposite sex.

historical linguistics The branch of anthropological linguistics that studies how languages emerge and change over time.

holism A perspective in anthropology that attempts to study a culture by looking at all parts of the system and how those parts are interrelated.

homosexual Having a sexual attraction to people of the same sex.

honor killing A euphemism referring to a practice found in various Middle Eastern cultures whereby women are killed by their own family members because they are thought to have dishonored the family.

horizontal function of kinship The ways in which all kinship systems, by requiring people to marry outside their own small kinship group, function to integrate the total society through marriage bonds between otherwise unrelated kin groups.

horticulture Small-scale crop cultivation characterized by the use of simple technology and the absence of irrigation.

housewife A traditional gender role in the United States that views females as responsible for child-rearing and domestic activities.

Human Relations Area Files (HRAF) The world's largest anthropological data retrieval system, used to test cross-cultural hypotheses.

human sexuality The sexual practices of humans, which vary from culture to culture.

Human Terrain System (HTS) A US Army, military intelligence support program in which personnel are hired from the social science disciplines—such as anthropology, sociology, political science, regional studies, and linguistics—to provide military commanders and staff with an understanding of the local population (that is, the "human terrain") in the regions in which they are deployed.

hydraulic theory of state formation The notion that early state systems of government arose because small-scale farmers were willing to surrender a portion of their autonomy to a large government entity in exchange for the benefits of large-scale irrigation systems.

hypothesis An educated hunch about the relationship among certain variables that guides a research project.

imitative magic A form of magic based on the idea that the procedure performed resembles the desired result; for example, sticking a doll-like image with pins will harm the person the doll represents.

incest taboo The prohibition of sexual intimacy between people defined as close relatives.

indigenous populations People who are the original inhabitants of a region, identify with a specific cultural heritage, and play no significant role in government.

individualistic cults The least complex type of religious organization in which each person is his or her own religious specialist.

inductive approach The act or process of reasoning that involves the development of general theories from the study of a number of specific cases; advocated by Franz Boas.

industrialization A process that results in the economic change from home production of goods to large-scale mechanized factory production.

infant mortality Infant death.

informant A person who provides information about his or her culture to the ethnographic fieldworker.

innovation A change brought about by the recombination of already existing items within a culture.

intensive agriculture A form of commodity production that requires intensive working of the land with plows and draft animals and the use of techniques of soil and water control.

intermediaries Mediators of disputes among individuals or families within a society.

interpreting data The stage of fieldwork, often the most difficult, in which the anthropologist searches for meaning in the data collected while in the field.

interpretive anthropology A contemporary theoretical orientation holding that the critical aspects of cultural systems are subjective factors such as values, ideas, and worldviews.

invention A new combination of existing cultural features.

Iroquois system A kinship system associated with unilineal descent in which the father and father's brother are called by the same term, as are the mother and the mother's sister.

jati Local subcastes found in Hindu India that are strictly endogamous.

kibbutz A communal farm or settlement in Israel.

kindred All the relatives a person recognizes in a bilateral kinship system.

kinship system Those relationships found in all societies that are based on blood or marriage.

kula ring A form of reciprocal trading found among the Trobriand Islanders involving the use of white shell necklaces and red shell bracelets.

labor specialization See *division of labor*.

language family A grouping of related languages.

law Cultural rules that regulate human behavior and maintain order.

legends Stories aimed at explaining local customs, which may or may not be based on historical fact.

Leopard-Skin Chief An intermediary between a murderer's family and the family of the victim; found among the Nuer of the African Sudan.

less developed countries (LDCs) Countries that have a relatively low gross national product and low annual family income.

levirate The practice of a man marrying the widow of a deceased brother.

liberation theater Theatrical production that uses high levels of audience participation and is aimed at bringing about social change.

liberation theology A form of Catholicism found throughout South and Central America in which priests and nuns are actively involved in programs that promote social justice for the poor.

lineage A unilineal descent group whose members can trace their line of descent back to a common ancestor.

lineality Kin relationships traced through a single line, such as son, father, and grandfather.

linked changes Changes in one part of a culture brought about by changes in other parts of the culture.

magic A system of supernatural beliefs that involves the manipulation of supernatural forces for the purpose of intervening in a wide range of human activities and natural events.

mahdist movements Revitalization movements in the Muslim world.

male gender bias A preference found in some societies for sons rather than daughters.

mana An impersonal supernatural force, inhabiting certain people or things, that is believed to confer power, strength, and success.

market exchange A mode of distribution in which goods and services are bought and sold and their value is determined by the principle of supply and demand.

masculinity The social definition of maleness, which varies from society to society.

matriarchy The rule or domination of women over men.

matrilineal descent A form of descent in which people trace their primary kin connections through their mothers.

matrilocal residence A residence pattern in which a married couple lives with or near the relatives of the wife.

mechanical solidarity A type of social integration based on mutuality of interests; found in societies with little division of labor.

millenarian movements Social movements by repressed groups of people who are looking forward to better times in the future.

modernization theory The idea that differences in economic development may be explained by inherent socio-cultural differences between the rich and the poor.

moieties Complementary descent groups that result from the division of a society into halves.

monochronic culture A culture in which people view time in a linear fashion, place great importance on being punctual and keeping on schedule, and prefer to work on one task at a time.

monogamy The marital practice of having only one spouse at a time.

monotheism The belief in only one god.

moots Informal hearings of disputes for the purpose of resolving conflicts; usually found in small-scale societies.

morphemes The smallest linguistic forms (usually words) that convey meaning.

morphology The study of the rules that govern how morphemes are formed into words.

multiculturalism A public policy philosophy that recognizes the legitimacy and equality of all cultures represented in a society.

multilinear evolution The mid-twentieth-century anthropological theory of Julian Steward, who suggested that specific cultures can evolve independently of all others even if they follow the same evolutionary process.

multinational corporations Large corporations that have economic operations in a number of different countries throughout the world.

myths Stories that transmit culturally meaningful messages about the universe, the natural and supernatural worlds, and a person's place within them.

nation A group of people who share a common identity, history, and culture.

nativistic movement A religious force for social change found among American Indians.

negative reciprocity A form of economic exchange between individuals who try to take advantage of each other.

negative sanctions Punishment for violating the norms of a society.

neocolonialism The process of developed nations continuing to exert economic, political, and military influence over less developed countries, even though the official period of colonization ended in the 1960s.

neoevolutionism A twentieth-century school of cultural anthropology, represented by White and Steward, that attempted to refine the previous evolutionary theories of Tylor and Morgan.

neolithic revolution A stage in human cultural evolution (beginning around ten thousand years ago) characterized by the transition from hunting and gathering to the domestication of plants and animals.

neolocal residence A residence pattern in which a married couple has its own place of residence apart from the relatives of either spouse.

nomadism The movement pattern of pastoralists that involves the periodic migration of human populations in search of food or pasture for livestock.

nonverbal communication The various means by which humans send and receive messages without using words (for example, gestures, facial expressions, and touching).

nuclear family The most basic family unit, composed of wife, husband, and children.

nutritional deprivation A form of child abuse involving withholding food; can retard learning, physical development, and social adjustment.

oath A declaration to a god to attest to the truth of what a person says.

obtrusive effect The presence of the researcher causes people to behave differently than they would if the researcher was not present.

occupational segregation The separation of different occupations in a society.

open system of communication Communication in which the user can create new sounds or words by combining two or more existing sounds or words.

optimal foraging theory A theory that foragers choose those species of plants and animals that maximize their caloric intake for the time spent hunting and gathering.

ordeal A painful and possibly life-threatening test inflicted on someone suspected of wrongdoing to determine guilt or innocence.

organic analogy The early functionalist idea that cultural systems are integrated into a whole cultural unit in much the same way that the various parts of a biological organism (such as a respiratory system or a circulatory system) function to maintain the health of the organism.

organic solidarity A type of social integration based on mutual interdependence; found in societies with a relatively elaborate division of labor.

paleoanthropology The study of human evolution through fossil remains.

paleopathology The study of disease in prehistoric populations.

pan-tribal mechanisms Mechanisms such as clans, age grades, and secret societies found in tribal societies that cut across kinship lines and integrate all the local segments of the tribe into a larger whole.

parallel cousins Children of one's mother's sister or father's brother.

participant-observation A fieldwork method in which the cultural anthropologist lives with the people under study and observes their everyday activities.

participatory action research A mode of research whereby the anthropologist and the community work together to understand the conditions that produce the community's problems to find solutions to those problems.

pastoralism A food-getting strategy based on animal husbandry; found in regions of the world that are generally unsuited for agriculture.

patrilineal descent A form of descent in which people trace their primary kin relationships through their fathers.

patrilocal residence A residence pattern in which a married couple lives with or near the relatives of the husband's father.

peasantry Rural peoples, usually on the lowest rung of society's ladder, who provide urban inhabitants with farm products but have little access to wealth or political power.

per capita gross national income A commonly used index of relative wealth among nations calculated by adding the output of goods and services in a country to the income of residents and dividing the sum by the total population.

phonemes The smallest units of sound in a language that distinguish meaning.

phonology The study of a language's sound system.

photography The use of a camera or video camera to document the ecology, material culture, and even social interactions of people during ethnographic fieldwork.

phratries Unilineal descent groups composed of related clans.

physical anthropology (biological anthropology) The subfield of anthropology that studies both human biological evolution and contemporary physical variations among peoples of the world.

plastic arts Artistic expression that involves molding certain forms, such as sculpture.

pluralistic societies Societies composed of a number of different cultural or subcultural groups.

political coerciveness The capacity of a political system to enforce its will on the general population.

political ecology Political ecology examines how unequal relations in and among societies affect the use of the natural environment and its resources, especially in the context of wide ranging ecological settings, and subsequent economic, policy, and regulatory actions.

political economy Political economy at its core examines the abstract issues of conflict, ideology and power.

political integration The process that brings disparate people under the control of a single political system.

polyandry The marriage of a woman to two or more men at the same time.

polychronic culture A culture in which people typically perform a number of tasks at the same time and place a higher value on nurturing and maintaining social relationships than on punctuality for its own sake.

polygyny The marriage of a man to two or more women at the same time.

polytheism The belief in more than one god.

population biology The study of the interrelationships between population characteristics and environments.

population transfer The physical relocation of a minority group from one area to another.

positive sanctions A mechanism of social control for enforcing a society's norms through rewards.

positivism A philosophical system based on observable scientific facts and their relationship to one another.

postmodernism A school of anthropology that advocates the switch from cultural generalization and laws to description, interpretation, and the search for meaning.

postpartum sex taboo The rule that a husband and wife must abstain from any sexual activity for a period of time after the birth of a child.

potlatch A competitive giveaway found among American Indians from the Northwest Coast that serves as a mechanism for both achieving social status and distributing goods.

power The capacity to produce intended effects for oneself, other people, social situations, or the environment.

praxis Integrating theory with practice and serves as a means to produce new knowledge.

preferential cousin marriage A marriage between either parallel or cross cousins.

prestige Social honor or respect.

prestige economies A category of economic institutions, such as the potlatch and big men or big women, in which wealth is distributed and prestige and status are thereby conferred.

primatology The study of nonhuman primates in their natural environments for the purpose of gaining insights into the human evolutionary process.

primogeniture The exclusive right of the eldest child (usually the son) to inherit his father's estate.

problem-oriented research A type of anthropological research designed to solve a particular societal problem rather than to test a theoretical position.

production The process whereby goods are obtained from the natural environment and altered to become consumable goods for society.

Project Camelot An aborted US Army research project designed to study the cause of civil unrest and violence in developing countries; created a controversy among anthropologists about whether the US government was using them as spies.

proletariat The term used in the conflict theory of social stratification to describe the working class who exchange their labor for wages.

property rights The Western concept of individual ownership in which rights and obligations to land, livestock, or material possessions reside with the individual rather than with a wider group.

proxemic analysis The study of how people in different cultures use space.

psychic unity A concept popular among some nineteenth-century anthropologists who assumed that all people, when operating under similar circumstances, will think and behave in similar ways.

psychological anthropology The subdiscipline of anthropology that looks at the relationships among cultures and such psychological phenomena as personality, cognition, and emotions.

public opinion What the general public thinks about some issue; when public opinion is brought to bear on an individual, it can influence his or her behavior.

purdah The Hindu or Muslim system of sex segregation, which keeps women in seclusion or requires them to wear clothing that conceals them completely.

qualitative data People's words, actions, records, and accounts obtained from participant-observation, interviews, group interviews, and relevant documents.

quantitative data The data that are counted and interpreted through statistical analyses.

race A subgroup of the human population whose members share a greater number of genes and physical traits with one another than they do with members of other subgroups.

rank societies Societies in which people have unequal access to prestige and status but not unequal access to wealth and power.

rebellion An attempt within a society to disrupt the status quo and redistribute the power and resources.

reciprocal exchange The equal exchange of gifts between the families of both the bride and groom to legitimize a marriage.

reciprocity A mode of distribution characterized by the exchange of goods and services of approximately equal value between parties.

redistribution A mode of distribution in which goods and services are given by members of a group to a central authority (such as a chief) and then distributed back to the donors, usually in the form of a feast.

reflexive or narrative ethnography A type of ethnography, associated with postmodernism, that focuses more on the interaction between the ethnographer and the informant than on scientific objectivity.

religion A set of beliefs in supernatural forces that functions to provide meaning, peace of mind, and a sense of control over unexplainable phenomena.

religious nationalism A trend toward merging traditional religious principles with the workings of government.

reproductive technologies Recent developments, such as in vitro fertilization, surrogate motherhood, and sperm banks, that make the reckoning of kin relationships more complex.

research clearance Permission from the host country in which fieldwork is to be conducted.

research design The overall strategy for conducting research.

research proposal A written proposal required for funding anthropological research that spells out in detail a research project's purpose, hypotheses, methodology, and significance.

revitalization movements Religious movements designed to bring about a new way of life within a society.

revolution An attempt to overthrow the existing form of political organization, the principles of economic production and distribution, and the allocation of social status.

rites of passage Ceremonies that celebrate the transition of a person from one social status to another.

rites of solidarity Ceremonies performed for the sake of enhancing social integration among groups of people.

role ambiguity Confusion about how one is expected to behave.

sanctions Any means used to enforce compliance with the rules and norms of a society.

Sanskritization A form of upward social mobility found in contemporary India whereby people born into lower castes can achieve higher status by taking on some of the behaviors and practices of the highest (Brahmin) caste.

Sapir–Whorf hypothesis The notion that a person's language shapes her or his perceptions and view of the world.

savagery The first of three basic stages of cultural evolution in the theory of Lewis Henry Morgan; based on hunting and gathering.

segmentation The process that takes place within a lineage whereby small subdivisions of a lineage oppose one another in some social situations but coalesce and become allies in other social situations.

separatist Christian churches Small-scale churches that break away from the dominant church to gain greater political, economic, social, and religious autonomy.

serial monogamy The practice of having a succession of marriage partners, but only one at a time.

sex The biological or genetic differences between males and females.

sexual asymmetry The universal tendency of women to be in a subordinate position in their social relationships with men.

sexual dimorphism The difference inform between men and women.

shaman A part-time religious specialist who is thought to have supernatural powers by virtue of birth, training, or inspiration.

shamanistic cults A type of religious organization in which part-time specialists called shamans intervene with the deities on behalf of their clients.

shifting cultivation (swidden cultivation, slash-and-burn method) A form of plant cultivation in which seeds are planted in fertile soil prepared by cutting and burning the natural growth; relatively short periods of cultivation are followed by longer fallow periods.

silent trade A form of trading found in some small-scale societies in which the trading partners have no face-to-face contact.

small-scale society A society that has a relatively small population, has minimal technology, is usually preliterate, has little division of labor, and is not highly stratified.

social control Mechanisms found in all societies that function to encourage people not to violate the social norms.

social mobility The ability of people to change their social position within society.

social norms Expected forms of behavior.

socialization Teaching young people the norms in a society.

sociolinguistics The branch of anthropological linguistics that studies how language and culture are related and how language is used in different social contexts.

soft money A form of political contribution not covered by federal regulation, which works to the advantage of wealthy candidates and their benefactors.

song duel A means of settling disputes over wife stealing among the Inui involving a public contest of derisive songs and lyrics.

sorcery The performance of certain magical rites for the purpose of harming other people.

sororate The practice of a woman marrying the husband of her deceased sister.

specialized political roles Specific tasks expected of a person or group, such as law enforcement, tax collection, dispute settlement, recruitment of labor, and protection from outside invasions.

standardized currency (money) A medium of exchange that has well-defined and understood value.

state A particular type of political structure that is hierarchical, bureaucratic, centralized, and has a monopoly on the legitimate use of force to implement its policies.

state system of government A bureaucratic, hierarchical form of government composed of various echelons of political specialists.

stock friendship A gift of livestock from one man to another to strengthen their friendship.

stratified societies Societies characterized by considerable inequality in all forms of social rewards—that is, power, wealth, and prestige.

structural functionalism A school of cultural anthropology, associated most closely with Radcliffe-Brown, that examines how parts of a culture function for the well-being of the society.

structured interview An ethnographic data-gathering technique in which large numbers of respondents are asked a set of specific questions.

subculture A subdivision of a national culture that shares some features with the larger society and also differs in some important respects.

substantivism A school of economic anthropology that seeks to understand economic processes in their role of maintaining an entire cultural order; often used when examining nonindustrial cultures.

supernatural belief systems A set of beliefs in forces that transcend the natural, observable world.

symbol Something, either verbal or nonverbal, that stands for something else.

synchronic analysis The analysis of data at a single point in time, rather than through time.

syntax The linguistic rules, found in all languages, that determine how phrases and sentences are constructed.

theory A general statement about how two or more facts are related.

transformational The quality of an artistic process that converts an image into a work of art.

transhumance The movement pattern of pastoralists in which some of the men move livestock seasonally.

tribal societies Small-scale societies composed of autonomous political units and sharing common linguistic and cultural features.

tribute See *chiefly redistribution.*

unilineal descent Descent traced through a single line (such as matrilineal or patrilineal) rather than through both sides (bilateral descent).

unilinear evolution A theory held by anthropologists such as Tylor and Morgan that attempts to place particular cultures into specific evolutionary stages.

universal evolution White's approach to cultural evolution, which developed laws that apply to culture as a whole and argued that all human societies pass through similar stages of development.

universal functions The functionalist idea that every part of a culture has a particular function.

universal male dominance The notion that men are more powerful and influential than women in all societies.

unstructured interview An ethnographic data-gathering technique—most often used in the early stages of fieldwork—in which interviewees are asked to respond to broad, open-ended questions.

varnas Caste groups in Hindu India that are associated with certain occupations.

vertical function of kinship The way in which all kinship systems tend to provide social continuity by binding together different generations.

vision quest A ritual found in some Plains Indian cultures wherein, through visions, people establish special relationships with spirits who provide them with knowledge, power, and protection.

voluntaristic theory of state formation The theory that stable systems of state government arose because people voluntarily surrendered some of their autonomy to the state in exchange for certain benefits.

warfare Institutionalized, armed conflict between nation-states or other politically distinct groups.

wealth The material objects that have value in a society.

Wicca A modern-day movement of witches and pagans.

witchcraft The use of inborn, involuntary, and often unconscious powers to cause harm to other people.

world systems theory The idea that differences in economic development may be explained by the exploitation of the poor by the rich nations of the world.

References

Abdo, Geneive. 2004. "Muslim Rap Finds Its Voice." *Chicago Tribune* (June 30): 1.

Abraham, Ebenezer Rajkumar, Sethumadhavan Ramachandran, and Velraj Ramalingam. 2007. "Biogas: Can It Be an Important Source of Energy?" *Environmental Science and Pollution Research* 14(1): 67–71.

Adams, Bert, and Edward Mburugu. 1994. "Kikuyu Bridewealth and Polygyny Today." *Journal of Comparative Family Studies* 25(2): 159–66.

Agosin, Marjorie. 1987. *Scraps of Life: Chilean Arpilleras.* Toronto: William Wallace Press.

Agyekum, Kofi. 2002. "Menstruation as a Verbal Taboo among the Akan of Ghana." *Journal of Anthropological Research* 58(3): 367–87.

Albright, Madeleine. 2009. *Read My Pins: Stories from a Diplomat's Jewel Box.* New York: HarperCollins, 2009.

Amadiume, I. 1987. *Male Daughters, Female Husbands.* London: Zed Books.

American Anthropological Association. http://www.aaanet.org.

American Anthropological Association Statement on Race. 1998. http://www.aaanet.org/stmts/racepp.htm.

American Medical Association. 2002. http://www.ama-assn.org/ama/pub/category/4867.html.

———. 2008. http://www.ama-assn.org/ama/pub/category/12912.html.

Anderson, Richard L. 2003. *Calliope's Sisters: The Role of Art in Human Thought,* 2nd ed. Upper Saddle River, NJ: Prentice Hall.

Andreatta, Susan L. 1998. "Agrochemical Exposure and Farmworker Health in the Caribbean: A Local/Global Perspective." *Human Organization* 57(3): 350–58.

Andreatta, Susan L., and Anne Parlier. 2010. "The Political Ecology of Small-Scale Commercial Fishermen in Carteret County, North Carolina." *Human Organization* 69(2): 180–91.

"Aral Sea Almost Dried Up: UN Chief Calls It 'Shocking Disaster.'" http://www.huffingtonpost.com/2010/04/04/aral-sea-almost-dried-up_n_524697.html.

Aunger, Robert. 2000. "The Life History of Culture Learning in a Face-to-Face Society." *Ethos* 28(3): 445–81.

Bailey, Benjamin. 1997. "Communication of Respect in Interethnic Service Encounters." *Language and Society* 26(3): 327–56.

Bakhshi, Vicki. 1999. "Gender Inequality Persists Without Exception." *Financial Times* (July 12): 4.

Balsam, John, and Dave Ryan. 2006. *Anaerobic Digestion of Animal Waste: Factors to Consider* (a publication of the National Sustainable Agriculture Information Services). Washington, DC: National Center for Appropriate Technology.

Balzer, Marjorie. 1993. "Two Urban Shamans." In *Perilous States: Conversations Amid Uncertain Transitions.* G. Marcus, ed., pp. 131–64. Chicago: University of Chicago Press.

Bamberger, Joan. 1974. "The Myth of Matriarchy: Why Men Rule in Primitive Society." In *Women, Culture and Society.* Michelle Zimbalist Rosaldo and Louise Lamphere, eds., pp. 263–80. Stanford, CA: Stanford University Press.

Barber, Benjamin. 1996. *Jehad and McWorld.* New York: Ballantine Books.

Barfield, Thomas. 1993. *The Nomadic Alternative.* Englewood Cliffs, NJ: Prentice Hall.

Barker, Holly. 2004. *Bravo for the Marshallese: Regaining Control in a Post-Nuclear, Post-Colonial World.* Belmont, CA: Wadsworth.

Barkun, Michael. 2000. "Millennialists and the State: Reflections After Waco." In *Conflict and Conformity: Readings in Cultural Anthropology,* 10th ed. James Spradley and David McCurdy, eds., pp. 332–40. Boston: Allyn & Bacon.

Barnes, Sandra T. 1990. "Women, Property, and Power." In *Beyond the Second Sex: New Directions in the Anthropology of Gender.* Peggy Reeves Sanday and Ruth G. Goodenough, eds., pp. 253–80. Philadelphia: University of Pennsylvania Press.

Barrett, Richard A. 1991. *Culture and Conduct: An Excursion in Anthropology,* 2nd ed. Belmont, CA: Wadsworth.

Barrett, Stanley. 1996. *Anthropology: A Student's Guide to Theory and Methods.* Toronto: University of Toronto Press.

Barrionuevo, Alexei. 2008. "A Tribe in Brazil Struggles at the Intersection of Drugs and Cultures." *New York Times* (December 6).

Barry, Dave. 1987. "Europe on Five Vowels a Day." *Miami Herald Tropic Magazine* (February 1): 7.

Barua, D. C. 2006. "Five Cents a Day: Innovative Programs for Reaching the Destitute with Microcredit, No-Interest Loans, and Other Instruments: The Experience of Grameen Bank." Global Microcredit Summit, Nova Scotia, Canada. http://www.microcreditsummit.org/papers/Workshops/7_Barua.pdf (accessed January 20, 2008).

Basso, Keith H. 1970. "'To Give Up on Words': Silence in Western Apache Culture." *Southwestern Journal of Anthropology* 26(3): 213–30.

Bauer, Jill. 2007. "Catching You a Catch Will Cost $$$." *Miami Herald* (October 27): E-l.

Beals, Alan. 1962. *Gopalpur: A South Indian Village.* New York: Holt, Rinehart & Winston.

Beals, Ralph L., Harry Hoijer, and Alan R. Beals. 1977. *An Introduction to Anthropology,* 5th ed. New York: Macmillan.

Beattie, John. 1960. *Bunyoro: An African Kingdom.* New York: Holt, Rinehart & Winston.

———. 1964. *Other Cultures: Aims, Methods, and Achievements in Social Anthropology.* New York: Free Press.

Beck, Casey, and Austin Blair. 2008. "Inundation." *Cultural Survival Quarterly* 32(2).

Beckerman, Stephen, and Paul Valentine. 2002. *Cultures of Multiple Fathers: The Theory and Practice of Partible Paternity in Lowland South America.* Gainesville: University Press of Florida.

Behar, Ruth. 1993. *Translated Woman: Crossing the Border with Esperanza 's Story.* Boston: Beacon Press.

Belson, Ken. 2004. "No, You Can't Walk and Talk at the Same Time." *New York Times* (August 29): 4.

Benedict, Ruth. 1934. *Patterns of Culture.* Boston: Houghton Mifflin.

———. 1946. *The Chrysanthemum and the Sword.* Boston: Houghton Mifflin.

Benet, Sula. 1976. *How to Live to Be a Hundred: The Lifestyle of the People of the Caucasus.* New York: Dial Press.

Bensman, Joseph, and Arthur Vidich. 1987. *American Society: The Welfare State and Beyond,* rev. ed. South Hadley, MA: Bergin & Garvey.

Berger, Joseph. 2005. "NooYawkese? Forget About It. The Dialect Today Is Global." *New York Times* (January 30).

Berman, Russell A. 2004. "Differences in American and European Worldviews." *Commentary* 117(2): 73.

Bernard, H. Russell. 1988. *Research Methods in Cultural Anthropology.* Newbury Park, CA: Sage Publications.

Bernstein, Nina. 2009. "Difficult Adjustment." *New York Times* (July 24): 15.

Besteman, Catherine, and Hugh Gusterson, eds. 2005. *Why America's Top Pundits Are Wrong: Anthropologists Talk Back.* Berkeley: University of California Press.

Betzig, Laura. 1988. "Redistribution: Equity or Exploitation?" In *Human Reproductive Behavior: A Darwinian Perspective.* Laura Betzig, M. B. Mulder, and Paul Türke, eds., pp. 49–63. Cambridge: Cambridge University Press.

Bilefsky, Dan. 2010. "Walls, Real and Imagined, Surround the Roma in Slovakia." *New York Times* (April 3): A-4.

Binford, Lewis. 1980. "Willow Smoke and Dogs' Tails: Hunter-Gatherer Settlement Systems and Archaeological Site Formation." *American Antiquity* 45(1): 4–20.

Bird, S. Elizabeth, and Carolena Von Trapp. 1999. "Beyond Bones and Stones." *Anthropology Newsletter* 40(9): 9–10.

Birket-Smith, K. 1959. *The Eskimos,* 2nd ed. London: Methuen.

Blanchard, Kendall. 1975. "Changing Sex Roles and Protestantism among the Navajo Women in Ramah." *Journal for the Scientific Study of Religion* 14(1): 43–50.

Boal, Augusto. 1979. *Theater of the Oppressed.* London: Pluto Press.

Boas, Franz. 1911a. *Handbook of American Indian Languages.* Bureau of American Ethnology. Bulletin 40.

———. 1911b. *The Mind of Primitive Man.* New York: Macmillan.

———. 1919. "Correspondence: Scientists as Spies." *The Nation* (December 20): 797.

Bodley, John. 2007. *Anthropology and Contemporary Human Progress.* Lanham, MD: AltaMira Press.

———. 2008. *Victims of Progress,* 5th ed. Lanham, MD: AltaMira Press.

Bohannan, Paul, and Philip Curtin. 1988. *African and Africans.* Prospect Heights, IL: Waveland Press.

Borden, Teresa. 2004. "In Chiapas, Cola Is Eng." *Atlanta Journal Constitution* (April 14): F-1.

Boroditsky, Lera. 2009. "How Does Our Language Shape the Way We Think?" In *What's Next: Dispatches on the Futures of Science.* Max Brockman, ed., pp. 116–29. New York: Vintage Books.

Bossen, Laurel H. 1984. *The Redivision of Labor: Women and Economic Choice in Four Guatemalan Communities.* Albany: State University of New York Press.

Bowen, Elenore Smith. 1964. *Return to Laughter.* Garden City, NY: Doubleday.

Boyd, Robert S. 2003. "A Case of He Wrote, She Wrote." *Charlotte Observer* (May 25): 7A.

Brady, Ivan. 1998. "Two Thousand and What? Anthropological Moments and Methods for the Next Century." *American Anthropologist* 100(2): 510–16.

Brettell, Caroline B., and Carolyn Sargent. 2005. *Gender in Cross-Cultural Perspective,* 4th ed. Upper Saddle River, NJ: Prentice Hall.

Brewer, Jeffrey D. 1988. "Traditional Land Use and Government Policy in Bima, East Sumbawa." In *The Real and Imagined Role of Culture in Development: Case Studies from Indonesia.* Michael R. Dove, ed., pp. 119–35. Honolulu: University of Hawaii Press.

Brooke, James. 1990. "Brazil Blows Up Miners' Airstrip, Pressing Its Drive to Save Indians." *New York Times* (May 23).

———. 2005. "Here Comes the Japanese Bride, Looking Very Western." *New York Times* (July 8): A-4.

Brown, Cecil. 2006. "Prehistoric Chronology of the Common Bean in the New World: The Linguistic Evidence." *American Anthropologist* 108(3): 506–16.

Brown, Donald E. 1991. *Human Universals.* New York: McGraw-Hill.

———. 2004. "Human Universals, Human Nature & Human Culture." *Daedalus* 133(4): 47–54.

Brown, Judith. 1970. "A Note on the Division of Labor by Sex." *American Anthropologist* 72: 1073–78.

Buckley, Cara. 2007. "Gays Living in Shadows in New Iraq." *New York Times* (December 18): A-8.

Buckley, T. 1993. "Menstruation and the Power of Yurok Women." In *Gender in Cross-Cultural Perspective.* Caroline B. Brettell and Carolyn F. Sargent, eds., pp. 133–48. Englewood Cliffs, NJ: Prentice Hall.

Bumiller, Elisabeth. 2010. "Female Troops Form a Bond with Afghans." *New York Times* (May 30): A1.

Burns, John F. 1998. "Once Widowed in India, Twice Scorned." *New York Times* (March 29): Al.

Burton, M. L., L. A. Brudner, and D. R. White. 1977. "A Model of the Sexual Division of Labor." *American Ethnologist A:* 227–51.

Byatt, A. S. 2002. "What Is a European?" *New York Times Magazine* (October 13): 46–51.

Callender, Charles, and Lee Kochems. 1983. "North American Berdache." *Current Anthropology* 24: 443–56.

Campbell, Bernard G. 1979. *Mankind Emerging,* 2nd ed. Boston: Little, Brown.

Canedy, Dana. 2002. "Lifting Veil for Photo ID Goes Too Far, Driver Says." *New York Times* (June 27): A-l, 6.

Carneiro, Robert. 1970. "A Theory of the Origin of the State." *Science* (August 21): 733–38.

Carpenter, Edmund. 1973. *Eskimo Realities.* New York: Holt, Rinehart & Winston.

Casagrande, Joseph B. 1960. "The Southwest Project in Comparative Psycholinguistics: A Preliminary Report." In *Men and Cultures: Selected Papers of the Fifth International Congress of Anthropological and Ethnological Sciences.* Anthony F. C. Wallace, ed., pp. 777–82. Philadelphia: University of Pennsylvania Press.

Chagnon, Napoleon A. 1983. *Yanomamo: The Fierce People,* 3rd ed. New York: Holt, Rinehart & Winston.

———. 1992. *Yanomamo: The Last Days of Eden,* 5th ed. San Diego: Harcourt Brace Jovanovich.

Chambers, John, ed. 1983. *Black English: Educational Equity and the Law.* Ann Arbor, MI: Karoma Publishers.

Chambers, Keith, and Anne Chambers. 2001. *Unity of Heart: Culture and Change in a Polynesian Atoll Society.* Prospect Heights, IL: Waveland Press.

Chambers, Robert. 1994. "The Origins and Practices of Participatory Rural Appraisal." *World Development* 2(7): 953–69.

Chambers, Veronica, et al. 1999. "Latino America: Hispanics Are Hip, Hot, and Making History." *Newsweek* (July 12): 48.

Chance, Norman A. 1990. *The Inupiat and Arctic Alaska: An Ethnography of Development.* Fort Worth, TX: Holt, Rinehart & Winston.

Charle, Suzanne. 1999. "A Far Island of Cultural Survival." *New York Times* (July 25, section 2): 1, 28.

Chatters, Linda M., Robert Joseph Taylor, and Rukmalie Jayakody. 1994. "Fictive Kinship Relations in Black Extended Families." *Journal of Comparative Family Studies* 25.

Chayes, Sarah. 2007. "Scents and Sensibilities." *The Atlantic Monthly* (December). http://theatlantic.com/doc/print/200712/afghans (accessed February 23, 2008).

Chen, Pauline W. 2009. "Bridging the Culture Gap." *New York Times* (July 16).

Childe, V. Gordon. 1936. *Man Makes Himself.* London: Watts.

Chomsky, Noam. 1972. *Language and Mind.* New York: Harcourt Brace Jovanovich.

Chura, Hillary. 2006. "A Year Abroad (or 3) as a Career Move." *New York Times* (February 25): B-5.

Cipollone, Nick, Steven Hartman Keiser, and Shravan Vasishth, eds. 1998. *Language Files: Materials for an Introduction to Language and Linguistics,* 7th ed. Columbus: Ohio State University Press.

Coates, Melissa. 2005. "Trends in Degrees and Dissertations in Anthropology." *Anthropology News* 46(4): 9.

Cohen, Eugene N., and Edwin Eames. 1982. *Cultural Anthropology.* Boston: Little, Brown.

Cohen, Margot. 2009. "A Search for a Surrogate Leads to India." *New York Times* (October 8): 1-D.

Cohen, M. N., and G. J. Armelagos, eds. 1984. *Paleopathology at the Origins of Agriculture.* New York: Academic Press.

Cohen, Roger. 2006. "Vive La Dolce Vita." *New York Times* (April 16, section 4): 1.

Coleman, Richard P., and Lee Rainwater. 1978. *Social Standing in America.* New York: Basic Books.

Collier, Jane F., and J. Yanagisako, eds. 1987. *Gender and Kinship: Essays Toward a Unified Analysis.* Stanford, CA: Stanford University Press.

Collins, Robert J. 1992. *Japan-think Ameri-think.* New York: Penguin.

Condon, John. 1984. *With Respect to the Japanese: A Guide for Americans.* Yarmouth, MA: Intercultural Press.

Confessore, Nicholas. 2006. "Spoonfuls of Culture Help Medicine Go Down." *New York Times* (June 4): 37.

Coote, Jeremy, and Anthony Shelton, eds. 1992. *Anthropology, Art, and Aesthetics.* Oxford: Clarendon Press.

Corbett, Sara. 2008. "Can the Cellphone Help End Global Poverty?" *New York Times Magazine* (April 13): 34–41.

Counts, David. 1995. "Too Many Bananas, Not Enough Pineapples, and No Watermelon at All: Three Object Lessons in Living with Reciprocity." In *Annual Editions: Anthropology, 95/96.* Elvio Angeloni, ed., pp. 95–98. Guilford, CT: Dushkin.

Coutsoukis, Photius. 2010. "Nobel Prizes by Country, Cumulative Prizes 1901–2009." http://www.photius.com/rankings/nobel_prizes_by_country_cummulative_1901_2009.html.

Cowan, Betty, and Jasbir Dhanoa. 1983. "The Prevention of Toddler Malnutrition by Home-Based Nutrition Education." In *Nutrition in the Community: A Critical Look at Nutrition Policy, Planning, and Programmes.* D. S. McLaren, ed., pp. 339–56. New York: Wiley.

Cox, Hillary. 2008. "The Tree of Life." *Cultural Survival Quarterly* 32(4).

Crampton, Thomas. 2003. "Cultural Gaffes: Bathing Rituals in Thai Village Aren't Always What They Seem." *International Herald Tribune* (September 27). http://www.iht.com/articles/2003/09/ 27rbath_ed3_.php.

Dahlberg, Frances. 1981. "Introduction." In *Woman the Gatherer.* New Haven, CT: Yale University Press.

Daly, Emma. 2005. "DNA Test Gives Students Ethnic Shocks" *New York Times* (April 3): A-18.

D'Antoni, Tom, and Alex Heard. 1998. "Subway Spirits." *New York Times Magazine* (October 25): 23.

Darian-Smith, Eve. 2004. *New Capitalists: Law, Politics, and Identity Surrounding Casino Gaming on Native American Land.* Belmont, CA: Wadsworth.

Dash, Eric. 2006. "Off to the Races Again, Leaving Many Behind." *New York Times* (April 9): 1.

Davis, Kingsley, and Wilbert Moore. 1945. "Some Principles of Stratification." *American Sociological Review* 10(April): 242–49.

———. 1988. "Wives and Work: A Theory of the Sex-Role Revolution and Its Consequences." In *Feminism, Children, and the New Families.* Sanford Dornbusch and Myra Strober, eds., pp. 67–86. New York: Guilford Press.

Davis, Shelton H. 1977. *Victims of the Miracle: Development and the Indians of Brazil.* Cambridge: Cambridge University Press.

Deardorff, Merle. 1951. "The Religion of Handsome Lake." In *Symposium on Local Diversity in Iroquois Culture.* W. N. Fenton, ed. Washington DC: Bureau of American Ethnology, Bulletin 149.

Dembo, Richard, Patrick Hughes, Lisa Jackson, and Thomas Mieczkowski. 1993. "Crack Cocaine Dealing by Adolescents in Two Public Housing Projects: A Pilot Study." *Human Organization* 52(1): 89–96.

Deng, Francis. 2009. *The Man Called Deng Majok: A Biography of Power, Polygyny, and Change.* Trenton, NJ: Red Sea Press.

DeVita, Philip R., ed. 1992. *The Naked Anthropologist: Tales from Around the World.* Belmont, CA: Wadsworth.

———. 2000. *Stumbling Toward Truth: Anthropologists at Work.* Prospect Heights, IL: Waveland Press.

DeVita, Philip R., and James D. Armstrong. 2001. *Distant Mirrors: America as a Foreign Culture.* Belmont, CA: Wadsworth.

Diamond, Jared. 1987. "The Worst Mistake in the History of the Human Race." *Discover* (May): 64–66.

———. 1995. "Easter's End." *Discover* (August).

———. 2001. "Death of Languages." *Natural History* (April): 30.

Digby-Clarke, Neil. 2007. "Marginalised Ju/'hoansi San at Nhoma Overcome Recent Setbacks." *Namibia Economist.* http://www.economist.com (accessed January 4, 2008).

Domhoff, G. William. 2009. *Who Rules America?* 6th ed. New York: McGraw-Hill.

Donnelly, John. 2006. "Study Suggests New HIV Infections Have Peaked." *Charlotte Observer* (March 3): 8A.

Dove, Michael R. 2009. "Dreams from His Mother." *New York Times* (August 11).

Downs, James F. 1971. *Cultures in Crisis.* Beverly Hills: Glencoe Press.

Dreifus, Claudia. 2001. "How Language Came to Be, and Change: A Conversation with John McWhorter." *New York Times News Brief* (October 30).

Dresser, Norine. 1996. *Multicultural Manners: New Rules of Etiquette for a Changing Society.* New York: Wiley.

Duncan, Greg J., Aletha C. Houston, and Thomas S. Weisner. 2007. *Higher Ground: New Hope for the Working Poor and Their Children.* New York: Russell Sage Foundation.

Dundes, Alan. 1965. "What Is Folklore?" In *The Study of Folklore.* Alan Dundes, ed. Englewood Cliffs, NJ: Prentice Hall.

Durkheim, Emile. 1933. *Division of Labor in Society* (G. Simpson, trans.). New York: Macmillan.

———. 2001. *The Elementary Forms of Religious Life* (Carol Cosman, trans.). Oxford: Oxford University Press (orig. 1912).

Dyson-Hudson, Rada, and Eric A. Smith. 1978. "Human Territoriality: An Ecological Reassessment." *American Anthropologist* 80: 21–41.

Dyson-Hudson, Rada, and Neville Dyson-Hudson. 1980. "Nomadic Pastoralism." *Annual Review of Anthropology* 9: 15–61.

Ebaugh, Helen Rose, and Mary Curry. 2000. "Fictive Kin as Social Capital in New Immigrant Communities." *Sociological Perspectives* 43(2): 189–209.

Eck, Diana. 2002. *A New Religious America: How a "Christian Country" Has Become the World's Most Religiously Diverse Nation.* San Francisco: Harper.

Eggan, Fred. 1950. *Social Organization of the Western Pueblos.* Chicago: University of Chicago Press.

Ekpo, Uwem F., Akin M. Omotayo, and Morenike A. Dipeolu. 2008. "Prevalence of Malnutrition among Settled Pastoral Fulani Children in Southwest Nigeria. *BMC Research Notes* 1: 7. http://ukpmc.ac.uk/classic/articlerender.cgi?artid=1628720 (accessed June 19, 2010).

Eller, Jack David. 2006. *Violence and Culture: A Cross-Cultural and Interdisciplinary Approach.* Belmont, CA: Wadsworth.

Emanuel, Kerry. 2009. "Phaeton's Reins: The Human Hand in Climate Change." In *World in Motion: The Globalization and the Environment Reader.* Gary M. Kroll and Richard H. Robbins, eds., pp. 168–85. Lanham, MD: AltaMira Press.

Ember, Carol R., and Melvin Ember. 2005. "Explaining Corporal Punishment of Children: A Cross Cultural Study." *American Anthropologist* 107(4): 609–19.

Erlanger, Steven. 2008. "100th Birthday Tributes Pour in for Levi-Strauss." *New York Times* (November 29).

Errington, Frederick, and Deborah Gewertz. 1987. *Cultural Alternatives and a Feminist Anthropology: An Analysis of Culturally Constructed Gender Interests in Papua New Guinea.* Cambridge: Cambridge University Press.

Ervin, Alexander M. 2005. *Applied Anthropology: Tools and Perspectives for Contemporary Practice.* Boston: Allyn & Bacon.

Etzioni, Amitai. 1993. "How to Make Marriage Matter." *Time* 142(10): 76.

European Commission. 2006. *Europeans and Their Languages* (Eurobarometer). http://ec.europa.eu/education/languages/pdf/doc62.

Evans-Pritchard, E. E. 1940. *The Nuer.* Oxford: Oxford University Press.

Everett, Margaret. 1998. "Latin America On-Line: The Internet, Development, and Democratization." *Human Organization* 57(4) (Winter): 385–93.

Faiola, Anthony. 2008. "Women Rise in Rwanda's Economic Revival." *Washington Post* (May 16). http://www.washingtonpost.com/wp-dyn/content/article/2008/05/15/AR2008051504035.html (accessed June 3, 2010).

Farb, Peter. 1968. "How Do I Know You Mean What You Mean?" *Horizon* 10(4): 52–57.

Faris, James C. 1972. *Nuba Personal Art.* Toronto: University of Toronto Press.

Fattah, Hassan M. 2007. "A Familiar Set Helps to Create a New Cultural Market." *New York Times* (August 2): A-4.

Fentiman, Alicia. 2009. "The Anthropology of Oil: The Impact of the Oil Industry on a Fishing Community in the Niger Delta." In *World in Motion: The Globalization and the Environment Reader.* Gary M. Kroll and Richard Robbins, eds., pp. 32–44. Lanham, MD: AltaMira Press.

Ferguson, B. 1984. "Re-examination of the Causes of Northwest Coast Warfare." In *Warfare, Culture, and Environment.* R. Ferguson, ed., pp. 267–328. New York: Academic Press.

Ferguson, Charles A. 1964. "Diglossia." In *Language in Culture and Society: A Reader in Linguistics and Anthropology.* Dell Hymes, ed., pp. 429–39. New York: Harper & Row.

Ferguson, R. Brian. 1995. *Yanomami Warfare: A Political History.* Santa Fe, NM: School of American Research Press.

Finke, Roger, and Rodney Stark. 2005. *The Churching of America, 1976–2005: Winners and Losers in Our Religious Economy.* New Brunswick, NJ: Rutgers University Press.

Finkelstein, Marni. 2005. *With No Direction Home: Homeless Youth on the Road and in the Streets.* Belmont, CA: Wadsworth.

Fish, Jefferson M. 1995. "Mixed Blood." *Psychology Today* 28(6) (November–December): 55–58, 60, 61, 76, 80.

Fishman, Charles. 2006. *The Wal-Mart Effect. How the World's Most Powerful Company Really Works—and How It's Transforming the American Economy.* New York. Penguin Press.

Forde, Daryll. 1967. "Double Descent Among the Yako." In *African Systems of Kinship and Marriage.* A. R. Radcliffe-Brown and Daryll Forde, eds., pp. 285–332. London: Oxford University Press (orig. 1950).

Fortes, M., and E. E. Evans-Pritchard. 1940. *African Political Systems.* London: Oxford University Press.

Fortmann, Louise. 1985. "The Tree Factor in Agroforestry with Particular Reference to Africa." *Agroforestry Systems* 2: 229–51.

Foster, George M. 1967. *Tzintzuntzan: Mexican Peasants in a Changing World.* Boston: Little, Brown.

———. 1973. *Traditional Societies and Technological Change,* 2nd ed. New York: Harper & Row.

Fox, Robin. 1967. *Kinship and Marriage: An Anthropological Perspective.* Baltimore: Penguin Books.

Freedman, Maurice. 1979. *The Study of Chinese Society: Essays by Maurice Freedman.* Stanford, CA: Stanford University Press.

Freedman, Samuel G. 2009. "Paganism, Just Another Religion for Military and Academia." *New York Times* (October 30).

French, Howard W. 2006. "In a Richer China, Billionaires Put Money on Marriage." *New York Times* (January 24): A-4.

———. 2007. "The Ship of State Shall Not Rock 'n' Roll." *New York Times* (October 25): A-4.

Fried, Morton H. 1967. *The Evolution of Political Society: An Essay in Political Anthropology.* New York: Random House.

Friedl, Ernestine. 1978. "Society and Sex Roles." *Human Nature* 1(4): 68–75.

Friedl, John, and John E. Pfeiffer. 1977. *Anthropology: The Study of People.* New York: Harper & Row.

Friedman, Thomas L. 1999a. *The Lexus and the Olive Tree.* New York: Farrar, Straus and Giroux.

———. 1999b. "Senseless in Seattle." *New York Times* (December 1): A-23.

———. 2002. "India, Pakistan, and G.E." *New York Times* (August 8): 13.

Fujita, Mariko, and Toshiyuki Sano. 2001. *Life in Riverfront: A Middle-Western Town Seen Through Japanese Eyes.* Belmont, CA: Wadsworth.

Fuller, Graham. 1999. "Islam Is the Answer to Indonesia's Crisis." *New Perspectives Quarterly* (Summer): 32–33.

Fuller, Thomas. 2007. "In Thai Cultural Battle, Name-Calling Is Encouraged." *New York Times* (August 29): A-4.

Galanti, Geri-Ann. 1991. *Caring for Patients from Different Cultures: Case Studies from American Hospitals.* Philadelphia: University of Pennsylvania Press.

Gallup. 2009. *State of the States: Importance of Religion* (January 28). gallup.com/poll/114022/state-states-importance-religion.aspx#1.

Gan, Lin, and Juan Yu. 2008. "Bioenergy Transition in Rural China: Policy Options and Co-benefits." *Energy Policy* 36(2): 531–40.

Gardner, R. Allen, and Beatrice T. Gardner. 1969. "Teaching Sign Language to a Chimpanzee." *Science* (August 15): 664–72.

Garfinkle, H. 1956. "Conditions of a Successful Degradation Ceremony." *American Journal of Sociology* 61: 420–24.

Garloch, Karen. 2006. "The Doctor Is in—Thailand." *Charlotte Observer* (December 10): 1.

Garson, Barbara. 2001. *Money Makes the World Go Around.* New York: Viking.

Geertz, Clifford. 1973. *The Interpretation of Cultures.* New York: Basic Books.

———. 1983. *Local Knowledge: Further Essays in Interpretive Anthropology.* New York: Basic Books.

Gibbs, James L. 1963. "The Kpelle Moot." *Africa* 33(1).

Gibson, Christina, and Thomas S. Weisner. 2002. "'Rational' and Ecocultural Circumstances of Program Take-up Among Low-Income Working Parents." *Human Organization* 61(2) (Summer): 154–66.

Gilbert, Dennis. 2008. *American Class Structure in an Age of Growing Inequality,* 7th ed. Belmont, CA: Wadsworth.

Gladwell, Malcolm. 2009. *What the Dog Saw.* New York: Little Brown.

Glossow, Michael. 1978. "The Concept of Carrying Capacity in the Study of Cultural Process." In *Advances in Archaeological Theory.* Michael Schiffler, ed., pp. 32–48. New York: Academic Press.

Gmelch, George. 1994a. "Lessons from the Field." In *Conformity and Conflict,* 8th ed. James P. Spradley and David McCurdy, eds., pp. 45–55. New York: HarperCollins.

———. 1994b. "Ritual and Magic in American Baseball." In *Conformity and Conflict,* 8th ed. James P. Spradley and David

McCurdy, eds., pp. 351–61. New York: HarperCollins.

Goldschmidt, Walter. 1979. "Introduction: On the Interdependence Between Utility and Theory." In *The Uses of Anthropology.* Walter Goldschmidt, ed. Washington, DC: American Anthropological Association.

Goldstein, Melvyn C. 1987. "When Brothers Share a Wife." *Natural History* 96(3): 39–48.

Goodall, Jane. 2005. *Harvest for Hope: A Guide to Mindful Eating.* New York: Warner Books.

Goode, William J. 1963. *World Revolution and Family Patterns.* New York: Free Press of Glencoe.

Goodenough, Ward H. 1956. "Componential Analysis and the Study of Meaning." *Language* 32: 195–216.

Goodman, Ellen. 2008. "Outsourcing Childbirth." *Charlotte Observer* (April 12): 13A.

Gorer, Geoffrey, and John Rickman. 1949. *The People of Great Russia.* London: Cresset.

Gottlieb, Alma. 1988. *Blood Magic: The Anthropology of Menstruation.* Berkeley: University of California Press.

Gough, Kathleen. 1959. "The Nayars and the Definition of Marriage." *Journal of the Royal Anthropological Institute* 89: 23–34.

Gouldner, Alvin. 1960. "The Norm of Reciprocity: A Preliminary Statement." *American Sociological Review* 25: 161–78.

Gray, J. Patrick, and Linda Wolfe. 1988. "An Anthropological Look at Human Sexuality." In *Human Sexuality,* 3rd ed. William H. Masters, Virginia E. Johnson, and Robert C. Kolodny, eds. Cambridge, MA: Addison-Wesley.

Gray, Robert F. 1960. "Sonjo Brideprice and the Question of African 'Wife Purchase.'" *American Anthropologist* 62: 34–57.

Gross, Daniel, and Barbara A. Underwood. 1971. "Technological Change and Caloric Costs: Sisal Agriculture." *American Anthropologist* 73(3): 725–40.

Guru, Gopal, and Shiraz Sidhva. 2001. "India's Hidden Apartheid." *UNESCO Courier* 54(9) (September): 27–29.

Gusterson, Hugh, and Catherine Besteman. 2005. "While We Were Sleeping." *Anthropology News* 46(4): 31.

Hall, Edward T. 1969. *The Hidden Dimension.* Garden City, NY: Doubleday.

Hall, Edward T., and Mildred R. Hall. 2009. "The Sounds of Silence." In *Classic Readings in Cultural Anthropology.* Gary Ferraro, ed., pp. 18–26. Belmont, CA: Wadsworth.

Hamamsy, Laila Shukry. 1957. "The Role of Women in a Changing Navaho Society." *American Anthropologist* 59(1): 101–11.

Hanna, Judith Lynne. 1979. *To Dance Is Human: A Theory of Nonverbal Communication.* Austin: University of Texas Press.

———. 2005. "Dance Speaks Out on Societal Issues." *Anthropology News* 46(4): 11–12.

Hardin, Garrett. 1968. "The Tragedy of the Commons." *Science* 162: 1243–48.

Harkin, Michael. 1998. "Whales, Chiefs, and Giants: An Exploration into Nuu-chah-nulth Political Thought." *Ethnology* 37(4): 317–32.

Harner, Michael J. 1973. "The Sound of Rushing Water." In *Hallucinogens and Shamanism.* Michael J. Harner, ed., pp. 15–27. New York: Oxford University Press.

Harris, Marvin. 1968. *The Rise of Anthropological Theory.* New York: Thomas Y. Crowell.

———. 1977. *Cannibals and Kings: The Origins of Culture.* New York: Random House.

———. 1979a. "Comments on Simoons' Questions in the Sacred Cow Controversy." *Current Anthropology* 20: 479–82.

———. 1979b. *Cultural Materialism: The Struggle for a Science of Culture.* New York: Random House.

———. 1979c. "The Yanomamo and the Cause of War in Band and Village Societies." In *Brazil: Anthropological Perspectives: Essays in Honor of Charles Wagley.* M. Margolis and W. Carter, eds., pp. 121–32. New York: Columbia University Press.

———. 1984. "A Cultural Materialist Theory of Band and Village Warfare: The Yanomamo Test." In *Warfare, Culture, and Environment.* R. B. Ferguson, ed., pp. 111–40. Orlando, FL: Academic Press.

———. 1999. *Theories of Culture in Postmodern Times.* Walnut Creek, CA: AltaMira Press.

Harris, Marvin, and Orna Johnson. 2003. *Cultural Anthropology,* 6th ed. Boston: Allyn & Bacon.

Hart, C.W.M., and Arnold R. Pilling. 1960. *The Tiwi of North Australia.* New York: Holt, Rinehart & Winston.

Hatch, Elvin. 1985. "Culture." In *The Social Science Encyclopedia.* Adam Kuper and Jessica Kuper, eds., p. 178. London: Routledge & Kegan Paul.

Hauswald, Lizbeth. 1987. "External Pressure/Internal Change: Child Neglect on the Navajo Reservation." In *Child Survival.* Nancy Scheper-Hughes, ed., pp. 145–64. Dordrecht, Holland: D. Reidel Publishing Company.

Hawkes, K., and J. O'Connell. 1981. "Affluent Hunters? Some Comments in Light of the Alyawara Case." *American Anthropologist* 83: 622–26.

Hecht, Michael L., Mary Jane Collier, and Sidney Ribeau. 1993. *African American Communication: Ethnic Identity and Cultural Interpretation.* Thousand Oaks, CA: Sage Publications.

Hecht, Robert M. 1986. "Salvage Anthropology: The Redesign of a Rural Development Project in Guinea." In *Anthropology and Rural Development in West Africa.* Michael M. Horowitz and Thomas M. Painter, eds., pp. 13–26. Boulder, CO: Westview Press.

Heider, Karl. 2006. *The Dugum Dani: A Papuan Culture in the Highlands of West New Guinea.* Piscataway, NJ: Aldine Transaction.

Heise, Lori, Mary Ellsberg, and Megan Gottemoeller. 1999. "Ending Violence Against Women." *Population Reports,* Series L, No. 11. http://info.k4health.org/pr/l11edsum.shtml (accessed July 14, 2010).

Hellinger, Daniel, and Dennis Judd. 1991. *The Demographic Facade.* Pacific Grove, CA: Brooks/Cole.

Herdt, Gilbert. 2006. *The Sambia: Ritual, Sexuality, and Change in Papua New Guinea*, 2nd ed. Belmont, CA: Cengage.

Hernandez, Daniel. 2003. "A Hybrid Ton-gue or Slanguage?" *Los Angeles Times* (December 27): A-l.

Hernandez Castillo, Rosalva A., and Ronald Nigh. 1998. "Global Processes and Local Identity Among Mayan Coffee Growers in Chiapas, Mexico." *American Anthropologist* 100(1): 136–47.

Hernandez Licona, Gonzalo. 2000. "Labor Market Transitions in Mexico: The Evolution of Household Businesses During Economic Crises." Paper delivered at conference, "Consequences of Financial Crises on Income: Distribution and Poverty in Latin America." Sponsored by ITAM (Instituto Tecnologico Autonomo de Mexico), May 19–20, 2000.

Herrnson, Paul S., Atiya Kai Stokes-Brown, and Matthew Hindman. 2007. "Campaign Politics and the Digital Divide: Constituency Characteristics, Strategic Considerations, and Candidate Internet Use in State Legislative Elections." *Political Research Quarterly* 60(1): 31–42.

Hersh, Seymour. 2004. "The Gray Zone: How a Secret Pentagon Program Came to Abu Ghraib." *The New Yorker* (May 24).

Herskovits, Melville. 1924. "A Preliminary Consideration of the Cultural Areas in Africa." *American Anthropologist* 26: 50–63.

———. 1967. *Dahomey: An Ancient West African Kingdom*, Vol. 1. Evanston, IL: Northwestern University Press (orig. 1938).

———. 1972. *Cultural Relativism: Perspectives in Cultural Pluralism*. New York: Vintage Books.

Hewlett, Barry, and Bonnie Hewlett. 2007. *Ebola, Culture, and Politics: The Anthropology of an Emerging Disease*. Belmont, CA: Wadsworth.

Hickerson, Nancy. 2000. *Linguistic Anthropology*, 2nd ed. Belmont, CA: Wadsworth.

Hicks, Kathryn, Nicole Fabricant, and Carlos Revilla. 2010. "The New Water Wars: Collective Action After Decentralization in El Alto, Bolivia." *Anthropology News* 51(1): 14–15.

Hill, Kim, Hillard Kaplan, Kristen Hawkes, and Magdalena Hurtado. 1985. "Men's Time Allocation to Subsistence Work Among the Ache of Eastern Paraguay." *Human Ecology* 13: 29–47.

———. 1987. "Foraging Decisions Among Ache Hunter-Gatherers: New Data and Implications for Optimal Foraging Models." *Ethology and Sociobiology* 8.

Hockett, Charles. 1973. *Man's Place in Nature*. New York: McGraw-Hill.

Hodge, Robert W., Donald J. Treiman, and Peter H. Rossi. 1966. "A Comparative Study of Occupational Prestige." In *Class, Status, and Power: Social Stratification in Comparative Perspective*, 2nd ed. Reinhard Bendix and Seymour Martin Lipset, eds., pp. 309–21. New York: Free Press.

Hoebel, E. Adamson. 1960. *The Cheyennes: Indians of the Great Plains*. New York: Holt, Rinehart & Winston.

———. 1972. *Anthropology: The Study of Man*, 4th ed. New York: McGraw-Hill.

Holloway, Kris. 2007. *Monique and the Mango Rains*. Long Grove, IL: Waveland Press.

Hossain, Ziarat, Beverly Chew, Sheryl Swilling, Sally Brown, Marcia Michaelis, and Sheila Philips. 1999. "Fathers' Participation in Childcare Within Navajo Indian Families." *Early Child Development and Care* 154: 63–74.

Hosseini, Khaled. 2003. *The Kite Runner*. New York: Riverhead Books.

Howard, Beth. 1991. "Ape Apothecary: Self-Prescribing Chimps Lead Researchers to Nature's Medicine Cabinet." *Omni* 13: 30.

Howell, N. 1986. "Feedbacks and Buffers in Relation to Scarcity and Abundance: Studies of Hunter-Gatherer Populations." In *The State of Population Theory*. D. Coleman and R. Schofield, eds., pp. 156–87. Oxford: Basil Blackwell.

Hu, Winnie. 2009. "Foreign Languages Fall as Schools Look for Cuts." *New York Times* (September 13): MB-1.

Hudson, Valarie, and Andrea M. den Boer. 2004. *Bare Branches: The Security Implications of Asia's Surplus Male Population*. Cambridge, MA: The MIT Press.

Hughes, Charles C., and John M. Hunter. 1972. "The Role of Technological Development in Promoting Disease in Africa." In *The Careless Technology: Ecology and International Development*. M. T. Farvar and John P. Milton, eds., pp. 69–101. Garden City, NY: Natural History Press.

Humphrey, Caroline. 1999. "Shamans in the City." *Anthropology Today* 15(3) (June): 3–10.

Hunt, Linda M., Jacqueline Pugh, and Miguel Valenzuela. 1995. "What They Do Outside the Doctor's Office: Understanding and Responding to Diabetes Patients' Strategic Adaptations of Self-Care Behavior." Paper given at the meetings of the Society for Applied Anthropology, Albuquerque, NM, April.

Hurdle, Jon. 2008. "A City Uses Murals to Bridge Differences." *New York Times* (October 7): 23.

Hymes, Dell. 1977. "Discovering Oral Performance and Measured Verse in American Indian Narrative." *New Literary History* 8(3): 431–57.

Igoe, Jim. 2004. *Conservation and Globalization: A Study of National Parks and Indigenous Communities from East Africa and South Dakota*. Belmont, CA: Wadsworth.

INCBS (Indian National Crime Bureau Statistics). 2007. http://mynation.wordpress.com/2007/07/01/Indian-National-Crime-Bureau-Statistics-1995–2005.

International Labour Organization. 2010. "New ILO Global Report on Child Labour: As Efforts to End Child Labour Slow, ILO Calls for 'Re-energized' Global Action." http://www.ilo.org/global/About_the_ILO/Media_and_public_information/Press_releases/lang–en/WCMS_126840/index.htm (accessed June 3, 2010).

Iqbal, Shamsi, and Eric Horvitz. 2007. *Disruption and Recovery of Computing Tasks: Field Study, Analysis, and Directions* (April 28–May 3). San Jose, CA: CHI.

Isaac, B. 1990. "Economy, Ecology, and Analogy: The !Kung San and the Generalized Foraging Model." In *Early Paleoindian Economies of Eastern North America*. B. Isaac and K Tankersley, eds., pp. 323–35. Greenwich, CT: JAI Press.

Ishii, Keiko, Jose Alberto Reyes, and Shinobu Kitayama. 2003. "Spontaneous Attention to Word Content Versus Emotional Tone: Differences among Three Cultures." *Psychological Science* 14(1): 39–46.

Jameson, Frederic. 1990. *Postmodernism, or the Cultural Logic of Late Capitalism*. Durham, NC: Duke University Press.

Jankowiak, W. R., and E. F. Fischer. 1992. "A Cross Cultural Perspective on Romantic Love." *Ethnology* 31(2): 149–56.

Janson, H. W. 1986. *History of Art* (revised by Anthony F. Janson). New York and Englewood Cliffs, NJ: Harry Abrams and Prentice Hall.

Jenkins, Henry. 2001. "Culture Goes Global." *Technology Review* 104(6): 89.

Jian, Li. 2009. "Socioeconomic Barriers to Biogas Development in Rural Southwest China: An Ethnographic Case Study." *Human Organization* 68(4): 415–30.

Joans, Barbara. 1984. "Problems in Pocotello: A Study in Linguistic Understanding." *Practicing Anthropology* 6(3/4).

———. 2007. "Anthropology Goes to Court: Problems in Pocatello, Infighting in Frisco, and Fiery Funerals." *Practicing Anthropology* 29(1): 35–40.

Johnson, Barbara Rose. 2010. "Water, Culture and Power Negotiations at the UN." *Anthropology News* 2010(January): 6.

Jonaitis, Alldona, ed. 1991. *Chiefly Feasts: The Enduring Kwakiutl Potlatch*. Seattle: University of Washington Press.

Jones, Maggie. 2006. "Shutting Themselves In." *New York Times Magazine* (January 15): 46–51.

Jordan, Cathie, Roland Tharp, and Lynn Baird-Vogt. 1992. "Just Open the Door: Cultural Compatibility and Classroom Rapport." In *Cross-Cultural Literacy: Ethnographies of Communication in Multiethnic Classrooms*. Marietta Saravia-Shore and Steven F. Arvizu, eds., pp. 3–18. New York: Garland.

Kaplan, David, and Robert Manners. 1986. *Culture Theory*. Englewood Cliffs, NJ: Prentice Hall.

Katzner, Kenneth. 1975. *The Languages of the World*. New York: Funk & Wagnalls.

Keenan, Elinor. 1974. "Norm-Makers, Norm-Breakers: Uses of Speech by Men and Women in a Malagasy Community." In *Explorations in the Ethnography of Speaking*. Richard Bauman and Joel Sherzer, eds., pp. 125–43. London: Cambridge University Press.

Keesing, Roger. 1992. "Not a Real Fish: The Ethnographer as Inside Outsider." In *The Naked Anthropologist: Tales from Around the World*. Philip DeVita, ed., pp. 73–78. Belmont, CA: Wadsworth.

Kelly, David. 2005. "'Lost Boys' Cast Out of Polygamous Enclaves." *Charlotte Observer* (June l9): A-23.

Kelly, Robert L. 1995. *The Foraging Spectrum: Diversity in Hunter-Gatherer Lifeways*. Washington, DC: Smithsonian Institution Press.

Kemper, Susan, and Tamara Harden. 1999. "Experimentally Disentangling What's Beneficial About *Elderspeak* From What's Not." *Psychology and Aging* 14(4): 656–70.

Kendall, Laurel. 1996. "Korean Shamans and the Spirit of Capitalism." *American Anthropologist* 98(2): 502–27.

Khanna, Sunil K. 2010. *Fetal/Fatal Knowledge: New Reproductive Technologies and Family-Building Strategies in India.* Belmont, CA: Wadsworth.

Khazanov, Anatoly M. 1994. *Nomads and the Outside World,* 2nd ed. Madison: University of Wisconsin Press.

Kilbride, Philip L. 1997. "African Polygyny Family Values and Contemporary Change." In *Applying Cultural Anthropology: An Introductory Reader.* Aaron Podolefsky and Peter Brown, eds., pp. 201–08. Mountain View. CA: Mayfield.

Kirsch, A. T. 1985. "Text and Context: Buddhist Sex Roles/Culture of Gender Revisited." *American Ethnologist* 12: 302–20.

Kluckhohn, Clyde. 1949. *Mirror for Man: Anthropology and Modern Life.* New York: Wittlesey House (McGraw-Hill).

Knauft, B. 1987. "Reconsidering Violence in Simple Human Societies: Homicide Among Gebusi of New Guinea." *Current Anthropology* 28: 457–500.

Kohls, L. Robert. 1984. *Survival Kit for Overseas Living.* Yarmouth, ME: Intercultural Press.

Kolenda, Pauline M. 1978. *Caste in Contemporary India: Beyond Organic Solidarity.* Prospect Heights, IL: Waveland Press.

Kourlas, Gia. 2010. "Playing Games with an Afro-Brazilian Leap into the Capoeira Circle." *New York Times* (March 25).

Krajick, Kevin. 1998. "Green Farming by the Incas?" *Science* 281: 323–29.

Kramer, Chéris. 1974. "Folk Linguistics: Wishy-Washy Mommy Talk." *Psychology Today* 8(1): 82–85.

Krause, Elizabeth. 2005. *A Crisis of Births: Population Politics and Family-Making in Italy.* Belmont, CA: Wadsworth.

Kroeber, Alfred L., and Clyde Kluckhohn. 1952. *Culture: A Critical Review of Concepts and Definitions.* Papers of the Peabody Museum of American Archaeology and Ethnology 47(1).

Kuczynski, Alex. 2004. "A Lovelier You, with Off-the-Shelf Parts." *New York Times* (May 2, section 4): 1.

Kulish, Nicholas. 2008. "Gay Muslims Pack a Dance Floor of Their Own." *New York Times* (January 1): A-4.

Kumar, Hari. 2005. "India's Harried Elite Now Turns, and Twists, to Yoga Lite." *New York Times* (February 1): A-4.

Kuper, Hilda. 1986. *The Swazi: A South African Kingdom,* 2nd ed. New York: Holt, Rinehart & Winston.

Kurtz, Donald V. 2001. *Political Anthropology: Power and Paradigms.* Boulder, CO: Westview Press.

Kuznar, Lawrence. 1996. *Reclaiming a Scientific Anthropology.* Thousand Oaks, CA: Sage Publications.

Labov, William. 1972. *Sociolinguistic Patterns.* Philadelphia: University of Pennsylvania Press.

Lacey, Marc. 2004. "Tribe, Claiming Whites' Land, Confronts Kenya's Government." *New York Times* (August 25): A-l.

———. 2005. "Victims of Uganda Atrocities Follow a Path of Forgiveness." *New York Times* (April 18): 1.

———. 2006. "The Case of the Stolen Statues: Solving a Kenyan Mystery." *New York Times* (April 16): 4.

La Fontaine, Jean. 1963. "Witchcraft in Bagisu." In *Witchcraft and Sorcery in East Africa.* John Middleton and E. H. Winter, eds., pp. 187–220. New York: Praeger.

LaFraniere, Sharon. 2007. "In Mauritania, Seeking to End an Overfed Ideal." *New York Times* (July 4): A-4.

Lakshmi, Rama. 2004. "Factory Orders Dropping? Astrologer Is Go-to Guru for Struggling Corporate Executives." *The Washington Post* (July 4): A-l 7.

Lamb, M. E. 1997. "The Development of Father–Infant Relationships." In *The Role of the Father in Child Development.* Lamb, M. E., ed., pp. 104–20. New York: Wiley.

Lamont-Brown, Raymond. 1999. "Japan's New Spirituality." *Contemporary Review* (August): 70–73.

Lamphere, Louise. 1974. "Stategies, Conflict, and Cooperation Among Women in Domestic Groups." In *Women, Culture, and Society.* Michelle Zimbalist Rosaldo and Louise Lamphere, eds. Stanford, CA: Stanford University Press.

Landler, Mark, and Michael Barbaro. 2006. "No, Not Always: Wal-Mart Discovers That Its Formula Doesn't Fit Every Culture." *New York Times* (August 2): Gl.

Lane, Beiden C. 1989. "The Power of Myth: Lessons from Joseph Campbell." *The Christian Century* 106 (July 5): 652–54.

Laumann, Edward O., John H. Gagnon, Robert T. Michael, and Stuart Michaels. 1994. *The Social Organization of Sexuality: Sexual Practices in the United States.* Chicago: University of Chicago Press.

Laumann, Edward O., and Robert T. Michael, eds. 2001. *Sex, Love, and Health in America: Private Choices and Public Policies.* Chicago: University of Chicago Press.

Lave, Jean, and Etienne Wenger. 1991. *Situated Learning: Legitimate Peripheral Participation.* Cambridge: Cambridge University Press.

Lederer, William J., and Eugene Burdick. 1958. *The Ugly American.* New York: Norton.

Lee, Dorothy. 1993. "Religious Perspectives in Anthropology." In *Magic, Witchcraft, and Religion: An Anthropological Study of the Supernatural,* 3rd ed. Arthur C. Lehmann and James E. Myers, eds., pp. 10–17. Mountain View, CA: Mayfield.

Lee, Richard B. 1968. "What Hunters Do for a Living, or How to Make Out on Scarce Resources." In *Man the Hunter.* Richard B. Lee and Irven DeVore, eds., pp. 30–48. Chicago: Aldine-Atherton.

———. 2003. *The Dobe Ju/'hoansi,* 3rd ed. Belmont, CA: Wadsworth.

———. 2007. "The Ju/'hoansi at the Crossroads: Continuity and Change in the Time of AIDS." In *Globalization and Change in 15 Cultures: Born in One World, Living in Another.* George Spindler and Janice Stockard, eds., pp. 144–71. Belmont, CA: Wadsworth.

Lee, Sharon M. 1993. "Racial Classifications in the United States Census: 1890–1990." *Racial and Ethnic Studies* 16(1) (January): 75–94.

Lehmann, Arthur C., and James E. Myers, eds. 1993. *Magic, Witchcraft, and Religion,* 3rd ed. Palo Alto, CA: Mayfield.

Lehmann, Arthur C., James E. Myers, and Pamela Moro, eds. 2001. *Magic, Witchcraft, and Religion: An Anthropological Study of the Supernatural,* 5th ed. Boston: McGraw-Hill.

Leighton, Dorothea, and Clyde Kluckhohn. 1948. *Children of the People.* Cambridge: Cambridge University Press.

di Leonardo, Micaela. 1991. *Gender at the Crossroads of Knowledge: Feminist Anthropology in the Postmodern Era.* Berkeley: University of California Press.

Lepowsky, Maria. 1990. "Big Men, Big Women, and Cultural Autonomy." *Ethnology* 29(1): 35–50.

Leung, Clint. 2007. "The Northwest Coast Native American Potlatch Ceremony." http://ezinearticles.com/?expert=Clint_Leung (accessed June 19, 2010).

Levin, Dan. 2009. "Shamans' Spirits Crowd Air of Mongolian Capitol." *New York Times* (July 21): A-6.

Levine, Ketzel. 2008. "Farming the Amazon with a Machete and Mulch." http://www.npr.org/templates/story/story,php.?storyId=18656632 (accessed February 4, 2008).

Lévi-Strauss, Claude. 1969. *The Elementary Structures of Kinship.* Boston: Beacon Press.

Levy, Becca, Martin Slade, and Stanislav Kasi. 2002a. "Longitudinal Benefit of Positive Self-Perceptions of Aging on Functional Health." *Journals of Gerontology Series B: Psychological Sciences and Social Sciences* 57b(5): 409–17.

Levy, Becca, Martin Slade, Suzanne Kunkel, and Stanislav Kasi. 2002b. "Longevity Increased by Positive Self–Perception of Aging." *Journal of Personality and Social Psychology* 83(2): 261–70.

Levy, Clifford J. 2009. "The Retreat of the Tongue of the Czars." *New York Times* (September 12): WK3.

Lewellen, Ted. 2003. *Political Anthropology: An Introduction,* 3rd ed. New York: Praeger.

Lewin, Ellen, ed. 2006. *Feminist Anthropology: A Reader.* Malden, MA: Blackwell Publishing.

Lewis, Oscar. 1955. "Peasant Culture in India and Mexico: A Comparative Analysis." In *Village India: Studies in the Little Community.* McKim Marriott, ed., pp. 145–70. Chicago: University of Chicago Press.

Lewis-Williams, J. D., and T. A. Dowson. 1988. "The Signs of All Times: Entoptic Phenomena in Upper Palaeolithic Art." *Current Anthropology* 29(2): 20–45.

Liebow, Elliot. 1967. *Tally's Corner.* Boston: Little, Brown.

Linton, Ralph. 1936. *The Study of Man.* New York: Appleton-Century-Crofts.

Loewe, Michael, and Edward L. Shaughnessy. 1999. *The Cambridge History of Ancient China.* Cambridge: Cambridge University Press.

Lohr, Steve. 2007. "Slow Down, Brave Multitasker, and Don't Read This in Traffic." *New York Times* (March 25): 14.

Loker, William M. 2000. "Sowing Discord, Planting Doubts: Rhetoric and Reality in an Environment and Development Project in Honduras." *Human Organization* 59(3): 300–10.

Lomax, Alan, et al. 1968. *Folk Song Style and Culture.* Washington, DC: American Association for the Advancement of Science.

Low, Setha M. 1981. "Anthropology as a New Technology in Landscape Planning." Unpublished paper presented at the meetings of the American Society of Landscape Architects.

Lowie, Robert. 1963. "Religion in Human Life." *American Anthropologist* 65: 532–42.

Lundgren, Nancy. 2002. *Watch and Pray: A Portrait of Fante Village Life in Transition.* Belmont, CA: Wadsworth.

Luo, Michael. 2006. "Preaching the Word and Quoting the Voice: An Evangelist Thrives in Manhattan by Embracing the City and Identifying with Its Culture." *New York Times* (February 26): 28.

Lutz, Ellen L. 2007. "Dam Nation." *Cultural Survival Quarterly* 31(4).

———. 2008. "Panama Dam Construction Steps Up the Pace." *Cultural Survival Quarterly* 32(1).

Lutz, William D. 1995. "Language, Appearance, and Reality: Doublespeak in 1984." In *Anthropology: Annual Editions 95/96.* Elvio Angeloni, ed. Guilford, CT: Dushkin.

MacFarquhar, Emily. 1994. "The War Against Women." *U.S. News & World Report* (March 28): 42–48.

Madigan, Nick. 2005. "After Fleeing Polygamist Community, an Opportunity for Influence." *New York Times* (June 29): A-14.

Mahbubani, Kishore. 2005. *Beyond the Age of Innocence: Rebuilding Trust Between America and the World.* New York: Public Affairs.

Malinowski, Bronislaw. 1922. *Argonauts of the Western Pacific.* New York: Dutton.

———. 1927. *Sex and Repression in Savage Society.* London: Kegan Paul.

———. 1944. *A Scientific Theory of Culture.* Chapel Hill: University of North Carolina Press.

Mandelbaum, David G. 1970. *Society in India,* Vol. 1. Berkeley: University of California Press.

Marett, Robert. 1914. *The Threshold of Religion.* London: Methuen.

Marksbury, Richard A., ed. 1993. *The Business of Marriage: Transformations in Oceanic Matrimony.* Pittsburgh: University of Pittsburgh Press.

Marshall, Donald S. 1971. "Sexual Behavior on Mangaia." In *Sexual Behavior: Variations in the Ethnographic Spectrum.* Donald S. Marshall and Robert Suggs, eds., pp. 103–62. New York: Basic Books.

Marshall, Lorna. 1965. "The !Kung Bushmen of the Kalahari Desert." In *Peoples of Africa.* James Gibbs, ed., pp. 243–78. New York: Holt, Rinehart & Winston.

Martin, Jodie. 2008. "Feminization of Poverty: Women Constitute the Majority of the World's Poor." http://poverty.suite101.com/article.cfm/feminization_of_poverty#ixzz0qfvaEh4s (accessed June 12, 2010).

Marx, Elizabeth. 1999. *Breaking Through Culture Shock: What You Need to Succeed in International Business.* London: Nicholas Brealey Publishing.

Marx, Karl. 1909. *Capital* (E. Unterman, trans.). Chicago: C. H. Kerr (orig. 1867).

Mascia-Lees, Frances, and Nancy Johnson Black. 2000. *Gender and Anthropology.* Prospect Heights, IL: Waveland Press.

Mauss, Marcel. 1954. *The Gift* (I. Cunnison, trans.). New York: Free Press.

Maybury-Lewis, David. 1992. *Millennium; Tribal Wisdom and the Modern World.* New York: Viking Press.

McCullough, Michael E., and Brian L. B. Willoughby. 2009. "Religion, Self-Regulation, and Self-Control: Associations, Explanations, and Implications." *Psychological Bulletin* 139(1): 69–93.

McFate, Montgomery. 2005. "Anthropology and Counterinsurgency." *Military Review* (March/April): 24–38.

McGee, R. Jon. 1990. *Life, Ritual and Religion Among the Lacandon Maya.* Belmont, CA: Wadsworth.

McKean, Erin. 2009. "Redefining Definition." *New York Times Magazine* (December 20): 16.

Mead, Margaret. 1928. *Coming of Age in Samoa.* New York: Morrow.

Mead, Margaret. 1935. *Sex and Temperament in Three Primitive Societies.* New York: Morrow.

———. 1950. *Sex and Temperament in Three Primitive Societies.* New York: Mentor (orig. 1935).

———. 1977. "Applied Anthropology: The State of the Art." In *Perspectives on Anthropology.* Washington, DC: The American Anthropological Association.

Meek, Charles K. 1972. "Ibo Law." In *Readings in Anthropology.* J. D. Jennings and E. A. Hoebel, eds. New York: McGraw-Hill.

Mehrabian, Albert. 1981. *Silent Messages,* 2nd ed. Belmont, CA: Wadsworth.

Mehta, Suketu. 2004. "Bollywood Confidential." *New York Times Magazine* (November 14): 60ff.

Melton, J. Gordon. 2002. *Encyclopedia of American Religions.* Detroit: Gale Research.

Mendonsa, Eugene. 1985. "Characteristics of Sisala Diviners." In *Magic, Witchcraft, and Religion: An Anthropological Study of the Supernatural.* Arthur C. Lehmann and James E. Myers, eds., pp. 214–24. Palo Alto, CA: Mayfield.

Merton, Robert K. 1957. *Social Theory and Social Structure.* Glencoe, IL: Free Press.

Michrina, Barry P., and Cherylanne Richards. 1996. *Person to Person: Fieldwork, Dialogue, and the Hermeneutic Method.* Albany: State University of New York Press.

Middleton, John. 1965. *The Lugbara of Uganda.* New York: Holt, Rinehart & Winston.

Middleton, John, and Greet Kershaw. 1965. *The Kihuyu and Kamba of Kenya.* London: International African Institute.

Middleton, John, and David Tait, eds. 1958. *Tribes Without Rulers: Studies in African Segmentary Systems.* London: Routledge & Kegan Paul.

Miller, Barbara D. 1993. "Female Infanticide and Child Neglect in Rural North India." In *Gender in Cross-Cultural Perspective.* Caroline Brettell and Carolyn Sargent, eds., pp. 423–35. Englewood Cliffs, NJ: Prentice Hall.

Miller, Lauren. 2006. "Selectively Importing Candomble: Through Americans' Capoeira Pilgrimages to Brazil." *Anthropology News* 47(5): 28.

Miller, Lisa. 1999. "The Age of Divine Disunity." *Wall Street Journal* (February 10): Bl.

Mills, C. Wright. 1956. *The Power Elite.* New York: Oxford University Press.

Mills, George. 1957. "Art: An Introduction to Qualitative Anthropology." *Journal of Aesthetics and Art Criticism* 16(1): 1–17.

Mohn, Tanya. 2006. "How to Become a World Citizen, Before Going to College." *New York Times* (September 3): 6.

Möller, V., and G. J. Welch. 1990. "Polygamy, Economic Security, and Well-Being of Retired Zulu Migrant Workers." *Journal of Cross-Cultural Gerontology* 5: 205–16.

Montagu, Ashley. 1972. *Touching: The Human Significance of the Shin.* New York: Harper & Row.

Morgan, Lewis H. 1871. *Systems of Consanguinity and Affinity of the Human Family.* Washington, DC: Smithsonian Institution.

———. 1963. *Ancient Society.* New York: World (orig. 1877).

Mortenson, Greg. 2009. *Stones into Schools.* New York: Viking.

Mortenson, Greg, and David Oliver Relin. 2006. *Three Cups of Tea.* New York: Penguin.

Mulder, Monique B. 1988. "Kipsigis Bridewealth Payments." In *Human Reproductive Behavior: A Darwinian Perspective.* Laura Betzig, Monique B. Mulder, and Paul Türke, eds., pp. 65–82. Cambridge: Cambridge University Press.

———. 1992. "Women's Strategies in Polygynous Marriage." *Human Nature* 3(1): 45–70.

Muraco, Anna. 2006. "Intentional Families: Fictive Kin Ties between Cross-Gender, Different Sexual Orientation Friends." *Journal of Marriage and Family* 68(5): 1313–25.

Murdock, George. 1945. "The Common Denominator of Cultures." In *The Science of Man in the World Crisis.* Ralph Linton, ed., p. 124. New York: Columbia University Press.

———. 1949. *Social Structure.* New York: Macmillan.

———. 1967. "Ethnographic Atlas: A Summary." *Ethnology* 6(2): 109–236.

Murphy, Dean E. 2004. "At War Against Dams, Tribe Turns to Old Ways." *New York Times* (September 14): A-13.

Murphy, R. F., and L. Kasdan. 1959. "The Structure of Parallel Cousin Marriage." *American Anthropologist* 61: 17–29.

Murray, Gerald F. 1984. "The Wood Tree as a Peasant Cash-Crop: An Anthropological Strategy for the Domestication of Energy." In *Haiti—Today and Tomorrow: An Interdisciplinary Study.* Charles R. Foster and Albert Valdman, eds., pp. 141–60. Lanham, MD: University Press of America.

———. 1986. "Seeing the Forest While Planting the Trees: An Anthropological Approach to Agroforestry in Rural Haiti." In *Politics, Projects, and People: Institutional Development in Haiti.* Derick W. Brinkerhoff and J. Garcia-Zamor, eds., pp. 193–226. New York: Praeger.

———. 1987a. "The Domestication of Wood in Haiti: A Case Study in Applied Evolution." In *Anthropological Praxis.* Robert Wulff and Shirley Fiske, eds., pp. 223–40. Boulder, CO: Westview Press.

———. 1987b. "Land Tenure and Agroforestry in Haiti: A Case Study in Anthropological Project Design." In *Land, Trees and Tenure.* J. B. Raintree, ed., pp. 323–28. Nairobi and Madison, WI: Land Tenure Center and International Council for Research in Agroforestry.

———. 1988. "The Wood Tree as a Peasant Cash Crop: An Anthropological Strategy for the Domestication of Energy." In *Whose Trees? Proprietary Dimensions of Forestry.* Louise Fortmann and John Bruce, eds., pp. 215–24. Boulder, CO: Westview Press.

Mwamwenda, T. S., and L. A. Monyooe. 1997. "Status of Bridewealth in an African Culture." *Journal of Social Psychology* 137(2): 269–71.

Mydans, Seth. 2008. "A Different Kind of Homework for Singapore Students: Get a Date." *New York Times* (April 29): 9.

Nakao, Keiko, and Judith Treas. 1990. "Occupational Prestige in the United States Revisited: Twenty-Five Years of Stability and Change." Paper presented at the annual meetings of the American Sociological Association.

Nanda, Serena. 1990. *Neither Man nor Woman: The Hijras of India.* Belmont, CA: Wadsworth.

———. 1992. "Arranging a Marriage in India." In *The Naked Anthropologist.* Philip DeVita, ed., pp. 137–43. Belmont, CA: Wadsworth.

Nathan, Rebekah. 2005. *My Freshman Year: What a Professor Learned by Becoming a Student.* New York: Penguin Books.

The Nation. 2010. "'Honour' Killings, Dowry Deaths." http://www.nation.com.pk/pakistan-news-newspaper-daily-english-online/Politics/08-Mar-2010/Honour-killings-dowry-deaths (accessed July 14, 2010).

National Association of Practicing Anthropologists (NAPA). 2010. "American Breakfast and the Mother-in-Law: How an Anthropologist Created Go-Gurt." http://www.practicinganthropology.org/learn/?storyid=4.

National Geographic and Roper Public Affairs. 2006. *National Geographic–Roper Public Affairs 2006 Geographic Literacy Study.* New York: National Geographic Society.

National Opinion Research Center. 1996. *General Social Surveys, 1972–1996: Cumulative Codebook.* Chicago: National Opinion Research Center.

Navarro, Mireya. 2005. "A Minder to Mind Your Manners," *New York Times* (August 14): 9–1.

———. 2006. "Many Families Are Adding a Third Generation to Their Households." *New York Times* (May 25): 1–22.

Nettl, Bruno. 1980. "Ethnomusicology: Definitions, Directions, and Problems." In *Music of Many Cultures.* Elizabeth May, ed., pp. 1–9. Berkeley: University of California Press.

Nettl, Bruno, and Philip V. Bohlman, eds. 1991. *Comparative Musicology and Anthropology of Music.* Chicago: University of Chicago Press.

Newman, Katherine S. 1988. *Falling from Grace: The Experience of Downward Mobility in the American Middle Class.* New York: Free Press.

———. 1999. *No Shame in My Game: The Working Poor in the Inner City.* New York: Knopf.

Newport, Frank. 2004. "A Look at Americans and Religion Today." *The Gallup Organization,* March 23. http://www.gallup.com/poll/content/default.aspx?ci511089&pg52.

New York City Department of City Planning. 2000. www.nyc.gov/html/dcp/html/census/nnyshtml.

New York Times. 2007. "Big Effort Under Way to Revive and Preserve Hawaii's Native Tongue." (April 15): 18.

Oberg, Kalervo. 1960. "Culture Shock: Adjustments to New Cultural Environments." *Practical Anthropology* (July/August): 177–82.

Oliver, Douglas. 1955. *A Solomon Island Society.* Cambridge, MA: Harvard University Press.

O'Meara, Tim. 1990. *Samoan Planters: Tradition and Economic Development in Polynesia.* Belmont, CA: Wadsworth, 2002.

Ortner, Sherry. 1974. "Is Female to Male as Nature Is to Culture?" In *Women, Culture, and Society.* Michelle Zimbalist Rosaldo and Louise Lamphere, eds., pp. 67–88. Stanford, CA: Stanford University Press.

Ottenheimer, Martin. 1996. *Forbidden Relatives.* Champaign: University of Illinois Press.

Pachon, Harry P. 1998. "Buenos Dias California." *UNESCO Courier* (November): 31–32.

Pape, Robert A. 2005. *Dying to Win: The Strategic Logic of Suicide Terrorism.* New York: Random House.

Paredes, Anthony. 1992. "Practical History and the Poarch Creeks: A Meeting Ground for Anthropologists and Tribal Leaders." In *Anthropological Research: Process and Application.* John Poggie, Billie R. DeWalt, and William Dressler, eds., pp. 209–26. Albany: State University of New York Press.

Parker, Arthur C. 1913. *The Code of Handsome Lake, the Seneca Prophet.* Albany: New York State Museum Bulletin, No. 163.

Parker, Patricia L., and Thomas F. King. 1987. "Intercultural Mediation at Truk International Airport." In *Anthropological Praxis.* Robert Wulff and Shirley Fiske, eds., pp. 160–73. Boulder, CO: Westview Press.

Parsons, Talcott, and Edward Shils. 1952. *Toward a General Theory of Action.* Cambridge, MA: Harvard University Press.

Patai, Raphael. 1973. *The Arab Mind.* New York: Scribner.

Patten, Sonia. 2003. "Medical Anthropology: Improving Nutrition in Malawi." In *Conformity and Conflict: Readings in Cultural Anthropology,* 11th ed. James Spradley and David McCurdy, eds., pp. 405–14. Boston: Allyn & Bacon.

Peacock, James L. 1986. *The Anthropological Lens.* Cambridge: Cambridge University Press.

Pear, Robert. 2008. "Gap in Life Expectancy Widens for the Nation." *New York Times* (March 23): 14.

Peterson, Valerie. 2008. *Peterson's Holiday Helper.* New York: Clarkson Potter.

Pew Forum on Religion & Public Life. 2010. "U.S. Religious Landscape Survey." http://religions.pewforum.org.

Polanyi, Karl. 1957. "The Economy as Instituted Process." In *Trade and Market in the Early Empires.* Karl Polanyi, Conrad Arensberg, and Harry Pearson, eds., pp. 243–70. New York: Free Press.

Porter, Justin. 2008. "In Williamsburg, Art Thrives Among the Wrenches." *New York Times* (July 6): 23.

Prestowitz, Clyde. 2003. *Rogue Nation: American Unilateralism and the Failure of Good Intentions.* New York: Basic Books.

Price, Sally. 2001. *Primitive Art in Civilized Places.* Chicago: University of Chicago Press.

Price, T. Douglas, and James A. Brown. 1985. *Prehistoric Hunter-Gatherers: The Emergence of Cultural Complexity.* Orlando, FL: Academic Press.

Prior, Ian. 1971. "The Price of Civilization." *Nutrition Today* 6(4): 2–11.

Pristin, Terry. 2002. "Behind the Legal and Private Worlds of the Veil." *New York Times* (August 11): L-4.

Pruzan, Todd. 2005. *The Clumsiest People in Europe: Or, Mrs. Mortimer's Bad-Tempered Guide to the Victorian World.* New York: Bloomsbury.

Puddington, Arch. 2010. "Freedom in the World 2010: Erosion of Freedom Intensifies" (Overview Essay) (www.freedomhouse.org).

Quigley, John M., Steven Raphael, and Eugene Smolensky. 2001. "Homeless in America, Homeless in California." *The Review of Economics and Statistics* 83(1): 37–51.

Rai, Saritha. 2004. "Short on Priests, U.S. Catholics Outsource Prayers to Indian Clergy." *New York Times* (June 13): 13.

Ramanamma, A., and U. Bambawale. 1980. "The Mania for Sons: An Analysis of Social Values in South Asia." *Social Science and Medicine* (14): 107–10.

Raphael, D., and F. Davis. 1985. *Only Mothers Know: Patterns of Infant Feeding in Traditional Cultures.* Westport, CT: Greenwood Press.

Rasmussen, Knud. 1927. *Across Arctic America.* New York: G. P. Putnam's Sons.

Real, Terrence. 2001. "Men's Hidden Depression." In *Men and Masculinity.* Theodore F. Cohen, ed. Belmont, CA: Wadsworth.

Renaud, Michelle L. 1993. "We're All in It Together: AIDS Prevention in Urban Senegal." *Practicing Anthropology* 15(4): 25–29.

———. 1997. "Applied Anthropology at the Crossroads: AIDS Prevention Research in Senegal and Beyond." *Practicing Anthropology* 19(1): 23–27.

Richtel, Matt. 2004. "For Liars and Loafers, Cell Phones Offer an Alibi." *New York Times* (June 26): A-l.

Rickford, John R. 1999. "Suite for Ebony and Phonics." In *Applying Anthropology: An Introductory Reader,* 5th ed. Aaron Podolefsky and Peter J. Brown, eds., pp. 176–80. Mountain View, CA: Mayfield.

Riding, Alan. 2004. "Babel, A New Capital for a Wider Continent." *New York Times* (May 2): 3.

Rizvi, Haider. 2005. "Development: Globalization Driving Inequality, U.N. Warns." Inter Press Service News Agency, August 25.

Robben, Antonius, and Carolyn Nordstrom. 1995. "The Anthropology and Ethnography of Violence and Sociopolitical Conflict." In *Fieldwork Under Fire: Contemporary Studies of Violence and Survival*. Carolyn Nordstrom and Antonius Robben, eds., pp. 1–23. Berkeley: University of California Press.

Roberts, J. M. 1965. "Oaths, Autonomic Ordeals, and Power." *American Anthropologist* 67: 186–212.

Robertson, Roland. 1992. *Globalization: Social Theory and Global Culture*. London: Sage.

Robinson, Linda. 1998. "Hispanics Don't Exist." *U.S. News & World Report* (May 11): 26.

Roesch, Roberta. 1984. "Violent Families." *Parents* 59(9) (September): 74–76, 150–52.

Rohner, Ronald P., and Evelyn C. Rohner. 1970. *The Kwakiutl: Indians of British Columbia*. New York: Holt, Rinehart & Winston.

Romero, Simon. 2007. "A Culture of Naming That Even a Law May Not Tame." *New York Times* (September 5): A-4.

———. 2008. "A Month to Conjure Luck with Sacrifices in Fire." *New York Times* (August 20).

Rosaldo, Michelle Zimbalist. 1974. "Women, Culture, and Society: A Theoretical Overview." In *Women, Culture, and Society*. Michelle Zimbalist Rosaldo and Louise Lamphere, eds. Stanford, CA: Stanford University Press.

Rose, Susan A. 1994. "Relation Between Physical Growth and Information Processing in Infants Born in India." *Child Development* (June): 889–902.

Rosenthal, Elisabeth. 2003. "Bias for Boys Leads to Sale of Baby Girls in China." *New York Times* (July 20): 1.

———. 2006. "Genital Cutting Raises by 50% Likelihood Mothers or Their Newborns Will Die, Study Finds." *New York Times* (June 2): A-l0.

———. 2009. "In Bolivia, Water and Ice Tell a Story of a Changing Climate." *New York Times* (December 14): 1–7.

Russell, Diana. 1990. *Rape in Marriage*. Indianapolis: Indiana University Press.

Rylko-Bauer, Barbara, Merrill Singer, and John Van Willigen. 2006. "Reclaiming Applied Anthropology: Its Past, Present, and Future." *American Anthropologist* 108(1): 178–90.

Rylko-Bauer, Barbara, Linda Whiteford, and Paul Farmer. 2009. *Global Health in Times of Violence*. Santa Fe, NM: SAR Press.

Ryu, Charles. 1992. "Koreans and Church." In *Asian Americans*. Joann Faungjean Lee, ed., pp. 162–64. New York: New Press.

Sahlins, Marshall. 1968. "Notes on the Original Affluent Society." In *Man the Hunter*. R. B. Lee and I. DeVore, eds., pp. 85–89. Chicago: Aldine.

———. 1972. *Stone Age Economics*. Chicago: Aldine-Atherton.

Salopek, Paul. 2004. "Southern Seas: The New Wild West." *Charlotte Observer* (September 5): P-1.

Samovar, Larry A., and Richard E. Porter. 1991. *Communication Between Cultures*. Belmont, CA: Wadsworth.

Samuels, Shayna. 2001. "Capoeira," *Dance Magazine* 75(12): 66–70.

Samuelson, Paul, and William Nordhaus. 1989. *Economics,* 13th ed. New York: McGraw-Hill.

Sanday, Peggy R. 2004. *Women at the Center: Life in a Modern Matriarchy*. Ithaca, NY: Cornell University Press.

Sang-Hun, Choe. 2007. "South Korea, Where Boys Were Kings, Revalues Its Girls." *New York Times* (December 23).

———. 2009. "Group Resists Korean Stigma for Mothers on Their Own." *New York Times* (October 8): 6.

Santos, Fernanda. 2009. "Musician Changes Tone of Impoverished Village." *New York Times* (October 13): A-10.

Sapir, Edward. 1929. "The Status of Linguistics as a Science." *Language* 5: 207–14.

Sarlin, Benjamin. 2008. "New York City Is No. 1 for Foreign Tourists." *New York Sun* (July 31).

Scaglion, Richard. 1987. "Customary Law Development in Papua New Guinea." In *Anthropological Praxis*. Robert Wulff and Shirley Fiske, eds., pp. 98–107. Boulder, CO: Westview Press.

Scarce, Rick. 2005. *Contempt of Court: A Scholar's Battle for Free Speech from Behind Bars*. Lanham, MD: AltaMira Press.

Scheper-Hughes, Nancy. 1989. "Death Without Weeping." *Natural History*, October.

Schwartz, Barry, Hazel Marcus, and Alana Snibbe. 2006. "Is Freedom Just Another Word for Many Things to Buy?" *New York Times Magazine* (February 26): 14–16.

Schwartz, John. 2006. "Archaeologist in New Orleans Finds a Way to Help the Living." *New York Times* (January 3): D-1.

Sciolino, Elaine. 2007. "French Dispute Whether Maori Head Is Body Part or Art." *New York Times* (October 26): A-4.

Scrimshaw, Susan C. M. 1976. *Women's Modesty: One Barrier to the Use of Family Planning Clinics in Ecuador*. Monographs of the Carolina Population Center, pp. 167–83.

Scudder, Thayer. 1999. "The Emerging Global Crisis and Development Anthropology: Can We Have an Impact?" *Human Organization* 58(4): 351–64.

Segre, Francesca. 2008. "Matchmaking, the Ultimate Government Service." *New York Times* (May 25): 14.

Selzer, Richard. 1979. *Confessions of a Knife*. New York: Simon & Schuster.

Semple, Kirk. 2007. "With Color and Panache, Afghans Fight a Different Kind of War." *New York Times* (December 15): A-6.

Sen, Amartya. 2001. "The Many Faces of Gender Inequality." *New Republic* (September 17): 35–40.

Sengupta, Somini. 2006. "India's 'Idol' Recipe: Mix Small-Town Grit and Democracy." *New York Times* (May 25): A-4.

Service, Elman R. 1966. *The Hunters*. Englewood Cliffs, NJ: Prentice Hall.

———. 1975. *Origins of the State and Civilization*. New York: Norton.

———. 1978. *Profiles in Ethnology*, 3rd ed. New York: Harper & Row.

Shahd, Laila S. 2005. *An Investigation of the Phenomenon of Polygyny in Rural Egypt* (Cairo Papers in Social Science, Volume 24, Number 3, Fall 2001). Cairo: American University in Cairo Press.

Sharff, Jagna W. 1981. "Free Enterprise and the Ghetto Family." *Psychology Today* (March).

Sheets, Payson D. 1993. "Dawn of a New Stone Age in Eye Surgery." In *Archaeology: Discovering Our Past*, 2nd ed. Robert J. Sharer and Wendy Ashmore, eds., Mountain View, CA: Mayfield.

Sheflen, Albert E. 1972. *Body Language and the Social Order*. Englewood Cliffs, NJ: Prentice Hall.

Shenk, Mary. 2006. "Models for the Future of Anthropology." *Anthropology News* 47(1): 6–7.

Shiva, Vandana. 2000. *Stolen Harvest: The Hijacking of the Global Food Supply*. Cambridge, MA: South End Press.

Shostak, Marjorie. 1983. *Nisa: The Life and Words of a !Kung Woman*. New York: Vintage Books.

Shweder, Richard A. 2007. "A True Culture War?" *New York Times* (October 27): op. ed. contribution.

Sieber, Roy. 1962. "Masks as Agents of Social Control." *African Studies Bulletin* 5(11): 8–13.

Simpson, George E., and J. Milton Yinger. 1985. *Racial and Cultural Minorities: An Analysis of Prejudice and Discrimination*, 5th ed. New York: Plenum.

Sklar, Holly. 2004. "Don't Outsource Workers, Bring in CEOs." *Charlotte Observer* (April 29): 9-A.

———. 2005. "Are CEOs Earning Their 54% Pay Increase?" *Charlotte Observer* (May 15): 2-D.

Slobin, Mark, and Jeff T. Titon. 1984. "The Music Culture as a World of Music." In *Worlds of Music: An Introduction to the Music of the World's Peoples*. Jeff T. Titon et al., eds., pp. 1–11. London: Collier Macmillan Publishers.

Smith, Aaron. 2009. "The Internet's Role in Campaign 2008." *Pew Research Center Publication* (April 15).

Smith, Bruce. 1998. *The Emergence of Agriculture*. New York: Scientific American Library.

Smith, Craig S. 2005. "Abduction, Often Violent, a Kyrgyz Wedding Rite." *New York Times* (April 30): 1-A.

Smith, E. A. 1983. "Anthropological Applications of Optimal Foraging Theory: A Critical Review." *Current Anthropology* 24: 625–51.

Smith, Jeffrey M. 2003. *Seeds of Deception: Exposing Industry and Government Lies About the Safety of the Genetically Engineered Foods You're Eating*. Fairfield, LA: Yes! Books.

Stack, Carol. 1975. *All Our Kin: Strategies for Survival in a Black Community*. New York: Harper & Row.

Stang, Veronica. 2009. *Gardening the World: Agency, Identity, and the Ownership of Water*. New York: Beghahn Books.

Statistical Abstract of the United States. 2006. http://www.census.gov/prod/www/statistical-abstract.html, Table 13 (Resident Population by Sex, Race, and Hispanic Origin Status, 2000–2004).

Stavans, Ilan. 2003. *Spanglish: The Making of a New American Language*. New York: Rayo (HarperCollins).

Steiner, Christopher B. 1990. "Body Personal and Body Politic: Adornment and Leadership in Cross-Cultural Perspective." *Anthropos* 85: 431–45.

Steinhauer, Jennifer. 2008. "I'll Have a Big Mac, Serenity on the Side." *New York Times* (March 2).

Steinmetz, David. 2004. "World Christianity Under New Management." *Charlotte Observer* (July 12): 11-A.

Stephens, William N. 1963. *The Family in Cross-Cultural Perspective*. New York: Holt, Rinehart & Winston.

Stille, Alexander. 2003. "Experts Can Help Rebuild a Country." *New York Times* (July 19): A-l 5 and A-l 7.

Stockard, Janice E. 2002. *Marriage in Culture*. Fort Worth, TX: Harcourt College Publishers.

Strathern, Marilyn. 1984. "Domesticity and the Denigration of Women." In *Rethinking Women's Roles: Perspectives from the Pacific*. Denise O'Brien and Sharon Tiffany, eds., pp. 13–31. Berkeley: University of California Press.

Sturtevant, William. 1964. "Studies in Ethnoscience." *American Anthropologist* 66(3) (Part 2): 99–131.

Sullivan, Thomas J., and Kenrick Thompson. 1990. *Sociology: Concepts, Issues, and Applications*. New York: Macmillan.

Sundkler, Bengt. 1961. *Bantu Prophets of South Africa*, 2nd ed. London: Oxford University Press.

Suskind, Ron. 2004. "What Makes Bush's Presidency So Radical Even to Some Republicans Is His Preternatural, Faith-Infused Certainty in Uncertain Times." *New York Times Magazine* (October 17): 44–51, 64, 102, 106.

Sutton, Mark Q., and Anderson, E. N. 2009. *Introduction to Cultural Ecology*, 2nd ed. Lanham, MD: AltaMira Press.

Tahmincioglu, Eve. 2004. "It's Not Only the Giants with Franchises Abroad." *New York Times* (February 12): C-4.

Takahashi, Dean. 1998. "Doing Fieldwork in the High-Tech Jungle." *Wall Street Journal* (October 27): B-1.

Talmon, Yohina. 1964. "Mate Selection in Collective Settlements." *American Sociological Review* 29: 491–508.

Tannen, Deborah. 1990. *You Just Don't Understand: Women and Men in Conversation*. New York: Morrow.

———. 1994. *Talking From 9 to 5*. New York: William Morrow.

Taylor, Brian K. 1962. *The Western Lacustrine Bantu*. London: International African Institute.

Terry, Don. 1996. "Cultural Tradition and Law Collide in Middle America." *New York Times* (December 2): A-10.

Thomson, David S. 1994. "Worlds Shaped by Words." In *Conformity and Conflict*, 8th ed. James P. Spradley and David McCurdy, eds., pp. 73–86. New York: HarperCollins.

Tierney, John. 2003. "Letter from the Middle East." *New York Times* (October 22): A-4.

———. 2008. "Hitting It Off, Thanks to Algorithms of Love." *New York Times* (February 9).

Tiger, Lionel, and Robin Fox. 1971. *The Imperial Animal*. New York: Holt, Rinehart & Winston.

Toffler, Alvin. 1970. *Future Shock*. New York: Random House.

Tollefson, Kenneth D. 1995. "Potlatching and Political Organization among the Northwest Coast Indians." *Ethnology* 34(1): 53–73.

Turnbull, Colin. 1981. "Mbuti Womanhood." In *Woman the Gatherer*. Frances Dahlberg, ed., pp. 205–19. New Haven, CT: Yale University Press.

Tylor, Edward B. 1958. *Origins of Culture*. New York: Harper & Row (orig. 1871).

———. 1889. "On a Method of Investigating the Development of Institutions: Applied to Laws of Marriage and Descent." *Journal of the Royal Anthropological Institute* 18: 245–69.

Udvardy, Monica, and Linda Giles. 2008. "Groundbreaking Repatriation of Two Kenya Memorial Statues." *Anthropology News* 49(l) (January): 30.

UNFPA (United Nations Fund for Population Activities). 2005. "State of the World Population." http://www.unfpa.org/swp/2005/presskit/factsheets/facts-vaw.htm.

UNICEF. 2009. *State of the World's Children—2009 Report*. http://www.unicef.org.sowc09.

Urbina, Ian. 2009. "Recession Drives Surge in Youth Runaways." *New York Times* (October 26): 1.

Urdang, Stephanie. 2001. "Women and AIDS: Gender Inequality Is Fatal." *Women's International Network News* 27(4) (Autumn): 24.

U.S. Census Bureau. 2008. *2006 American Community Survey (S2301), Empoyment Status*.

———. 2008. *Current Population Reports (Series P-60-236)*.

U.S. Department of Labor. 2010. "Employment Status of the Civilian Population by Sex and Age." http://www.bls.gov/news.release/empsit.t01.htm (accessed July 14, 2010).

Vallardes, Danillo. 2010. "Central America: Women Eke Out a Living." http://ipsnews.net/news.asp?idnews=50352 (accessed June 3, 2010).

Van Esterik, Penny. 1989. *Beyond the Breast-Bottle Controversy*. New Brunswick, NJ: Rutgers University Press.

Van Gennep, Arnold. 1960. *The Rites of Passage*. Chicago: University of Chicago Press (orig. 1908).

Vanneman, Reeve, and L. W. Cannon. 1987. *The American Perception of Class*. Philadelphia: Temple University Press.

Van Willigen, John. 2002. *Applied Anthropology: An Introduction*, 3rd ed. Westport, CT: Bergin & Garvey.

Wagner, Gunter. 1949. *The Bantu of North Kavirondo*. London, published for the International African Institute by Oxford University Press.

Wallace, Anthony F. C. 1966. *Religion: An Anthropological View*. New York: Random House.

Waring, Marilyn. 1989. *If Women Counted: A New Feminist Economics*. New York: HarperCollins.

———. 2004. *Counting for Nothing: What Men Value and What Women Are Worth*. Toronto: University of Toronto Press.

Weber, Max. 1946. *From Max Weber: Essays in Sociology* (Hans Girth and C. Wright Mills, trans. and eds.). New York: Oxford University Press.

———. 1958. *The Protestant Ethic and the Spirit of Capitalism*. New York: Charles Scribner's Sons (orig. 1904).

Weiner, Annette. 1976. *Women of Value, Men of Renown*. Austin: University of Texas Press.

———. 1988. *The Trobrianders of Papua New Guinea*. New York: Holt, Rinehart & Winston.

Weiner, E. 1994. "Muslim Radicals and Police Hunt Feminist Bangladeshi Writer." *Christian Science Monitor* (July 26): 6.

Weismantel, Mary. 1995. "Making Kin: Kinship Theory and Zumbagua Adoptions." *American Ethnologist* 22(4): 685–709.

Whelehan, Patricia. 1985. "Review of *Incest: A Biosocial View* by Joseph Shepher." *American Anthropologist* 87: 677.

White, Leslie. 1959. *The Evolution of Culture*. New York: McGraw-Hill.

Whitehead, Neil L., and R. Brian Ferguson. 1993. "Deceptive Stereotypes About Tribal Warfare." *Chronicle of Higher Education* (November 10): 48.

Whiting, John W., and Irvin L. Child. 1953. *Child Training and Personality: A Cross-Cultural Study*. New Haven, CT: Yale University Press.

Whiting, Robert. 1979. "You've Gotta Have 'wa.'" *Sports Illustrated* (September 24): 60–71.

Whyte, M. K. 1978. *The Status of Women in Preindustrial Societies*. Princeton, NJ: Princeton University Press.

Williams, Florence. 1998. "In Utah, Polygamy Goes Suburban." *Charlotte Observer* (February 28): G-3.

Wilson, Monica. 1960. "Nyakyusa Age Villages." In *Cultures and Societies of Africa*. Simon and Phoebe Ottenberg, eds., pp. 227–36. New York: Random House.

Wines, Michael. 2007. "In a Land of Homemade Names, Tiffany Doesn't Cut It." *New York Times* (October 1): A-4.

Wisconsin v. Yoder, 406 U.S. 205 (1972).

Witherspoon, Gary. 1975. *Navajo Kinship and Marriage*. Chicago: University of Chicago Press.

———. 1977. *Language and Art in the Navajo Universe*. Ann Arbor: University of Michigan Press.

Wittfogel, Karl. 1957. *Oriental Despotism: A Comparative Study of Total Power*. New Haven, CT: Yale University Press.

Wolf, Arthur. 1968. "Adopt a Daughter-in-Law, Marry a Sister: A Chinese Solution to the Incest Taboo." *American Anthropologist* 70: 864–74.

Wolf, E. 1964. *Anthropology*. Englewood Cliffs, NJ: Prentice Hall.

Wolf, Margery. 1972. *Women and the Family in Rural Taiwan*. Stanford, CA: Stanford University Press.

Wood, Julia T. 1994. "Gender, Communication, and Culture." In *Intercultural Communication: A Reader*, 7th ed. Larry Samovar and Richard Porter, eds., pp. 155–65. Belmont, CA: Wadsworth.

Wood, Lamont. 2010. "Office Technology: Productivity Boost or Time Sink?" *Computer World* (March 30). http://www.computerworld.com/s/article/9174223/Office_technology_Productivity_boost_or_time_sink_?taxonomyId=12&pageNumber=1 (accessed June 3, 2010).

World Health Organization. 2009. "What do we mean by 'sex' and 'gender'?" http://www.who.int/gender/whatisgender/en/index.html (accessed July 14, 2010).

Wright, Melissa W. 2006. *Disposable Women and Other Myths and Global Capitalism*. New York: Routledge.

Yardley, Jim. 2005. "Fearing Future, China Starts to Give Girls Their Due." *New York Times* (January 31): A-3.

Yellen, John. 1990. "The Transformation of the Kalahari !Kung." *Scientific American* (April): 96–104.

Yellin, Emily. 2004. *Our Mother's War: American Women at Home and at the Front during World War II*. New York: Free Press.

Credits

Chapter 1

page xxi: © Bill Bachmann/DanitaDelimont.com; page 4: © Marie Riene Mattera; page 5: The Dian Fossey Gorilla Fund International; page 6: © REUTERS/El Comercio/Landov; page 8: © Shannon Lee Dawdy/University of Chicago; page 10: Image copyright Sam Cornwell, 2010. Used under license from Shutterstock.com; page 11: © Susan Andreatta; page 12: © Photoshot/Landov; page 19: Courtesy Bron Solyom; page 20: © Tom & Dee Ann McCarthy/Corbis; page 21: © Jose Luis Pelaez/Corbis

Chapter 2

page 26: © John Warburton-Lee/DanitaDelimont.com; page 28 left: © Charles and Rosette Lenars/Corbis; page 28 right: © Alex Grimm/Reuters/Corbis; page 31: © Gerrit de Heus/Alamy; page 32: © David Young-Wolf/PhotoEdit, Inc.; page 36: © Photoalto/Alamy; page 37: © Reuters/Fred Prouser/Landov; page 38 left: © DPA/The Image Works; page 38 right: Courtesy of Gary Ferraro/Photo by Ginger Wagner; page 40: © Galen Rowell/Corbis; page 44: © Chicago Tribune/MCT/Landov; page 45: Photo Courtesy of NEW PEOPLE; page 46: © Monica Almeida/New York Times/Redux; page 50: © Travel Ink/Getty Images

Chapter 3

page 52: © Joerg Boethling/Peter Arnold, Inc./Photolibrary; page 54: © Robert Brenner/PhotoEdit, Inc.; page 56: © Jesper Jensen/Alamy; page 57: © Guy Cali/Corbis; page 58: © Michael Pole/Corbis; page 59: © Wolfgang Kahler/Corbis; page 60: © Tina Manley/Central America/Alamy; page 61: © Lorne Lassiter; page 63: © Penny Van Esterik; page 64: © Susan Andreatta; page 66: © Charles Gupton/Getty Images; page 68: Tom Brownold

Chapter 4

page 72: © John Warburton-Lee/DanitaDelimont.com; page 74: © Brown Brothers; page 76: © Jack Stein Grove/PhotoEdit, Inc.; page 77: © Brown Brothers; page 79: Professor Gerald Murray, University of Florida, Gainesville; page 80: © Mary Evans Picture Library/The Everett Collection; page 81: © Bettmann/Corbis; page 82: © Corbis/SuperStock; page 83: © Sophie Bassouls/Sygma/Corbis; page 85: © Michael Ventura/PhotoEdit, Inc.; page 86: Courtesy of Dr. William E. Mitchell; page 87: © Jerry Bauer; page 89: Professor Clifford Geertz, Institute of Advanced Study, Princeton

Chapter 5

page 92: © Richard Lord; page 94 top: Courtesy of Gary Ferraro; page 94 bottom: © Jorgen Schytte/Peter Arnold, Inc./Photolibrary; page 99: © Susan Andreatta; page 101: © Peggy & Yoram Kahana/Peter Arnold, Inc./Photolibrary; page 102: © Mel Konner/Anthro-Photo; page 107: © Martin Alipaz/epa/Corbis; page 108: © Jenny Matthews/Alamy; page 109: © Edward Tronick/Anthro-Photo; page 110:

© Images of Africa Photobank/Alamy; page 111: © Associated Press

Chapter 6

page 120: © age fotostock/First Light; page 124: © Cultural Survival, photo by Polly Laurelchild Hertig; page 125: © Susan Kuklin/Photo Researchers, Inc.; page 131: Image copyright Ilja Masik, 2010. Used under license from Shutterstock.com; page 132: © Maxpp/Landov; page 133: © Joel Gordon; page 134: © Jim West/age fotostock; page 137: © MIXA/Getty Images; page 138: © design pics/First Light; page 139: © Richard Cummins/SuperStock; page 140 top: © Studio Wartenberg/Zefa/Corbis; page 140 bottom: © Dennis MacDonald/fotostock; page 142: © Reuters/Nikola Solic/Landov; page 143: © Todd Heisler/The New York Times/Redux

Chapter 7

page 148: © Adrian Weston/Alamy; page 150 left: © John Warburton-Lee/DanitaDelimont.com; page 150 right: © Arcticphoto/Alamy; page 151: © Peter Langer/DanitaDelimont.com; page 152: © Robert Harding Picture Library, Ltd/Alamy; page 153: © 1998 Peter Menzel/*Man Eating Bugs*/www.menzelphoto.com; page 156: © Richard Lee/Anthro-Photo; page 158: © Bryan & Cherry Alexander Photography/Alamy; page 159: © Frans Lemmens/Lonely Planet Images; page 160: © Susan Andreatta; page 161: © Lee Celano/Reuters/Landov; page 162: © Susan Andreatta; page 165: © Jacques Jangoux/Alamy; page 167: © Arcticphoto/Alamy; page 169: © John Warburton-Lee/DanitaDelimont.com; page 170: © David Austen/Stock, Boston; page 172: © SambaPhoto/Eduardo Barcellos/Getty Images

Chapter 8

page 176: © Thomas Kelly/Peter Arnold, Inc./Photolibrary; page 180 left & right: © John Warburton-Lee/DanitaDelimont.com; page 181: © Jon Arnold Images Ltd/Alamy; page 184: © DPA/The Image Works; page 186: © Pablo CorralV/Corbis; page 187 left: © Charlotte Thege/Peter Arnold, Inc./Photolibrary; page 187 right: © Dan Vincent/Alamy; page 190: © Washburn/Anthro-Photo; pages 191 & 193: © Irven DeVore/Anthro-Photo; page 194: P208-109 Alaska State Library Lantern Slides of Alaska Photograph Collection; page 197 top: © Alison Jones/DanitaDelimont.com; page 197 bottom: © Bill Bachmann/Alamy; page 198: © David R. Frazier/DanitaDelimont.com; page 200 left: © AFP/Getty Images; page 200 right: © Bob Daemmrich/The Image Works; page 201: © Shehzad Noorani/Peter Arnold, Inc./Photolibrary

Chapter 9

page 206: © Stuart F. Westmorland/DanitaDelimont.com; page 208: © Rick Friedman/Corbis; page 210: © View Stock/Alamy; page 211: © Mary Evans/Photo Researchers, Inc.; page 213: © Karl Mondon/mct/Landov; page 214: © Michael

S. Yamashita/Corbis; page 216: © Charles Pertwee/HT-The New York Times/Redux; page 219 left: © Reuters/Bazuki Muhammad/Landov; page 219 right: © AFP/Getty Images; page 222: © Arco Images/GmnH/Alamy; page 224: © John Eastcott/Yva Momatiuk/Woodfin Camp & Associates; page 225: © Maxpp/Landov; page 226: © Michael S. Yamashita/Corbis; page 227: © Preston O'Berry; page 228: © Art Directors & TRIP/Alamy

Chapter 10

page 232: © Chuck Savage/Corbis; page 234: © Schuler/Anthro-Photo; pages 235 & 240: © Gary Ferraro; page 242: © Nativestock Pictures/Photolibrary; page 250: © Bettmann/Corbis; page 251 left: Courtesy of Nancy Sheper-Hughes; page 251 right: © Blair Seitz/Photo Researchers, Inc.; page 252: Courtesy of Mami Finklestein

Chapter 11

page 256: © Paul Conklin/PhotoEdit; page 258: © Louise Gubb/The Image Works; page 259: © 1999 Serena Nanda; page 264: © Augustus Butera/ABStudio/Getty Images; page 265: © Ranier Jensen/epa/Landov; page 267: © Sylvan Grandadam/age footstock; page 268 left: © ML Harris/Getty Images; page 268 right: © Banana Stock/Photolibrary; page 270: © Jalil Rezayee/epa/Landov; page 272 left: © Lindsay Hebberd/Corbis; page 272 right: © John Elk/Stock, Boston; page 275: © Dominic Harcourt- Webster/Robert Harding Picture Library; page 279: © Robin Nelson/PhotoEdit; page 281: © Alaska Stock/LLC/Alamy

Chapter 12

page 284: © Christopher Pillitz/Getty Images; page 286: © Fernando Castillo/Landov; page 289: © Photostock-Israel/Alamy; page 292 top: © Daniele Cati/Iconotec/Photolibrary; page 292 bottom: © Ghislain & Marie David deLossy/Getty Images; page 293 top & bottom: © Associated Press; page 295: © Friedrich Stark/Alamy; page 296: © Ariel Skelley/Corbis; page 298: © Martin Marencin/HT/New York Times/Redux; page 301: © Matt Sullivan/Reuters/Landov; page 303: © Bettmann/Corbis; page 305: Lions Gate/The Kobal Collection; page 306: © Michelle D. Birdwall/PhotoEdit; page 309: © Bruno de Hogues/Getty Images

Chapter 13

page 312: © Lewis Whyld/PA Photos/Landov; page 315: © Wendy Stone/Corbis; page 318: © J.Anthony Paredes; page 319: © Brooks Kraft/Corbis; page 321: © China Features/Corbis/Sygma; page 322: © David Turnley/Corbis; page 323: © Jayanta Shaw/Reuters/Landov; page 324: © Corbis; page 327 left: © Washington Post/Getty Images; page 327 right: © Dennis McDonald/Alamy; page 331: © Jeff Greenberg/PhotoEdit; page 333: © David Gillisin/Peter Arnold, Inc./Photolibrary; page 336: © Chip East/Reuters/Corbis; page 337: © L. O'Shaughnessy/Roberstock.com; page 339: © Jerry Lampen/Reuters/Corbis

Index